110
Livingston

Street

❧

pupil's achievement and national standards widens as he remains in school. In the past ten years reading scores have gone down, dropout rates have gone up, community protest has increased, and the middle class has been steadily withdrawing its children from the public schools. In 1966, 12,000 pupils were suspended, 30% of the teachers were "permanent substitutes" without standard licenses; 89,227 pupils attended overcrowded schools while 99,872 were in underutilized schools.[4] Teacher strikes, deteriorating community relations, and increasing criticism from business of student unpreparedness are further indications of the schools' failure. In 1967, Superintendent Donovan made a public statement of hope that soon all high school graduates would be reading at or above eighth grade level.[5] Many businessmen in the city were reportedly shocked at such a statement; they are angry at the school system's failure to produce an employable black and Puerto Rican population.

The fact that the New York City school system has an annual expense budget of well over $1 billion and keeps producing more and more welfare clients makes the failure of the schools a significant public issue. Many of the city's taxpayers increasingly feel that they have a right to expect more for their money than the schools are giving them. Furthermore, city residents and institutions are often double and triple taxed for the schools' failures, paying for welfare, correctional institutions, crime, delinquency, and narcotics addiction. Under increasing pressure from the government and civil rights groups to hire more Negroes and Puerto Ricans, big business in New York City, as elsewhere, has begun to hire "qualifiables" rather than "qualified" people. It takes the cripples from the public school system—for example, ghetto high school dropouts and graduates—and gives them the training the schools were unable to give. Indeed, a parallel school system is beginning to emerge in such training programs,[6] but business strongly resents the fact that the schools' failures have forced it into these programs.*

Effecting a Change: Concepts and Method

The New York City school system is flooded with demonstration projects and piecemeal innovations, most of which are uncoordinated, overlapping, and often inadequately evaluated.

---

* This is not to suggest that such training programs are extensive or that big business is necessarily altruistic. Some of its job training programs are partly underwritten by the federal government.

reformist outlook that has been typical of the city's political life. Yet, desegregation is not taking place in New York City, nor are the schools providing adequately for the education of minority group populations. It is important to know why this is, because if public education fails in New York City, there is serious question whether it can succeed in any other large northern city. In the words of one cynic, the New York City school system is the nightmare toward which many others are moving.

The Politics of Education

Plans for changes in the public school system, and the implementation of such plans, are affected by the actions and attitudes of many "constituencies," ranging from professional groups inside the school system to community groups, real estate interests, and politicians. The Board of Education and the superintendent act within what students of administration call "zones of acceptance" or "conceptions of legitimacy." [2] If the board is to implement new plans, it must mobilize support within the school system and in the community. This is a political problem, and an explanation of public education decisions such as "we're doing what is educationally right and that's the only consideration" fails to describe how such decisions are made. Though such statements may be necessary for public relations purposes, they obviously cannot be used as substitutes for political realities.

Furthermore, one cannot assume that presumably "technical" education decisions are apolitical. All administrative decisions are based on assumptions of value. They involve priorities; and they involve conceptions of alternative costs. A technocratic bias has long dominated the education profession, though educators are of course not alone in this regard. More than most others, however, they are being forced to recognize that personal, professional, and institutional interests, rather than technical judgments alone, shape their decisions.[3]

Thus there arises a serious question of public policy regarding the amount of insulation the education profession should have from its clients—that is, pupils, their parents, and the taxpayers as a whole, and from city, state, and federal officials.

The Record

In New York City public schools, one out of three pupils is a year or more retarded in arithmetic, and the gap between a

The controversies that the issue of desegregation raised have illustrated the more general problem of the failure of our schools to educate children. Though desegregation *per se* is now much less of an issue, the question of how to improve education for Negro and Puerto Rican pupils still remains. There are some astute students of the New York City school system who claim that it has functioned poorly for several decades, and that the notion that it was a top-grade system until the vast influx of Negroes and Puerto Ricans is a myth. Louis Yavner, for example, a lawyer who co-authored a pioneering two-volume study of the system in 1951 and did others before then, holds to this view.[1] Administratively, the system may never have been a viable one, and it may have suffered from many pedagogical shortcomings as well—regardless of how much better it was than other big-city school systems.*

Why New York City?

New York City's experiences make it a strategic case for several reasons. Its school system, viable or not, has often been a model for those in other large cities. It is generally farther along in the formulation of desegregation, compensatory education, and decentralization plans and their implementation on a selective, local basis than any other large northern city. The successes and failures of New York's school and political officials and of various civic groups are taken into account by their colleagues elsewhere and become guidelines for action.

Furthermore, New York City has long been a center of cosmopolitan values, progressive politics, and innovation. The present Board of Education is dominated by people with long records of support for progressive causes; they share an egalitarian,

---

* David Alison's *Searchlight: An Exposé of New York City Schools,* New York City, The Teachers Center Presses, 1951, documents the system's many weaknesses in the 1930s and forties. Political patronage in board-member selection, corruption among board members overly responsive to real estate and construction interests, anti-Semitism and racism among school officials, the Red-baiting of school officials (many of them highly competent and committed to improving ghetto schools), and the pedestrian nature of curriculum and instructional methods were among the system's main features.

"The schools were good for the Jews and for them only," recalled an old-time New Yorker, "and mainly because of what Jewish kids and their parents brought to the schools rather than because of the system itself. For every Westinghouse scholar, there were dozens of kids who didn't graduate from high school or ever even get there, and most of them were white."

INTRODUCTION:
THE NEW YORK CITY
SCHOOL STRUGGLE

A political struggle has been waged over the adequacy of the New York City school system since the 1954 Supreme Court decision that outlawed segregation. Until the middle of the 1960s the issue centered on the nature, speed, and scope of the Board of Education's efforts to desegregate the schools. The New York City Board of Education, like its counterparts in other cities, has been caught between civil rights groups' protesting that it was not moving fast enough, and white neighborhood school groups' claiming that it was moving too quickly.

But more is at issue in New York's school system than its rate of desegregation: the extent of professionalism and the accountability of the school system to the public it serves; the ability of its administrative structure to achieve its announced goals of quality education; and its relations with the mayor, with city, state, and federal agencies, and with the community. This study examines the political and social forces that have affected the school system. My primary concern is with innovation and reform, and ultimately with the politics of school administration in large cities. I chose to analyze the board's handling of desegregation as a means of studying the operations of the total system.*

* The term "board" has several meanings. Sometimes, it refers to the immense staff at 110 Livingston Street, the system's headquarters. At other times it refers to the non-salaried, appointed policy makers (lay board). At still other times, it refers to the total institution, field and headquarters staff as well as the lay board. More often than not, I have used "board" to refer to any of the three, and have depended on the context to make its meaning clear.

110 *Livingston Street*

CONTENTS

by the editorial work of Jason Epstein and Alice Mayhew. Both deserve credit for helping to shape a long manuscript into a more sharply written book. Usually, copy editors get little if any mention. I am pleased to publicly thank Cicely Nichols.

I made many friendships in the course of writing this book, and one that has taken on special meaning for me is with Cyril Tyson. I have learned more from him about social change and ghetto problems than I can readily recall, and I never cease being amazed at the vitality with which he goes about trying to make New York City a more humane and livable place for its many ghetto residents.

I also want to thank Deans Clifford Clark and Joseph Taggart and Dr. Norman Martin of the Graduate School of Business Administration at NYU for permitting me the research time to complete this study; Mitchell Sviridoff, who supported it in its final stages; Rhoda Howard, who provided many valuable insights into the workings of the Board of Education, and Valerie Moolman, who read and skillfully edited several early drafts.

Finally, I want to thank my wife, Terry, and my two sons for their patience over the many years that I worked on the study. Terry's quiet but persistent questioning of many of my assumptions and values in the course of this study has helped enormously in sharpening my thoughts.

DAVID ROGERS

Kenneth Lenihan. The help that Mrs. Benjamin gave, reading successive drafts and helping to clarify some of the workings of the Board of Education, was of special value.

Many officials and activists in the civil rights movement gave enormous amounts of their time, patiently explaining the inner workings of the movement and enhancing our insights into their communities' dealings with the Board of Education. Of special help were Carl Fields, Dorothy Jones, James Jones, Edward Lewis, Ellen Lurie, Irving Levine, Doris and Roy Innis, Thelma Johnson, June Shagaloff, John Silverberg, and Cyril Tyson. These people spent literally hours and days with us, invited me to their private meetings, and conferred a trust and confidence in me that I hope I have lived up to in this book. I cannot disguise my affection and admiration for all these people, and I hope that the book may be of some small help in forwarding the cause for which they are fighting.

Others who shared their insights into the school system's workings included Dick Bader, Florence Flast, Fred McLaughlin, Monsigneur Raymond Rigney, Albert Shanker, Harold Siegel, and numerous teachers, principals, district superintendents, school headquarters officials, and board members. Given the critical judgments I make of the Board of Education, I will not thank publicly by name those school officials who helped us, and I am sure that most would prefer it that way. We interviewed seven of the nine board members (as of May, 1968), and several others who had served on the board or in the professional hierarchy in previous years.

I regret that I was unable to reach Superintendent Bernard Donovan, who was unavailable the several times I tried to reach him, both by phone and personal letter.

I am continually reminded of how big a contribution my two research associates, Faith Kortheuer and Roslyn Menzel, have made in this study, both in the field work and in developing the ideas for the book. Their loyalty, good humor, and research skills made it possible for us to undertake and complete the enormous task of studying the administration and politics of the New York City school system with literally a skeletal work crew. I believe in an informal, small research team, and they have helped to reinforce that belief. I would also like to thank Jean Murphy for her seven months of intensive field work on parent attitudes and conditions in ghetto schools.

Successive drafts of the manuscript benefited tremendously

ACKNOWLEDGMENTS

The sheer number of people we interviewed, some several times, makes it impossible to thank each separately. Many officials and members of the organizations mentioned in this book gave generously of their time and insights. Indeed, almost everywhere we went within the city, either on official field trips or social occasions, we met somebody who was connected with the New York City schools, indicating the pervasiveness of 110 Livingston Street, the Board of Education headquarters, in the lives of the city's residents.

I owe a special thanks to Robert Dentler, Director of the Center for Urban Education, who literally made this study possible. He was interested enough in the study in its early stages, to offer to support it through the Center, where I worked for two years while the bulk of it was done. Not only did he support the study, but he gave generously of the Center's staff and facilities, granting most of my requests for more resources, and giving me autonomy to pursue the research in directions that my judgments and interests indicated. I could not have hoped for more sympathetic and professional support than he gave. Needless to say, the views presented in this book are not necessarily those of the Center.

The research- and policy-oriented climate at the Center were a source of constant stimulation, and several Center colleagues generously read early drafts and made critical comments. Herbert Gans, Mortimer Kreuter, Annie Stein, and Mary Ellen Warshauer, in addition to Robert Dentler were especially helpful.

Other friends and colleagues who read sections of the book include Margaret Benjamin, Ivar Berg, Robert Dreeben, and

For Edward, Alex, Terry
AND
for Cyril D. Tyson

Library of Congress Catalog Card Number: 68-14499

Manufactured in the United States of America

Acknowledgment is gratefully made
to the following publishers,
who have granted permission to reprint
excerpts from copyrighted publications:

Renewal, Chet and Dot Fulmer,
"The Board and the Bus,"
October–November, 1966.
Women's City Club of New York,
Performance and Promise, 1966.

110

Livingston

Street

---

*Politics and Bureaucracy in
the New York City School System*

DAVID ROGERS

RANDOM HOUSE
New York

But virtually none of the techniques that have been tried have worked. The multiple, piecemeal experiments have been in part a technique to absorb protest, whether consciously planned that way or not, and they help to maintain the bureaucratic structure by isolating innovations and not letting them affect the broader system.[7]

But the structure of the school system itself must be changed if public education is to fulfill its functions in our society. Centrally administered public education has failed in New York City. In order to reverse that failure and change the structure to one that allows success, it is, of course, necessary to understanding the existing structure and its contributions to the failure, and the political and social forces that affect and are dealt with by that structure.

The conceptual scheme I have used to study such forces and their effects is a very simple one. It brings to bear a particular kind of social science analysis, namely, the analysis of formal, bureaucratic organizations. One way to look at big-city school systems is to look at them as bureaucracies—engaged in numerous kinds of tasks; structured and administered in particular ways to carry out these tasks; with informal codes and traditions and an internal politics; and confronted with a variety of outside clients.[8] These clients often make conflicting demands. To the extent that their demands are frustrated, the clients often increase them. They want more and better educational services and greater responsiveness of school officials to citizen complaints.

This study begins with a consideration of the significance of *ecological and situational* factors for the failure of public education in the New York City schools. These include demographic and housing patterns, conditions of poverty and social pathology in the ghetto, and the availability of staff and funds. Changing neighborhood patterns, for example, affect the composition and cohesiveness of various constituencies making demands on the board. They also effect prospects for desegregation and improved educational quality.

The main part of the study deals more directly with the administration and politics of educational decision-making, and the three general sources of pressure and constraint that the board faces. One is *interest group politics:* the alignments of civic groups into various coalitions, the positions they take, the political resources they have, the skill with which they use such resources, and the degree of access they have to board and city officials, all place upper and lower limits on the board's programs and on the speed and efficiency with which they are implemented.

Another center of power is the *school system* itself. The Board of Education does not passively reflect public opinion. The board's own strategies for dealing with various interest groups and coalitions affect the prospects for innovation; the timing of the board's decisions and its attempts at consulting and bargaining with civic groups affect their willingness to support particular reforms. The resources of its top leadership, the power and influence of various professional groups, and the administrative structure and codes of the board, have a major effect on the implementation of innovation and reform. The chapters dealing with these issues are perhaps the most important part of the study, since my main concern is to interpret how educational decisions are made.

School decisions are also made within the broader political context of a number of *city, state, and federal agencies* that review the board's capital budget for school construction, that are responsible for housing, urban renewal, and poverty programs, and that serve as mediaries between civic groups and the board. They include the mayor, the Board of Estimate, City Planning Commission, Site Selection Board, City Commission on Human Rights, Housing Authority, and Housing and Redevelopment Board—among others.

I have found it useful to view the controversies over public education in New York City as a kind of "ecology of games," a concept that suggests that the municipality is a kind of territorial or ecological field, composed of many social structures, each of which tends to confront a particular issue in terms of its own interests, maintenance needs, inner agendas, or what Norton Long calls its separate games.[9] The agendas of each organization provide the logic for its actions. In many instances, the result may be contrary to the stated interests of the parties. They may all be involved in a game that nobody wins and everybody loses—an outcome, incidentally, that is often characteristic of public-education controversies in New York City. Since nobody wins, the behavior of each participant may seem irrational. In fact, however, if one interprets the participants' behavior in the context of their stated interests, they are acting rationally.

More generally, I have tried to interpret public-education controversies in New York City through the use of sociological models of the "mass society." [10] The term "mass society" has many technical meanings in sociology; I am using it here to refer to the institutions of urban, industrial societies, and especially to the power relations between decision makers and the citizenry. One of these models suggests that social and political changes in large urban centers are hampered because power is in the hands of a closed élite of public officials and civic groups, supposedly insulated from the masses and with a vested interest in maintaining the status quo. The other model suggests that change is hampered because of the increasing vulnerability of public officials in mass democracies to pressures and counter-pressures from leaders representing various publics. Many of my interpretations of the relations between board and city officials and their constituencies are partial tests of each point of view. These are not just abstract, sociological notions. They are relevant to interpreting how and why large cities are governed the way they are and what some of the levers for social change may be.

One of the advantages of a case study is that one can explore in depth the style and workings of an institution, and I have tried to do that for the New York City schools and their politics. Fred M. Hechinger, education writer for the *New York Times,* has coined the term "the New York City syndrome" to characterize the city's lack of genuine innovation. The course of the New York City school struggle reflects this condition. On controversial issues like desegregation and decentralization, there have been many studies, public exchanges and "dialogues" between contesting parties, hearings until all participants are in a state of acute exhaustion, advanced policy statements and actual programs for reform, promising action, and then very little if any implementation. This study examines the validity of such a view and suggests how the politics might be changed.

I am not interested in simply recording events, or as one sociologist used to say, in "telling the news." Journalists do that, and in many cases they do it much better than a sociologist might. I concentrate much more on interpreting the news, in the hope that a sociological analysis of controversies over public education may suggest better solutions for the future than there have been in the past. The policy implications of this study are discussed throughout the book.

My investigation concentrated most heavily on the period from May, 1963, through February, 1968. I began with 1963 because it coincides with the sharp rise of militant civil rights activity and with a query from the State Education Commissioner to all local school boards throughout the state asking for reports on their plans for increasing the amount of racial balance in their schools. My sources for data were extensive interviews, observation at meetings and hearings, press coverage of events, newsletters and documents of interest groups, and studies done by and for the Board of Education.* Since New York City politics is an "over-organized" and "factional" one, and since all interest groups often articulate their views in public, there is no lack of data for a study of this nature.

Fortunately, my staff and I were able to interview most of the influential leaders and activists on the desegregation issue, at least for the period I was most interested in interpreting. So much of the controversy since 1963 has been so intense that it was not difficult to reach the key participants.

The one place where it was most difficult to get data was the school system itself. Many headquarters officials were reluctant to talk freely about how decisions got made. This reluctance is common to officials in many other public and private institutions; this institution, however, has a particular style that makes it even more resistant to study than most. Its officials have been isolated for decades from the city and from any outside review, and now they are under constant attack and tend to be inordi-

* There have been so many studies of the New York City schools that it is important to distinguish what this one purports to do that previous ones have not. Many administrative-effectiveness studies have been commissioned since the late 1930s, and they have been helpful to me in many ways—to provide some orientation to understanding a system that has not changed much, fundamentally, since these studies started accumulating; and to understand how and why reports with useful recommendations for reform get shelved. They have not looked at the schools in the context of the entire city—its demography, interest group politics, and government—nor have they generally been based on the intensive field work (interviewing, observation) that I have pursued.

One social science study should be mentioned as well. Dr. Marilyn Gittell and Dr. Theodore Hollander of The City University of New York have done a comparative study of innovation in six big-city school systems, one of which was New York; and Gittell published a separate monograph, *Participants and Participation,* dealing with decision-making in the system and its informal power structure. Though there is some convergence between this study and mine, there are substantial differences in scope, conceptualization, and some in findings. References to such convergencies and differences are made at appropriate sections in the text.

nately suspicious of any outsiders. The institution has taken on an almost "paranoid" tone in recent years. To illustrate: One headquarters official recounted that when he moved to a professional post, all his relationships at the board changed. Colleagues began asking him why he ate lunch with particular people, why he was or was not present at particular meetings. The system is a "total institution" for its officials and they are preoccupied with its internal politics and status order. They are at the same time withdrawn from and often suspicious of or arrogant toward outsiders. Such comments as: "We're tired of studies by people who have never taught in the system," and "Nobody could be effective as a superintendent unless he had been in the system for many years," reflect this attitude.*

My data on the Board of Education come much more from the interviews than from personal observation. School officials may, of course, contest its validity on such grounds, but they would do so anyway. I have checked all the observations and reports I could and have only included in the book those that stood up under such continued attempts at cross-validation.

This study does not assume that desegregation is necessarily the answer to the shortcomings of the school system, nor does it propose to answer important pedagogical questions. I am not a specialist on matters of instructional methods and curriculum development, nor am I trained in relevant fields of psychology. I assume, however, that many of the problems of public education are administrative, social, and political. Even matters of instruction and curriculum involve sociological questions. Indeed, one of the basic questions to which I address the study is how a white middle class institution can provide adequate educational services to lower class black and Puerto Rican populations.

The reader should be clear about my views on what desegregation can do for quality of education and on what came out of the desegregation movement. There is increasing evidence from the Coleman Report, the U.S. Civil Rights Commission Report, and studies of the effects of school desegregation in such suburban communities as White Plains, Evanston, and Berkeley, confirming the argument that desegregated education does not necessarily hamper the achievement of white middle

* It is important to add that all the board members and a few professionals were most cooperative.

class pupils and does substantially upgrade that of black pupils from the ghetto.* [11]

I believe that on balance, despite its many failures, the desegregation movement brought many benefits, the most important of which was that it made more visible the many inadequacies of the school system and helped to mobilize civic groups to question the entire institution of public education more than they had in the past. If the desegregation controversy led only to a greater realization that the way to reform public education is to take some of the monopolistic power away from school professionals and the wider educational establishment—teacher training institutions, professional associations—it will have served a significant social purpose.

It is difficult in a study of this nature to say how much each of the discussed factors contributes to the failure of public education in New York City. It would be absurd to suggest that the schools are the primary cause of many social problems with which they must deal, or that they alone can provide solutions. There are pathologies in the ghetto and in relations among races and classes, just as there are in the interest group politics and in the governmental agencies. The demographic, social, and technological changes of the past twenty years may have created problems in metropolitan centers that cannot be solved through existing institutions. But one of my main points is that much controversy on public education reflects problems inside the New York Board of Education. Bureaucratic pathology within the school system—in addition to pressures from its clients, their escalating demands, conditions within the ghetto, the fragmented structure of city government, and the limited planning —is a key factor in the school system's failure. Furthermore, this condition of bureaucratic pathology often contributes to these pressures, these ghetto conditions, and these other problems.

Two recent books, Richard J. Whalen's _A City Destroying Itself_ and Barry Gottehrer's _New York City in Crisis_, have

---

* The single most important factor affecting the extent to which desegregation helps both middle and lower class pupils is the _social climate_ of the school. Desegregation works when it takes place in a predominantly middle class milieu. This is why it is more successful and feasible in white middle class suburbs than in large inner cities. When at least 60–70% of the pupils are middle class (mostly white), there is little immediate danger of the school tipping, and slower pupils can be dispersed throughout the school in a way that does not hamper instruction in any single classroom.

argued that New York City government cannot deal with the municipality's mounting social problems.[12] It seems to me that the struggle in New York City over school desegregation and the quality of education in the ghetto is in many ways a microcosm of the cities' crisis, directly related to the general questions not only of desegregation but of the departure of the white middle class, problems of unemployment and manpower, the departure of business and industry, poverty, urban renewal, and housing.

I hope that this book communicates quite clearly my own sense of urgency about the schools. I believe that the schools are critical to the city's future, and that drastic and radical solutions are needed immediately. Solutions must be worked out in collaboration with such other institutions as city hall, business, labor, universities, foundations, and civic groups.

I believe further that the past two decades have seen little if any educational reform, despite the best intentions of some school and city officials. Now that the decentralization of the school system has been proposed as a solution, there is the possibility that it, too, may undergo the same fate as the policy of desegregation. The civic groups I will be describing are still fragmented and unable to form a strong coalition for change. And the Board of Education is still able to discredit decentralization through poor administrative communications and through protectionist power blocs (administrators, supervisors, teachers) inside the system.

Of great significance is the Board of Education's active role in shaping and promoting a "politics of futility" that exists in New York City around the public schools. The institution has *organizational defenses* that allow it to function in inefficient, unprofessional, undemocratic, and politically costly ways without evoking more of a revolution or push for radical change than has yet emerged. It has an almost unlimited capacity for absorbing protest and externalizing the blame, for confusing and dividing the opposition, "seeming" to appear responsive to legitimate protest by issuing sophisticated and progressive policy statements that are poorly implemented, if at all, and then pointing to all its paper "accomplishments" over the years as evidence both of good faith and effective performance.

The board continues to be successful in these strategies. The fact that no strong change-oriented coalition has yet emerged is proof enough of this fact. The system is much like a punching bag. Protest groups can hit it in one place, and it simply returns to an old equilibrium. Even hitting it in several places has not helped to effect basic structural change. It has been able to maintain its archaic programs, not solely for protectionist motives, but just by its normal cumbersome workings.

One purpose of the book is to help new participants from falling into the same nonproductive relationships with one another and with the board that past participants have done. An analysis of the desegregation struggle is more than just history, then. It is meant to portray the major actors, coalitions, and strategies in that controversy to alert more people to present and future versions. Though the slogans and goals of the school protest movement have changed—from desegregation to community control and decentralization—the political dynamics are the same. And what happened to desegregation may happen again and again, unless people are aware of the political dynamics and act on such an awareness.

The consequences of such a repetition are very ugly to contemplate. I believe that if school officials and the other involved interests fail to decentralize in such a way as to produce an effective and responsible public school system, community protest may grow so intense as to tear the social fabric of the city apart. This crisis must not be allowed to continue for much longer, since everybody involved is losing. My purpose is to suggest how it developed and present some recommendations for reform.

Social scientists differ in how strongly they feel about the phenomena they study. At one time, the notions of "value neutrality" and "objectivity" reigned supreme among sociologists.[13] There are now many within the profession who feel they should take a stronger stand on major social problems. I am part of this group. This is not to forsake the tools of sociological analysis, which often help us understand social phenomena. Nor is it to search in any moralistic and partisan way for scapegoats to account for the pathologies that now characterize our cities. Rather, I take the position that analysis of complexity is not enough, and that the social scientist has a moral obligation to devote much of his energies to suggesting remedies for the many social problems in the cities of mid-twentieth century America.

❧

THE FAILURE OF DESEGREGATION: A BRIEF HISTORY

New York City's Board of Education responded immediately to the 1954 Supreme Court decision, stating in December of that year that "It is now the clearly reiterated policy and program of the Board of Education of the City of New York to devise and put into operation a plan which will prevent the further development of such segregated schools, and would integrate the existing ones as quickly as practicable." [1] Since then it has formulated many desegregation plans, issued policy statements, done studies, and established committees, commissions, and subcommissions on desegregation. Some of the most advanced policy statements ever written on school desegregation were developed by New York City's Board of Education. And they recommended basic, not diversionary, strategies, including site selection, rezoning, changes in feeder patterns, pairings, and educational complexes and parks. Yet, in the more than twelve years of such policy statements there has been little implementation. [2]

The number of predominantly Negro and Puerto Rican schools, according to Board of Education figures (90% or more Negro and Puerto Rican pupils at the elementary level and 85% at the junior high and high school level), increased from 118 in 1960 to 201 in 1966. [3] In 1960, they accounted for 15% of all schools, in 1965 for 23%—indicating an increase in segregation. At the same time, the number of predominantly white schools has decreased from 327 to 237, a decrease from 42 to 31% of the schools. Finally, the number of mid-range schools (between 10 and 90% Negro and Puerto Rican pupils at the elementary level and 15 to 85% beyond that) increased slightly during this period from 337 to 387, accounting for 43% in 1960 and 46% in 1965. The data thus suggest a mixed trend, with more segregation among Negro and Puerto Rican pupils and less among whites.

The pattern becomes clearer if we look at the figures for Negro–Puerto Rican pupils and whites separately. In 1960, 41% of Negro–Puerto Rican pupils were in segregated schools as defined above, compared with 49% in 1965. And although the proportion of mid-range schools has risen slightly, the proportion of Negro and Puerto Rican pupils in such schools actually declined from 56 to 48%. Where there was less segregation, it was because Negroes and Puerto Ricans were increasingly moving into predominantly white neighborhoods.

Furthermore, two ways in which the data are grouped by the Central Zoning Unit at school headquarters may well disguise the actual trend toward increased segregation for Negro pupils. First, Puerto Rican and Negro pupils are lumped together in the statistics.* Since Puerto Rican pupils attend mid-range and predominantly white schools more than Negro pupils do, reflecting the wider dispersion of the Puerto Rican population throughout the city, lumping the two groups together only obscures the trend toward segregation for Negroes. Second, if headquarters officials had broken down the category of integrated schools into smaller subgroups, the distribution would have become bi-modal, that is, most of the Negro pupils would turn up at one end, in schools that are 70–90% Negro–Puerto Rican, and most of the whites at the other.

This picture contrasts sharply with the situation in 1960, when many more white and Negro–Puerto Rican pupils were in the middle of the distribution, in schools with 30–70% of each ethnic category. In short, there has been a substantial increase in segregation for minority group populations in the last five years.

The standard interpretation of this phenomenon is that it reflects a change in the city's population and the increased housing segregation. The continued departure of the white middle class, the continued withdrawal from the public schools of whites who stay in the city, the increase in young, low income

---

* Certain ethnic groups—Cubans, Haitians, etc.—are often categorized as Puerto Ricans or Negroes. Many are in the Upper West Side and Central Harlem schools in Manhattan.

Negro and Puerto Rican families whose birth rates are much higher than those of whites, and the growth of low income housing projects in ghetto areas, further ghettoizing them and spreading the ghetto out across the city all make it hard to improve the racial balance of the schools.

The increase in housing segregation is a special obstacle. It limits the number of fringe areas,* thus limiting the prospects for a mixed pupil population, without resort to transfer programs involving long-distance traveling for large numbers of children. Even the most militant civil rights leaders generally accept the argument that housing segregation has contributed, in part, to school segregation. But they do not agree that it is so great a problem as the board says it is.

Even if the housing pattern allowed for more school desegregation—so the argument continues—there are further obstacles: chronic scarcities of trained and committed staff, building space, and funds.

There can be no question about the importance of such conditions. Their impact seems to corroborate the view that the board is held responsible for failing to bring about change that it has neither the authority nor influence to implement. This study is in part a test of that conventional view.

Data that I gathered early in this study on the increasingly wide gap between the board's many advanced policy statements and their implementation suggested to me that there might well be more reasons for the increasing segregation than the conventional view implies. The city's experience on Open Enrollment—a voluntary pupil transfer plan designed to promote both desegregation and more even utilization—the first desegregation technique it tried, is a case in point: fewer than 3% of the pupils to whom the plan was applicable in the first years of its operation (1960–1964) actually transferred.[4] As the authors of the Allen Committee Report of 1964 on prospects for desegregation in the city stated:

> The (Board of Education's own) Commission on Integration recommendations on the redistribution of pupils through "permissive zoning" and busing were not implemented.[5]

The board's policy statements, however, went well beyond such voluntary plans. They included rezoning, changes in

---

* Fringe areas are those neighborhoods located on or immediately adjacent to the "racial frontier," which separates black and white communities.

feeder patterns, and fundamental changes in the construction program so that schools would be built in fringe areas wherever possible. On balance these plans were not implemented. For example, 39 of the 106 projects in the board's 1964–1965 building program were for local school areas where it was estimated that 90% or more of the pupils would be Negro and Puerto Rican. Thus, more than one-third of the planned schools were guaranteed to be segregated. Many might have been located in fringe areas to prevent that. The board's most recent construction budget provides that well over 55% of its funds will be spent on segregated schools.[6] In one instance, in southeast Brooklyn, the board planned to build seven segregated elementary and intermediate schools, rather than accept the request of many local and citywide civic groups, backed by State Education Commissioner Allen, that it build those schools in desegregated educational parks. To quote the Allen Report once again:

> The school building program as presently set forth reinforces substantially the historic pattern of building on sites within the most segregated areas. This is the case chiefly in Negro residential areas, but it is also true in some mainly white neighborhoods, and thus helps to intensify both forms of segregation.[7]

The consistent board practice has been to "build the schools where the children are," despite continued pressure from civil rights groups and continued encouragement from the State Education Department to do otherwise. The board's actual school construction and site selection decisions are at wide variance with its stated desegregation policies.

Why is it, then, that even in New York City, though the Board of Education at least got to the policy-making stage, there has been so little implementation? Why has the board tended to zone and build schools in a way that followed rather than offset the segregated housing pattern? And why in some areas has the board zoned so as to counteract an integrated housing pattern? To answer these questions is to suggest some of the political forces that have contributed, I think substantially, to the increasing segregation of New York City's schools.

The Academic Stage

The New York City school desegregation struggle has gone through several stages. During the first, from 1954 to 1960, the board made studies, formed committees, issued reports and policy statements. Nevertheless, it maintained its commitment to the neighborhood school concept, giving in to civil rights protest groups only when they seemed to have strong local or city-wide support, and often not even then. The board's main changes were some rezonings, fringe-area school construction, and voluntary transfers to relieve overcrowding. Meanwhile, pressures were continually building up from ghetto groups for more desegregation.

A report by the Public Education Association, a civic agency concerned with educational reform, submitted in October, 1955, and commissioned by the Board of Education, pointed to marked differences in quality between predominantly Negro–Puerto Rican schools and white schools. This led to further reports and recommendations for reform by the board's Commission on Integration, formed in May, 1955.[8] An early commission statement that "it is a desirable policy to promote ethnic integration in our schools as a positive educational experience of which no child in the city should be deprived" expressed its mission. This reflected the board's policy statement of December, 1954, that segregated education is inferior education.

The commission was divided into six subcommissions: zoning; teacher assignments and personnel; community relations and information; guidance, educational stimulation and placement; physical plant and maintenance; and educational standards and curriculum. During the next three years, the board held public hearings on the reports of each subcommission, approved some of their recommendations, and adopted further policy resolutions.[9]

The two most controversial reports—on teacher assignment and zoning—were the last to be submitted.[10] The first recommended transfer of experienced teachers to ghetto schools and was nullified by the teachers' union. The zoning report recommended setting up a zoning unit at headquarters to develop a comprehensive plan for maximum integration. It even recommended that elementary schools be built in so-called fringe areas. Though the Central Zoning Unit was established in 1957, Superintendent Jansen did not give it any authority to implement the report's recommendations. He announced in July, 1957, that authority for zoning would continue to be

vested in district superintendents and that permissive zoning*
for integration would not be allowed. He reasserted his intention of following the neighborhood school concept in zoning
and site location.

Other commission recommendations were quashed, also. Dr.
Kenneth Clark† stated publicly that Superintendent Jansen was
"deliberately confusing, delaying, distorting, and sidetracking
the reports of our commission." Some Negro members of the
commission threatened to resign. And Mrs. Rose Shapiro, its
chairman and now a member of the Board of Education, said
the zoning report had been altered substantially after the public
hearing.[11]

In September, 1957, Superintendent Jansen announced that
an experiment in permissive zoning was under way, and was intended to determine whether Negro students would be willing
to travel a long distance to reach integrated schools. He allowed
thirteen Negro pupils to travel from Bedford–Stuyvesant to
Abraham Lincoln High School in the Coney Island area. Since
this involved two to three hours of busing each day, many civic
groups regarded it more as an endurance test than an expression of commitment to desegregation as board policy. By early
1959, it became clear to all interested groups that the board was
not implementing any of the recommendations of its own commission and subcommissions. One civic leader has correctly referred to this period as the "academic stage."

Civil rights groups, meanwhile, responding to the board's
inactions and delaying tactics, became more militant. Bedford–
Stuyvesant in Brooklyn and Harlem in Manhattan were the
main centers of protest. Rev. Milton Galamison and his close
associate, Mrs. Annie Stein, led the Bedford–Stuyvesant protests.

---

* "Permissive zoning" is a procedure that allows parents to transfer
their children from segregated neighborhood schools to underused schools
outside the immediate area. Parents may transfer their children, but they
are not forced to.

† Dr. Kenneth Clark is a nationally known Negro psychologist and
professor at the College of the City of New York. His research and testimony
on the psychological and educational damage to Negro children attending
segregated schools was one of the main bases for the 1954 Supreme Court
decision in the Brown case, outlawing segregation. Clark was very active in
the desegregation struggle in New York City, especially in the 1950s and
early sixties, and he is now active once again in the decentralization movement as a member of the State Board of Regents. Clark is now director
of the Metropolitan Applied Research Corporation (MARC), which supports action programs in ghetto areas.

Their first action was in 1956, and was an attempt to integrate a new junior high school (JHS 258) in Bedford–Stuyvesant that was three or four blocks north of Atlantic Avenue, the racial frontier at that time.[12] He had the support of a citywide integrationist coalition—the Intergroup Committee, the Urban League, Dr. Kenneth Clark, local parent associations, and labor unions and religious groups—but the board refused to move. The board opened 258 as an all-Negro school, though it later compromised on another junior high in the area (JHS 61) and tried to integrate it. Reverend Galamison's organization, Parents Workshop, representing the Brooklyn branch of the National Association for the Advancement of Colored People (NAACP), got citywide support for its protests from many white as well as Negro groups, and even Mayor Wagner promised to help. In a public speech before an annual state NAACP convention, Wagner was quoted as saying: "Today is Sunday and I cannot do anything about it. I'll take care of it tomorrow." [13] He was running for the Senate then. But despite all the announced support for integrating 258, the board opened and maintained it as a segregated school. School officials, real estate interests, and white and Negro middle class parent groups prevailed.*

There were many other cases of the board's subverting its own policy statements, and they all followed a similar pattern. New schools would first be placed badly for desegregation, away from fringe areas. Then the board would zone for segregation, and when civil rights groups and their allies protested, the board would try unworkable compromises that often discredited the whole desegregation concept. The history of school desegregation controversies throughout the city, and especially in Brooklyn, is full of such stories.

One of the most significant was PS 289 in Crown Heights, then a white area. When 289 was about to open, Parents Workshop, working together with twenty parent associations of surrounding schools, demanded zoning for desegregation. The Board of Education gave them information on the number of black and white children, block by block, in Crown Heights, the

* Upward mobile Negroes who had moved out of the Bedford–Stuyvesant ghetto to white residential areas did not want their children forced to attend schools with poor Negroes from the ghetto. They also wanted to limit the number of Negroes in their new communities, so that whites would not panic and move out.

Eastern Parkway area to the south, and Bedford–Stuyvesant to the north, and the parents worked out a plan integrating all the schools in the area. "That was one time when we worked through so many tensions," explained a parent leader, "and got the support of all the white schools involved. Mrs. Sands, the board member from Brooklyn, was for it. But Frank Turner, the head of Central Zoning, opposed the plan. He wouldn't let the middle class Negro kids from the other side of Eastern Parkway who had made it go 'back' to 289, where they'd be with another element of blacks. He held a secret meeting with the black *nouveaux riches* which was written up as a story in the *Amsterdam News* [14] through information provided by one of our people. Anyhow, we lost. They zoned 289 so that it opened 90% black. There was a determined campaign to hold the line at Eastern Parkway, the racial frontier. This was a case where the white community was ready to desegregate and the board stopped it." *

Other cases, PS 41, 45, 61, 270—the details of which are repetitions of PS 289—are further illustrations of conscious gerrymandering for purposes of segregation, in areas of Crown Heights and Bedford–Stuyvesant where desegregation was physically possible. Gerrymandering was especially rampant at the high school level. One of the most dramatic cases was Erasmus Hall High School in Flatbush whose zone lines were shaped like a finger, including white pupils from a mile or two away—above Prospect Park—but excluding blacks who lived much closer (to the north), and who traveled several miles by bus to Eastern District High School. Much of the Brooklyn protest related to cases like these.[15]

Similar protests began in Harlem during this period. Militant parent groups, under the leadership of Paul Zuber, a Negro lawyer, and Ella Baker, an NAACP branch official, organized several strikes and boycotts in the late 1950s to protest the board's unwillingness to implement its own permissive zoning plans. They wanted their children transferred from overcrowded and inferior ghetto schools. In one court case brought by striking parents against the board, Judge Justine Wise Polier

---

* The pattern of the board's actions on PS 289—first selecting a site deep in the ghetto, and later locating it near the white community, only to zone it for segregation—was repeated in many other contested cases at a later time, the most dramatic of which were JHS 275 in Canarsie, Brooklyn, and JHS 8 in Rochdale Village, Queens, both of which are discussed below.

ruled in favor of the parents on grounds that the quality of teaching in their schools was markedly inferior to that in predominantly white schools.[16]

The community's mood in 1958 and 1959 was reflected in strikes and boycotts over the inability of Negro parents to send their children to schools outside their district. Zuber represented a group called the "Harlem Nine," which staged a 156-day boycott in 1958. The board finally zoned their children to schools outside. A similar protest in Bedford–Stuyvesant by a group led by Reverend Galamison, which called itself the "Brooklyn Seven," took place at the same time. In 1959, there was a further protest by twenty-five Harlem mothers demanding that their children be allowed to transfer to Washington Heights and Riverdale schools. At a court hearing, Superintendent Theobald, who had succeeded Jansen, granted their request, but said that it set no precedent. The board did, however, transfer the first group of Negro pupils into predominantly white schools in September, 1959; 302 eight- and nine-year-olds were bussed from Bedford–Stuyvesant in Brooklyn to the Ridgewood–Glendale section of Queens. White residents of the area staged a brief boycott in reaction.[17]

The two main issues at this time were transfers for relief from overcrowding and the construction of schools in fringe areas. Ghetto groups, with some support from white liberal groups, were attempting to make the board live up to the recommendations of its subcommission on zoning and to its own policy statements.

In 1960, after limited board implementation, leaders of Parents Workshop decided to take the initiative once again and develop a new strategy, asking for rezoning for desegregation. Up to that time, there had been no transfers for desegregation but only, as Superintendent Theobald stated repeatedly, for more even utilization of school facilities.

The Voluntary Stage

The second stage, from 1960 to 1963, was characterized by the limited implementation of Open Enrollment, a voluntary transfer plan designed specifically to promote desegregation. Parents Workshop had threatened a citywide strike for the opening of school in September, 1960, if the board failed to come up with a plan. By 1962, Open Enrollment had been mandated on a citywide basis for elementary, junior high, and high school levels. Yet, Reverend Galamison told the board during this period that he wanted a timetable, and considered Open Enrollment only a first step.

Whatever success the Open Enrollment program had was due mainly to efforts of civic groups. Local civil rights leaders reported that the board rarely gave detailed instructions to parents as to what schools their children could attend and how they might get there. Many parents whose children were eligible for transfers never knew about it.*

Superintendent Theobald was negotiating all the while to make just enough concessions to keep the level of protest down, without at the same time activating the neighborhood school opposition. He maintained what he called his "Black Cabinet," a group of civil rights leaders including Judge Hubert Delaney; Dr. Frank Horne of the Mayor's Commission on Human Rights; Dr. Edward Lewis, Arthur Wright, and Alexander J. Allen of the Urban League; Dr. Kenneth Clark; Richard Plaut of the National Negro Scholarship Fund; the Honorable George Gregory, Jr., from the Civil Service Commission; Thomas B. Dyett, attorney; and Robert Weaver, then at the Housing and Redevelopment Board.[18]

It was after conferring with his Black Cabinet that Theobald implemented his first Open Enrollment plan, transferring elementary school children from Bedford–Stuyvesant to Ridgewood–Glendale in Queens, in September, 1959. He defined that transfer as a unique situation, however, not to be construed as setting any precedent. He waited for the build-up of pressure from local civil rights groups, from his Black Cabinet, and from the mayor before implementing Open Enrollment, and he played down its relevance for desegregation, always stressing that Open Enrollment would relieve overcrowding.[19]

A new reform board was appointed in 1961 in the wake of some construction scandals, and Theobald left in 1962, but there was little more implementation of Open Enrollment. The civil rights movement did have a few isolated successes, for ex-

---

* The highest percentages of transfers were in Brooklyn, due largely to Parents Workshop. They had tooled up for the task in earlier years, having persuaded many parents from Brooklyn Heights, Fort Greene, Williamsburg, and Bedford–Stuyvesant to transfer their children to underused white schools. They continued this work by telling parents of transportation routes and taking them on tours. They took Brooklyn and Queens maps and developed transfer plans within the framework of the board's programs. Thus, parents took over th ejob the board was supposed to be doing.

ample, in the rezoning of East Harlem pupils to predominantly white schools in Yorkville and the silk stocking, upper Park Avenue area (PS 6).[20] But there were many failures, the most publicized being the zoning and site-location controversy over JHS 275 in southeast Brooklyn that was built on the edge of the black (Brownsville) and white (Canarsie) communities and then zoned to include few (12%) whites.[21] The movement failed, however, to prevail against the board's poor and limited implementation of Open Enrollment.

The Non-Voluntary Stage

By 1963, civil rights leaders had become convinced that Open Enrollment would never appreciably desegregate the schools. The struggle moved on to what might be called its non-voluntary stage. It began in May, 1963, with State Education Commissioner James Allen's request that the New York City Board of Education submit a report to him on the racial composition of its schools, including a statement of plans to redress "racial imbalance" in schools that departed markedly from a 50–50 Negro–white ratio.[22] Allen's actions came when civil rights leaders were formulating new demands and his actions reinforced their pressures for better desegregation plans.

The next two years were characterized by intensified conflict between civil rights groups and the board and between both and the neighborhood school movement. Indeed, a series of self-generating conflicts was set in motion that polarized and stalemated relations among key participants in the struggle, while the board still refused to implement any but the most limited desegregation experiments.

In July, 1963, the NAACP threatened a boycott and called a meeting to form a coordinating body of civil rights groups, the Citywide Committee for Integrated Schools.[23] The boycott was called off when the board agreed to develop a citywide plan and timetable by December. When the December report contained neither a plan nor a timetable and few plans for non-voluntary desegregation techniques, civil rights leaders charged that the new superintendent, Dr. Calvin Gross, had acted in a "spineless and vacillating manner." [24] They made immediate plans for a boycott, which took place, as scheduled, on February 3rd, under the leadership of Reverend Galamison and Bayard Rustin, the national civil rights leader, who helped to organize the boycott during the last week. About 464,000 pupils or 44.8% of the total enrollment were absent that day, well above the normal 100,000. Though board president James Donovan referred to it as a "fizzle," it was clearly not that. A week later Reverend Galamison announced that the civil rights coordinating group of which he was chairman, the Citywide Committee for Integrated Schools, would conduct another one-day boycott in March or April, "whenever it will hurt the board the most economically." * He said he would call it "Fizzle No. 2." 25

Soon after the first boycott, the board asked State Education Commissioner James Allen to appoint a group to do a study of New York City, suggesting specific desegregation proposals that would be possible there. Allen appointed a committee composed of Dr. Kenneth Clark, psychologist at CCNY, Dr. John Fischer, President of Teachers College, and Rabbi Judah Kahn of New York City. Some civil rights groups wanted to wait until the Allen Committee Report before conducting another boycott, while others did not want to wait, and clear differences emerged as to appropriate strategy.

Liberal groups then stated publicly their opposition to some of the civil rights demands and tactics.† The Anti-Defamation League, the American Jewish Committee, the Liberal Party, and the New York Civil Liberties Union all expressed their opposition to the bussing of white children for purposes of desegregation. Only the American Jewish Congress had backed the demand of civil rights groups for citywide pairings and other non-voluntary plans.26

Galamison met additional resistance within the Citywide Committee. A CORE representative expressed dissatisfaction with his leadership. NAACP pulled out right after the first boycott, followed later by national CORE, though the Urban League maintained a tenuous tie.‡ Officials in all these groups objected to Galamison's tendency to speak out unilaterally and to announce decisions not yet agreed upon or even discussed by the entire coordinating group.27 Many felt that a second boycott

---

* State aid to the city schools is made partly on the basis of pupil enrollment, based in turn on attendance figures.

† They had privately expressed their opposition to non-voluntary school desegregation plans and to civil rights demands on many previous occasions.

‡ Nine of the thirteen local CORE chapters, however, supported the second boycott.

at that time would be a tactical mistake and might jeopardize the progress they had already made.*

The second boycott, on March 16, 1964, drew roughly 300,-000 pupils.[28] The board announced that 268,000 stayed out but later stated that it had compiled the figures in haste and that there might have been more absentees. It didn't really matter, though, because a backlash had already started to set in. Civil rights groups attempted to heal some of their differences.† NAACP officials announced that their organization was not opposed to another boycott, but this did not prevent the board from continuing to backtrack on its original plans, as it sensed the growing opposition from white parents and the lack of unity among the Negro leadership.‡

On May 28 the board announced its desegregation program, calling for four pairings, the rezoning of eight junior high schools, shifts of sixth and ninth graders into new junior high and high school arrangements, and a redesign of four high schools to make them comprehensive schools.[29] Gross negotiated with civil rights leaders to defer their demands for more changes for another year, while he sat down with them in private meetings to work out further reforms.

Meanwhile, in April, 1964, a set of recommendations for desegregation was released by the Allen Committee. This group called for four-year comprehensive high schools and integrated four-year middle schools—both organized in educational complexes and parks so as to draw on large, heterogenous populations—and much more fringe-area construction.§ The private meetings between Gross and civil rights leaders focused on these recommendations, and civil rights leaders abandoned any further pressure for pairings.||

Despite the new show of civil rights unity around the Allen

---

* Galamison and his followers regarded the Citywide Committee as a coalition with a single chairman and strategy. Headquarters officials of the NAACP, CORE, and Urban League regarded it as a coordinating group that should try to follow a single strategy but should use several if necessary, as various organizational interests demanded.

† NAACP and CORE officials approached the Urban League's representatives in private and attempted to form a new coalition without Galamison, but this was turned down.

‡ By this time, the Citywide Committee was no longer the coordinating body it was set up to be.

§ Dr. Robert Dentler and his staff, then at the Institute for Urban Studies at Teachers College, did the research for the Allen Committee.

|| Some had given up on the idea months before.

Report and the private meetings with Gross, the board gave no indication of embarking on any significant desegregation program, and meetings with Gross broke down in the fall of 1964.[30] In January of 1965 Galamison led a shutdown of segregated junior high schools and of special "600" schools for delinquent and retarded children, which drew between 4,250 and 4,500 students out of a total registration of 18,000 in the schools he selected. The shutdown was in direct protest against the board's failure to begin desegregating the junior high schools, a key recommendation in the Allen Report which Gross had agreed in private meetings with civil rights leaders to implement. It went on for six weeks, accompanied by the arrests of Galamison and many of his followers, and ended because Galamison ran out of resources. Demands for improvement of the "600" schools and for more supervisory positions for black people were also pressed in this boycott, and they remain important issues to this day.[31]

Just after the shutdown ended, the board dismissed Gross. His integration report was nevertheless presented and referred to by the board as the Gross Blueprint. It involved more transfers of sixth and ninth graders and the beginnings of a grade reorganization plan to effect more desegregation. Most civil rights groups condemned it, and NAACP representatives led a demonstration protesting it as a watered-down Allen Report.[32]

On April 22, 1965, the board announced its new policy statement, committing itself to a major reorganization of the school system along the lines of the Allen Report for new four-year intermediate schools, four-year comprehensive high schools, and some pre-kindergarten programs in minority group areas. All civil rights groups commended the statement.[33]

But little has been done to implement these policies, and there has been much backtracking. Superintendent Donovan, who succeeded Gross, promised at the time to come up with more specific plans in a year and asked for that time to "do studies" and "re-tool." The plans he and the board came up with in early 1966 so antagonized civil rights groups that they staged a protest at board headquarters in April to express their disappointment with the report.[34]

Meanwhile, the board planned to build most intermediate schools in the ghetto or in segregated white communities rather than in fringe areas. It hedged on whether these schools should have three or four grades. And it built them all at only 1,800 capacity, thereby limiting their enrollment to a narrow area and precluding the possibility of desegregation. Just as Open Enrollment had been the battleground in earlier stages, so junior high school desegregation was the issue at this stage, and the results were roughly the same, namely, little was done.

Civil rights leaders were so demoralized by this time and so tired after their long series of defeats that many of them temporarily retired from the desegregation struggle. A number went to work in anti-poverty agencies or in the new Lindsay administration,* where they felt they might see more tangible results. The movement had reached its greatest influence at the time of its first boycott. After the fruitless 1964 summer negotiations with Gross, the leadership lost the support it originally had from parents. In Galamison's 1965 boycott, relatively few parents came out, and a new mood was in the air.† With leaders talking behind closed doors and getting no results, parents turned away from programmatic action and toward Black Power with its emphasis on community participation and control.‡

The Decentralization, Community-Control Phase

Some carried on the desegregation battle with a new strategy. Several court suits were brought against the board for expanding segregation.§ But the black community has temporarily given up on pressing the New York City Board of Education for more desegregation.

The school struggle entered a new phase in September, 1966, with the Intermediate School 201 controversy.[35] Parents in the East Harlem community where 201 was to open at the start of that school year said the board should choose between either desegregating the school as it had promised on numerous occasions, or giving much more control over the school to local

* John V. Lindsay took office as mayor on January 1, 1966.
† Children were most active in the 1965 boycott, not parents.
‡ September, 1966, marked the beginning of this development.
§ The main cases were demands for an educational park in East Brooklyn, and for junior high and high school rezoning in Queens. The East Brooklyn suit, brought by Galamison and local parents, is still pending in Queens; the board announced in March, 1968, its plans to rezone Queens high schools, in a case brought by a confederation of civic groups (white and Negro), the Tri-Community Council; the junior high school suit has not been resolved.

parents and community groups. This controversy spawned others throughout the city, as parents, community groups, and often teachers themselves protested against inadequate facilities, and demanded greater control. A Peoples' Board made up of Negro, Puerto Rican, and white leaders was formed in December, 1966, at board headquarters, when a group of irate parents carried on after the lay board had walked out on its own public hearing.[36] It left on finding itself in the midst of clamor and protest from the public in attendance, when it refused to allow a Brownsville mother to speak.

The emphasis within the movement has thus shifted from desegregation to quality and local control, and there is much political logic in the shift. Frustration over the inability of the schools to educate their children and the power of school professionals to subvert desegregation plans, convinced militant civil rights leaders that they would have to dilute that power before they could ever hope to realize any of their goals. This development coincided with the Black Power movement, and also with the state legislature's request that the board produce a decentralization plan by December, 1967, and with Mayor Lindsay's creation of a panel to come up with his own separate plan.

Desegregation Techniques and Their Non-Implementation

The political logic for the community control movement is self-explanatory, but it becomes even more obvious from a brief analysis of how the board handled every new desegregation technique. The board's political caution, basic flaws in administration, in addition to outside political and demographic constraints, contributed to the failure of every plan.

Open Enrollment. Under Open Enrollment, pupils who chose to were allowed to transfer from overcrowded ghetto schools into underutilized white schools. By May, 1966, the total number of pupil transfers under the plan was roughly 22,300—14,440 in elementary grades and 7,860 in the seventh grade. Dr. Jacob Landers, former assistant superintendent in charge of integration activities, reported that "the percentage of applicants has been consistently below 5% of the total eligibles."[37]

The board's explanation for the limited success of the program is that Negro parents did not want to transfer their children out of their local schools. Undoubtedly some parents felt this way and always will. On reviewing the history of how

Open Enrollment was introduced, however, I found that it was inaccurate and unfair to place the responsibility on parents for the small numbers who took advantage of the program.

The problem with Open Enrollment, similar to that in almost every other innovation the board adopted, was an administrative one. The board did develop elaborate instructions to teachers, principals, and district superintendents, and centralized the administration of the program to ensure compliance with directives. However, it stopped far short of effectively monitoring how the plan was carried out, and it did not exert the leadership necessary to actually ensure compliance.

Many parents whose children were eligible for transfers never knew it. And when people were informed, it turned out that local school officials and some headquarters personnel were opposed to the plan. Parents rarely got sufficient information about what schools their children could attend and how they might get there. The school system did little to counteract false statements by "neighborhood school" groups, quoted widely in the press, that described bussing as involving long and arduous trips that would deposit children on the school steps too weary to concentrate in their classes.

Extensive reports furnished to me by some civil rights leaders and school officials, as well as studies done on the program, suggest a widespread pattern of undermining by principals, teachers, and field superintendents, and very limited support for Open Enrollment from headquarters.*

Free Choice Transfer Plan. A test of the hypothesis that more Negro and Puerto Rican pupils would have participated in Open Enrollment if the plan had been implemented, was provided in June, 1964, with the board's Free Choice–Open Enrollment Plan. This was an extension of Open Enrollment that gave graduating fifth-grade pupils moving into grade six of a junior high school (under the board's grade reorganization plan) a choice of transferring to underused white junior highs or of going on to segregated junior high schools within the ghetto. Superintendent Gross ordered the plan, after being pushed to do so by civil rights leaders who had been meeting with him in private.

The civil rights leaders who had negotiated the plan with Gross and his staff were well aware of the limited implementa-

* Unpublished studies by The Urban League and The City Commission on Human Rights.

tion of Open Enrollment. They set up a monitoring system in all the sending schools, to check on the degree to which teachers and principals pushed the plan. As expected, school officials did not publicize it in many cases. As also expected, principals gave lectures to parents on the many costs to their children of transferring out, urging them not to participate in the plan. Civil rights leaders systematically collected all the information they could on these incidents and presented the data to Gross.

He responded at first with disbelief. One of his top headquarters officials told him that principals are professionals and wouldn't act that way. They were so swayed by the data, however, that Gross called a special meeting at headquarters of all principals involved in the program and told them that he really meant what he said in his original order from headquarters: that the plan should be implemented. According to final board estimates,[38] roughly 30% of those pupils eligible for transfer availed themselves of the opportunity, in contrast to the 3% who had participated in Open Enrollment. That first year, 942 pupils transferred, and another 852 did the second. As civil rights pressures diminished, the percent of transfers likewise went down, to 14.8% the second year; this plan, like Open Enrollment, was implemented as much as civil rights pressures were felt.

Pairings. The civil rights movement demanded school pairings, when it became clear that the board was not implementing Open Enrollment. Civil rights leaders assumed that if the board adopted a non-voluntary desegregation plan, this would take the burden off the parents and would force the field superintendents, principals, and teachers to comply with headquarters directives. While there was more compliance than under Open Enrollment, many administrative and planning problems seriously hampered the effectiveness of programs in the schools involved.

Princeton plan pairings* involved the rezoning and consolidation of two contiguous elementary schools, one predominantly Negro and the other predominantly white. All the pupils would attend one of the schools for the first three grades and the other for the last three grades. The New York City Board of Education "experimented" with five such pairings. Initially, in January, 1964, under the pressure of an impending civil rights

---

* The technique was first instituted in Princeton, New Jersey.

boycott, the board had announced that it had a list of twenty-
odd pairings. When faced with counter-pressures from white
civic groups and from school officials at all levels, the board
eliminated all but five from this list.* The board has no plans
for more pairings, and all participants in public education affairs in the city generally agree that future pairings are very unlikely, especially at the elementary school level.

Grade Reorganization, 4-4-4, The Allen Report. When the
Allen Report recommendations for a complete grade reorganization were made public in April, 1964, civil rights groups
warmly endorsed them. Even though Open Enrollment had
failed and few pairings were being planned, the prospect of
integrated four-year middle and high schools, built in consolidated educational complexes and parks † gave a sense of hope
to civil rights leaders after their years of limited success. But
the same pattern prevailed—limited implementation, poor
planning, and chaos in the schools where the program went
into effect.

The general record since April, 1964, on the Allen Report
recommendations has been one of continued delays and of continued inefficiencies in the preliminary experiments that went
into effect. The four-year comprehensive high school is a case
in point. Many middle class white organizations, as well as civil
rights groups, supported the concept as a way to upgrade the
city's high schools and provide for more ethnic and class desegregation. Some of the system's trade high schools are among
the most successful in the nation—in terms of the training they
provide. Other vocational high schools, however, have badly
outdated curricula, and there is much consensus on this point
among civil rights and moderate groups.

Furthermore, the comprehensive high school has gained
more national acceptance among professional educators. It was
in this context that the Allen Committee recommended basic
changes in the high school system in New York City in 1964.
Yet the board delayed for three and one-half years before even

* The politics of those board decisions are discussed in many of the
succeeding chapters.

† Educational complexes and parks are clusters of schools at all levels,
located in a consolidated campus arrangement, and drawing pupils from a
wider geographic area than traditional neighborhood schools. Complexes
are generally conceived on a smaller scale than parks, and as transitional
arrangements from neighborhood schools to parks.

announcing the comprehensive high school as policy, and finally did so only in December, 1967.[39]

The record on intermediate schools is not much more impressive. One of the reasons civil rights groups were so receptive to the Allen Committee recommendations was that they proposed the desegregation of the junior high schools and their conversion to four-year middle schools, to provide a desegregated education from the fifth grade up.

Though the board adopted this recommendation in policy, it did not implement the policy. It deliberated over the next three years on whether the middle school should include three or four years, fearing that middle schools might become too big, thereby depersonalizing relationships within the schools and between them and the community. To ensure that middle schools would be small, the board limited their capacity to 1,800, the same size as the old junior high schools. This gave the middle schools less potential for desegregation than the old junior highs, since those with four grades would have to draw pupils from a smaller geographic area.

As if to ensure that middle schools would not be desegregated, almost all the ones built since 1964 have been located away from fringe areas, toward the center of ghetto or white communities. Furthermore, the board referred site-selection decisions to the nearest local school board,* a move that could only emphasize narrow neighborhood needs. Zoning also has followed neighborhood lines. An evaluation of the middle school program by the Center for Urban Education in 1967 indicated that in nine of the fourteen intermediate schools, the feeder patterns from elementary schools did not achieve ethnic balance.[40]

The Allen Report recommended that educational complexes as well as parks be set up for desegregation after the first four grades, but the board failed to implement these ideas either. Dr. Robert Dentler, a sociologist, who with his colleagues then at the Institute for Urban Studies at Teachers College did the demographic research for the Allen Report, worked for the board under contract to develop plans for complexes in Queens and Brooklyn, but his recommendations were not incorporated in the board's later desegregation efforts—which were them-

* Local school boards are citizen groups selected by the central board to act as a buffer between it and local residents, and represent local residents' interests to field and headquarters school officials.

selves quite modest. The educational complex concept was used later, in 1967, to set up decentralized demonstration units, but these were segregated.*

Educational parks have met a similar fate.[41] The board announced in September, 1965, that it was adopting the educational parks concept as policy, following a June conference at which there was virtual unanimity among the "experts" present—Dentler; Dr. Max Wolff, educational sociologist and research director at the Commonwealth of Puerto Rico; Dr. Dan Dodson, and Dr. Frank Riessman, social scientists at New York University—that parks would make a major contribution to New York City. Once the concept was accepted as policy, it was subject to the same fate as most others—namely, non-implementation. As of March, 1968, the board has developed preliminary plans for three sites, one in the Bronx and two in Brooklyn. All are in middle class white areas and generally preclude the prospect of desegregation without a great deal of long-distance travel for black students. The present mood in the black communities throughout the city, is not conducive to desegregation on such terms or, by now, on any terms.

This is the history, then, a dismal record of increasing segregation, despite a long list of policy statements adopted by the board, endorsing various desegregation techniques. Now let us turn in greater depth to the question of why desegregation failed, what new reform demands it spawned, and what the prospects are for success in getting them accepted.

* See Chapter Eleven for a discussion of the complex educational study.

DEMOGRAPHIC AND HOUSING
PATTERNS

The changes in population experienced by New York City over the past twenty years are the same as those going on in all large northern cities. There has been an exodus of the white middle class from Manhattan and, increasingly, from the outlying boroughs of Brooklyn, Queens, and The Bronx; and an influx of younger, minority group populations with higher birth rates than the remaining whites. The construction of low income housing projects in ghetto areas has further ghettoized the minorities. There has also been extension and hardening of segregated residential patterns.

These demographic and residential changes began in the 1920s, when the first waves of Negro migrants from the South started reaching Harlem, Bedford–Stuyvesant, and other ghetto areas of the city, in substantial numbers. The changes have accelerated since 1946, when more Puerto Ricans and Negroes began to move into New York City.

A recent trend has been the upward mobility of a second or third generation Negro population and their movement to outlying boroughs or to adjacent suburbs. This trend is so far no more than a trickle, but it is likely to accelerate over the next few decades, and its acceleration would directly affect the city's many social problems. If the population of Negro ghettos were to decrease, the task of providing more and better services might be easier. There might even be limited prospects for desegregation in some parts of the city where few such prospects have existed before, but if this meant that the ghettos lost their middle class, however, conditions would worsen. Federally promoted public housing in adjacent suburbs for low income Negroes would ease ghetto conditions much more than the exodus of the black middle class. There is some likelihood that the federal government may try such programs, despite the political resistance they would encounter.*

Another recent trend has been the in-migration of older middle class whites, people with grown children, who return to the inner city to escape the costs of commuting, of local taxes, and of maintaining suburban homes that they no longer need. They move into middle income and luxury housing, on Manhattan's East Side or Upper West Side, to enjoy the amenities and cultural advantages of the city. They are an older, middle class population who have no substantial effect on school desegregation. They are joined in this respect by many older, indigenous, white middle class populations in Queens, The Bronx, and Brooklyn.

Data based on the 1950 and 1960 censuses, supplemented by a New York Department of Health survey in 1964, indicate more precisely the nature of these trends. From 1950 to 1960, while the total population of the city decreased ever so slightly (down only 109,973 from 7,781,984), the total white population decreased by 836,807. Meanwhile, there was an increase of 366,268 Puerto Ricans and 360,566 Negroes.[1]

This change in the ethnic composition of the city continued and may even have accelerated between 1960 and 1964. There was a decline of roughly 539,000 whites during that time, and increases of 285,600 Negroes and 98,600 Puerto Ricans.[2] The Puerto Rican influx has leveled off as employment opportunities expand in Puerto Rico.

The main trend, then, is an accelerating pattern of movement out of the city as the middle class whites leave for the suburbs and as Negro and Puerto Rican middle class populations start to do the same. Even a few lower and lower middle

---

* Furthermore, since New York, like most other large inner cities, has been losing blue collar jobs to the suburbs as industry has moved out, it makes little sense to keep black people bottled up in ghettos while white suburbs maintain their exclusiveness. There is no moral justification for expecting that Negroes will always fill the lowest level jobs, but over the short run they will, and they should not be burdened with the problem of having their homes so far from work if that is not their choice. It would only be a further commentary on the sick racism of our society if we forced poor Negroes to stay in the inner city slums while many jobs moved out.

class whites are now participating in this trend, as they move into small homes in New Jersey, Long Island, or South Westchester.

The flight of the white middle class undoubtedly has many causes. More space, a home of one's own, better schools, and an escape from the many annoyances of the inner city (air pollution, narcotics, crime), are all reasons for leaving the city. Two sociologists, Seymour Sudman and Norman Bradburn, found in a recent study that "among community facilities which attract and keep residents, schools are considered most important." [3] As one of the persons interviewed in the study said: "The kind of people we want here will be attracted by schools only. As long as our schools are overcrowded we can't attract or keep them."

This was a pilot study, and systematic data on why white families leave inner cities do not exist. My interviews and observations at parent and civic association meetings suggest that there may be different motivations for different categories of whites. Lower and lower middle class whites who moved from such outlying boroughs as Queens to adjacent suburbs may well have done so to get away from Negroes and Puerto Ricans and from integrated schools. This was probably less likely for middle and upper middle class whites; if they were in search of better schools, it was perhaps more because of what they saw as the deteriorating quality of the New York City schools than the threat of desegregation. Many upward mobile, liberal, middle class whites moved away from Manhattan's Upper West Side for that reason.*

Age and birth-rate differences between the whites who stay (or move back in) and incoming minority group populations also affect prospects for school desegregation. The remaining whites are a much older population than Negroes and Puerto Ricans, and many are long past the age of having children in school. In 1964, roughly 35% of the whites living in the city were fifty years old or more, compared with 17% for the Negro population and only 13% for Puerto Ricans.[4] Many areas of the

---

* Evidence from surveys, to be presented in Chapter Three, indicates consistent differences in attitudes toward school desegregation between lower and middle class whites, with the latter much more receptive. The local white parent groups in The Bronx, Manhattan, Queens, and Brooklyn who tended to favor desegregation and send their children to desegregated public schools were middle and upper class, college educated—usually Reform Democrats. See source citation no. 29 in Chapter Three.

city where minority group populations have moved in recently have disproportionate numbers of such an aging white population—Washington Heights, the Upper West Side, and the Lower East Side in Manhattan; the Grand Concourse, Tremont, and Pelham Parkway communities of the Bronx; and Bay Ridge, Coney Island, and East Flatbush in Brooklyn.

The difference in birth rates is also marked. Estimates based on the 1964 Department of Health survey indicate that 14% of the white families in the city have five or more members in the household, compared with 24% of Negro families and 34% for Puerto Rican families. These differences are a reflection of social class and religious and ethnic factors, among others. Negroes and Puerto Ricans generally have much lower socioeconomic status than whites. Puerto Ricans have a large Catholic population and a tightly knit family structure as well. All these factors further limit possibilities for school desegregation, since an increasing percentage of the school-age population are poor Negroes and Puerto Ricans.[5]

The Department of Health's sampling techniques are probably adequate enough so that the estimates made in the study correspond roughly to the city's total population. They indicate the tremendous numbers of Negro and Puerto Rican children of school age, relative to the proportion of minority groups in the city's total population. The fact that Puerto Ricans and Negroes so outnumber whites among families with five persons or more is indicative of the trend. Furthermore, those whites with larger families probably include disproportionate numbers of Catholics who, in turn, send their children to parochial schools much more often than other whites.

All these patterns are reflected in the city's public school population. For a more specific picture of ethnic changes in residential patterns and public schools, one must look at each borough. Each borough is at a different stage of ethnic evolution in what may, over the long run, be a common demographic experience.

Staten Island

Staten Island, accounting for only 3% of the city's total population, is at the earliest stage of ethnic change. It has had only gradual, though accelerating, increases in the proportion of Negroes, and corresponding decreases in whites. Whites constituted 97% of Staten Island's population in 1950, 95% in

1960, and 90% in 1964.[6] Since the new Verrazano–Narrows Bridge has connected Staten Island with Brooklyn, Negroes will undoubtedly move to Staten Island at a greater rate. Staten Island's Negro population increased from 3 to 9.3% between 1950 and 1964 and soon may constitute a large part of the borough. Many planners have suggested to the Board of Education that it anticipate this inevitable change and develop consolidated school facilities, that is, clusters of schools with shared facilities that draw on a larger geographic area than traditional neighborhood schools. Typical of its perennial non-planning posture, the Board of Education has not yet developed such plans or any plans for Staten Island's anticipated population changes.

The white population of Staten Island includes large numbers of Italian, German, Irish, and English homeowners. Italians account for roughly 20% of its total population, and these other ethnic groups together account for another 15%.[7] They tend to vote as a bloc and more conservatively than all other ethnic groups on such issues as public housing and the proposed civilian review board (which was to have listened to citizens' complaints against police brutality but was voted down by a coalition of conservative votes). The vote in Staten Island against the civilian review board was roughly 5 to 1, by far the highest per cent against the board of any borough in the city.[8] There are areas on Staten Island's south shore with large numbers of John Birch Society members and sympathizers with various right wing causes.*

This suggests how the population of Staten Island might respond to plans for school consolidation and desegregation. Unless the Board of Education were willing to provide active leadership to persuade the community to integrate its schools, the white residents of Staten Island would probably develop strong grass-roots support for neighborhood school programs opposing desegregation. Though the borough's Negro population is not yet so large as to have brought this issue to the fore, controversy over it may not be more than five to ten years off.

PTA and civic leaders in Staten Island are now much concerned about the quality of services in their schools. They refer

---

* Some Staten Island residents do favor decentralization, much to the chagrin of middle class liberals who fear that Birchites may try to eliminate courses and textbooks (for example, on the UN) that conflict with their values.

to their borough in public hearings and private communications with the Board of Education as the forgotten land.[9] Their main concern is that the board will not plan for the tremendous population increase they expect within the next few years. They also express a grievance common to many white middle class PTA groups, that too much of the board's budget goes to schools in disadvantaged areas, at the expense of their children. As one leader of the Staten Island Federation of Parent–Teacher Associations complained: "You must not overendow one group, however worthy, at the expense of another. Many children are denied basic needs, while others are showered with special services." Many Staten Island parents now refer to the "poverty of the privileged"[10] and they have become increasingly vociferous and angry in public hearings. They are, in this regard, following the lead of white parent associations and parent–teacher associations from other boroughs.

Yet, as of now, Staten Island has not been the site of any major controversies relating to school desegregation and the education of minority group children. For that reason, I give it little attention. Furthermore, it still accounts for only 3% of the city's total population.*

Queens

Queens, the fastest growing borough in the city, is next along the continuum of ethnic succession. It now houses 25% of the city's total population, compared with 19% in 1950.[11] An increasing number of Negroes have moved in, and to a smaller extent, Puerto Ricans, in the past few years. Such communities as South Jamaica (just below central Queens), St. Albans and neighboring areas (to the east), Corona, parts of Astoria and Flushing (northwest), and parts of the Rockaways (southwest), now have large and increasing concentrations of Negroes.[12] Some are a homeowning Negro middle class, as in St. Albans, Corona, and the fringes of South Jamaica, as well as neighboring Laurelton, Rosedale, and Springfield Gardens. Like middle

---

* Staten Island is a borough with large numbers of poor whites, a majority of them (68%) Catholic, who tend most often to go into the blue collar trades. Only 30–35% of the high school graduates in Staten Island receive an academic diploma. Ironically, a delegation from the Staten Island PTA visited Andrew Jackson High School in Queens in 1967, a school with 50% Negro students, mostly middle class, to find out why it had been so successful in sending its graduates on to good colleges. Their all-white high schools in Staten Island had not done so well as Jackson.

class white homeowners, some of them are conservative politically. They occasionally even protest the Board of Education's attempts to provide integrated schooling for their children through rezoning or locating schools in fringe areas, that is, areas between concentrated Negro and white settlements. They resent the assumption that they have the same problems as lower class Negroes and sometimes interpret programs for school desegregation in this vein.* What they resent most is having their children bussed out to integrated schools for which additional services have not been provided, and which have generally not been prepared for the incoming students. Many of them have thus given up on desegregation. For example, Randolf Rankin, executive director of Allied Democrats in Jamaica, spoke out at a City Planning Commission hearing in late 1965 against having an intermediate school zoned out of the area for purposes of desegregation. He said: "We just want quality schools, unless we get an integration policy that works." [13] Rankin was followed by a number of speakers making the same point.

The substantial growth of Queens from 1950 to 1960, an increase of almost 260,000, has now perhaps started to taper off. Furthermore, the nature of the growth has changed markedly. More than half the increase from 1950 to 1960, or 146,000, were white, an overwhelming majority of whom were probably Jews, who moved into new, middle income apartments. Most of the remainder—100,000—were Negro.† [14]

Since 1960, there has been a decrease of whites (25,000), while 83,000 Negroes moved in.[15] The whites who have been leaving are generally an upward mobile, college educated, liberal group, who settled in such areas as Jackson Heights, Flushing, Astoria, Kew Gardens, or Forest Hills, before moving on to Westchester, Long Island, or Connecticut. This left a predominantly lower and lower middle class white population—Irish,

---

* Several Board of Education hearings on desegregation included testimonies of middle class Negro groups from such areas as Bedford–Stuyvesant and South Jamaica, asking for more schools in their local neighborhoods. Interviews with civil rights leaders suggested that the Negro middle class generally was not active in the desegregation fight. See Chapter Four discussion of Galamison and NAACP on this point.

† In 1950, Queens had a population of 1,550,849; 96% or 1,492,666 were white; 53,347 (3.8%) were Negro; and the remainder, 4,836, were Puerto Rican. In 1964, its population had risen to 1,872,000, with 1,603,500 whites (85%), 235,000 Negroes (12%), and 28,500 (3%) Puerto Ricans.

Germans, Italians, and Slavs—who tended to be less receptive to housing and school desegregation. Even some of these have recently moved out to such places as Hicksville, Levittown, and neighboring communities on Long Island.

Data on the ethnic composition of public schools in Queens indicate the nature of the changes outlined above. The percentage of whites declined from 87.7 in 1957, the first year the Board of Education took any systematic ethnic census, to 72.8 in 1967. Negroes increased from 10.9 to 22.7%, while Puerto Ricans increased from a negligible 1.4 to 4.5%.[16] Queens is still a predominantly white borough.

If demography and residential patterns were the prime considerations, Queens would offer many possibilities for desegregation. The residential patterns in many parts of the borough, especially in the southeast and to the north, have not hardened along segregated lines to nearly the same degree that they have in Brooklyn and are hardening now in the Bronx. The large Negro middle class, for example, while somewhat boxed in in the Corona community from Jackson Heights on the south, have moved to the south and east from the Jamaica area, into such attractive residential neighborhoods as St. Albans, Hollis, and the surrounding communities. Furthermore, the only Queens ghetto, South Jamaica, has a much smaller poverty population than other ghetto areas of the city. There are fewer low income projects, fewer high-rise buildings, more space, and less density. Also, bussing is not new to many Queens whites. There is much more space in Queens than in most other boroughs, and many families live beyond the prescribed walking distance from schools. They have been bussing their children for years.

Yet, much more than demography and housing patterns is involved. Local homeowner, self-titled "taxpayer," and civic groups have much political power in Queens. By working through the borough president and local politicians, they have successfully prevented the location of many low income housing projects in most residential areas of the borough. The Board of Education has hesitated to buck their power and press vigorously for desegregation, even in communities where the residential pattern was favorable. Most of the citywide controversy over bussing originated in Queens, illustrating the determination of many whites there to keep their schools as segregated as possible.

Indeed, for all the openness and flexibility in housing pat-

terns of some communities in Queens, many others are completely under the control of Irish, German, Italian, or Slavic
groups. Many such communities hold to their ethnic traditions—German beer halls, Sunday afternoon soccer matches—
and are quite insulated and ethnocentric in outlook. The College Point German community to the northwest, near the
Throgs Neck Bridge, the Ridgewood, Glendale, and Maspeth
German and Irish communities to the west, and the Italian
community in Jackson Heights, are cases in point. There are
parts of Ridgewood and Glendale where Irish and German
mothers still get out and scrub their sidewalks and stoops.
Many of these groups are determined to keep their schools and
communities closed to Negroes and Puerto Ricans.

In addition to its politics, there is a physical obstacle to
school desegregation in Queens. Almost all the bus routes run
east and west. To desegregate, it would be essential to have
more north-to-south transportation. Jamaica Avenue, which
runs east to west through the center of the borough, is the
racial frontier in Queens. North of that thoroughfare Queens is
essentially white, with the exception of Corona. To the south
there is South Jamaica, and to the southeast are the middle class
Negro communities.

Civil rights and white integrationist groups have petitioned
the Board of Transportation for new bus routes, which have
yet to be established. But the Board of Education has not
pressed for these routes. Many integrationist leaders feel that
the Board of Education should do so, given its advanced policy
statements on desegregation. As one white integrationist leader
noted: "I feel that the Board of Transportation's attitude is
strictly a business one. I don't sense any racist consideration
there at all. They just get their best return on the east to west
routes. I have a different feeling about the Board of Transportation than I have about the Board of Education. They are not
as obligated as the Board of Education is to break segregated
school patterns." [17]

There are some white areas in Queens—College Point, Little Neck, and Douglaston, for example—that are not linked via
public transportation to communities with large Negro populations. When civil rights leaders were engaged in discussions
in 1964 with Board of Education headquarters officials about
plans for desegregation that might include these communities,

Adrian Blumenfeld, director of the School Planning and Research Unit, suggested that such plans were simply impractical. Bus lines didn't run that far out. When asked if he would make an effort to extend the bus routes, he expressed some interest and then never followed through. Neither, however, did the civil rights leaders who asked him.

Even these transportation problems are not insurmountable, if city officials chose to create new bus routes. But these officials tend to act only if enough pressure is brought to bear by the citizenry. Since they have so far chosen not to act, they apparently feel that there is not enough community support for such changes.

A small group of white parents who are integrationists have formulated plans for educational complexes in parts of central and southeast Queens and presented them to headquarters officials at the board. These plans have not been acted upon. Dr. Robert Dentler, director of the Center for Urban Education, was commissioned by the board in 1964 to develop plans for educational complexes. Dentler and his colleagues, working out of the Institute of Urban Studies at Teachers College, formulated a number of "educational complex" proposals for Queens as well as for Brooklyn. The Board of Education did not act on these proposals.

Some headquarters staff in the Central Zoning Unit have developed their own plans for educational complexes in Queens. As one member of the unit said in 1965: "We're just waiting for word from upstairs." Word has yet to come.

As the Dentler papers and Central Zoning Unit plans indicate, there are many plans that might work in Queens, given the fluid demographic and housing pattern there. But they would work only if the Board of Education were willing to face the political opposition that their implementation would provoke. The Board of Education has not only failed to run this risk, it has actually created segregated schools in some integrated residential areas. In one such instance, in a middle income project called Rochdale Village, white pupils were zoned into JHS 8 near South Jamaica.[18] There were no overt protests, since JHS 8 was generally regarded as a good school. But then the board made plans to build a junior high school (JHS 72) in Rochdale itself, resegregating JHS 8. Ironically, the white parents from Rochdale who send their children to JHS 8 are generally satisfied with their children's integrated school experience and are behind any plans that are likely to keep on giving their children such an experience, whether they are shifted to 72 or kept in 8.

The main reason for the board's rezoning 8 was that many conservative white parents from the wealthy Jamaica Estates community and outside the Rochdale area had also been zoned into that school. They demanded that their children be allowed to go to another school, JHS 217, which was in their neighborhood and was almost exclusively white. To appease these whites, the board decided to rezone JHS 8, build 72 in the Rochdale community, and integrate it by bussing Negro children in from South Jamaica.

Liberal white parents now have a suit pending before State Education Commissioner James Allen, that he direct the board to present a plan that prevents JHS 8 from becoming a segregated school.[19] These parents and some civil rights leaders developed a number of plans for rezoning all three schools for purposes of desegregation. Meanwhile, Superintendent Donovan and officials at the Central Zoning Unit have not come up with a plan of their own that would attempt to desegregate the three schools.

A different group of Queens parents brought suit on a related matter, demanding that the board either rezone white pupils from two high schools that are now on triple session into an underused, predominantly Negro high school, Andrew Jackson, or develop an overall plan for rezoning all Queens high schools.[20] There are strong local, political pressures against desegregation; this suit is the result of another case of the board's unwillingness to buck such pressures even where desegregation is physically practicable. In this instance, utilization considerations alone merit a rezoning, since the board is making inefficient use of its existing school space.

Superintendent Donovan proposed a rezoning plan on February 13, 1968, to change attendance areas of all seventeen Queens academic high schools to promote desegregation, partly in response to pressure from State Education Commissioner James Allen. One would hope that this might be implemented, but past experience leads to skepticism. The proposal affects students who will be entering high school in September, 1968.[21]

The uneven school utilization pattern in Queens is a significant issue for city planning officials and some school officials as well as for integrationist groups. As of 1965, there were 5,500 more pupils than seats in one cluster of elementary schools and 2,700 more in junior high schools, while there were 19,800 empty seats in other elementary schools and 3,300 in other junior highs.[22] The general pattern, in contrast to that of the high school example I have just cited, is for overcrowding to exist in Negro and Puerto Rican communities, while there are empty seats in white areas. This pattern exists in other boroughs as well.

Brooklyn

Brooklyn is even farther along in this pattern of ethnic change. It is now the most populated borough in the city, with 2,606,000 inhabitants in 1964. It also has the most Negroes— 529,000 (1964).[23] There has been a marked influx of Negroes and Puerto Ricans and an exodus of whites. The percentage of whites in the public schools declined from 72.3 in 1957 to 45.1 in 1967, while Negroes increased from 17.5 to 33.5% and Puerto Ricans from 10.2 to 21.4%.[24]

The residential pattern in Brooklyn has shifted considerably since 1950. Many low income projects have been placed in a few ghetto areas—Brownsville, Crown Heights, East New York, and more recently, Williamsburg and Coney Island. At the same time, real estate interests have engaged in massive blockbusting activity in fringe areas. The racial frontier has moved south from Fulton Street, the southern edge of Bedford–Stuyvesant in northern Brooklyn, all the way through Crown Heights, Flatbush, and Brownsville, to Linden Boulevard, which divides Brownsville from Canarsie to the south. Even parts of East New York have had an influx of Negroes and Puerto Ricans.

Minority group populations have also started to move in a southwesterly direction to include areas like Sheepshead Bay and Coney Island. They have, in addition, spread north to the communities of Williamsburg, Park Slope, Fort Greene, and Brooklyn Heights. Indeed, many parts of north, central, and southeast Brooklyn now have densely populated Negro and Puerto Rican settlements. The largest and most continuous ghetto in the city has begun to take shape on a boroughwide basis in Brooklyn. Private real estate interests—banks, developers, brokers—have been permitted to dispose of property and engage in blockbusting in a way that has rapidly tipped large sections of the borough. Neither city officials nor the Board of

Education have tried much to stem the tide. Some schools and neighborhoods have tipped almost overnight.*

One of the reasons Brooklyn changed so much from 1950 to 1964 was that there were already ghetto areas that qualified for low income housing. Negro and Puerto Rican populations dislocated by urban renewal moved to Brooklyn in large numbers. One informant in the housing field suggested that each month as many as 1,200 Negroes and Puerto Ricans have moved into Brownsville alone in recent years. Another reason was Brooklyn's more liberal politics. There were many more Jews in Brooklyn than in Queens, and they were somewhat more receptive than other groups to Negroes and Puerto Ricans. Also, there were more communities of apartment dwellers, and residents of these areas were more favorably disposed toward low income project populations than homeowners.

Some of the remaining all-white areas of Brooklyn, however, are similar in important respects to those in Queens. Bensonhurst, Borough Park, Bay Ridge, and Fort Hamilton, to the south and west, have predominantly Italian, Norwegian, and Irish populations, many of them homeowners. There is a sprinkling of lower middle and middle class Jews as well, who are not very receptive to integration.[25]

Many of the controversies over desegregation that have started up in Queens during the last few years had been raging in Brooklyn since the late 1950s. They usually involved site location and zoning decisions, with integrationist groups fighting a losing battle on any number of schools, and white parents, real estate interests, and civic leaders holding the line. The Board of Education, meanwhile, was engaged in its own series of holding actions, responding to pressures from whites who were generally more organized than integrationist groups.

The two most publicized of these controversies were over the construction and zoning of schools in the Brownsville,

* A typical example of a Brooklyn community now undergoing change is Flatbush, the former home of the Brooklyn Dodgers. The last dramatic ethnic change in Flatbush was in the World War One years when Jewish immigrants from Williamsburg and Manhattan's Lower East Side moved into the farmlands of southern Brooklyn, alongside the old Protestant élite. In the mid-1960s, more middle class Negroes started moving in. As a recent *New York Times* report notes: "White residents also complain that they have been harassed by blockbusters using 'scare' tactics—spreading rumors of lower property values and higher insurance rates—to get them to sell cheaply and move quickly. Real estate agents phone them daily, they say, to ask if they are ready to sell." *New York Times*, February 14, 1968, p. 49.

Canarsie, and East Flatbush area of southeast Brooklyn.[26] One such controversy, lasting for four and a half years, concerned JHS 275. Civil rights and white integrationist groups wanted it built on the boundaries of the Negro and white communities and zoned for integration, while whites from East Flatbush and Canarsie wanted their own junior highs, preferring to have JHS 275 located in the Brownsville ghetto to serve that population. The school was finally located on the boundary line and then zoned in such a way that it was segregated. This struggle went on from 1960 to 1964.

Another followed soon after, resulting from a request from the same integrationist groups for an educational park in Canarsie to serve the four communities of Brownsville, Canarsie, East Flatbush, and East New York. They protested the Board of Education's plan for the construction of seven segregated, neighborhood schools and suggested instead a consolidated educational park facility that would draw on several neighborhoods. The integrationist group, called Parents for an Educational Park, brought their case to Commissioner Allen in the summer of 1966. He issued an order to the Board of Education to stop construction of the segregated schools it had planned. Actually, the construction had not yet begun, and Allen's order was to make sure that nothing would be built until the board came up with a desegregation plan. The case has still to be decided.*

The main centers of controversy, then, have been central and southeast Brooklyn in recent years—Brownsville, Canarsie, East Flatbush, and East New York—and Crown Heights and Bedford–Stuyvesant in northern Brooklyn in the 1950s and early sixties when the racial frontier was farther north. In these areas, integrationist groups were led by the Rev. Milton Galamison, minister of a middle class Negro Presbyterian church in Bedford–Stuyvesant. Since 1957, Galamison and his white, very able parent organizer and planner, Mrs. Annie Stein, fought endless battles for desegregation through their grass-roots organization—Parents Workshop for Equality.

They were struggling against highly organized and powerful real estate, white parent, and political interests; nevertheless,

---

* Dr. Cyril Sergeant of CCNY has developed a new concept for a linear city in Brooklyn that would use an abandoned Long Island railroad track to transport pupils to consolidated campus schools located along the track through Southeast Brooklyn.

they had a number of partial victories. In 1959, for example, they were able to mobilize close to five hundred Bedford–Stuyvesant parents to send their children under Open Enrollment to the Ridgewood–Glendale community in Queens. Later, they were able to influence a few zoning and school-construction decisions. On balance, however, the forces for maintaining the status quo were much too powerful.

One example is the fight that took place in Crown Heights, a largely white Jewish community where a number of Negroes and Puerto Ricans had begun to move in in the early 1960s. Parents Workshop was able to mobilize officials in twenty parent associations to support a plan for dispersing Negro children throughout the elementary schools in the community, thus integrating them all and perhaps preventing any of them from tipping suddenly. The dispersal plan was purposely formulated to keep the percentage of whites well above the tipping point. Informants who participated in developing the plan and pressing for its implementation report that the Board of Education refused to cooperate.[27] It was reportedly responding to pressures from real estate interests, parents, and school officials to keep the schools and neighborhoods segregated. Civil rights and parent association leaders report that the board followed the strategy of trying to keep the percentage of whites as high as possible in as many schools as possible by sending all the Negro children to just a few schools in the ghetto. Eventually, the board gave up on many of the schools with increasing Negro enrollments by failing to provide adequate services, thereby abandoning its holding actions. Those schools tipped within a few years.

A big part of the Brooklyn story, then, is the emergence and growth of two massive Negro ghettos, Bedford–Stuyvesant and Brownsville. Before 1920, Bedford–Stuyvesant had been a somewhat fashionable middle and upper middle class white community. Many middle class Jews and some Protestants lived there. In the 1920s and 1930s a middle class Negro population moved in. Gradually, with the increased migration from the South and the exodus of middle class whites from New York City, Bedford–Stuyvesant became more and more working class in composition. The housing there has deteriorated, and the area has become increasingly impoverished and ghettoized.

Brownsville's decline followed hard on that of Bedford–Stuyvesant. Before 1950, it was a community of working class

Jews. Just after the turn of the century, it became a center of Jewish migrants, many of them members of various trade union and leftist movements. Their children and grandchildren went on to college, moved into the professions, business, and academic life, migrated to other areas of the city, and became part of the city's Jewish intelligentsia.* The tenements and small two-family houses that they and their parents lived in are now occupied mainly by a lower class, minority group population. And since 1950, Brownsville has become primarily a Negro and Puerto Rican low income project area.

This same general pattern of evolution has taken place in Crown Heights and Williamsburg to the north, both predominantly Jewish communities until the 1950s and sixties and still housing many older generation orthodox Jews. Coney Island is just starting to undergo the same changes, as low income projects have begun to proliferate.

The population shifts have been so extensive and at times so rapid that they have produced severe overcrowding in some schools and comparable underuse in others. A 1965 City Planning Commission estimate indicates that the schools were overcrowded by 19,600 pupils at the elementary level and 5,900 at the junior high level, while there were 25,100 available seats at the elementary level and 3,500 at the junior high level in other parts of the borough.[28] The overcrowding was usually in the ghetto, and the empty seats were in white areas.

Bronx

The Bronx is the most rapidly changing borough of all. It is changing so fast that it may even skip a few stages in the demographic succession pattern. The Bronx, along with Brooklyn, has increasingly become the refuge for Negro and Puerto Rican families from Manhattan, displaced by urban renewal. It has received, in addition, an overflow of Negro and Puerto Rican populations from Central and East Harlem. They have moved into the south Bronx and Morrisania, along with dislocated families from Manhattan. They are now moving to the north and east along a few main thoroughfares—Bruckner Boulevard, the Grand Concourse, and Tremont Avenue—into such previously all-white communities as Throgs Neck and

* Norman Podhoretz, editor of *Commentary,* and Irving Kristol, editor of *The Public Interest,* are two prototypes. Podhoretz's book, *Making It,* is an autobiography depicting his mobility experience.

Clason Point. Meanwhile, many lower and lower middle class whites, mostly Jews, have moved out of The Bronx to Queens, Brooklyn, or adjacent suburbs. The Concourse Village community in the mid-Bronx is one such area where the exodus has proceeded extensively. It is now changing so rapidly that the community may become a ghetto in the next five to ten years. The same blockbusting pattern so characteristic of parts of Brooklyn may well take place there.*

The percentage of whites in the public schools of The Bronx has decreased since 1957 from 64.6 to 33.0. Puerto Ricans have increased from 19.8 to 36.1%, while Negroes have increased from 15.6 to 30.9%.[29] The largest increase, reflected in the school population, has been that of Puerto Ricans. Indeed, The Bronx now has more Puerto Ricans—242,000—than any other borough, even though its total population is less than that of Manhattan, Queens, or Brooklyn. It elected the city's first Puerto Rican borough president, Herman Badillo, in 1965. Badillo barely beat out Joseph Perricone in an election that was symbolic of the decline of conservative Italian, Irish, and other homeowner interests. Badillo was elected by a coalition of Puerto Ricans, Negroes, and Reform Democrats. Many of the latter were middle and upper middle class Jewish professionals.†

The racial frontier, previously located just south of the Concourse Village area of the mid-Bronx, near Yankee Stadium, will move north very rapidly in the next few years. Until quite recently, the bulk of the borough's Negro and Puerto Rican population was concentrated in a very small but densely populated section in the southern tip.

Most of the white areas of the borough are similar in ethnic composition and in their degree of ethnocentrism to their counterparts in Queens and Brooklyn. To the north and east are lower middle class Irish and Italian homeowners. There are also some older Jewish populations in high-rise apartments. The Jewish settlement extends north in a pencil-shaped pattern

---

* Recent studies of the Grand Concourse area by the American Jewish Congress and Bronx Borough President Herman Badillo reveal these dramatic changes and suggest remedies to arrest them. Badillo has tried to plan for a substantial upgrading of shopping centers and city services in the area.

† In 1950, the Bronx had a population of 1,451,277; 1,292,623 (89%) were white; 96,730 (7%) were Negro; and 61,924 (4%) were Puerto Rican. By 1964, its population had declined slightly to 1,306,000, with 872,000 whites (62%), 192,000 Negro (14%), and 242,000 Puerto Rican (24%).

along the Grand Concourse, and then east along Pelham Parkway, Tremont Avenue, and Fordham Road.

The most affluent part of the borough, called Riverdale, is an area of large private homes, luxury and middle income apartments, and some co-ops. It faces the Hudson River on the west and Van Cortland Park and its golf course on the east. This is a community of upper middle class professionals and executives, many of them Jewish, and some active in civil rights and liberal causes. They are isolated from the rest of the borough, and have been able to maintain zoning patterns that place sharp limitations on housing and school desegregation. As one cynical politician related: "They can afford their liberalism. They are so far away from all the problems."

As one moves to the east and then south of Riverdale, white homeowners predominate. Much to the dismay of local residents, there has been a gradual trickling in of Negroes and Puerto Ricans, as low income projects have been built in such communities as Throgs Neck and Clason Point. One Democratic state senator who supported a project in the Throgs Neck area was spat upon and physically threatened as he left the public hearings on the matter. Bronx liberals refer to white residents of such communities as the "know nothings" of the borough. Politicians and populations in these communities, resentful of plans to build more projects, have caustically referred to Borough President Badillo as a patsy for minority groups. Racial and ethnic tensions thus occasionally run high in this part of the borough, just as they do in similar communities in Queens and Brooklyn. The Board of Education and other city officials face strong opposition to desegregation from such populations.

One reason for the pessimism of many planners regarding the likelihood of maintaining residential desegregation in the mid-Bronx area, and therefore of stemming the trend toward the ghettoization of a large segment of the borough, has been the development of a middle income project, Co-Op City, to be completed in a couple of years in the northeast Bronx. On last count, it had already signed up 5,500 white middle class families from the Concourse area. They had been a significant stabilizing force there. The projection is that as many as 11,000 families (the majority of them white, middle class Jews) will move into the co-op from the Concourse community. It is estimated that another 40 to 50,000 families might later leave the

Concourse area, because of changes in its ethnic composition.

Prospects for school desegregation in The Bronx, as in Queens and Brooklyn, would then be contingent on a decision by the Board of Education to build schools away from ghetto communities in the south and mid-Bronx, anticipating demographic changes. If the board were to hold the line against a further white exodus from the public schools, it would have to overbuild in these integrated, fringe areas, and in all-white areas that will soon have expanded minority group populations.

Yet the board has planned to build several middle and elementary schools in the south Bronx in the next few years. That area is already seriously overcrowded, and the pressures to build in the ghetto, from Puerto Rican populations in particular, are strong. Puerto Ricans tend to have tightly knit families and many Puerto Rican parents are reluctant to have their children attend schools outside the local community. In addition, many Puerto Ricans and Negroes have become disenchanted with the idea of bussing their children any distance for purposes of desegregation. They don't like to bear all the burdens of travel; and many of them have been disappointed by the minimal services and discourteous treatment their children received in the schools they attended under Open Enrollment.

A serious problem in The Bronx, though not peculiar to that borough, has been an acute shortage of vital services. Since 1950, the south Bronx has had great numbers of new Negro and Puerto Rican residents in low income projects. Yet schools were planned to take care of a much smaller population. The population changes have been recent and very rapid, but the planning of school construction hasn't begun to keep pace. The school needs in the south Bronx are almost unbelievably acute, and the tremendous lag between major population shifts and school construction indicates that a close examination of school planning is necessary. The south Bronx recently got clearance for a new high school, but from the point of view of local residents, it was long overdue, and they shouldn't have had to fight for it as hard as they did.

There has been a lag between population and housing changes and school construction in other parts of the borough as well. In a development along Bruckner Boulevard, where middle income and public (low income) housing are built together, children from the middle income developments were forced to cross an eight-lane highway to get to school. Whites were put off by this, and left the area in great numbers. The lack of planning has not been confined to schools. In the Co-Op City project there was little planning for any services—transportation, parks, or schools—until Borough President Badillo took office. Officials in the State Division of Housing approved the project without ever consulting citizen groups. In all these cases public officials said that the City Planning Commission had abdicated its function and might well be held responsible for the inadequate services and exodus of whites that often followed. Again, the problem is a citywide one, but The Bronx has been unusually hard hit in this regard. It faces more acute shortages of services than almost any other borough.

Manhattan

Manhattan's total population has been declining steadily since 1950, as has that of The Bronx, mainly because the whites have been leaving. There has been a decline in Manhattan's Puerto Rican population as well. There were 25,000 fewer Puerto Ricans in Manhattan in 1964 than in 1960.[30] One of the reasons has been the dislocation of large numbers of Puerto Rican families in the Lincoln Square and Upper West Side urban renewal programs. Some have returned to Puerto Rico.

Actually, Manhattan's ethnic and racial composition has stabilized since 1960. The percentage of whites is likely to continue to hold up and perhaps even increase, as long as rent control and the influx of an older middle class population continue.*

Manhattan has the lowest percentage of whites in the public schools of any borough in the city. The decline has slackened since 1957, but this was largely because Manhattan had already undergone the changes that Brooklyn, Queens, and The Bronx have experienced more recently. The proportion of whites in Manhattan's public schools was 36.9% in 1957 and only 28.7% in 1967. The proportion of Negroes increased from 32.7 to 36.6%, while that of Puerto Ricans increased from 30.4 to 34.7%.[31] Many people who are skeptical about prospects for

---

* There is always the possibility, however, that more whites would leave Manhattan if there were riots that were not confined to the ghettos of Harlem, East Harlem, and the Lower East Side.

school desegregation in New York City point to Manhattan as
an illustration of how hopeless the cause is. There aren't
enough whites to go around.*

The fact that whites account for only 28.7% of the public
school enrollment while they are 60% of Manhattan's total
population, does, indeed, seem to argue against school desegregation. There are several reasons for the difference. One is the
increasingly older white population. Another is that many middle and upper middle class whites who remain in Manhattan
send their children to private schools. While this was always the
case for those living on the Upper East Side, it has become increasingly the pattern for West Siders as well.†

Many Reform Democrat, liberal Jewish professionals
living on the Upper West Side (along Riverside Drive, West
End Avenue, and Central Park West from 66th Street to 122nd)
have given up on the city's public schools and send their children to such private schools as Walden, Dalton, Agnes Russell,
Collegiate, Columbia Grammar, New Lincoln, Ethical Culture,
and Fieldston, among others. Even some of the militant, civil
rights activists among them do so, despite their supposedly
strong commitment to desegregation. These people may not be
running away from the Negroes and Puerto Ricans. They are
simply convinced of the inferior education in public schools.

As discriminatory barriers against Jews have been lifted in
private schools in the postwar years, they have flocked to such
schools, even though the expense strains budgets. For those
who aren't subsidized, the financial and psychological strains of
using the private school system are sometimes very great. Children are required to take entrance examinations. There are
many more applicants than there are openings.

Now even private schools are very much concerned about
having some semblance of ethnic balance. Dalton, for example,

---

* In 1950, Manhattan had a population of 1,960,101; 1,431,895 (74%)
were white; 389,699 (19%) were Negro; and 138,507 (7%) were Puerto
Rican. In 1964, its population had declined to 1,545,00, with 934,500 (61%)
whites, 411,000 (27%) Negroes, and 171,500 (12%) Puerto Rican.

† The estimated private school enrollment in Manhattan in the 1967–
1968 school year was 23,000, up more than 50% from the 14,300 of 1952.
Grace and Fred M. Hechinger estimate that soon there will be 26,000 private
school students in the borough. The enrollment at non-denominational private schools in most of the other boroughs except in Riverdale in the Bronx
is negligible. The total public school population in Manhattan is 173,730 (as
of October, 1967).

has recently given a number of scholarships to Negro pupils from Harlem. This has become a more prevalent and accepted practice in private schools.

The Upper West Side is one of the city's most integrated areas and contains some integrated schools. Rent control, for all its imputed costs in the form of reduced repairs and services, has contributed to the holding power of the area for the white middle class.* So have some of the urban renewal programs in Lincoln Square, Park West Village, and Morningside Heights, and the presence of Columbia University and the various religious and cultural institutions surrounding it. They have done so, however, only at tremendous cost to many low income Negro and Puerto Rican populations who have been dislocated and forced to move to other parts of the city. Columbia University is now trying to live down its reputation of attempting to control as many of the resources of its area as possible.†

Though many school officials have reportedly given up hope, there are some who feel that Manhattan's Upper West Side might keep the white middle class in the public school system. A few West Side principals, in collaboration with white middle class parents and civic leaders, have actually been moderately successful in maintaining or even raising white enrollments. It may be argued that these trends are at best only temporary, but some schools have at least demonstrated their holding power. They often do so by maintaining fast-track classes and homogeneous groupings in which the more successful children are separated from the others, thus segregating

* Since late 1966, however, rent control has been under increasing attack, and controls are gradually being lifted, initially in middle income apartments with rents above $250. Since these are the apartments most likely to be leased to young families with children, one would expect them to leave the area in increasing numbers.

† Columbia has been vying with the Harlem and Morningside communities over its desire to have a gymnasium in Morningside Park, just below the campus. When it received a $10 million Ford Foundation grant in late 1967 to contribute to the revitalization of Harlem, there was much resentment among Harlem leaders and residents that they were not consulted or brought into the planning, and that most of the money would go to Columbia-employed people. In late March, 1968, a faculty committee formed at Columbia, protested the administration's limited actions on civil rights matters and its insensitivity to the needs of the Harlem and Morningside communities. The campus protests of April and May of 1968 indicate how alienated some of the students and faculty had become from the university administration.

the schools internally. If the district superintendent and principals actually go through with a plan, announced in the spring of 1967, to establish heterogeneous groupings, the commitment of middle class whites to the public schools of the area will be more directly tested.

If any white population were to be attracted back into the public schools, it might well be this one. They do have some limited commitments at least to acting out their egalitarian ideologies. But they are also acutely concerned about the intellectual development of their children, and would not want to sacrifice the latter for the former. Attracting the white middle class back into the public schools depends on the extent to which headquarters and local school officials are able to improve their educational programs; so far there is no evidence of such improvement.

A further obstacle is the limited school space and overcrowding, especially in the high schools. The Louis D. Brandeis High School opened on the Upper West Side in September, 1966, for example, at almost 200% capacity. Many parent groups and the local school board had urged the Board of Education to plan for at least 4,000 pupils. The board claimed that its projections indicated that no more than 2,300 seats were needed. The school went on triple sessions a year after it opened. Combined with its annex, it has a capacity of 3,800 students; the September, 1967, enrollment was 5,229.[32] The community is now so outraged that many more parents may be turning away from the public school system than in the past. The problem of overcrowding is not limited to Manhattan's West Side. It is even worse in ghetto and fringe areas. Yet it discourages community support among a white population who might contribute in a small way to upgrading the school system.

Increased numbers of Puerto Ricans and Negroes in formerly all-white or predominantly white areas are common in Manhattan. One of the areas where the most rapid demographic changes have taken place is East Harlem, which runs north from 96th Street to 132nd Street and east from Fifth Avenue to the East and Harlem Rivers. In 1950, the area was still 45–50% white. Now it is closer to 20% white, 50% Puerto Rican, and 30% Negro.[33] The die may actually have been cast for East Harlem in 1940 when financial institutions, such as the Bowery Bank, decided that it was no longer a profitable place in which to carry on their activities. It soon became a community without a source of financing, even for the most basic needs. Deterioration, especially in housing, proceeded quickly. The area is now extremely poor, with predictable political consequences. A nationally publicized controversy over the desegregation of one of its intermediate schools (IS 201), where community leaders demanded that the school either be desegregated or that they be given much more authority and power in its operations, was one result of more than two decades of frustration over conditions in the area.

Many Negroes and Puerto Ricans have also moved into the Upper West Side, above 66th Street, and into the Lower East Side. They were preceded on the Lower East Side by a large Jewish population, mostly low income, blue collar, or small shopkeepers. There is still a large second and third generation who have remained there, in what was once the main center for recently migrated Jewish populations from Eastern Europe. On the West Side, minority groups followed a middle class Jewish population, some of whom moved to the Upper East Side or to the suburbs, though many of them remained.

The Parochial Schools

Though private school enrollments have not cut into those of public schools, except in some areas like Manhattan's Upper West Side, the operations of the parochial school system have. Catholic parochial schools in the five boroughs accounted for roughly 450,000 pupil enrollments in 1967, close to 30% of all those in the city; the large Catholic schools enrollments in the Bronx (73,000) and Brooklyn and Queens (326,000) have drained off many white Catholic pupils from the public schools.[34] Many civil rights and liberal white groups charge that the parochial schools have hampered desegregation programs in the public schools.

Conflicts between liberal groups and the archdiocese have always been a part of New York City political life, and have been largely Jewish–Catholic conflicts. They have become intensified since 1965, with the passage of the Elementary and Secondary Education Act (ESEA) and its Title I provisions for federal funds to go to parochial as well as public schools, and with the debates at the 1967 State Constitutional Convention at Albany over the repeal of the Blaine amendment, which had previously prohibited public funds from being used for parochial schools. White and Negro liberal groups charge that Catholic schools are the segregated refuge for white racists; that they have pre-empted strategic sites in the outlying boroughs of the city that might better have been used for public schools; and that they have been asking for more public funds since Title I money first became available in 1965 for exclusively parochial school programs, even though those funds were to have been made available to public and parochial schools on a shared basis only.*

One of the reasons for the heavy parochial school enrollment is the large Catholic population in New York City.† Catholics are the largest religious group in the city, comprising an estimated 47% of its total population, compared with 27% Jewish, and 24% Protestant[35] (the rest are not affiliated with a religion or do not report an affiliation).‡

Some Catholic parochial schools are just beginning to become concerned about desegregation, after much adverse publicity. Their ethnic enrollments reflect the neighborhoods where they are located, and it is probably accurate to say that the increasing number of Catholic schools that are mixed ethnically (fewer than 90% white or Puerto Rican–Negro) is more a result of white Catholics' moving increasingly to the suburbs, leaving space for more Puerto Ricans and other Latin American pupils, than of any active desegregation programs the archdiocese has underway. On desegregation, they are roughly at the stage that the public schools were at in the early 1950s.[36] As one top Catholic leader related: "I pushed the Bishops' Commission on Race for an unqualified statement endorsing the concept of quality integrated education and repudiation of anything contributing to segregation, and I wanted this as a policy statement of the Archdiocese. This would have had a secondary effect of strengthening the hand of the Board of Education in its policy stand. It was promised me but I never received it. The Archdiocese has no blueprint for race relations at all. It is not knowledgeable in that area and is unsure as to the kind of

---

* See Chapters Seven and Eight for a discussion of these funds.

† The Catholic population includes many Puerto Ricans as well as whites. There are some blacks who are Catholic—mostly middle class, and probably less than 10% of the total black population.

‡ Jewish parochial schools had an enrollment of 87,713 in 1967, 79% of which were in elementary schools, 15% in high schools, and 6% in preschool programs.

leadership it should provide in the whole spectrum of inter-racial programs." [37]

Thus there is a clear demographic trend in New York City's recent history. Negroes and Puerto Ricans have moved into decaying areas of Manhattan and the other boroughs that were formerly occupied by Jews, Irish, Italians, and other ethnic minorities. The racial frontier, marking the outer perimeters of minority group concentration, kept shifting as transitional, fringe areas tipped. In time, as more urban renewal took place, dislocating many Negro and Puerto Rican families, as the Negroes and Puerto Ricans continued to come to the city, and as Negro and Puerto Rican birth rates maintained their high level relative to those of whites, the ghetto populations overflowed.

Whites who have remained in many parts of the city are more often than not an older, more conservative, lower or lower middle class population. They have been less tolerant of Negroes and Puerto Ricans than the upward mobile, middle class liberals who left.

Some parts of the city have become physically integrated—though the integration has little social meaning: the diverse racial, ethnic, and generational groups live in separate worlds in such places as the Upper West Side of Manhattan. There still remain, however, many areas of upper middle or upper class white concentration. Manhattan's Upper East Side, for example, contains most of the city's rich whites, who send their children to private schools. There are, in addition, some exclusive communities in Queens and Brooklyn. They have generally held the line against housing or school desegregation.

Real Estate Interests and the Board of Education

These trends are not inevitable. They are perpetuated by numerous institutional and political forces. Though they were not concerned mainly with education, private developers, local homeowner groups, slum landlords, and even city housing agencies, acting in their own interests or in the interests of their tenants, or in accordance with housing codes, have contributed to school desegregation by perpetuating segregated housing. They also exerted direct influence on the Board of Education to build schools and zone them to preserve homogeneous student populations.

The housing politics of Queens, Brooklyn, and The Bronx is full of examples of the success of local real estate interests in keeping low income projects out of white, middle class areas. The borough president's office is a center for such pressures, and historically the borough presidents of The Bronx, Queens, and Brooklyn have been aligned with and politically indebted to, developer and homeowner interests. Constance Baker Motley and Percy Sutton of Manhattan, and Herman Badillo of The Bronx, are among the few borough presidents who have worked actively for desegregated housing.

The objections to low income projects in white, middle class areas are the conventional ones that property values will go down and "problems" will come into the neighborhood. Often, large real estate interests—brokers and developers—feed these fears by spreading rumors that one project will be followed by many others. Generally, most real estate interests, whether operating in the ghetto (for example, slum landlords) or in white residential areas, see little profit in desegregation.

State legislation (the Mitchell–Lama Act) has been enacted to put some profit into interracial housing by providing subsidies, low interest loans, and tax abatement. Taxes are levied on the property on the old base, rather than on the improved one. The state, in turn, has the right to prevent racial discrimination in such housing. The law encourages builders to invest in land that would ordinarily be too expensive for them to develop. Though the state partially regulates the profits, developers do stand to benefit. Even so, most still promote segregated, one-class housing as a way to encourage more rentals, especially by white middle class families.

The real estate market is much affected by banks and other financial institutions which may inadvertently also promote segregation. Large banks that float mortgages in white, middle class homeowner areas may rig them to discourage Negro applicants. Some engage in "blockbusting," contributing to a spreading of the ghetto. Rumors are often circulated that large numbers of Negroes are about to move in, with the supposed planning of low income projects. Banks sometimes encourage large lower class Negro families to move into white residential areas, after denying that opportunity to middle class Negroes. They later make a big profit by buying out the remaining white residents at a depressed price and selling to incoming Negroes at a very high one.

There are other forces working for segregated housing as well. Federal money for low income housing projects has been rendered only if the projects were located in decaying, slum areas. City housing agencies have reinforced this pattern, by building low income projects in slums. They are under continued pressure to do so from homeowner groups, developers, and many politicians who act as their intermediaries. All these interests contribute to a furtherance of slum crystallization rather than to desegregation.

One reason city officials have not resisted the trend toward segregation more vigorously is that it has many payoffs. There are votes for politicians and profits for landlords and developers. And there is grass roots support among homeowners, taxpayers, and civic improvement associations that is hard to overlook. Local groups of this nature have been organized for many decades in the four outlying boroughs of the city and have acted in their own best interests. And their pressures reinforce the effects of private economic decisions by developers, brokers, and banks. The result of these alliances is increased housing segregation.*

Sometimes overlooked is the fact that these real estate and propertied groups also influence school officials on school construction and zoning decisions. Historically, the board has always been under pressure from such interests to locate and zone schools according to their needs. Sometimes the board has even cooperated with landlords and tenants in zoning to preserve segregation. In one area of the mid-Bronx, for example, along the Grand Concourse, landlords and the Board of Education developed a plan whereby landlords provided free bus service for children of their tenants to schools outside the neighborhood, while the board cooperated in its zoning practices. This cooperative venture began around 1952, when the neighborhood school concept was considered sacrosanct. It involved bussing white children away from integrated neighborhood schools.[38]

A conventional interpretation of school and city officials, and of social scientists and urban planners, is that housing segregation is the primary cause of school segregation. It is assumed that school segregation was not deliberately planned,

---

* Racism is thus built into the underlying economic structure of the city, reflecting a national pattern.

but just came about as a result of residential patterns. My evidence suggests that this is not totally the case in New York City and that the Board of Education's own actions contributed to the tipping of some residential areas that had previously been integrated. I am suggesting that school construction and zoning practices of the board were a cause not only of increased school segregation but of housing segregation as well.

One typical example is at a middle income housing development called Concourse Village Co-Op in the mid-Bronx.* In late 1965, the co-op had a minority group population of about 35%. To the south and east was a densely populated area, almost all Negro and Puerto Rican, called the south Bronx. There were about half a dozen low cost public housing developments with inadequate facilities in that part of the ghetto most adjacent to the co-op. The board had built a two-story school with roughly 1,200 seats, to service an area of 1,500 low income Negro and Puerto Rican families. Co-op officials secured an appropriation for a school to the southeast of their development to relieve this overcrowding. It was to be an elementary school in the fringe area and was to be integrated by white middle class children from the co-op. The school was to be about 80% Negro and Puerto Rican. The strategy of the integration-minded co-op officials was to make the school a good one and then press for zoning changes to increase its white enrollment. The biggest immediate need, however, was for the south Bronx children.

The Board of Education did build a new school, but at much less capacity than the co-op officials requested, and as a replacement for another school that was over one hundred years old. Since the new school was overcrowded when it opened, the hundred-year-old facility was reopened and used as an annex. This was the last straw for the middle class white parents. Up to that point they had not raised any significant complaint about sending their children to the new school. They did refuse, however, to send their children to a hundred-year-old "firetrap." They won their point. Their children were zoned elsewhere, and the minority group children attended the firetrap, in conjunction with the new building. The board refurbished two floors of the old school, connected the two schools with a tunnel, and they are now almost 100% segregated. Within

---

* Distinct from Co-Op City, discussed earlier in this chapter.

a few months two buildings in the co-op went from 30% to 65% minority population, as the whites gave up on the school.

Another fringe area example, illustrating in this case the board's failure to zone for desegregation where the housing pattern permitted it, was JHS 275 in the Canarsie–Brownsville area of southeast Brooklyn. A group of liberal white parents in the Butchers' Union's Jimerson and Gorman co-ops, recognizing the possibilities for desegregation there, asked that the school be placed right on the main thoroughfare, Linden Boulevard, which divides the ghetto from the white community. Lower middle class whites from Canarsie led a four-year fight against the desegregation of this school.*

Headquarters staff and the lay board acknowledge that they bungled in capitulating to the district superintendent and white civic groups who opposed having 275 desegregated. Admittedly, the white community was divided, but the board helped fan the conflict by its hesitation and vacillation and got itself into a difficult cross-pressure situation. JHS 275 wasn't even a threat to the neighborhood school concept. Most of the white children who might have been zoned in from Canarsie could have walked to school. Yet well-meaning Canarsie parents actually believed that their children would be bussed deep into the ghetto if they went to 275.

The board changed its mind about the location of 275 on three separate occasions, finally locating it on Linden Boulevard. The first two sites were closer to the heart of the Brownsville community than to Canarsie, but the third and final site, forced by the mayor and other city officials, was right on the racial frontier. By that time, the segregationist opposition group was well-formed and its leadership was feeding on fears based on the first two sites. The board made little attempt to explain that the new site would not involve traveling into the ghetto for whites. In the end, the board built an additional junior high for whites, and zoned 275 so that it was 90% Negro and Puerto Rican.

To build schools in fringe areas for desegregation would require strong board leadership. The board would have to fight many white parent, homeowner, and real estate groups. It has

* The lay board is the citizens group theoretically responsible for policy making. They act as watchdogs and trustees of the citizenry and are appointed for seven-year terms on a staggered basis. See Chapter Seven for a more extended discussion.

preferred not to do this, and it has tended to retreat in the face of mounting pressure from the white community against fringe-area schools. Real estate developers, brokers, bankers, and homeowners, as well as numerous city agencies, have contributed to this increase in segregation. The latter have tended to shape their policies mainly in response to pressures from their constituencies. Since the white community was much more highly organized than the minority groups, housing and school projects were located and zoned to maintain and expand patterns of segregation. More political pressure from minority groups and more leadership from city officials might at least minimize these trends. There have been a number of efforts in housing—scattered siting of low income projects, subsidized low income families in middle income apartments and projects, and mixed income housing, indicating that some reversals of past policies are possible. The Negro community's understandable disenchantment with integration, after the experience of the past few years, might make many city officials unwilling to incur the political risks of pressing too vigorously for it.

The politics of the situation and administrative constraints within the school system militate against desegregation. Many school officials and parent groups are opposed to it. The main question is why they have been so opposed. Is their opposition based on sound educational arguments, or are these factions motivated by other considerations? What do they see as the rewards of maintaining the status quo, and why do they fear desegregation? And how do they go about influencing the decisions of city officials? I shall deal with these issues in the remaining chapters.

❦

THE NEIGHBORHOOD SCHOOL MOVEMENT

One of the main obstacles to school desegregation in New York City has been a loosely joined coalition of powerful professional groups inside the school system, including teachers, principals, field superintendents, divisional heads, and key headquarters staff personnel; local parent associations, homeowner, taxpayer, and civic groups; and public and private real estate interests. The "neighborhood school" became the slogan around which such status-quo-oriented interests united.

Local, neighborhood schools, which were developed nearly three generations ago to counter the impersonality of urban life, became multipurpose institutions. Many became community centers for the newly arrived ethnic groups who settled in such neighborhoods as the Lower East Side, Yorkville, Hell's Kitchen, Inwood, Brownsville, Crown Heights, Bensonhurst, Bay Ridge, Flatbush, Maspeth, Ridgewood, Glendale—each with its own distinctive ethnic identity and traditions. The neighborhood school was an essential part of these settlements. In some instances, neighborhoods had their own style of architecture, often reflected in the schools. High schools especially became symbols of enduring loyalties and traditions.

Although the public school was supposed to be the great leveling institution, training diverse groups in the virtues of democracy and equality, confining a school's enrollment to its neighborhood limited the mixing of pupils from diverse ethnic and class backgrounds. Yet, the neighborhood school was the gateway to citizenship and participation in American society.

As the most important institution for acculturation, it was in many instances the first place where the child of immigrant parents heard English spoken.

To urban and educational planners, the benefits of the neighborhood school were assumed to be self-evident. To some extent they were, though the neighborhood school has clearly been a strong barrier to mobility and achievement for the ghetto child today. Even today, however, the idea of the neighborhood unit remains among the favorite values of urban planners.

A further argument for the neighborhood school was that relations between the school and the community would be close if schools were near home. Parents and school officials would come together more easily; they would develop deeper and more enduring relations; parents would participate more in school affairs; and teachers and principals would understand the culture of the parents. Pupils would have a more integrated social experience with school friends as the school became a center of social and recreational activity.[1]

Another benefit of the neighborhood school had to do with transportation, a point that white parent groups who oppose non-voluntary desegregation plans always make in their resistance to "bussing." They argue that traveling is minimized under a neighborhood school arrangement, thus avoiding fatigue and danger for young children, while the children know that their mothers are near in case of illness or emergency. Advocates of neighborhood schools also argue that it is much more important to spend school funds on salaries, buildings, books, and other facilities that will improve the quality of services, than on transportation. Basic to all these arguments is the belief that neighborhood schools provide better education, all other things being equal, than schools that draw pupils from a much wider area.

A final argument supporting the neighborhood school concept is that it is much easier to maintain close, informal relationships between teachers and pupils in small, local schools than in those that draw pupils from a very wide area. Many educators are convinced of the presumed benefits of small, local schools, even if no studies bear out their judgments. The only literature on the relation between school size and quality deals with total districts, and the general finding is that quality does increase with increased size, up to a certain point (50,000 to 100,000 pupils per district), after which quality declines. These are only correlational studies, however, and the mere association of bigness with lowered quality does not mean that one causes the other. Big-city school systems, after all, have the largest poverty populations, another significant factor affecting quality.

This is not the place to review all the evidence that tests some of the assumptions of the neighborhood school and questions its benefits. It is possible, for example, that the distance between school and home is not the major factor determining the extent of parent participation in school affairs. More important is the receptivity of local school officials, and the race and social class of parents.

There are many commentaries by urban planners and social scientists on the advantages of school consolidation in educational complexes and parks rather than in neighborhood schools. Indeed, a voluminous literature has accumulated on the administrative, economic, educational, and desegregative benefits of school consolidation in large cities.[2] Much of the discussion is based on logic and argument by analogy—using consolidated rural schools as a model—since there aren't many examples of urban educational complexes and parks from which to derive any generalizations. Nevertheless, even the unvalidated arguments that support consolidation and sharply condemn the neighborhood school are compelling. But the New York City Board of Education still shows little sign of taking them seriously enough to want to try them out. Instead, the board is in the forefront of the neighborhood school coalition.*

A direct confrontation of civil rights leaders with board officials in 1964 on school construction indicated how firmly wedded the board was to the neighborhood school.[3] Dr. Adrian Blumenfeld, director of the School Planning and Research Unit, told protesting civil rights leaders time and again that he only followed board policy, which was "to build the schools where the children are." He and the board refused to re-evaluate or modify their construction program.

---

* One has to distinguish between neighborhood elementary schools and consolidated middle and upper schools. Broadening the geographic area for zoning may have more educational and social justification for grades above the elementary level than in the elementary grades, for many of the reasons cited above. Even at that, however, educational complexes and parks would include the primary grades, with those children not being required to travel very far to school.

A recent example of the board's unwillingness to change is its location of middle schools.* One recommendation of the Allen Committee Report was that middle schools be located in fringe areas.[4] But the board's April, 1965, policy statement on desegregation indicated an intent to do so only where practicable.[5] Apparently, it has not been practicable for at least nine of the fourteen intermediate schools the board has built since 1965. Furthermore, the board is building four-year middle schools at a maximum capacity of 1,800 pupils, the same size as its old three-year junior highs, only large enough to draw pupils from a local population. The desegregative purpose of the middle schools, both as indicated in the Allen Report and in the board's own policy statements, is therefore defeated.

The same failures occurred with rezoning plans. In September, 1966, the board began a new plan to decrease overcrowding in ghetto schools, by sending children into underused schools in white neighborhoods—they called it their "equalization–utilization" plan. Principals in receiving schools have objected to the plan, just as they did in the past to Open Enrollment, and headquarters has not pressed for compliance. In late 1966, Superintendent Donovan reportedly told one of his headquarters staff who was responsible for administering the program that if principals balked at participating, they should not be pushed.[6] The neighborhood school, then, is still the guiding principle for zoning and site location, even though the board's policy statements say otherwise.

The board defends this inertia with two arguments: First, it says it has a responsibility as a public agency to respond to its constituencies. Public opinion must necessarily shape many of its decisions and, according to its top officials, there has not been much grass roots support for fringe area construction and rezoning. But this is only part of the story; it ignores civil rights pressures to build and zone for desegregation, which reached their peak in 1964 and early 1965. The pressures have eased up since then, as it became increasingly clear that regardless of what the board's policy statements said, it would not change its practices. Many school officials have welcomed such an easing of pressures, and they point to the absence of demands for rezoning to justify maintaining the

---

* Middle schools are new intermediate schools for pre-adolescent children, replacing the old junior highs and including the fifth through eighth grades. They were recommended in the Allen Report.

neighborhood schools. But their own inactions have had much to do with the civil rights leaders' shift of pressure to community control.*

The board's second argument is that fringe areas change too rapidly for construction to have any lasting effect on desegregation.[7] They are often defined as transitional areas that will become predominantly Negro and Puerto Rican by the time schools get built. Sometimes this is true, but the process is not inevitable. Sometimes it is a self-fulfilling prophecy, insofar as the board's policies affect demographic trends. Failure to provide school facilities in integrated neighborhoods contributes to their tipping, as many whites leave in search of uncrowded and better schools.[8]

The board's zoning and construction policies thus may help accelerate the very white exodus that, according to the board, prevents desegregation. The lay board does not admit this. One of its members, Morris Iushewitz, persistently attempts to push through more fringe area construction, but has been consistently overruled by his colleagues and most of the top professional staff.

Though the neighborhood school concept is often defended on pedagogical grounds, there is reason to think that, for the board, it is really a device to prevent desegregation. School officials typically succumb to real estate and white parent pressures and deliberately gerrymander school boundaries to maintain the class, racial, and ethnic homogeneity of pupil populations in ways that make a farce of the label "neighborhood school."

Several examples of gerrymandering come to mind. Manhattan's Upper West and Upper East Side, the mid-Bronx, and the Canarsie section of southeast Brooklyn are all areas where schools have been zoned to maintain segregation. The pattern was most prevalent in fringe areas—along the so-called racial frontiers. PS 6, one of Manhattan's Upper East Side schools in the "silk stocking" area, provides a historic case. This school, on 81st Street, drew children from as far south as 45th Street and all the way north to 96th. Its district extended more than three miles, well beyond the distance the Board of Education

---

* In a television appearance of the board just after the Bundy Report was released (1967), Mrs. Rose Shapiro, one of its senior members, exclaimed that she hoped there would not be any more public pressure for bussing, implying that New York City had had enough.

generally accepts as desirable. The district line zig-zagged from west to east in such a way as to exclude working and lower middle class Irish and German populations in nearby Yorkville. The areas these pupils came from could hardly be considered a neighborhood. Indeed PS 6 was the "private" public school for an upper middle class, white Protestant and German Jewish population, scattered throughout the fashionable East Side. The Board of Education did rezone PS 6 in 1964, under strong pressure from civil rights groups and the Commission on Human Rights, a city agency concerned with race problems— much to the chagrin of some of the PS 6 parents, who took their case to the courts and lost.[9]

Deliberate gerrymandering of a new high school in Canarsie, in East Brooklyn, was equally blatant.[10] Canarsie is an isolated area, populated mainly by lower middle class, homeowning whites, most of whom recently migrated from slums and were anxious to keep Negroes out of their schools and neighborhood. A large portion of the population is Jewish, with a significant minority of Italians. The Italians in the area are the old-timers, who play an important role in local politics. Only recently have the Jews begun to move into positions of civic leadership and power.

Both groups wanted to preserve segregated schools. They were able to force the zoning for Canarsie High School so that it deliberately excluded Negroes from neighboring Brownsville on the north, but included whites from more distant areas. This was done against the will of the new principal of the school, a man dedicated to desegregation. He had developed a zoning plan that included many Brownsville students, but he was caught in a squeeze between local Canarsie groups and headquarters. His zoning plan was rejected.[11]

There are such instances in most fringe areas throughout the city, which cast doubt on the board's continued protests that it could desegregate more if the segregated housing pattern would only change. Furthermore, the board's argument that rezoning in fringe or integrated areas would cause schools to tip does not always hold. A number of schools throughout the city have held their white middle class students, despite increased numbers of Negro and Puerto Rican pupils. The quality of school programs, and especially abilities of the principal, may affect the willingness of white middle class parents to keep their children in such desegregated schools, as shown in Manhattan's

Upper West Side.* It may be possible, then, to maintain desegregated fringe area schools without losing most of the whites.[12]

To go one step beyond the board's arguments, rezoning and fringe area construction are essentially political questions. They bear on the issue of how free the board is to change the neighborhood school tradition. Did the constraints the board faced limit its options? Or did it have more freedom than it cared to exercise? On one hand, the board has been pressed by civic and real estate groups, and by many school officials. On the other, interest-group pressures are in varying degrees a product of board actions and inactions, even if that is not their only source.

Civic Groups

There had never been any organized neighborhood school movement in New York City until the desegregation controversy intensified in 1963. Until then, the board's attempts at desegregation had been limited, never exceeding plans for voluntary pupil transfers. Even these modest plans were poorly implemented, so there was no occasion for an anti-integration movement to arise.

One of the few exceptions, when a well-organized opposition group did develop, was in the summer and early fall of 1959, when the Board of Education transferred the first group of Negro pupils into predominantly white schools. In September, 1959, 302 Negro pupils were transferred from overcrowded elementary schools in the Bedford–Stuyvesant area of Brooklyn to underused schools in the Ridgewood–Glendale section of Queens.[13] Ridgewood and Glendale were among the most conservative white communities in New York City, composed mainly of lower and lower middle class German and Irish homeowners. Both communities were physically insulated from the rest of the city by a broad belt of cemeteries. They were socially insulated as well.

Local groups coalesced to block the plan. They protested on

* PS 145, 75, 87, 9, and 166 on Manhattan's Upper West Side are all examples. Dr. Carl D. Ergberg, then of 145, rang doorbells to get more white middle class parents to send their children to his school, which was in danger of becoming all black and Puerto Rican in the early 1960s. He was quite successful and was able to stabilize the white enrollment at 40 to 45%. He spent much time working with white, Puerto Rican, and black groups in the community.

the grounds that real estate and property values would go down, school standards would be lowered, delinquency and crime rates would increase, and that local white children would become "contaminated" by incoming Negro pupils. Opposing parent and civic groups (and many opponents were not parents) urged the neighborhood school concept, suggesting that it was not necessary to transfer Negro children out of their local schools. They recommended faster construction of more schools in Bedford–Stuyvesant.[14]

These groups represented as resistant a white population as one could choose for the first attempt at school desegregation. There were threats and indications of possible violence, even though the incoming Negro pupils were only eight and nine years old. White residents in the area staged a boycott of five elementary schools to which Negro children had been transferred, keeping 42% of the white enrollment out of school the first day.[15]

Yet, through the skillful intervention of the Mayor's Commission on Intergroup Relations and the Catholic Inter-Racial Council, which mobilized neighborhood leadership to counter the agitation of the local "taxpayer" associations, violence and continued resistance were avoided. Clergymen mingled with the crowds at the schools on opening day and finally persuaded many reluctant mothers to send their children to school. Superintendent John Theobald's strong leadership also contributed to acceptance of the plan.

This event marked the beginning of Open Enrollment in New York City, and while some white communities were not enthusiastic at first, the idea was gradually accepted as inevitable.* Few open, organized protests occurred over the next four years. One could hardly say that any kind of active neighborhood school, anti-integration movement existed.

In 1963, things changed—a reflection, largely, of the Birmingham riots and the new Negro militancy. Voluntary Open Enrollment plans were now increasingly seen to have little effect on desegregation and nonvoluntary transfer began to seem a more effective desegregation strategy.

Two developments in the late spring of 1963 contributed to this change. In May, State Education Commissioner James Allen requested that the New York City Board of Education

---

* The Open Enrollment program actually did not get underway until 1960, but this helped pave the way.

report on the extent of "racial balance" in their schools and on their plans for change where imbalance existed.[16]

The other development was the new attitude of civil rights groups: their disenchantment with Open Enrollment, their movement toward a potentially powerful coalition within the Citywide Committee for Integrated Schools, and their demand for a citywide desegregation plan.[17] The rising militancy of the national civil rights movement stimulated this development, as did a policy statement by the lay board in June, 1963, applauding President Kennedy for his increased civil rights efforts and announcing that it was going ahead with new plans for desegregation on its own.[18]

As many Negro and white integrationists hoped that more school desegregation might now be possible in a liberal city like New York, they increased their demands on the board.

But in September a critical event occurred that both spurred the opposition movement and marked the beginning of the end for the emerging school desegregation coalition, almost before it was formed. This was the announcement in September, 1963, of a possible Princeton Plan pairing of a predominantly white elementary school in the Jackson Heights area of Queens (PS 149) with a segregated Negro school in nearby Corona (PS 92).* The idea for the pairing was developed by some liberal white parents on the executive committee of the PS 149 parent association, in collaboration with top officials of the United Parents Association (central headquarters agency for most of the parent associations in the city). The plan would never have been announced so early in its development, but for a leak to the New York *Herald Tribune*.[19]

PS 149 and 92 finally were paired, but only after a controversy that shook the entire city, contributed to the development of a powerful opposition coalition, and effectively discouraged the Board of Education and top city officials from ever entertaining any significant plans for school desegregation in the future.

As soon as word of the possible pairing got out, a number of lower and lower middle class Jackson Heights parents, most

---

* Pairing is a desegregation technique that rezones two contiguous elementary schools, one predominantly white, the other predominantly black, so that all pupils go to one for the first three grades and to the other for the next three. The schools are usually on either side of the racial frontier of the area.

of them residing in one large co-op, and with children in PS
149, protested that a few parent association leaders had developed this plan during the summer without ever consulting the
community. They strongly objected to the pairing idea, although the schools were only six blocks apart, and despite an
informal promise by the Board of Education that both schools
would get many additional services. School officials and many
progressive white parents in the area agreed that 149 was a
mediocre school and had continually been denied needed staff
and services over the past few years, on the understandable
grounds that schools in ghetto areas had a much greater need.
Nevertheless, several white parents claimed that the Board
of Education had no legal right to transfer their children away
from their neighborhood school.

The community immediately became polarized into pro-
and anti-pairing groups, the neighborhood school movement
was formed, and the conflict expanded to draw in parents and
communities from the entire city.[20] Only Staten Island and
parts of Manhattan were relatively uninvolved in the struggle.
Even at that, some councilmen and legislators from Staten Island entered the struggle by pressing for anti-bussing legislation. And many areas of Manhattan—for example, Washington
Heights–Inwood, Harlem, East Harlem, Yorkville, and Lincoln
Center—became sites of desegregation plans and controversies.

An organization which called itself Parents and Taxpayers
(PAT) was formed a few days after the announcement of the
pairing, in the rumpus room of the Jackson Heights co-op,
where most white parents with children in PS 149 lived. PAT's
leaders decided that the only way to fight the Princeton Plan
was to organize on a federated basis in local communities
throughout the city. Many feared that the Board of Education
might try to institute citywide pairings.

The leaders of PAT were adept at dramatizing that possibility, thereby feeding the anxieties that were developing in
many white communities. With no clear statements from the
board on just what its intentions might be, it was relatively easy
for a hard core of activists and a few leaders to mobilize a large
following quickly.[21]

The press also helped by dramatizing the bussing issue, even
though the superintendent and lay board had no immediate
plans for the mandatory bussing of children, and certainly not
of white children. Internal divisions, however, kept the board

from speaking out. The confusion that followed reinforced the fears of parents, and the neighborhood school movement picked up a large following. Even Robert Kennedy, campaigning for senator in 1964, came out against bussing.[22]

As soon as word got out in September, 1963, that the board might, indeed, pair 149 and 92 and perhaps other schools (information on the latter was never corroborated until many months later), Parents and Taxpayers formed a citywide coalition of white citizen groups, formed on a taxpayer, parent association, and civic base, including organizations from white communities in Queens, Brooklyn, and even from the neighboring city of Malverne in Nassau County on Long Island.[23]

Later, a separate group formed in The Bronx, calling itself Parents and Citizens (PAC), under the leadership of Mrs. Lynette Teich, a middle class Jewish housewife.[24] Most of the Brooklyn organizations, led by Gerald Dallek, an accountant and also Jewish,[25] split off and formed their own confederated group, the Joint Council for Better Education. I emphasize the fact that Mrs. Teich and Dallek were Jewish to highlight the uneasiness of many Jewish members of PAT with what struck them as the Nazi-like, demagogic atmosphere of the meetings,[26] though their views on the neighborhood school and mandatory pupil transfers remained similar to PAT's and still do. Their differences did not, however, hamper the movement's political effectiveness.

The communities represented in the PAT's Coordinating Council at this early stage were invariably composed of lower and lower middle class, second generation white homeowners who lived in fringe areas or in communities with an expanding Negro population; many of these communities were rumored to be facing school desegregation plans in the near future. They included Canarsie, Flatbush, East Flatbush, Bay Ridge, Sheepshead Bay, and Bensonhurst in Brooklyn; Ridgewood, Glendale, Maspeth, Hollis, Middle Village, the Rockaways, Rockwood Park, Woodside, Astoria, Jackson Heights, Bergen Basin, and Howard Beach in Queens; and Washington Heights–Inwood in Manhattan.*

---

* There was also a representative present from Malverne, a community ridden with conflict over school desegregation, and located in nearby Nassau County, adjacent to Queens. A group called Taxpayers and Parents had formed in Malverne and was fighting State Education Commissioner James Allen's order to desegregate.

Two main coalitions emerged in the Jackson Heights pairing controversy.* The pressure to take sides was so intense in the single co-op where most of the involved parents resided that it was difficult for a moderate group to form and mediate between the two parties.

The integrationists were organized and led by an articulate lawyer, Harry Ansorge,[27] who was active in Reform Democrat circles, and had worked for the New York State Commission Against Discrimination. He and his followers were primarily middle class, upward mobile, college educated, liberal Jews. They formed an organization called Citizens Committee for Better Schools (CCBS), composed almost equally of Negroes from Corona and whites from Jackson Heights. Ansorge and other whites assumed leadership in the organization, though not without some conflicts with the Corona Negroes. Ansorge and his colleagues felt this was a fight in which the white community had to show leadership.

The opposition was also led by a lawyer, Bernard Kessler, who, like Ansorge, lived in the co-op, though he had previously been inactive in school and civic affairs.[28] Kessler had lived on a farm in the upstate village of Hyde Park through high school, and later attended St. John's College and law school. Parents called him in to represent them in the very first meeting on the pairing question, partly because they felt there were many legal issues involved.

The controversy between PAT and CCBS ran from September, 1963, through the following fall, when the pairing went into effect. Since the controversy took place almost exclusively within this single co-op, this led to abrasive personal relations between residents, and to a hardening of lines and positions. It was carried on primarily as a leaflet war between CCBS and PAT, with the local school board, district superintendent, and other school officials, who tried to play a mediating role, generally supporting the pairing.

Relations among residents were so strained that people wouldn't talk when they came together in elevators and on the co-op grounds. In some cases, even their children could not play together, and to this day some deep divisions remain.

---

* The Jackson Heights controversy and the people involved should be seen as prototypes of a citywide and, indeed, a nationwide pattern, and not as unique or idiosyncratic to that area.

Socio-Economic Status, Mobility Experiences, Values, Life Styles

One explanation for the different responses among white residents to the pairing is their differences in social background, present circumstances and values.[29] Jackson Heights has a large lower middle class, homeowner population who became the most committed followers of PAT. In occupation, education, and income they may be classified at the lower margins of the middle class. Many of these homeowners are clerical workers, salesmen, or small businessmen, with little to distinguish them from blue collar workers except their occupational status and residential area. They are an upward mobile group: many had moved out to their present communities from ethnic ghetto areas closer to the central city. Some came from The Bronx, others from parts of Manhattan or Brooklyn. For many, their upward mobility had more to do with a change of residence than with changes in occupation or income. They had moved from overcrowded apartment dwellings to single and two-family homes or co-ops in outlying areas.

Many felt they could not easily afford to move again. Moreover, their limited occupational skills and education probably precluded further occupational mobility. Although they have often threatened the Board of Education that they will move out in large numbers if their schools are desegregated, many have strong ties to the local area and probably intend to remain where they are. Finally, they look with some scorn on private schools—which they cannot afford in any case. Some have sent their children to parochial schools, and there are sections in The Bronx, Queens, and Brooklyn, where even Jewish families who do not regularly attend synagogues have tried to open their own religious schools; they do not necessarily want religious education, but rather to avoid sending their children to what they see as poor quality schools with lower class Negro and Puerto Rican pupils.

There are at least two "social types" among the opposition in these fringe areas—the new residents I have just described and the old-timers who have lived in their neighborhoods for many years and who now have children of school age and also fear that the schools and neighborhoods will be overrun by lower class Negroes. Many of them nourish fantasies about the 1930s and forties when their communities had few Negroes and the city had no "race problem." Both these social types are somewhat similar in class and ethnic characteristics, though the old-timers may be of a slightly higher socio-economic status.

Supporters of such integrationist groups as the Citizens' Committee for Better Schools in Jackson Heights are much more likely to be middle and upper middle class, and more highly educated than most PAT followers. In Jackson Heights, for example, the basic split was between a "college" and "non-college" group. The two groups had never had much social contact before the pairing controversy and obviously had much less afterward.[30]

This middle class, liberal group is more cosmopolitan than the PAT followers. Its range of social contacts is broader than that of neighborhood school people, who are primarily locals. Many of them lived in such communities as Jackson Heights as an interim move, before going out to Connecticut or Westchester. They are much more upward-mobile than PAT followers. One of the things that PAT followers in Jackson Heights most resented was that the pairing was pushed by a group that clearly intended to leave the neighborhood in the next few years. Neighborhood school advocates throughout the city resented the fact that upper middle class "white liberals" had placed them on the firing line while sending their own children to private schools or while planning to move out. Many leaders in the school desegregation movement had their children in private schools.*

Furthermore, many of the neighborhood school group, as members of ethnic minorities, are acutely conscious of how they or their parents were able to "work their way" out of poverty and slums "the hard way," without any artificial props and government support. It seems more than reasonable to them that since they have improved themselves through "self-help," why can't the Negro? As one upward-mobile person from an old Jewish community once said to me: "I left Brownsville. Why can't they?"

That this lower middle class group is largely second-generation affects its view of school desegregation in at least two ways.

* Peter Schrag suggests that the same pattern existed in Boston. The working class Irish there were forced by the middle class Yankees and Jewish liberals who had long since moved out, to desegregate with the Negro. Furthermore, the Yankees had kept the Irish down in Boston for over a century, and this new pressure was viewed with much resentment. Peter Schrag, *Village School Downtown,* Boston: Beacon Press, 1967.

First, many are highly ethnocentric, having moved so recently from ethnically homogeneous areas. Just one step removed from an ethnic ghetto, they maintain the residue of distrust toward outsiders that their parents felt.[31] Outsiders in this instance are the new Negro residents in their communities and pupils in their schools. These patterns of ethnocentrism and prejudice are prevalent among Irish, Italian and German populations, as well as among Jews, though somewhat less so among the latter. These tendencies are of great concern to liberal Catholic and Jewish leaders. The Anti-Defamation League, the American Jewish Congress, the American Jewish Committee, the Union of American Hebrew Congregations, and the Catholic Inter-Racial Council have all attempted to counter such fears and prejudices.

Another consequence of their second generation status is their self-consciousness about being minorities and their interest in becoming bona fide Americans. They are frequently ambivalent about their ethnic identity when it conflicts with an equally strong need to be accepted by the majority. Typically they project their doubts about the worth of their own ethnic group onto the Negroes.[32]

These characteristics are frequently associated with a number of social attitudes—intolerance of "outgroups," stereotyping, rigid moralism that sees the world as made up of "good guys" and "bad guys," an exaggerated preoccupation with status, and a limited tolerance of alternative values.[33]

The neighborhood school movement may be interpreted as a form of status politics,[34] whose followers are concerned that if Negroes move into their schools and neighborhoods there will no longer be a group whose status is lower than their own. Many of these whites are homeowners who are concerned about declining property values if Negroes move into their area; they believe this will contribute to a general deterioration of living conditions. Many may be concerned about protecting their jobs against competition from Negroes. They want to preserve hard-won status advantages and maintain the respectability of their local area. They are also concerned about keeping the community free from control by Negro pressure groups and politicians. Finally, they are concerned about the upward mobility of their children, which they feel is threatened by forced desegregation and, they reason, a decline in the quality of their education.

A kind of scarcity psychology underlies these fears.* These people assume that there is a fixed amount of rights, rewards, power, and opportunities, and that if Negroes get a larger slice of the pie, whites will get less. This is what the civil rights movement means to many of them, and they are unwilling to tolerate demands for school desegregation. These views were expressed in their most extreme form by a group of young men from parts of Queens and Brooklyn who called themselves SPONGE (Society for the Prevention of Negroes Getting Everything) which demonstrated at the World's Fair in the spring of 1964 against civil rights. SPONGE never had more than a handful of followers, but the sentiments they expressed were in line with those of many neighborhood school zealots, even though the latter did not express such views quite so openly.

This difference in the political attitudes of lower and higher status whites has much to do with how white communities react to desegregation plans. In Brooklyn Heights, for example, the site of one pairing, Parents and Taxpayers could not mobilize much local support. Neither could the Joint Council or any other neighborhood school group. Some parents opposed the pairing there, and so did some real estate interests, but they were overruled by most white parents and civic leaders. Brooklyn Heights is a college-educated, upper middle class, white community.

In Lincoln Center, the site of another pairing, Parents and Taxpayers leaders tried to organize white parents but were similarly unsuccessful, though an opposition group, the West Side Parents League, formed there. It was unable to carry much weight in the community, however, and the pairing went through. Eight of the nine local school board members voted for it. The tone of this Upper West Side neighborhood was set by its upper middle class, Reform Democrat, predominantly Jewish, professional population.

Yet, it is important to keep some perspective on how receptive to school desegregation even this white liberal group was. In other areas they did not always respond as favorably as they did in Jackson Heights, Brooklyn Heights, and Lincoln Square.

---

* This scarcity psychology is a classic lower middle class ideology, characteristic of homeowners and of small businessmen who feel increasingly oppressed by big labor, big business, and big government. See: Svend Ranulf, *Moral Indignation and Middle Class Psychology*, Copenhagen, 1938, and Arthur J. Vidich and Joseph Bensman, *Small Town in Mass Society*, Princeton: Princeton University Press, 1958.

For example, there was a rumor in early 1964 that PS 84, a predominantly white elementary school on Manhattan's Upper West Side (West 92nd Street, near Central Park West), would be paired with a nearby segregated Negro and Puerto Rican school. Many West Side Reform Democrats from the FDR–Woodrow Wilson Club called an emergency meeting. Some were very upset and organized to beat the proposal down. As one disappointed member of the club stated: "All their old liberalism went by the boards. They are liberal in the abstract, and when the problem is far away, say in Selma, Jackson, or Birmingham, but not for their children or their schools and neighborhoods." [35]

Nevertheless, Italians, Irish and Germans dominated neighborhood school groups, particularly in Queens, and to a lesser degree in The Bronx and Brooklyn. A large Irish and Italian group led the activist wing of PAT in Jackson Heights, parts of Elmhurst, South Ozone Park, and East Queens. They were active in the Inwood section of Washington Heights in upper Manhattan, in the mid- and northeast Bronx, and Bensonhurst and Canarsie in Brooklyn. William F. Buckley and Rosemary Gunning, both Irish Catholics, running on the Conservative Party ticket in the 1965 mayoralty campaign, appealed to those ethnic groups. Mrs. Gunning was a leader in Queens PAT.

Voting Patterns

Data compiled from returns on the 1965 mayoralty election and the 1966 civilian review board referendum support all these interpretations.[36] Throughout the campaign, Buckley and Gunning emphasized their strong support of the neighborhood school and their opposition to bussing. The 1966 civilian review board vote became in part a test of attitudes toward Negroes. Buckley received his strongest support in Staten Island (25%), which has large lower middle class, homeowner, Italian and Irish populations. Queens, which gave him 17%, The Bronx 12%, and Brooklyn 11%, have more of these populations than does Manhattan, which gave Buckley 7% of its vote.

To test the hypothesis that class and nationality characteristics within the white community relate to race attitudes, I have computed the Buckley vote in those election districts where he did best and worst, deliberately excluding from consideration those districts with large Negro and Puerto Rican populations.

Looking first at The Bronx, three of the districts where he polled his highest vote—Parkchester–Pelham Parkway, Eden-wald–Westchester Heights, and Clason Point–Soundview—are in the northeast. They are centers of Parents and Citizens (PAC) strength. Until very recently they were areas of almost 100% white population, but Negroes and Puerto Ricans are gradually moving into low income projects. Those neighborhoods that remain all white have receiving schools under Open Enroll-ment. Some are adjacent to communities whose Negro and Puerto Rican populations have increased in recent years.

The 1960 census data indicate marked nationality differ-ences in subcommunity populations with highest and lowest Buckley votes. Roughly 30% of the Parkchester–Pelham Park-way population, for example, with the highest Buckley vote (28%), were Italian, Irish, and German, with Italians (15%) predominating. A majority of this group were homeowners. The Port Morris–Mott Haven district, by contrast, with the lowest Buckley vote (6%), has a much smaller representation of these ethnic groups (10–15%) and many more East Euro-pean Jews. The same general pattern holds for Queens and Brooklyn.

The civilian review board vote of 1966 further corroborates the ethnic and class hypotheses. The same voting pattern ex-isted as in the 1965 election. In The Bronx, for example, the highest vote against the board (80%) was in the Parkchester–Throgs Neck district, with the highest percentage of Italians of any election district in the borough (15%). Italians, Irish and Germans account for 28% of the total population in the district, compared with 3% of Russian (and most of them Jewish) background. This is in contrast to Riverdale, which had the lowest vote against the board of any district in the borough (57%), and where the numbers are literally re-versed.

In Brooklyn and Queens, the ethnic pattern is if anything even more pronounced. Those districts where the vote against the board was highest (75% or more) were also the ones with the highest Italian, Norwegian, Irish, or German population. Bay Ridge–Fort Hamilton, Gowanus–Downtown Brooklyn, Bay Ridge–Borough Park, and Park Slope–Borough Park are all ex-amples. By contrast, Flatbush and Midwood, where the board was outvoted by a somewhat lower percentage (60–65%) contained up to four times as many residents of Russian origin as Italian, Irish, and German.

In Queens, Italians, Irish and Germans also accounted for the high vote against the board—as in the Elmhurst–Maspeth, Sunnyside–Maspeth, Ozone Park–Woodhaven, South Ozone Park–Howard Beach, and Cambria Heights–Hollis districts. There were few Russians and Poles in these districts. The low vote districts—Forest Hills–Rego Park and Kew Gardens–Jamaica—contained more German and East European Jews, and also had many more middle and upper middle class people.

The two votes are one indication of which class and ethnic groups are attracted to PAT and related neighborhood school groups. There were, to be sure, many voters opposed to school desegregation who would never vote for Buckley. A number of old-line, conservative Bronx, Queens, and Brooklyn Democrats voted in great numbers for O'Connor, the Democratic candidate for City Council president, and some voted for Beame, the Democratic Party candidate for mayor, both products of the party machine. Actually, this is another indication of the college versus non-college, blue- versus white-collar split within the white population. The non-college, blue-, and lower white-collar groups often tended to be old-line Democrats who backed machine candidates. The college-educated, upper middle class, many of whom were Jewish professionals and executives, tended to gravitate more toward the Reform Democrat movement and voted in greater numbers for Lindsay, the Republican and Liberal Party candidate who provided the only alternative to the traditional Democratic slate.

Grass Roots Power, Patterns of Political Participation

Feelings of alienation and powerlessness of many citizen groups who were unable to reach school officials or participate in school decisions have also contributed to the strength of the neighborhood school movement. These sentiments apply equally to the Negro and Puerto Rican populations and to the lower-class and lower-middle-class whites. The recent Black Power movement and demands for greater local participation in the running of schools in ghetto areas are perfect examples. Indeed, at a June, 1967, public hearing held in Harlem by the education committee of the Constitutional Convention, Mrs.

Gunning even acclaimed a plan of Roy Innis, then head of Harlem CORE, for the creation of a separate Harlem school system, indicating how much militant ghetto groups and PAT can have in common.[37] Conservative upstate legislators endorsed the Innis plan during the summer of 1967. Middle class liberals are of course concerned that "extremists" on both sides endorse decentralization and such liberals define this as a regressive move into parochialism and separatism. Parents and other interested citizens, with few if any channels of access to the Board of Education, face a large, amorphous, distant bureaucracy that seldom responds to citizen demands. Many parents with legitimate complaints have no place to take them. Their local school boards are powerless. The principal and the district superintendent often pass the buck to headquarters.* And headquarters officials, in turn, often pass it on to other headquarters colleagues, to state officials, or back down to the field. PAs and PTAs are sometimes of help, but there are many ghetto and white parents whom they don't reach.

In short, despite the continued existence of the neighborhood school, many parents feel they are dealing with a faceless bureaucracy which is not accountable to the public.

The setting in which the neighborhood school movement developed is in many ways typical of the "mass society" discussed in so much contemporary sociological writing.[38] Intermediate community organizations between the citizenry and city government are almost completely lacking. Though Mayor Wagner set up community planning boards throughout the city in the late 1950s, and the Board of Education set up its revitalized local school boards in 1961, neither institution eased the fears of white parents over school desegregation. Citizens had no way to express their resentments through continued public discussion.[39] This both strengthened the opposition and polarized the sides in Jackson Heights and elsewhere. Furthermore, the attitudes and values of the lower middle class that contributed so many followers to the neighborhood school movement were not conducive to civic participation. Typi-

---

* A controversy over the desegregation of JHS 115 in December, 1967, illustrates this. District Superintendent Schapp told angry parents who did not want their children transferred that this was a headquarters decision. Executive Deputy Superintendent Nathan Brown told parents that district superintendents had the option to develop plans. A Bronx politician representing the parents pointed out on a TV news report that this was another example of how the board constantly lies to the community.

cally they lived in relatively private worlds, experimenting with their new leisure in a family-oriented way—avoiding community organizations; spending their evenings, weekends, and vacations with their families; looking at television; visiting friends and kin; cultivating their gardens; pursuing personal hobbies or participating in sports.[40]

Where the neighborhood school movement was strongest, a socio-political vacuum existed, reminiscent of Mannheim's and Ortega y Gasset's view of the alienated, powerless, and privatized citizen, adrift in a mass society where power is increasingly held in a few hands.[41] As the pairing controversy developed, local parents experienced a sense of anomie or shattered expectations. As they saw it, there was no longer any close relationship between expected and actual conditions in their communities. Many felt they had done so many of the "right" things for which society is supposed to reward people: they had worked long hours, saved enough money to move into a respectable neighborhood, bought their own homes, and established residence near a supposedly good school. Suddenly it seemed to them that many of these rewards were being taken away or debased as a result of social forces they could neither understand nor control. The many placards they carried in boycotts and marches on city hall, calling attention to "socialist and communist schemes" concocted by city officials, to the mayor's "irresponsibility" in letting Negro groups take over to push through desegregation plans, and calling for an end to "grand timetables to integrate the schools," indicate the resentments of this group.

Had these people been able to express their grievances through established political institutions, they would have had a safety valve to ease their fears and feelings of alienation. Their resistance might have been tempered and perhaps they would have felt some stake in improving the public schools for all children, as they met other groups, heard other points of view, and had some of their questions answered.

Instead, they developed negative and distorted views of what city and local education officials were doing about desegregation. For example, PAT leaders in many areas stated publicly that board officials were closing schools for the intellectually gifted, planning to bus white pupils in increasing numbers into predominantly Negro areas, and formulating a citywide desegregation plan and a timetable for its implementation—

none of which was true. Some implied that there was a conspiracy of school officials and civil rights leaders to move thousands of white children into the Negro ghetto in the next few years.

As word got around that the Board of Education might implement pairing plans in different areas, many lower middle class white populations changed almost overnight from an apathetic mass into a highly politicized activist movement. Actually, the apathy and sudden activism are closely related. They reflect a condition of mass society described by sociologists James Coleman and William Kornhauser. As Coleman noted:

> These movements operate by mobilizing a previously apathetic mass and demanding responsiveness from an administration at these points in the decision-making process which have heretofore been shut off from public pressure.[42]

Kornhauser points up the affinity of apathy and activism:

> In the absence of proximate sources of gratification and restraint, individuals may become highly responsive to the appeal of mass movements. . . . On the other hand people may respond to their lack of proximate relations with apathy; as a result, their availability for mobilization may be hidden. Apathy born of alienation from community may persist under more or less stable conditions. However, the underlying disaffection of which apathy may be an expression readily leads to activism in times of crisis, as when people who have previously rejected politics turn out in large numbers to support demagogic attacks on the existing political system.[43]

Many Queens, Brooklyn, and Bronx mothers suddenly found themselves working together on boycotts, demonstrations, and vigils at city hall or the mayor's mansion. They had become active in community affairs for the first time in their lives.

In Brooklyn Heights and Lincoln Square, on the other hand, there was a well-organized white community in both neighborhoods, long before pairings became an issue. Lincoln Square is almost overorganized with a variety of political organizations—Reform Democrat clubs, a West Side Civil Rights Committee, and special committees on school integration formed by a local community planning board. Long before school officials had announced pairing plans, these white groups had actively sought to improve opportunities in housing, employment, and education for Negroes and Puerto Ricans. The same situation existed in Brooklyn Heights. The white community there simultaneously developed a pairing plan and even recommended that the two schools and parent associations be merged into a single unit. In January, 1967, the parents asked for the same kind of local community council and extra services that had been urged by Harlem parents for IS 201.

These upper middle class liberals were not an alienated, powerless population, suspicious of politicians and "socialist schemes" from city hall. They were much less ethnocentric and insulated from Negro and Puerto Rican communities, and they were much more oriented to social reform.

Residential Patterns, Organization and Leadership

Militant group action is possible only when people in similar circumstances have opportunities for sustained contacts.[44] Jackson Heights, a homogeneous community along class lines, illustrates this point. Though there was a small middle class minority in Jackson Heights, there was a majority of lower middle class homeowners, either in co-op apartments or single family dwellings. Ethnically too, Jackson Heights consisted of a few closely knit groups. Furthermore, many residents, being second generation, had interests that cut across whatever ethnic differences there were, especially based on a common set of experiences with regard to their assimilation into the middle class. In addition, these lower middle class homeowners were a fairly stable population. Many had lived in the same area for several years, and those who had moved in recently had strong local ties and intended to stay.

In the co-ops, living conditions led easily to the quick formation of a militant and well-organized opposition group. People of similar background lived close together, and the physical layout where meetings, demonstrations, and the establishment of private schools took place encouraged close friendships.[45] The park bench, the low walls where people would sit and chat, and the co-op rumpus room were all centers of continued discussion about the issue.

Brooklyn Heights and Lincoln Square—where pairings gained wider acceptance—were different. The population was more heterogeneous. More residents had recently moved in from outside the city (8% in Lincoln Square as compared with 3% in Jackson Heights, according to 1960 data). In Jackson Heights there were large numbers of a few ethnic groups, while in Lincoln Square there were many ethnic groups. For the most part, the tall buildings in Lincoln Square provided less opportunity for contact than in Jackson Heights. The play-grounds and parks along Riverside Drive provided some opportunity, but they were too far away from the residences to allow for more than limited and sporadic discussion. There was one co-op that later became a center for opposition activity; but for the many reasons I have already discussed, this opposition group did not gain nearly so much support as its counterpart in Jackson Heights.

Throughout the city PAT, PAC, and the Joint Council mobilized support from already existing taxpayers and homeowner groups, as well as from neighborhood improvement, and similar civic organizations. But even these militant groups were not given to sustained political activity. They would come together only on particular issues that affected their communities—zoning, prospects of low income housing projects, site location controversies on schools, taxes, and neighborhood renewal plans. In the absence of such issues, only a very small cadre of activists would keep the organizations going.

Yet, these organizations became the constituent groups of PAT, PAC, and the Joint Council. A list of the organizations that formed the citywide Coordinating Council for PAT at its inception (October 3, 1963) includes, for example: the Community Council of Rockaway, the Flatbush Park Civic Association, Bergen Basin Civic Association, Rockwood Park Civic Association, Howard Beach Civic Association, East Flatbush Civic Association, Bay Ridge Civic Association, the Washington Heights PTA, Malverne Taxpayers and Parents, and PAT of Ridgewood–Glendale, Woodside, Middle Village, Maspeth, and Jackson Heights.

This is one reason for the strength of neighborhood school groups compared with that of civil rights groups. The ghetto areas did not have the organization that white areas had. There were some local church and civil rights groups—NAACP and CORE branches, block associations, and some community organizations, but generally, the civil rights movement suffered from a more atomized population whose leadership could never quite organize. Despite all their efforts, they were beaten decisively by the neighborhood school movement in the desegregation struggle.

The neighborhood school movement organized on a citywide basis soon after the Jackson Heights pairing, in the fall of

1963. The coalition was loose, and local chapters had a high degree of autonomy, but a citywide show of strength was seen as important: it would keep board officials from thinking that they might successfully desegregate the system on any scale in the future; and it gave the movement more access to the board, which often insisted at this time that it meet only with citywide, not local, organizations.

Mayor Wagner, under increasing pressure from PAT leaders and intermediaries, finally agreed in September, 1964, that neighborhood school groups could be present at private meetings between school headquarters officials and other civic groups discussing future desegregation plans. The civil rights movement was allowed only one representative at these meetings, but PAT could send a representative from each of its several groups.

All the PAT leaders were Queens or Brooklyn lawyers who had represented homeowner groups and often were in the real estate business as well. Their alignment with homeowner and taxpayer groups on political controversies—for example, keeping low income housing projects out of the neighborhood, opposing fluoridation, opposing school bond issues, opposing high taxes—gave them a strong power base. The best known and most active PAT leaders were Mrs. Rosemary Gunning of the Ridgewood–Glendale area; Bernard Kessler of Jackson Heights, whom I have already described; Frederick Reuss of East Queens; and Alfred Polizotto of Brooklyn. Mrs. Gunning, an Irish Catholic, was a lawyer and had been a member of the Ridgewood Property Owners and Civic Association.[46] Mr. Reuss and Mr. Polizotto had similar backgrounds and careers: Reuss was a lawyer from East Queens who had led many homeowners' fights, and Polizotto was a lawyer and real estate dealer from Brooklyn. Reuss, Kessler, and Mrs. Gunning had run unsuccessfully for political office in the past.[47]

The separation of Mrs. Lynette Teich's Parents and Citizens in The Bronx and Gerald Dallek's Joint Council for Better Education in Brooklyn was very important, illustrating differences in political style, ideology, and ethnic identification. Mrs. Teich had said publicly that she resented some of PAT's leaders' using the organization for personal political gain.[48] Dallek and his associates were offended by some of the "rabble-rousing tactics" of Queens PAT. After the two-day boycott of

September 14–15, 1964, PAT said that it might continue indefinitely. Dallek said that his organization, a co-sponsor of the boycott, thought that "the children belong in school tomorrow"; his organization planned to "fight some of these pairings in court." [49] He actually went much further and pointed out that the two organizations were completely separate and had only cooperated for the boycott and for a demonstration the previous March at the Board of Education and City Hall.

PAT was very sensitive about its image and was especially concerned about being portrayed in the press as a segregationist organization. Its leaders made many statements that they were not against desegregation. Mrs. Gunning insisted, for example, that PAT was doing "a more sincere and sensible job towards integration than anyone else." [50] One top PAT leader suggested to me that his organization had been one of the initiators of preschool programs. So concerned were PAT leaders about being called segregationists that several once spent a long evening at the home of a civil rights leader, protesting that they really believed in desegregation.

Tactics and Strategy

The neighborhood school movement went through at least two stages in its political activity. At first it engaged in public protests. After the pairing controversy died down in early 1965, and it became clear that the Board of Education would probably not try any more pairings, it adopted a different strategy. Though it always operated in private as well as through public demonstrations, it changed its priorities in the late summer and fall of 1965 and made fewer public protests. Instead it campaigned in the 1965 elections, supporting candidates favorable to its cause.

This is not to say, however, that neighborhood school groups couldn't draw demonstrators when they needed them. In late June of 1965, for example, a few hundred parents from The Bronx picketed a decentralization hearing at board headquarters for several hours, after they had been led to believe that the board was redrawing district lines to include more Negroes. They convinced the board that they could still draw a big following when a particular issue arose. [51]

At City Planning Commission or Board of Estimate hearings on the Board of Education's capital budget, PAT of Canarsie could attract busloads of parents, protesting plans the board might have for an educational park in their area. Several public hearings were devoted to the issue, and Canarsie PAT had as many as fifty speakers ready to testify each time.

PAT, PAC, and the Joint Council's political influence has been apparent since the pairing controversy began. City officials still recall the first public protest in March, 1964, when these groups drew an estimated 15 to 20,000 demonstrators at city hall.[52] Throngs of ladies, many of them wheeling baby carriages, walking across the Brooklyn Bridge, and literally storming city hall, made a profound impression on Mayor Wagner and other city officials. The board's reduction of its pairing program from twenty to five sets of schools was partly a response to this show of political strength. The two-day boycott in September, 1964, accounting for 27% absentees the first day and 23% the second, also impressed board and city officials.[53] Both these displays were so effective that neighborhood school advocates haven't had to resort to such tactics again.

One of their few defeats was in court, where they contested every pairing; in each case the court ruled that the pairing was constitutional. Yet even this defeat was not a serious one, since the board implemented only five pairings in all.

PAT's most vigorous activity since 1965 has been keeping a paid lobbyist in Albany for anti-bussing legislation.[54] Their lobbyist works with a broad-based coalition of conservative legislators from opposition areas in New York City, from many communities on Long Island such as Malverne and Freeport, and from many upstate areas. The presence of this coalition and the threat of passage of one or another of their neighborhood school bills has limited the State Education Department's willingness and ability to intervene in local situations.*

Another of the movement's tactics has been to press for an elected board. They have urged the mayor and state officials to institute new procedures for board selection, but with no more success than their efforts to pass a neighborhood school bill.

* When he came into office, Superintendent Donovan appointed a colleague as the board's liaison with Albany and the state legislature who was reportedly in strong sympathy with New York City neighborhood school groups. When board president Lloyd Garrison finally had this brought to his attention. the man was transferred. The fact that board members were unaware of the man's actions and sympathies is indicative of how removed they have been from the actual operation of the system.

They are continuing this battle and may win a partial victory if at least some local board members are elected, as planned in recently formulated decentralization programs.

Neighborhood school groups work informally on non-legal matters as well. They are in constant communication with board officials and politicians at every level. They continue to be more organized and effective than civil rights groups in this regard. One liberal councilman from East Brooklyn told us that he received more calls and letters from PAT and its affiliates than from civil rights groups about desegregation plans such as pairings and parks. PAT leaders regularly contacted all politicians, especially those they thought were integrationists, with the result that politicians and other city officials paid more attention to them than to civil rights groups. I should emphasize, however, that civil rights groups have just begun to develop a local leadership, have faced extreme shortages of funds and personnel, and have had less experience than PAT in negotiating with white politicians. PAT's success was partly a result of these factors.

Another strategy that neighborhood school groups have used successfully has been to take over key positions in parent associations and on some local school boards. The moderate United Parents Association, a citywide confederation of local PAs and PTAs, has lost a number of members and chapters to PAT, PAC, and Joint Council since 1964. Leaders of Jackson Heights PAT, for example, drew up a petition to impeach the parent association leaders at PS 149, after they had developed the pairing plan. The UPA was able to beat that down, but in an election conducted in the spring of 1964, most of the PAT candidates were voted into office. The same pattern held for other areas of Queens, The Bronx, and Brooklyn.

The selection of local school board members was still another means by which the neighborhood school coalition gained power. Over the last two years, some PAT members and sympathizers have gained positions on local school boards. Integrationists have also been appointed, but the trend may be to appoint moderates and segregationists.

This pattern of control at the local level extends to community planning boards as well. Community planning boards are citizen groups appointed by the borough president to meet with local residents to discuss neighborhood problems and develop programs. In many areas where PAT is strong, these boards were composed of the same interests as local school board and parent associations, and together constituted a kind of interlocking directorate. In a few areas, the same local real estate interests serve on community planning boards and local school boards, and their decisions clearly reflect such concerns.[55]

It is in this way that the neighborhood school movement has influenced public education and taken power from moderate liberal groups.

Board of Education Strategies and Opposition Strength

The movement might not have been so successful, however, had the board handled desegregation controversies differently. One militant PAT leader in Jackson Heights said: "The Board of Education could easily have mandated many more pairings throughout the city if they had not been so secretive about it. Even our well-organized groups wouldn't have made nearly as much noise if we had been included in discussions earlier and not had the thing sprung on us so suddenly." [56]

This judgment may be inaccurate, but the board's vacillation did contribute substantially to the fears of white parents.[57] Rumors and press leaks were widespread in 1963 and 1964. Parents in areas rumored to be sites of pairings tried to get further information on the board's intentions, but they got little from headquarters, local school officials, or the local school board. Parents had legitimate fears that should have been answered. They wanted to know how far their children might travel, what kind of school program they would have in a new setting, what provisions would be made for maintaining standards, and when and how the community would be consulted, but the board kept its counsel, and many of these parents ended up supporting PAT.

The board's reticence was made to order for the leaders of PAT. Though they knew no more about the board's intentions than any other parents, they could nevertheless stir up their communities by saying that they didn't want the board to bus white children into ghetto schools, and shouldn't the community rise up to ensure that this would not happen? Board officials who point to the grass roots support of the neighborhood school movement as one reason for not implementing more desegregation plans overlook the way in which their own inaction contributed to that support.

IV

❧

CIVIL RIGHTS ORGANIZATIONS

The neighborhood school movement developed in response to the civil rights movement's demands for desegregation and might have been less influential if the latter had been more effective. New York City's increasing segregation, however, indicates that the civil rights movement failed on that issue. There were many reasons for the failure, many of which had nothing to do with the movement itself. The power of *a minority* to influence public policy, even when surrounded by an aura of constitutional respectability, depends on winning over or neutralizing large segments of majority opinion. In New York City, with its liberal traditions, this was a reasonable expectation. However, events proved otherwise, and the pervasive racism in the city that was activated on the school desegregation question became far stronger than could have been anticipated.

The obstacles to integration were so great that no matter how well organized the movement might have been, it probably would not have made much difference. The objective circumstances clearly favored the status quo. Nevertheless, the movement's internal characteristics affected to some extent the degree of its success. The movement was unable to mobilize any *sustained grass roots support*. Though civil rights leaders could always demonstrate a groundswell of protest against inferior ghetto schools, they could not maintain this protest at a high level over a long period. The movement was also unable to achieve any degree of *unity within its leadership*. Internal differences over strategy, mostly between national and local groups, wasted much of the movement's scarce resources. Furthermore, the pursuit of a *conflict strategy*, emphasizing racial balance alone, without reference to goals that might have appealed to a wider public, also hurt the movement. Its inability to muster a broad coalition from labor, business, and other publics with a stake in quality education, limited its power. All these conditions plus the fact that PAT's goals were very simple and for the status quo, while civil rights goals were much more complex, limited the movement's success.*

Many civic groups have pressed the Board of Education for more school desegregation. There were Negro organizations, both national and local, the most influential being the NAACP, the Urban League, CORE, Parents Workshop for Equality, and Harlem Parents Committee. A militant white parent group, EQUAL, supported and helped lead the struggle in ghetto communities. Then there were Puerto Rican organizations that participated in a much more limited way, including the Commonwealth of Puerto Rico, Puerto Rican Forum, ASPIRA, National Association for Puerto Rican Civil Rights, and some purely local groups. Other liberal organizations joined the struggle early, including the American Jewish Congress, the Anti-Defamation League, the American Jewish Committee, the Protestant Council, the Catholic Inter-Racial Council, the Citizens Committee for Children, the American Civil Liberties Union, the Liberal Party, the Reform Democrat groups, ADA, and a few unions. Finally, there were others involved more as individuals than as members of organizations, including activist academicians and planners, and city and school officials.

To forge a strong coalition among these groups would have required more astute political leadership than one might ever find for any cause. These organizations had markedly different constituencies (racial, ethnic, class, religious, geographic), scopes of operations (national, citywide, borough, local), structures (centralized *vs.* federated), and durability (permanent, ad hoc).

The result has been fragmentation and conflict within and among these organizations, limiting their effectiveness. They had to resolve internal differences over appropriate strategy before they could influence board decisions. Only in an extreme

---

* Civil rights groups were also asking for more services, better education, and more power to influence board policy, and this was very threatening to whites, including school officials, for reasons outlined in the last chapter.

crisis or when the board inadvertently stated its preference for the status quo more clearly than it intended did these groups come together. But the coalition rarely endured for any length of time.

Grass Roots Mobilization and Support

"We cannot divorce our discussions of school integration from ghetto culture, conditions, and housing. The reason we have had so much difficulty in moving on school integration is that we have had so little political strength at the grass roots. We will become politically effective only when we get white and black parents who are taxpayers and voters to present a united front. Black people in Harlem are not organized." So spoke a New York City civil rights leader who had lived in Harlem and knew its culture well—at a public conference where political strategies were being reviewed.[1]

No political movement can succeed without a strong local following. Yet civil rights leaders were unable to maintain sustained grass roots organization and protest, for several reasons. One reason is the inherent nature of parents organizations, whose leadership changes as the children of each group of leaders move into the upper grades.

A second is that Negro and Puerto Rican communities have not had as many local and political and social organizations on which to build their movement as did other coalitions—for example, the neighborhood school movement. The latter could mobilize a following through already established homeowner, taxpayer, and civic groups. This was not possible in such recently developed ghettos as the south Bronx, Morrisania, and Brownsville. It was even difficult in Harlem and East Harlem.

Many ghetto residents were disenfranchised. They were neither homeowners nor registered voters. Until very recently, their communities were atomized, powerless, and alienated from the wider society, for obvious historical reasons. Efforts of the civil rights movement, the city administration, and federal government, through the poverty program, have begun to change this condition. Their effects are only beginning to be felt, however, and they are still limited.

Newly formed anti-poverty groups like MEND, the East Harlem Tenants' Council, Youth-in-Action, the Central Brooklyn Coordinating Council, HARYOU-ACT, Mobilization for Youth, and community corporations established through the city administration's Council Against Poverty, are attempting to develop community organizations, a sense of ethnic solidarity, and group consciousness. However, these anti-poverty groups face many obstacles, including bureaucratic entanglements with city and federal officials, attempts by the latter to limit their funds and power if they seem to be too critical of existing governmental agencies, and local leadership struggles. Though the Lindsay administration is strongly committed to the organization of ghetto populations, by the time these communities get organized into effective power blocs there may not be enough whites left with whom to integrate. And minority group populations may not want integration by that time. Many don't much want it now.

A third reason, then, for the desegregation movement's limited political base, is the outlook of ghetto populations. Some Negro and Puerto Rican parents associations have the same neighborhood school outlook as whites. Some saw no relationship between desegregation and quality or they had no experience with the benefits of integrated education for their children. Like other lower class populations, they see the world in concrete terms, and conceive of solutions for inferior schools as local ones—in the upgrading and renovating of their neighborhood schools.

One board strategy that further reinforced this neighborhood school preference within the Negro and Puerto Rican population was to provide more services in ghetto schools than in receiving schools under Open Enrollment. Minority group parents often testified at public hearings that they would rather send their children to segregated ghetto schools, with their extra services, than to Open Enrollment schools where their children were placed in segregated classrooms and not given the compensatory programs they could get in the ghetto. Many minority group parents became convinced that as bad as conditions were in ghetto schools, they might be even worse in receiving schools under Open Enrollment.

It has been difficult, then, for civil rights leaders to maintain a strong, broad-based organization under such conditions. To be sure, there have been some significant exceptions to this Negro and Puerto Rican disinterest in school desegregation. Parents Workshop organized many parents to transfer their children under the board's equalization–utilization and Open Enrollment programs. As we have seen, the movement drew large numbers of absentees in both boycotts. And Brownsville mobilized a large parent and civic group in 1965 and 1966 to protest the board's plans for building more segregated schools. These parents asked for a desegregated educational park instead.* [2]

The battle for community support for desegregation, however, seems to be lost. Neither civil rights leaders nor minority group parents have confidence any more that they can push the board toward desegregation through public demonstrations. They have seen too many plans subverted through non-implementation, and they no longer have much faith in the integrity of the board to mandate reforms of any kind. In addition, few ghetto parents are yet involved in the politics of education to anywhere near the degree that middle class white, Negro, and Puerto Rican parents are.

There were doubts that the board would implement its desegregation plans before the IS 201 controversy broke out in September, 1966.[3] But 201 crystallized these doubts and since then, decentralization has become the movement's main effort, supported by the same discontent but this time with a harder edge.

The same problems of community mobilization, of unity, leadership, and organization remain to be solved, however. Though the movement has adopted a few key slogans—for example, accountability, responsiveness, and community control—and knows that the central bureaucracy must be broken up, through some form of decentralization, there is no agreement over how decentralization should proceed and how the schools should be run once the bureaucracy is out of the way. Many approaches for community participation are being considered. When local groups were mobilized for desegregation, there were fewer differences within the movement over the merits of particular plans.

As long as the New York City school system continues under a citywide central board, local groups must unite if they expect to have their way. Otherwise, they will be out-maneuvered by a board with many more political resources than any single community can muster. This is not to say that the community should necessarily unite behind a single plan, but rather that they should support one another's separate plans, formulated to fit

* See Chapter One for a discussion of the protests around the board's inactions in 1965 and 1966.

the unique conditions of their respective areas. There has to be some overall coordination by a committee of citywide leaders who provide political and technical help to the leaders of each subcommunity. Such leaders must be willing to delegate authority and power, while at the same time convincing local groups that coordination of their protests and programs is essential if the board is not to deal with isolated local groups which it can easily defeat.

The "Peoples' Board," [4] which sat-in for three days at a board hearing in December, 1966, was set up to coordinate the various community movements, and it has tried to organize local parent groups and protests ever since. Ironically, this board faces some of the same problems that the regular board does, in that it must deal with numerous local groups and factions, each with its own demands, which makes it difficult to come to any consensus about strategy or to reconcile the different local demands in a unified policy. In addition, there has been continued conflict among the leadership of the Peoples' Board over strategy. Reverend Galamison, its president, has favored a citywide approach under unified leadership, while other leaders have favored a much more local one. Such differences are common to all social movements, but they have weakened the effectiveness of the ghetto groups just as the failure to maintain a sustained grass roots organization did.*

Parents Workshop: Rev. Milton Galamison

Though the Urban League and the NAACP were the first Negro civil rights organizations to become involved, in 1953, the first significant local protests took place in Brooklyn and were led by Reverend Milton Galamison, then President of the Brooklyn branch of the NAACP. Galamison was from Brooklyn's Bedford–Stuyvesant community and a minister in the Siloam Presbyterian Church, one of the established Negro middle class churches in Brooklyn.

* At first, the impetus for school desegregation in New York City came from both national and local groups, though in different ways. These differences were symbolic of conflicts in values and political style that have persisted throughout the struggle. Typically, the national officials were moderate in strategy while the local groups were more radical, and sometimes their goals were different as well—local groups tended to demand much more than the national ones. Numerous interviews with civil rights leaders indicated that the inability of national and local groups to stay together for any length of time was one of the movement's major problems.

Negro parent groups from ghetto communities throughout
the city had been protesting conditions in their local schools
since the early 1950s, and Galamison led the Brooklyn groups
to force remedial action by the Board of Education. He and his
associate, Mrs. Annie Stein, formed the Parents Workshop of
the NAACP in 1956.[5]

Parents Workshop conducted an unrelenting campaign
from 1956 through 1965 and were the avant garde of the movement, initiating the most progressive desegregation plans and
engaging in the most vigorous protest actions to see that the
plans were implemented.* They, more than any other single
group, were the ones who kept the pressure on board and city
officials, though in recent years they have been joined by Harlem Parents Committee and EQUAL, two equally militant local
parent groups. Galamison is regarded within the movement and
among some liberals as a prophetic figure with great vision and
a deep commitment to desegregation, but it also is widely agreed
that his strong views and his aggressive leadership have alienated him from many other groups within the movement and in
the liberal community, thus adding to its problems of unity. He,
more than any other single person, was the leader of the school
desegregation fight in New York City, and when the coalition
around him dissolved in 1964, no other leader emerged to take
his place. Given the factional politics in New York City, it is
easily conceivable that nobody ever will.†

Signs of disunity appeared early. Though Galamison was
the president of the NAACP's Brooklyn branch in the late 1950s
and Mrs. Stein was an active member, Parents Workshop spent
almost as much time fighting the NAACP national office as it
did the Board of Education.

Many middle class Negroes had moved out of Bedford–
Stuyvesant and neighboring ghettos into white residential areas.
Parents Workshop had often urged that schools be rezoned so
that the upward mobile Negro middle class would have to send
its children to schools with lower class Negroes. The middle

---

* A citywide coalition, composed of Negro and white groups, the Intergroup Committee on the New York City Public Schools, was also active
during this period but not nearly as militant or locally based. See my discussion of the committee in the next chapter.

† Galamison is now heading the City-Wide Coalition for Community
Control of Public Schools, organized around the Board of Education's
demonstration projects for decentralization. See Chapter Twelve for a
further discussion of these projects.

class group consistently opposed such plans [6] and were supported by the national office as well as by some Brooklyn officials. They prevailed, since they were supported not only by elements of the NAACP but by real estate interests, white parent groups, and board and city officials.

There were personal differences between Parents Workshop and some NAACP officials as well.* By 1959, Reverend Galamison decided that he had better subordinate his involvment in the NAACP, and he declined to run again for president of the Brooklyn branch, though he remained on its board.†

The strategy of Parents Workshop was to demand that desegregated plans be implemented, and then if the Board of Education failed to respond, to threaten strikes and boycotts. Most of their demands were for the board to implement its own policy statements. Reverend Galamison and his associates were not opposed, however, to negotiation, and had engaged in it with limited success on many occasions. More often, however, they were frustrated. They turned to demonstrations as the only way to get the board to move, and their experience validated this strategy.

By the early 1960s, Reverend Galamison and his associates began to see the need for a citywide coalition, even though their earlier relations with the NAACP had not always been amicable. One of the main reasons for coming together was that local and national organizations each had essential resources that the other did not have: Parents Workshop and other local groups had little money and no professional staff (with the exception of Mrs. Stein), and few sustained contacts with top city and board officials, while the NAACP and the Urban League had limited popular support in ghetto communities.‡ Civil

* Galamison and NAACP headquarters officials split sharply over his public statement in 1957 demanding the dismissal of Superintendent Jansen when Jansen refused to desegregate JHS 258. At that time, the NAACP was not ready to make such a demand, and felt that it was tactically harmful.

† A Parents Workshop official recalled: "Reverend Coleman, the first Negro board member, visited us in 1956 with Shockley, then president of Brooklyn NAACP. He told us to lay off on integration, saying it was bad for the Negroes. Milton Galamison finally said to Coleman: 'Do you mean to tell me that you are really for separate but equal schools?' Coleman did not answer. This was how bad it was then."

‡ The NAACP had local branches throughout the city, and some of them were militant, for example, Brooklyn, The Bronx, Jamaica, Astoria, and Corona–Elmhurst in Queens. Galamison's Parents Workshop, however, was generally the most active and militant local group on school desegregation matters.

rights leaders often commented that the NAACP had the money, while Galamison had the people, a comment made with much sadness, since it was obviously so hard to maintain relations between them. This observation was sometimes made, with some modifications, about the Urban League as well.*

Harlem Parents Committee and EQUAL

The only other local groups representing ghetto parents were Harlem Parents Committee and EQUAL. Neither could ever attract nearly so large a following as Galamison did, and both were generally strong supporters of Galamison. Harlem Parents Committee was formed in the summer of 1963, in protest against conditions in Harlem schools and against what its leaders still refer to as the apartheid nature of the New York City school system.[7] It came out of the New York branch of the NAACP, and included middle class black militants—lawyers, artists, community workers—who felt that local NAACP branches were constrained by headquarters officials.† This group, led by Mr. Isaiah Robinson, head of the parents association of JHS 139 in Harlem, and Mrs. Thelma Johnson,‡ a community organization specialist and now a top education official in the Lindsay Administration, has been unable to mobilize a large following. It does, however, publish a monthly newsletter and a widely circulated document, the *Harlem Black Paper,* presenting its critical view of expanding segregation and the deteriorating quality of the school system.[8]

Harlem has always been a difficult area to organize because of its large population (400,000), and the diversity of factions and points of view therein. Clergymen, politicians, activists, and local businessmen are its main civic leaders. Adam Clayton Powell occasionally offered his support, but he was not deeply involved with school desegregation. Indeed, his separatist in-

---

* When Galamison pulled Parents Workshop out of the NAACP in 1959, for example, some civil rights leaders acknowledged that the NAACP lost most of its local parent activists.

† "The local branches here in New York City are right under national's eye," reported a Harlem Parents Committee official. "National will often send in 'observers' to local meetings who are always of a more reactionary point of view than the local."

‡ Assistant Commissioner of the Education Action Division in the city's Human Resources Administration.

terests and baronial style may have helped to keep Harlem from organizing behind school desegregation.*

Many Harlem politicians had little interest in school desegregation. Indeed, they had a vested interest in maintaining their power base by keeping Harlem a segregated community, as did many of the bankers and businessmen there. The Board of Education had often been able to get statements from Harlem political leaders that they were not very committed to school desegregation. The board used such statements against desegregation activists. Often the board did not have to solicit these statements. They were offered freely.[9]

Local support for desegregation from within the Negro community also came from CORE and NAACP chapters.[10] CORE was often militant, especially in The Bronx, Harlem, and Brooklyn, but it had few members; its funds were limited, its leadership divided, and its programs poorly organized. The NAACP had fourteen local chapters in the city, all of whom participated in the first boycott, but many of them were not very active before 1963, nor have they been active since late 1964. Harlem was one of the communities where the NAACP was weakest of all, partly because Powell prevented local leaders from emerging and because he opposed the NAACP—its board, its top officials, and its program.

EQUAL, the militant white group, did give much assistance to ghetto organizations. Formed in early 1964, and led throughout most of its history by Mrs. Ellen Lurie, an activist and former social worker who had previously participated in East Harlem housing controversies, EQUAL rallied a small but intensely committed group of white middle class parents who sent their children to ghetto and integrated schools,† led many demonstrations, and published numerous newsletters and reports

---

* Powell did, however, march with Galamison in the second boycott and helped whenever Galamison asked. He had previously organized a leadership conference which included Paul Zuber as its education head, a group that was formed to push for more school desegregation.

† One of the most celebrated recent cases was that of the late Mrs. Dorothy Fulmer from the white area of Sheepshead Bay in Brooklyn, who sent her children to an almost all-black segregated school in Bedford–Stuyvesant. She organized seventy-five parents to do likewise, and they pressed for a Reverse Open Enrollment program—which the board finally set up, though only after considerable resistance on their part and harassment of Mrs. Fulmer and her friends. See Chapter Eight for a brief discussion of the harassment.

on conditions in the schools. Mrs. Lurie initiated most of these actions and was widely regarded as one of the best informed people in the city on school matters. EQUAL had a very small following, however, in the white middle class community. Many white liberals objected to EQUAL's vigorous line, and dismissed Mrs. Lurie as an "extremist."

National Association for the Advancement of Colored People

The NAACP became involved in the northern school desegregation struggle in the late 1950s, after its Legal Defense Fund began to take on some de facto school segregation cases.[11] Local NAACP branches throughout the city had also become involved, though many were inactive on desegregation matters.

Some NAACP headquarters officials opposed getting involved in New York City school matters for fear that they might undermine their desegregation efforts in the South. Since they were pressing southern courts and school officials to be "color blind," they did not see how they could then turn around and ask northern officials to be "color conscious."

Thus, when the NAACP intervened in the late 1950s, it tended to react to rather than encourage the demands of local parents for desegregation. They did not fully accept the activism of parent groups, though they did engage in negotiations with board and city officials.*

Though the NAACP became much more militant in the 1960s, the conflict remained between the preference of some of its headquarters officials for negotiation and that of local parent groups from Brooklyn and Harlem, including some local NAACP branches, for boycotts and demonstrations. However, the difference was more a matter of strategy than goals.

The NAACP's increased militancy in the 1960s and its adoption of a strategy of selective demonstrations "when necessary," was partly the result of an organizational decision to press strongly in the North for school desegregation. An education office was established in August, 1961, to pursue that strategy, and led by Miss June Shagaloff, who had worked in the NAACP Legal Defense Fund and had been active in the school

---

* Some exceptions included the Jamaica branch under William Booth, the Corona–Elmhurst branch under Reverend Sherard, and, of course, the Brooklyn branch under Reverend Galamison.

desegregation movement in New York City since 1953. Since 1961, she has serviced local branches throughout the nation on education matters.

It should also be noted, however, that the NAACP's decision to press for school desegregation in the North came after Paul Zuber, a Harlem lawyer, had taken on cases in Englewood, New Jersey, and a few other northern cities where NAACP locals begged its national headquarters to come in. Initially, it did not, but after Zuber started taking on more cases, the NAACP adopted a more aggressive policy in the North, taking on cases of its own in Gary, Indiana, Cleveland, Ohio, and other cities.

Since 1963, the publicly stated positions of the NAACP on desegregation have been virtually as progressive as those of ghetto parent groups. For example, in the December, 1963, showdown between civil rights leaders and board officials where Gross presented his progress report, the NAACP urged the board, as it had a few months earlier, to adopt citywide desegregation plans based on pupil assignments rather than on the voluntary choice of Negro parents and with a timetable for their implementation.[12] In March, 1965, it urged implementation of all the recommendations of the Allen Report, including the integrated, four-year middle school, and educational complexes and parks.[13] NAACP officials and members staged a public demonstration a month later at board headquarters, protesting the limited proposals in the Gross Blueprint.

Thus, the NAACP's demands had become not much more moderate than those of Parents Workshop or Harlem Parents Committee. Their differences had other sources, rooted in personality conflicts, leadership struggles, and differences in organizational style. To be sure, the militants were often disenchanted with the public statements of Roy Wilkins, the NAACP's executive secretary, for example, when he criticized Galamison's demand for a new school system, a month before the boycott, and when he expressed his skepticism of the boycott's value. As one top NAACP official said: "Wilkins exerted some pressure on us to disaffiliate from the committee. He'd had grave misgivings anyway about the first boycott, but he cooperated then, since it became clear that the branches would do so." His first response to the Gross Blueprint the following March (1965) was to characterize its recommendations as "a giant step forward." [14] Many of the NAACP's branch presidents in New York City, as well as professional staff, informed Wilkins of their dismay over that statement. Another NAACP official noted: "The branches weren't too happy with this giant step forward business with Gross's Blueprint—nor did Wilkins remain happy with it for any length of time." [15]

Some local ghetto groups, many of whom had always been suspicious of the NAACP as an organization controlled by "white liberals" and conservative Negro leaders, became even more so when the conflict with Galamison flared up and the NAACP temporarily withdrew from the coalition. Negative stereotypes abounded about the NAACP headquarters and its supposed pressures on the branches, and these stereotypes were reinforced by the fact that the day after the first boycott a dramatic meeting of the branches was held at the NAACP headquarters. Several headquarters officials were present, gave speeches condemning Galamison's leadership, and urged that he be removed. The branches then voted 11–2 to withdraw from the Citywide Committee.

Some NAACP officials, however, deny such headquarters influence. As one NAACP official said: "There was one painful meeting of all civil rights groups after the first boycott. Two people raised the charge that Wilkins was running the organization, and that he was influenced in turn by his board. The president of one of our branches got up and made an impassioned rebuttal. Now his branch is one of our most militant ones, and he pointed out that NAACP branches functioned within a national policy adopted at the convention, and were not run by Wilkins. He was enraged." This militant faction often prevailed.*

It apparently prevailed, however, only under some duress, as indicated by another NAACP official who reported: "New York City is always a special problem for the national office, with its being located right here. The location often makes them feel impelled to take action on an issue more appropriate to local action. And unless they're extremely careful, they'll get involved in actions and issues more appropriate to local

---

* Many active civil rights leaders throughout the city still have this feeling about headquarters interference, which suggests how fragmented the movement still is, and how limited are the communications between the NAACP headquarters and local leaders. This, along with other personal and organizational differences, continues to hamper the movement.

branches. National tried hard to keep out, and didn't always succeed, and there was some animosity about this." *

The NAACP is one of the few Negro civil rights organizations still actively pursuing school desegregation programs in the North. In September, 1967, Robert Carter, its legal counsel, announced a new campaign to desegregate large, inner cities by setting up educational parks and urban–suburban interchanges and consolidation, a position also taken by the U.S. Civil Rights Commission.

Urban League

The Urban League tried hardest to mediate conflicts between the NAACP and local groups.[16] It had played a major part in the school struggle from 1954 through 1964 through the research and negotiating skills of its professional staff and education committee, headed by Dr. Edward Lewis, experienced educator, social worker, and consultant to city and school officials, and Mrs. Ethel Schwabacher, an artist, author, and tireless worker for school desegregation.

The Urban League always had a full-time professional working on educational matters. Dr. Ofelia Mendoza, a community organization specialist, gathered much material on the implementation of Open Enrollment and prepared the original pamphlets, which the board initially refused to prepare or distribute, encouraging minority group parents to transfer their children out of the ghetto. Her work helped mobilize grass roots protests against non-implementation in Brooklyn and Harlem, documenting as it did the board's failures to pursue Open Enrollment, and it also served to bring Negro and white liberal organizations into a coalition that also pressed the board. From 1961 to 1963, Bert Phillips, now dean of students at Tuskegee Institute, gathered material that went into the writing of the Urban League's 1963 report, summarizing the

* A top NAACP branch official described branch–headquarters relations: "Branches are not autonomous in setting policy. The national office sets policy in an annual meeting. The resolutions committee prepares the resolutions for adoption by local branches, and then that policy governs the whole organization for the year. When a branch has been defiant, it's been corrected by the State Conference or the national office. Sometimes both." On the question of who at national made policy, he suggested: "June Shagaloff was in a position where she was not always supported by Wilkins. He has not supported everything she or we did. We knew she was in a ticklish position all the time. She still is."

history of the desegregation controversy in New York City and criticizing the board for its actions. In 1964, Carl Fields, director of student affairs and counsellor at Princeton, played an important role as chairman of the civil rights negotiating team that met with Superintendent Gross and his staff. All these people were highly competent professionals, and they enabled the Urban League to play a role that few other civil rights organizations had played during those years.

The Urban League, like the NAACP, had access to the mayor and was regarded as a respected organization in the city. It also had close ties to the Democratic Party and to top board and city officials. Charles Silver, president of the Board of Education from 1955 to 1961, was also president of the Urban League's board in the late 1950s. Despite these contacts, and despite the Urban League's reputation as a responsible organization, it could not appreciably move the mayor or the board on desegregation. Some militant civil rights leaders believed that it was unable to do so because of its relations with top city officials.

As dedicated to change as the Urban League's specialists were, the pressures on them from the national board not to push the Board of Education were tremendous, like those sometimes exerted by NAACP officials on its education staff. One Urban League official said: "One board member and I were at daggers' points. He was interested in employment and housing rather than education. He wanted me to keep my hands out of stuff like picketing, and we had a running battle. My local New York City board backed me, and I got into it in spite of him." [17]

Some members of the Urban League's board were especially active in trying to limit its alliances with the militants. They did not succeed but the internal pressures on its education committee were strong. Its staff always had to maneuver carefully between the militants, including some NAACP officials, who wanted more intervention, and their board, who wanted less. Both sides were sometimes suspicious of the staff.

Though the Urban League's by-laws prevented it from participating in any public protests, its education officials attended private meetings as observers where boycott preparations were being made, and offered their support where they could.[18] Thus they were able to interpret the movement to their board members and officials, some of whom were removed from the ghetto and its problems.

There was not nearly the suspicion toward the Urban League from ghetto groups that there was toward the NAACP, largely because of the informal relations between its beleaguered local officials and the participants in the movement. The Urban League never became polarized from Galamison the way the NAACP headquarters and the national CORE office did. Yet, the contributions it was able to make—through research, negotiation, and by interpreting diverse groups to one another, both within the Negro movement and between Negro and white organizations—were insufficient to move the Board of Education toward reform.

CORE

The relationship of CORE, the other national civil rights organization, to the movement, was completely different from that of either the NAACP or the Urban League. Unlike the NAACP, CORE had a very decentralized structure, which permitted much more conflict between the national office and local branches, and among and within the branches themselves. Furthermore, CORE had no rationalized national policy on school matters such as NAACP had. It had no consistent program or guidelines, and it tended to move into critical situations in somewhat unpredictable ways.

Furthermore, CORE had nothing like the membership in New York City that NAACP had. One civil rights leader estimated that, in early 1964, CORE had roughly 300 members in the city compared with nearly 30,000 members of NAACP. CORE also tended to encourage public protest and had its greatest strength in the ghetto where the NAACP was weakest. Ironically, CORE may have been more subject than the NAACP to pressure from its national officers who had to please their white liberal benefactors. Local CORE branches were generally more suspicious that their national office was afraid of offending white benefactors than NAACP branches seemed to be.[19]

While particular CORE branches worked closely with Galamison, especially in Brooklyn, Harlem, and The Bronx, the fact that there were so many factions within CORE and so few constituents led the Board of Education and city officials to pay little attention to their protests.* One civil rights leader said: "Your picture of CORE's position depends on whom you talk to. You get a different one with every major figure there." [20]

CORE's problems within the movement reflected its organizational difficulties. It withdrew from the coalition in 1964, partly because some of its officials feared that Galamison would continue to be the most militant New York City civil rights leader where the schools were concerned. In addition, by late 1965, some CORE officials had begun to adopt a Black Separatist strategy for dealing with civil rights—a result of their cynicism about the Board of Education's willingness to ever desegregate the schools.† Roy Innis, then head of Harlem CORE, takes this position. He is not against desegregation, but is more committed to revitalizing the self-image and power of the Negro in his own community. Mr. Innis is now leading an action to form a separate board for Harlem schools and has enlisted the help of legal, educational, and fiscal experts.‡ [21]

CORE's power has been limited in the city. It has never been so close to board and city officials as the NAACP and the Urban League, partly because it was never so much interested in bargaining and negotiation as in public protests to bring about radical change. But it could never really agree on what these changes should be, and so it was an organization without a consensus.

Citywide Committee for Integrated Schools

The first major coalition within the movement was the Citywide Committee, set up in August, 1963.[22] From the start the national offices of the NAACP, the Urban League, and CORE were uneasy about joining such a coalition partly because of obvious differences in organizational styles.

The doubts of some national officials were reinforced in

---

* Although the national office of CORE withdrew from the Citywide Committee, nine of the thirteen local CORE chapters supported the second boycott in March, 1964.

† CORE had serious internal problems in early 1964, especially within its Harlem branch, and was approaching an all-black point of view even then. Some of its unpredictable behavior and its ambivalence about Galamison was symptomatic of those problems.

‡ Indeed, this is a joint project of Harlem CORE and several university and public education people, including Dr. Edward Gottlieb, a former Upper West Side principal well known for his positive stands on desegregation and decentralization.

December, 1963, when Reverend Galamison, who had been appointed the committee's chairman, began to follow what was
generally agreed to be a unilateral strategy. Press coverage of
his sharp exchanges with Board President James Donovan, his
commentaries about the failures of the New York City school
system, and his announced plans to stage school boycotts
throughout the North reactivated those forces within the national organizations who either wanted him deposed as leader or
wanted to withdraw from the coalition.* They felt Galamison
wanted personal power. Their attitudes were partly affected by
Galamison's unfavorable press coverage which hurt his image
considerably within the movement. One ally of Galamison suggested: "Some of the moderates in the movement have to read
the *New York Times* before they decide how well they are
doing."

Before the first boycott, national CORE was the organization that most wanted to get rid of Galamison.[23] They tried to
get the NAACP to join them in deposing him, but the NAACP
refused to go along, not because it felt that CORE's complaints
were unfounded, but rather for reasons of political strategy.
According to one NAACP official: "We felt as CORE did, but
we thought and pointed out that to call a meeting for that
purpose at just that time would be devastating in terms of
planning for the boycott, about which, mind you, there was
unanimous agreement. You see, we weren't divided on the basic
issue at that point."[24]

After the boycott, complaints increased that Galamison was
representing himself as chairman of the Citywide Committee
without ever clearing his actions with the other members. When
he unilaterally announced a second boycott, all participating
organizations met to establish new procedures governing the
chairmanship that they hoped would be acceptable to the entire committee, especially Galamison. One civil rights leader
said the problem was to "keep Galamison from destroying our
concentration on the issue by his own personality needs." While
the issues were often more complicated, this was how many

---

* Galamison, as the chairman of the Citywide Committee, got a lot of
publicity during this period, and his supporters felt that the NAACP, CORE,
and to a lesser extent the Urban League, resented this, especially since the
NAACP at least was footing the bills. Galamison's partial answer to the
charge of unilateral action was that he had always wanted an indefinite
boycott rather than for one day and had been overruled by other civil
rights organizations.

national organization officials saw them, and since perceptions affect behavior, these views were significant.[25]

There was also increasing concern about Galamison's political skills. Some civil rights leaders felt that his organizing ability was limited and that he had not developed plans for conducting the second boycott before he announced it. One of his critics said: "A number of us raised questions when Milton was charging ahead with the second boycott. There was nothing like the organization that went into the first. He just went charging off with the bit in his teeth, and when we asked about the organization, the money, the community backing, whatever, his response was something like, 'of course, of course, let's move ahead.' But there was no thinking it through at all." [26]

Apart from personal criticism of Galamison, there were sharp disagreements about the boycott itself. Many civil rights leaders felt that a second boycott was unwise at that time, that it might create a strong backlash, and that they should sit back and take stock, waiting to see what the board would do, and perhaps attempt to negotiate. These leaders were more optimistic than Galamison about the board's willingness to move.[27]

There were organizational reasons for their position. The NAACP, the Urban League, and CORE were all worried about the coalition. The NAACP and CORE, especially, wanted more control over it. They wanted to be seen as co-participants with Galamison, rather than as followers, which was complicated by the fact that the press regarded Galamison as the leader. The NAACP had often staged protests on its own, which was one reason that it had been able to build itself into the strongest civil rights organization in the nation. Furthermore, some NAACP officials and board members did not believe in Galamison's form of militancy. They favored negotiation and legal solutions to the problem, supported by selective demonstrations. When the press attacked Galamison during the boycott period, it became easier for these national officers to prevail in discussions of the NAACP's status within the Citywide Committee.

CORE reacted differently to the coalition and its problems. Though its headquarters officials were the first to urge an open break with Galamison, they didn't follow through, partly because they couldn't get many local branches to go along. Some of the local branches agreed with the national office, but they resented its intrusions on their autonomy. As one local branch leader noted: "We were never too strong for Galamison, but we were closer to him than to the national office position. We've always had more trouble with the national office than with Galamison."

Ironically the Urban League, though it was the most moderate of the three, had less of a problem with Galamison. Since its by-laws prohibited it from taking part directly in the first boycott, except to endorse it, it had less of a commitment to withdraw from. Moreover, one of its lay leaders, Mrs. Ethel Schwabacher, had been able to maintain good working relationships with the main contending factions within the movement, and she continued to try to mediate among them. Its education director, Alexander J. Allen, was also strongly supportive of Galamison's boycott efforts throughout.

From Galamison's side, of course, the unity problem seemed quite different. When he saw how successful the first boycott was, at least in the number of students who stayed out of school, he may have become more convinced of his own strength. Since the board failed to respond favorably after the boycott, Galamison felt it was necessary to have a second boycott soon, especially since his popular support was so strong. Board President James Donovan's reference to the first boycott as "Fizzle No. 1" only confirmed his decision.

Galamison was also afraid that another boycott might well be delayed if the Citywide Committee became too carefully structured. He was uncomfortable with an arrangement that allowed national organizations to go through their established channels for review and approval of particular plans. He had had long experience with the NAACP, and was skeptical of its commitment to militant protest, unless prodded by grass roots pressure. He apparently felt that the success of the first boycott gave him leverage for a second. And he allegedly interpreted the many plans to change the structure of the Citywide Committee as attempts to buy him out.

All civil rights organizations wanted a share in the leadership. Galamison combined his deep knowledge of the problem, his ten-year leadership at the local level, and his personal charisma, to move into a commanding position, and this made some of the other groups uneasy, especially when they disagreed with his tactics. The press gave him tremendous publicity and generally ignored the other leaders, which may have added to their resentment.

The tragedy of this split was that Galamison and the national civil rights organizations had similar commitments to school desegregation, regardless of the personal and organizational interests that divided them. Yet, these interests kept interfering with their relations.*

Since the demise of the Citywide Committee in 1964, the civil rights movement has suffered from limited unity. Later boycotts were in part tests of power within the movement, as well as protests against the Board of Education. Galamison may have been hoping through the second boycott, for example, to make such a show of strength that his leadership would be confirmed.† One of the problems of that March, 1964, boycott, however, was that divisions within the movement had already been announced in the press. And the fact that NAACP and CORE headquarters pulled out carried great weight with many influential whites. Furthermore, opposition groups had begun to show their local and citywide strength. The board and city officials were thus less intimidated by the second boycott than they had been by the first, and it became clear that Galamison would be better off to wait awhile before leading a third one.

The Civil Rights Negotiating Team

The next attempt to build a coalition came shortly after the second boycott of March, 1964. As the board began to backtrack on its pairing proposals, civil rights leaders worked once again for unity.[28] NAACP officials even suggested that they would consider another boycott, if the board continued to vacillate. But it took more than the board's stalling to unify the movement a second time. In April, Superintendent Gross decided to begin meeting in private with civil rights leaders. A month later, the Allen Committee released its desegregation recommendations.[29] When Gross tried to develop his own report, partly to counter the Allen Report, civil rights leaders unanimously rejected it. They agreed on the virtues of the Allen Report, and Gross' counterproposals brought them together again in an uneasy truce. A civil rights negotiating team

* Ironically, at some meetings Galamison could not attend, or had not been informed about beforehand, Parents Workshop officials present would say that they could not ratify an agreed-on strategy until they cleared with their organization, meaning Galamison.

† Though obviously not as successful as the first, this boycott did draw close to 300,000, as estimated by the *New York Times,* March 17, 1964.

was formed in late May, 1964, to bargain with Gross and his staff.[30]

Civil rights leaders still might not have come together but for the intervention of the Urban League, the perennial neutral party in their conflicts. Alexander J. Allen, the league's education committee chairman, went to Board President James Donovan to ask permission, on behalf of all civil rights organizations, to meet as a group with Gross. Donovan agreed to the meetings, which Gross himself had already helped instigate by individual communications with civil rights leaders. All civil rights groups were represented—the Urban League, the NAACP, CORE, Parents Workshop, Harlem Parents Committee, and EQUAL, as well as two Puerto Rican groups—Commonwealth of Puerto Rico and the Puerto Rican Civil Rights Committee, and one white and Negro coalition—the Conference for Quality Integrated Education.

But the negotiating team had the same problems as the Citywide Committee, despite ground rules set up to minimize internal conflicts and many caucuses called to build agreement on strategy. The ground rules were that there would be no leader, that each representative would maintain autonomy for his organization and accommodate himself as well as he could to the interests of the coalition, and that any group that dissented had to clear its public statements with the other members of the coalition. Otherwise, the press would once again play up their disunity, the board would get the message, and the political consequences would be self-evident.[31]

This arrangement worked through the summer and early fall for everybody except Galamison, who attended few of the sessions. He was concerned that they might miss their chance to build mass support while negotiating with the board. He felt that the board was stalling, and subsequent events proved him right.

Nevertheless, the result of these ground rules was that civil rights leaders finally represented a unified bloc. They met with Gross and his top staff for several months, and though the meetings turned out to be largely useless, their dynamics revealed how the board handled protest from which subsequent negotiating groups may learn a lesson.

The first meetings were in late May, 1964. At first the civil rights groups had many successes. They got Gross to back the Allen Report rather than his own, pushed him to mandate a free choice transfer plan for the next fall,[32] and began to find out much more than they knew before about how decisions were made at the board, and how field and headquarters staff related to Gross, and Gross to the lay board. They also learned more about the inadequacies of the board's own data, as, for example, on school utilization.

They made an agreement with Gross that they would call off any public protests that summer and fall if he and they could develop, in private, some plans for implementing the Allen Report recommendations starting in September, 1965. Civil rights leaders defined the meetings as "bargaining" sessions. Whatever they were, their results did not support this definition. After some initial successes, the civil rights leaders won few other concessions. They had no way of knowing in advance, however, that Gross would be either unable or unwilling to implement the seeming "promises" he made at the meetings.*

There were degrees of unity within the negotiating team depending in part on the success of their negotiations and compounded by the militants' view, based on long, painful experience, that negotiation was a waste of time. But when Gross mandated the Free Choice Transfer Plan, and when school officials began to reveal how the system really worked, the militants went along with the negotiations. Success unified the coalition.

The unity started to break down, however, in July and August, when a couple of meetings were held with board staff in Gross's absence. At these meetings Dr. Adrian Blumenfeld, director of the School Planning and Research Unit, denied that he and Gross had agreed to modify the school construction program to bring about more desegregation. He repeated that board policy was to build the schools where the children are and that he was only carrying this policy out. Civil rights leaders couldn't believe their ears. Though they then walked out of a couple of meetings where Blumenfeld presided. Gross never reversed Blumenfeld on school location.[33]

By September, moderates and neighborhood school groups had influenced board and city officials to enlarge the representation of organizations at these meetings. From that point on, the meetings were of no further significance.

The more it became clear that Gross was not honoring the

* See Chapter Seven for an analysis.

so-called "agreements" made at these meetings, the more difficult it was to keep the coalition together. Each time it appeared that he might not deliver on his promises, the militants in the negotiating team grew more opposed to those who favored going through with the sessions.

Two factions emerged, one favoring continued negotiation and the other, public demonstrations. The first group feared that public demonstrations would reactivate the opposition and re-polarize what might still be a fluid situation. They were especially concerned about the effects of demonstrations in an election year, with Goldwater running, and with the prospects of an emerging white backlash.[34] They maintained that the commitments Gross had made were the best that had ever been made anywhere in the nation and that if carried out, they would lead to major reforms. While the negotiating team should drive a hard bargain, they continued, it should keep meeting with Gross and his staff. They argued that if Gross did not carry out his commitments, then all the responsibility could be placed on him and they could publicize his broken promises. They felt, however, that Gross was bargaining in good faith, regardless of attempts at sabotage by his headquarters and field staff. The NAACP, the Urban League, the Commonwealth of Puerto Rico, and the Conference for Quality Integrated Education all seemed to endorse this position.

The other position, held mainly by Galamison, the Harlem Parents Committee, EQUAL, and other militants, was that discussions, studies, and board-initiated negotiations were merely delaying tactics. They had doubts about Gross's integrity, and were not sure that it even mattered how much integrity he had, since they were convinced that board and city officials would subvert any private commitments he might make with civil rights leaders. They argued that the negotiating team should make greater demands than had been made so far.[35] Since this was an election year, they continued, the negotiating team had much more bargaining power than it had used.*

Conflict developed around this point. The more moderate faction argued that to increase the demands would upset the

* Galamison was especially concerned about frittering away the grass roots support (already mobilized by the boycotts) through secret negotiations, in his view only a stall. He demanded speedy board approval of the Allen Plan and the desegregation of the junior high schools. Actually the board did not approve the Allen Plan until a year later, and the junior high school issue was stalled, resulting in the strike of 1965.

"good" relationships they had established with Gross, saying to him, as one of them noted, that "you made a commitment to one set of demands, but now we are brushing those demands off the table and establishing stronger ones, and we can do it because we have a lot of power in this election year." They feared that he would probably pull out, and instead of getting all the changes they wanted, as the militants suggested they should try for, they would get nothing.

The coalition might have been maintained, however tenuously, had Gross given any indication that he could deliver. But starting with the undermining by field personnel of the Free Choice Transfer Plan, and continuing with Blumenfeld's refusal to change the construction program, it became obvious that Gross had little support from his own bureaucracy. Had civil rights leaders any inkling that Gross's power within the board was so limited,* they would not have invested the resources they did in these meetings with him. There was no way for them to have known beforehand. The secrecy of the board's internal politics prevented their finding out. As a result this strategy was ineffective in proportion to Gross's limited influence within the system.

The decline of the civil rights negotiating team may have hurt Gross almost as much as it hurt the team itself.[36] He implied to civil rights leaders that they were one of his last hopes for survival in a situation where he was at odds with his lay board and generally isolated from his professional staff. One of the things that threw him off most was the tendency on the part of several members of the negotiating team to call him or board members individually, without clearing it with other members. When he inferred from this that some members of the movement might not trust one another, he may have begun to doubt that they would ever trust him, or that he could ever trust them. He expressed disappointment that they hadn't showed up at the joint meetings with moderate and opposition groups. In one of his last private sessions with some of the negotiating team, a civil rights leader quoted Gross as saying: "You let me down when I needed you, by not attending the joint meetings. If you cannot accept the idea that I always acted in good faith with you, then what do you ever expect from me?"[37] The reply was that he had not delivered on his commitments.

* See Chapter Seven.

The coalition finally dissolved in November, 1964, a few days after the elections. Galamison was the first to withdraw,* announcing a shut-down of selected junior high and "600" schools for January.† [38] Shortly thereafter, Mrs. Thelma Johnson of the Harlem Parents Committee and Mrs. Ellen Lurie of EQUAL also walked out, without consulting the others on the negotiating team, [39] which showed how difficult it was for the coalition to agree even on the most general ground rules.

Since then, all attempts to form a citywide coalition have failed. A group calling itself the Harlem Confederation for Integrated Quality Education was formed in March, 1966, and stayed together for only a few months. The Peoples' Board, formed in December, 1966, has been relatively ineffective. As of this writing (September, 1967), there are renewed attempts to form a citywide coordinating body to organize parent groups to develop decentralization plans. Without such citywide organization, the movement can hardly be effective.

Puerto Rican Organizations

Negro and white civil rights groups might have been more successful in their efforts to desegregate the schools and get the Board of Education to make other reforms, had they formed a united front with the city's Puerto Ricans, but such a coalition never developed. In fact, relations between Negroes and Puerto Ricans have been getting worse in New York City since the end of the desegregation fight in 1965, as both groups have been fighting for control, jobs, and money in the anti-poverty agencies and for positions in the city administration. [40] The Human Resources Administration, for example, Mayor Lindsay's super-agency administering poverty, manpower, education, and welfare programs, has been a focal point of these conflicts, as Negro and Puerto Rican leaders have each charged top officials in the agency with favoritism toward applicants from the other group in making appointments.

The Negro and Puerto Rican poor in New York City seem to face similar problems. They live in largely the same ghetto areas, attend the same segregated and poor quality schools, and are in a similar position of powerlessness. But the fact that they

---

* Actually, Galamison never participated actively in the negotiating team, having attended only one meeting. Mrs. Thelma Johnson, who did attend, acted as his representative.

† The "600" schools are for pupils with emotional and learning problems.

live in the same areas only leads to conflict, and their many cultural differences further limit the prospects of their forming a viable coalition.

Puerto Ricans had been integrated among themselves in Puerto Rico and many simply failed to see the point of the Negroes' fight for desegregation in New York City. They had no race problem. Furthermore, many Puerto Ricans did not want to be identified with the low status of the Negro, since they had their own problems. In addition, they came from a culture that emphasized the virtues of deference to authority. "Social protest is just not the Puerto Ricans' style of life," a prominent Puerto Rican spokesman in the city explained. "They are far more used to going in with hat in hand and saying please. This is their feudal heritage." [41]

Puerto Rican spokesmen identify at least three separate categories of Puerto Ricans, each with different ethnic attitudes. There is first a middle and lower middle class who maintain that Puerto Ricans are not Negroes, do not face the same problems, and have cultural rather than racial difficulties in America. They feel they have been "making it" faster than many other ethnic groups, and that therefore the way to proceed is quietly, with dignity, negotiating problems, educating themselves, and progressing into the mainstream of American life.

A second, lower class group, feel that they have problems different from those of Negroes, but that their solutions lie along the same path, making it necessary to work together politically, applying strong pressure on city officials and, if necessary, engaging in official protest. Their goal is not complete integration, but to establish the Puerto Rican culture as an entity within American culture, as the Irish, Italians, Jews, and other ethnic groups have done.

A third and much smaller group, an upper middle class and semi-aristocracy within the Puerto Rican population, not only fail to identify with the Negro but dissociate themselves from any Puerto Rican identity. They tend to be light skinned, often blond and blue-eyed, buy homes in the suburbs, and claim to be Spaniards. "I was shocked to find out how many Puerto Ricans earn over $100,000 a year, but they are for the most part people who came with small fortunes, made more, often have ties to the Spanish aristocracy, and don't acknowledge the fact that they are Puerto Rican. You could almost say, using the

Negro expression, that they pass," said a middle class Puerto Rican leader.[42]

Several Puerto Rican organizations have come into existence since the 1940s. The first, the Commonwealth of Puerto Rico, is financed and operated through Puerto Rico's Department of Migration, and was influential from the late 1940s when it was established, through the late fifties. At first it was concerned with employment, and later got into housing, social services, and education. As the migrants began to have to deal with the Board of Education, the commonwealth began speaking for local Puerto Rican groups to top school officials, and interceding on such questions as suspensions, pupil transfers, encouraging instruction in Spanish, and improving school–community relations by interpreting Puerto Rican culture to school officials. The commonwealth is widely regarded among local Puerto Rican leaders as an establishment organization, having too limited contact with local problems, though maintaining very good ties with powerful citywide groups and board officials.

Around 1955, a second locus of power emerged, the Puerto Rican Forum, composed of middle class intellectuals and professionals—and including Herman Badillo, now the borough president of The Bronx; Dr. Antonio Pantoja, professor at the New York School of Social Work; Manuel Diaz, social worker, former regional director of the Equal Employment Opportunity Commission and now Deputy Commissioner of the Manpower and Career Development Agency of HRA; and Dr. Frank Bonilla, now a professor of sociology at MIT. It had the great advantage over the commonwealth of being an overtly political organization. Forum backed Mayor Wagner in 1961, as part of his reform coalition, and got many political appointments as a result.

The early 1960s saw the emergence of a third set of local groups, from the Parade Committee and the Congress of Home Town clubs. They began to get involved in civil rights activity, protesting police brutality, quality of schools, and wages. By this time, the commonwealth had lost stature among Puerto Ricans, the forum had begun to pass its peak, and this third confederation of local groups came to the fore.

Despite the differences in interest between Puerto Ricans and Negroes, some Puerto Ricans did participate in the protest movement for desegregation. Negro leaders, mainly Bayard

Rustin, approached four leaders in the Forum and the Parade Committee to participate in the first boycott of February, 1964, offering them four seats in a committee of twelve. The four rejected the offer, on grounds that they could not maintain unity among Puerto Ricans if decisions were being made mainly by the Negroes, if they held no veto, and could be outvoted 3 to 1. They went back to Rustin and proposed instead that there be two groups, the four of them and a Negro group of eight, but that basic decisions had to be ratified by both. The night before the boycott, Rustin gave a speech to the effect that there was not one army but two, ready to do battle. That was the high point of Negro–Puerto Rican cooperation in the educational politics of New York City. The areas where Puerto Ricans predominated had the highest absenteeism rates during the boycott—East Harlem, the south Bronx, the Lower East Side of Manhattan, and Williamsburg; Harlem and Bedford–Stuyvesant had lower rates.

Puerto Rican groups lost interest in the desegregation fight after that boycott, for many of the same reasons that some Negroes and many whites did. The bussing solution did not appeal to Puerto Ricans, with their very close family ties and the strong protectiveness of many Puerto Rican parents. Second, *El Diario*, the main Puerto Rican paper in the city, charged that the Citywide Coordinating Committee for Integrated Schools was being led by communists, including a Puerto Rican leader, and even the forum became restive about staying in the coalition. Finally, there was great disaffection among Puerto Rican spokesmen with Galamison and the small cadre of people around him in the Citywide Committee. The more moderate Puerto Ricans preferred the consensus politics of a Rustin to the vanguard leadership of a Galamison. Though Gilberto Valentin, one of the more radical Puerto Rican leaders, supported the second boycott, most Puerto Ricans did not.[43]

They then tried to salvage the coalition by going to the Negro leaders with a proposal for a silent march across the Brooklyn Bridge. The parade was the Puerto Rican style, and they wanted to have more of a leadership position. It was defined as a Puerto Rican affair and drew only 3,000 Puerto Ricans and 700 Negroes, far short of the 15,000 that its leader, Valentin, had promised; many Puerto Ricans inferred that they could not mobilize a large following, and that the Negroes were not willing to go along. "Galamison only joined halfway through—he was not at the rally first," reported a Puerto Rican leader, "and Rustin didn't show up until they were already at Livingston Street. This said to the Puerto Ricans that the Negroes want and expect us to help them, but they are not willing to reciprocate. This was the high-water mark of Puerto Rican social protest, and the beginning of the loss of confidence that the Negroes would go down the line on Puerto Rican issues."

Later, during the negotiating sessions with Gross and his top staff, Puerto Rican leaders did attend, but they did not feel part of the negotiating team. "Usually the basic decisions had already been made when we got to a meeting and they were essentially asking us to react," said one Puerto Rican participant. "I did not have any objections to any of the decisions, and I would suggest one or two points to be added, like compulsory Spanish in the elementary schools, and they always added them on, but without any discussion. I would have liked it better if they had developed their demands at a meeting with everybody there, instead of in a smaller meeting beforehand."

Puerto Ricans have also lagged behind the Negroes on the community participation controversies. Though IS 201 is roughly 40% Puerto Rican, for example, Puerto Ricans never participated to any degree. Ted Velez, director of the East Harlem Tenants' Council, an anti-poverty agency, attended the first few meetings of the IS 201 parents group and was asked to leave. This reflected the deep conflict between Velez's group and MEND.[44]

The community participation movement is just as alien to the interests of many Puerto Ricans as desegregation was, reflecting once more their disinclination to engage in social protest. "It is difficult to convince Puerto Rican parents that they have any basis or right to challenge the school system," a Puerto Rican leader explained. "From all their experience they hold a great confidence in the public schools and a general attitude of respecting authority. 'How could I possibly know more than the teachers and principals?' is the attitude of many. Negroes are more militant about rights they feel they have not been able to get, while Puerto Ricans withdraw instead of getting angry. They have a hope the Negroes don't have. Their reaction to a poor school is when I can earn a little more money, we'll move to a better area or go back to Puerto Rico. They have the dream that the Negroes do not have—a little education, a better job, and you are equal."

The important exception to this pattern is the Puerto Rican Development Corporation, a coalition of the anti-poverty agencies of Puerto Ricans in the city, but mainly concentrated in the south Bronx, under the leadership of Mrs. Evelina Antonetty. Mrs. Antonetty is now in the process of trying to mobilize a following. She is one of the few active integrationists among Puerto Ricans and has developed the Negroes' style of political protest, participating in the Negro coalition and now developing parent training programs and local community organizations to enable local groups to take over more power in the administration of schools and other city agencies.

Even if Mrs. Antonetty succeeds in her local area, no mean feat, the pattern of Puerto Rican organization, though more centralized than that of Negro groups from the ghetto, is still quite localistic and fragmented. Unless these diverse local organizations—community corporations and other anti-poverty agencies—coalesce, there is little likelihood that they can exert enough power on even a sympathetic city administration to secure more services for their people.

Meanwhile, the Negroes and Puerto Ricans are farther apart than ever before, and their conflicts have become a political issue in emerging pre-mayoralty-election politics.

Tactics and Strategy

There are many parallels between the civil rights movement and other peoples' movements during the period of early organization. The same struggles between moderate and militant leaders, the same factionalism, the same strikes as tests of leadership were common in the labor movement, for example, in its early stages.

It is hard to see how local civil rights groups can ever work with national organizations which regard the problems of New York City in the light of their national policies and strategies. They prefer going through structured channels to review particular proposed actions, developing a plan and strategy, securing general agreements within their own organization, presenting the plan to the Board of Education and then, given its response, reviewing what action they should take.[45]

Social action groups cannot easily proceed that way. Their problem is to hold a large mass following, and their leaders often feel that demonstrations are one of the only ways to keep their followers together. Furthermore, they are freer to plan protest actions quickly, since they have no established organizational procedures or board. Their strength lies in being in close touch with the masses. The two groups thus face different and seemingly incompatible imperatives. It is difficult to conceive of more divisive relationships than the ones that existed in New York City's civil rights movement on the school desegregation issue. One civil rights leader noted: "At one point there were meetings to decide whether we should have further meetings to decide whether we should have meetings with Gross. A fantastic amount of tension seemed to be created during these meetings." [46]

It is perhaps unfair to expect the civil rights movement to be different from other such movements at such a stage of evolution. Its disunity was part of an inevitable process of crystallization, and more than most such movements', this one's disunity was reinforced by the diversity of organizations and interests involved, and the geographic spread of the city. The board's actions were a great factor, and this point merits special mention.

Board Actions and Civil Rights Unity. The Board of Education capitalized on divisions within the civil rights movement, much as management had taken advantage of rival union factions. The board could easily "whip-saw" one faction against another. Any public agency must develop strategies of defense in the face of mounting popular criticism, and this was one of the strategies the Board of Education sometimes used. When James Donovan was president there was much debate at top levels within the board over whether to deal with national or local leaders. Important communications were sometimes sent only to national organizations, excluding people like Galamison or Harlem Parents Committee representatives. Private meetings were sometimes set up with national leaders, in the hope that agreements could be made on limited reforms, thus playing moderate elements off against the militants. [47]

NAACP and Urban League officials who understood this tactic agreed that a national official should never attend a meeting without a local representative. Even so, the Board of Education adopted the tactic on a few occasions. One civil rights leader recalled: "The board called a meeting with Wilkins, Farmer, and Whitney Young, but each took one other person with him." Another said: "James Donovan always wanted me to talk to Whitney Young or Wilkins. He always knew that the national office would take a more conservative approach." Still another reported: "When Galamison withdrew from the NAACP in Brooklyn, he was bitter and set out to out-militant the militants. The board plays on these weaknesses to the hilt. I don't underestimate their ability to play both ends against the middle." [48]

In many cases, it wasn't necessary for the board to try to divide the movement. It had only to function as usual, which meant delaying for many months before announcing its plans. Civil rights leaders would then grow uncertain of the board's commitments and would debate among themselves on what the delays meant. The militants would argue that the board was simply stalling, in the hope that community pressure for change would wane.[49] They would urge another boycott to show the board that there was still popular discontent. The national civil rights organization officials would argue that the board should be given more time to complete its investigations and that further demonstrations should await the release of its plan. They favored private communications and negotiations with the board, indicating at the same time their demands for far-reaching plans. This was what happened in 1964 and 1965, giving conservative white groups the chance to consolidate their power.

Leadership. Though civil rights leaders faced many external obstacles in their struggle to mobilize support, some of their own strategies may also have contributed to their difficulties. Many civil rights leaders characterized some of the grass roots militants as "leaders without followers," suggesting from personal experience and with some dismay that the same small cadre of activists kept vying for control, without actually mobilizing a large local following or drawing in moderate civil rights organizations. Some of the militants themselves sometimes characterized their many meetings as a "liberal monologue" where the same people ended up talking to each other, rather than to a wider audience. As one moderate civil rights leader noted, referring to the coalition that formed in early 1966: "Now, once more, a small cadre is attempting to take over. They will never be able to do anything. There are many newcomers and they know what they want to happen. The militants have refused to learn from past experience."

Some militants within the ghetto had the same view. It was expressed by one Harlem leader: "The trouble with the confederation and the 'Peoples' Board' has been the same, time and time again. The concentration of leadership, or the artificial formation of a few handpicked people, always leads to the same old story. There's no looking to the community, no wish for changing or expanding leadership. They pull a big crowd on an issue, but it remains inert, not activated." [50]

While this observation held for much of the period since Galamison's last shutdown in early 1965, it is becoming less true as decentralization becomes the issue, which, by definition, requires increasing community participation. The problem, in part, has been that a small group of activists are far more experienced about the issues than the rest of the ghetto communities. They know more about how reform has been scuttled and about the operations of the school system than most others in the movement and are impatient with the board's stalling. But in failing to broaden their leadership, they cut themselves off, both from other local leaders and local followers. They also leave themselves open to charges by many board officials and moderates that the movement consists only of a handful of "outside agitators" with no interest in education.

Unless the problem of developing new leadership and getting much more parent participation in the movement is solved, the movement will continue to founder and repeat past failures. There were times when public demonstrations were held, as one civil rights leader put it, "before the generals got their troops prepared." Then, as he added: "They were easily outflanked." [51] This strategy of not staging public protests until the movement had many followers would, of course, pose further problems, since public protests are one of the only ways to mobilize followers in the first place. They dramatize the issues more than most other strategies.

Limited Follow-Through. The movement's effectiveness was also limited by its tendency to withdraw pressure and limit protest after the board announced a desegregation plan. Since so much resistance to reform came from within the school system itself, which often refused to implement changes that the board proposed, the movement's inability to police the system contributed to maintaining the status quo. There were some attempts to check on Open Enrollment, the Free Choice Transfer Plan, and pairings [52]—but there weren't enough, largely because of the movement's limited resources and staff. Continued monitoring of board programs at every stage of implementation is essential, even though the civil rights movement might never undertake technical evaluations and audits. Some groups within the movement have increased their vigilance in this regard.*

At the peak of the desegregation controversy, some civil rights leaders felt that it was the board's responsibility alone to implement plans, evaluate them, and increase community participation and improve school–community relations in areas where the plans were implemented. The view that boycotts and public demonstrations for new plans do not ensure their efficient implementation has greater support now within the movement, which is now more politically sophisticated than it used to be.†

Morality and Conflict Strategies. Some of the ways in which civil rights groups tried to project their demands for school desegregation also hurt that cause, or at least failed to help it. One was to appeal to the social conscience of the white community by arguing that desegregation had been federally mandated, that Negro children do not learn and are psychologically damaged by segregated schools, and that whites as well benefit from desegregation. The white community, however, had its own morality, usually defined by its constitutional rights, its children's needs, and the many other interests the neighborhood school movement articulated. In the early stages of the conflict, some civil rights leaders felt that it might be possible to get many whites to accept desegregation, since New York City was such a "liberal" town, but this judgment proved wrong. This is not to say that the effort shouldn't still be made, and with much more leadership than board and city officials have exerted in the past. But appeals to morality alone are ineffective as a political strategy.

Moral arguments were often accompanied by another tactic

---

* The Office of Economic Opportunity has funded a few groups in poverty areas to train parents in how to evaluate school programs, deal with school officials, and develop curricula and proposals. Mrs. Evelina Antonetty, co-chairman of the education committee of the New York City Urban Coalition, and now leader of the Puerto Rican community in the south Bronx, is one such leader. Mrs. Ellen Lurie of EQUAL, who has worked with her, is another.

† The goal within the movement now has become *gaining* power, rather than winning concessions *from* power. Winning particular battles (getting policy statements) and losing the war (implementation) happened so often that civil rights leaders finally realized they had to break the power of the headquarters and field professionals to push through any reforms.

that didn't work either. Civil rights leaders, using the slogan "racial balance," assumed that the benefits of desegregation would become evident to whites as well as to Negroes. They did not: whites feared that school standards would be lowered, and they were unwilling to risk desegregation to find out if their fears were justified.

The issue was thus posed as one of Negro self-interest, without much attempt to ease the fears of whites and without an effective strategy to deal with their racism. The board had a responsibility to press for more white acceptance of desegregation, but since it did little to fulfill that responsibility, civil rights leaders might have tried to do more than they did. At times, they categorized all whites who resisted desegregation in the most negative terms. The charges may have been valid in some cases, but to make them openly was bad politics.*

The effects of this strategy were to alienate many white liberals and moderates and further polarize the opposition to civil rights groups. To categorize people as "friends" or "foes" so rigidly discourages potential allies. It was bad politics to write off some politicians as "typical white liberals" or as "sellouts," as sometimes happened at the peak of the controversy. The reaction was understandable, but politically it was not productive. A better strategy might have been an appeal to the pocketbooks of white taxpayers: "How can you afford to support a school system that turns out an illiterate and unemployable Negro population?" "You are being double- and triple-taxed for the schools' failures by having to pay for welfare, crime, narcotics, correctional institutions."

The powerful teachers' union, the United Federation of Teachers, was one moderate group with which the movement rarely aligned itself. Civil rights groups were in conflict with the union on key issues—the transfer of teachers to ghetto schools, provision of a bonus system for ghetto teachers, and increased community participation. The union wanted more job rights for teachers, and ghetto parents felt that its demands on the board were against their children's interests.

But while the UFT was certainly not a civil rights organization, and it never will be, teachers and parents have many common interests, and since the union had progressive leader-

---

* The public statement of the Conference for Quality Integrated Education of August, 1964, condemning all parents who supported PAT and the boycott as racist, is an example. See Chapter Five.

ship, there might have been more collaboration than there was. Throughout the 1966–1967 school year, the union staged many demonstrations with parents for better services and conditions in ghetto schools.[53] Previously, the union had honored the first boycott by not condemning teachers who refused to walk across the picket line. Yet, no rapprochement between the teachers' union and ghetto parents ever took place, nor does one seem likely in the near future. As liberal as the union's top leadership was, some of its positions have antagonized parents, and for good reason: for example, the union's demand in 1967 that teachers be given more say in expelling pupils who are disciplinary problems. The gulf between teachers and ghetto parents is wider now partly because plans for community control are regarded by teachers as a threat to their status and job rights.*

The difference between a conflict strategy and a "consensus" strategy is that in the latter, there is somewhat more room for the needs and organizational imperatives of groups that take more moderate positions—accepting the fact that the NAACP and the Urban League will be less action-oriented, and that the United Federation of Teachers will want to protect the job rights of teachers and its own power even though it may also want to respond to the demands of parents. Such tolerance, in turn, makes it easier to develop a viable coalition where alliances can be struck on particular issues that may further everyone's interests. This is not to justify the positions of the moderates but only to suggest the preeminance of "politics" over "morality" as an organizing strategy.

Yet, the obstacles civil rights groups confront are often too great to suggest that an alliance with white liberals would really increase their political effectiveness. They have often been caught in such a bind that they could not win either way. When they were too militant, they alienated potential allies. But if they formed too many alliances within too broadly based a coalition, they would have trouble agreeing on any but the most moderate programs. Their only successes, after all, had

---

* This analysis of the UFT treats the period before early 1967. The UFT-ghetto community conflict over decentralization and community control worsened as this book was going to press. See Chapter Six for a discussion of the buildup to the recent decentralization fight between the UFT and the community. See also *Epilogue* on their confrontation over the Albany legislation of May, 1968.

come through militant activity of a kind that white liberals generally did not approve.*

But there may be a consensus strategy based on goals that will not alienate other groups from the movement. However offensive the term consensus politics is to radicals, it need not take on the pejorative connotations they ascribe to it. One tactic might be to present new ideas in terms of benefits that liberal or even conservative white groups will welcome.† The educational park is one such new idea, provided it is not presented only as a technique for desegregation, but also for its economic as well as its educational virtues. This is not to play down its significance as a desegregative device, but only to suggest a tactic that makes it difficult for conservative parents and real estate groups, in alliance with rightwing interests, to defeat such a potentially valuable innovation.

Irving Levine, of the American Jewish Committee, has suggested what he calls a technological approach, which involves showing citizens the many benefits—federal money, new instructional devices, neighborhood renewal—that will accrue if they adopt certain innovations and learn about the federal legislation that qualifies urban centers for funds for such purposes. Levine has shown the variety of federal programs under which a school district could apply for money if it adopted such innovations as educational parks.‡ Other urban affairs specialists have also used this tactic.[54]

.   Such an approach de-politicizes discussion about innovations that might lead to conflict and resistance, in contrast to public protest strategies, which have failed in the past. When innovations are presented with such a set of inducements, it is hard to oppose them, though ultra-conservative groups probably will anyway, as long as they sense that Negroes may be mixed with them. These groups might be isolated, however,

---

* And it must be emphasized that back-door negotiations were rarely successful unless backed by a strong show of strength, something that was often possible only through public demonstrations. Furthermore, it is difficult to mobilize the black community, or any other dispossessed group, except through public protests, which may be much more "moral" than private negotiations made by leaders with limited accountability to their constituents.

† Social scientists interested in conflict resolution have coined the term "integrative symbols" to describe one mechanism for easing stalemated conflicts, so that all parties may win at least a partial victory.

‡ See Chapter Five for a somewhat fuller discussion of this approach.

as a minority who are against "spending more money on our children's education," by a large coalition of moderate and liberal whites, along with Negroes and Puerto Ricans.

A Totalism, No-Win Strategy. Another civil rights tactic was to set very advanced goals, rarely waver from them except to raise them still higher, and then suffer defeat after defeat as potential allies fell away. Sometimes these goals were advanced for purposes of bargaining rather than as a liberal expression of demands. They were interpreted literally, however, by such widely read education reporters as Fred Hechinger of the *New York Times.**

Stubbornly following such a hard line hurt the movement in many ways—often demoralizing even the most dogged and committed activists. It is hard to sustain a movement when the goals are set so high that no action by the public agency under attack can be considered a victory. Meanwhile, the opposition feels even more threatened. It mobilizes for a long struggle. The moderates drop out, and the militants are once more isolated from the rest of the community. Hard bargaining for more limited objectives, rather than unrealizable demands, might have won more victories on a few occasions.

Lest I seem to place too much responsibility on the civil rights movement for its limited political effectiveness, it must be kept in mind that the movement did not have nearly the money, the personnel, the experience, nor the access to board and city officials that other civic groups had, which made the struggle that much harder. Furthermore, the most powerful civil rights organizations, the NAACP and Urban League, are multipurpose organizations, with housing, employment, and voter registration on their agendas, as well as education, and with limited resources to deal with all these problems. The location of their national office central headquarters in New York City made it still harder to mobilize their support on local school problems.

Finally, the Board of Education itself was a formidable foe. Its inefficiencies, the power of its professionals to sabotage whatever innovations seemed to threaten, and its insulation from its constituency, made it hard to introduce changes. The civil rights movement in New York City functions under the most

* See Chapter Six for a development of this point.

trying conditions. While its strategies might well be improved, other groups as well will have to join it if there is to be any reform.*

There will have to be a fundamental alteration in the balance of political power in the city. The board itself cannot preserve the status quo, without the continued support of many moderate groups like the Public Education Association, the United Parents Association, and various boroughwide and local parent associations, which pour all their resources into public education. Their success in shoring up the board or limiting reform shows how powerful they have been; an analysis of their role is essential in filling out the picture. First, however, I should like to interpret the role played by liberal white groups that have more interests in common with the civil rights movement. There is more prospect for securing their support, and it is important to know why they have not given more support than they have.

* It is of great political significance that factions within the board, or among neighborhood school groups, never were dramatized in the press and never hampered the status quo politics of these interests—while much attention was drawn to civil rights divisions, which the board clearly did take advantage of. When the Citywide Committee was still together in December, 1963, it had clearly become a political threat in the city, and something had to be done to dilute its effectiveness. This is not necessarily to say that influential board and city officials were deliberately trying to divide the movement, but simply to suggest that most "power structures" and advantaged groups develop mechanisms for diluting protests that appear to threaten their position. Beyond this, the diversity of groups and pluralism within the movement and the autonomy and maintenance needs of every civil rights organization contributed as well to disunity.

THE WHITE LIBERALS

White liberal organizations participated in the school desegregation movement, usually in collaboration with national office staff of the NAACP, the Urban League, and CORE. In New York City they contributed money to these organizations, and some served on their boards. Such Negro spokesmen as James Baldwin, Adam Clayton Powell, and Floyd McKissick have sometimes claimed that white liberals had too much control over the movement and that they had maintained a form of colonial rule over civil rights organizations, especially in New York City.[1]

Apart from civil rights groups, the most active white liberal organizations were the American Jewish Congress, the American Jewish Committee, the Anti-Defamation League, EQUAL, the Protestant Council, and the Citizens Committee for Children. Others included the Catholic Inter-Racial Council, Lutheran Human Relations Association of Greater New York, the Liberal Party, Americans for Democratic Action (ADA), the Ethical Culture Society, the Jewish Labor Committee, the National Council of Jewish Women, the American Civil Liberties Union, and District 65 (Union of Wholesale and Retail Clerks). Organizations in this latter group were either latecomers to the struggle or participated in a much more limited way than the others.

Coalitions

There were also two loose coalitions of white and Negro organizations. One, the Intergroup Committee, was formed in

1954 and helped to prod the Board of Education to make plans and policy statements on desegregation. The Intergroup Committee was most active in the implementation of Open Enrollment, in the late 1950s and very early sixties. By 1961, it had all but disbanded, and repeated attempts to revive it over the next few years failed.

The other coalition, called the Conference for Quality Integrated Education, was formed in March, 1964, to gain support for Negro civil rights organizations from the white liberal community for non-voluntary desegregation plans. The conference did give some support, though it was unable to agree on an appropriate strategy among its diverse member organizations. Indeed, both coalitions fell apart for many of the same reasons that the civil rights movement itself faltered. And they faced the additional problem of mediating between conflicting interests of Negro and white organizations.

Since the failure of both coalitions shows how hard it is to keep even the most progressive white organizations allied with civil rights groups, it is worth recounting their activities in some detail. The story of their failure provides further evidence of the obstacles to forming a strong integrationist coalition in New York City. Needless to say, decentralization coalitions will face the same obstacles.*

Intergroup Committee. The first coalition of school desegregation groups, the Intergroup Committee, played an important part in moving the Board of Education to do studies and develop desegregation plans in the 1950s. It was composed of a broad cross-section of liberal organizations, including the Urban League, the American Jewish Committee, the American Jewish Congress, the Anti-Defamation League, ADA, The NAACP, the Citizens Committee for Children and a number of others. Dr. Kenneth Clark, who charged in 1954 that the board was maintaining inferior, segregated schools, was the first chairman, from 1954 to 1955. He was followed by Israel Laster who was chairman from 1956 to 1960. Judge Hubert Delaney succeeded Laster, but he resigned in 1961 when it became apparent that the coalition could no longer move the board toward reforms.

* A conventional liberal interpretation for this political failure is that desegregation in New York City is impractical and is irrelevant to the problem of educating ghetto children. To some extent this is true, though perhaps for reasons other than those liberals generally use—for example, the racism of the whites and the incapacity of the school system to manage innovation of any kind.

The committee held numerous public meetings throughout the 1950s on particular controversies and also met with the board to get it to implement its policy statements and recommendations more quickly. But as it became increasingly clear that the board was delaying in implementation, the organizations within the committee could not agree on an appropriate strategy.

Some groups argued that the committee should take a stronger stand in support of rezoning and building schools in fringe areas, rather than push for more studies and meetings with the board.[2] Some even urged that the committee endorse the citywide boycott that was being proposed by Reverend Galamison and Parents Workshop.* Other, more moderate groups demurred, however, arguing that the board was acting in good faith and that its many administrative problems kept it from implementing reforms more rapidly or in more schools.

There was also much conflict over how the committee would relate to militant local groups, for example, whether Galamison's Parents Workshop should be allowed to join. The moderates kept winning out, but not without contributing to major differences within the committee and between it and the civil rights movement.

One of the committee's main contributions was its research on school programs and particularly on the implementation of Open Enrollment.[3] Dr. Ofelia Mendoza of the Urban League had done much of her research under the Intergroup Committee, and her data sustained the involvement of its member organizations. Many meetings of the committee were called to review her studies and to try to use them to prod the board. She was the only full-time professional working for the committee, and when she left in early 1961, the committee soon collapsed. Delaney resigned as chairman soon thereafter.

The circumstances of her leaving revealed some of the committee's problems. Her research had been supported by grants from the Taconic Foundation to the Urban League. In late 1960, the grants ran out, and Urban League officials refused to be the sole supporting agency for her research. But no other organizations within the committee felt they could share the cost, even on a limited basis.

Even before 1961, however, divisions within the committee had become clear; and it lost much of its effectiveness as the

* The 1960 boycott

moderate faction, led by Israel Laster, Clark, NAACP representatives, and UPA and PEA, continued to avoid the activist strategies offered by the militant groups. The Harlem and Brooklyn strikes alienated these moderate groups, who felt that the board was moving ahead on desegregation and would continue to do so in the face of "responsible" pressures and protests. Several participants in the committee were also members of Theobald's Black Cabinet,* and felt he could be counted on to move the board toward more school desegregation. Clark's later characterizations of "white liberals" in his book, *The Dark Ghetto*,[4] reflected his deep disappointment with the board's inaction on desegregation.

Ironically, the few times the committee met in the 1960s to revive the coalition, it discussed the very matters that the militants chided it for not taking seriously enough.[5] The agenda of a meeting in late 1962,[6] for example, included such items as the failure of the board to implement the reports of the Commission on Integration; the doubling of segregation† since the 1950s; and the failure of the board to take active steps to prevent this. They were discussing the key problems, but they weren't doing much about them.

A major reason for the committee's inaction, in addition to its internal divisions, was the attitude of some of its moderate leaders, especially Israel Laster, the person most responsible for its continued operation. Laster defined the committee as a "professional" coordinating group, set up to gather data on school programs and to maintain communications between protest groups and the board.[7] This was like the approach taken by some Urban League officials, understandably, since Laster had served for many years on its board.

Laster, like many other "human relations" specialists, felt that the way to get educational reform was to interpret the interests of all participants in school controversies to one another, and to keep communication lines open. This method is based on the assumption that many board officials were qualified professionals who wanted to respond to legitimate protests, and that there was actually much common ground between the board and the community. As later chapters will show, there was little basis for Laster's optimism.

Conference for Quality Integrated Education. The next serious

* See Chapter One.
† Twice as many segregated schools.

attempt at building a coalition began in March, 1964, soon after the two civil rights boycotts. Many white liberal groups who felt committed to the cause of school desegregation had sat on the sidelines while the controversy raged between the board and civil rights groups. They wanted to join the conflict, and a few leaders among them formed the conference.

One goal of the conference was to mobilize support for Negro civil rights groups from white liberals. A more important goal was to develop and maintain unity among the many Negro and white groups that were active participants in the school desegregation controversy.[8] The conference included all the Negro organizations and numerous white ones, and its leadership tried to keep them working together.

Yet, the conference fell apart. Though its two chairmen, David Livingston, president of District 65, and Reverend Donald Harrington, presiding minister of the Community Church and later chairman of the New York State Liberal Party, were astute leaders, the conference petered out after little more than a year. The same factions had become polarized once more. The board's advanced policy statement of April, 1965, adopting many of the Allen Report recommendations, left the conference without a mission, and the leadership became involved in other activities. It was only later that they realized how little the board was implementing its own recommendations. Militants, meanwhile, lost faith in the conference, while moderates saw it as a captive of Galamison.[9]

The conference's first few meetings indicated how limited its active following was to be. The first meeting drew several hundred people, most of them white, and most of them concerned with bringing the Negro and white liberal communities together. Many old-line liberals of the thirties were there—for example, Dwight MacDonald and Waldo Frank—as well as a younger generation of white, civil rights activists. It was one of the largest informal turnouts of whites for a civil rights cause in recent New York City history.

The only segment of the liberal community that was conspicuously absent was the leadership of the New York City labor movement. Livingston and a few representatives of such unions as the longshoremen and teamsters were there, but the most powerful labor leaders—such as Harry van Ardsdale, chairman of the Central Labor Council, David Dubinsky, president of the International Ladies Garment Workers Union, Alex Rose of the Hatters Union, and Jacob Potofsky of the Amalgamated Clothing Workers Union—were all absent, and their organizations were not represented. Albert Shanker of the United Federation of Teachers was the only other major labor leader present, and he later served on the conference's steering committee.

The purpose of the meeting was to develop a dialogue between Negro and white groups, but many whites, especially the old-line liberals, felt they were not given a fair hearing. Several, on raising questions of a critical nature regarding the tactics of civil rights groups, were cut off.[10] The chairman argued that the meeting was not to criticize particular civil rights groups or tactics, but rather to try to find grounds on which white organizations could join the Negro community in its quest for desegregated schools.

One result of what some who were there defined as a restricted dialogue was that many who did not get a hearing started to drift out. Many white liberals refused to become involved in the conference's activities. These liberals had never participated in school desegregation controversies in the past, however, and most of the Negro and white organizations that had an interest in the issue stayed in the conference.

The conference held a series of meetings from March, 1964, through April, 1965. A final meeting was held in March of 1966 to decide if the conference should reconvene, and it was decided that it should not.

The main thing the conference did was negotiate with Gross and his staff, but after the meetings with Gross broke down in December, 1964, there was nothing left for the conference to negotiate. It had already lost the moderates, however, several months before, through two critical actions. The first was a conference press release in late August, referring to the impending PAT boycott as "racist and reactionary in essence." The moderates resented the implication that all boycotters should be labelled as racist and reactionary, feeling it was impolitic to do so and would further activate the white opposition. And they objected that the statement was made on behalf of the conference, with the names of all its constituent organizations included, even though many had not been consulted about it beforehand.[11]

The other action was the unwillingness of the conference to expand the representation of the civil rights negotiating team to include such moderate organizations as the Anti-Defamation League, the American Jewish Committee, and PEA. Conference leaders took this position on the grounds that too broadly based a representation would ruin any chance of unity, a view that Negro groups held strongly. Some moderate leaders were embarrassed that their organizations were represented in such an activist coalition. They were dubious of its strategies, and were not willing to let Negro and radical white groups take over.

So went one more attempt to form an integrationist coalition. Though the leadership tried many times to bring together white moderate, liberal, and Negro groups, it was an almost impossible task. There were two ways to proceed, neither very satisfactory. One was to get as broad a representation of groups as possible, which made it difficult to reach a consensus on any but the most limited goals. The other was to unite the militants and try to bring in as many moderates as would come, but the moderates wouldn't budge and the militants became isolated politically.

Particular white liberal organizations did participate in the desegregation controversy on an individual basis, but their influence on board decisions was not nearly so great as if they had been part of a larger coalition. The most active participants in this group have been the Jewish community relations organizations—the American Jewish Congress, the American Jewish Committee, and the Anti-Defamation League, which share interest in intergroup relations and civil rights. Their importance lies in the fact that Jewish children still represent the largest remaining white ethnic group in the New York City school system. Catholic parents have the option of sending their children to parochial schools and the inducements to do so have increased, with the federal money now available for parochial use alone, and with the threat of desegregation in public schools. White Protestants have moved out of the city in great numbers, and those who have stayed have tended to send their children to private schools. Jews and low income Catholics are the only remaining white groups of any size.[12]

Though increasing numbers of Jewish parents have been sending their children to private schools, there are many more who still use the public schools.* Desegregation on any scale

* The total proportion of pupils in private schools in New York City is still less than 5%.

would have to involve Jewish children and many Jewish leaders see the conflict over school desegregation as a battle between Jewish and Negro groups.[13] This is, of course, an exaggeration: the homeowner movement in New York City, which became the basis for PAT, was primarily a Catholic movement. Nevertheless, Jews and Negroes confronted each other directly on school desegregation.

At the peak of the desegregation controversy, in early 1964, Jews were of little help to the Negro. No Jewish organization supported the first boycott, and all condemned the second. As one Jewish official stated candidly: "New York City's Jewish groups are good on abstract thinking, ideology, and the rest of it, but policy agitation is done by others. Unfortunately, the school system doesn't duplicate the thinking of liberals, and liberals are too easily satisfied with symbolic victories and diverted from real ones." [14]

Jews differ among themselves on the school desegregation issue, along class, generational, and organizational lines, with the younger generation and higher status Jews much less likely to label Negro action groups as "extremist" and thus cut off communication with them. These differences are often reflected in Jewish organizations.

American Jewish Congress

The most progressive Jewish organization has been the American Jewish Congress, representing a lower middle and middle class population, East European, traditional in their religious practice, yet generally liberal in their politics. Its leaders reflect a tradition of East European socialism, with close ties to peoples' movements, in contrast to the political conservatism of many middle and upper class German Jews.

The congress has roughly 50,000 members nationally, and in the New York area they have 300 chapters, each with at least 25 members who meet monthly. Congress officials estimate that they have as many as 10,000 members in the metropolitan area. The congress is set up so that local chapters cannot contradict national policy. At the same time, the leadership of the congress is sensitive to the views of local chapters for fear of losing its following, and this has been one of its greatest problems. Local chapters come together in a body called the Metropolitan Council, where they make their views known.

The New York City organization of the congress has been actively involved in school desegregation since 1954, when it filed the first brief in the North against de facto school segregation, in Englewood, New Jersey, where it took a much more advanced position than national civil rights organizations held at that time. In fact, congress representatives had numerous discussions with NAACP officials in the mid-1950s, trying to get the NAACP to be more active in the New York City school situation. In 1959, Naomi Levine and Will Maslow, the congress officials closest to education, published their short monograph, *From Color Blind to Color Conscious*, a history of the New York City experience. Partly an attempt to awaken the conscience of more white liberal groups, it also tried to reassure NAACP officials that the pursuit of racial balance in the North would not hurt its legal efforts to eliminate de jure school segregation in the South.

Later publications and positions taken by congress officials were equally advanced. In early 1964, while most white liberal organizations were refusing to take a positive stand on pairings, the congress issued a well-publicized document suggesting the feasibility of more than eighty pairings throughout the city.[15] The document was not taken seriously by the Board of Education and—more important—was rejected outright by local congress chapters, the children of whose members would have been affected, but it did give notice of the strong commitment to desegregation of at least some top officials in the organization.

Yet, the congress did not participate in the two boycotts and played a smaller role immediately afterward, when Negro leaders demanded that the negotiating team meeting with Gross not include any white liberal groups other than the Conference for Quality Integrated Education. One congress official said: "At one time we were the leadership, with NAACP and other groups along behind. Now we are the tail of the movement, and it is sometimes difficult for some who don't understand the importance to the Negro movement of asserting its own leadership to accept this change. We understand it, though with many regrets." [16] But officials in other Jewish organizations refused to accept Negro leadership so easily and actively tried to prevent the negotiating team from monopolizing the board's time. When they failed to win representation on the negotiating team by trying to influence the national offices of the Urban

League and the NAACP and the conference, they went to top board and city officials, where they got their way.* As a result, Gross was forced to hold two sets of meetings, one with the moderates and liberal white organizations and one with Negro leaders.

Meanwhile, the congress was faced with a revolt from its constituency, and its officials clearly saw their situation in such terms. "We miscalculated on what our members were thinking, but they were a little bit schizophrenic. They always went along on Open Enrollment, and they talked in favor of pairings and other plans. But, when the chips were down, and we started talking about implementing pairings in particular schools, *their schools*, then they suddenly backed off, and many of us were quite embarrassed. Unfortunately, we hadn't prepared our members for the pairings, but we didn't realize that before-hand." [17] After this disappointment, congress officials tried harder to get their members to accept desegregation.

But why this sudden backing off among lower middle and middle class Jews after they had apparently endorsed desegregation? One reason was their fear that standards would be low-ered with integration. "Our members are almost psychotically concerned with education," reported one congress official. The typical congress member—a salesman, small businessman, or lower white collar person—though more liberal politically than members of most other white groups, shared the fears that many whites had about sending their children to school with lower class Negro children. "It was not the movement of children alone that upset many of our people," continued this official, "but rather exposing their children to a slum environ-ment, with all that that implied for them—immorality, knifing, urinating in the halls, the sex codes of Negro children. I realize now what an education job we really have." [18]

When congress officials attempted to counter these fears, they had little success. "I am convinced that I will be able to get our parents to understand that integrated schools and het-erogeneous classrooms won't necessarily lower educational stan-dards. But our parents can accept this only on an intellectual rather than emotional level at this time," said a congress offi-cial.[19]

* This informal exercise of influence was reported in interviews with leaders of civil rights and Jewish organizations.

Congress staff have tried hard to change the attitudes of their constituents, conducting many human relations workshops in which they discussed research that questions the many negative stereotypes of Negroes, and the fears of declining standards in desegregated schools. They also took their members to communities where desegregation plans had "worked," such as Greenburg, N.Y., Montclair, N.J., and West Orange, N.J.

It would have taken a vast educational program, however, to change the attitudes of this population appreciably. Congress members harassed their leadership at meetings held to dispel community fears about desegregation. The political implications of this revolt were not lost on the mayor and the board. When organizations like the American Jewish Congress, the Anti-Defamation League, and the United Parents Association were unable to mobilize membership support for nonvoluntary desegregation plans, the board and mayor took notice, and scaled their plans down accordingly. "The Mayor and the board have been counting noses," remarked one liberal organization official, "and when they found so many against desegregation, they were not about to buck the tide."

This was not just a problem for the American Jewish Congress, then. Many other Jewish, Catholic, and Protestant groups were even more strongly opposed to non-voluntary plans. Except for the efforts of the Catholic Inter-Racial Council, there was nothing like the attempt by Catholic leaders that there was from Jewish organizations to mobilize support for desegregation, and the Catholic Inter-Racial Council had only the most limited resources to carry on such a campaign.

One of the biggest problems the American Jewish Congress and other Jewish groups faced was the large Jewish leadership and following in neighborhood school organizations. Not only were the Joint Council for Better Education in Brooklyn, and Parents and Citizens in the north Bronx mainly Jewish, but so, too, were some PAT chapters, in such areas as Canarsie and East Flatbush. Officials in Jewish organizations tried to show how PAT strategies were like those of right wing extremist groups,[20] but while this may have had some impact, many Jewish parents and local community groups still remain very much opposed to any compulsory transfer plans for purposes of desegregation, much like lower and lower middle class groups of other religious faiths.

Yet, whatever white support there was for desegregation came largely from Jews. The American Jewish Congress group in Jackson Heights supported the pairing there, and Rabbi Myron Fenster, who lived in that community at the time, was one of the leaders of the white integrationists. Other congress chapters, in the Jamaica and Hollis communities in Queens, also worked hard for integration, urging the board to establish educational complexes and rezone the junior high and high schools. Thus far, however, they have been outnumbered and defeated in these efforts.

Though its troubles with its chapters cut the American Jewish Congress off from the civil rights movement for a while and limited the support it could give, its officials did not abandon their efforts to promote more harmonious Negro–white relations, or to press their membership to accept desegregation. In 1965 and 1966, they tried to mobilize the rabbinate, which had been reluctant to get into the controversy—a campaign that is still going on.*

The fears of Jewish parents were not just a reflection of their prejudices. Some of these parents had experienced integration in receiving schools under Open Enrollment.[21] They saw how inadequately prepared the schools were and how limited were their services. Some of their fears were justified, not because desegregation necessarily lowers standards, but because of the way desegregation programs were implemented in New York City.†

Since late 1965, the American Jewish Congress has renewed its involvement in school desegregation. Mrs. Naomi Levine of the congress was the chairman and one of the main organizers of the citywide educational parks movement in New York. Congress lawyers gave much assistance to east Brooklyn parents in their educational parks suit against the Board of Education. The parks movement has not been successful, however, since there has not been enough political pressure to force the board

---

* In early February, 1968, the Central Board of Rabbis issued a strong statement condemning the mayor's plan for decentralizing the schools, on grounds that it would lead to separatism and segregation. One can reasonably ask where the rabbis were when desegregation was being contested. The answer is that most of them sat on the sidelines, by and large, failing to provide leadership.

† See Chapter One.

to move ahead. Parks are not an issue now, but they may become one if the federal government and State Education Department offer inducements for the setting up of parks linking New York City and adjacent suburbs.

American Jewish Committee

The membership of the American Jewish Committee is much more upper middle class and upper class than that of the congress, more German than East European, more conservative politically, and less so in its religion. It also differs in organizational structure, in that it is exclusively a citywide and national organization and has no local chapters or branches within the city. It is thus free of pressures from a local constituency. The committee is generally referred to as the "aristocrat" of the Jewish organizations. The typical committee member is a wealthy businessman, real estate developer, or professional. One has only to look at the annual budgets of these organizations to see the tremendous wealth of the committee compared to the others.

The committee's participation goes back to 1954, mainly through the efforts of the same Israel Laster who later was to become chairman of the Intergroup Committee. He also helped get the PEA study underway, had served on the board of directors of PEA and the Urban League, and helped establish PEA's coordinating committee and expand its membership to include national civil rights organizations.

That the wealthy and conservative committee was concerned with desegregation suggested to the board and city officials that important white elements in the city were allied with Negro civil rights groups. The committee helped the desegregation cause in more concrete ways, too: in 1959, when ways to implement Open Enrollment were being discussed, it was Israel Laster who helped make the plans a reality. One moderate civil rights leader who was very close to the situation recalled: "When the Board of Education dropped Open Enrollment in our laps, I don't think they had any idea of implementing it. There was no money for carfare or bussing. Israel Laster went to the American Jewish Committee and the Urban League, and he really saved the whole idea. He gave us some money to put out pamphlets and really let the parents know what it was all about. We were too poor to do it ourselves.

At this time, we had unity. We had to have unity to battle this gigantic bureaucracy."

The committee's financial contribution to the publicity campaign was partly responsible for raising the number of transfer applications under Open Enrollment from 337 the first year, 1960–1961 (there were over 12,000 openings), to approximately 8,000 the next, when the board expanded the plan. At the same time, the committee preferred to work behind the scenes. "While the committee gave us funds to distribute pamphlets," a civil rights leader recalled, "we could never get them to come out and announce publicly their approval of the program. I feel the upper class Jewish parents did not buy this program, not so much out of racism as out of fears for quality education. In any case, they didn't support it with enthusiasm." [22]

More than most civil rights groups, the committee was committed to working with rather than against the board in 1960–1964. Along with PEA, UPA, and other moderate groups, it was so committed to gradualism that it was not about to make strong public protests that the board had moved too slowly, and it didn't. Civil rights leaders saw these organizations as representing the board's view, and as early as 1960, when local civil rights groups were calling for strikes and citywide boycotts to implement Open Enrollment, the American Jewish Committee became known within the protest movement as part of the "enemy camp." On the other hand, some committee leaders and moderates applaud the board's Open Enrollment program to this day, and attribute its failings to the many administrative and political problems it faced in implementation.

A moderate civil rights leader referred to the committee as "dormant" and as "Janus-faced" after Open Enrollment began, and reported that while it sounded as if it were committed to the plan, it did not follow through when Open Enrollment became a reality.[23] Thiis was probably accurate; the committee all but dropped out of the school desegregation movement after 1960, when it became necessary to press the board more vigorously for implementation. The committee's withdrawal coincided with the increasing militancy and expanding demands of the civil rights movement. The mutual estrangement was all but inevitable when committee officials assumed the task of "explaining" the board to Negro groups and lauding its efforts.

The split, however, was not permanent, and the committee

has fundamentally changed its role on desegregation and civil rights since 1964. Though it remains an establishment organization, it has played a distinctly non-establishment role, moving away from its close alignment with the moderates as it takes a more critical view of the board. This is largely the effort of Irving Levine, its new education director, who took over in early 1964 and worked to re-establish the committee's ties to the civil rights movement and enlarge its participation in school issues. Levine, a longtime activist, had previously worked as a community relations specialist for the Mayor's Commission on Intergroup Relations where he participated as the Queens field man on the Ridgewood–Glendale project. He had also worked for the committee on school desegregation problems in Cleveland. Levine's interest in educational parks, in citywide educational planning, and in pursuing a technological rather than a civil rights tack, moved the committee back into a position of leadership.

The committee has maintained its ties with the Board of Education, but in quite a different way from what they had been. "We were actually an establishment group," said one of its officials, "playing a non-establishment role, which may have heightened the anxieties of the establishment. Our joining the critics really bothered the respectables. We'd suddenly pulled out from the front door crowd, although we were never denied entrée there. It was a strategy on our part to continue criticism of a liberal establishment we were close to. Many liberals on the Board of Education couldn't move within the bureaucracy, and this was one way we strengthened their hand." [24]

At the same time, Levine and other committee officials worked to develop and maintain ties with Negro protest groups. They worked through the Conference for Quality Integrated Education and later through an *ad hoc* group of citywide organizations to promote the educational park. As one committee official related: "It was a strategy designed to bring about a new contact with the protest movement. The school system was failing so miserably that protest, no matter how irrational, had to be supported." [25]

Yet, because of the committee's former role, the militants didn't completely trust it. One committee official said: "They would call on us for help, but we were not within their fold. Our heart was generally with the militants, but they didn't trust us." [26]

The action that finally re-aligned the committee with the protest groups was its all-out support of educational parks. It helped an east Brooklyn parents' group get a hearing with top city officials and made sure that their request for an educational park was given responsible attention.[27] It also gave the group technical advice on developing their own plans.

In fact, the committee became so critical of the Board of Education's lack of planning on another park site, at Co-Op City in The Bronx, that several district superintendents demanded the resignation of a committee official, angrily accusing him of "irresponsible agitation" against the school system. As one informant said, recalling this incident: "In their view, we were crazy, supporting the wrong horses, a respectable organization like us. What were we doing hob-nobbing with such radical outfits like EQUAL and the NAACP? They felt we were interfering with good education. They were older men, in their fifties and sixties, very much educational establishment. Our position was that there is no such thing as good education in New York City." [28] John Slawson, the head of the American Jewish Committee, backed this official, and the superintendents who were members of the committee threatened to withdraw.

One of the committee's main contributions has been to develop Levine's so-called "technological strategy." This involves advocating the construction of many new educational facilities in inner cities and adjacent suburbs, largely with federal aid, and the conversion of older buildings to a variety of different educational uses. The new educational forms would include educational parks and laboratories, arts centers, half-day children's academies, five-day boarding schools, country camp schools, computer centers, science and technology centers, suburban–urban exchange, therapeutic and library centers. Children would have a home base, but they would also have a wide choice among these other institutions. These new planning concepts provide federal aid and educational benefits for all children in school districts that adopt them, while at the same time contributing to desegregation. The strategy is, in Levine's words, one of breaking out of "the old semantics and tactics of the civil rights movement," and battling for desegregation and priority services for disadvantaged minority groups "within a new context that offers some recognizable benefits to the majority group."

The committee's most recent activity has been to set up a

national Department of Education and Urban Programming to mobilize support for a wide variety of educational innovations. The committee has the resources to make an important contribution to educational reform in urban centers throughout the nation.

Anti-Defamation League

The Anti-Defamation League participated in the controversy through its interest in intergroup relations, discrimination, and civil rights. Harold Schiff handles ADL's school activities, with special emphasis on in-service training for teachers and other school staff. His interest in the New York City school situation is part of a general program of intergroup and community relations that he directs in the metropolitan area.

The ADL is similar to the American Jewish Congress in organizational structure, though its constituency is a lower status one and more conservative politically. During the pairing controversy this constituency staged the same kind of revolt, and perhaps an even stronger one; local B'nai B'rith chapters supported PAT and other neighborhood school groups.* Schiff and his colleagues have tried to discourage this support and the negative attitudes toward Negroes that give rise to it.[29]

But ADL never took the advanced positions that the congress did on pairings or that the congress and the committee later took on educational parks. Furthermore, its officials rarely acknowledged in public their members' opposition to desegregation, and when the question came up they tended to be defensive about it in the presence of civil rights groups.†[30] In these respects they shared the "educationist" point of view held by the moderates. They supported the neighborhood school, questioned the advantages of educational parks, and generally felt that they had fewer values and interests in common with civil rights groups than either the congress or the committee. ADL is much more "quality" conscious, and often takes the position that desegregation plans, unless implemented very gradually

---

* Lists of organizations in Brooklyn, for example, that opposed pairings and openly endorsed PAT, included local B'nai B'rith chapters in Bay Ridge, Bensonhurst, Canarsie, and east Flatbush, among others.

† Congress staff would state openly at civil rights meetings that they had lost their constituency, but Anti-Defamation League officials withdrew more from the movement and initially tended to rationalize and justify their members' participation in neighborhood school groups.

and with much more preparation than there has been thus far in New York City, will lower educational standards.

ADL still feels that many local civil rights leaders are irresponsible "extremists." Though they regret the polarization between white and Negro groups, they have tended to withdraw from sustained communications with many Negro leaders and from active participation in protest group coalitions. This posture reflects the influence of their board and professional staff as well as their constituency. The latter, through their fraternal B'nai B'rith lodges, are sometimes aptly characterized as a kind of Jewish Elks Club.

The questions of educational parks and the relation of desegregation to quality are complex. The evidence is certainly not in regarding the conditions under which parks and desegregation contribute to quality education. But the positions taken by ADL and other moderate organizations are not based primarily on the available evidence. They are largely political positions, reflecting the interests of their membership, many of whom are members of PAT and other neighborhood school groups, and oppose desegregation.

Though the wealthy real estate and other business interests that dominated the board of the American Jewish Committee were generally liberal, they might not have agreed to such advanced ideas as educational parks without constant pressure from their professional staff. ADL might have supported its staff too, but its professionals were less innovative and less committed to radical change than those in the congress and the committee. A couple of older-generation professionals made a try for broader representation in the civil rights negotiating team's meetings with Gross and his staff: they worked through the Urban League, the Board of Education, and the mayor to influence Gross in this way. This attempt illustrates the resentment this group felt at being excluded—from a movement whose "exclusiveness" they had actually helped develop, by limiting their responsiveness to its protests in the past.

People were hired who were far to the left of Jewish organizations' stated policy on school desegregation, in order to keep them aware of progressive ideas. Annie Stein of Parents Workshop, for example, was the chairman of the American Jewish Congress's education committee, even though many officials within the organization were far more moderate than she. The congress consistently refused to let her testify for it at public hearings, but it did accept her as education director.[31] It was the same with Irving Levine and the American Jewish Committee.* These organizations were trying to help the movement, even though they had sometimes failed to do so before.†

Protestant Council

There are few white Protestants left in New York City, though there are many Negro Protestants. The single most active Protestant agency has been the Protestant Council, the delegated agent of Protestant churches within the city which has generally supported school desegregation and decentralization, but its power has been very limited.‡

The response from ministers of local parishes to a statement sent out by Reverend Norman van Meter, the council's education director, in June, 1964,[32] which supported quality integrated education indicated how little power the council had over its members. The ministers resisted—on grounds that the church should not involve itself in such political matters, especially since the demands of civil rights groups limited certain freedoms which the church had no right to do.

In September, 1964, the council urged local ministers to give sermons in support of school desegregation, and again they resisted. Many suggested that such sermons would violate the old American tradition of the separation of church and state, claiming that this was a secular matter only. Others objected to the Protestant Council's request as an intrusion on their local autonomy.[33]

---

* Stein and Levine differed in their radicalism. She was more a community organizer and activist, while he was more interested in planning.

† Other Jewish organizations have participated in the school issue periodically, as, for example, the Central Board of Rabbis and the Union of American Hebrew Congregations. UAHC, the social action arm of Reform Jewish groups, has attempted to infuse a spirit of progressivism among the Reform rabbinate and Jewish populations. The Central Board of Rabbis has played a less active role than UAHC, but it has encouraged rabbis all over the city to support desegregation plans and participate in intergroup relations programs in local communities to dampen racial and ethnic tensions.

‡ According to estimates made by the Protestant Council, Protestants accounted for roughly 23.5% of the city's total population in 1967. Since most Negroes (perhaps more than 90%) are Protestant, and since Negroes accounted for 18% of the population, one can see how few WASPs are left in New York City. Most of them probably live on Manhattan's Upper East Side, and a large majority of those with children of school age probably send them to private schools.

Yet, in the past two years, the views of Protestant clergymen on this issue have changed considerably, in line with those of the Protestant Council. The change has been so pronounced that one has only to go over the list of speakers at public hearings to notice the Protestant clergy's increased involvement. Many ministers in ghetto or fringe areas not only testified in support of the civil rights movement, but led and participated in many public demonstrations. White Protestant clergy from East Harlem, for example, participated in the "tear-in" protest in April, 1966, against the board's inadequate desegregation proposals.[34] But increased participation may not necessarily lead to increased influence over the board. Thus, when in January, 1965, a group of white Protestant ministers formed the Temporary Committee to Forestall the New York City School Crisis,[35] and held an emergency breakfast meeting at a downtown hotel, the ministers decided to send a delegation to the mayor and the board; Mayor Wagner was not available to meet with them and the Board of Education was almost as inaccessible. They barely made the press. After the "tear-in," one board official referred cynically to them as "naive men trying to save all our souls."

The Protestant Council, however, has become more powerful in recent years. It has a separate Church and Race Secretariat, under Mrs. Dorothy Jones, a middle class Negro professional. Mrs. Jones is one of the most experienced and informed people in the city on school matters, having served on her Harlem local school board, on the Mayor's Commission on Human Rights, and as an active member of the Harlem Parents Committee. Through the offices of the Protestant Council, Mrs. Jones has rallied support for many protest groups.[36]

The council has also maintained communication with the Public Education Association, one of the few public education interest groups to which wealthy white Protestants belong. Council officials have tried to acquaint PEA's board with the many problems of ghetto communities, and have occasionally been able to neutralize PEA's negative effects on the civil rights movement.

Citizens Committee for Children

The Citizens Committee for Children, an organization of professional and lay experts in various fields of child care, seeks to initiate and improve services for children. It was founded in 1944 by Eleanor Roosevelt, Stanley M. Isaacs, and

Adele R. Levy. The committee, a powerful white liberal organization, functions mainly as a "watchdog," examining budgets, legislation, programs, institutions, and city departments
that affect children.[37] Inevitably, it became involved in school
problems, especially as board and staff are interested in problems of poverty in New York City. Mrs. Trude Lash, its executive director, has served on Mayor Wagner's Anti-Poverty board,
and later as chairman of the education committee of Mayor
Lindsay's Council Against Poverty.

Though some civil rights leaders link the Citizens Committee with more status-quo-oriented moderate groups, one
must distinguish its outlook and positions from those of such
organizations as PEA and UPA. Despite its many ties with PEA
and UPA, the committee is more closely tied to the civil rights
movement, through various poverty programs, and such community action agencies as HARYOU-ACT and Mobilization
for Youth, than PEA or UPA. CCC sees poverty as a political
problem whose solutions depend on radical alterations in municipal institutions.

CCC, like the American Jewish Committee, saw itself as an
intermediary between the civil rights movement and moderate
establishment organizations. It had a foot in each camp and
frequently tried to interpret one to the other. Unlike some of the
moderates, it always sent a staff person to meetings of the Conference for Quality Integrated Education, no matter how radical
the conference seemed to be. It tried to play such an intermediary role on the bussing issue, reportedly by trying to talk many
moderate leaders out of their anti-bussing position. "We thought
the whole bussing issue was unnecessary," a CCC professional
said, "and that it wasn't even an issue, but rather a red flag that
some of our friends had been waving. We have had mass bussing
for a long time, and it is not a revolutionary concept. We have no
evidence that children are hurt by it. Besides, it does not apply
to New York City. We ought to play it down and try to talk about
what's really going on." [38]

CCC took many pro-civil rights positions. In late 1963, it
supported a statement through the Intergroup Committee that
future desegregation plans should be citywide, with a timetable
for their implementation, that they should be board-mandated
and beyond voluntary techniques. CCC pointed out to the
Board of Education the "sabotage" (their phrase) by field superintendents and principals of Open Enrollment, urging

stronger central leadership by the board. It was an early supporter of educational parks, high school rezoning, and the establishment of specialized integrated schools in the ghetto. It
criticized the board for not revising its construction programs
to fit the Allen Report recommendations. And it endorsed those
recommendations, taking the board to task, both in private
communications and in public, for its delay in implementing
them.[39] Mrs. Lash, in a speech at a public conference in March,
1965, attended by then United States Education Commissioner
Francis Keppel, charged that the board had not shown any
leadership, that not one of its announcements of intentions to
implement the recommendations had ever been followed up,
and that this had created an unhealthy state of confusion in
the city. This was one of the most critical public statements an
official of a white liberal organization ever made about the
board.[40]

Yet, CCC was not a significant agent of educational reform.
Like the American Jewish Congress and the American Jewish
Committee, its professional staff were under strong pressure
from their more conservative board to tone down their public
criticisms of the school system, and this pressure was reflected
in many CCC statements. In late 1963, for example, CCC
strongly endorsed an interim desegregation report of Superintendent Gross as "the most comprehensive effort to achieve
maximum integration thus far." Yet, this report contained little that was new and was rejected outright by civil rights
groups. The statement went on to express agreement with the
board that "compulsory bussing would not make a contribution to school integration and should not be instituted." [41]

These statements were in direct conflict with civil rights
groups, as well as with private statements of CCC officials. Later,
a few days before the first civil rights boycott, CCC expressed in
a private memo to the board its confidence in the board's actions. It referred to the board's report (intended to head off the
boycott) as indicating "substantial progress." At a key point in
the controversy, then, CCC joined the moderates in endorsing
the board's stand.

Another reason for CCC's failure to press more for educational reform was the fact that it had many other priorities, for
example, in the fields of mental health, hospitals, and handicapped children. Since it had limited resources, it could not
always follow up on school matters, at least not to the same de-

gree that other, exclusively educational organizations could. Its officials also feared that too radical a position on school desegregation might hurt their ability to bargain with the city on hospital or mental health facilities.

This hurt the desegregation cause, because CCC was a very influential organization in New York City politics. Its top officials—Mrs. Max Ascoli, the late Mrs. Adele Levy, and Mrs. Trude Lash—had very close relations with Mayor Wagner and the Democratic Party in the city. They were highly regarded and feared by school officials, precisely because of their influence, and the progressive positions they sometimes took. Members of the lay board have sometimes called CCC officials, pleading with them not to appear and testify at public hearings, knowing how informed and critical they might be. The election of Mayor Lindsay, a Republican Liberal, in 1965, appreciably lessened CCC's power.

Yet, because of its ties with moderate groups, and as a result of pressures from its conservative board, CCC did not swing the weight it might have on the desegregation issue.[42] It gave large contributions to the Democratic Party in the city and to Mayor Wagner's campaigns, and thus could have contributed to educational reform. Yet, it chose to play a more temperate role on desegregation, though it was less moderate on other matters. Its power, however, was clear. "These people contributed a lot to the mayor's campaign," reported a top board official. "When they want to see someone, you can bet they see him. I've seen issues decided professionally in the morning and completely shifted around by the afternoon, with a phone call in between from one of those ladies at CCC." [43]

EQUAL

The one white liberal group that did not have to worry about a conservative board was EQUAL, founded in March, 1964, by Harry Ansorge, who had participated in the Jackson Heights pairing controversy. When Ansorge and his associates in their pro-pairing group were told by the board officials that they would not get a hearing because they weren't a citywide organization, he decided to make them one, as a countervailing force to PAT. One of EQUAL's first public meetings was advertised in an EQUAL circular entitled *Don't Stand PAT*.

EQUAL formed separate units in each borough and became a citywide grass roots group, most of whose members were white, middle class, college-educated, Jewish professionals. Its chairman from 1964 to 1966 was Mrs. Ellen Lurie, a middle class mother of five, who was one of the city's most informed, dynamic, and militant activists. She was trained as a social worker and had been active in the housing and school politics of East Harlem for many years. She also served on the local school board in the Washington Heights–Harlem district. Mrs. Rosalie Stutz, a middle class mother on Manhattan's West Side, is now chairman. She also has participated in many public school controversies and is unusually well-informed about the school system.[44]

EQUAL didn't have any problems with its board because it didn't have one. It was an activist group that could respond immediately to local controversies as they arose. Unlike any other white liberal group, EQUAL identified with the most militant Negro groups, supporting Reverend Galamison's strikes and shutdowns, and has assisted ghetto residents in East Harlem, Harlem, Brownsville, and the south Bronx in their recent demands for more community participation in school decisions.

EQUAL has made many contributions to the protest movement, including newsletters and fact sheets on the board's programs, public vigils and other demonstrations, attempts to enlist the aid of religious leaders and liberal civic groups, and testimony at public hearings. Mrs. Lurie's testimonies at such hearings were often acclaimed by forward-looking planners, and at one hearing in 1966, Mayor Lindsay left his office part way through her testimony, entered the city chambers, and congratulated her on her remarks.[45] (He had been listening to the hearings on the radio.) When the pairings were implemented, she and her colleagues helped to prepare the parents and communities involved. Her recent papers on evaluations of the board's programs under Title I and reading score data have served to galvanize the movement.* [46]

These actions inevitably split EQUAL from the white liberal community, as Mrs. Lurie and her colleagues knew they

* The many EQUAL newsletters, testimonies, and research reports are probably among the most detailed and sophisticated treatments of the New York City schools that any civic group has ever compiled, though obviously reflecting EQUAL's radical activist interests. The fact that EQUAL was so radical meant that most moderates and school officials paid little attention to its reports. A kind of "halo effect" set in, and since the materials were drawn together by Mrs. Lurie and EQUAL, they were discounted almost before they were read.

would. The split involved a number of costs: if EQUAL did not represent more than a minority of white liberals, whom did it represent? The Negro movement is increasingly committed to its own black leadership. Yet, EQUAL plays an important role, furnishing information and advice about strategy. If it can continue to relate to the movement in this way, it will make an important contribution to the movement's effectiveness.

But in taking such a militant position, EQUAL of course cut itself off from board and city officials, as well as from white groups. Mrs. Lurie and other EQUAL leaders wanted to make certain that they spoke for the interests and problems of ghetto groups and were not just another well-meaning white liberal organization. They thus had a difficult decision to make: to cut themselves off from either the Negroes or the white liberals. The experience of other groups has shown that it was impossible to have it both ways.

Negro–Jewish Relations

Underlying the fruitless attempts at forging an integrationist coalition were the difficult relations between Negroes and Jews in the city. Many Jewish leaders, as we have seen, are ambivalent about the Negroes' demands and protests, especially when they seem to threaten local Jewish communities. They may be genuinely sympathetic to the civil rights movement, but they are also sympathetic to the fears of their constituents, and they know how hard it is to convince these people that they should support Negro demands.

The Harlem community, meanwhile, sees itself exploited by the Jewish shopkeeper on 125th Street who makes his living from the ghetto, takes his money outside where he lives, and until recently employed few Negroes; or by the peddler who overcharges Negro customers and garnishees their wages; the slumlord who refuses to provide services; and the paternalistic Jewish social workers and the welfare officials. Jewish "white liberals" who contribute to NAACP and Urban League and sit on their boards, where they limit their participation in Negro protest, have also made few friends among the more militant Negroes. Negro anti-Semitism may not be nearly so prevalent as James Baldwin suggests in his *Notes of a Native Son,* where he writes that he never met a Negro in Harlem who was not anti-Semitic, but it would be wrong to deny its existence, particularly

among some Black Nationalist groups and lower class Negroes.*
Jews represent not only exploitation. They also represent success. They are one of the wealthiest groups in the city, while Negroes are one of the poorest. They control much real estate in the city, both as individuals and through corporations. Many large developers are Jewish, and so are some homeowner associations, though the homeowner and taxpayer movement is now predominantly Catholic in New York City and was formerly Protestant. Jewish developers as well as Jewish homeowners protest loudly at the prospect of low income projects in such communities as Forest Hills, Elmhurst, and Canarsie.

The New York City labor movement is still another symbol of protectionism. Negroes have moved into such unions as the ILGWU, the Amalgamated Clothing Workers, and the Hatters' Union in increasing numbers, but as Herbert Hill of the NAACP has noted, they do not hold many positions of leadership within the unions.†

More important, many school officials are Jewish, including the majority of teachers, principals, and district superintendents, as well as headquarters officials. There may be as many as 35,000 Jewish public educators in the New York City school system, and they set the tone as much as the Irish do in Boston. The "Jewish principal" stands for oppression and failure in Harlem, Brownsville, and other ghetto communities, if only because so many principals there are Jewish and so many schools are inferior. The Anti-Defamation League has brought complaints to the Mayor's Commission on Human Rights against such groups as Brooklyn CORE for its allegedly anti-Semitic attacks on school officials. The "bad" principal sometimes gets identified as the bad Jewish principal.

The situation is made worse by the fact that many old-line liberals (Jews are prominent among them) have become intolerant of militant ghetto leaders. They identify such leaders with the Stalinists they knew in the thirties, and accuse them of the same obstructionist tactics. A nationally publicized event had much symbolic significance in this regard: Will Maslow of the American Jewish Congress resigned from CORE's board

---

* A recent study by sociologist Gary T. Marx, *Protest and Prejudice*, N.Y., Harper and Row, 1967, however, indicates that Negro anti-Semitism is quite limited.

† All these unions were composed mainly of Jewish workers until quite recently, since Jews went into the garment fields in great numbers.

when a CORE official shouted at a public meeting, in a fit of
rage, that Hitler should have finished off all the Jews. As one
high-ranking Jewish leader commented: "I don't know what
was wrong with Maslow, because he knew, as many of us did,
although the newspapers didn't report it, of a number of anti-
Negro cracks made by some of the Jews at that meeting before
the CORE man's outburst. What a time for the congress to
break with CORE." [47] Maslow's reaction was of course understandable. But so was the CORE official's rage, if not his specific
comment, after hearing the bigoted slurs about Negroes from
Jews. This tragic meeting reflects the tensions between Negroes
and Jews that have so hampered the civil rights movement nationally as well as in New York City.*

Jews have become a main target for Negro hostility and for
their impatience with the slow pace of change. This is probably—at least in part—an ironic result of Jews' involvement
in civil rights. They have been the main victims of the Negroes'
anti-liberal attack even though they joined the civil rights
movement out of unpolitical, humanitarian motives.

Yet, Jews have contributed to conflicts between the two
groups. The lower middle and middle class Jewish homeowners who follow the neighborhood school movement are one
source of the problem, as are certain Jewish leaders. One Jewish
organization official said: "My experience has been that there
are four questions abroad in the Jewish community when I try
to discuss improving Negro–Jewish relations. They are:
'Why are they so loud? Why can't they do things our way?
What more do they want? And isn't preferential treatment discrimination of another sort?' " Such candor is not uncommon.†

Jews are at a crossroads on civil rights issues, and Negro
and Jewish leaders increasingly recognize that new strategies
are needed to re-involve Jews in the civil rights struggle. Part
of the American Jewish Committee's urban affairs program, for
example, is a move in this direction; it attempts to mobilize

---

* The racist slurs by whites at the meeting (Jews and Italians) characterized Negroes as not valuing education, being unable to learn, and being
uncivilized.

† This is a very common phenomenon. Ethnic minorities, subject to
discrimination and prejudice by a majority group, tend to assimilate and
subject the next ethnic minority to the same treatment that they received.
Negro sociologist Franklin Frazier's study, *The Black Bourgeoisie*, indicates
how some upward-mobile Negroes subjected poor Negroes to similar treatment, or at least related to them with much ambivalence.

Jewish businessmen—real estate developers, department store owners, small merchants, and industrialists—to participate in economic and social development programs for the ghetto. They participate as businessmen, not only as Jews, and this strategy may increase the participation of many Jewish businessmen in the urban coalitions, both in New York City and nationally.

Problems of Jewish identity in America, however, may continue to hamper such efforts. Jews still have memories of Nazi Germany and have a pervasive fear of anti-Semitism—which may be increasing in the ghetto, and to which Jewish liberals do become vulnerable when they work on civil rights. They need some reassurance that they won't be subject to such scapegoating.

Also, many Jews have been successful in business and the professions and have become accepted in prestigeful circles. They do not want to give up the power, status, and wealth of their present positions, and are therefore reluctant to participate in a movement that aims to do so.

Despite the risks and costs, it is obviously essential that Jews stay in the civil rights, anti-poverty, and urban affairs movements. They are primarily an urban as well as liberal group whose whole mentality was shaped in the city and whose general style is a cosmopolitan one.

The one strategy they might do well to avoid emphasizing too much is the intergroup relations approach of some Jewish agencies. Poverty, segregation, and other problems of the ghetto are historical and institutional in origin, and they cannot be effectively handled by the meliorist, human relations approach of old-line social workers. Improved communications and "dialogues" between Jews and Negroes are important, but they must be accompanied by imaginative urban and metropolitan area-wide planning, and by substantial commitments of money and other resources. Many Jewish agencies are beginning to recognize this and are reacting accordingly.

Jewish leaders in the forefront of these developments still lack a large constituency, however, and time is running out on the cities. The most recent reason for Jewish non-involvement in civil rights activity is the Black Power movement and anti-Semitism. Albert Vorspan, director of the Social Action Committee of the Union of American Hebrew Congregations, and active in the civil rights movement, has scored those Jews who use Negro anti-Semitism "as a cop-out from the civil rights movement," [48] but the fact is that some do. Conversely, some Negro leaders have contributed to the problem as well. "Those black nationalists who seek to preempt the civil rights struggle for themselves are among the most pathetic victims of the virulence of American racism," says Dr. Kenneth Clark, and he has a point.[49] Joint problem-solving between Jews and Negroes on the problems of education, housing, and employment in the nation's largest cities is imperative in the coming years, if we are not already too late.

The problem for liberals is that they see few practical programs as alternatives to the present mess in urban education and in the cities. Without practical alternatives, there cannot be a liberal program, and the militants take over by default. This seems to have happened in New York City, and it has taken place throughout the nation. Hopefully, the critical nature of the present situation will force liberals, moderates, and conservatives alike to develop some programs. It is in their best interests as well as those of black people to do so.

THE MODERATES

Even though the opponents of desegregation were better mobilized than the Negroes and white liberals, there might have been more movement had the city's powerful moderate organizations helped out. But the moderates, who held the balance of power and were influential with the board, did little to press desegregation.

The most powerful moderate groups are the United Parents Association (UPA), representing as many as 430 local parent associations and 400,000 mothers and fathers throughout the city;[1] the Public Education Association (PEA), representing through its board and coordinating committee some of the most influential professional and civic groups in the city;[*] and various borough-wide or citywide parent groups. These groups represent the professional and civic élite in the city, and they have close ties both with one another and with top city and board officials. Since their activities did not include boycotts and demonstrations, they got considerably less press coverage than neighborhood school and civil rights groups. Their influence over board decisions was known mainly by informed insiders.[2]

Collectively, these groups represented a pattern of white, middle and upper middle class, predominantly Jewish and Protestant control of the New York City school system. PEA and

[*] The Citizens Budget Commission, Citizens Union, Bar Association, League for Industrial Democracy, and Men's and Women's City Clubs were active on PEA's coordinating committee. These organizations are sometimes referred to as conservative liberals, or as the liberal establishment.

UPA had both become highly politicized and had built up their private access to board and city officials through years of experience.

UPA was the more influential of the two, partly because of its larger membership. "The board is a highly political structure," one civic leader reported. "They have their roster of ins and outs. UPA is one of the ins. They have always had a direct relationship with all levels of the structure. They are absolutely politically oriented. Out in the open or under cover, they act like the politician on the beat. They use their numbers boldly, politically. PEA is respected, but they're not like UPA. They don't have the troops. UPA got power by helping Wagner in his campaign. They can always get in to see him. When they call up to see someone there, they jump around."

In some ways, PEA and UPA were extensions of the lay board, participating directly in its policy deliberations. Board members regarded them as the most professional, informed, and public-regarding civic groups in the city.

The scheduling of groups to speak in public hearings reflects this: the moderates were always first on the list. "We find it hard to listen after the groups give their presentation at the beginning," said one board member. "After we hear from UPA, PEA, CCC, and the National Congress of Parents and Teachers, we've heard all the good, new ideas we're going to hear, and it's a parade after that. We hear everybody who wants to speak, but everybody gets very tired after the hearings drag on, and little that's new comes out after these groups have had their say. That's why we put them at the beginning."

The middle class thus controls the New York City school system, even though as many as 50% of the pupils are from low income Negro and Puerto Rican families. Why don't civil rights organizations have nearly the power of these other, more moderate groups?

One reason has been the factionalism among civil rights organizations. The board was not always certain who was speaking for whom in the Negro and Puerto Rican populations; but the moderates usually had a clearly stated position on which they all generally agreed. And it is easy for the board to see their large following.

A more important reason was that civil rights groups did not have the money, professional staff, facilities, or accumulated experience in dealing with the board that the moderates had;

thus they, unlike the moderates, could not monitor the day-to-day operations of the school system and check on whether the board's policy statements were implemented. Most civil rights and liberal white organizations had other commitments. In contrast, both UPA and PEA are primarily education-oriented organizations which devote virtually all their resources to the schools. Both are rich enough to have either full-time staff professionals or volunteers who spend all their time just on school matters. And both have participated in school affairs for decades. Their professional staff are experienced in dealing with the board, and know much about the system's operations, especially the many defensive strategies the board uses when it is confronted with citizen groups like themselves who demand more services. It is little wonder, then, that they have so far been more powerful than civil rights organizations.*

The political power of moderate groups is further increased by their representation on the selection board that nominates people to serve on the Board of Education. The Public Education Association, the United Parents Association, the Citizens Union, the Citizens Budget Commission, the Commerce and Industry Association, and the Association of the Bar of the City of New York are among the members of that panel.

The moderate groups have only occasionally supported the school desegregation movement. UPA and PEA officials claim that they are in favor of desegregation, but not to the degree or with the speed of implementation that civil rights groups demand. In the early years of the desegregation controversy, the moderates endorsed civil rights demands more than they have since 1964. PEA, for example, sponsored the first major study on segregation and equality in New York City schools.[3] Though the study's findings were radical in their implications, PEA never pressed for the reforms suggested in its own report. Thus, in 1959, it opposed Judge Justine Polier's decision that, since the teaching staff in segregated Harlem schools was inferior to that in white schools, parents should be allowed to transfer their children out. Her decision was based on the spirit, if not the precise findings of the PEA Report.[4]

* One of the few major board programs in recent years that directly contradicted UPA demands was its use of Title I money. Much more of those funds went to parochial schools and on a non-shared basis than UPA and many other public school groups wanted. Even in this case, however, UPA, in collaboration with most civic groups, has forced the board to recast its programs.

UPA took similar positions, and though it urged some fringe area schools and rezoning, by 1960, it was starting to backtrack on Open Enrollment. One informed civil rights leader with ties to UPA said: "This whole business of attacking the problem of school segregation split the white community wide open. We found we couldn't depend on any white liberals to carry on our battle. The Citizens Committee for Children,* the United Parents Association, and the Public Education Association were all good allies, but we had to carry through on our own, and this was a good thing in the long run. The so-called white liberals were very divided on issues like bussing and Open Enrollment. The civil rights group could mobilize the whites once we got out there in front, but we couldn't really depend on them to see our point of view in the most basic terms of equality."

The moderate organizations were in the ambivalent position of favoring both quality and equality, but they did not want to sacrifice the former for the latter. They feared that desegregation might lead to a decline in quality, and they were afraid of supporting many desegregation plans for this reason. They ended by straddling the fence on the issue, never coming out openly and opposing any desegregation plans, but never really supporting them strongly either. One civil rights leader with ties to all these groups said: "They never discussed the issue of Open Enrollment as such, but always latched on to auxiliary issues. That's the way these groups—UPA, PEA and CCC—would express themselves."

PEA officials, for example, rarely discussed the merits of the board's particular pairing plans until after they were finally announced. Neither did they discuss the merits of pairing in general for New York City. Instead, they debated with civil rights leaders on the issue of "long-distance bussing," much as the neighborhood school spokesmen did. Long distance bussing was not an issue, however, either in the board's projected pairings that were later dropped, or in pairings as a desegregation technique, since the pairings were based on the rezoning of contiguous schools along the racial frontier.

UPA took a similar position on bussing. "UPA also really played politics with that bussing issue," recalled a civil rights leader. "The middle class women were not straight on the bus-

* See the preceding chapter on the white liberals for a discussion of the Citizens Committee for Children (CCC).

sing issue themselves and couldn't be effective as leaders. They always said they were for integration but were adamantly opposed to long-distance bussing. Now long-distance bussing was never at issue. That was just a way to label it so as to kill integration." Like most moderate organizations, UPA often took the position that many new desegregation concepts had not been clarified, nor had the problems of implementing them been worked out in advance. These organizations thus opted for limited local experiments to see if particular plans would really work. The board encouraged and welcomed such an approach.

The moderates were concerned with more than a decline in quality. They also feared that if desegregation plans were implemented on a large scale or too rapidly, this would lead to further opposition from white parents and to more withdrawals of white pupils. They stressed the importance, then, of planning, of orderly implementation, and of gradualism. Furthermore, they gave other goals a higher priority—for example, increased funds, more services for schools in transition, teacher training, neighborhood school centers, and more citizen participation in school affairs. They favored compensatory programs for ghetto schools—Headstart, All Day Neighborhood Schools, More Effective Schools—as the strategy to follow.* They felt that there would be more chance for desegregation when quality education was provided, and they were especially concerned with "stabilizing"† schools and communities as a way to get more desegregation.

As reasonable as these attitudes seem, the main political effect of the moderates' position was to undermine the civil rights groups' demands for desegregation and strengthen the neighborhood school opposition by contributing to board inaction and caution. The moderates gave an appearance of legitimacy to the board's limited desegregation program by suggesting that only those plans that were "educationally sound" should be implemented. Thus, UPA and PEA presented, in a reasoned, respectable, and "professional" way, the neighborhood school point of view. They didn't use slogans, nor did they demonstrate

* Even on such programs as the More Effective Schools, however, top UPA officials initially resisted the idea, complaining that it helped just the ghetto schools and not those in white middle class areas.

† By "stabilizing" they mean preventing the schools from tipping, from losing more of their white middle class pupils.

or boycott, but the result of their actions furthered the interests of the neighborhood school movement.

The moderates' advice to integrationist groups and to the board to limit public meetings on controversial plans may also have contributed to the strength of the opposition. There is much to be said for the view that public meetings only stir up community tensions, but the board's decision not to inform parents of its plans, as the controversy over pairings increased, intensified the concern of whites over the board's intentions to desegregate their schools and bus their children into ghetto schools. The board met mainly with the moderates, further alienating civil rights and neighborhood school groups.

Since the moderates had so much power, it is important to know more about how they exercised this power and what interests it served. The UPA and the PEA, the two most influential moderate organizations, took similar positions on desegregation, but there were important differences between the two groups that are worth discussing.

United Parents Association

UPA is the most powerful moderate organization. Its political base, its experience, its money, its many parent volunteers who reported conditions in particular schools and districts, and the technical and political sophistication of the staff, all place UPA in a position to influence the board. Harold Siegel, UPA's executive secretary from 1952 to 1965, knows more about the New York City school system than almost anyone else in town. Siegel had been a confidential secretary to James Marshall, former board president, had intimate knowledge of the internal politics and administration and technical workings of the system, and used his knowledge to further UPA interests. If civil rights leaders had known what he knew, they would have been far more effective than they were. In September, 1965, Siegel began to work for the lay board and is now board secretary, an indication of how highly the board regarded his expertise.*

UPA represents mainly middle class parents, though with an increasing proportion of Negro and Puerto Rican members,

---

* Some informed insiders at the board feel that Siegel still furthers middle class interests in this new position.

reflecting changes in the ethnic composition of public school enrollments and the increased participation of minority group parents in school affairs. Some of these parents have already moved into high positions within the organization, but most minority group members of UPA are middle class and dissociate themselves from the demands and tactics of lower class ghetto populations. Many identify less with the plight of the lower class Negro then some middle class whites, in keeping with the compulsive assimilationist tendencies of the Negro middle class, documented by the Negro sociologist Franklin Frazier and others.[5]

UPA has least representation in ghetto and lower middle class white communities, and throughout the 1960s it was under considerable attack from both the left and the right for its moderate desegregation stand. Negro groups felt UPA had capitulated to neighborhood school interests, and neighborhood groups felt UPA had given in to civil rights movements in many instances. UPA reported a drop in membership during this period from roughly 450,000 to 400,000.[6] The attacks from neighborhood school groups were strong and often well organized, with PAC, PAT, and Joint Council leaders attempting to take over local PAs throughout the city. In many instances they succeeded, as, for example, at PS 149 in Jackson Heights.

One reason that the UPA did not take a strong stand on pairings was its fear that PAT might prevail on more PAs to disaffiliate. Within UPA itself, there were sharp differences on pairings, with some members much more in favor of the plan, as they had been of Open Enrollment, than others; and UPA's delegate assembly meetings reflected these conflicts. UPA's tendency to relate obliquely to the desegregation issue was partly a consequence of these divisions and organizational problems.[7]

The neighborhood school groups could have decimated UPA's local organizations if the latter had endorsed pairings too strongly. One counter-strategy of UPA was to go out into those communities where neighborhood school groups were well organized and calm the hysteria that was being created. "We had orientation sessions for speakers to go out to communities and nail down PAT lies," a UPA official recalled. "What we did and continue to do is to nail down the PAT lie whenever and wherever we can. They would twist the fearful questions of parents about school deterioration." Other strategies were taking less advanced positions than some liberal parent associations would have liked. Though UPA officials had many nonpolitical reasons for their moderate position on pairings and other non-voluntary desegregation plans, they were also concerned about protecting the organization from further attack by the right.

The strongest ethnic representation within UPA—and New York City politics are, after all, mostly ethnic politics—is Jewish. One school official suggested that UPA was run by "Jewish WASPs." This is exaggerated, but it correctly points to UPA's upper middle class, moderate outlook, its disdain for direct action, and its unwillingness to support radical changes in the schools. "I see here by looking down the administrative list that we have a preponderance of Jews and a large number of Negro Protestants and Roman Catholics," reported a top UPA official, "but very few white Protestants. And we don't have any chapters on Staten Island, while our most recent growth has been in Queens." The conservatives in Staten Island have so far felt little need for UPA, but UPA's recent growth in Queens includes some conservative Catholics who are perhaps more opposed to school desegregation than UPA's predominantly Jewish members, and these newcomers will push UPA even farther away from any desegregation movements by civil rights groups.

As with most moderate organizations, UPA's leadership were reformers in the 1930s and forties, and perhaps even a little later. But by the 1950s and sixties, when desegregation, decentralization and the abuse of power by school officials became the issues, they were for the status quo. The moderate groups were part of an "educationist" coalition to maintain standards and preserve professionalism by protecting school officials from political interference—when the time for such protection was over, and, in fact, the insulation, power, and autonomy of school officials were contributing substantially to public education's failures in the city.

Furthermore, beneath this façade of good intentions, UPA had many political interests that its positions on desegregation reflected. It was protecting some informal bargaining and consultation "rights" that it had won through many years of struggle, and that were threatened by the civil rights movement at the peak of the desegregation fight. It was also protecting the essentially "private" character of public schools in white middle class communities.* UPA members felt they had almost proprietary rights over the schools they had controlled and had helped upgrade over the years, and attempts to desegregate or rezone such schools were viewed with much disfavor.

At the same time, however, the fears of UPA members were sometimes validated by their experiences. Some of "their" schools were declining in quality under Open Enrollment, in cases where the board provided only a bare minimum of services, either for incoming minority group pupils or for the white children. In addition, much more money per pupil was being spent in ghetto schools, after years of neglect, and many white middle class parents, whose schools had been so favored in the past, felt deprived as conditions changed in the 1960s. They were committed to a kind of "holding action" at a time when they feared that the increasing power of Negro groups, combined with the board's guilt about the past neglect of ghetto schools, might contribute to a deterioration of conditions in middle class schools. This is the context, then, in which UPA's positions must be interpreted.

Localism. UPA wanted the board to adopt an experimental, community-by-community approach to desegregation. It felt that system-wide desegregation would be too disruptive and would lower standards and drive white families out of the city. It demanded that local parent groups be consulted about any plans the board finally implemented, realizing how little headquarters knew about local conditions, how tenuously it controlled field operations, and how inefficiently even the most limited innovations were implemented. It felt that some fringe-area schools had tipped in the past because of faulty implementation of desegregation plans, and it wasn't about to let that happen again.

Political interests were served by this position as well, since UPA and local PA officials feared that their power might be usurped by headquarters, responding to rising pressures from

---

* By "private" I mean that these schools reflect the aspirations and values of the white middle class (predominantly Jewish) communities in which they are located. The Parent Associations have worked hard since the 1930s to improve the schools and reform them. Now they are very reluctant to give up the power (as well as the high standards, they fear) that they have gained, by acceding to Negro demands.

civil rights groups.* They were determined, therefore, to force
the board to include local parent groups in any future desegregation decisions, even so far as to say that if such groups
were not consulted, the board's desegregation plans would not
work. This view was perhaps most clearly spelled out in a
UPA report on integration, developed for discussion at its October, 1963, delegate assembly meeting.[8] The report said:

> While recognizing that communities and parents do not have the
> final decision . . . we insist that the communities and parents
> *must* be consulted in a *meaningful* way on matters which affect
> their children and their schools . . . .
> The thinking of UPA is that mandates imposed from above
> without the involvement of the community in seeking solutions
> simply will not work.

Though this position had much merit, it also reflected
UPA's fears that Negro groups were taking away its power. As
it finally turned out, since civil rights groups were not as well
organized as UPA and did not have as many sources, UPA
won in the end as the board acceded to many of its expressed
demands in its desegregation decisions.

The main issue on which UPA and local parent associations
won out was pairings. The board's deliberations on pairings
were conducted within the consultative framework that UPA
had requested. Thus, in January, 1964, UPA sent a memo to
all local PA presidents, stating that "Parent Associations can
expect to be increasingly involved in community consultation
for the purpose of working out feasible ways of achieving more
integration in their schools." [9] This was to suggest, then, that
the board was going to call them in to discuss all the sites it
had considered for possible pairings, and this was precisely what
happened.

The board had a list of twenty proposed pairings and held
private meetings with district superintendents, local school

---

* UPA and local PA officials have similar fears about black and Puerto
Rican groups taking over power locally, in decentralized schools. An
example is in Manhattan's Upper West Side area between 90th Street and
110th, where Negro, Puerto Rican, and liberal white groups proposed
a decentralization plan in the spring of 1967. White middle class parents
from PS 75, calling themselves the Responsible Committee for Decentralization, feared losing to black and Puerto Rican parents in vying for local
control. PS 75 is a gerrymandered school and whites who controlled the
local parent association may have feared that they would lose some of that
control under decentralization.

board members, and PA representatives at headquarters to discuss the feasibility of each. Harold Siegel, who was still executive secretary of UPA at the time, prepared demographic data for discussions regarding sixteen of the twenty. The UPA was thus given access to the decision-making and policy deliberations of the board before any public hearings. A further memo from Mrs. Adele Tunick, the president of UPA, describes the role the UPA and local PAs played:

> UPA is prepared to help parents groups, both those immediately involved and others, to analyze their own situations and to decide on future procedures. School pairing might be one way to effect integration. In some instances, it might work; in others it clearly would not. The Board has the unmistakable obligation to encourage local communities to develop plans that best suit that community. Community consultation, which involves public hearings alone, without the opportunity for an exchange of ideas and for give and take among people of varying points of view, is not the answer. *Prior to public hearings,* more productive consultation might result when the Assistant Superintendents and the Local School Boards meet in small groups with identifiable community and parent leaders . . .[10]

The results of these private meetings showed UPA's power to affect board decisions. UPA's argument that the sixteen pairings would hasten the tipping of the predominantly white elementary schools involved, resulting in more rather than less segregation,[11] convinced the board to drop plans to pair all sixteen of them. One UPA official said that the only reason the other four pairings were left on the books was that the PA representatives failed to mobilize enough support in those communities for the UPA position. Otherwise, he said, they might have wiped the slate clean.

Civil rights groups did not have their own technicians to dispute the UPA assertions about demographic trends in communities where the sixteen pairings had been proposed, nor did the board's technicians dispute UPA's judgments.* Since, in other instances, civil rights groups did have the weight of demographic research on their side and still lost—the east Brooklyn educational parks case being the best single example—one can only conclude that politics as well as educational criteria affected such decisions.

---

* See the discussion and data on the tipping of these white schools in Chapter Eleven.

As a logical extension of its demands for local experiments rather than citywide reform, UPA strongly opposed the demands of civil rights groups for citywide desegregation to be implemented according to a timetable. Instead, it argued that the board should carry out only those plans it felt would work.[12] The board, however, had no idea of what would or would not work.

UPA did more: it evaluated new board programs so that they would be implemented efficiently.* One of its most publicized studies was an evaluation of the board's first steps toward a grade reorganization plan, begun in September, 1964, which involved shifts of sixth grades from elementary to junior high schools and of ninth grades to a new four year high school. Taking sixth graders out of neighborhood elementary schools and putting them into the more heterogeneous (because larger) middle schools would increase the number of children in integrated situations by one full grade. UPA's informal study documented the many ways the implementation went awry, showing the confusion among the staff as to whether the sixth grade was the responsibility of the elementary school division or the junior high school division.

It also reported that hasty implementation left the staff unprepared for the change, with no time for preparation or planning and no consultation with the administration. With minimal direction from the board, the field staff was not sure of what to do. In the confusion, morale declined.

Though the UPA did the board and the city an important service in documenting these problems, some of its conclusions are questionable. It generalized from such experiences that change must take place in an orderly, limited, step-by-step way, and that the city cannot desegregate overnight by administrative order. But it did not consider that this conclusion was based on a "given" of the present structure of the school system; it never seriously questioned the soundness of the present structure—which is what distinquishes UPA from the radicals. It never asked whether the gradual approach was not a requirement of an inefficient bureaucracy. This is quite different from saying that desegregation as such is not possible in New York

---

* These UPA evaluations, while useful, may also have dampened the board's inclination to move faster on desegregation. Given UPA's caution about implementing desegregation, one might reason that its evaluations were a way of undermining that cause.

City. It isn't the demand for desegregation that creates the problem. It is the school system's inability to make even the most limited innovations. Recognizing this, civil rights groups have now turned their attention to changing the administrative structure of the board.

UPA does not yet share this position, though its own reports (the one on grade reorganization that was cited above and its Title I study) provide much documentation for it. If UPA had a strong commitment to educational reform, its officials might have suggested and even demanded such basic changes in the structure and operations of the school system as decentralization, a stronger superintendent and lay board, and the elimination of the Board of Examiners.* They have the resources and influence to do so. One important reason why they have not is that they fear that standards will decline even further if any more changes are made at this time. This position commits UPA unwittingly to a strategy that may only contribute to the very deterioration it most fears. The school system is not working. Resisting bold reforms will not arrest its present decline.

The Concern for Quality over Equality. UPA has issued many statements over the years that indicate a seeming ambivalence between its interest in desegregation and in maintaining standards and quality. On its commitments to desegregation, consider the following:

> We are committed to a belief that one of the main objectives of a good education is to prepare the child to live, work, and function effectively in a pluralistic society. . . . *Yet* physical integration is not enough to accomplish this.

> We are concerned that ways be found to provide integrated education for much larger numbers, in spite of the complexity of the problem. . . . *Yet* in ways which will retain as many white children in schools as possible.[13]

These statements were issued in late 1963, at the height of the desegregation controversy; they were clearly reasonable in themselves, but their effect was to block change and protect white middle class parent interests. Civil rights groups were never interested in physical integration alone, but were as com-

---

* See Chapter Eight for a discussion of the Board of Examiners, the agency that administers the tests for teaching, supervisory, and administrative appointments.

mitted as UPA to desegregation in "educationally sound" ways, with adequate preparation. The difference was that they did not accept UPA's implicit assumption that poor preparation was inevitable.

The second statement cautions the board against driving out more whites,[14] but desegregation need not inevitably lead to this. Surely it is possible that both planning, preparation, and headquarters leadership would encourage many white middle class parents to keep their children in desegregating schools. Though some white middle class parents will continue to take their children out of such schools, this is not necessarily to say that desegregation itself makes them move. It may only be that the way desegregation is implemented in New York City will drive the white middle class out, suggesting once more the need to examine closely how the Board of Education handles innovation.

The board's poor performance in preparing parents, students, school officials, and the wider community for desegregation makes one wonder why even more whites didn't leave. The only true test of whether desegregation drives whites out would be to compare those instances where the board did an effective job at implementation with those where it did not. Unfortunately, there have been too few cases of the former.

UPA's concern with quality extended to its concern with limiting desegregation within the classroom as well as within the schools themselves. It often argued for homogeneous classes and the single-track system, as part of its proposed program to keep the white and Negro middle class in the public schools. Many local parent association officials felt that classroom desegregation might retard advanced students. Having worked so hard to upgrade services and programs in the 1940s and fifties, UPA did not want to lose ground in the face of civil rights demands for classroom desegregation. Its members were reformers who had suddenly become protectors of the changes they had helped create.[15]

Even in the 1940s and fifties, when UPA was more reform-minded, it primarily served the white middle class. Since the Negro community was not well organized then, UPA had no direct conflict with it. Recently, however, the demands of civil rights groups for desegregation and equality inevitably conflicted with the protectionist interests of UPA. Because UPA exercised its power in private, some ghetto communities have not understood the conflict. Also, many UPA public statements suggested that it supported civil rights demands. But there was frequently a conflict between UPA's publicly stated support for desegregation and its private actions to limit the board's programs. Its approach to reform was much like that of headquarters technicians, and it was correct as far as it went, in the sense that nobody can argue with the importance of maintaining standards.

UPA's solution, to provide more and more services, assumes that aspirations, reading levels, and intellectual and social skills of minority group children will be raised through conventional methods and within the traditional structure of the system. It offers an individualistic, middle class solution to a problem that is institutional in nature. The most important contribution of the civil rights movement was to dramatize the failure of the school system—the many characteristics that would have to be changed if it were ever to provide quality, desegregated education. UPA has steadfastly refused to share this position, partly out of the fear that public confidence in the capacity of public education in New York City would decline even more than it has.

Factionalism Within UPA. I have implied thus far that UPA had a single position, with a high degree of consensus among its local chapters. This was generally true, but not completely true. A minority of more progressive parent asssociations favored more reforms than UPA traditionally did. Some UPA delegate assembly meetings were torn with dissension as a result of this highly vocal minority. It was the PA leaders in Jackson Heights, for example, who initiated the idea of pairing schools there, and there were other parent association members with such a liberal outlook. Yet, many more UPA members felt otherwise.

At a session of the 1967 UPA conference, one parent asked a top UPA official if the organization had had trouble with dissident parent groups. The question was asked in such an open-ended way that the UPA official had an opportunity to answer it as she saw fit. She could have spoken of PAT and other neighborhood school groups, but, instead, she replied unequivocally that their biggest problem was a handful of outside agitators who were stirring up a small number of ghetto parents. She went on to suggest that the protests over IS 201 were consistently led by the same small group with a limited following and an even more limited interest in improving public schools. This judgment was not only inaccurate, given the developments since September, 1966, but it also affected the board's perceptions and increased the likelihood of conflict between the board and ghetto communities throughout the city.[16]

Though I have portrayed UPA as a status quo, tradition-oriented organization, this judgment has to be interpreted in a broader perspective. It was generally progressive on some issues, especially compared to other parent associations throughout the nation. It should not be lumped, for example, with the wide range of fiscally conservative parent groups in small towns and suburbs who perennially vote down school bond issues and protest against higher taxes for public schools. On the contrary, one of UPA's major activities has been to justify the board's pleas for budgetary increases for more schools and services. It has led the fight in New York City in this regard, joining the pilgrimage to Albany every year to ask for more state money. Furthermore, on matters of upgrading services, it is militantly progressive. And it provides the important service, as well, of evaluating programs that the board implements.

Its positions on major issues in the mid-1960s, however, have lacked a sense of the challenges that public education is having to confront. Relative to the new problems posed by such social changes as the civil rights revolution, automation, urbanization, and poverty, UPA has come up with few solutions.

It is easier for an outside observer to recommend changes in UPA's positions than it is for the parents themselves, who directly experience the declining quality of education in their children's schools. Obviously, it is hard for these parents to want anything more than to maintain or improve educational standards, especially in cases where their experience with desegregation has been so negative. Consider the following comments: "We are an Open Enrollment school with two hundred kids coming in," said one parent in an Upper East Side Manhattan school. "We are not given the services we need. Our teachers are without adequate supervision—which has resulted in racial incidents. There are two standards of discipline. Nothing constructive is being done with the Open Enrollment program. We have pleaded for urban readers. We have demanded a double lunch hour to service more kids. Our school is homogeneously grouped. There is a different level of expectation for the Open Enrollment kids by teachers and principals, and this makes a different level of education and discipline. There is nobody on the busses with the kids."

Another white middle class parent, from the Midwood community in Brooklyn, said: "We have 240 children who come in from out of the neighborhood and 200 who are retarded in reading. The board gave us one extra teacher. I decided to find out what exactly were the board's guidelines for Open Enrollment schools and I never at any time got any response on paper. When I asked Superintendent Donovan at the Title I hearings, he said that the federal funds had been allocated for Open Enrollment schools and I should ask my principal about the matter. I started then in September to find out what was happening—and it took five and a half months to discover that Donovan knew damn well that the funds went to the district and how much. The board is still operating under its old assumptions that parents don't understand anything."

Such distrust of school officials by white middle class parents is deep. "The board's handling of the whole Open Enrollment program was atrocious," another parent said. "Their response to any demands was one of professionalese. The principal often divides us, by taking our complaints and turning them as if we had complained against the teachers. Our district superintendent knows about our principal—but yet he does nothing. At the recent annual principals' conference, you could see so clearly the hostility that principals feel for the community and teachers. They took smacks right and left. They are scared stiff of decentralization and having to be accountable to the community. They don't think that parents have a right to know or say anything." Another noted: "The Board of Education has a very ambivalent attitude toward parents. The principal is the only one who has to deal with parents. The district superintendent is a company man. His attitude is that parents are not to be told anything more than they have to be. The board lost too many parents in this community by lack of faith. Everyone lied when we tried to get extra services to help take care of our overcrowding. The biggest problem is the little faith people have in the word of the board. Individuals are nice, but the system is distasteful to work with."

Again, these are moderate, middle class, parent association officials. Their grievances are based on months and years of frustration at being unable to secure needed services for their schools. The grievances are minor, compared with those that minority group parents have experienced for decades, but in the context of their experiences and expectations, many of these white middle class mothers are alienated enough to want to give up fighting the Board of Education. Many are ready to move to the suburbs or to send their children to private schools. Thus, one can understand the conservative outlook of many UPA and local parent association officials. They know at first hand how poorly the board implements even the most minor innovations and so, rightly or wrongly, they learn to be skeptical of bigger changes.

Public Education Association

The other powerful moderate organization is the Public Education Association, a small, élite group that was spawned by the New York City reform movement in 1895. PEA's main purpose has been to advance the cause of reform in the city's public school system by urging administrative efficiency and professionalism, and by protecting professional educators from outside political pressures. According to a recent historical study of PEA, it represented the "good government" point of view* in public education. As the study also points out, PEA showed all the inconsistencies of most good government organizations that mask their self-interest with the claim of serving the public interest.[17]

Membership and Staff. PEA is organized in three units. It has a board that theoretically establishes general policy; a professional staff, many of whom participate in the formulation of that policy; and a relatively powerless coordinating committee, which includes a wide range of moderate interests and relates to particular school issues within the context of PEA's policy positions.

Historically, PEA's board was limited to a small, élite membership—the most prestigious, influential, and affluent interests in the city, and virtually all Manhattan-based. They included Wall Street financiers; industrialists and heads of large distribution firms; successful lawyers, frequently with close links to business; philanthropic socialites; and some civic leaders and professional educators. It is on the basis of this kind of board membership that Sol Cohen's study portrays PEA as tradition-

---

* The term "good government" is often used to characterize middle class liberal reformers (often WASPs and Jewish liberals) who have fought against machine politics.

ally representing a single class interest. It has taken its tone from this small, relatively homogeneous leadership of wealthy, upper class, well-educated Yankee Protestants and German Jews. Recently, its board has somewhat expanded to include representatives of the city's newly rising middle classes, children of the last waves of East European Jewish immigrants, and representatives of the city's most important civic, social, and philanthropic agencies. But this has not seriously altered PEA's élite character, its oligarchic structure, or its special interests.

"They are all well-meaning," said one civil rights leader, "some more intelligent than others, some more sympathetic to us and compassionate than others, but all of them pretty removed by the comfortable padding of their lives from contact with the real, raw problems. They're nice people, you know, but not very real."

Most of the people on PEA's board did have a genuine concern with improving public education in New York City, and since they represented the city's élite, they had much potential power to do so. "These people gave money and time because many were doing penance for not sending their children to the public schools. Some of them actually saw it this way," explained one top moderate official. They used their power in limited ways, however, though they felt they were playing a role as reformers.

PEA's professional staff often make policy for the organization. Dr. Frederick McLaughlin, the executive secretary, plays the most important role on PEA's professional staff, as leader and policy-maker for the organization. According to him, PEA takes "the middle position," on desegregation, "striking a balance between the two extreme groups, PAT and most civil rights groups." Since he was so much better informed than his board members, he often set policy on controversial issues like desegregation without having to clear it with them. PEA could thus respond much more quickly to events than UPA, which had to consult parent association representatives.

PEA's coordinating committee is more broadly based than its board, and is composed of liberal and civil rights groups as well as the traditional interests its board represents. The traditional groups include such good-government organizations as Commerce and Industry Association and Citizens Budget Commission. Moderate and liberal groups include religious, community relations, labor, political, parent, professional, child welfare, and civil rights organizations, and miscellaneous other civic groups.*

Until the late 1950s even PEA's coordinating committee was limited to élite groups. At that time, officials from the committee's more progressive organizations worked to expand its membership base. One noted: "PEA was always a very high status, aristocratic type organization. Their Jewish members were the really wealthy German Jews—the Lewisohns, the Loebs, and Guggenheims."

Even now, the coordinating committee's most liberal groups are not active participants, due largely to the position PEA took on pairings and educational complexes and parks. Its broad representation is thus more of a façade than a true representation of liberal and civil rights interests in the city. The élite membership of both its board and the coordinating committee explains in large part PEA's moderate stands on desegregation. And though the coordinating committee's membership is more broadly based than that of PEA's board, the committee has no power to set policy. It merely provides political endorsement for positions already arrived at by PEA's board and professional staff.

Outlook, Positions. Until school desegregation became such a contested issue, PEA was generally regarded as progressive on most public education controversies. Like UPA, it wanted expanded services. It was particularly interested in the education and assimilation of the "tenement child," during the period of substantial immigration of ethnic minorities to New York City from the 1890s through the 1920s. It wanted to transform the public school system into a multipurpose child welfare agency, through the creation of after-school neighborhood centers, and by merging many institutions into a more coordinated program.

Many of the progressive public education causes of the early twentieth century, then, were PEA's causes. It devoted much of its organizational resources to improving the situation of the poor, new immigrant groups. PEA always took an élitist approach to these problems. Its progressivism was the middle class kind that dominated much municipal reform during this period.

* Specifically, this includes the American Jewish Committee, the Anti-Defamation League, the League for Industrial Democracy, the United Parents Association, the Protestant Council, the Urban League, and the National Conference for Christians and Jews.

It was in this spirit that PEA first confronted the school desegregation problem. Its 1955 study on segregation in the New York City schools and on the differences in quality between segregated minority group schools and predominantly white schools was in keeping with this reformist spirit.[18] Since then, however, PEA's commitments to reform, at least on the desegregation issue, and at times on others as well, have been moderate and selective, in line with UPA's. One PEA official said: "Our positions are much the same as those of UPA. Since we are a citywide organization with no local branches, we rely on UPA for grass roots information and activity."

PEA has supported some desegregation reforms and in a few instances has led the fight for their implementation. It did a lengthy study of the vocational and academic high schools, for example, and urged the Board of Education to eliminate most vocational high schools, whose curricula had become increasingly dated, pointing out as well that most of these schools were a dumping ground for Negro and Puerto Rican pupils.[19] It referred to a pattern of "unintentional social stratification and de facto segregation as a result of the dual high school system" in its 1963 report, *Reorganizing Secondary Education in New York City*. Though some civil rights and white liberal leaders would have preferred that the term "unintentional" be dropped, or at least the first two letters, this report furthered their interests. PEA is still committed to high school reorganization and eliminating de facto segregation by race and class at that level. It strongly criticizes the general-education curriculum* in the academic high schools, referring to it as "little more than a holding operation." [20] This program serves lower class Negro and Puerto Rican pupils primarily and fails to train them for anything—either future schooling or jobs. PEA has pushed instead for a four-year comprehensive high school that would include Negroes and Puerto Ricans as well as college-bound whites. This is one of the only issues on which it has differed from UPA, whose members want to protect their white middle class high schools. It has also worked to establish post-high school programs and job training centers. All these efforts certainly put it in the reformist camp.

The same can be said of its decentralization proposals, which accept as valid the claims of ghetto parents about the

---

* The general-education curriculum is the alternative to the academic, commercial, and vocational curricula.

indifference of the school system to the needs and grievances of the community. PEA's proposals ask that authority for the selection of district superintendents and principals be vested in local school boards that would represent the communities they serve. As one PEA statement recommends: "We believe that the way to decentralize the school system is to give local community representatives a sense of participation in the critical decisions to be made with respect to their public schools. Certainly the appointment of school principals and the superintendent are the most important acts in relation to the well-being and improvement of district schools, and present and potential board members are bound to recognize this." [21]

The statement even goes so far as to suggest that new district superintendents may be needed, precisely the view of many ghetto leaders. As it reads: "It has been our feeling that the problem will be to get district superintendents willingly to take the full measure of risks that go with leadership. A new breed of superintendent as well as strong local school boards will be necessary, and the Board of Education should be prepared to find or develop them." This again places PEA on the side of the many parent groups who have agitated since the IS 201 controversy for much more local community participation and control.

PEA's other actions on behalf of causes minority groups favor include its continued lobbying in the state legislature against the enactment of any of the numerous "neighborhood school" bills that have been introduced at every session since 1963, when the issue of "mandatory bussing" first became so controversial. PEA has helped to defeat every bill proposed so far.

One may wonder, then, why I have placed PEA among the moderates, rather than among the liberals. Besides the fact that its officials and other civic leaders speak of it as moderate, PEA's actions on the desegregation issue opposed civil rights demands at many points, just as UPA's did. It felt that desegregation was important, but not so important as reduced class size, teacher and staff retraining, and preschool programs for minority group children. It kept pointing up the many costs and risks in rapid, citywide desegregation. One top PEA official noted: "We need a better mixing of ethnic groups, to be brought about in every way possible. But possible means that you don't do some things."

The strategy of PEA urged on the board was one of "orderly change," taking into account the inequities that minority group pupils have faced, and rectifying them in a reasonable way. They supported Open Enrollment, limited pairings, and rezoning, though they were very hesitant, as was UPA, to support such techniques as educational complexes and parks. The main strategy they recommended was a compensatory one that would bring minority group pupils up to a level where they could compete with white middle class pupils. This, they argued, would help facilitate desegregation in the long run by posing less of a threat to standards, causing less fear among whites than it would, and creating fewer tensions among minority group pupils in desegregating schools. PEA officials often cite Dr. Kenneth Clark as one Negro leader whose research supports their own position, and their citations of Clark are inaccurate and out of context. It was only after many disappointments with the board's inaction on desegregation that Clark turned to the compensatory education strategy.*

Their view, then, was that the problems of desegregation and quality, though related, should be considered separately, suggesting that much progress could be made toward equality of opportunity by saturating ghetto schools with services. They supported Headstart programs and were in favor of extending them into the elementary grades. Long before Headstart had become a reality, PEA had sponsored a teacher-aide and parent-volunteer program to improve instruction in ghetto schools, a program in keeping with its philanthropic, child welfare traditions. All these strategies were opposed by many civil rights groups at the time of the desegregation controversy as a "separate but equal" approach. They are now accepted, though in more radical form.

Events surrounding PEA's estrangement from civil rights groups show how hard it was to maintain an alliance throughout the desegregation controversy. As we have seen, opposition to "long-distance bussing" had become the rallying cry for all the groups on the right and was the slogan, along with the "neighborhood school," that they used most successfully to mobilize their large following. PEA was opposed to the goals and tactics of the neighborhood school movement. Indeed, its top

---

* PEA's is not a reformist position, because it ignores the structural defects within the system that make quality education impossible. See Chapters Seven through Eleven for a discussion of those defects.

officials referred to the movement's followers as "near bigots," as New York City's version of "white citizens' councils," and as spreading "the big lie." Yet, on this issue, PEA became identified by Negro and white liberal integrationists with the neighborhood school side.[22] This was unfortunate, because, as I have said, bussing was really a "non-issue." PEA nevertheless took a public position on bussing that enabled integrationists to lump PEA with the militant opposition, which contributed to a further estrangement between the moderates and the civil rights movement. The public position may have been a partial misrepresentation of PEA's commitments—at a time when unity between civil rights groups and moderates was sorely needed. Some board members and officials in PEA recognized this, but they were overruled.

Most PEA officials felt that the expense of bussing might better be diverted to improving classroom instruction, especially in ghetto schools, a reasonable position, given the way desegregation was implemented, and one that Negro groups take today. It was in this sense that they argued that exclusive or major attention by civil rights groups to "racial balance" as a goal might defeat their efforts both to increase desegregation and to upgrade quality.

This notion that desegregation plans might divert scarce school funds away from school improvement was basic to PEA's position. PEA reflected in this regard the fiscal conservatism of their élite board and of some of their professional staff. While they had always pushed the Board of Education for an expansion of services and continually supported its attempts to secure more money, they were not about to support what they referred to as "untested and unvalidated" plans, forced on the board by special interest pressure groups whose leaders had no professional competence to assess the educational merits of such plans. PEA did not take the position that it might cost more in the long run to maintain segregated, neighborhood schools. Neither did it dramatize the fact that the board was running an inefficient operation and might have pruned many poorly formulated programs from its budget through administrative and personnel reforms. If PEA had been genuinely interested in the wise use of funds, bussing was hardly the place to begin. In fact, PEA, more than any other civic group, supported the board's annual requests for additional funds. PEA was shortsighted on this matter, since more money spent in the same traditional ways, for programs implemented by the usual archaic procedures, would promote neither reform nor administrative efficiency, and might even reinforce inefficient procedures.

PEA's own studies of the board's budgetary planning, and the board's failure in recent years to give any public accounting of how it allocated its funds, should have shown that more money alone would not lessen the system's problems and might make them worse.[23] Yet, PEA never chose to make organizational questions the public issue they have recently become— through efforts of the Lindsay administration, Mayor Wagner's Temporary Commission on City Finances, and ghetto groups. PEA did not lead the fight for greater efficiency, though it castigated civil rights groups for demanding fiscally questionable desegregation programs.

Indeed, PEA conflicted sharply with civil rights groups on the matter of school funds. PEA officials were upset when major civil rights leaders refused to join in its pleas for more state aid. Civil rights leaders said that campaigning for more money to perpetuate and expand segregated education was in direct conflict with all their goals. They suggested that desegregation could be mandated in some fringe areas at no additional cost. Regardless of the merits of these arguments, though I believe that the first, especially, has much merit, the issue further separated PEA and civil rights groups from one another.

An added source of conflict between PEA and civil rights leaders was the PEA officials' strong disapproval of the personal behavior and tactics of the militants. Privately, PEA officials characterized them as "irresponsible extremists, agitators, publicity seekers, without a large following, and unreliable as a steadying and balancing influence." These views were widely shared within the liberal white and moderate community, among education officials and board members of such organizations as UPA, ADL, CCC, the American Jewish Committee, and even the American Jewish Congress. The hostility ran so deep that one white moderate went so far as to say that he would never want to sit in the same room with these militants. Another declared that he would never go to a meeting in Harlem.

Such judgments had a profound effect on the alliances that PEA formed. They explained its unwillingness to participate in such coalitions as the Conference for Quality Integrated Education, for example, which PEA officials felt was controlled by the militants. Civil rights leaders were just as disenchanted with the moderates. As one said: "This PEA man says a lot of things and they appear in the papers. If he doesn't mean it 'that way,' he shouldn't say it 'that way.' But how many meanings can the word 'rabble' have?" [24]

The tendency of moderates to complain that most public protests are led by "outside agitators" reinforced the attitudes of the mass media, the board, and many top city officials toward the civil rights movement. The moderates' perceptions of school controversies, reflected in the *New York Times* and *Herald Tribune*, have shaped, in turn, public opinion.

Ironically, though PEA officials were dismayed at the polarization among groups on the desegregation controversy, they did nothing to end it. Their position was as inflexible during the heat of the controversy as those of civil rights and neighborhood school groups. *

Underlying its perennial conflict with the civil rights movement was PEA's view that the movement represented the legitimate but special interests of Negroes, while good-government organizations like itself represented the entire city. PEA officials thus tended to see their own positions and those of many board professionals as "above politics," as if they had no class and ethnic interests of their own. But the history of PEA's efforts in public education contradicts its claims to be above politics. As Sol Cohen points out in the study cited above, PEA had traditionally tried to keep control of the public schools out of the hands of outside political pressure groups and politicians—the clubhouse and political machine of the past, and the increasingly militant civil rights movement in recent years. Cohen suggests that PEA really meant that "control of the schools was to be lodged in the hands of 'good people' or the 'better element,' the city's educated, cultured, civic-minded community, the Yankee Protestants and the wealthy, assimilated German Jews, or their spokesmen or representatives, the 'experts.' " [25] The "good government" line served this group interest.

The issue, then, was not to keep politics out of the public schools, but rather to keep any politics but that of PEA and its

---

* The civil rights leader PEA officials felt most in sympathy with was Roy Wilkins, especially in his public statements condemning boycotts, mass bussing, and adventurist demonstrators.

associates out of the schools. Thus, Cohen reports that since 1930 PEA spent much time cultivating the new "professional" class of school officials and turned more and more control of school affairs over to school "experts." This fit its own interests, since PEA, more than any other civic group, had established private, informal ties with key school officials. Cohen notes: "PEA has become an intimate part of the machinery of educational decision-making in the city . . . and has established itself as the city's dominant non-governmental group, exclusive of the religious groups, in the public school field." [26]

PEA clearly helped insulate school officials from review and from any outside controls other than PEA's. Cohen observes: "The consequences have included not only an increase in conventional rationality and competence in the administration of the schools, but the creation of a school island of power. The school bureaucracy, deeply involved in questions of policy and value, has won a peculiar freedom from democratic controls. The two school boards [the Board of Education and the Board of Superintendents] each operate in an environment of low visibility approaching complete privacy." [27]

Recent PEA statements, however, especially the one on decentralization noted above, indicate that PEA has become aware of this situation. PEA officials now see more clearly the dangers of the board's insulation from the community. They realize that the gulf between the community and the board, and the diminishing faith of parent groups in the system's integrity, are largely a product of the board's own doing. They see that the concentration of power in the hands of professionals at the board, who are answerable mainly to each other, and who have a vested interest in preserving an inert status quo, should not be permitted to continue. If PEA follows through on this important insight, it may play a significant reform role in the future. It certainly has the power to do so.

Examples of its power are legion. In 1961, it was reportedly PEA officials who prevailed on Mayor Wagner to fire the lay board, and later proposed a committee system for the nomination of board members in which PEA played an important role. PEA has also been responsible for the selection of particular board members and has helped to get rid of at least one. Its power in Albany is even greater than it is in the city. Albany will be the key arena in which legal and administrative reforms are effected, since so much of the present bureaucracy is mandated by state laws that will have to be changed if there is to be any reform at all, and so PEA could play a significant role in such efforts.*

But until recently, PEA's power has been used to buttress the board. No other civic group has endorsed the board's plans and programs to the degree that PEA has. A review of its testimonies at every public hearing in the past four years—on desegregation, on decentralization, and on the board's capital budget—indicates as much.†

United Federation of Teachers

The United Federation of Teachers (UFT) had ties with all three camps—Negro civil rights groups, white liberals, and moderates. It had been an important progressive force in the New York City school system; for example, it has bargained for decreased class size, more teacher preparation time, a More Effective Schools program for ghetto schools, and improved salaries and fringe benefits for teachers—all in the interests of both teachers and pupils. The union has been especially concerned with professionalizing the role of the teacher, giving the teacher more autonomy and responsibility and pressing for a career-line in classroom teaching that concentrates more of the rewards of the system at that level rather than in administration.

The UFT now represents more than 50,000 teachers and has begun to organize guidance counselors, secretaries, and psychologists. Most likely, its power will increase as the school system becomes more vulnerable to attack. Some union officials make the most of the system's inadequacies, pointing up the academic retardation of ghetto pupils and the non-teaching in ghetto schools as justification for their demands on the board

* Evidence on these illustrations of PEA's influence came from interviews with PEA officials and other civic leaders.

† One cannot help but be skeptical, then, of PEA's intention to push in the same reformist (and sometimes radical) direction as its public statements, for example, on decentralization. Liberal and civil rights leaders are able to influence its board enough to get strong statements for reform, but the organization then tends to backslide in the face of pressure for action. When the Bundy Report on school decentralization came out, for example, one top PEA official tried to persuade leading city university officials to join him in condemning it, as one such official related.

for better working conditions. At the same time, the union is attacked by ghetto groups for some of its demands—for example, to have disciplinary-problem pupils removed from classrooms, and to give teachers more preparation time.

The union's general position on desegregation and ghetto school problems has been sympathetic. It has supported many civil rights protests, while protecting the hard-won job rights and improved working conditions of teachers. Its positions have sometimes aligned it with civil rights groups, and at other times with liberal white and moderate groups. It has come into direct conflict with civil rights groups on such issues as the mandatory transfer of experienced teachers to ghetto schools, the handling of disciplinary-problem pupils, instituting bonus pay and salary increments as inducements to attract teachers to ghetto schools, and its actions in the IS 201 controversy. At the same time, top union officials have close ties with many liberal and civil rights leaders and have supported, both privately and publicly, ghetto parent fights for desegregation, improved services, and increased community participation and control. The union wants to make sure, however, that teachers are not hurt by these parent demands.

Despite the union's support for some ghetto causes, it is held in low regard by some civil rights leaders who see it as still another enemy that is miseducating their children and as a reactionary force within the school system. Some white groups feel the same way, as reflected by Senator Robert Kennedy's public reference to the union in May, 1965, as "a new voice of intolerance in the North," when it refused to accept a unilaterally imposed mandatory transfer plan.[28]

The UFT has been the exclusive bargaining agent for the teachers since 1961. Before, there were many teacher organizations within the New York City school system, organized along divisional, borough, religious, and other lines. One union official reported that there were 106 different teacher organizations in 1960. Historically, the two main groups were the Teachers Union and the Teachers Guild. The former was founded in 1917, and the Teachers Guild split off in 1935 over the issue of communist domination of the Teachers Union. The anticommunist guild later evolved into the UFT, in 1961, and the Teachers Union went out of existence two years later.

The union's main concern, along with getting more money

for its members, has been to increase their autonomy and power, in the schools as well as in the system. Collective bargaining agreements have attempted to replace what the union considers a private patronage system in principal–teacher relations with general rules that give teachers rights and benefits they never had before, on a system-wide basis.*

The leadership of the UFT have close alliances with the liberal, intellectual community in New York City as well as nationally. "We have grown," said a union official, "not just because we have increased salaries and decreased class size, but because of the endorsement of the professional, liberal, and intellectual community. We are winning the struggle not on narrowly based issues but because of our more general concerns with civil rights, progressive social legislation, and improving public education. We consider ourselves part of a civil rights–liberal coalition."

Nonetheless, many teachers are more provincial and ethnocentric than their leadership, as data on teacher attitudes and expectations about minority group pupils indicate.[29] Some teachers endorsed the neighborhood school movement and openly expressed their sympathies. Yet, the union leadership has successfully pushed the organization toward progressive stands on many civil rights and social issues. The union's executive committee, for example, voted 30–2 to urge rank-and-file members to endorse the civilian review board. The union gave substantial financial help to civil rights demonstrators in Selma, Alabama, in 1965. Recently, some union officials have urged that the union take a public position opposing escalation of the war in Vietnam.

Union officials believe in the importance of developing a viable coalition of civil rights and traditional liberal groups (labor movement, intellectuals, clergy) as the best way to deal with civil rights and poverty problems. Albert Shanker, the union's president, was an active member in both Negro–white coalitions, the Integroup Committee and the Conference for Quality Integrated Education. He was a member of the steering committee of the conference, and was genuinely in favor of desegregation. Although the UFT is now in direct opposition

---

* These benefits include seniority rights, more preparation periods, smaller class size, less punitive monitoring by principals, more sick days, relief from clerical chores, and a grievance machinery that permits teachers to get a hearing when they feel their rights have been violated.

with ghetto parents, it was not in such conflict with them a few years ago.

Unlike the Council of Supervisory Associations, which played a consistently obstructionist role, the union supported the school pairings, and the first civil rights boycott, and it later endorsed the board's policy statement favoring either a 5–3–4 or a 4–4–4 organization in the interest of more desegregation. It also opposed the PAT-sponsored boycott. "We do not claim to qualify for any medals or badges," said a union official, "but we have not obstructed most civil rights demands and have in fact tried to smooth the way. We are not a civil rights organization, but we believe strongly in integration and try to promote it."

During the first civil rights boycott the union privately encouraged its members to honor the picket lines of civil rights protesters, with the result that Board President James Donovan threatened to withhold their pay for the days they were out, but the union made him back down. Union officials have also mobilized support from members for accepting extra teaching duties in schools where desegregation plans were being implemented. And since the fall of 1966, teachers have joined ghetto parents in Brooklyn, Manhattan, and The Bronx in public picketing and demonstrations, protesting inferior conditions within their schools. Indeed, the union organized protests with parents in poverty areas and later joined with those in the decentralization experiments in Brownsville, East Harlem and the Lower East Side in late 1966 and 1967.[30]

Yet despite the many cases where the union has seemingly been on the side of ghetto parents, the gulf has widened. All the issues that have periodically led to conflict—staffing of ghetto schools, handling disciplinary cases—keep coming up, and prevent the two groups from working together as much as they might on matters where they clearly have many common interests.

The union periodically tries to reconcile these differences. In the December, 1966, *American Teacher*, Shanker wrote:

> The conflict between teachers and parents in the ghetto is most tragic. It is tragic because the parents do not see that massive educational failure cannot be explained by a single good-teacher–bad-teacher theory, for the truth is that both teachers and students are being destroyed by a rotten system. It is tragic because that system can be changed only if parents and teachers

enter into a partnership for educational revolution—a partnership which is made impossible if parents blame educational disaster on bad teachers and teachers blame it on bad parents.[31]

But Shanker's message did not get through, and civil rights leaders continue to feel that the union is more concerned with rights, salaries, fringe benefits, and a shorter work week, than with the needs of children.

A question of teacher transfers has been another source of conflict between the union and civil rights groups since it was first raised in 1957 as a recommendation of the board's Subcommission on Teacher Placement.[32] The union has defeated all attempts to transfer experienced teachers, though the issue arises periodically, sometimes when the union is in the midst of hard bargaining with the board over a new contract.[33]

The union has argued against mandatory teacher transfers on several grounds. Its officials feel that experienced teachers from white middle class schools may be ill-trained to teach in a ghetto school, that transfers imply invidious comparisons between already demoralized ghetto school teachers and their colleagues from white middle class schools, and that the plan deals only with a symptom and not with any basic causes of the high teacher turnover and "non-teaching" * in ghetto schools. They blame these problems on the lack of training and commitment of many ghetto school principals and the limited support they give their teachers.

The union also argues that it has already done a lot to ease staffing problems in ghetto schools by bargaining for seniority rights and central placement for substitutes, thus minimizing incentives for transfers; by pressing for a teacher internship program; and by urging the board to send most of the teachers working at headquarters back to the classroom. It has also recommended that principals not be allowed the privilege of rejecting schools, that those assigned to ghetto schools not be promised that they can transfer out after a few years,[34] and that each principal be given a business manager, freeing him to concentrate more on pedagogical tasks. These numerous rec-

---

* Inadequately trained and motivated teachers who get no supervisory help in ghetto schools often resort to running their classes in a purely custodial way to keep order, and order becomes an end in itself. Teachers and union officials readily admit that little actual teaching goes on in most ghetto school classrooms.

ommendations do not protect the union from attack, however, on the question of mandatory teacher transfers.

The other staffing issue on which the union sometimes came into conflict with civil rights leaders was a plan to give as many as 2,000 teachers extra pay for transferring to ghetto schools.* The union attacked the offer as "combat pay," and finally secured so much support from civil groups that some board officials denied the plan was ever meant to go into effect, even though it was put down in writing.

In 1963, the union, working with Superintendent Gross, came up with a More Effective Schools plan for saturating ghetto schools with compensatory services. It involved smaller classes and extra school staff and was installed in twenty schools. Some civil rights leaders resented the fact that though the plan was supposed to encourage desegregation, it went into effect only in segregated ghetto schools. Furthermore, separate evaluations of the program by the board and the Center for Urban Education indicated that the program failed to attract experienced teachers and did not raise reading levels.[35] Yet, in 1967, the union repeated its demand for the expansion of the program.

Since late 1966, there has been a marked deterioration of relations between the union and ghetto parents, and the single incident that triggered this development occurred in the IS 201 controversy. When the parent boycott was still going on at that school, the board offered to open neighboring PS 103, pending the outcome of negotiations. The IS 201 teachers refused to work at the school, claiming that it had few if any facilities, while their colleagues in JHS 164 in the same district willingly served under much more trying conditions—as renovations were still being made.† Later, the teachers expressed a vote of confidence in Principal Stanley Lisser, after Superintendent Donovan had decided to remove him. Their vote of confi-

---

* This bonus plan was the board's idea and kept getting proposed every year or two.

† It was not clear how the opening of 103 would have affected the boycott. It might have given the boycotters or the board more bargaining power, or it might have made no difference at all in the negotiations. A more significant question is how the UFT's refusal to have 103 open was viewed by the board and by the community. Each generally felt the refusal would help the other party; the union was caught in the middle between these contending forces, a position it usually occupies.

dence was not the main reason for his reinstatement, but it was a symbolic act that was not lost on the parents, reinforcing their view of the union as the enemy.

Events leading up to the collective bargaining of 1967 further strained union–parent relations. In March, 1967, the union had a full page ad in the *New York Times*,[36] asking for the right to remove "disruptive children" from classrooms, and Negro and Puerto Rican parents realized that the union meant their children.

The conflict got still worse during and after the union's two-week strike in September, 1967. The disruptive-child issue remained salient for the union, which continued to handle it in a way that alienated ghetto parents. Teachers complained that "problem" children prevented any learning from taking place in ghetto schools, initially demanded the right to unilaterally remove these children from their classes, and charged the board with having failed to provide adequate treatment and services for these children.

Underlying the strike were such questions as how to account for the ghetto schools' failure, what to do about it, and who should have the power to run the system. The union was caught in the middle between the parents and the board, and the teachers' vulnerability as the system's front line officials made them the most visible target for angry ghetto parents. At the same time, teachers feared the increased parent power that was starting to emerge with preliminary decentralization programs, and they made demands for much more power for themselves.

During the strike, attempts by parents and community leaders in some ghetto schools to "screen" teachers added to the conflict. Now that decentralization has become the issue, it is clear that teachers have become increasingly anxious about what they define as intrusions on their professional autonomy and integrity. The idea of having para-professionals in the schools and classrooms, of having parents on local school boards select a district superintendent and evaluate teachers, and of opening up teaching positions to more outsiders, including Negroes and Puerto Ricans, frightened many teachers. They feared Black Power, and many felt that their authority would be completely undermined under decentralization, with "extremists" taking over.

It is unfortunate but true that the union has thus moved from being a potentially reformist force to a largely protectionist one. But even before decentralization became a possibility, relations between teachers and parents in the ghetto areas were bad. It is clear that a sizeable number of teachers share in the wider society's racism, and many in ghetto schools are incompetent.* One top union official reports that over the past couple of years, there have been numerous protests from local union officials to the UFT headquarters, asking for more police protection in ghetto schools. The union leadership was usually able to cool them off, suggesting that more police would probably lead to more violence against them, but it seems increasingly evident that relations have completely broken down in many instances.

The UFT has thus moved away from any present alliances with liberal and civil rights groups into the educational establishment, protecting "professional" rights against community pressures. The conflict has reached the point where the union brought a court case against the Board of Education in the fall of 1967, asking that its decentralization experiments in three ghetto districts be eliminated. Something close to all-out war between teachers and ghetto parents has thus emerged, prompting one top city official who was well informed on the subject to remark that he had visited many cities throughout the nation and had never seen one with any worse relations between teachers and community. It is unfortunate that teachers and parents, who are both victims of the school system, should become so involved in power-seeking that they take it out on one another.

Both the union leaders and many rank-and-file teachers were ready to move in this direction, away from working together with groups from the poverty area communities, as a result of past differences with civil rights leaders on desegregation. Some union officials see a similarity between the tactics and strategies of civil rights leaders and those of the radical, leftist groups whom they had fought for control of their own union. And they were sometimes disenchanted with the movement's unwillingness to bargain or compromise, its inattentiveness to the educational implications of the plans it demanded, and its failure to capitalize on board offers, however limited, when such offers were made. One top union official suggested: "Civil rights leaders keep snatching defeat from the jaws of victory," referring to instances where they had maneuvered the board into a com-

* See Chapter Eight for a discussion on this point.

promising position on desegregation, only to fritter away their superior bargaining position by not making compromises. Civil rights leaders answer that they are only successful with the most militant strategy.

There were other reasons for the union's being critical of civil rights groups' demands. Its officials were concerned about what might happen to quality and standards if desegregation or decentralization were not well planned; they knew how oppressive their working conditions could become when hasty implementation took place; and they had to be concerned about teacher reactions. The union had fought hard to upgrade the teachers' working conditions—through such devices as providing more preparation time, free periods, autonomy from oppressive supervision, and smaller class size—and civil rights groups' demands seemed to imply a restoration of some of the burdens teachers used to have.

Board officials were aware of this potential conflict between teachers and parents, and many union officials felt the board tried to exploit the situation. This was the gist of the union's interpretation of the timing of the board's announcement of a mandatory transfer plan in April, 1965: they considered that the board's purpose was to limit their power in collective bargaining by once more turning civil groups and the press against the union.

The mutual interests that could be served by a coalition of the union and civil rights groups are quite substantial. Unfortunately, for all the progressive views of some top union leaders, such a coalition may never develop. A majority of teachers, even in New York City, may well have the same civil service mentality and the same lower middle class ethnocentrism that their superiors in the school system do. "If it were not for the UFT," explained a top union official, "the teachers would take the same position on desegregation and other race issues as all civil servants. They would want to remain as tied to the status quo as PAT."

This perennial conflict between the union and the Negro and Puerto Rican populations is, as Albert Shanker correctly points out, one of the many tragedies of contemporary urban education, and certainly of the New York City schools. The civil rights movement would benefit tremendously from having at its disposal all the "inside" experiences of teachers and union officials with bureaucratic ineptitude and sabotage, and it would also have access to relevant judgments on the educational complexities of instituting new programs. It is even conceivable that a union–civil rights coalition could build into the union's contract with the board those parent demands that are acceptable to the union. The union is doing well at the bargaining table, but it could benefit by having more ghetto parent support than it has for some of its demands for improved classroom conditions. However, unless there is a dramatic shift in events and political interests, such a development is very unlikely.

The Press

A significant participant in the politics of education is the press. Several different points of view are represented in the various metropolitan New York newspapers.* The most reform-minded has been the New York *Post,* which generally reaches a lower and middle income (trade union, Reform Democrat, liberal) audience. The *Post* has consistently given the most coverage to civil rights demands and activities and to the many shortcomings of the board. For example, in the spring of 1966, the *Post* had many articles on the civil rights confederation, the protests over the board's building of segregated intermediate schools, the East Brooklyn educational parks suit, the board's continued delays on its four-year comprehensive high school program, and the educational parks movement. Many of these matters were not adequately covered in the *New York Times,* and when they did get limited coverage, the tone was much more apologetic for the board.†

In the period from September, 1967, through April, 1968, when decentralization and community control were the issues, the *Post* was consistently more critical of the board—for example, reporting its sabotage of the demonstration units, and indicating that they had still not been given any powers—than the *Times.*‡

* These judgments are made on the basis of a thorough reading of education coverage of all the major newspapers. A quantitative content analysis would be necessary to completely validate these assertions, but knowledgeable informants agree on them.

† Though the *Times* is written for a national audience more than the *Post* is, it has much local and metropolitan education coverage.

‡ Civil rights leaders are almost unanimous on these points, and they often observe that Bernard Bard, the *Post's* education writer, is much more accurate and fair in his reporting than the *Times* reporters.

The next most liberal was the *Herald Tribune,* whose two education reporters, Terry Ferrar and Joseph Michalak, while not as anti-board as Bard, gave more ghetto coverage than the *Times* reporters. I am referring here not to editorials, but to regular news reporting and to the nature of its selectivity. The *Post* and *Herald Tribune* reporters have been more likely to report the shortcomings of the school system and the bureaucracy than reporters on the *Times.* The *Herald Tribune* closed down in 1966, handing over to the *Times* a virtual monopoly on the college-educated, upper middle class readers. "The *Tribune* kept the *Times* a little more honest than it would have otherwise been," reported a prominent civil rights leader. "If I called in to the *Times* desk with a story or press release and said I had already called the *Trib,* they were much more likely to print it than otherwise. We don't have that protection any more, and we're hurting as a result."

The most status-quo-oriented papers were the *Long Island Daily Press* (which reached many poor whites and homeowners in Queens, the PAT group) and the *World-Telegram.** They tended to represent the neighborhood school point of view. On the other side, the *Amsterdam News,* the largest black paper in the nation, was the most supportive of the civil rights groups' positions, and the most critical of the schools.

The most important paper by far is the *Times,* and its role in shaping public discussion and affecting the perceptions of white liberals (many of them out of touch with the ghetto) is very far-reaching. The distortion in its reporting is equally far-reaching; a serious question is raised about the "social responsibility" of the press, and about the extent to which its "all the news that's fit to print" dictum has much reality in the public education field.† Consider the following examples, and they are meant as illustrative only: (1) During the peak period of integration controversy, Fred M. Hechinger made constant references to civil rights leaders as "instant integrationists," even though not even the most militant like Reverend Galamison ever had any hopes or designs for desegregating the New York

---

* The *World-Telegram* had a full school page in its early edition that was widely read by school officials and civic groups in the city.

† This view is expressed by liberals and radicals in both labor and civil rights as a *Times* official acknowledged at a meeting of several civic leaders who came together to protest its biased and limited public education coverage.

City schools quickly. This was a way of characterizing the movement and its leaders that discredited them with the white community, and it probably had a profound effect on their capacity to mobilize more white support. (2) In late 1963 and early 1964, civil rights leaders had urged Leonard Buder, *Times* education reporter, to do an article on Dr. Max Wolff and the educational park. No such article was done during this period, and Buder reportedly commented at the time that Wolff was "too controversial" a figure to write about then. (3) City Planning Commission officials have called the *Times* on numerous occasions over the last five years, asking that it give the commission's side as well as the board's when the commission cut the board's construction budget. "They wouldn't give me the right time," reported a top commission staff person, "and we tried for several years running." The *Times* would print only the board's view, that the commission was hampering the education of children by cutting the school construction budget.* (4) In a heated controversy between civil rights leaders and Superintendent Donovan over the poverty area communities' rejection of his plan to have an Intensive Teacher Training Program in the summer of 1965 and send those newly trained and inexperienced young teachers to ghetto schools in the fall, responsible and influential civil rights leaders were unable to get Buder to do a story on their side. Their side was widely supported in ghetto areas.

The recent decentralization controversy indicates similar bias and distortion, almost always in support of the board. For example: (5) Leonard Buder had front-page articles on February 2, 1968, on the "jungle-like conditions" at IS 201, and on February 22, 1968, on expressions of violence by Negro speakers at a Malcolm X memorial service, and many similar pieces had appeared since the fall on chaos in decentralization experiments. What Buder failed to report, except in a couple of sentences buried in the middle of his articles, was that the governing council at 201 had no powers, and that this was not a decentralization experiment at all. The common reaction of legislators and white liberals to decentralization, shaped by the *Times* reporting, was that it was not working and probably

---

* The commission maintained that the board was holding immobile millions of dollars of city tax monies by vacillating on construction policy and engaging in cumbersome bureaucratic procedures that delayed decisions on school sites, planning, and actual construction.

never would. Buder in the *Times* failed to point out clearly that it had not yet been tried.*

Many other errors in reporting were also in evidence. Had the *Times* reporters spent more time visiting ghetto schools, they would have realized that the "jungle-like conditions" that Buder decided were worthy of front-page coverage have existed in ghetto schools throughout the city and the nation for thirty to forty years. "It is only now, when black people are struggling to correct these conditions, that the press sees fit to explode the situation," wrote John Bell and fifteen other IS 201 teachers in a letter to the editor that the *Times* did not print, "with the unjustified effect of implying that the source of such chaos is in 'community control' rather than in the existing school system."

(6) The misreporting at 201 actually has a longer history. In September, 1966, when the parents and community boycotted the school, the *Times* indicated that the Black Panthers and other black nationalist groups had taken over the fight. In fact, when the board refused to meet with local groups and finally when the board forced Superintendent Donovan to renege on his promise to the community to remove Principal Lisser, parent and community leaders called in these more militant groups to help in the struggle against the board. The *Times'* account was grotesquely inaccurate on this point.

Times officials maintain that though some articles that perhaps should be printed must be cut in deference to other priorities (national news, particular emergency stories), they do cover all major public statements of such key city officials as the mayor or the president of the Board of Education. Yet, Mayor Lindsay gave a very significant policy speech on education at a February 14, 1968, meeting of the Civic Assembly, a citywide citizens group including a broad cross-section of organizations, and the *Times* never printed it. The speech condemned the school system, strongly urged support for decentralization, and was one of the first major public speeches given by the mayor indicating his views on decentralization. Leonard Buder attended, sat in a front row, and followed the speech carefully. It got coverage on several television channels, but some-

* Paradoxically, the *Times* editorials are in direct contradiction to its reporting. For several months, in the spring of 1968, it carried editorials asking for meaningful decentralization of the schools, and making the point that in 201 and the two other demonstration projects, decentralization had not really been tried.

how the *Times* omitted it. In answering a criticism of their omission, *Times* officials suggested that the garbage crisis of that week (a strike by sanitation workers) pushed several articles out of the paper—but one would hope that such a significant speech on school decentralization would get at least limited attention.

Traditionally, the *Times* has been a vehicle for the Board of Education's press releases. Whenever the board wanted to announce a new program or its position on some controversial policy matter, Buder would print it, and often he would get a reaction from PEA, UPA, and perhaps one or two other groups like the teachers' union. It was more difficult to get any single ghetto area reaction, because many different factions and points of view prevailed. But the *Times* often did not meet its responsibility of comprehensive coverage by even trying. When it does try occasionally, the widespread resentment against the *Times* among ghetto leaders makes it difficult to reach them.

The existence of close, informal relations between Buder and many white liberals (in PEA and UPA) and board officials is well known. *Times* officials point out in all honesty that reporters have an entrée problem. If Buder or some other *Times* education reporter were to be too critical of the board or too sympathetic to protest groups, they might suddenly have more trouble in getting the inside story and the first crack at printing a board announcement. If this is a factor affecting, however subtly, the *Times'* education reporting, the political implications seem quite clear. An institution that no longer merits shoring up, and a movement that does not merit continued discrediting, in fact get such treatment. Surely, this does not fall under the rubric of "responsible" reporting; though it does indicate what social scientists and political analysts have known for a long time—that the press is a significant element shaping political events.

There is a widespread consensus among civil rights and militant white leaders that the *New York Times* version of the city's school controversies is not only quite distorted, but discredits the movement and acts as a continual damper on badly needed school reforms. My interviews with many white liberals and moderates tend to confirm this judgment: many seem greatly influenced by the *Times* reporting. If the *Times* does influence these interests that much, its role in shaping the politics of public education in New York City seems quite clearly unconstructive. The *Times* is one of several institutions that has dampened prospects for educational reform.

Coalition

A centrist coalition does exist in New York City, led by UPA, UFT, PEA, and CCC, closely tied to board and city officials, and committed as most liberal groups are to limited reform. They are ideologically in favor of desegregation, but the improvement of services within the existing structure comes first. While this commitment posed serious problems for the civil rights movement a few years ago, it no longer does, since most leaders within the movement have now given up on desegregation within the present structure of the school system and have moved, in some ways, closer to the position the moderates and white liberals have held all along.*

One might expect, then, that after civil rights leaders have come to accept the depressing fact that the desegregation of the New York City schools is not now possible, for all sorts of political as well as demographic reasons, there are nevertheless some prospects for the development of a powerful coalition, oriented to change. As disheartening as it is to contemplate, I don't believe that the prospects for forming such a coalition are any better now than they were before. The Negroes and Puerto Ricans want much more power, but they can only get it by taking some away from PAT, the moderates, the white liberals, the UFT, and the board. This is what the struggle over decentralization really means, and it is why the white groups have been so reluctant to endorse the ghetto leadership's demands for community participation in the schools. As oppressive and unsatisfactory as the school bureaucracy may be, the white groups have developed techniques for influencing and/or overruling decisions from Livingston Street and from the district or principal's office.

The moderates and white liberals rose to power in the 1940s and fifties on a wave of municipal reform from the LaGuardia and Wagner administrations, displacing the Catholic power of Tammany Hall and the political clubhouse, and even sharing in that of the Protestant élite—the Rockefellers, the Astors—who still own much of the city. Now, however,

---

* The moderates differ from civil rights groups on the question of community control, however, and fear taking as much power away from the professionals as many civil rights leaders want to.

there is a shift of power away from these predominantly Jewish liberals toward new groups and coalitions, reflecting the waves of ethnic succession of the postwar years. The struggles over desegregation and decentralization are merely symbolic of these larger historical changes.

Until now, this loose coalition of moderates and liberals has been able to maintain its position, and it has done so in more sophisticated and humane ways than the Irish in Boston, the Poles in Buffalo, or other lower and middle class groups who have become part of the white backlash in the North. Some of the positions they took on desegregation were sensible, though hardly revolutionary, but their positions have always been protectionist. They want to maintain their élite high schools, they want to induce the middle class to stay in the city, and they want to maintain standards—all holding actions. This coalition has had the support and sometimes strong endorsement of the mass media, a potent political force. Key officials in moderate and liberal groups, along with education reporters for the *Times,* defined the issues for the middle class liberals, established upper and lower limits for the board's plans, and ultimately helped it make its final decisions.[37] Such cynical comments as "the board waits for the morning edition of the *Times* to find out how it is doing," or "a phone call from CCC or UPA can really turn things around at the board," or "the board's idea of reaching the public is to call the PEA and announce some program," may be exaggerated, but they are not entirely false.[38]

Officials in one organization in this coalition have close relations with those in others, and most have attended the PEA Coordinating Committee. One board member, Mrs. Rose Shapiro, significantly the chairman of the board's Community Relations Committee, is a former president of the UPA and chairman of the PEA Coordinating Committee.

All these people have conducted a somewhat narrowly based dialogue. Some of them have tried to reach out to ghetto parent groups or national civil rights organizations, but the exchanges have been limited. There might be more prospects for reform, despite inevitable differences in point of view, if these contacts were deepened and institutionalized.

Since the IS 201 controversy in September, 1966, the moderates and liberals have been more openly critical of the schools than they had been. PEA's forceful statements on decentralization, for example, and *New York Times* editorials condemning the school bureaucracy, reflect such a change in position, though in each instance there are people in these organizations who demur. As long as decentralization is not well planned and supported politically, the moderates will not resist the temptation—guided by what they feel are the noblest of motivations— to defeat it as they did desegregation.

That would be a "no win" strategy, however, because the ghetto community will not give up its fight for better education and more local control over the schools. It may be years before we really know how to educate the city's ghetto populations, and there is always the dismal prospect that the New York City school system will increasingly become a one-class, Negro and Puerto Rican one, provided services by the same poorly trained and often unsympathetic lower middle class whites in supervisory positions and in the classroom who have contributed so much to the mis-education and massive academic retardation that now exist.

Civic groups alone cannot reverse all the schools' failures, but they can help if the white coalition begins to realize that without basic structural changes the school system will continue to fail and breed more community tensions than it already has. The white groups must accept the inevitable historical changes that are now unfolding, give up some of their power and outdated commitments to professional autonomy for school officials, and work with rather than against an insurgent Negro population. Given the times in which we live and the problems that the schools confront, holding actions no longer hold.

The story of the moderates' failure recapitulates that of the white liberals and civil rights groups. None of these sets of interest groups appreciably furthered educational reform. One main reason for their ineffectiveness was that with such diverse interests and constituencies they could rarely come together.

Factional Politics

In addition to this "organizational pluralism" was the pluralism within particular ethnic and socio-economic groups that prevented any full-blown social movements from developing. Neither a consistent "class" or "race" politics could emerge in New York City because people within any given group (Negroes, Puerto Ricans, the poor) had too many other differences. There was no piling up of interests all converging in the same direction; peoples' loyalties and affiliations diverged as they belonged to many different groups holding different values; and they tended to dissipate their energies fighting among themselves rather than against the Board of Education and the city. The Negroes and Puerto Ricans were obviously split, as pointed out in Chapter Four, and even within each population there were many factions, divided along class, ethnic, and neighborhood lines, and committed to one or another leader. Among the poor, Negroes and Puerto Ricans were both at odds with the whites. Among the Negro civil rights groups there were the many conflicts I have described, and similar differences in point of view among Jewish groups, white middle class, and parent groups. Within each of the sets of organizations that existed, from the most militant integrationist groups on the left to most militant neighborhood groups on the right, different goals, styles, tactics, and strategies existed, making it difficult to mount a concerted attack for any reforms. Political resources were so dispersed, in addition, that no one group or set of groups had the potential to move the board, making reform little more than a pleasant fantasy.*

For many of these groups, the more they found they could not work together productively, the less they kept up close communications, and their misperceptions of one another became rampant. Even within a set of like-minded organizations—for example, Negro civil rights groups—a process of limited contact, leading to misperceptions by each side of the other, to polarization, and to increasing mistrust and negative stereotypes, was set in motion. This further decreased the likelihood that these groups could ever get together in the future in any coordinated action. The local grass-roots people regarded the NAACP and the Urban League headquarters officials as "moderates," "sellouts," and even "reactionary," while some NAACP and Urban League officials regarded local leaders like Galamison as "extremists," "irresponsible," and "power mad."

The same kinds of differences characterized relations between Negro groups and liberal white organizations. Many white liberals tended to get lumped as part of the "white power structure," "the establishment," and "downtown groups," while white leaders saw Galamison and other local civil rights leaders as "extremists" and "instant integrationists."

* For some sociological discussions of pluralism and factional politics, and of the conditions that give rise to them, see William Kornhauser, *The Politics of Mass Society*, pp. 76–84; Seymour M. Lipset, *Political Man*, New York: Doubleday, 1959, pp. 88–90; Robert A Dahl, *Who Governs?*, New Haven: Yale, 1961, pp. 89–103; and James Coleman, *Community Conflict*.

It was therefore impossible to develop a civil rights movement or a liberal coalition in a situation like this. The best reform groups could do was to form limited alliances, make public protests where possible, and be of nuisance value to the board. Clearly, that wasn't enough.

The interest group politics cannot be considered in isolation, however, from the actions and inactions of the Board of Education and the mayor, as I have already indicated in passing. We turn now to an examination of the role that these participants played.

THE BOARD AND ITS TOP
DECISION MAKERS

Demographic changes in the city, extreme poverty in ghetto communities, and acute neighborhood and family disorganization among lower class Negro populations, are hard social facts. Few educators know how to cope with these conditions, and the New York City Board of Education, like its counterparts elsewhere, obviously cannot be held responsible for all the social problems and pathologies it has to deal with. Yet, the school system is the one institution that must find ways to educate and help these people to overcome the neglect and oppression they have suffered. The schools have come under more attack than any other institution for failing to meet these challenges.

The Institution: Some General Facts and Highlights

The New York City school system is by far the largest in the nation, employing more than 56,000 teachers, several thousand administrators and technicians, and serving close to 1,100,000 pupils.[1] It is spread over the five boroughs of the city and services many different populations and communities. The problems and needs of its many clients are often quite different, yet a single citywide board is responsible for the whole system. Historically the system has become progressively more centralized, with central headquarters officials responsible for decisions on even the most trivial matters—from providing light bulbs, doorknobs, and erasers, to deciding on transportation facilities.[2] The board's legal and political structure, developed originally to maintain high levels of performance and professionalism and to protect the system from political interference, have not counteracted the harmful effects of overcentralization. And the trend toward increased centralization, which complicates administrative and pedagogical problems even in white middle class areas, makes it much harder to run the schools in ghetto communities. It is in such areas as Harlem, Brownsville, and Bedford–Stuyvesant that the pathologies of the centralized board have become most obvious.[3]

The main disadvantage of the present system is the privacy with which the board operates, in isolation from large elements of the population and from the city government, and the limited provision for outside review and control. The board does not have its own taxing powers, but has to subject its capital and expense budgets to such city agencies as the Board of Estimate, the City Planning Commission, the Site Selection Board, and the mayor. These agencies can and often do delay school construction decisions,* though the board's basic policy position as to where schools should be located, at what capacity, and in what order of priority is rarely questioned by city agencies.

One characteristic of the New York City school system that distinguishes it from many others in large northern cities is its insulation from machine and party politics. The lay board is appointed, rather than elected,† and patronage plays less of a role in board appointments than it did a generation or two ago. Nevertheless, the composition of the nominating committee is part of the reason why the lay board is responsive to only a narrowly based constituency,‡ and some board members and their sponsors still engage in active campaigning for office.

While this independence from party politics should have

---

* These agencies delay things because each one of them is subject to pressures from different constituencies and each has different standards in making site location decisions.

† Appointed boards may be less vulnerable to external political pressures than those that are elected, and less likely to develop polarized factions that prevent their acting on controversial issues.

‡ Mayor Lindsay's decentralization panel, set up in April, 1967, hopes to enact legislation to enlarge the nominating panel to include more organizations that represent the interests of Negroes, Puerto Ricans, and the poor. While it may help some to make the board more aware of conditions in poverty areas, I do not believe that simply changing the composition of the board is going to do much at the level where it counts—namely, the local school and classroom.

led to more professionalism, it has not. Under the guise of professionalism, a number of protectionist practices that are distinctly nonprofessional have begun to affect the system—for example, the resistance of principals, district superintendents, and other supervisory groups as well as teachers to desegregation, decentralization, and such procedural changes as the abolition of the IQ test. A new form of "educational politics" has evolved in which established professional groups now resist many proposed innovations by arguing that they would lead to a decline of standards. Often these innovations, like the four-year comprehensive high school, for example, had already achieved national acceptance within the academic and educational community, yet they were initially rejected in New York City because they threatened one or another power bloc within the system.[4]

Furthermore, there are many headquarters positions not subject to review by the Board of Examiners, and they are often filled on the basis of personal friendship and loyalty rather than on technical competence.* While the two need not always be incompatible, they sometimes are. Appointments to divisional offices, bureaus, and as directors or administrators on special projects often go to people who follow tradition, who have been in the system for years and even decades, and have always taken politically safe positions on pedagogical and social issues. Since the examination system contributes to the recruitment almost exclusively of local New Yorkers for teaching posts and New York City teachers for supervisory positions, a pattern of inbreeding has developed that limits the capacity of the system for innovation. It is no different in this regard from most big city school systems.[5]

Yet, the New York City school system has many other characteristics that potentially encourage innovation and reform. One is its liberalism, shaped in large degree by the political climate of Manhattan. New York City has long been a center of cosmopolitan values, progressive politics, and innovation in many fields. In some ways, the schools reflected this progressivism in the past, with their many new programs, their nation-

---

* At this level (divisional, bureau, administrative appointments), people inside the system acknowledge that they "make the exams to fit the man," meaning that there is no open competition for posts. People are generally chosen who are "compatible" with others in the unit, and that usually means that they are members of the club or at least have the "right" points of view.

ally renowned high schools, and their many scholarship and award winners. The present board still reflects this progressive spirit; it is dominated by people with a long record of support for progressive and civil rights causes, who share an egalitarian, social reformist outlook that has been the mark of the city's political life. But absence of effective programs for desegregation and for improving the quality of education in ghetto and integrated schools—and throughout the system—suggests that the progressive outlook of the lay board and some members of the professional staff are not enough.

The problem is not the lack of a liberal ideology, but rather the many bureaucratic impediments that prevent the liberals in the school system from implementing their ideology. They have been so caught up in trying to win over a resisting professional staff, while at the same time defending the staff and the system against outside attack, that they have not been able to provide the leadership for needed reforms. One civic group informant suggested: "The lay board was afraid to joust with the professional staff. The administration was more powerful. That's really the whole story." [6]

Actually, the New York City Board of Education's policy statements and programs for desegregation and upgrading ghetto schools are among the most extensive of any city in the nation. It was the first large city to have an Open Enrollment plan, fringe area construction, or rezoning for desegregation and pairings. It was also the first to develop such advanced policy statements and to set up separate headquarters units on zoning, community relations, and integration.[7]

The board's numerous programs for compensatory education for ghetto schools are equally impressive.[8] Starting with a demonstration guidance program in a West Harlem–Washington Heights junior high school, the board has tried several plans to raise reading and achievement levels in ghetto schools. More than three hundred such schools have been labeled "special service" schools, and the board spends $150 more a year per pupil there than in middle class schools, with slightly smaller class size, and many more remedial reading and other specialists.* It developed a program called Higher Horizons, and

---

* Since this was written, data prepared and analyzed by the United Bronx Parents indicate that, by and large, expenditures per pupil in ghetto schools are considerably less than those in white middle class schools. This suggests that the board unevenly implemented its compensatory education programs.

spread the procedures to thirty ghetto schools; set up a More Effective Schools program, developed in collaboration with the teachers' union, in twenty-one more ghetto schools, with smaller class size and more staff. The All Day Neighborhood Schools program, begun in 1936, provided remedial help in ghetto schools. The after-school programs, special programs for Puerto Rican pupils, and programs to absorb Negro teachers displaced by school desegregation in southern cities are other experiments. The new College Bound program helps minority-group high school students and encourages more of them to go on to college. The preschool programs were underway before the federal government started financing Operation Headstart. Ungraded and heterogeneous classes have been instituted on an experimental basis. Group IQ tests, seen as a discriminatory device to segregate minority group and white children, have been eliminated. The board has developed African-studies curricula, textbooks on Negro history, and urban readers. It has many in-service training programs in intergroup and race relations for teachers. It has after-school-studies centers, programs for the training of nonprofessionals in poverty areas for careers in the system, a "college discovery" program to find high school students in poverty areas to go on to college, and a number of teacher training and reading institutes in poverty area school districts, among others. It has been developing plans to eliminate some outmoded vocational high schools and to replace them with four-year comprehensive high schools. It also has plans for a 4–4–4 grade organization, with four-year middle schools, and zoned to permit more desegregation than has been possible in the junior high schools. And these are just a few of the many plans the board has developed.

They constitute a very impressive list, and they all seem to indicate a strong positive commitment to change on the part of the board. The plans are especially impressive compared to what many other big city school systems have done. But they haven't produced any results, because the system itself doesn't work.* Higher Horizons failed according to the board's own

* Unfortunately, some liberals on the board don't see this, and they keep pointing to their policy statements and "paper accomplishments" as evidence of how much they have done, without realizing the numerous ways in which the "system" has subverted all these programs. This may well be a reflection of the mentality of white liberals. They are good at conceptualizing problems, but they are very weak when it comes to action— partly because they see so much complexity in situations that they are not

evaluation data and was quietly phased out in 1966.[9] New York City was the first to implement Open Enrollment, but it was also one of the first to kill it, and it did the same with pairings.

The Lay Board

One of the board's major characteristics is a pattern of *weak leadership*. Those in top positions have limited power to effect change. This is a structural and political condition rather than a psychological one. Most of the liberals on the lay board have been no more effective than the moderates or conservatives, or even than the four superintendents in the past couple of decades. Even when they choose to exercise power they are limited in what they can do—by the professional staff, outdated laws and traditions, and the enormity of the problems they confront.[10]

The lay board and the superintendent might have mandated more change if they had been able to work together effectively. They rarely have, regardless of who was in office, because of a number of conflicts, ambiguities, and lack of trust in their relationship, that are built into the system, compounding the weakness of each party.

Recruitment. The lay board is selected on an ethnic and geographical basis to include three Protestants, three Catholics, and three Jews, a tradition referred to by one school official as "the Noah's Ark principle of board selection," and reflecting the pattern of ethnic politics in the city. There is also an accepted code that boroughs should be represented in proportion to their populations.

Since 1961 a selection board* has been the nominating

---

sure what to do; and partly, perhaps, because they sometimes take words and symbols (policy statements) as realities. One spokesman for a liberal white group explained: "The board's progressive policies have become an albatross. They hang on their necks and these liberals can't get out from under. We've won too many policy battles and lost on the implementation. Liberals are too easily satisfied with symbolic victories—diverted from real ones."

* The selection board includes presidents of major universities in New York City, the City Bar Association, the Commerce and Industry Association of New York, the PEA, the UPA, the League of Women Voters, the Citizens Union, the Citizens Budget Commission, and the New York City Central Trades and Labor Council. These organizations represent a narrow segment of the city; none is primarily attuned to the interests of the ghetto populations; and none tends toward radical changes. PEA has

panel for board members. As specified by law, the selection board is required to send the mayor at least three names of qualified candidates for membership on the board for each vacancy. Lay board members are appointed for seven-year terms, which are staggered.

There has been a Negro member since the late 1940s, but there has never been a Puerto Rican board member. The first Negro was Rev. John Coleman of Brooklyn, selected, reportedly, because O'Dwyer was running for mayor and was worried about the Negro vote, and Coleman "wouldn't ruffle too many people." The next, Rev. Gardiner Taylor, was much more highly regarded. The most recently selected Negro, Dr. Aaron Brown, a former college president and educational researcher, has served since 1961. Brown was backed by the Urban League. Most civil rights leaders have viewed him negatively. One said: "His battlecry is, 'Now I'm not speaking just for the Negro community.' "[11]

Board members respond to pressures from the organizations that put them in office—not only Reverend Coleman and Dr. Brown, but many liberal whites who have served have done so. They have gone along with some of those who have often refused to accept militant ghetto parent groups as "legitimate" spokesmen for the Negro. In the late 1950s and early sixties the lay board often refused to meet Rev. Milton Galamison and his Parents Workshop group.[12]

The one liberal board member who took a very critical posture about board practices and procedures angered some board colleagues and members of the professional staff by questioning unwritten board codes: do not interfere in administration (bringing in outsiders to evaluate board programs, suggesting new curricula), do not bargain with militant civil rights leaders over desegregation, do not question the ability of headquarters professionals to make meaningful innovations and evaluations of programs.[13] Mrs. Kohler served for six months, filling an unexpired term that was not renewed. A few key

tremendous power within this group, as suggested by Mrs. Rose Shapiro in a letter to PEA, in February, 1968, protesting its support of Mayor Lindsay's decentralization proposals: "In a very real sense, members of the Board of Education since 1961 have been selected by the Public Education Association through its president, William B. Nichols." This expression of what might be called "the white liberals' nostalgia" indicates the main constituency of a powerful element of the board.

members of the selective board and lay board impugned her qualifications and character. The attack was preceded by an informal investigation of Mrs. Kohler's credentials and an inquiry into her status in the California Bar Association. Mrs. Kohler had been a Referee in the Children's Court in San Francisco, and the attack mounted against her was personal and unfounded. Liberal members of the lay board did not come to her defense. The incident of Mrs. Kohler is perhaps the most dramatic example, but there were others, too, where former activists and liberals were subjected to such strong pressures to limit their aspirations toward reforming the system that their effectiveness was diluted. One exception is John Lotz, a member who is strongly committed to reform, and who was renewed for a seven-year term in May, 1967.*

Membership on the lay board is highly prestigious, and some people spend much time and energy campaigning informally for office, securing signatures and gaining the support of influential organizations in the city.[14] The Catholic members were generally selected by the Chancery, often in collaboration with Mayor Wagner. One informant said: "The Cardinal names them and that's that."

Organizations representing three of the major religious groups press for board appointments. Sponsoring organizations hope that the lay board will play an innovating role. Several informants suggested to me that a kind of "politics of gratitude" existed, whereby board members would orient their actions primarily to the organizations who helped put them in.[15] Some may be interested in a larger view, but still pay conspicuous attention to particular interests. Morris Iushewitz, secretary of the Central Labor Council represents the interests of unions and the labor movement, as Mrs. Rose Shapiro represents UPA and PEA. Thomas Burke, a Catholic member, invariably "votes the Roman position," as one board official put it, and Dr. Aaron Brown, for all his earlier protest, now represents the middle class Negro.[16]

It does seem clear, however, that the personality and political style of the board president affects its functioning to a certain extent. Different boards have adopted slightly different

---

* Lotz had the firm support of Mayor Lindsay, who is much more strongly disposed to encouraging educational reform than Mayor Wagner was. Had Wagner given Mrs. Kohler his support, she might have fared better.

positions on controversial policy questions, and have had some-what different relationships with particular interest groups.

The Donovan board was the one during which all the major desegregation controversies took place. It could be character-ized as run by a man whose own colleagues regarded him as tactless, and who embarrassed them in public on a number of occasions. His consistent capacity to insult civil rights and union leaders, both in private meetings and in public, finally convinced his board colleagues to ask him to resign, which he did in June, 1965.[17]

The Garrison board was a much more "humane" one in re-lations with the poverty area communities, but little leadership was demonstrated on either of the major issues it faced—de-segregation and decentralization. Toward the end of Garrison's term (in early 1967) some of his colleagues were increasingly anxious about his leadership; that Garrison had taken so long to develop a policy paper on decentralization disturbed them to the point where they encouraged him to step aside. The burdens of the office were so great that he did not need much urging, especially since he, like Rubin and Donovan, had given up much of his law practice to tend to board duties.

The Giardino board is generally a middle-of-the-road one, with Giardino making a show of strong leadership in public ap-pearances and on particular issues like labor negotiations and decentralization.

Of great significance is the fact that it is very difficult for a reform-minded board member like Garrison to get the necessary votes. "Lloyd might count on one or two votes," explained one headquarters official, "but he rarely did better than that on many issues." For middle-of-the-road and status-quo positions, it was much easier for a board member to garner votes.

The board president leads his colleagues, and this fact affects how the system works. James Donovan, for example, clearly led the anti-integration faction while he served, and he set the rigid, nonbargaining, and insulated tone that the board had during this period. Garrison gave the office a more humane quality and tone, though without moving the system forward, and now Giardino gives it a determined middle-of-the-road and melioristic one.

Despite the many personality and ideological differences among these men, the cliché that "the office shapes the man" has great relevance in such an established and tradition-bound institution as this. "It doesn't matter who the board president is," remarked an insider and civic group leader, "he always acts the same and says the same things. He has to defend the system, while giving the appearance of moving forward. More and more people are getting tired of the rituals and charades."

It is unlikely that changing the composition of the selection board and consequently of the lay board is going to change things appreciably. Liberals have not accomplished much, and the lay board is not where the power is. Nevertheless, there is much to be said for including more spokesmen for the poor in the selection process and on the board itself.

Legal Mandate and Activities. As trustees of the citizenry and as watchdogs over the school system's operations, the lay board is responsible for establishing basic policy and seeing to it that the policy is carried out. The board members are the system's top decision makers, and the superintendent is ultimately responsible to them. In fact, however, the lay board merely goes through the motions of making policy and monitoring its implementation. Many school officials and civic leaders feel the present lay board is not very powerful, perhaps even less so than the boards of the 1950s.*

The lay board is generally organized into committees, with each member acting as a chairman of one committee and as a member of two others.[18] The committees cover such matters as integration, business affairs, law and legislation, educational affairs, community relations, buildings and maintenance, city, state, and federal programs, and liaison with other cities and states. Each board member tends to become a specialist on a particular set of problems, but most know little about education or about the school system, outside their particular fields of interest.

The board's priorities over the past few years have been desegregation and administrative reorganization. There have been so many crises, however, that there has been little time for long-range planning. Since late 1966, the board's priorities

---

* The boards of the 1950s were at least highly "political" and they had many close contacts throughout the city, both inside and outside the administration. This board, striving to be reform-minded, tried to stay "above politics" (a grotesquely irrelevant aspiration in New York City), thereby isolating itself from centers of power. The fact that there were such poor communications and information flows, and so little monitoring and systematic evaluations of most board programs, left this relatively apolitical board almost powerless.

have shifted because of the shift in community demands. Desegregation has become a minor issue, and decentralization and community control have become the new rallying cries of protest groups. The board now has three decentralization experiments underway, and is investigating the possibility of setting up others.

Some of the other long-range issues that the board has been working on with limited success are reforming personnel and recruitment procedures; establishment of harmonious relationships with the mayor and his administration; and setting up federally funded programs for poverty areas. Changing procedures for the selection of teachers and supervisors has had high priority, at a time when there is a desperate need for more personnel, and preferably some outsiders with a sense of daring and risk. Recommendations to update examination procedures and eliminate the Board of Examiners had been made as early as 1951,[19] and the lay board has made efforts in this direction since 1962, but it is still struggling with the problem. Against strong opposition from the Council of Supervisory Associations,* Board President Alfred Giardino succeeded in cutting the size of the Board of Examiners, streamlining the placement and testing procedures, and opening up teaching and supervisory appointments to out-of-city and state applicants, in February, 1967. His reforms fell far short of those of an NYU study team commissioned to investigate the matter and of many civic groups.[20]

One of the reasons for the board's ineffectiveness is the magnitude of the problems it inherited. The legal and political structure of the system prevents the lay board from taking even the minimum steps necessary to revamp itself, not to speak of the apparent reluctance of members to engage in the massive political struggle necessary to move a professional bureaucracy toward reform. Some board members hold strongly to the view that head-on public collisions with their professional staff and its powerful lobby in Albany would only be self-defeating, and they may be right. They have committed themselves to a slow, reformist strategy, under which the schools have not improved much. The lay board has acquired a widespread reputation for weakness among headquarters professionals, field supervisors,

---

* A powerful organization of principals, district superintendents, department chairmen, assistant principals, and other professional groups.

numerous civic groups, and city officials, and this further limits
its ability to lead.

Activities, Resources, and Influence. The lay board does not
have the staff, money, expertise, time, or energy to do an effective job. Its members are unpaid, and all except one have
outside careers. Former Board President Max Rubin, who was
on the board from 1961 until the end of 1963, practically gave
up a lucrative law practice to tend to board duties.[21] He was
forced to resign, ill and demoralized by the system's many problems.*

A simple activities analysis of how the board members
spend their time clearly indicates that they are not doing what
they are supposed to do—namely, set policy and establish broad
guidelines for the direction of school programs. Most of their
time is spent on endless, petty details, from school maintenance
and construction contracts to the purchasing of supplies, and
they have little time left to think about important policy
questions.[22]

One established board institution is the "informal," a weekly
meeting of all members of the lay board and the superintendent.
Each Wednesday, it begins around noon, and it may run until
after dinner. An agenda is usually provided beforehand, and as
many as forty or fifty items may be on it, none of which can be
easily covered in a few minutes. Some items may relate to broad
policy questions like decentralization, and others to such trivia
as how much envelopes should cost.†

Every four weeks there is a "formal," where board members
go over the items that will be included in the monthly public
meeting and decide what positions the board as a body will take,
sometimes even to the point of deciding beforehand who will
speak and what views will be expressed. The average agenda for
one of these monthly meetings includes as many as fifty or sixty
items, and detailed materials on contracts for books, other
supplies, repairs, and new construction are included.

Whether planned that way or not, it is useful for the pro-

---

* Rubin reportedly told a friend that he took time off to regain his
health, after leaving the board, and that he almost had a relapse one day
when he chanced to see his successor, James Donovan, on television. Rubin
said that the mere thought of the job and its many attendant strains
was so distressing that he came close to getting sick just thinking about it.

† No minutes are taken at these meetings, and the general public therefore has no record of what its public servants and representatives have been
doing in their inner councils.

fessionals that their lay board is bogged down in trivia. This keeps the lay board so busy that it doesn't have time to set policy, let alone find out what is going on in local schools, districts, or headquarters.*

Another factor limiting the lay board's influence is the ponderous style with which it proceeds on broad policy questions.[23] Rubin was not alone in his concern for attention to detail, and his successors have done the same. Both the president and the entire board often spend days, weeks, and even months working on the precise language of new policy proposals. "After the IS 201 controversy, when we were trying to work out a task force paper," related a board member, "Garrison sat for weeks, writing and rewriting the thing." "Giardino sometimes does his homework so thoroughly that he rewrites memoranda ten or fifteen times, until he feels he has them perfect," related another headquarters official. Even when they work on policy, then, they get so bogged down in successive drafts and rewordings, not to say working to develop a consensus, that the board members develop the same cumbersome and ponderous way of responding to events that their professional staff has. It seems unnecessary for the board to have to do this. Many top professionals at headquarters are aware of the board's ponderous style, and those who favor reform get quite discouraged. "They vacillated so much on desegregation," a headquarters official said, "it is no wonder that civil rights groups got impatient. We need them to keep us honest."

Between time the board must spend on trivia and time they spend pondering over their prose, there is little left for thinking about important policy questions. When the board does develop new ideas for curricula, instructional methods, staffing and administrative procedures, it must hand over to the professionals the responsibility for refining the ideas and carrying them out, all the while having to bargain with them to accept even the most limited reforms. The lay board has almost no staff of its own. It is very much aware of the need for more staff, but state education laws and pressures from the Board of Examiners have prevented it from acquiring one, lest it become too powerful. What else should it be but powerful in a

---

* One top school official described the informals: "It's like Grant at Appomattox," he suggested, "worrying about how much canteen money the soldiers have and how many calories are in their diets, while outside a war is going on and people are dying."

school system as large and with so many problems as New York City's, and with as insulated and tradition-bound a professional staff? If the board remains as powerless in the future as it has been lately, perhaps it should be disbanded as a vestigial institution that no longer serves any purpose, and be replaced by local boards that set policy for their own districts.

The issue of the lay board's research staff and committees recurs, which may indicate that something is radically wrong with the present arrangement. An obvious reason for the fact that it does not have a larger staff is the professionals' fear that they will lose power, and they still have enough support from state education officials and civic groups to prevail. The pattern has been for the board to set up staffs, which come under attack, are dismantled, and resurrected by the next board. The cycle has recurred for the past ten to fifteen years.

The present reform board came into being in 1961, and its predecessor had been criticized for meddling in administration. The new board recognized almost immediately the absurdity of staying out of administration, and it became more and more involved in running the system.[24] In 1964, after the board decided that Superintendent Gross was not providing any leadership, it told him it wanted an independent research staff. Gross seemed to consider the request, as had previous superintendents, as a threat to his authority. He opposed the lay board and won his case, gaining the support of the same coalition of state officials and local civic groups that had always beaten down the board in the past.[25] However, after Gross was dismissed in March, 1965, the lay board set up its own committees once more, and they have been at work ever since.[26] Harold Siegel was hired for full-time research and liaison, with a few researchers to work with him.

The lay board has attempted to do informally what it has been prevented from doing formally. It has worked with various consultants who serve at the board's pleasure, despite objections from the Board of Examiners and other inside professionals. Nevertheless, it is cautious about expanding its staff, because such a move would require a change in state education laws and incur the wrath and opposition of city and state education officials, as well as their civic allies. This is an untenable situation for a lay board committed to reform and innovation.

The solution to this problem would be for the lay board to rally support from the mayor and various civic groups for the legislative changes that are needed to set up and expand its professional staff. Informal, makeshift arrangements, such as having experts serve as consultants, must eventually be replaced by a legally institutionalized procedure that enables the board to employ its own staff without fear of reprisal.

In 1966, a large coalition of civic groups protested against gross inequities in Superintendent Donovan's distribution of federal funds provided by Title I of the Elementary and Secondary Education Act of 1965 to parochial and public schools.[27] The specific complaints, outlined in a letter from UPA officials to United States Commissioner of Education Harold Howe, were that some funds were going to parochial schools with middle class pupils, who did not qualify for aid under the poverty provisions of the law; some public school teachers were assigned to parochial schools in daytime, after-school, and summer remedial programs without public discussion; and many planned special services (in music, art, library, reading, and health education) were provided to parochial schools, in violation of the law.

Though the services were supposed to be allocated to public and non-public school children on a shared basis, this was not done. Parochial school children were put in separate programs with a different time schedule, and many newly established after-school centers were actually closed to public school children. "I don't have room for my own children," a public school director of a center said to parent group representatives. "If someone came in from my own school, I would have to tell him there is no room. The allotment of staff was based on the enrollment expected from the feeding parochial school." There were many reports of preferential allocation of Title I funds to parochial schools and of the failure to integrate public and parochial school students in the programs.

The lay board subsequently overturned some of the superintendent's recommendations, especially on the matter of mixing the children. Yet, UPA representatives who had done much research on the programs reported: "Despite the board's resolution, when the programs were implemented, our investigations indicated that this master plan was not working out as devised. There had been a breakdown in communication."

The issues are complex and involve judgments of the constitutionality of a federal law that seems to violate legal guarantees of separation of church and state. I use the example only to illustrate how the lay board was often unable to represent the interests of its civic group constituencies—in this case the moderates, white liberals, and minority groups—and had limited control over the actions of its professional staff. Many civic leaders felt that Superintendent Donovan had given in too easily to parochial school interests, and that he had defied his board.*

Another case involved an informal investigation by a board member of how Title I money was actually spent.[28] The board member found out that the professional staff had followed its conventional budgetary procedures of continually modifying the money allocations to particular programs as contingencies developed. It soon became apparent that it was very difficult to obtain an accounting of how the money was finally spent, making it impossible to evaluate the programs. He sent off a strongly worded memo to the superintendent and the official responsible for administering the programs, suggesting that the lay board could never justify such budgetary procedures. The agenda for the next private executive session of the board included a discussion of this issue. Superintendent Donovan took the initiative and gave a long and spirited defense of a modifiable budget, in view of all the contingencies that any school programs face. On this occasion, as on many others, the lay board capitulated to his point of view.

The lay board, then, has the difficult responsibility for policy and implementation, without the resources to do either well. Its policy decisions depend on studies provided by headquarters technicians, many of whom want to protect their own interests and careers and are hesitant to incur the wrath of supervisory groups. In cases where the board's policy statements and programs may seem too advanced to the headquarters and field staff, they can be watered down or subverted in implementation. And since the board does not have its own

* There is a widespread consensus among school professionals and highly informed civic groups that the present (1968) board is "Donovan's board." "He is able to manipulate them on many important day-to-day affairs," a civic group leader reported, "and though Giardino makes the big public ploy on policy questions of high visibility, like the teachers' strike, IS 201, and decentralization, people inside know that Donovan runs this system, and the way he wants to run it." "Donovan is shrewd, a slick politician, a fast thinker," related another inside informant. "He is smart enough to sense the road of the future, thus he has formed alliances, an internal machine, and an administrative structure is being built in his image."

staff to monitor the various programs and knows so little about local conditions, it must rely upon the professionals inside the system. Finally, evaluations of programs were, until very recently, done by insiders. The system is locked in and self-reinforcing at every turn.

The superintendent and his staff actually make policy. They have all the research staff, all the data, and much of the expertise. Many of his staff have a vested interest in maintaining the system the way it is.* Their initial advice to the board on the feasibility of particular new programs is likely to be replete with judgments presented as facts. This is one reason for the gap between the board's advanced policy statements on desegregation and their implementation.

If the board is criticized by civic groups about particular programs, its own examination of what has been done turns out to be a public disavowal of the superintendent and his staff. But the professionals feel they can disregard lay board and civic review: the lay board cannot possibly keep track of all the administrative decisions that are made as particular policy statements and programs become progressively specified for final implementation. Of course, if a policy is too blatantly sabotaged there is the possibility that civic groups will complain to board members. But the complainants will probably be referred to the professional staff and sent from unit to unit, each of which typically abdicates responsibility. The lay board will pick it up, only if the complaint is loud, is backed by moderate groups, has citywide implications, appeals to the board's collective social conscience, and is politically threatening. This combination of circumstances is rare.

Backgrounds, Outlooks, and Codes. In addition to the legal, administrative, and political constraints on the lay board's powers to innovate, there are some self-imposed constraints, relating to the backgrounds, outlooks, and codes of its members. The present board, which still includes a nucleus of four persons from the original group set up in 1961, is probably one of the most liberal and progressive in the nation. Outwardly, they look like a perfect antidote to a tradition-bound officialdom. Consider their liberalism and credentials: [29]

> *Lloyd Garrison,* board president from 1965 to 1967, and great-grandson of the famous abolitionist, has given a lifetime to public service and liberal movements. He was a former dean of Wisconsin

---

* See Chapter Eight for a full discussion of this interest.

Law School, legal counsel for the War Production Board, a founder and organizer of the National Labor Relations Board, a leader of the Reform Democrat movement in New York City, and national chairman of the Urban League in the 1950s. He is one of the members most sympathetic to problems of ghetto and poverty area communities but unable to get the votes, and generally regarded by colleagues and professionals as an idealistic liberal. He has concentrated much of his energies on housing and school planning, having sponsored a state law for dual occupancy of buildings that links school construction with housing in such a way that state loans and financing for schools are increased substantially.

Dr. Clarence Senior, internationally respected sociologist, and former research director of the Commonwealth of Puerto Rico, has also devoted many years of service to liberal causes. Senior is now chairman of the Sociology Department at Brooklyn College; board member of Youth-in-Action, a large anti-poverty agency in Brooklyn; consultant for the federal and Puerto Rican governments on the social and economic development of Puerto Rico and other Latin American nations, and he is still active in the poverty and civil rights fields. He has a general reputation on the board as one who "reads voraciously everything he can get his hands on in urban education," but he seems to have lost all the zest he used to have for action. He is most active in the board's educational affairs committee, covering a multitude of problems connected with upgrading instruction through teacher training, new textbooks and curriculum materials, special programs, and grade reorganization.

Morris Iushewitz, secretary of the Central Labor Council, has spent much of his career furthering the causes of the labor movement and civil rights, and is also a board member of numerous hospital, welfare, and youth agencies. He has worked primarily on desegregation and labor problems and is one of the board members most committed to fringe area school construction and educational parks, along with Garrison.

Dr. Aaron Brown, a Southern-born Negro educator, was formerly president of Albany (Georgia) State College, and was the research director and a consultant for the Phelps–Stokes Foundation before joining the board in 1961. He is now a professor and dean at the Brooklyn branch of Long Island University, and serves with Senior in Youth-in-Action. He is the board's liaison with outside school systems, and has worked informally for many years to secure more Negroes in supervisory positions and to recruit outstanding Negro educators from the South.

All these people joined the board in 1961 and have been its integrationist faction, though not strong enough to vote for many desegregation programs or to swing the votes of their colleagues for others.

Mrs. Rose Shapiro, now vice president of the board, was selected in 1963, having come up through the ranks of various parent, civic, and governmental groups concerned with public education. Starting as the president of a parent association in an integrated community adjacent to Harlem, she went on to become president of UPA, vice president of PEA and chairman of its Coordinating Committee, and education staff person for the Mayor's Commission on Human Rights. She knows more about how the school system actually works than many of her colleagues. Wife of Morris Shapiro, prominent liberal lawyer, and among the early militants in the civil rights movement, she trained some civil rights activists and professionals, whom she encouraged to agitate for school desegregation. Some of her strongest support for selection to the board came from ghetto parents and liberal white groups, as well as from the moderates. Like other board members, she was much more effective before she got on the board than since. Defensive, bewildered by recent poverty-area demands; generally regarded as the prototype of the old-line liberal of the thirties who does not understand or sympathize with the recent protest movement, her main interests are school–community relations, early childhood education, and the status of local school boards. She is now regarded in the Negro and liberal white community as only marginally committed to reform.

Alfred Giardino, now president of the board, is a Catholic, lawyer, arbitrator, and supporter of the Reform Democrat movement. He was formerly executive secretary of the New York State Labor Relations Board and now arbitrates for the Federal Mediation and Conciliation Service, State Mediation Board and American Arbitration Service. He has taught at several city colleges. Mr. Giardino is one of the most energetic and effective members of the board. Much tougher than Garrison, and much less progressive in social outlook, especially on desegregation and decentralization, he always does his homework. He is a strong debater, but generally regarded as somewhat authoritarian, middle-of-the-road, ritualistic, and not capable of moving the system to reform; a better debater than mover. Not committed to anything more than meliorist solutions, he has been most active on matters of decentralization and the licensing of teachers and supervisors, two of the most vital issues of the late 1960s. He is especially concerned with enacting new legislation that will further reforms in these fields. He is somewhat conservative on many social issues, for example, board–union relations and civil rights, but quite iconoclastic on some others. A very active board member.

Thomas Burke, also a Catholic and lawyer, was appointed to the board in 1964, as was Giardino. He comes from a family that has long been active in board service. His father, the late John S. Burke, served as a member of the Board of Higher Education in 1942–1943, and his maternal grandfather was president of the Board of Education from 1913–1917. His main interest is in the building and maintenance fields, traditionally dominated by Catholics. Generally regarded as representing Catholic interests.

Joseph Barkan, a Jewish businessman from Queens, is executive vice president and treasurer of the Prudential Steamship Corporation and was appointed to the board in 1963. He has also served in federal posts for the Maritime Administration and the General Accounting Office. His main interests are in business affairs and he has promoted performance budgeting and the use of computers in programming the board's operations. Generally conservative on civil rights and labor issues, like Burke and Giardino, Barkan is one of the least active members.

John Lotz, a liberal Catholic from Staten Island, is the newest member of the board, appointed in 1965 to fill the unexpired term of former Board President James B. Donovan, and for a full term in 1967. He is widely regarded by activists and City Hall as "by far the best man there" ("The only guy who will level with you"). Lotz is intelligent, direct and radical, but he can't get enough votes. He was formerly a longshoreman and social worker; long active in the labor movement and radical social work circles, a teacher, and now an insurance executive. He has concentrated most heavily on evaluating how state and federal funds are used and has been especially active in monitoring the board's use of Title I money.

The board follows a number of codes* that reinforce its weaknesses.[30] These codes include not meddling in administration; moving only after a consensus and making a public posture of unanimity; not bargaining with civil rights groups, especially the militants; maintaining tight, centralized control over policy making, rather than giving local boards some powers; not offending the professional staff by bringing in too many outside consultants to develop new programs; and maintaining their autonomy as a state agency by steering clear of political involvement and interference by the mayor. These codes were stronger in 1964 and 1965 when James Donovan was president than they have been since then, but they still set the pattern for the board's actions. Given these codes, the board defines a number of practices as highly questionable; for example, visit-

* By "codes" I mean basic assumptions about what is appropriate or inappropriate behavior.

ing schools, or bringing in outside experts. One board member announced to friends and colleagues when he was appointed that he was there to do something and not just to sit. He started making visits to ghetto schools and holding meetings with principals on compensatory programs, but was prevailed upon to curtail such visits, after numerous complaints from principals and headquarters staff. Another board member also made many field trips, riding busses with Open Enrollment children, and taking copious notes on conditions in schools, and was denounced by many school professionals.[31] To be a board member acceptable to the professionals, then, was to be uninformed about school conditions, except as reported by a field supervisory staff who are dependent for promotions on the board, the superintendent, and other top headquarters officials. Principals and district superintendents wanted to "look good" to their bureaucratic superiors, and only reported on local school programs and conditions in a very selective way.*

The more the lay board followed this code and avoided going into the field, the more it handed over to the professional staff the freedom to ignore board policies. One board member, for example, expressed surprise at the agitation by ghetto groups in the early months of 1967. Had he and his colleagues been better informed about conditions in the schools and the political climate in ghetto communities, he would not have been surprised at all.

Over the past few years, board members have come to realize the futility of this posture. They are now somewhat less reluctant about making an occasional visit to local schools and meeting with local board members and civic leaders, especially on matters of rising community tensions. Yet, the board is still far removed from local situations.[32]

The code of unanimity and consensus, which school boards follow throughout the nation, was also followed in New York City during the heat of the desegregation controversy. When Board President James Donovan was in office, many executive sessions of the board were held at which only Donovan did the talking. The trouble with such a consensus strategy was that it

* Many Human Relations Unit Staff members at headquarters, for example, reported to us that principals and district superintendents only called them in when a school–community conflict had gone long past the boiling point, reflecting in part the supervisors' concern with not letting headquarters know what was going on.

made the board members almost completely subject to the dictates of Donovan, who was not sympathetic to desegregation. It also led to numerous delays in coming to any final decisions. Ideological differences among board members gradually became known to civic groups through articles in the press, and a spirit of dissent to Donovan's judgments finally arose. At last his colleagues encouraged him to resign. However, before then, the board's attempt to present a united front on desegregation to the general public mystified many civil rights leaders. They found it hard to understand where the liberal members on the board stood on desegregation, and were especially disturbed that there wasn't more protest from the liberal faction when one of its members was kept off the board's desegregation committee. A common observation made by representatives of many liberal and Negro groups that this board "is not of the people" reflected the distrust that had built up.

Another code that the board followed during James Donovan's presidency was refusal to bargain with civil rights groups. The intention was to be sensitive to the needs of the entire city, and not be carried away by the desires of any single interest group. Ironically, civil rights and moderate leaders with some access to the board noticed that it succumbed readily to pressure.

The board's nonbargaining strategy was largely attributable to Donovan, though neither Gross nor many other headquarters professionals was willing to bargain on the desegregation issue either. When Donovan became president in December, 1963, he appealed to the sympathies of his colleagues and asked them to stand behind him, since they were all under attack. This took place publicly, and there was a show of unanimity, even though they didn't all believe in his positions.[33] The liberal and conservative factions described their differences by periodic press leaks, and the liberals especially resented being put on the defensive by civil rights groups. They had to defend Donovan and the system, while not believing in either, but not knowing what possible political strategy might ease community tensions and move the system toward more desegregation. Some remained unconvinced that acceding to many civil rights groups' demands for desegregation was any solution to the schools' shortcomings.

Donovan, however, became a source of increasing embarrassment to his colleagues. One top civic official who knew him quite well suggested that his actions had contributed substantially to community conflicts over desegregation. "Jim Donovan had done some liberal things in his life," he suggested, "but he was completely inept in race relations."

The board's relations with the Mayor's Commission on Human Rights illustrated how tenaciously it held to this non-bargaining code. After the commission's officials had successfully negotiated a truce between civil rights groups and the board in September, 1963, with the understanding that Gross would come up with a desegregation proposal in December, one of its representatives tried to continue meeting with the board to ensure that the understanding would be honored. "Our community relations unit and education committee tried to keep in contact," a commission official said, "but that is one thing that was difficult with the board. They didn't drop one big gate down. Just little by little, they didn't get around to seeing us. Or they never really said anything at meetings." Since the commission was a mediator between civil rights groups and the board, and the board made little attempt to communicate with civil rights groups on their own, this position amounted to a refusal to bargain.

Meanwhile, bussing had already become an issue, and opposition groups were organizing. Civil rights groups were ready to engage in public demonstrations by December, and by January the boycott was in preparation. Commission representatives saw what was going to happen and attempted to intervene once again as mediators. There were two meetings, one with and one without civil rights leaders. At the first meeting, a commission spokesman pleaded with the board to take a public position endorsing some desegregation plans and to meet with civil rights groups. As he reported his comments: "I'm not asking you for instant integration, I said. You have a series of possible integration measures. You have a policy position on integration. Use these measures. Use them sensitively. Use them combined. Use them one after another. Use them however you want to, but make clear where you stand. Make clear that you are going to use them." The board refused to make any commitments.

The commission representative recalled, "They heard us saying that we wanted them to bus large numbers of children for miles and miles, which we never said. That wasn't even relevant."

The plans the board was asked to endorse were flexible and moderate, as some liberal board members admitted in private. But the board was supporting its president, and it continued to give the appearance of unanimity while refusing to bargain. Donovan believed in neighborhood schools, and the liberals on the board were forced to defend an institution that they themselves did not completely believe in.[34] While the board tried to give the appearance of being above politics, that was not the case. They were a political body and had supported their president's judgment that the white community would not tolerate mandatory desegregation.

Commission officials and civil rights leaders were often bewildered by their liberal friends on the board. "I don't know what happened to Rose Shapiro," a commission official commented. "There is something about getting to that position at the board that produces the most profound and the most ominous changes in people. It was as if Donovan's blindness was catching. How Rose changed. That's a story in itself. When she got on the board, we just rubbed our hands with glee and said, oh, we've finally got a person of our own there now—and we really felt that something was going to happen. After a few months there, you talked to Rose Shapiro and she would come out with things like, well, we must support our president. I don't know what happened to the woman there."

The liberals on the board say that they became more aware of the difficulties in mandating desegregation once they saw how the school system worked and what pressures it was under from inside and outside groups. Furthermore, the liberals could not muster enough votes for desegregation from their own colleagues.[35]

The second meeting which took place in late 1963 included some civil rights leaders. Rev. Milton Galamison presented James Donovan with a list of demands and Donovan refused to respond. One person present described it: "I can only describe Donovan as if he hadn't heard a word Galamison said. Finally, he spoke: 'Why don't you people go to Albany. We're really a state agency. We operate under Commissioner Allen.'" A commission representative asked Donovan, "If you would only say one definite thing. You know that an educational park in the Bronx would reduce segregation there. You've got some Princeton Plans. Put up some new construction somewhere else. Nobody is asking for miracles. Outline a ten-year program and they'll agree. Say that it may take as long as twelve years. But if you tell them the things you're going to do, it doesn't even matter how much time you ask for to do it in. If you would only say something definite about what you'll do, they'll accept." Donovan refused to budge.

However, one liberal board member did speak up, suggesting that the argument presented was reasonable, and that the board should try to work something out. This was a violation of the board's non-bargaining strategy and an exception to its presumed unanimity: Donovan was upset. One person recalled: "If looks could kill, you should have seen the look Donovan shot at the board member. 'We'll discuss this in executive session,' he said."

At times, the board abandoned its nonbargaining strategy and made periodic attempts to deal with national civil rights leaders, in the hope of forging a consensus through them. Donovan actually followed this strategy. "He always knew that the national office would take a more conservative approach," a civil rights leader explained. "This question of bargaining with national or local leaders was kicked around a lot at the board during the pairing discussions. We did have a meeting with Wilkins and Young and they talked. Both told him that they might disagree on some matters with their local people but they would never undercut them in any way. They said that they would not take over the role of meeting and bargaining with the board on school integration."

To be fair to the board, Superintendent Gross had little interest in negotiating from September, 1963, through April, 1964. "I kept telling Jack Landers* at headquarters," a civil rights leader said, "that there was no way to resolve some of the basic civil rights questions except by negotiation. He and Gross and the top brass took the position that they would not negotiate."

The nonbargaining posture was more pronounced when James Donovan was president than it has been since then. Nevertheless, the board continues to follow it in a number of critical situations. In the IS 201 controversy, for example, East Harlem leaders had tried to meet with the lay board for several months before Board President Lloyd Garrison finally sat down with them.[36] In the PS 125–PS 36 controversy involving a similar

* Jack Landers was the assistant superintendent in charge of integration activities.

issue of community participation, in the Columbia University–Morningside Heights area, the board refused to meet with a delegation of parent representatives until they ended their boycott. In the end there was no meeting at all. Superintendent Donovan and his staff met with parents in both of these controversies, but he was given no authority to negotiate for his board. Though I suggested earlier that the board responded to pressure, at times even overresponding, that needn't be in contradiction to its nonbargaining posture. Nonbargaining was a code that was selectively applied. Moderate groups could and did sway board decisions, civil rights groups could not, except when they made a show of local and citywide strength. Even when they did, at the time of the first boycott, James Donovan held the line.

Nonbargaining was not the board's posture with its professional staff; the board tried to mobilize the greatest degree of receptivity to innovation.[37] It is difficult to conceive of any strategy other than negotiation for winning over the professionals to change. There is no doubt that the professionals are fixed in their attachment to such traditions as the neighborhood school, and that they know how to wreck plans with which they don't agree. The lay board might well have moved the professionals faster than it did, but it was unwilling to do so because of its own lack of agreement on desegregation. The board also saw the risks in pushing its professionals too hard, fearing that they might rebel and subvert its plans and that they might take their case to the public through the press, undermining the community's already flagging faith in the public schools.

One way the board could have become more responsive to local interests was to have campaigned vigorously to increase the power of local school boards, through changing state education laws. But the board was very reluctant to do that, and it was only after Mayor Lindsay's decentralization panel developed such recommendations that the central board seemed to make much of any move in that direction.[38] Many local school board members and chairmen had become quite demoralized by their powerless, buffer position between a central board and headquarters—whose workings they could not comprehend, let alone influence—and community groups.*

---

* See Chapter Ten for a fuller discussion of local school boards.

The board might also have worked more closely with the mayor, to ensure that it would not be too isolated from the city, but they never did that either. Mayor Wagner clearly preferred to have as little to do with education as possible, and the board's harmonious relations with him were based on little contact. When Mayor Lindsay made clear his intention to reform the schools and set up a decentralization panel to come up with some recommendations, relations between him and the board gradually deteriorated, and by April, 1968, when the state legislature was about to select a decentralization plan, they had completely broken down.[39] Board members resented the mayor's interference in educational policy making that was clearly their legal prerogative, and some reportedly felt that he was using the schools for his own political career and national image. Since the schools do affect the city, and since Lindsay was elected as a reform mayor, the board's attempt to maintain its legal and de facto autonomy in the face of increasing citizen pressures for reform had little relevance to the situation it faced.

Instead of being responsive to a wider variety of local and citywide interests and needs through these means, the board continued to call on its narrowly based constituency, the moderates, before formulating new plans and policy statements and before public hearings—for support, information, and advice. However, most of the moderate organizations were unwilling to endorse plans for changing the structure and operation of the school system. They were especially opposed to decisions that might redistribute power within the system and in its relations with civic groups.

Not all the moderates, though. Even some established groups such as the Women's City Club were considered too radical to be invited to key private meetings. Mrs. Blanche Katz, education director of the Women's City Club, had taken progressive positions on pairings and the role of local school boards. On one occasion, she was not supposed to be invited to a private board meeting on its policy deliberations regarding local boards, but due to some slip-up had been invited. Two board representatives were angry about the mistake.[40]

Recently, the lay board had expanded the roster of organizations invited to pre-hearing and policy meetings. During the first Title I controversy, in 1965, the NAACP, the Urban League, the Catholic Inter-Racial Council, and the Protestant

Council were asked for their evaluations of board programs. But with the exception of the Protestant Council, these organizations did not participate. This pattern of withdrawal extended to other matters as well. Civil rights and liberal groups were contacted in late 1966 to evaluate the capital and expense budget, and most of them refused to do so. They had lost faith in the board's capacity to develop meaningful programs, having decided to try for large reforms, and therefore not to use their energies for whatever small changes they could make in the budget.

Outlook on School Desegregation. Board members are deeply pessimistic about the prospects of desegregating the New York City school system, partly because they have carried on a narrowly based dialogue with moderate, centrist groups and tended to view the desegregation issue as these groups did, and partly because of the obvious fiasco that resulted from previous efforts to desegregate. There are factions for and against desegregation on the board. Members who have supported desegregation include Garrison, Senior, Iushewitz, and Brown. The other board members are generally committed to other priorities. This was illustrated by the board's vote on an educational park for East Brooklyn: the vote was reportedly 5 to 4, with the integrationists losing out.* Rose Shapiro had always been regarded as an integrationist before she became a member of the board, but now she tends to vote conservatively, under pressure from her moderate UPA and PEA constituency.[41]

Although most board members are not strongly committed to desegregation, they tend to suggest otherwise in public statements. For example, Alfred Giardino, who is generally on the moderate side and often votes that way, announced publicly in November, 1966, that segregation—along with dropouts, bigness, and the difficulty of getting experienced teachers—was one of the major problems of the schools.[42] This suggests once again a gap between the board's stated intentions and its actions.

The actions and words of the liberal board members, especially, justify deep pessimism regarding the prospects for school desegregation. Sometimes, their views appear to be formed without reference to the realities of how desegregation plans had been implemented in the past. One board member said: "We have tried Open Enrollment across the board and it hasn't had much effect on segregation." Could this board mem-

* A top school official reported this.

ber have known how poorly Open Enrollment was implemented? [43]

Another liberal board member, aware of the necessity for citywide planning for desegregation, noted: "The desegregation problem will only be solved through the commitment to an open city policy, and that will have to come from the mayor. We would like to participate." Unfortunately, this very positive attitude toward desegregation gets lost in the bureaucratic entanglements of the Board of Education and the city, state, and federal governments, which have not yet worked effectively together in planning for desegregation.

There has not been strong leadership from the liberals on the lay board for desegregation, even in instances where such planning might be possible. When a leader of a neighborhood school group asked one of the liberal board members, for example, what he thought the justification was for the board's four pairings, he said: "Faith." When a local school board from east Brooklyn met with the board in private, and one of its spokesmen asked why the central board felt the educational park was one solution to the city's educational problems, there was silence, after which a liberal board member suggested that this person read some articles on the subject, thus abdicating direct responsibility for having to justify the educational parks idea.

It is not that the liberal board members are unwilling to set up some educational parks if the politics of the situation warrant that, but that they are overwhelmed with their many tasks and are ill-equipped to make technical judgments about such innovations as parks.

The capacity of liberal board members to line up enough votes is also critical. Unless a board member is genuinely committed to a particular cause and can mobilize support from his colleagues for it, there is little likelihood of reform. Furthermore, the superintendent's refusal to go along is equal to a veto.

The Superintendent

Many of the forces that limit the authority of the lay board also limit the superintendent, who is controlled by the same power blocs at headquarters and in the field: the teachers' union, principals' associations, department chairmen, divisional and bureau heads, the Board of Examiners, and the

Council of Supervisory Associations. This, combined with poor communication and coordination across units, makes it difficult to institute reforms with even a modicum of efficiency. Each unit within the system is oriented more toward its own needs than toward overall goals of the system. At the policy level, any new programs that represent significant departures from the old structure are almost automatically resisted. Professional associations function as protectionist organizations, rather than as agencies to develop, maintain, and enforce professional standards.

That the New York City school system suffers from weak leadership has much less to do with the abilities of particular superintendents and lay boards than it does with the many *structural constraints* they face, and the stringent *cultural traditions* and *operating codes* within the system.* If personality and leadership ability had much to do with the extent of innovation in the system, one would expect some variation under different administrations. Yet, the system has had four superintendents and three lay boards in the past twelve years, with little change in its operations.

These bureaucratic and structural conditions are not unique to the New York City school system. All big city school systems face internal and external problems, and no others have handled them much more successfully than New York City, with the possible exception of Philadelphia. Lay boards and superintendents are weak in all big cities because they confront the same protectionist interests among teachers and supervisors, and this condition is characteristic of public education as a national institution. Educators in big cities remain insulated from the massive social changes of the past twenty years and have become protectionist in the face of new demands by citizen groups.

What is unique about New York City is its size and ethnic diversity. Its size alone differentiates it from any other city, contributing to the growth of a mammoth bureaucracy and large professional organizations. The Board of Superintendents (which was made up of the eight associate superintendents, the deputy superintendent, and the superintendent) was the system's major decision-making body until 1961, when it was formally abolished, although it still functioned informally un-

---

* One of the most significant sets of constraints the board faces is state education laws and the by-laws of the New York City system.

til 1966. The superintendent could be outnumbered, and his only power was through building his own coalition within the group.

The most powerful organization of the professional groups is the Council of Supervisory Associations (CSA), which has successfully blocked numerous plans for desegregation and administrative change over the past several years. When it has not been able to prevent new policies from being formulated, it was able to subvert their implementation, thereby helping to discredit them. The Board of Examiners is another powerful group inside the system.* Any superintendent who had plans for innovation was defined as an "outsider" and readily cut down by these groups.

The limited authority and power of the superintendent to innovate is best understood through a brief review of the experience of the last four. None has mandated any significant innovations, despite differences in political skills and the climate of the city.

Jansen. William Jansen was superintendent from 1947 to 1958. He, more than any of his successors, fought against desegregation and reaffirmed his strong commitment to the neighborhood school. In 1954, when Kenneth Clark charged that the New York City school system had become more segregated and that segregated schools were inferior, Jansen denied that this was so.[44] When the board's Commission on Integration completed a number of reports with recommendations for reform, Jansen tried to rewrite them and delayed putting them into effect until the end of his administration.† "Jansen held back progress on those reports for the rest of his term," a civic leader reported. "He had techniques for undercutting, even after the report was adopted. For example, on teacher movement, he pulled in the top power structure to show how it was not feasible. He called for so many proposals that they became, in effect, counterproposals, and so we wound up with no implementation at all. He could always prove that under certain circumstances Negro parents were clamoring for their own schools and not for any new concepts of zoning. He would deny that a situation existed in the first place and then present expert opinion that nothing could be done about it in the second place."

* See Chapter Eight for a lengthy discussion of their role.
† The reports were completed in 1956 and 1957, and Jansen left in June, 1958.

Jansen, more than any of his successors, was a captive of his powerful lay board, and constrained by his professional staff; the professionals prevented him from instituting new programs.* His continued refusal to implement the recommendations of the Commission on Integration for fringe-area construction, rezoning, and transfers of teachers to ghetto schools illustrate how tied to tradition and how constrained by inside professional pressures Jansen was.

Progressive school officials comment on the demoralization that some of them felt existed in the 1950s under Jansen. "There simply was no movement," one of them said. "He sat at his desk like a sphinx. Jansen was strictly nineteenth century, and he didn't want to do anything to push the system ahead."

His departure was partly the result of his unwillingness and inability to innovate on desegregation.

Theobald. Dr. John Theobald, his successor from 1958 to 1962, was chosen only after he had met privately with civil rights leaders and gained their approval. "Charles Silver (the board president) got people together with Theobald one day at the Empire State Building," a civil rights leader recalled. "That was Roy Wilkins, Hubert Delany, and the other top people. We faced him across the table and asked questions. We questioned him thoroughly. He was like most politicians and promised us everything. He really did a job on all of us. He convinced us he was going to work for what we wanted. The whole Negro community, potentially Theobald's greatest opponents, well, he just took the wind right out of our sails, and if we hadn't been won over, Silver wouldn't have endorsed him."

Theobald had resources that Jansen never had. He had been deputy mayor under Wagner. He had political skills, developed as he moved up the ranks of higher education politics in the city to become president of Queens College before coming to the Board of Education. He was an outsider, far less constrained than Jansen by loyalties to board professionals. As a result, Theobald was able to press for some reforms. He pushed through Open Enrollment, against the wishes of some board members, and he developed a pupil transfer program to effect more even use of school space. However, these were all marginal changes and were subverted in their implementation by the professional staff.

* The Board of Superintendents was the main policy-making body during this period, and they, rather than Jansen, made key decisions.

One of Theobald's most significant political actions was to gather many civil rights leaders into his Black Cabinet.* The purpose seems to have been to get Negroes of distinguished stature so that the populace would believe in the board. Theobald regularly met in private with this group, with the understanding that they would furnish him with information about conditions in ghetto communities, while he would maneuver some desegregation measures through the board. Open Enrollment was worked out in part through this group, though Reverend Galamison's threat of a citywide boycott was what really forced the board to put it into operation.

However, the influence of the Black Cabinet waned rapidly after 1961. The new board expressed its disapproval of Theobald's continuing to meet with that group, and many militants. within the Negro movement began to feel that Theobald was using the group to keep the lid on protest while mandating only the most limited reforms. Soon, Theobald himself was out of favor with his board and was encouraged to resign by a coalition of the board, moderate groups who felt threatened by his gestures toward desegregation and negotiation with Negro leaders, and professionals. The final incident involved the building of his private boat by students in a vocational high school, but he had been maneuvered out well before.

If Jansen was an insider, Theobald was a political outsider who was at least more sensitive to the need for change than his predecessor. But Theobald couldn't mandate many changes, and he never won the respect of his board. Max Rubin, the incoming president, met with Theobald daily to go over all key policy and administrative matters, reflecting the lack of confidence Rubin and his board had in Theobald.

Gross. In 1962, the lay board looked for an outsider to replace Theobald, on the assumption that he would be more receptive to innovation and better able to withstand the resistance of the vested interests than somebody from inside the system. This reform board felt they had the perfect opportunity to push the system forward with an outside superintendent.[45] In theory they were right, while in fact, they could not have been more wrong.

Several circumstances contributed to Gross's failure to mandate innovations. A few top insiders were angry about being passed over for the position; all the professional groups were skeptical and distrustful of an outsider; and the lay board had

* See Chapter One for a discussion of the Black Cabinet.

become used to dealing with administrative problems and was not willing to relinquish the powers it had accumulated since 1961. In addition, there was the threat of a school boycott and a teachers' strike for September, 1963, when Gross was to begin his duties.

The position clearly demanded a person with more political and administrative astuteness and bargaining and leadership skills than Gross had. It was essential that the superintendent have the ability to mobilize a broad-based consensus, given the factional politics of the board and the city. He would have to strengthen the superintendency and the system by reaching some understandings with the lay board on his authority; he would have to cajole professionals into supporting innovations that they would inevitably resist; and he would have to gain wide, community-based support. Gross was unable to do any of these things. He never took the board or civic leaders into his confidence, and he completely lost the support of his professional staff. Some headquarters officials feel that he never had it to begin with.

The job demands educational vision as well. The New York City school system, like all other big-city systems, was confronted with many social and demographic changes that demanded organizational, curriculum, staffing, and instructional reforms. It needed an educational leader who could formulate new programs to adapt to these changes. In educational expertise, Gross came especially well recommended: he had instituted many new programs in Pittsburgh for ghetto pupils, and worked effectively with foundations to secure financial support for such programs. But he couldn't use these skills in New York City because of political and administrative problems. Gross was quoted as saying in a private meeting, when told of the sabotage by principals of his Free Choice Transfer Plan: "In Pittsburgh, when I gave an order, it was carried out. Why doesn't that happen here?" [46]

Gross's problems began the day he arrived. The three top officials at headquarters had reportedly expressed the view that they should have had his job. Bernard Donovan, whom Gross immediately appointed as executive deputy superintendent, had been one of the board's top choices, but they did not select him because they felt that an outsider with more educational credentials and a national reputation might do a better job.* Both Donovan and Dr. John King, the system's top Negro, indicated to the board and their colleagues that they were looking for other positions. Dr. Joseph Loretan, deputy superintendent in charge of curriculum and instruction, also felt that he should have been appointed, since he was the best trained educator of the three. Loretan made numerous references to Gross's lack of ability at private meetings with board professionals.†

Gross's own administrative style and political strategy also hurt him. He had what board members referred to as "extreme sensitivities" about the powers and prerogatives of the superintendent.[47] He laid down a number of rules to establish a strong superintendent system. However, they served to undermine him more rapidly than if he had been willing to give the board more powers and to take it into his confidence. He seemed to distrust the board as one of his main adversaries, although most board members claimed they only wanted him to work with them to move the entire institution toward more reform. Since Gross, as an outsider, had so few allies, he made a tactical error in refusing to work with his board.

Gross did this because he felt that lay boards should not encroach on the professional prerogatives of superintendents.[48] This couldn't work in New York City, where the superintendent was so weak politically that he needed all the allies he could muster, especially from the group that was legally empowered to make policy for the system. Initially, most board members seemed willing to compromise with him on many issues, because they were insecure about their own political posi-

---

* One might question the wisdom of appointing as "crown prince" a man who was passed over. When a new top executive takes over, in most large organizations, there is a purging of officials from the old order. Co-option may not work under such circumstances.

† A further example of the power conflicts: from May, 1964 through December, Gross met regularly with civil rights leaders to discuss the implications of the Allen Report for junior high and high school desegregation. Bernard Donovan was not present at those meetings, after the first few sessions. He was, however, working as the chairman of a headquarters committee formulating its own recommendations for junior high and high school reorganization. In late December, shortly before Gross was to announce his own recommendations, Donovan reported out those of his committee. They were for little change, justifying the existing 6–3–3 grade organization and warning against any change that would alter this arrangement. The next day, Gross appeared on television to announce his commitment to a four-year comprehensive high school.

tions, and would have supported Gross had he worked more closely with them.*

One of Gross's first actions was to inform both his board and professional staff that any communications they had with one another could take place only through him. He was wary of any possible attempts by his staff to undercut him by going straight to the board, and was equally afraid that board members would undermine him by cultivating informal ties with his staff, thus intruding into his authority. Gross was in an admittedly difficult situation, as an outsider in a highly political organization. However, in attempting to establish his own power base by working alone, he alienated many potential allies.

Gross undermined himself rather quickly, creating the very conditions he most feared. One board member who was sympathetic toward Gross remarked: "Because of his rule about staff members only communicating with us through him, and his lack of accessibility to most of us, his desk was piled so high that it looked like a big cargo had been dumped on him. He started complaining about the demands and work load of a superintendent in this system. Even his own staff, after a while, couldn't get through to him."

Gross's relations with his top staff and with the lay board indeed became strained.[49] Some of his staff could not get in to see him for important business. The lay board had almost no relationship with him at all. They did try to interfere in administration, but only after he bypassed them and failed to follow through on their requests. Informal alliances did develop between the board and the professional staff, but mainly to fill a leadership vacuum. Headquarters and field sabotage of efforts by the superintendent and lay board to innovate, especially on desegregation, did continue.

The communication breakdown became so complete that Gross left town for several weeks without submitting a capital and expense budget, which then had to be presented in his absence at Board of Estimate hearings. "Gross was extremely difficult to reach in times of crises," said a top headquarters official. "Landers, Donovan . . . couldn't reach him. They

---

* A public controversy between Gross and his board in which he demanded a higher salary and more fringe and pension benefits reportedly helped turn them against him after he had been in New York City less than a year.

didn't know what he was thinking. There was never a sense of any relationship with Gross. Nobody felt any contact. You couldn't see him. You invite disaster when your staff can't get to see you."

Gross developed a number of strategies for responding to his board, staff, and civic groups. He tended to agree with his board's requests in personal encounters, but then did not initiate the proposals. Sometimes he would follow through in ways that were contrary to their requests and understandings with him, as illustrated by the expense budget he drew up in late fall, 1964, for the following year. Although the board requested that he come up with a decentralization plan that would pare down the headquarters bureaucracy, Gross's expense budget had provisions to expand it. In an unprecedented move, board member Joseph Barkan, a businessman and accountant, released to the press a sharp critique of Gross's budget, communicating clearly the lay board's general disenchantment.[50]

Gross handled the problem of desegregation in the same way that he tried to cope with other questions. His first major action was in August, 1963, when he and his top professional staff wrote a report on the board's progress toward desegregation, in response to State Education Commissioner Allen's request of May, 1963, to every school board throughout the state for an ethnic census and projection of plans to redress racial imbalance.

The correspondence between Gross and Allen that summer indicated Gross's reaction to the request. Gross asked Allen numerous questions calling for further clarification. He wanted to know if Allen really expected that by a given date there would be an end to de facto segregation in New York City; that the neighborhood school concept should be dropped; that the school system should set up a program for compulsory bussing of white children into Negro neighborhoods; and that all schools that were 50% or more Negro should be closed. The questions indicated that Gross and his top advisers did not believe that Allen could have meant the request to be taken seriously, that they thought desegregation was not possible in New York City.

The report of August, 1963, reflected Gross's disinterest in complying with Allen's demands.[51] It was written by Gross's top advisors, though he had to take responsibility as superintendent. His board was never consulted before the report was sent on to Allen, although as the system's main policy makers they had to assume ultimate responsibility on the issue.

The report was a repetition of old programs—for example, Open Enrollment and Higher Horizons, neither of which had contributed to either desegregation or upgrading ghetto schools. Like many board reports, it was a product of a small committee that rewrote old reports and included as much public relations rhetoric as seemed likely to satisfy groups protesting on all sides.

Gross was then attacked from all sides. The lay board resented his not taking it into his confidence on such a highly contested issue that involved basic policy matters. Civil rights groups rejected it as a "do-nothing" statement and started preparing for a school boycott, and lower middle class white parent groups started growing restive about the prospects of the board's expanding Open Enrollment and mandating pairings. Gross and his staff produced another report in December, but it contained few new plans and violated in all major respects the September agreement that it include a timetable, be citywide in scope, and go beyond voluntary measures. Furthermore, it too was written without consulting the lay board.

During the fall, Board President Rubin prevailed upon Mayor Wagner to provide the board with sizeable funds for desegregation and called an executive session, with Gross included, to discuss these transactions. Rubin was stunned when Gross announced that he had gone to Wagner himself, after developing a plan with his top advisor, Dr. John King. Rubin asked Gross why he had not consulted with the board before going to Wagner. The same could of course have been asked of Rubin in relation to Gross.

When the December report was released, the board was again outraged that it had not been consulted, but it issued a public statement supporting Gross and the report. When civil rights groups rejected the report for not including the agreed-upon criteria, and announced their intention to conduct a citywide boycott in early February, the lay board undercut Gross publicly and denounced his report, developing their own.[52]

Gross then left the city for the West Coast and was gone for several weeks. Some board members beseeched him to evaluate and endorse publicly their plan before he left, but he refused to do so. He was away during the peak of the controversy and past the time of the first boycott. The New York City press reported that he had given a public address to school administrators in Los Angeles on the eve of the boycott, although he was supposed to be convalescing from pneumonia. Gross apparently felt that the board had got itself into the desegregation crisis and after criticizing him they could not expect him to get them out of it.

In April, 1964, theNew York State Board of Regents called a conference at Greystone Mansion in Riverdale, New York, for a review by educators and social scientists of northern school desegregation trends. One purpose of the conference was to explore New York City's problems, and Gross was asked to give his views. At first he turned down the invitation, but he was prevailed upon to attend. Early in the conference, one of the chairmen turned to Gross and asked him to comment on the prospects for desegregation in New York City. He told the assembled group that his advisers had suggested to him that this problem had been brought on New York City, not by the school professionals, but rather by the lay board itself, going on to suggest that it was their problem and they would have to handle it. He was reportedly taking a position urged on him by top board professionals, who were his advisers.[53]

This position was inconsistent with Gross's interest in establishing a strong superintendency. Actually he wanted to preserve his prerogatives as superintendent, except on highly controversial issues, and then he was willing and even eager to abdicate responsibility to his board.

Gross was challenged after he finished his short summary of the New York City situation. One participant at the conference suggested to Gross that the press had given the impression that he was in favor of only a quality program for ghetto schools and did not want to move ahead on desegregation. Two editorials in the *New York Times* in late 1963 and early 1964 referred to a "saturation" program that Gross claimed he was developing for ghetto schools. Gross never answered the question.[54]

In May, 1964, the Allen Committee released its desegregation report on the New York City schools. As if to indicate his displeasure with the report's sweeping recommendations, Gross issued his own plan to the press a few days later. When civil rights groups rejected his plan—popularly called the Gross

Blueprint—and embraced the Allen Report, Gross accepted the latter.[55]

Gross then conducted a series of private negotiating sessions with civil rights leaders from May through December, for the purpose of coming to some agreements about specific plans the board could implement, but little came of the meetings, which were his last major activity. When they had petered out and he still delayed in coming up with any decentralization or desegregation plan, the board decided to dismiss him. While his meetings with civil rights leaders were still going on, the board had been hesitant to dismiss him, for fear that such an act might be interpreted as indicating their displeasure at his desegregation views or at his attempt to negotiate. They actually dismissed him because of their general dissatisfaction, and not for his views on desegregation. But they were especially disappointed that he did nothing on decentralization.

Gross's inactions on the problems that were plaguing the schools were a product of his own ineffective strategies and of the many pressures he faced. While he did not attack the major issues confronting the system, he showed a complete lack of confidence in his board, thus turning them against him. Since they had the authority to dismiss him, such a strategy made little sense. Gross's only way to maintain his position would have been to mobilize a strong coalition to support him, but he never attempted it. A statement released by the Council of Supervisory Associations in April, 1964, opposed Gross's desegregation plans and criticized him for not exchanging ideas with them or keeping them informed. Gross might have looked for support from the moderates and civil rights groups, but he never courted the moderates, and his contact with civil rights groups failed.

Every time Gross met with resistance, he reaffirmed a posture of trying to be above politics and preserving his professional autonomy, but this got him into many difficulties and weakened his position. His final public statement condemned the board for encroaching on his professional domain, and for intruding crass political considerations into the administration of the schools. This indicated how far removed from the political realities of the city he was. The fact was that he had taken on a supremely political job, had consistently not handled it as such, provided little leadership, and got himself fired. Of course, he inherited enormous problems and was confronted by many people within the professional staff who wanted to oust him. Even if Gross had been a more astute political strategist, this would have placed a heavy burden on him and seriously limited his capacity to manage the system.

Furthermore, the lay board was no more committed to change on desegregation than Gross, and its strong anti-integration faction, led by James Donovan, had serious doubts about going beyond Open Enrollment. Many of the charges they made against Gross, such as procrastination, inaction, failure to come up with a plan and to show leadership in developing a coalition could equally be made against them.

Donovan. A comparison between the performances of Calvin Gross and Bernard Donovan, his successor, is a good test of the proposition that the superintendency of the New York City schools is a weak position that precludes much possibility for innovation. There are substantial differences between Gross and Donovan in background, training, outlook, experience, and political and administrative skills. Yet, neither was effective in mandating needed innovations. Both were engaged in dealing with numerous crisis situations and never had time to embark on any significant planning and reform.

Calvin Gross was handicapped by being an outsider and by not having the necessary political and administrative skills, but this cannot be said for his successor. One might argue that it is too soon to judge Donovan's performance, since he is still in office at the time of this writing and may yet shake the system loose from its inertia. I feel, however, that he has had enough time to demonstrate that he cannot implement any innovations on the key problems of the system. If Donovan is incapable of mandating major changes, perhaps nobody can, for he has many political and administrative skills and knows the system and New York City politics well.

Donovan had served in the system for more than thirty years before he was appointed superintendent in March, 1965, having come up through the ranks. He had been acting superintendent the year before Gross came, had previously served as associate and executive deputy superintendent, and had held a top position in the school construction field, one of the most central and sensitive spots in the entire organization.[56] He was also familiar with New York City politics, having served on the advisory board of several city agencies and developed working relationships with various Catholic, professional, and parent groups. The only segment of the populace he had few contacts with were the civil rights and white liberal groups. Of great importance was the fact that the high school division regarded him very highly, and they were one of the groups that had given Gross so much trouble on desegregation.

The lay board and officials at the State Education Department were optimistic about Donovan's capacity to run the system when he took office. Though he had strong ties to conservative Catholic interests and to many inside professional groups who had resisted reforms, it was widely believed that he would favor more innovation as superintendent.

However, the results of his first three years in office give no indication that Donovan is more able to move the system toward desegregation and basic administrative reorganization than was Gross. By early 1967, there had been some sign of innovation on decentralization and budgetary questions, but this is related to strong pressures from Mayor Lindsay, who gives every indication that unlike Robert Wagner, his predecessor, he will intervene in educational policy matters.[57]

Gross had made no progress at all on decentralization. When Donovan became superintendent, there was hope that plans that had stalled in their implementation would finally be revived. But in the next two and a half years, little decentralization took place. Following two hearings in June, 1965, and a brief statement by the board of its preliminary plans, there was to be an increased delegation of authority to district superintendents and an elimination of divisional offices at headquarters, but this did not take place.[58] Had the mayor, the Ford Foundation, universities, and civic groups not become increasingly involved in decentralization, and had the IS 201 incident and other controversies over community participation not taken place, the board and Donovan would probably have done little to decentralize. By 1968, they have begun to institute three demonstration projects and have some general plans on paper for the entire system, but the pace of change is slow and its scope is limited.* Considering the inefficiency of implementation in the past, there is no reason to expect that Donovan alone will be able to depart significantly from this pattern, unless he has strong political support.†

---

* Donovan may have had little choice on the decentralization projects, so great was community pressure. And when the local school board of Lower Manhattan asked that Dr. Elliot Shapiro, nationally known former

Principals, for example, were still reporting to a divisional office at headquarters in 1967, although divisional offices were supposed to have been abolished two years before. Principals and district superintendents are still hesitant, in 1968, to innovate without securing headquarters clearance. Divisional offices and bureaus at headquarters still function as focal points in the flow of communications and influence, and information sifts through their functionaries selectively.[59]

The progress toward desegregation was almost nonexistent in late 1967, and it is still nonexistent. Donovan became superintendent just when the board developed its policy statement to implement the Allen Report. Two key recommendations were for four-year middle schools, to be built in fringe areas where practicable, and for four-year comprehensive high schools. The comprehensive high school concept had wide support from civic groups, though not from neighborhood school groups or the UPA. The four-year middle school was acceptable even to the UPA, although local parent organizations did not want them located in fringe areas.

Even on a preliminary basis, Donovan has not been successful in implementing these two concepts, although they have some civic support. Both vocational and academic high school principals associations have a vested interest in preserving the structure the way it is, as do the middle class parents in UPA who want to maintain control over the élite high schools, and both have contributed substantially to the delays.[60] Donovan is caught in the cross fires between these groups and the ones who

---

Harlem principal, be their district superintendent, Donovan initially turned down the request. One reason Donovan gave was that Shapiro, whose community relations probably surpassed those of any New York City principal over the past seventy years and who has become a legendary figure in Harlem, did not have the required courses in community relations. Donovan later reversed his decision under pressure, and Shapiro took some community relations credits.

† Superintendent Donovan generally favors decentralization and is looking to future reforms. The following incident is revealing: Just after the Bundy Report (McGeorge Bundy's report to Mayor John Lindsay) on decentralization was released, Bundy himself was invited to present his staff's ideas to the top administrators in the system, at a week-end retreat in Sterling Forest in New York State. One person present reported: "Bundy got the kicking around that he and everybody else expected, given the resentment of most of the New York City school administrators toward change. But the next day Donovan really gave it to them and knocked their heads together, telling them that they had better do something fast or they'd all be in trouble."

want reforms, though his own committee's report of late 1964 came out against comprehensive high schools.

Donovan has an additional problem on this issue, resulting from his strained relations with the high school principals. He had come up through the ranks as a "high school man" and always had the support of this group, until the fall of 1966. "The high school principals decided to make a test case at Forest Hills High School of this long hair business," related an inside informant, "and the principal there wouldn't let some of the long-haired boys in regular classrooms. Bernie was supposed to back the principal, but he had outside pressures telling him not to, and he refused to do so. Since then, high school principals and others have been down on him for not taking them into his confidence and consulting with them on what he wanted to do." [61] One might agree that the high school principals exhibited limited professionalism here.

Middle schools are being planned for three as well as four grades, and most of them are scheduled for construction and zoned in a way that maintains or increases segregation. The board has concluded that the city has only two types of subcommunities—segregated white and Negro–Puerto Rican areas, and transitional integrated areas that will soon tip, and it therefore builds few schools in integrated areas in an attempt to stabilize them. Donovan has not countered this view. [62]

When the board was criticized by civic groups and conservative councilmen at a 1967 Board of Estimate hearing on its capital budget for its integration program, Donovan announced that if the 4–4–4 system did not work out, the board could convert back to the old system. He said that all the proposed middle schools were only experimental and for only three grades. "This is just an approach," he said, "and if we find that it is not what we want, we can convert back to the old system. We will still be able to use the new buildings, and the size of the intermediate schools is 1,800, which is the same as the present junior high school, so it will be easy to convert." Because of the increase in strength of segregationist, neighborhood school sentiments, in the Negro as well as white populations, Donovan felt obliged to modify his remarks to suit the political climate that confronted him.

Donovan has taken the same stand on educational parks. There is no plan to develop parks throughout the city, nor are the two projects the board has proposed actual parks as that concept is defined. At the same Board of Estimate hearing, Donovan testified: "We will have to look into the tremendous costs of bussing in regard to educational parks, but now we have no plans for another park, besides the one in Co-op City, and we are reviewing the transportation costs." [63]

I believe that the same interests that blocked Gross have also inhibited Donovan from pressing for innovations. Although Donovan is more highly regarded by the professionals than Gross was, he is ultimately as constrained by them. As superintendent, he has had to accommodate to a much wider circle of publics than he did earlier, and any progressive positions he may want to take may alienate him from the professionals, too. Despite all his skills, Donovan has been little more successful in mobilizing a consensus around new ideas than Gross.[64]

The authority and powers of the superintendency in the New York City school system are simply too limited for him to play a decisive leadership role. He must spend so much time meeting with various interest groups, tending to particular crisis situations, and playing a purely public relations role, that he has little time to think. This is not to say that the superintendent is bereft of all authority. He can use the power of his office to formulate and issue new programs, but he cannot enforce their acceptance among the professionals.

However, the superintendent may be able to define some innovations as administrative matters and maneuver limited reforms. Theobald did this with Open Enrollment and transfer plans for better utilization, but this was only instituted after mounting civil rights protests, a threat of a citywide boycott, numerous recommendations from the board's own Commission on Integration, and orders from Wagner that the plans be instituted.

Gross did this on a Free Choice Transfer Plan in June, 1964. Civil rights leaders pushed him into mandating this plan by asking him straight out why he couldn't define it as an administrative question. He was sensitive on this issue, since he had been battling with his board on his prerogatives. His professional staff was amazed when he announced to civil rights leaders that he had all the authority he needed to mandate such a plan.

Gross was soon removed, though. If the superintendent uses what little power he has, he gets stopped before he can carry out his plans. Neither his personal ideology nor his past experience as a school administrator seem to affect the outcome. Theobald and Gross, who came in as outsiders, were as constrained as the insiders Jansen and Donovan.

There are some features of the superintendent's position that transcend the characteristics of individual men, and contribute to their incapacity to innovate. The superintendent is always in conflict with his board, and must negotiate with them in distinguishing between administrative and policy issues. He must face power blocs within the system that will try to thwart him. He must always work within a centralized bureaucracy with notoriously poor communications internally and little coordination of activities, leading to inefficiencies in implementation.* He must rely on his inside experts, who tend to present their own limited and conservative judgments as facts and who do so to preserve their own tenuous position.

The superintendent cannot make any changes without communicating with local schools and districts. He requires data on local conditions before deciding upon the desirability of certain innovations. Later, he must be provided with evaluations and measurements of how well the programs were implemented. Virtually all the information he does get from the field is filtered before it reaches him, because principals and district superintendents often distrust headquarters. They resent its lack of responsiveness to their requests, its tendency to mandate changes without adequately consulting them, and its general posture of insulation from field problems. They are also anxious about transfers and promotions.

The superintendent's powers to effect change are thus constrained by his limited communications with the field. Principals and district superintendents who felt their schools would be downgraded by desegregation might sabotage plans in a manner not visible to headquarters. For example, a principal in a mid-Bronx elementary school had never explained the Free Choice Transfer Plan of June, 1964, to parents. When some found out, they went to their district superintendent, who had encouraged their taking such grievances to him. He claimed

* See Chapter Eight for a more extended discussion of the professional bureaucracy and its many power blocs.

to have passed on word to headquarters but in fact withheld this information for two months—which disqualified the pupils involved from transferring. When headquarters was finally informed, they sent a person from the Human Relations Unit to speak with the principal, but this took place long after the deadline for applying for transfers.[65]

The superintendent has to mobilize support from civic groups as well as from his professional staff and board to endorse particular programs. Schisms and factions would soon develop within their ranks, even if the superintendent were willing to align himself with reform groups, as Gross's experience confirmed.* Of course, the civil rights movement might not have become so divided if he had shown any signs of being able to innovate. But even if civil rights groups were united, Gross would have had to win over the moderates and placate the neighborhood school movement.

Thus, a superintendent in the New York City school system, like his counterparts elsewhere, is surrounded by pressures. Even if he were able to mobilize a coalition endorsing change, the numerous routine tasks and crisis situations he confronts make it difficult for him to develop long-range plans. Years of neglect of the problems in minority schools, and the rising expectations of all citizens as to what the public schools should be doing, make him a target for more demands than he or his staff can handle. The superintendent is forced into conducting a chronic holding action.

But this is not inevitable. If the board and superintendent were willing and staffed to maintain open communications throughout the city, they would be informed of trouble spots before they boil over. Part of the reason for the increased community agitation has been that most low income minority groups have been unable to secure a hearing and impartial handling of their grievances. The board had always operated as a highly insulated institution.

Paradoxically, if the board and superintendent maintained freer communications with all citizen groups, they could then devote more of their energies to long-range planning and to mobilizing support for new programs. While the board and superintendent are right in saying that community pressures move them from crisis to crisis and that short-run problems

* See Chapter Four.

take up much of their time, they are wrong in assuming, as many of them do, that this limitation on their capacity for longer-range planning is something they cannot control.

Conflicts and Ambiguities in the Superintendent—Lay Board Relationship

The limited authority and power of the board and superintendent are compounded by the fact that there is much conflict and ambiguity in their relationship. The conflict reached its greatest intensity in relations between Gross and his board, especially between Gross and Board President James Donovan. This helped stalemate all board programs, including desegregation. Many board members now point to Gross as having delayed all their plans for innovation, but many of the tensions that divided Gross from his board and James Donovan had existed before and continue to exist under Bernard Donovan's superintendency. Struggles for power and conflicts over prerogatives have not abated, and it seems that there are ambiguities and strains built into their relationship regardless of the personalities involved.

Theoretically, the lay board, as a citizen "watchdog" body, is responsible for making policy, while the superintendent and his staff are responsible for administration. It is difficult in many instances, however, to draw a line between policy and administration, and some boards, in an attempt to ensure that their general policies are put into effect, get into administration. The professional staff finds them obtrusive and may then refuse to give out certain information. They may also sabotage the lay board in their implementation of programs. And the superintendent may simply veto some board proposals or suggest that they involve administrative matters. Gross reportedly did this in a more passive way by informally acquiescing to board requests in private meetings and then not acting on them. Donovan is much more direct and tells his board outright when he feels they are encroaching on his authority.

Any superintendent with a sense of professional competence would find it disturbing to be designated merely as "implementer" of policies set down by a board that is made up of laymen with little technical expertise and is subject to a variety of political pressures. There is every indication that Gross felt this way.

The degree of conflict between superintendents and boards

may be largely a function of how they define their roles. Lay boards may see themselves as playing either a fiduciary or managerial role. Superintendents, in turn, may view themselves as agents and subordinates of their board, as a senior colleague of teachers and supervisors, or as a specialist in school administration. There has been little complementarity in role definitions in the New York City school system, and this may well be a pattern common to many large cities. The board wants to play an active role in administration, while the superintendent does not always see himself as their subordinate.[66]

At crucial points in the desegregation controversy, when the mobilization of civil rights groups created a promising atmosphere for change, the conflict between the superintendent and board increased, and contributed substantially to board inaction. The pattern is evident from the time of the previous superintendency of Dr. John Theobald, when the desegregation issue started to become highly contested, to the present.

Theobald had many fights with his board over high-level appointments, desegregation, and what he regarded as their constant attempt to usurp power and take over administration. He especially objected to their use of committees and "confidential secretaries," essential devices through which the board kept itself informed. Confidential secretaries were private research and administrative assistants, but were untrained in research, education, or administration. The principle of the board's having its own staff was sound, but the limited qualifications of its confidential secretaries left the board open to justifiable criticism. Though having its own staff was the only way the board could have any independent source of information and expertise, all superintendents since Jansen have interpreted such a watchdog tactic as an unwarranted intrusion on their autonomy and authority.

Theobald, as an experienced politician, was able to manipulate his board on some occasions, thereby temporarily enlarging his authority. His long experience in New York City politics gave him a number of contacts, which he used at opportune moments. Through his ties with the top officialdom in the Catholic Church, he was able to push through the appointments of Dr. John King and Dr. Bernard Donovan, although both were strongly opposed by some of his board members.[67]

Theobald's adoption of Open Enrollment, against the will of several board members, was another example of his capacity to maneuver. He was able to usurp power from the board by relegating Open Enrollment to the sphere of administration, presenting it as a plan for effecting a more efficient use of school facilities and therefore a more economical use of the educational tax dollar. Some board members saw Open Enrollment as a basic change in policy because it involved a departure from the neighborhood school tradition. One even threatened to have Theobald removed, but he was unable to mobilize the necessary support to do so.

The main issue, then, was who had what powers. Each side was strong enough to prevent the other from prevailing, but instead of a functional balance and separation of powers, a pattern of mutual stalemate predominated.

As a result, the board came under increasing attack. Mayor Wagner believed that it was important to keep outside politics out of education and supported the professionals, as did the State Education Department and moderate groups. The professionals had a powerful lobby in Albany to outmaneuver the board in power struggles that reached the legislative stage, aided by such organizations as the Public Education Association.

The issue of who should have what powers among the system's top decision makers has been the subject of many investigations.[68] Most studies recommended curbing the powers of the board and increasing those of the superintendent. They pointed out that the board was overburdened with administrative trivia that should be delegated to the professional staff. They also accurately noted that there was no clear distinction between the board's functions and those of the professionals, and they criticized the board for interfering in educational matters that were legitimately the province of the professionals. They failed to note, however, that many of the professionals were neither competent nor motivated to do an effective job (see the following chapter).

Because of the conflict among the board, the superintendent, and the professionals, and the increasing power of the latter, the New York City school system gradually evolved into a cluttered and leaderless institution. It did not matter who held top positions, because the system was increasingly geared to undermine their power, authority, and effectiveness.

A key event in deteriorating superintendent–board relations was the removal of the lay board in 1961, after construction scandals in which the entire lay board was suspected of corruption and political meddling.* The removal of the board was followed closely by the departure of Superintendent Theobald. Neither change was much more than a changing of the guard, and they did little to alter the distribution of power at the board, since it had long since left the top leadership.

The lay boards that served in the 1950s were considered strong. They had close ties to the city administration and knew their way through the complexities of New York City politics. In fact one of the reasons given for the removal of Charles Silver's board in 1961 was that it had become too strong and was threatening professional groups and their supporters in state education and political circles. The charges of corruption had much support, but a big issue was also made of the fact that this board was seen as meddling too much in matters that should have been under the jurisdiction of the superintendent and his staff.[69]

The new board that took office in late 1961 included a number of distinguished and civic-minded people. It came in as a reformist and progressive board that was advised to avoid outside interference, not to intrude their own politics into the school system, and to move it toward needed innovations. Many liberal members of the board saw their mission as dealing primarily with problems of poverty.

At this time, the school system was in bad repute, and had been declared in a state of crisis by the State Board of Regents, so the city board inherited a heavy burden.[70] With the exception of their president, Max Rubin, who had previous board experience in Great Neck, Long Island, this board was, in the words of one of its most prominent members, "as green as could be."

Despite the fact that the old board was criticized for meddling too much in administration, the new board had no intention of letting the professionals make key decisions. Their first major action was to encourage Theobald to leave, because they were convinced that he was a weak superintendent. They joined forces with other interests to effect his resignation, and they then tried to solidify their power base so that badly needed changes might get underway.†

* Mayor Wagner removed the board, on the strong advice of Dr. Frederick McGlaughlin of PEA, who disagreed with some of Wagner's other advisers.

† Several school officials and board members recounted these events.

To ensure that they would not become victimized like their predecessors by inside professional interests, they decided to recruit the next superintendent from outside the system and eventually settled on Gross. In the year before he arrived many board members felt they had started to consolidate their position and were ready to mobilize the system. They began moving into administration in ways similar to those that caused the removal of the former board. "I must say in all fairness," a board member recalled, "that the board got spoiled in that period, as we moved into administration in a much bigger way, convinced as Max Rubin and the rest of us were that Theobald was only temporary. After he did leave, we were used to certain kinds of controls that we weren't going to give up that easily." This set the stage for their later conflicts with Gross.

Though Rubin believed strongly in the importance of separating policy from administration and told his board that they should follow this dictum, he took over single-handedly many administrative duties, demonstrating the board's general lack of confidence in Theobald.[71] He made almost superhuman attempts to redirect the system from its flagging course, and still was unable to do so—which indicates how weak the top decision makers at the board had become.

Gross had no intention of letting the board go on as it had before, and this led to conflict almost from the day he arrived. His relationship with the board then deteriorated so markedly that in early 1964, the board decided to hold a private meeting, outside the city, and without his presence, to formulate a strategy. One member suggested that two of them should meet privately with Gross and speak candidly about their disappointments over his performance and his tendency to resist working with them.

That meeting with the two board members took place at Gross's home. They felt that he took their criticisms well and seemed to indicate a willingness to work more closely with them. However, subsequent events indicated little change in their relationship.

Shortly after the meeting, Gross and his board came into direct public confrontation. The board insisted that they "have special assistants working to deal in depth with situations as they arise." The *Times* carried a report of a five-hour meeting of the board and Gross, which was held in an effort "to resolve a dispute over school administration." [72] A few weeks later, the board issued another press release indicating their dissatisfaction with Gross's performance on decentralization and desegregation.

The conflict between Gross and the board pertained less to ideological differences than to a struggle over his authority. Neither he nor the majority of board members were in favor of more than limited desegregation measures. They agreed that non-voluntary desegregation plans were not politically feasible, and doubted the educational merits of such plans.

Their conflict did, however, affect the course of the desegregation controversy, contributing to long delays in making decisions and increased buck passing. Gross and his staff often told civil rights leaders that they were ready to move but were waiting for a policy statement from the board. He would then explain his inaction by saying that "a study is being done on that now," or "a committee is looking into it." When civil rights leaders went to the board, they would be told that Gross had failed to produce the studies and data that they needed before deciding policy.

Each side vacillated on the question of what its appropriate role should be on desegregation. Gross saw community protest as a direct result of the board's failure to exert leadership, a view he took over from his top advisers, and justifying his decision not to take the responsibility for a problem he had not created. He thus abdicated responsibility, despite his sensitivities about his prerogatives as superintendent, but he would not let the board take complete authority on the issue either.

In April, 1964, when it became apparent to Gross that his position in the system was tenuous, he started to assume leadership on desegregation. Apparently he realized that establishing an alliance with civil rights groups might be one of the only ways he could build a coalition and keep his job. When Gross was asked why he had not told the board about the first meeting he called, or invited them to attend, he replied: "It would be very weak of me, indeed, if I felt it necessary to check with the president of the board and the whole board before establishing such a meeting." Gross's belief in the importance of breaking the stalemate on desegregation and thus improving his own position was sound. But it made no political sense to try it without including the board, and this action was doomed to defeat.[73]

Neither the board nor Gross knew who was ultimately responsible for formulating a desegregation plan, and since neither really wanted to do so, they blamed each other for inaction. The fact that desegregation was such an explosive issue contributed to this mutual failure of Gross and the board to work together on a common plan, as did Gross's sensitivities about his prerogatives and the personal conflicts between him and Board President James Donovan. Their personality clashes were certainly in evidence at numerous private meetings with state officials.*

However, one cannot dismiss situational factors—they affect all superintendent–board relations, and certainly are reflected in Bernard Donovan's relations with his board. Though Donovan handles his board more skillfully than Gross, the outcome is not substantially different in terms of their ability to effect change.

A few months after Donovan became superintendent, the board hired Harold Siegel, the former executive director of the United Parents Association, to act as liaison between the school system and community groups and between the board and the superintendent. This was done without consulting Donovan, and Siegel eventually hired three researchers who worked with him and the board in gathering information about the system. Donovan was understandably concerned that such appointments would undermine his authority, and reportedly informed the board that he was going to resign if there were the equivalent of two or three other quasi superintendents serving at its pleasure. The board accepted this, only to change Siegel's status to secretary of the board, and Siegel still has much informal power, because of his vast knowledge of the school system. He sometimes challenges Donovan's judgments on key matters.†

Donovan is a much more able and astute administrator–politician than his predecessors, and has taken over much power from the board. Many top headquarters officials and civic leaders have suggested that Donovan has been able to manipulate his board on key issues, as he has done on budgetary matters and on the allocation of federal funds to parochial schools. Yet, on most policy issues, as in the IS 201 incident and other controversies over decentralization, Donovan accedes to the board's final judgment. His conflicts with the board are less intense and less debilitating to the school system than were those between Gross and his board.

---

* Several people present at these meetings reported in detail on how Gross and Donovan argued at length before other people.

† Siegel still has a small research staff, though the original three people he had all left.

A main question for the future is how this superintendent–board relationship will evolve. One suggestion is that the board enlarge its own professional staff—the problems of big-city school systems are too complex and unmanageable for a board to understand without the assistance of a research staff—and change the superintendent's role solely to that of chief educational administrator, unequivocally responsible and subordinate to his board. The dual authority that now exists in practice would thus be replaced by a more unilateral authority, and there might be less buck passing than in the past. If the New York City school system does evolve in this direction, the difficulty will be in the superintendent's acceptance of such an arrangement. But such a change might well increase the resources of both parties to mandate innovations by forcing more coordination and harmony in their joint efforts.

One explanation for the New York City Board of Education's inertia and failure to innovate, then, is the limited authority and resources of the lay board and superintendent, and their tendency to dilute what authority they have in a power struggle. Another explanation is that the lay board and superintendent are involved in a complete reversal of roles. While the lay board is mandated to make policy and set general standards and guidelines, it is bogged down in administrative minutia. Meanwhile, the superintendent, who is supposed to carry out the board's policies as the chief administrator, moves into the leadership vacuum and takes on the policy-making role himself. The board is not entirely happy with such a situation, however, and it periodically makes an effort to prevent him from usurping such a policy role. A fuller analysis of the system's administration and internal politics must come from a close look at the resources and interests of those groups within the system who do have the power that the lay board and superintendent so sorely lack.*

* The New York City experiences raise a general question about the actual benefits of a board of education in its present form. It is in many respects an archaic and ancient institution. It was originally conceived to rid public education of politics in New York City, but why shouldn't the mayor have more power than he does? It's his city: he has the ultimate responsibility for how well the schools work. It was also meant to be a buffer between the schools and the citizens, but is it really that? When the policy makers spend all their time worrying about petty administrative details, are they making any contribution that low-level clerks couldn't make? And if not, why is it that all the state education laws and board by-laws that oblige board members to tend to such trivia have never been changed?

CHAPTER

VIII

❧

THE PROFESSIONAL BUREAUCRACY

School officials desperately need more explanations for their failures and more suggestions for reversing such failures than they have received thus far. Some are beginning to realize that time is running out on them, and that they had better reform the schools quickly before ghetto unrest leads to rioting, to demands to take over the schools, and the white middle class exodus contributes to the final downfall of big-city public education.

The temptation in diagnosing how the schools have failed is to search for scapegoats. Actually, the entire institution of public education is to blame, as are the present conditions of urban life that it confronts.

Nobody can make the system work if the bureaucratic structure is not radically altered. State education laws, traditions, rules, and interlocking administrative relationships victimize anybody who comes into contact with the system—parents with legitimate complaints, people applying for teaching licenses, city officials developing community renewal programs, publishers struggling to get their textbooks and readers into the classrooms even after the principals and teachers have accepted them, teachers and principals waiting months to receive needed supplies from headquarters, and pupils in the classrooms. To maneuver through the bureaucratic maze of the New York City school system takes more patience and political connections than most people can ever hope to have.

It is almost impossible to innovate in the institution. Policy statements are only the beginning of the process. Those who make the decisions, even if they were more eager for reform, must negotiate with the professional staff to secure compliance with their directives. They must secure efficient coordination of the actions of all units carrying out the plans, and they must provide rewards and punishments that will ensure compliance, institute performance measures, and evaluate how the plans actually worked. Legal and bureaucratic constraints, however, limit the power of the superintendent and the board over the headquarters and field staff, and reforms mandated from above are seldom carried out as they were intended.

Chester Barnard, a distinguished writer and theorist on administration, has noted that an order is never an order unless it is obeyed.[1] Barnard was pointing to a central component of administrative authority, namely, that it exists only when it is regarded as "legitimate" by those in subordinate positions.

A Model of Bureaucratic Pathology

The New York City school system is typical of what social scientists call a "sick" bureaucracy—a term for organizations whose traditions, structure, and operations subvert their stated missions and prevent any flexible accommodation to changing client demands. It has all those characteristics that every large bureaucratic organization has, but they have been instituted and followed to such a degree that they no longer serve their original purpose. Such characteristics as (1) overcentralization, the development of many levels in the chain of command, and an upward orientation of anxious subordinates; (2) vertical and horizontal fragmentation, isolating units from one another and limiting communication and coordination of functions; (3) the consequent development of chauvinism within particular units, reflected in actions to protect and expand their power; (4) the exercise of strong, informal pressure from peers within units to conform to their codes, geared toward political protection and expansion and ignoring the organization's wider goals; (5) compulsive rule following and rule enforcing; (6) the rebellion of lower-level supervisors against headquarters directives, alternating at times with overconformity, as they develop concerns about ratings and promotions; (7) increasing insulation from clients, as internal politics and personal career interests override interests in serving various publics; and (8) the tendency to make decisions in committees, making it difficult to pinpoint responsibility and authority are the institution's main pathologies.[2]

Such characteristics are exaggerations of a number of administrative patterns that may not be bad if they are not carried too far. In the New York City school system, however, they are carried to the point where they paralyze the system in the face of rapid social changes that demand new administrative arrangements and programs.

Though the term "bureaucracy" usually has negative connotations in popular usage, I am using it here in a neutral sense, referring simply to social patterns associated with large scale organizations. There can be "good" and "bad" bureaucracy, and much of my analysis of the New York City school system, using the social science model of bureaucratic pathology, will include examples of "bad" bureaucracy.

The school system is set up to function as a "professional" bureaucracy, manned by more than 59,000 teachers and several thousand administrators and technicians. But the term "professionalism" has been given so many meanings, especially in school–community controversies, that little meaningful communication any longer occurs when school officials and community groups try to resolve their differences.* If we use the term in its conventional sense to refer to a combination of expertise and service to clients, the bureaucratic structure of the New York City school system clearly undermines the professionalism of its personnel. Service to clients and to the community are often secondary considerations for school officials who are more preoccupied with their own careers.†

This is to suggest, then, that "bad" bureaucracy is often associated with "bad" professionalism in the New York City school system, as, indeed, it is in many large civil service

---

* The term has been used as a slogan by school officials to defend themselves against outside attack ("We are professionals, and you, as laymen, have no right to tell us what to do").

† Political scientist Victor Thompson observes in his *Modern Organizations*: "When officials are caught between demands or "rights" of clients and tight administrative controls from above, dissociation from the clients and disinterest in their problems may seem to be the only way out of the dilemma. Client hostility, generated by what appears to be official emphasis on the wrong goals, creates tension. Inconsiderate treatment of the clients may become a device for reducing tensions and maintaining the cohesion of the officials." *Modern Organization*, New York: Knopf, 1961, p. 162.

bureaucracies.[3] While it may be appropriate for teachers and supervisors to want a degree of autonomy from client pressures, as many professionals do, on grounds that they are better equipped to do the job of educating than laymen, they may use their autonomy for personal ends that do not include service to the community. Further, professionals who are protected from their clients are likely to be unaware of changes in their clients' needs. And bureaucratic pressures to follow particular curricula, texts, instructional methods, and administrative procedures, may prevent teachers and principals from actually educating. Bureaucracy and professionalism may be incompatible in the New York City schools.

If arresting the failure of the schools were just a question of revamping the bureaucracy, there might be more hope for improvement than there really is. But the situation is much more complex. The entire institution of public education, including teacher training, the professional associations, and the technology of teaching, contribute to the schools' failures. While teachers and principals may know more about education than most laymen, they don't know very much. There is no codified body of knowledge that educators can learn and apply, as there is in medicine and law. Teacher training institutions reflect this in their curriculum, which is based on questionable and unvalidated principles of education, learning, and child development. The fact that these institutions often disregard the rapid demographic and social changes of the city, incapacitates their graduates further. There is little expertise to apply, despite any myths to the contrary.

Furthermore, the quality of people who go into public education careers is not very high. The situation may well be changing, but traditionally education has attracted the mediocre students in the colleges, often of provincial, lower middle class outlook, a large proportion of whom were women marking time before getting married.* [4]

This combination of poor training and personal mediocrity is reflected in the limited confidence that many college edu-

---

* It is unlikely, however, that the situation will change that much, given the irrelevant and tedious education courses that are required for licensing and later promotions, and given the fact that New York City school teachers are at the mercy of the bureaucracy and given little autonomy and responsibility.

cated, upper middle class people have in the public schools. Many regard Board of Education personnel as culturally and intellectually inferior, and send their children to private schools.

One has only to review the frustrating and tragic experiences of the system's many victims to realize how bad it is. Consider the case of a Puerto Rican mother with two children in schools on Manhattan's West Side.[5] Anyone who cares to can collect hundreds of case histories like this one:

> In the 5th grade, Billy did not seem to me to be reading as well as he should. In the Spanish Mothers Club at the school, we asked if remedial help could be given. There was only one remedial reading teacher so that only a few children could be helped. Then the Club asked if Columbia students could help. In the meantime I took Billy to Columbia myself for reading assistance. In March I went to see the teacher to find out how Billy was doing. The teacher said "very well." He will soon be reading a 5th grade book. In May I received a letter from the Assistant Principal asking me to come to school about Billy. I was told that Billy could not go to the 6th grade because he was reading on a 3.0 level. I was very upset and angry because it seemed to me that the school had done nothing for Billy. He stayed in the 5th grade for another six months. We continued the tutoring but the school gave him no additional help. If I had not found a way to help him, nobody else would have helped him. He is now in 10th grade and still has a reading problem which hurts his other studies.

> When he went into the New York School of Printing, he needed algebra and science in order to take an academic program. The junior high school had told him that he would have an academic program. But when he got to high school, they refused to give it to him because he did not have these subjects. It was only through his and my persistence that they finally permitted him to take the academic program.

> In kindergarten, Grace could read Billy's first grade reader. When she went to the first grade, she never received a reader. When I asked the teacher why, she said that Grace wasn't ready yet. In the first half of second grade, she had a good teacher and books. In the second half, a new teacher came in. She did not give her much work. In the third grade, the teacher told me that she was a brilliant child and warned me to be careful. She feared that Grace might be hurt by other teachers. She tried to help her and told me to get her help at Columbia. . . . For 4th grade the teacher tried to have Grace put into a "good" class. She was not successful. Instead, she was put into a class where she fell behind—she read the same books she had read in the 3rd grade. When the 3rd grade teacher asked the 4th grade teacher why she was using the

same books, the 4th grade teacher became angry with Grace. In the 5th grade Grace seemed to do better. She had a teacher of Puerto Rican background and read 5th grade books. But in the 6th grade she tested at 4.6. The teacher did not give too much work. When I saw the teacher, he said Grace was "blocked." He seemed to feel it was because we spoke Spanish at home. In February, I noticed that Grace had nothing written in her notebook. She said that they were doing nothing in class. I spoke to the Assistant Principal about it. He looked at two notebooks from the class and saw that I was right. He was sorry about it but seemed to have no reason for it. I asked to have Grace's class changed. They asked me which class I wanted her in. I said a "good class" and they transferred her to a class with a teacher who taught. But this teacher told Grace that she didn't belong in her class. I told her not to worry and she remained in the class, where she did well. In March, the teacher in charge of a new program of teaching Spanish, asked Grace to take the program. Her 6th grade teacher said Grace could never make it. Grace insisted upon taking the program because she reads Spanish. She took the test for the program and passed it. She went on to the 7th grade even though her reading test showed a 4th grade level. She was never given any remedial reading in school.

She is now in the 9th grade and studies Spanish. Grace wants to be a teacher. We've been struggling not to make any mistakes so that she will be able to go to an academic high school. The junior high school wanted her to take General Math. She had to fight to get algebra. We knew enough to fight because of what happened to Billy and we won the fight.

WHY HAVE I HAD TO TAKE MY CHILDREN FOR OUT-SIDE HELP? AND WHY DO THEY HAVE TO FIGHT TO GET THE KIND OF EDUCATION THEY WANT? I HAVE LEARNED HOW TO PROTECT MY CHILDREN AND IT IS STILL BAD. BUT WHAT ABOUT THE THOUSANDS OF MOTHERS WHO DON'T KNOW WHAT IS HAPPENING TO THEIR CHILDREN IN THE SCHOOLS?

Bureaucratic Centralism

Many of the pathologies of the New York City school system can be traced to the overcentralization of decisions, combined with the proliferation of specialized administrative units. Most decisions on such matters as curriculum, staffing, budgeting, supplies, construction, and maintenance are made by professionals at central headquarters, several layers removed from the schools themselves.[6] The headquarters personnel who make decisions do not know the problems directly, while district superintendents, principals, and teachers who do have some direct knowledge have never had the authority to adjust, experiment, and innovate, though a few adventurous types have taken it upon themselves to run their schools or classrooms as they see fit, without reference to headquarters.

Like any large bureaucracy that has to establish generalized rules for its field units, the Board of Education has a system of formulas and applies programs to schools as the schools fit into particular classifications—special service, transitional, segregated Negro–Puerto Rican, mid-range, segregated white. The system does not take into account gradations within each category, and so it minimizes its flexibility and effective use and distribution of supplies and personnel. While it may be important for large bureaucracies like this one with so many field offices and operating units to categorize and generalize about situations, they do so here with disastrous results. The categorizations are too gross, and many local variations and problems are overlooked.[7]

The NYC Board of Education is thus the prototype of what students of administration call "top down" rather than "bottom up" management.[8] Instead of looking at the particular school and community (with particular ethnic, socio-economic groups, local resources and institutions) and saying "here is a school and community, now let's work with parent and community groups to set up an appropriate program," they say "here is a program, now let's see where it can go." Too many schools and communities have their own particular problems that do not fit into standard formulas and programs.

Originally there were valid administrative reasons for centralization—to guarantee uniform standards across the city, to preserve professional autonomy from outside political interference at the local level, to prevent ethnic separatism, and to maintain headquarters control over field officials.[9] Also, the sheer size and geographic spread of the system contributed to centralization. Many headquarters officials distrust field personnel and hesitate to delegate authority.

Another reason for centralization was the complexity of the social and psychological problems the system faced. Numerous agencies have been formed over the years—such as the Bureau of Child Guidance, the Bureau for Children with Retarded Mental Development, the Bureau of Physically Handicapped, the Bureau of Socially Maladjusted Children, the Bureau of Speech Improvement, the Bureau of Visually Handicapped, the Bureau of Community Education, the More Effective Schools Program, the Bureau of In-Service Training, the Offices of Zoning, Integration, and Human Relations to deal with these problems. These bureaus in themselves may be necessary, although they often may obstruct education.

The school budget has also led to increased centralization. The difficulties of getting allocations in the budget for more staff led to the practice of transferring more and more teachers to headquarters. Many were eager to escape the trials and stresses of the classroom and, in some cases, the authoritarian rule of the principal. This practice is now reportedly being reversed, but the net effect of the policy change is still limited. There are still nearly 700 teachers on assignment at headquarters, and federal programs will add to the number.[10] Many teachers at headquarters are engaged in tasks for which they are not trained, in auditing, business affairs, programming, human relations, and demographic analysis. There are also cases of teachers at headquarters who direct and monitor research studies, and some teachers perform jobs that could be done by a lower level clerical person. The existence of such headquarters positions helped drain away many competent people from the classroom, while contributing to incompetent and inefficient administration.*

The centralized set-up created other obstacles to efficient administration too. The grouping of units and personnel at headquarters violates many basic principles of rational administration, creating little unity of command, much duplication and overlapping of responsibilities, and confusion on who should report to whom.

Positions and tasks were simultaneously grouped along both divisional (elementary, junior high, high) and functional (curriculum, instruction, staffing) lines.[11] Field officials often receive numerous directives, some of them contradictory, from different sources. A publisher finds, for example, that his curriculum materials are welcomed by the board, the superintendent, and the divisions, yet they are not acceptable to some curriculum official who invokes a state education law to justify his authority. A music teacher wants to serve in a ghetto school, but instead gets assigned to a white, middle class school in Queens. When

---

* It may also be true, however, as many informants in the system suggested, that putting teachers into headquarters jobs was one of the few ways to unburden the classrooms of incompetents.

an opening appears in a southeast Bronx school, the Queens principal will not let her go, threatening to give her a bad rating if she leaves. When she goes to headquarters to plead her case before the deputy superintendent in charge of personnel, it takes her a day before she can reach his secretary, and she never does get to see him. Parents who go to headquarters to inquire about zoning regulations are often shunted from office to office without getting any clear answer to their requests.[12]

This pattern of multiple authority hampers the efforts of field personnel to integrate various programs, confronted as they often are with buckpassing when making requests at headquarters for information, facilities, and support. It results in considerable frustration in securing services and much resentment among community groups, local school board members, and field officials.*

Securing Services. In many experimental programs, most of which are in ghetto schools, there are long delays in securing textbooks and supplies.[13] Teachers report that they sometimes get supplies several months or a year late; if they want to receive them in time to coordinate them with their programs, they pay for them out of their own pockets.†

There is a special problem for teachers who want to experiment with new books. They are required to follow prepared

---

* These pathologies have all been discussed in the many management studies on the New York City school system. Consider the following: "The major problems in the functioning of the existing organization are lack of organizational clarity, multiple assignment of functions, and lack of assignment for some important and vital functions." (Cresap, McCormick, and Paget, 1962, chapter II, p. 16); "At present, communications within the school system contribute to considerable confusion. Field Assistant Superintendents, principals, and teachers complain about the plethora of memorandums, directives and requests, some of them conflicting, which flow from many different organizational units." (Cresap, McCormick, and Paget, *op. cit.,* chapter II, p. 18).

† A recent study on the Bureau of Supplies by the UPA documents these points well. They found that it frequently took a year, and sometimes up to four years, to deliver supplies requisitioned by the NYC schools. They cited the following illustrations: "In one school movable blackboards ordered for a team-teaching project arrived 2½ years later. In another school, 1,500 library books lay unused because there were no shelves in the library on which to place them. When a school sent a letter to the supply bureau requesting certain order forms, the bureau replied that these forms could not be requested by letter, but had to be requisitioned on a form that the school did not have." (*New York Times,* March 6, 1968, p. 30.)

book lists that are sometimes out of date, and requests for new books are often turned down for unexplained reasons. A music teacher in an élite high school asked the assistant principal to permit her to order some new books that she felt should have been on the list but were not. "Some of the books on the list were out of date ten or twenty years ago," she reported. But the assistant principal told her that it was not within his authority or that of the principal to honor her request.

New materials are essential for curriculum change, and the present system makes it almost impossible to introduce such new materials. Curriculum officials have taken no initiative in encouraging publishers to create new materials, and the bureaucratic difficulties that publishers encounter discourage them from risking their capital in programs for urban children.

Many teachers complain that they can't get simple things like paper or chairs when they need them. "A school representative went to headquarters," one teacher reported, "to get some chairs. We needed them badly. He knew the size he wanted. Instead, they led him into a room with undersized chairs, for much younger kids and said 'take your pick.' He had no choice and finally took the chairs, and the kids have been putting their feet up on the desks ever since. There is no room for them to sit comfortably." [14]

Securing Staff. Staffing is an even worse problem. An NYU report on teacher mobility concludes that the present examination system and personnel procedures are in many respects relics of the past.[15] Methods that produced an adequate supply of trained teachers in the 1930s and forties no longer work in the sixties, when teachers are scarce, and the use of those methods produces ever-increasing percentages of substitute teachers: one-third were in this category in 1967.

Bureaucratic entanglements at headquarters made the problem worse. Several headquarters units were involved in staffing decisions, and principals often had great difficulty in getting teachers and supervisors. Dr. Paul Warner, principal at a newly opened, segregated junior high school in The Bronx, JHS 145, tells the followng story: [16] "Upon my designation as principal," he wrote, "I conferred with this bureau [the Bureau of Appointment] and was assured that the new school would receive top priority." Despite the many visits to the bureau he made throughout the summer as the desperateness of his situation became more and more apparent, procedural confusions at headquarters prevented him from making any headway. The bureau assigned him only eight regular teachers for the whole school. The rest were substitutes who had not been highly enough regarded by their principals to be asked back.

An indication of the bureau's inefficiency in the matter was that two teachers requested appointments at 145 but were instead reappointed to their current schools, even though there were many regular teachers serving in these schools in their subject areas. Headquarters thus unwittingly subverted Warner's efforts to open his school fully staffed.

His supervisory situation was also critical. Although it was informal board policy to provide three or four assistant principals to ghetto schools, only one woman, who had served for only one year in another school, was assigned to 145. Warner notes further that "two assistant principals applied for transfer and their applications were properly endorsed, but they were rejected by the bureau because of the current 'freeze' on transfers. The freeze has the clear and tenable purpose of impeding an exodus of assistant principals from special service schools until another list of eligibles appears. However, the freeze should not apply to new schools—particularly special service ones."

Principal Warner's dealings with the junior high school division were even more bizarre. He met with a representative of the division in the spring and inquired about transfers and available substitutes. He went back in July, but Holmes, the division official, did not know at the time what appointments would be made. Holmes was away in August, and when he returned on September 11 he was cooperative but was confronted with the impossible task of sorting out lists of available substitutes and making assignments in the week before school opened.

"I learned," Warner went on to say, "that some high school substitutes might not be assigned. After reviewing the addresses of all substitutes not likely to be reached for high school assignment, I mailed about one hundred letters. Some twenty substitutes responded and most of them indicated a desire to join us. However, under the contract, assignment had to be made by Mr. Holmes. It was impossible to reach him by telephone, and he informed me subsequently that he was swamped with a backlog of mail. At one point, I sent him a telegram.

Because I was unable to hire these substitutes, all of them took positions elsewhere, many in other school systems." *

Warner did receive help from the Board of Examiners, which gave emergency examinations; from the district superintendent; and from the elementary school division, which furnished twelve substitute teachers. Nevertheless, his school had thirteen vacancies as late as October 19. Many people Warner considered competent could not be licensed because they did not meet the minimum course requirements.

Principal Warner understood some of the causes of his difficulty. "Nothing that I write is intended to reflect adversely on the personal qualities or cooperative spirit of the people charged with responsibilities concerning personnel. I found them to be friendly in spirit and cooperative in attitude. I am convinced that our school's extreme difficulties arose from organizational and procedural problems." The fundamental pathology of the system, then, is the source of the trouble, not just the incompetence of particular units or people.

All the pathologies of the system get played out most dramatically in the ghetto schools. Teachers and principals, as well as pupils and the wider community, are beaten down and demoralized by experiences there.

The PEA study of 1955 and the Urban League study of 1963 showed that ghetto schools got fewer services than the others in New York City. The recent Sheldon-Glazier fact book, *Pupils and Schools in New York City*, documents this with reference to staffing.[17] Only 8% of the Negro–Puerto Rican segregated elementary schools had more than 65% regularly licensed teachers, while 68% of the segregated white elementary schools did.† While ghetto schools have many more compensatory programs and more expenditures per pupil than segregated white schools, the bureaucracy prevents the coherent, integrated use of these "special services," as extra teachers and staff don't understand each others' role and the fragmentation is even worse than before. In New York City, compensatory programs for ghetto schools usually mean more of the same. But these

---

* Numerous interviews with principals, teachers, and parents suggest that Warner's experience was quite common.

† Board data on educational resources in Bronx schools, analyzed by the United Bronx Parents, indicate that ghetto schools consistently get a higher proportion of inexperienced and substitute teachers than schools in middle class white areas.

schools don't need more of the same. They need innovation, which is what the bureaucracy won't permit.

Many headquarters people and board members still don't know how poorly staffed and equipped ghetto schools really are. Board members have visited some schools with the worst conditions and where critical conflicts blow up, but they don't have the time or inclination to do this regularly. They tend to feel that they should not meddle in administration or get too close to particular problems, because this might limit their capacity to serve the entire city. One member of the board with a special interest in ghetto populations told a civil rights leader that he was appalled at conditions in the ghetto schools he visited, adding that he had always discounted the many complaints of Negro leaders as a political tactic to mobilize a following. Few members of the headquarters professional staff know the conditions in these schools either. They know only what field supervisors choose to tell them. There is no established procedure for headquarters officials to make regular visits to local schools, to see how facilities are being used.

One example of how little headquarters is aware of local conditions came during the crisis over the possible closing of JHS 139 in Harlem, a focus of continued community complaints. In early 1965, Isaiah Robinson, chairman of the Harlem Parents Committee, asked the Board of Education to close the school. The board agreed, but toward the end of the school year, after the board had repeatedly refused to say where the children would be going in the fall, the parents changed their minds about wanting the school closed, and the board reversed itself at their request. By that time, however, the principal and many teachers had already been given other assignments. The school opened in the fall of 1965 twenty-eight teachers short, with close to 50% substitutes, and at least twenty teachers teaching out of license,* while many of the experienced ones were appointed to non-teaching positions or to other schools. Teacher morale was low, as teachers were constantly called upon to double up for absentees.[18]

Headquarters blamed the confusion on internal leadership struggles within the Harlem community. Some officials felt that a new Harlem faction had taken over and demanded that the school reopen. These officials simply did not know what really

* Junior high school teachers are trained and licensed to teach particular subjects.

had happened and were unaware of the parents' fears about the board's failure to relocate the children.

Local Innovation. In many instances, principals, district superintendents and teachers who wanted to make changes and experiment were discouraged from doing so. One headquarters official told of her gloom at coming back to the city after a conference on teaching the disadvantaged.[19] She said that she came back with many new ideas but couldn't talk to Superintendent Donovan about them "because he is so overloaded with emergency matters. And if I went to principals and district superintendents, they wouldn't do anything without Donovan's approval. So that is where we are in New York City." She said she was confident that a few district superintendents might be interested and willing to try out some of the programs that worked in other cities, but "most superintendents have acquired the habit of looking over their shoulder and approaching new ideas with extreme caution."

Decisions on curriculum and instruction are made by headquarters officials, who are often removed from local conditions, insulated from national developments, and not in a position to implement new ideas.[20] Field supervisors have become so used to their limited authority that many won't assume responsibility for innovating and thus subjecting themselves to questions and criticism from curriculum and instruction officials at headquarters. "What's wrong with the system," says one principal, "is the teachers who won't take any responsibility for trying anything new. The reason they won't do so is that assistant principals, principals, and district superintendents won't either, and this goes all the way up the chain of command."

The problem is that the professionals are concerned about their careers and do not want to alienate their bureaucratic superiors by instituting new programs; and at the same time, headquarters does not always provide support for school officials who want to attack the problems of limited services and low reading levels. "It is known by everyone," said a school official with many years of experience, "that headquarters doesn't know what's going on. Information does not get back from the field and they don't even care. To some extent, field people don't even know what policy actually is. They get no help from headquarters, only a mass of paper directives. It is set up like a machine, and the basic set throughout the system is not in any way toward experimenting or even pushing at a rule. A

coherent plan has to aim at loosening up the central bureaucracy to begin with, and you have to build in rewards to innovate."

Martin Mayer, former chairman of a local school board on
Manhattan's Upper East Side, tells how he wanted to try out
some new methods for reading instruction that had become
nationally recognized.[21] It took a while before he could get his
district superintendent to go along, but he finally did. Later
they had some battles with headquarters curriculum and instructional officials, and it was only the persistence of Mayer,
later backed by his superintendent, that let them keep the
program.

Occasionally one finds a principal who simply ignores the
board, does not fill out all its forms, and does what he wants.
Dr. Seymour Gang, principal of a Harlem elementary school,
and one of the few who strike out on their own with new programs, is an example, and he has the respect and admiration
of the Harlem community.

There are countless incidents involving professionals with
imaginative new curricula who have not been able to get their
materials into the classrooms or have been harassed when they
did. Herbert Kohl tells of teaching in a Harlem school and
starting a newspaper in which the students write poetry and
articles in their own "street language," often describing conditions in their community. The principal of the school eventually refused to allow the paper to continue and even sent a
Negro school official to talk with Kohl and his class, questioning
the educational worth of what they were doing.*

Random House developed a weekly newspaper, *New York,
N.Y.*, with materials for reading instruction, and it was used in
ghetto schools throughout the system in 1966–1967. (It included pictures, project suggestions, and instructional guides
for teachers and was developed by Jason Epstein, Vice President of Random House, and several highly trained educators,
including Dr. Madelon Stent, Professor at the City University of
New York, and Dr. Allen Cohen, Professor at Yeshiva.) Despite the fact that parents, students, teachers, and principals

---

* Herbert Kohl is a teacher and author. He taught for one year in a
Harlem school and prepared a booklet entitled *Teaching the Unteachable*,
containing materials prepared by his pupils. He has also served as Director
of Teachers and Writers Collaborative, a group undertaking a revision of
the English curriculum in elementary and secondary schools.

widely acclaimed the paper, Random House was informed in March, 1967, that it could not be used in elementary schools for the following school year. The reason given was that a state education law prevented the use of textbook funds for this purpose. Yet, when Random House officials went to state education officials, they were told that this was sheer nonsense. After six months of lobbying, Random House got its paper back into the schools, though almost every top school official contacted passed the buck to somebody else.

Headquarters and field people differ in their view of how much freedom there actually is to innovate locally. "I can't even blow my nose without permission from headquarters," says one principal, who claimed to reflect the views of many of his peers as well. "They are afraid to take the initiative, not deprived of it," says a top headquarters official in reply. Both are partly right, but that is less important than that both sides agree on how little initiative is actually taken in the field.

The pressure of informal peer group controls, then, is an important reason why more principals do not ignore the board and do what they want. It exists at every level and is especially prevalent among teachers in ghetto schools, where the rewards are often for "keeping order." "I went to teach in a Harlem school," a teacher said, "from formerly all middle class white communities. What a shock. Teachers in a special service school can get to a pretty intolerable state. When I was in this junior high school, other teachers complained of my overstimulating the kids. It made it tough on them. The kids would never settle down to quiet, unthreatening behavior after a class of mine. Throughout the ghetto schools you'll find this avoidance of overstimulation. It does real harm to the teachers too, only they don't realize it. When you stimulate a child, who needs discipline?"

Overcentralization has contributed to what headquarters officials themselves refer to as a pattern of "over-administration" and "under-supervision." [22] Headquarters officials are preoccupied with forcing field personnel to conform to numerous rules and directives.* "There is pressure from the top down in this system," reported a board member who had made visits to

* This is widely recognized as an organization that runs on fear. Officials are afraid to assume reponsibility for any action that may become "controversial," and the safest thing for somebody who wants to maintain his good standing within the system is to follow established rules and traditions.

ghetto schools before being discouraged from doing so, "and by the time it reaches the teacher it gets pretty strong, and the teacher sometimes takes it out on the kids."

Authoritarian and paternalistic supervision are as prevalent in principal–teacher relations as at higher levels.[23] Many teachers and union spokesmen report that ghetto principals run their schools in a custodial way.* Teachers may be subjected to such administrative sanctions as extra chores, assignment to special classes, or continued visits to their classes by the principal. There are also informal sanctions from one's peers, such as those imposed on the former Harlem junior high school teacher whose colleagues resented his "overstimulating" the pupils.

The pattern of tight supervision rather than professional support is perhaps most acute in principal–teacher relations. Teachers feel that principals are often authoritarian, coercive, and paternalistic, and union spokesmen describe principals as similar to old-line foremen, who talk of "my" school and "my" teachers. The teachers want a more egalitarian and professional relationship, suggesting that decisions about school policy and procedures should be made jointly with teacher representatives, rather than unilaterally by the principal.

Principals and teachers come into greatest conflict on the formers' use of observations and ratings, which many teachers claim are artificial standards, often used as weapons to intimidate teachers who disagree with them.[24] Some union spokesmen have campaigned to include in the collective bargaining contract the elimination of ratings and observations, arguing that if teachers are incompetent, principals should eliminate them in the probationary period.†

One local school board chairman, a sharp critic of the system's authoritarian style, sides with the teachers in pointing out how principals' ratings actually discourage creativity in instructional methods.[25] "Official observers who go to see how a

---

* By custodial I mean that the principals seem content just to keep the pupils off the streets, and devote little time and resources to education.

† The teachers do not have tenure until after their third year and may be removed by the principal for "poor performance." Though union leaders state publicly that they favor eliminating incompetent teachers, many ghetto parents are impatient with their failure to accept a procedure for doing so, suggesting that there are at least as many "problem" teachers as there are pupils. The union has not yet acted on this request. Admittedly, there are few agreed-on criteria for deciding whether a teacher is "good" or "bad", except reading scores which can easily be "rigged" in the present system, by giving the tests several times.

teacher is doing in the class," he explained, "are as inflexible as machines. A good teacher will really come off badly, because he disregards many old traditions." The same point has been made in the many administrative studies on the system.*

The ways in which teachers are hampered by an authoritarian, bureaucratic system have been reviewed by Dr. Mortimer Kreuter of the Center for Urban Education.[26] Kreuter suggests that teachers have become "infantilized" by a system whose functionaries grade and inspect them much like children. "They literally have no time to go to the toilet," he reports, "and when they must, they are obliged to summon a next door teacher to keep an eye on the classroom. They must punch time clocks daily and file affidavits when ill."

Principals are in a difficult position too. They are the middle men in the system, and they feel they are increasingly ignored in headquarters policy decisions. They see the powerful union and headquarters encroaching on their authority through collective bargaining, they bear the brunt of community protests, and they have the major responsibility for the operation of the schools. They can't hire or fire regular teachers, either. Their desire to control their staff in the ways they can is at least partly a reflection of these pressures.

If principals had got more professional assistance from field superintendents, they might have been under less pressure and performed better. Dr. Marilyn Gittell suggests, however, in a recent study of the New York City schools, that "individual conferences with principals were rare, evaluation scanty, and services to principals limited." [27] Superintendents, as well, are ground down by the system, due partly to their insufficient staff, their limited authority to direct and organize their staff according to the needs of their schools. Here again authority was in the hands of headquarters people who were generally out of touch with local situations.

Though the system hampers teachers, principals, and field

* "The greatest failing of the schools today is the failure to use the creative ability of teachers. Too often little or no opportunity is given teachers to contribute to the development of the educational program or to the management of the school. Supervision is never creative unless the people being supervised are given responsibility commensurate with their professional competence." Strayer and Yavner, *op. cit.*, ch. 4. The same criticisms appear in the board's studies of the 1960's and continue to be voiced by teachers and their union spokesmen.

superintendents, so does the authoritarian and petty civil service outlook that many of them have. The system attracts people with such an outlook, and of those who don't have it when they come in, most soon acquire it. Survival and promotion within the institution all but demand that they acquire it. And it contributes to their inflexibility in adapting to new programs and situations.

This is indicated in some of the reports on the controversial More Effective Schools program, set up by the board, the union, and the Council of Supervisory Associations in 1964, and now covering twenty-one ghetto schools. The program was in part the union's rejoinder to the charge that it had forsaken the needs of the ghetto child in favor of more power, higher salaries, and less classroom time. Despite smaller class size and several hundred dollars more money spent per pupil, the program has not yet significantly raised the reading levels of these children. The administrative structure of the system and the "trained incapacity" of many school officials in the program may be among the primary reasons. A Center for Urban Education evaluation, for example, indicates that many MES teachers use the same methods in a class of 22 pupils as they used in a class of 40.* Gloria Channon, a teacher in the program, writes in *The Urban Review* [28] that "some of the most essential aspects of the More Effective Schools program have not been used: the flexibility, the democracy of staff participation, the freedom to depart from the curriculum in new ways, the research and evaluation process and the interaction with the community. The fault is not with the paper program, but with the people." †

The apparent need of many school officials to maintain the same militaristic atmosphere that they had in more traditional programs is particularly striking. "The drive for discipline is as obsessive in More Effective Schools," she writes, "as it is in others. Here too one hears early childhood teachers complain: 'They haven't learned to sit still or stand in line.' Our district superintendent on his first visit to our school was seen to be gesturing with imperious disapproval at the shocking spectacle of children talking to each other as they moved from one class-

---

* David J. Fox, *Expansion of the More Effective Schools Program*, Center for Urban Education, New York, Sept., 1967.

† More radical changes are needed in the schools than just decreasing class size, but the class size reductions in the More Effective Schools were dramatic. See Chapter Thirteen for a discussion of other factors that may influence teaching effectiveness.

room to another. . . . Again and again the fault seems to lie not so much with the machinery as with the people using it, or afraid of using it, or ignorant of the ways in which it can be used. Solutions are sought in administrative terms. Gimmicks, such as overhead projectors, become the substitutes for genuine change of curriculum content. And in a showdown, the conforming unquestioning acceptance of the board's definitions of the problem, of the curriculum, and of the methods, prevails."

Recruitment and Promotion Procedures

Inside the temple, at the top of the bureaucratic pyramid, is the Board of Examiners. The Board of Examiners is the one institution that would have to be radically changed for any meaningful reforms, such as decentralization and performance budgeting, to be effective.* It administers the examinations for teaching, supervisory, and staff positions, and zealously defends a system that has led to much in-breeding and to the promotion to supervisory positions of some people with a minimum of daring, imagination and innovativeness. Until the examinations are changed, other reforms will probably be meaningless, and they may be discredited for trying and failing. If school personnel as well as the administrative structure contribute to the system's failures, it is the Board of Examiners that is largely responsible for both. No other single agency within the system contributes so much to a perpetuation of the status quo.

Until early 1967, the Board of Examiners had nine members, all of whom had come up through the ranks. They were selected by examination, but it was generally understood that examinations at that level were tailored to the applicant, and that it helped a lot to have political connections among top headquarters officials. The Board of Examiners was widely regarded within the system as one of its most powerful bodies, and its members were considered gatekeepers and maintainers of high standards of professionalism against periodic political pressures from outsiders to break in without adequate training.

The examination system has been under attack by public administration specialists, the lay board, and various civic groups for nearly two decades, largely because the tests were too limited in scope, favored insiders, and subtly discriminated against minority group applicants. Yet, there has been little

---

* See Chapter Nine for a further discussion of budgeting.

change in the Board of Examiners' procedures or power. Created by an act of the state legislature, it has enjoyed great influence in city and state educational circles. And though nominally subject to directives from the superintendent and lay board, it has operated under its own by-laws and enjoyed considerable freedom of action.

Strayer and Yavner observed in 1951, for example, that the Board of Examiners acted independently, that its efforts were not coordinated with the school system, and that it was responsible and accountable to nobody.[29] They suggested changes to make it administratively accountable to the superintendent and the lay board, and also questioned the life-tenure appointments, suggesting legislative changes to eliminate this.

In 1959, political scientists Wallace Sayre and Herbert Kaufman spelled out some of the implications of the Board of Examiners' powers, characterizing the institution as "a civil service reformer's dream, a bureaucrat's delight, and an official's nightmare." [30] They noted that the "promotion from within" doctrine was so zealously pursued that it made the New York City school system more tightly closed than any other in the United States. In 1966, an NYU research team, headed by Dr. Daniel E. Griffiths, dean of the School of Education, commented on the archaic nature of the examination system, on bureaucratic inefficiences in recruitment and promotion procedures, and on the favored position of insiders.[31] They recommended that an entirely new personnel system be set up.*

None of these recommendations was acted upon until February, 1967, when Alfred Giardino pushed through legislation and changes in administration to reduce the size of the Board of Examiners from 9 to 5, increase the recruitment of outsiders, and provide for more flexibility in promotion procedures.† [32]

The Griffiths Report suggests that in-breeding has been pro-

---

* Professional, collegial criticisms of examination procedures by social scientists and public administration specialists have not always evoked a collegial response. When the Griffiths Report came out, the Board of Examiners received a foundation grant and did a study that defended existing personnel procedures. The study contained some valid criticisms of the sampling techniques of the Griffiths Report, but failed to negate its many recommendations for change.

† The NYU report also recommended completely abolishing the Board of Examiners, setting up a personnel commission, and using the National

moted in three ways, among others.[33] Little effort was made to recruit people from outside the city; examinations stressed localized knowledge, available only to insiders; and an informal system of "prepping" for examinations brought inside candidates under the tutelage of other insiders who were already members of the administrative hierarchy. At the teacher level, outsiders have traditionally been excluded by the Board of Examiners' refusal to use the National Teachers Examination or the New York State Teaching Certificate as criteria of eligibility for the regular teaching license.

Dr. Gittell found in her study that of the 26 field superintendents, 19—or 76%—had been in the system more than thirty years, and only one had been in less twenty years.[34]

No wonder so little innovation has taken place, or that the examiners have enjoyed such prestige among school officials. Nor is it surprising that the Council of Supervisory Associations has lobbied so strenuously to protect the Board of Examiners from attack and to retain the present system. The Board of Examiners literally has the keys to the temple, and everybody else, including the superintendent and the lay board, has been at its mercy, that is, everybody except the professionals within the system whom it put there. Furthermore, the parochialism, the generally patronizing attitude toward outsiders, the insulation, and the pedantic tone of the school system are due largely to the influence of this agency.

The Board of Examiners even has its own legal and public relations divisions, duplicating functions and encouraging and reinforcing what one board member referred to as a "psychology of independence." They were so independent, in fact, that they were accountable to nobody in their appointments of assistant examiners.

An incident illustrating this last point occurred in late December, 1966, when a principal wrote to Board President Lloyd Garrison, complaining that he could not find out how people were chosen for that position.[35] Suggesting what many people inside the system have known for a long time, that these appointments are intramural plums, given out to friends, and now cost more than $1.5 million, he wrote: "I have tried to get a

Teachers Examination (NTE) as a basis for recruiting teachers instead of the local New York City exam then given. These recommendations were not instituted, and the examinations have not changed that much since Giardino's compromise reforms.

statement from the Board of Examiners regarding established criteria for the selection of examination assistants and proctors, the number of such people employed in each category and the average number of hours assigned to these people. I am told that these questions cannot be answered because it violates the confidentiality between the examination assistant and the Board of Examiners. It appears to me that the Board of Examiners should answer to some educational authority before the situation is put before the fiscal authorities and the public." As a top headquarters official acknowledged in response: "The cry of integrity [on the part of the Board of Examiners] seems to be a little bit marred."

Despite the Board of Examiners' defense of testing procedures on the ground that they eliminated patronage, civil rights groups, the chairman of the Mayor's Commission on Human Rights, the Negro Teachers' Association, and even the mayor himself have attacked the institution for discriminating against Negroes. Nobody has produced much hard data to demonstrate this beyond particular cases here and there, but suspicions certainly abound, and there is certainly evidence that Negro applicants have not been very welcome in the past. Until 1967, for example, there were only 4 Negro principals out of 865 principal positions (a little less than .5%) and only 12 Negro assistant principals in the 1500 positions at that rank.[36]

Many Negro applicants reportedly used to be ruled out on oral examinations because of so-called "Southernisms" in their speech, and one board member became so concerned about this that he suggested that all interviews be tape recorded to allow further review, and that there be three interviewers instead of one. "People had been flunked because of their accents," he reported. "Some very able Negro educators from the South with a lot of teaching and supervisory experience have been turned down on this basis in New York City." Some civil rights leaders further claim that applicants with local dialects—e.g., "Brooklynese"—had not all been subjected to similarly discriminatory treatment. Yet, some old-timers within the system suggest that many whites were ruled out on the oral exams. "What happened previously was an open scandal," reported one. "People were failed for New York accents, Jewish accents, minor speech impediments. I remember trying to perfect an innocuous Mid-Western flatness in old exams just after the war."

Regardless of the motives and social outlooks of the examiners, the fact is that few Negroes passed the supervisory exams. "Forty years ago, you had to be Irish to pass," said a member of the Board of Examiners when pressed on the matter. "Over the past generation it helped a lot to be Jewish. I would not deny that some unconscious discrimination may have existed." *

Particular ethnic groups have been the gatekeepers of the system at different historical periods, reflecting an ethnic politics that existed throughout New York City government. Now that Negroes are becoming more powerful, they are starting to gain more access. Over the past couple of years, for example, forty to fifty Negro applicants have passed the assistant principals' exam and have been assigned to ghetto schools.†

The system abounds in coaching courses, usually given by principals, department heads or district superintendents.‡ The courses are recognized by people inside the system as "really a big business. People really make money with coaching," a school official said. "They have coaching schools that charge $300 to $500, taught by principals or department heads who have been examiners before," reported an NYU researcher. "There are as many as thirty teachers in each group. One supervisor in The Bronx made several hundred thousand dollars giving those classes over the years. Also, there are informal study teams. They have printed books on how to pass the exams. Would-be principals take their vacations together in the Catskills. They sit around and play 'twenty questions,' and they are all on the exams."

Many Negro teachers and civil rights leaders feel that the prepping courses are open mainly to insiders. "Not only is this coaching a big business," reported a headquarters official with Negro friends in the system, "it is also a fairly closed system. Principals often invited only their friends, and Negroes rarely got into the courses. There were always some, but only a few, not because they didn't want to, but because they were not asked and felt they were not welcome."

* The waiting list in now eight years long.

† Civil rights leaders are divided on the question of where these people should be assigned. Some resent the fact that they are placed in segregated ghetto schools, while others see it as essential for the pupils in those schools to have more black teachers and principals.

‡ Coaching courses are for people preparing to take the assistant principal and principal exams.

In 1963, however, some people at headquarters started their own coaching seminars for Negro applicants "This would not hurt business," reported one participant. "Business could go on as usual." While the fee was smaller, some principals voluntarily gave up their coaching business and participated in these courses, set up in ghetto locations to encourage Negro applicants. In the first year, some 1,700 teachers applied, including 500 Negroes and Puerto Ricans. "The papers were bad on that," a participating administrator related. "The *World-Telegram* had some bad headlines, suggesting discrimination in reverse. So we put some in fringe areas."

For whatever combination of reasons, Negro teachers had been reluctant until the past couple of years to take the test for promotion to supervisory positions. Many of them felt the Board of Examiners wouldn't pass them anyway.

Finally, an informal investigation was begun. "We went to Negro teachers wherever we could and to the Negro Teachers' Association," said a school official, "and asked, 'Why aren't you taking the tests?' The things we heard were so discouraging in terms of the tremendous distrust, sensitivities, wounded egos still to be bridged. We heard: 'Why prepare and study when they'll knock you out as soon as you show up for the interview?' Or even—'They put a special mark on the back of an exam paper so they can tell they're marking a Negro's exam.' All kinds of things like that. I protested. I mark these exams, too. I'd never do a thing like that. They told me: 'I know you wouldn't, but about the others, you're just naive.' "

A further charge was that the supervisors who prepped people for exams had friends and close colleagues who actually wrote and gave them. "The coaching club extended to the Board of Examiners," an NYU researcher said. "It's an insider's edge, and the questions on the exams are loaded in terms of New York City." The insiders' edge extended beyond the prep courses and friends of friends on the examining board, to include the "exam savvy" of New York City candidates. "An education major in the city colleges is prepping for the exam from the junior year of college on," explained a former principal. "In addition, the city colleges are part of the education apparatus, and since the ed profs are assistant examiners for the board, they can't help but be prep agents too. The Negroes who were principals were products of the city colleges."

The coaching courses are essentially memorization exercises, both in subject matter and administrative codes. Coaches would use mimeograph machines to produce standard answers to standard questions and would suggest mnemonic formulas to help applicants prepare for the tests. "The whole trick to pass the exams is to memorize all the answers, and you can't lose," explained an insider. "The prepping courses are given via mnemonic techniques, and once you catch on and can reel the answers off quickly, you're in."

Not only are insiders favored in the supervisory exams, but little attempt has been made to select insiders with relevant skills. Though one of the strengths of the system is that it tests for subject matter mastery, high academic competence in subject matter or unusual abilities at memorization may not be correlated with leadership ability or a capacity for innovation.[37]

Strayer and Yavner suggested many years ago that exams, seemingly set up for easy scoring and to preclude charges of patronage, rather than to set good teachers and supervisors apart from bad, had not rewarded applicants for creativity, imagination, and leadership skills. Many traits identifying potential innovators were not only excluded from consideration in the exams, but people who had them might consistently fail, at least in the written, short-answer parts, because of the way they were set up. Traits that lend themselves to easy measurements rather than those identifying leadership potential are often the ones tapped. These points deserve much more public discussion and debate than they have had thus far.[38]

To protect themselves against charges of patronage, the Board of Examiners has tried to develop written and oral examinations whose norms can be explicitly specified. But the question is not how accurate the measures are, but how relevant they are. The Board of Examiners has developed the most standardized and elaborate measures imaginable, but the measures have little to do with identifying a competent supervisor, mainly because they have not thought enough about what qualities a competent supervisor needs, especially in ghetto and integrated schools. Meanwhile, the examiners keep developing more exams.*

* The Board of Examiners had developed 1,050 different licenses (and examination positions) by 1966, and headquarters officials starting discussing how they could reduce the number by combining similar licenses. This would obviously help reduce the cost of examinations as well.

Part of the problem lies in the nature of testing and personnel management as fields of scientific inquiry and application. Many psychologists themselves make the valid point that these disciplines are scientifically bankrupt. The main criticisms of selection techniques are that there is limited sensitivity about the work settings that people are being recruited for, and that there is a preoccupation with standardizing tests without thinking through what the tests are good for. These criticisms can all be made of the Board of Examiners. Their claims for the "scientific" nature of their testing procedures reflect a limited concept of that term.[39]

Actually, the Board of Examiners has never even tried to validate its tests and its personnel are not trained to do so.* Thus, the tests can hardly be more than a ritualistic device to promote insiders. "They have been urged repeatedly to validate," an NYU researcher reported, "from the Kandel Report in the late 1930s, to Strayer–Yavner in 1951, to Shinnerer in the late 1950s. But to validate tests implies you have some outside yardstick, and you would need an outside crew of psychometricians. There is no move to get either. From the technical angle, there is little point if you change exams every year. I cannot see it being done when tests have become so ritualistic and costly, and so they avoid it."

Until quite recently, anyone who wanted to be a New York City teacher had to prove himself in a speech test. "If the guy could speak well enough in the first test to pass it," an NYU researcher put it, "he must speak well enough to not need further speech exams. There is no reason for speech exams to be given with each exam in the series."

Furthermore, the licensing process is unnecessarily complex. Few examinations are given outside the city. Neither the National Teachers Examination nor the New York State teaching certificate is allowed as a basis for eligibility. To become a regular teacher in New York City one must take a series of sequential exams that are given over two years, and there is no feedback until the entire sequence has been completed. Yet, if a candidate fails a single part, he is out completely. There are further delays in getting the lists of eligibles completed and published. Some people undergo three years of tests to become principals. Many get discouraged and go elsewhere.

* That is, they have never checked to see if there is any correlation between test scores and later performance.

The people who administer the exams are mostly principals and department heads, many of them brought in when needed and paid $15 and more an hour. "This is just legal moon-lighting," explained an outside researcher. "In the course of a year more money is spent on exams than on the whole civil service system." * A civic group professional told the following story: "I made up two questions once. You are entitled to make out expense accounts according to the number of your questions that find their way onto an exam, and by the amount of time it takes you to make them out. Within the law, you can make out a bill for $100 or $150, as I discovered when I made up my questions. Now I get regular letters from the Board of Examiners telling me how necessary they are. I am part of their constituency, and they keep in touch with me."

Board members are aware of these points, and in 1962, Board President Max Rubin developed plans to change examination procedures.[40] He and his colleagues wanted to abolish the Board of Examiners, develop a new personnel unit that would be less autonomous, and improve test procedures. He went to Albany to try to enact the legislation necessary for such changes.

Just after he took office, Rubin spoke at a dinner of an association of influential New York City school administrators, including members of the Board of Examiners, about the importance of recruiting from outside. During the question-and-answer period, one assistant superintendent who later rose to a top headquarters position reportedly said: "Since you were so frank with us, I would now like to be very frank with you. I think it would be a disservice to our system if you were to suddenly change the procedures for selecting people to supervisory positions."

An informant who was present described what followed as a free-for-all during which Rubin was criticized in sharp terms by one of the members of the Board of Examiners. Finally, he posed a question to his critic and to the entire audience: "If I were to find some outstanding men from outside the system, say in California or Illinois, shouldn't I think seriously about inviting them here?" A loud and seemingly unanimous "No" resounded through the hall. Several prominent headquarters administrators made brief speeches criticizing Rubin's views.

---

* The Board of Examiners had a $2 million budget in the 1966–67 school year.

He then threw out another question to one of his most vociferous critics: "If you are so sure that only insiders can do the job in New York City, please show up at my office at your leisure and before coming pull out the names of the three superintendents from big-city school systems you feel are among the best and three from smaller systems—and you show me whether they are all insiders." That person never produced the data, though he and many of his colleagues did produce apologies.

Rubin and his lay board were overwhelmingly defeated, however, in their attempts to change the state education laws that protected the examination system, and to open supervisory appointments to outsiders. He had the support of most of his board and of such powerful civic groups as PEA, CCC, and UPA. But the Board of Examiners had the support of headquarters and field supervisors, teachers, other civil service groups in the city such as the police and firemen, and many state education and political officials. The board was so demoralized by this defeat that it all but gave up trying to reform personnel procedures until 1966.

In early 1967, Alfred Giardino pushed through a number of compromise reforms and got the necessary legislative changes to put the reforms into effect. Unlike Rubin, who declared his position unilaterally in a public confrontation with supervisors, Giardino negotiated privately, continually explaining to the Board of Examiners why change was necessary, without arousing their defenses. Only the Council of Supervisory Associations objected strongly in public to Giardino's reforms.*

The changes that Giardino negotiated in addition to those mentioned earlier were as follows: improved training and teaching conditions; liberalization of eligibility for promotion, and modification of evaluation procedures to permit more rapid advancement of qualified people; a concentration of all recruitment functions in the office of personnel, with administration by one person, not nine; and a discontinuance of the practice of granting substitute teacher licenses. None of these

* Without detracting from Giardino's efforts, conditions were in his favor. Four of the examiners had just died or retired, recommendations from the NYU Griffiths Report had just been published in the fall of 1966, and the mayor and Negro groups were increasingly critical of the examination system.

changes has gone into effect yet, however, and many other changes urged in the NYU Griffiths Report were discarded.*

Ethnic Politics

The Board of Examiners was the legal and political arm of inside professional groups, protecting the careers of teachers and supervisors against competition from outside. And it reflected a particular kind of ethnic politics, perhaps not planned, though it sometimes seems to be so, that discriminates against Negro and Puerto Rican applicants.[41]

The politics of the Board of Examiners is not the politics of the political clubhouse, of Tammany Hall, or the party machines, but a professional politics that reflects the interests of whatever ethnic groups are in power. A generation ago they were the Catholics, and now they are the Jews. The New York City school system in the 1950s and sixties has been largely a Jewish school system, in the sense that Jews hold power in the professional associations and the Board of Examiners. They have tended to protect themselves against outsiders much as the Catholics tried to protect themselves against the Jews in previous generations.†

Historically, the Catholic ascendancy was due largely to the tie-ins between the political machines and school appointments. Catholic influence, however, has been gradually waning over the past decade, and Jews are the next emerging ethnic group.

---

* The most important included the complete elimination of the Board of Examiners, with the creation of a Personnel Commission in its place; the transfer of selection, screening, and testing to a new Bureau of Selection in the Office of Personnel that would be directly responsible to the superintendent; and granting authority to the superintendent to make each year up to 5% of his appointments to administrative and supervisory positions on an exempt basis, outside of normal selection procedures.

† Anti-Semitic Negroes sometimes make this point, and I do not wish to imply as they do that the Jews in the New York City schools are any more racist than other ethnic groups before them were, or are now. In fact, as I indicated in Chapter Three, Jews are generally more liberal (though not much more so) on race matters than other ethnic groups. Jews just happened by historical accident to move into the school system in the thirties, and they are now the dominant ethnic group. They have been the gatekeepers of the institution who have, along with the minority of Catholics, kept out others, for many reasons. One Jewish principal suggested that many of his colleagues feared they would not get jobs if there were no exam, a fear based on their personal experience with anti-Semitism and discrimination in the 1920s and thirties.

They have placed great value on civil service reform and have certainly benefited from it. They are now at middle and upper middle levels in the hierarchy, as the Catholics were twenty to thirty years ago, and they will probably move into greater power and prominence where they will come into periodic conflict with emerging Negro and Puerto Rican groups who would like retribution for past discrimination and do not want to wait any longer for their turn. They stake their claims on the grounds of the increasing number of minority-group pupils in the schools and, for the Negro, the teaching tradition within their middle class population. Civil rights leaders claim there is a significant pool of Negro educators, both in New York City and throughout the nation, who would qualify for teaching and supervisory positions here.*

I do not suggest that ethnic politics should not affect personnel decisions in the New York City schools, simply that they do, and that justifications of the "merit" system and of "professionalism," especially by insiders in favored positions, evoke understandable resentment from Negroes and Puerto Ricans because they are excluded. Neither am I saying that those within the system necessarily do not deserve their positions. The point is that whether so planned or not, minority group candidates have been at a disadvantage.

A real merit system should not be compromised, but for white middle class groups such as UPA and PEA or school professionals to defend it—as they did in the IS 201 controversy—without recognizing its history of ethnic politics, was unrealistic. The ethnic politics are that the examination system has always favored whatever ethnic group was in power. Irish power up to the 1930s was gradually replaced by Jewish power through the late 1960s, and it will soon be replaced by black and Puerto Rican power. If the politics of the "merit" system are not recognized, ethnic conflicts and school–community tensions will only be exacerbated. A wiser course would be to recruit more Negroes and Puerto Ricans: not just to ease tensions or to be fair but also because many of them have needed skills and experience. One obvious way is to broaden the narrow standards that now apply and ask candidates to show social and psychological skills other than just verbal ones. Many Ne-

---

* Teaching has been a perennial occupation for upward-mobile Negroes in the past, though increasing white collar opportunities may change that.

gro and Puerto Rican applicants have experience and skills that are badly needed in ghetto communities.*

But the monopolistic control by the Board of Examiners and inside professionals over definitions of "professionalism" has prevented this change.

Furthermore, at job levels above principal, exams in the strict sense are not used; and informal judgments prevail.[42] "At levels above the principal, they really tailor the exams to fit the guy," an NYU researcher reported. "An associate superintendent can't be defined by exam. What is very important is how he and the other guys fit. A standard exam does not work." Often, only one person is groomed for a top headquarters job and an "exam" is made up to suit him.† If old-line administrators who are reluctant to recruit outsiders have this "appointive" power, the practice can only contribute to a perpetuation of existing power blocs and traditions, as it has so far.

The Board of Examiners has also stifled innovation by hamstringing the superintendent. Superintendents are not allowed to bring in their own loyal staff when they take office.‡ Giardino rejected the NYU report's recommendation to give the superintendent the authority to make up to 5% of his appointments on an exempt basis, outside normal selection procedures.

Compulsive Rule Following

The civil service mentality, reinforced by the examination system, has hampered the schools at every turn. Many headquarters staff often hesitated to formulate advanced desegregation plans, for example, for fear of offending some of the administrators and supervisors and losing what little influence they had to effect even minor reforms.[43] After a while, they too,

* The board has started to recruit more Negroes to supervisory positions, in response to continued pressure from civil rights groups. There are still fewer than one hundred Negro supervisors in the field, out of more than two thousand positions. There are even fewer Puerto Rican teachers and supervisors.

† Headquarters officials acknowledge that this is always done.

‡ Calvin Gross, for example, would probably have fared much better if he had been allowed to bring with him a staff of competent and loyal colleagues. Instead, he came in with only his personal secretary. Donovan, on the other hand, has managed to place his friends and associates in key positions (for example, as special assistants), and this has allowed him to build a machine inside. These were people already in the system, however, indicating once again how much easier it was for insiders than outsiders to function in it.

and this includes staff personnel in those headquarters units most directly involved in desegregation planning, would feel obliged to retreat behind one or another legalism that supposedly prevented them from recommending more far-reaching desegregation proposals. Sometimes, the tendency to invoke particular rules or by-laws as a justification for inaction was not so much a matter of being against a desegregation plan as it was an attempt at personal and organizational survival. And the more tradition-bound officials were, the more attached they were to rules.*

One top-level commissioner in the Mayor's Commission on Human Rights, who had dealt with the Board of Education on the desegregation issue for many years, described some of the professionals he encountered: "When Gross came in we told them what they need is leadership. There is no flow in that kind of bureaucracy. The Board of Education is like an old man with arteriosclerosis. They make a good statement and it sits there like a heart pumping, but there are no veins or the veins aren't working. They are hardened. The bureaucracy is so paralyzed. They are slaves of their own past frame of mind. In other words, they set up ideas and lose sight of the fact that if they set the ideas up they could change them too. They became enslaved by the structure that they themselves had been responsible for setting up."

It was on the desegregation issue, perhaps more than on any others, that this bureaucratic outlook prevailed. The neighborhood school was an axiom, basic and unshakeable; many of the rules that were cited to justify the status quo followed logically from this axiom. Questioned about school construction and zoning, the educators recited the old rules. Even after the board had made numerous policy statements on construction to the effect that schools would be built in fringe areas where possible or where practicable, headquarters professionals continued to quote the old policy to justify building them as neighborhood schools.

On zoning, though the board had added integration and

---

* Social scientists have coined the term "bureaucratic personality" to characterize such forms of behavior, and suggest that they are prevalent in large civil service organizations. A preoccupation with rules, procedures, and traditional ways of solving problems is generally seen as the hallmark of this personality type. The New York City schools have more than their share of such people; the board recognizes this fact, but civil service laws preclude doing much about it.

utilization in 1957 as criteria for zoning decisions, particular plans were sometimes evaluated on the basis of other, more traditional criteria. For example, some plans were rejected because they violated the rule that there be no skip zoning—that is, that pupils not transfer across a contiguous school district.

One leader of a white civic group reported her conversations with Central Zoning Unit staff over feeder patterns they had developed for junior high schools in several boroughs. They told her with some pride how they had rearranged zoning patterns without violating traditional Board policy. "They kept trying to show me how they could break with the old without breaking with the old," she recalled. "It was a little bit like verbal gymnastics, because there wasn't much desegregation coming out of their plans. Many of them wanted to desegregate and it wasn't their fault, because they were bound by old zoning rules. It was sad to see them try to do something they couldn't do within the framework they followed and try to make themselves feel good about it. If it were up to them alone, at least some of them would have discarded old zoning rules."

Fragmentation, Field Rebellion, and Protectionist Politics

Two other key features of the system are its lateral and vertical divisions. The fragmentation of headquarters into various power blocs and cliques, and the rebellion and non-compliance of field officials with headquarters directives, contribute substantially to the school system's failures.

Despite the formal and legal centralization, the school system is in fact informally decentralized and quite anarchic. Invariably, when authority is centralized in large, bureaucratic organizations and dispersed across numerous headquarters units, the ranks become alienated and rebel. This has happened in the New York City schools.

Flooded with so many directives from so many bureaus, angry at how little headquarters knows about local conditions, and frustrated by the red tape, many field personnel of the New York City schools concluded that headquarters could usually be disregarded. This was not just a minority view held by a few rebellious field officials, but was part of their shared outlook, and one was a deviant if he did not follow it.

One field superintendent who had formerly been a high-ranking headquarters official said: "At the field superintendents' association meetings you'd see this distinct division between the district men and the headquarters men. The latter were regarded as in an ivory tower by the men in the field. Anything coming out of headquarters from someone of peer rank they regarded with a jaundiced eye. Now I'm out in the field, I'm one of the boys, and I'm also somewhat infected with their attitudes. I often find myself grumbling: 'Why don't they consult with us?' "

Field superintendents and principals often reinterpret directives to mean that they should do what they can to implement them in the light of their own superior knowledge of local conditions. Such reinterpretations could be anything from "passive sabotage" (as in Open Enrollment, when Negro and Puerto Rican parents were not informed of transfer opportunities) to more active efforts (such as telling parents at the end of the school year of the many costs and hardships involved in bussing their children out of the district or local school). If the directive was on a relatively noncontroversial matter, it might simply be filed away and disregarded.

The fragmentation comes about as a result of the elaborate vertical and horizontal differentiation of the system, dividing it up into a series of separate power centers.

Divisions. In both desegregation and decentralization, the significant power blocs have been the elementary, junior high, and academic and vocational high school divisions. Innovation threatens the position or even the survival of these units.

By 1965, when the board formulated its first decentralization proposals, the divisional offices had become solidified within the system with much authority and informal power. They added to their staff at headquarters and took over decisions on staffing, curriculum, budgeting, and basic pedagogical and administrative matters for their units. At the least, they had strong veto power over decisions made by higher level officials.

Each divisional office was generally supported by its principals' association in the field. Occasionally, the associations were even informally encouraged in their opposition to reforms by headquarters officials.

The divisions were a focus of strong loyalties. At headquarters especially, one was known as a high school or a junior high school man and often identified as a protegé or ally of a strong personality within a division. Appointment to the superintendency, as well as to other top administrative and field posts, involved the influence of particular cliques formed within the divisions.[44] Superintendent Donovan, for example, was known as a "high school man," partial to other high school men in his selection of people to serve on key committees. The late Dr. Joseph Loretan was a "junior high school man." There were constant clashes between these divisions and personalities.

These loyalties, cliques, and internal power struggles were an essential element in headquarters politics, with respect to routine matters as well as innovation. Administrative studies of the system indicate that the divisions were often insulated from one another and tended to approach routine staffing, curriculum, and budgetary questions from the perspective of their own specialist logics.[45] They functioned as separate baronies that just happened to be part of a larger structure. Predictably, the divisions competed in trying to secure larger shares of the scarce resources of the system. "What will this do to our unit?" was the usual question when reforms were discussed.

The high school division was generally regarded as the most powerful unit. "There's an old saying around the board," explained a headquarters person, "that there is the New York City school system, and then there is the high school division." Some academic high schools had achieved a national reputation over the past several decades for their programs; many of their award-winning students went on to top colleges, where they won more honors. Some of the vocational high school programs had a similar reputation, though some were justly criticized for their outdated curricula, and for ethnic and class segregation.

The junior high school division perhaps had the most problems, the result of its ambiguous position. It was the most recently established of the four divisions, and it had trouble getting accepted as a bona fide unit. The New York City school system used to be organized in an 8–4 arrangement and there was resistance to the 6–3–3 organization introduced in the late 1920s. Some elementary and high school officials held out to the bitter end.

This division's officials have felt for many years that they have never been given the status, power, and salary scale that they merited. Junior high school staff, and especially principals, have been lobbying for a long time to get salaries equivalent to those of high school principals, on grounds that they have equal responsibilities and training. They say that they deal with pupils at an especially difficult period in their growth and development, and they resent the "stand-offishness" of high school officials and the unwillingness of the latter to see this.

The junior high school division was often viewed as the stepchild of the system.[46] And its curriculum and programs were often poorly coordinated with those of elementary and high schools. Furthermore, the concept of the four-year comprehensive high school, discussed publicly since the early 1950s, and the middle school, threatened its future.*

Elementary school principals were allowed, sometimes encouraged, to move up to junior high school posts, but the same opportunity had not generally been granted the junior high school principals to move up to the high schools. Junior high school spokesmen demanded equal salaries, perhaps partially to compensate for their lower status, and were denied that as well. They were constantly told in these symbolic ways that their division was the weakest in the entire system.

Personal factors contributed to the division's problems, too. The junior high school division needed a strong and able administrator, given its anomalous position within the system. Instead, it suffered from weak leadership in its early years. Later, in the 1950s and 1960s, its leaders began to struggle among themselves and alienated many other headquarters officials. They were in a difficult position and compounded their difficulties by their inability to maintain amicable working relations with administrators outside the division.†

Salary scales preoccupied officials in all divisions. Elementary

---

* See my discussion below on these concepts in the context of desegregation controversies.

† Students of administration note that the status of "middle" groups in organizations is often a source of much strain, both within the range of middle status occupations themselves and in their relations with lower and higher ranking groups. Dr. Leonard Sayles suggests that this problem is endemic in both blue collar and professional hierarchies. Middle groups often face an ambiguity of status that leads to attempts at monetary, political, and status improvement. They feel that their training and skills are virtually the equivalent of those of top-level people, and resent the fact that this goes unrewarded. A vicious cycle often gets established: failure to secure more rewards and status reinforces doubts about the importance of the job, leading to more efforts to gain recognition, new evidence that the job is not appreciated, and renewed efforts to raise one's status through pressure tactics and grievances. Among unionized blue collar workers, wildcat strikes are quite common from within this group. Professionals often respond by rebellion and behind-the-scenes struggles for status and power. This characterization fits the situation and behavior of many junior high school officials in the New York City schools. See his *Behavior of Industrial Work Groups*, New York: Wiley, 1958, pp. 49–56.

school principals received the least, followed by the junior high and high school staffs. The difference in salary between the junior high school and elementary school staff was only about $600, which led to much resentment among junior high school officials. The status hierarchy and tensions that existed generally affected the response of people in the divisions to headquarters pressures for desegregation and decentralization.

The commitment to their divisions often took on a remarkable intensity. "If you just said the word 'junior high school,'" a headquarters official said, "some of these people would literally have a religious experience. This is an interesting question of semantics, the way a particular word or concept would evoke such feelings. People would tell you the wondrous things their division had done in New York City. Their division was their whole way of life. They meant it in a professional as well as political sense."

The other major blocs, in addition to the Board of Examiners and divisions, were the Board of Superintendents,* the Council of Supervisory Associations, particular bureaus, the district superintendents, and the principals' associations.[47]

The Council of Supervisory Associations is a major symbol of traditional bureaucratic politics. Formed in 1963 to represent all the field supervisors—principals, department chairmen, district superintendents, administrative assistants, and various staff personnel—it has opposed virtually every suggested innovation on desegregation or administrative reform. The Council upholds the neighborhood school, and it defends it against all demands for desegregation, even to the point of having led open rebellions against Calvin Gross and the lay board during the controversy over pairings and implementation of the Allen Report recommendations for junior high and high school desegregation. When Alfred Giardino presented his proposed reforms in February, 1967, concerning examination procedures, the CSA went to Albany to prevent the necessary legislative

---

* The Board of Superintendents included divisional and bureau heads, all of whom had associate superintendent rank, plus the superintendent. This group was abolished in 1961, when the Board of Education underwent some organizational changes in top positions, though it continued to function informally for a few years after that. It made major policy decisions on pedagogical and administrative matters and reportedly hemmed in the board and superintendent with precedents and traditions whenever there was any discussion of possible innovations. It was a symbol of much of the status quo politics that had existed before Calvin Gross arrived in 1963.

changes, even though the Board of Examiners itself came to accept, however reluctantly, Giardino's proposals.

Field supervisors, especially district superintendents and principals, who are the backbone of CSA, resent the unilateral way in which the lay board and top headquarters officials usually propose innovations.[48] The field supervisors felt threatened as civil rights and other integrationist groups began to influence top decision makers at headquarters, and when headquarters formulated actual desegregation plans without consulting them, the field supervisors revolted.

District superintendents obstructed desegregation, both in policy-making and implementation. They strongly resisted most of the original pairing plans, not only because they were attached to the neighborhood school idea, but because many of them resented the fact that headquarters had taken over much of the authority that they used to exercise informally. The district superintendents made most zoning and site location decisions, even though these decisions were supposed to be made at headquarters.* When Gross was superintendent, he rarely communicated with them and didn't take them into his confidence, nor, apparently, did the lay board. Many district superintendents as well as principals have made the same complaint, however, about Superintendent Donovan as well, whom they condemn for "not touching base with us, but making the big decisions on impulse," as one of them put it.

At a private meeting of the lay board in 1964 attended by representatives of local school boards, parent associations and district superintendents, for purposes of discussing the proposed pairings, the revolt took place in dramatic fashion. "A district superintendent got up," recalled an informant who was present, "and shouted at Gross in anger, saying that he didn't care what happened to him for making the speech, but that he would absolutely refuse ever to be a party to such a bunch of trumped-up and politically inspired and expedient plans that were so educationally unsound. He accused Gross of becoming a tool of civil rights leaders and suggested that this could hurt the schools. This meeting included all the district superintendents, and after he finished, they gave him resounding applause. I was

---

* The Central Zoning Unit staff at headquarters were therefore only reacting to suggestions made locally, rather than initiating rezoning plans themselves. See below, Chapter Nine, on the Central Zoning Unit for a more extended discussion of these points.

surprised to see this insubordination before a group of outside citizens."

Desegregation

These bureaucratic pathologies are not unique to the New York City school system. They are present to one degree or another in many other school systems, and are characteristic of most large civil service organizations, in this country and elsewhere. But the New York City schools fit the bureaucratic pathology model in virtually every respect.

The pathology is indicated most clearly in the way the bureaucracy and the professional staff handled the desegregation question—which did more to dramatize the system's failures than any other issue in recent decades and provoked the public outcry for change.

Open Enrollment. Many headquarters staff worked hard to make the board's first major desegregation plan, Open Enrollment, a success. There was an Open Enrollment Committee, composed of field supervisors and top headquarters personnel, and they developed various programs to make it work—for example, elaborate instructions to teachers, principals, and district superintendents, and centralized administration to ensure compliance with directives regarding the plan.[49]

Despite these efforts, however, Open Enrollment is the one desegregation technique for which the evidence of field sabotage is most extensive. Less than 5% of the total eligibles ever participated in the program. While some board officials concluded from this that Negro and Puerto Rican parents don't want to transfer their children, and that this was the main reason for the limited effect of the program, the evidence of sabotage in the field suggests other reasons.

My previous discussion of the increase in percentage of transfers in the Free Choice Transfer plan over Open Enrollment indicated how much effect headquarters controls and policing could have.* Landers reports that 30% of the eligible pupils selected to transfer under the plan did so in September, 1964, while 14.8% transferred the following year, both figures well above the 3% for Open Enrollment. He neglects to report, however, that civil rights groups' pressures contributed substantially to the strong headquarters control over implementa-

* See Chapter One.

tion in 1964.[50] On the other hand, civil rights groups' pressures were not nearly so strong in 1965, and principals could subvert the plan with more impunity.

The techniques principals used in sending and in receiving schools to discourage pupil transfers were varied. The following comments are illustrative of what went on in the sending schools: [51]

Human relations staff person in field, Bronx
Open Enrollment proposals were always announced at the last minute, with a notice sent home the last two weeks of school with an invitation to visit new schools. They know that the parents don't have time on two weeks notice to get involved. So in a way, it was doomed to failure before they started.

Local school board member, Brooklyn
PS 20, the Reverse Open Enrollment school, was really the exception. This is the only time I have seen the board go into a white sending school and press their plan. Usually, they just file the plan and let it go at that. . . . They don't tell you what school you will be going to, or how much space is available at their list of choices. Nor do they publicize, for instance, that one parent may go in each bus every day. Mrs. Dorothy Fulmer got that concession from the board on the Reverse Open Enrollment situation, and it eventually was extended over the district superintendent's strong resistance.

Civil rights leader, Brooklyn
I don't know that the board or principals tried to get parents not to transfer, but they certainly never promoted the plan. With the complete lack of information coming from the board, it is inevitable that both apathy and general negative attitudes about the whole thing will spread through the community; and that is what happened.

Local school board member, Manhattan
The principals tended to discourage it. Those that I heard about said things like, of course, it will be impossible for the kids to go home for lunch and that's a big disadvantage. It is possible that some principals or teachers encouraged the program, but I haven't heard of any. Any promotion was done by other community agencies and organizations.

Civil rights leader, Brooklyn
In almost every school I have anything to do with, Open Enrollment was not only not pushed but talked against. Parents got lectures about how hard it is to travel and go to a school far away. This was usually how it went and I can only remember one school where it was not true. I made many trips to the board with parents from several schools asking why their kids were not

included. They were told their slips got in too late. Livingston
Street people said the parents should get after the principals, because they were supposed to give out the slips a week ahead
of time.

Former headquarters official
Principals and teachers often did not inform parents about Open
Enrollment options. When we checked up, principals would say
that they had announced it in class but that the child probably
did not tell his parents. Some principals told parents about the
plan in ambiguous or technical language that they could not understand—and parents would sometimes withdraw for fear of
exposing their inability to understand, or simply out of fear of
getting their children involved in anything so complicated. Another technique was to discourage parents by telling them of all
the difficulties involved—from bussing their children to segregated
classes in receiving schools.

These six witnesses are well-informed people, who know the
system on a district- or borough-wide basis. The last informant
knew about how the plan was implemented throughout the
city.*

From the comments it is clear that the board put a tremendous burden on Negro and Puerto Rican parents to find out
about the transfer options themselves, even after the plan was
mandated from headquarters. As the Brooklyn civil rights
leader said, she had constantly to fight school officials just to
give Negro children rights that the Board of Education itself
had decreed. It was experiences like hers throughout the city
that led civil rights groups to the position in 1963 that voluntary desegregation plans place too great a burden on Negro
parents and should be supplemented if not replaced by non-
voluntary plans.

The story of sabotage in receiving schools under Open Enrollment is much the same. Indeed, principals and teachers in
receiving schools may, if anything, have been even more anxious than their colleagues in sending schools about the effects
of Open Enrollment. They had many techniques to discourage
transfers. Incoming pupils would often be placed in slow
and/or segregated classes; more disciplinary measures would be
used; they sent in false data to headquarters; and sometimes
principals would show little interest in securing extra services

---

* I have so many more similar reports from parents and school officials
that there seems little question about the "representativeness" of the ones
cited above.

for the incoming pupils. These techniques embittered Negro parents who would often withdraw their children from Open Enrollment schools. Consider the following comments:

Human relations staff person in field, Bronx
In one elementary school, the principal always referred to the Negro kids as "our bussed-in children." The coordination between headquarters and the school was particularly bad, and school opened before the school received either books or records of the new kids. The attitude of the principal and teachers at that point was not to complain about the lack of books and records but to use the line, "If the kids weren't there there would be no problem."

Civic Leader, Manhattan
I have been involved in several cases of suspensions and severe disciplinary action for kids who opted to go to schools in white areas in The Bronx. Some were suspended or disciplined for little justifiable cause.

Civil rights leader, Brooklyn
Several years ago, an elementary school principal who has since been transferred was quoted in the school newspaper as saying that he lacked money for textbooks because he had to provide notebooks and pencils for the underprivileged kids from Brownsville. He spoke about how harmful this all was and could be prevented by rezoning the school within the immediate area.

Local school board member, Brooklyn
One of our elementary schools has kids bussed in. This necessitated a lunch program, additional supervision, and the problems of playground activity. The school tried to avoid many of them. The kids are kept under tight wraps and they sit and read and are told to stay quiet.

UPA official, Queens
Some Harlem kids were given an Open Enrollment option into one of our elementary schools. Our local parent association wanted to contact their Harlem schools and express our welcome, encouraging them to send their children. This was all done against the principal's wishes. His major objection was a fear that the school would get too large for his assistant principal status and he would be replaced.

Civil rights leader, Brooklyn
I always make it a point to look in the classroom windows whenever I am in an Open Enrollment school. Nearly all the classes are almost all white or all black. The principals of the junior high schools claim the Negro kids are all so far behind, but in the elementary schools the principals claim they are not homogeneously grouped. They often are.

Civic Leader, Bronx
A few years ago, about 30–35 kids were bussed into an elementary school here. They went on one bus and were deposited at a particular door, never in the school yard where the rest of the kids were. They went directly to their room and from 8:30 until 3:00 they stayed there. They ate their lunch in the room and did exercises there rather than recess. They left the room only to go to the bathroom and were taken directly to the bus and home at the end of the day.

We conducted interviews in all boroughs except Staten Island and found the weight of evidence on the negative side on the implementation of Open Enrollment, though there were a few cases where the program was pushed by principals and teachers.

The behavior of principals and teachers was quite rational, given their interests. Principals from sending schools feared that large numbers of pupil transfers might reflect adversely on the quality of their schools. Many were oriented toward making a good showing to their district superintendent and toward headquarters, in the hope of being promoted or transferred. If too many Negro parents transferred their children out, some principals and teachers understandably feared the board might assume considerable parent dissatisfaction. Teachers had similar fears. Teachers and principals were also against Open Enrollment because they wanted to keep at least a few potentially "high achievers" in their schools. Understandably they felt that such children might inspire the others. Meanwhile, principals and teachers in receiving schools feared that standards would decline, intergroup tensions might increase, classes might be disrupted, and middle class parents might object and even pull their children out of the school. The problem is how to change some of the assumptions within the system that spawn such fears and behavior.

Some principals appeal to the sense of pride that Negro parents should feel for their ghetto schools, suggesting that sending large numbers of children out of the school would imply that it was not as good as schools in white middle class areas. This argument carries more and more weight with Negro parents, now that their commitment to desegregation is waning. An indication of how little they care about desegregation now is that there was barely a ripple when the board announced in

June, 1967, that it was discontinuing most of its Open Enrollment programs.

A final justification field officials sometimes gave for rejecting headquarters directives to implement the program was that
they were "professionals" who should be given autonomy commensurate with their training and knowledge of local school
conditions. Some felt it was unfair and unnecessary for headquarters to do more than recommend that they push the
program, subject to their own professional judgement. This
self-conscious professionalism of school officials at all levels
helped justify their strategies of independence in rejecting many
headquarters plans.

It would be inaccurate to suggest that headquarters was
completely unaware of this noncompliance or that the board
did nothing about it. As time went on, the Central Zoning
Unit took over more of the responsibility for mimeographing
and circulating Open Enrollment notices to parents.[52] It also
collected their replies. Thus, principals could no longer say
that they had sent notices when they hadn't, or had arranged
transfers for those parents who had opted for them when they
hadn't.

Headquarters went even further. An Open Enrollment
Committee was formed in 1960 to brief principals, field superintendents, school–community coordinators, divisional and
bureau representatives, and other staff. Suggestions and recommendations were solicited in these meetings during the pilot
stage of the program from 1960 to 1963.

One result of these meetings was a board progress report,
published in September, 1963, which summarized the experiences of the previous three years. It contained a comprehensive
listing of suggestions offered to principals participating in the
program, covering virtually every conceivable administrative
contingency.[53]

The report also included certain moral exhortations: "The
program, to succeed, must be presented as an official policy and
as a moral obligation. Principals must set the tone because it is
morally right, not merely because it is official policy. . . . After
careful examination of records and administration of new
tests, if necessary, placement should be made so as to avoid
segregation in any one class." The New York City Board of
Education probably surpasses any other big city school system in
such liberal policy statements, but, as we have seen, the bureau-

cracy and the interests of its officials responsible for implementation lead to the widespread subversion of the best laid plans.*
Pairings. The five pairings mandated in 1964 are still in operation as of this writing. Pairings provided fewer chances for field sabotage than Open Enrollment, since the board had to take the responsibility for rezoning and give local school officials no options in this regard. There were inefficiencies, but informal evaluations by parent groups are generally positive. The board's own evaluation indicates that while white pupils have left, especially in Jackson Heights where PAT groups opened their own private school and recruited about seventy pupils, the plan has worked satisfactorily, measured by conventional pupil achievement, attitudinal, and sociometric tests.† [54]

Nevertheless, some principals flagrantly maintain segregated, homogeneous classes in many of the paired schools, as other principals had done under Open Enrollment, partly as a way to keep the white middle class in the school. The most conspicuous instance of this practice was the so-called model pairing of PS 7 and 8 in Brooklyn Heights which alienated both Negro and white parents. [55]

I have already referred to the spontaneous development of the pairing idea in Brooklyn Heights, within the upper middle class white liberal community there as well as among Negroes.‡ The Negro and white groups were especially anxious for the pairing to get rid of two principals with whom the board was reportedly unhappy as well, mainly for their anti-Negro attitudes. The community knew that if the pairing went through there would have to be a new principal, since the school would then be too big for only an assistant principal, which is what PS 8 then had.§

But then headquarters made the mistake of choosing as principal a woman who had served for some time in a ghetto

---

* This is not to deny the many administrative problems in carrying out such a program, especially given the limits of available staff, space, and money. But sabotage is sabotage, even given such problems.

† The board's own evaluations indicated that 5,200 pupils participated initially (October, 1964) in the Queens and Brooklyn pairings, 52% of whom were white, 41% black, and 7% Puerto Rican. After the first year, there were 48% whites in the program, but that decline seems to have levelled off since 1965.

‡ See Chapter Three.

§ They didn't like the assistant principal and embraced the pairing as a way of getting him out.

school. She dampened the community's enthusiasm for the pairing so rapidly that she left the school after one year. "She turned out to be arrogant," one civic leader recalled. "She made kids wear ties to school and infuriated parents by refusing to let them in the building with slacks on. If Johnny forgot his lunch, a mother would just run down to the school and get a lecture on dress and not be allowed to give him the lunch. She had obviously been assigned to ghetto schools all her life and was used to treating parents this way and getting away with it. There was tremendous antagonism between parents and the principal, to the extent that more than one mother got into actual screaming fights with her in the halls of the school. It was so bad that one parent who was also a *New York Post* reporter referred to her in his column as the 'abrasive principal of the PS 7–8 pairing.' "

"[That person] was chosen, partly because she had wanted to be a district superintendent," an informed headquarters person reported. "It was thought that this might be a way of mollifying her." But if the board had really wanted to make this pairing work, it should not have let internal political considerations affect its choice of a principal. It should have selected a person who was committed to pairing to handle this difficult situation. It should also have selected a principal who was committed to maintaining desegregated classrooms, which this one was not.

Integrationists also wanted the board to retain a middle school for the area, so that the graduates of PS 7 and 8 would continue to have an integrated school experience beyond the elementary level. Instead, the PS 7 and 8 graduates are all zoned into Rothschild Junior High School in Bedford–Stuyvesant, further discouraging the whites.

The next principal who was assigned to the paired schools also maintained homogeneous, segregated classes. "I couldn't integrate everybody," she explained, "and I didn't want the white kids to feel like a minority." One white parent reported that whites still get better treatment in the school. "The board strives to keep the whites happy," he said. "My wife can get almost anything from the teachers or principal. It makes her sick, though she sometimes takes advantage of it. Basically, the board interprets integration to mean preventing the alienation of whites."

By now, the Negro community is largely zoned into the

new PS 307.* These parents are among the most militant Black Power advocates, partly because of their experience with the pairing, partly because of their resentment that the white community did not unite and protest more against the building of 307. Some parents are still trying to save the pairing by asking for a broad community participation program, similar to what the IS 201 parents asked for. Their distrust of the board continues.

The board's limited preparation of the community, parents, school staff, and pupils for the pairings contributed to many problems in implementation. Too many orientation meetings on pairings might have led to more community conflict than there was. The controversy over pairings raged throughout the city, and it would have been senseless to fan it any more. But the board withdrew from the essential task of preparation much more than was necessary.

In fact, Dr. Fredrick Williams and his staff from the board's Human Relations Unit were busily visiting the offices of various civic groups the week before school opened.[56] Williams decided that it would be helpful for his staff to know what the citywide groups were up to. Meanwhile, community tensions in Queens, where three pairings were instituted, were explosive, and Williams and his staff were not there. A top official in one citywide organization—who was not enthusiastic about pairings, but who wanted those that were implemented given as much headquarters support as possible—said: "Williams and his staff were leisurely sipping tea and killed most of a day hanging around our office, while Parents and Taxpayers were busily spreading fear among the white parents in Queens and organizing their boycott and private school."

Principals, teachers, and district superintendents in the paired schools, whom the board interviewed in its own evaluation study, complained that they had to spend much of their time dealing with community tensions at the beginning of the school year, and they had little time left over for instruction and internal school matters.[57] The evaluation indicated that the decision for particular pairings was made so late (it was made in late May, 1964, for the following school year) that there was literally no time to plan for extra space, supplies,

* PS 307 was built in the ghetto community in 1965.

and staffing for the schools; there was no provision for securing community and staff acceptance of the plan; and there was poor coordination of efforts between headquarters and the schools to equip the schools, once the decision was made. In other words, the school system functioned as usual.

Since pairings were tried in only eight schools from the first to the sixth grades, and in two more for the first three grades, it might be assumed that headquarters would have tried hard to make them work, as "showcase schools," to be cited as examples of how well desegregation worked. The board's evaluation indicates that the program did well in many respects, despite numerous bureaucratic inefficiencies. There were inceased interracial contacts and friendships among pupils and parents, and a softening of negative attitudes toward Negroes among some teachers and principals. Furthermore, while there was no marked change in academic performance for white middle class pupils, there was some slight improvement for Negro children.

The comments of principals and district superintendents show how the system has habitually implemented new desegregation plans. Everyone agreed that the program was poorly planned and that last-minute efforts to get facilities and set up the schools was demoralizing. The three superintendents in the districts where pairings were instituted were interviewed in January, 1965, and asked to enumerate the major problems they had encountered. They replied:

> There was so little time between the final decision to proceed with the program and the actual commencement, that complete organizational and administrative steps could not be taken.

> The inception or increase of bussing created confusion. In the case of the younger children, so much time had to be spent on bussing routines that some parents complained of a shortened school day.

> The movement of books and materials from building to building and within buildings was a monumental task.

These administrative matters should have been handled better. Some of the complaints by parents, especially those involving bussing, were justified, in view of the board's chaotic implementations.

Principals of the paired schools were interviewed in the fall of 1964 and again in the spring of 1965, and were asked to comment on the main accomplishments of the pairings, the problems they encountered, and their recommendations for improving the program. They all agreed that the planning could have been much better. "All new equipment and materials should be sent to newly paired schools in June, and all school repairs should be done in the summer before the September opening of schools," one principal recommended. In two cases, repairs and renovation went on well through the school year. "More time should be allowed for pre-planning," recommended another principal. "The decision to pair our schools came so late in June that the interchange of materials of designated grades and the assigning of personnel had to be accomplished in the last few weeks during the summer and early in the fall."

Several principals said that their responsibilities were increased, but that they got no additional assistance. One, for example, reported that he received no help in recruiting personnel for the newly created positions, nor was he able to recruit the experienced teachers the school needed. Of the 37 classroom teachers on his staff, only 10 were permanently appointed, and 15 were substitutes. Hence a great deal of his time had to be given to teacher training.

It was the inefficient implementation of pairings and other desegregation plans that led some civil rights leaders to feel that the board was implementing these plans in such a way to insure their failure. Board officials often claim that such views reflect the Negro's paranoia, but Negro experiences with desegregation have not been pleasant ones.

One of the most striking omissions was the lack of plans to prepare the community, the staff, the pupils, or the parents for the change. The board was as inefficient in this case as it had been earlier with Open Enrollment. The board's unofficial policy which had become a tradition was that if there was too much controversy in the community, school officials should stay away. "We often get word about how hot things are out in the community," a headquarters staff member said, "and if we are asked to come and speak, we don't go unless we have some assurance that the meeting won't get too far out of hand." No matter what practical advantages followed from this procedure, it was hardly a way to encourage innovation in keeping with the wishes and needs of many in the community, nor was it a way to gain the community's support.

This strategy undermined the whole concept of pairing,

in the eyes of some parents and school officials. It demoralized many of the school staff in paired schools who had to spend so much of their time on community relations. Though it was enlightening for them to have to meet the community head on, it was unfortunate that they had to do so without support from headquarters. "A more concerted effort should be made, in advance, to supply the community with information regarding the school as it will be," said one principal. Another complained: "An exorbitant amount of time was devoted to dealing with parent–school and community–school relations. There should be an intensive program, in advance, to win the acceptance of the pairing plan by the community." A superintendent recommended: "Headquarters should assign one person to each field superintendent's office to work only with the pairing program, especially in the areas of community relations and curriculum implementation."

These comments came from school officials who were generally insulated themselves from the community and headquarters. If they had become so desperate as to request more help from headquarters in community relations, then the situation must have deteriorated to a considerable extent.

Grade Reorganization, The 4–4–4 Plan. The reorganization proposal* activated all the old status anxieties and internal political rivalries that have existed among the divisions for years, and they fought with all the resources they could muster. They protested publicly, mobilized support from their principals' associations, lobbied with the board and civic groups, and engaged in work slowdowns as well as open subversion of the early pilot plans.[58]

When the board announced its intention to change to a four-year comprehensive high school and phase out many vocational high school programs, for example, it met great resistance. Vocational high school staff were concerned about the extinction of their division, and pointed to the career opportunities that their programs provided for many low income, minority-group pupils. The academic high school division was worried about losing its influential position in the system† if vocational and academic programs were merged.

Headquarters and field officials from each division followed

* See Chapter One.
† Due in part to the prestige gained from award-winning pupils, as described earlier.

several strategies to inhibit change. A committee chaired by Superintendent Donovan submitted a report in December, 1964, praised the 6–3–3 system, and called for a continuation of the status quo.[59] In 1966 and 1967, when the board was pressed by a coalition of civil rights and moderate groups to show some minimal attempts at implementation of its 1965 and 1966 policy statements about the four-year comprehensive high school, representatives of the academic and vocational high school principals' associations moved to block any changes. A headquarters official said: "One way the high school principals have sabotaged the comprehensive high school and clusters plan is simply to refuse to develop curriculum and staffing ideas for them. There is a system-wide slowdown and inaction on this. In fact, the Council of Supervisory Associations and high school principals' association are leading this campaign."

In May, 1967, Donovan opposed the board's recommendations to phase out the archaic vocational schools and to absorb many vocational programs in comprehensive high schools, even though two years earlier Donovan himself had recommended that the changeover to comprehensive high schools be completed by 1970.*

Donovan's statement infuriated even the usually moderate Public Education Association, which had supported the high school reorganization. Dr. Frederick C. McLaughlin, director of the PEA, declared: "When all the talk contained in the superintendent's fourteen points is sifted and studied, it becomes clear that he is proposing to do business at the same old stand. A few obsolete vocational high schools will be phased out—how many is not stated—but for the rest it will be business as usual. . . . Two years have been wasted while the policy of the Board of Education for a single system of comprehensive high schools has been talked to death. Now the Board of Education is beng asked to ignore its own decision and to reward the delaying tactics and obstructionism of the staff by repudiating its own policy decision of two years ago." [60]

JHS 38, in the Bronx, was one of the schools selected for the change to a 4–4–4 plan in the fall of 1964.[61] But in the spring of that year, the teachers and their principal rebelled. The complaints of the teachers were summarized in a letter

---

* In 1966, he asked for a delay until 1973 because of problems of time, space, and money. He also proposed a compromise cluster plan to consolidate some vocational and academic schools.

from Albert Shanker, president of the United Federation of Teachers, to Superintendent Gross, dated June 12, 1964. He reported that a substantial part of the plan was being sabotaged through poor implementation and cited the following examples: (1) Teachers in new sixth grade classes were being forced to teach out of license; (2) Principals told the teachers that they would have to go on an increased teaching schedule (more periods) because they were involved in an integration experiment; (3) Principals also told teachers that class size would be increased; (4) Many teachers were told they would have to leave the school with the changeover—for example, shop teachers—but they were not informed as to their rights in seeking new positions; and (5) added clerical burdens were imposed on the teachers. As Shanker concludes:

> These problems have arisen because there was *no* consultation on the implementation of the plan. Furthermore, an analysis of the above would indicate that there is a definite effort on the part of the Junior High School Division and Junior High School principals to undermine the integration plan by proceeding along lines calculated to create the greatest hostility among teachers and produce the least effective education possible under the circumstances.

Data from minutes of meetings held with Mrs. Martha Finkler, acting associate superintendent of the Junior High School Division, Assistant Superintendent Max Rubinstein of the Division, and teacher representatives, indicate that Shanker's charge of sabotage accurately reflected the actions and motivations of the division's heads. A few excerpts from those meetings provide such evidence. They are Mrs. Finkler's answers to questions of teacher representatives:

QUESTION: Can we assume that the Board of Education is mandating that teachers teach out of license, i.e., social studies, teachers teaching language arts?

ANSWER: These are enough common branch people in the junior high schools to handle the sixth grade program. [When it was pointed out that these ten schools lack a sufficient number of common branch people, Mrs. Finkler did not readily respond.]

It was clear, then, that the bulk of the sixth grade teaching program would be carried out by JHS teachers not trained in language arts.

QUESTION: Would it be possible to assign common branch teachers to the junior high schools to teach the sixth grade?
ANSWER: No.
QUESTION: What rationale is behind the lack of departmentalized program for sixth-grade students?
ANSWER: Sixth grade students are not junior high school students but are elementary school children being held in the JHS. Therefore, they will follow the normal elementary school programs as presented by Dr. King and converted into periods by the JHS division.

In other words, there was to be no real change. Sixth graders were merely defined as elementary school pupils who happened to be housed in a junior high school building, rather than as part of a new grade structure.

QUESTION: Would it not work better to immobilize sixth grade classes in one room and have the subject teachers travel to the classroom to teach the various academic subjects, i.e., language arts, social studies, math, etc.?
ANSWER: The basis of a self-contained program is to keep the children in one room with one teacher for as many hours as is possible and only to allow departmentalization for specialized subjects.
QUESTION: Are we to assume that language arts is not a specialized subject?
ANSWER: That's correct. Language arts is not a specialized subject.

Another complaint by teachers was that many shop teachers in these junior high schools had been phased out without being given any information on where they could go for new positions. There were strong objections to excluding sixth graders from shop courses, as reflected in the following exchange:

QUESTION: Why aren't the sixth graders being given industrial arts, since there have been many experiments in the suburbs and in other cities, as well as in our own city that have been successful?
ANSWER: Since this is not part of the normal elementary school program, it will not be done in the 6–7–8 school.
QUESTION: What will be done about the objections of the teachers involved in this experiment?
ANSWER: If the JHS teachers object too vigorously, they may find themselves losing their positions.

Furthermore, Mrs. Finkler and her associates in the division aso implied that the desegregation plan would have an adverse effect on quality, as indicated in a further exchange:

QUESTION: Is this a program for quality education and integration?

ANSWER: No, it is for the desegregation of certain junior high schools and for sending ninth grade students into integrated high schools a year earlier.

This view was spelled out by Mrs. Finkler and Mr. Rubinstein at the end of one meeting, as recorded by teacher representatives who were present: "Mrs. Finkler and Mr. Rubinstein stated candidly that they were opposed to this plan and that it was handed to them readymade from above. They had no choice but to see that it is followed as mandated by Dr. King, Dr. Loretan, Dr. Donovan, and Superintendent Gross. Any change in the basic structure of this plan can only come from those above Mrs. Finkler. As far as the ten experimental schools are concerned, they will receive no additional services." There was at best a limited commitment to this plan, then, from the divisional heads, and they were in fact subverting it by imposing undue hardships on teachers and principals in its implementation.

It wasn't just teachers who were outraged by the way the Junior High School Division had chosen to implement the plan. Leonard F. Littwin, principal at JHS 38, sided with his teachers in complaining about conditions planned for his school. In a letter to Mrs. Finkler, written during the teacher uprising, he expressed his support for the desegregation plan, also indicating his dismay at the increased class size, the elimination of the school's interscholastic athletic program, and the increased pupil load for its guidance counsellors and secretaries. He also commented on the lowered teacher morale as a result of larger classes and on the community's shock at hearing that no new services had been listed for the school. It is hard to imagine any bureaucratic unit at the board or anywhere else which would not resist its own extinction. The heads of the Junior High School Division were no exception.

The board transferred 2,134 sixth grade children into 8 junior high schools, and 4,486 ninth graders into 29 academic and 7 vocational high schools, at the same time that it instituted the pairings.[62] The pupils were transferred from schools with 85% or more minority group children, as a preliminary step toward establishing four year middle and high schools.

Though the board did not evaluate the program in its first year, just as it did not evaluate Open Enrollment initially, the UPA did.[63] It visited all of the junior and senior high schools that had received the majority of these children, and concluded that the program was poorly implemented:

> There was some confusion as to which division was in charge of these sixth grade children. Three principals said the elementary division was in charge. Two said both divisions were in charge. Two were not sure. One principal felt that no one was taking charge; it was left to him. To quote another: "the sixth graders are guests in the school."

Their summary statement included a stronger indictment of the board's failure to implement even this pilot project effectively:

> The hasty implementation of the program left the staff completely unprepared for the change. There was no time for proper preparation or planning. There was no consultation with the administration responsible for implementing the program. The principals were handed a *fait accompli*. The result was a decline in morale and a heightened feeling of insecurity . . . The lack of direction from the Board of Education, coupled with the resistance of staff are great deterrents to the success of this program. Obviously there is much confusion and little direction from the Board of Education.

These are very strong charges, especially from a moderate organization like the UPA which is not nearly so anti-board and anti-establishment as militant groups on the left or right.

The UPA evaluation reported similar problems at the high school level. Overcrowding and inadequate preparation of students, staff, and parents led to much confusion. The board had been burdened with overcrowding at the high school level before embarking on these reforms, but planning for supplementary space might have been undertaken and generally was not. Many ghetto high schools that are overcrowded have used supplementary, extra facilities—annexes, portable classrooms, for example. For various political and administrative reasons—e.g., white students resent being displaced by incoming Negro and Puerto Rican students—such facilities were not used extensively in newly organized high schools. The price the board paid for this poor planning and preparation was that desegregation plans like Open Enrollment, pairings, and grade reorganization are discredited in their initial stages of implementation. This contributes to greater resistance from community groups and school officials, and the board can then say that it has tried such plans, but that they have not worked well. They have not worked in part because of the way they were implemented.

The four-year comprehensive high school concept got increasingly delayed, partly as a result of this early experience. The delay was also prompted by strong resistance from academic and vocational high school officials and from the United Parents Association, which wanted to maintain standards and privileged opportunities for middle class pupils at academic high schools.

Civic groups forcefully expressed their resentment over this delay—most forcefully at a public hearing in May, 1967. A representative from the Women's City Club, for example, suggested that the school professionals had successfully challenged the board's authority, noting further that no line of authority existed to assure that policy statements adopted by the board were carried through.

These delays on the comprehensive high school had broader ramifications, holding up high school construction throughout the city, as the board continued to vacillate on what kind of high school system it wanted. Even though money had been appropriated for construction, the schools were not being built very rapidly, worsening an already overcrowded situation. Many high schools operated at well over 125% capacity, making it difficult to have any viable educational programs.* The situation became so acute that Mayor Lindsay formed a high school construction task force in March, 1968, to get more schools built faster than the board was building them.†

All the desegregation techniques the board tried, then, were discredited in their initial stages, and both whites and blacks were understandably aggrieved. The board could then say that it had tried desegregation, but that the plans were not acceptable to the field staff or the community and did not work. They did not work because the bureaucracy and the staff made them fail. Chances are that they would never work in the New York

---

* As of October, 1966, the following utilization pattern existed at some typical high schools around the city: Midwood–177%; Lincoln–144%; Taft–132%; Flushing–141%; Columbus–127%; Washington–130%.

† See Chapter Nine for a more extensive discussion of school construction.

City schools, because the structure is so defective that school officials have enough trouble just handling routine questions, let alone innovation. The desegregation controversy indicated beyond much question how and why the system didn't work; some alternative system is essential if the schools are not to continue their downward trend.

❧

ADMINISTRATIVE CONTROLS

One administrative perspective that helps to further clarify the many pathologies I have described is what social scientists now refer to as "systems analysis." [1] Any organization may be viewed in terms of the flows of information, personnel, and materials that affect its capacity to realize its announced goals and adapt to changing conditions. An organization is healthy if its information flows, evaluations, and monitoring systems are adequate for top decision makers to formulate meaningful programs that meet local needs. In other words, the healthy organization has built-in self-corrective and feed-back mechanisms so that its key decision makers are always in touch with what is going on in the field, can make necessary changes in programs and policies as conditions indicate, and can engage in long-range planning.

The New York City school system does not have these necessary kinds of administrative controls. One school official with more detachment about the institution than his colleagues suggested that a part of the system could have stopped functioning and headquarters might not even know about it for several months, so slowly does information pass through the institution. It has no good information system, nor indeed does it have many of the feed-back mechanisms necessary for meaningful programs in its wide range of local schools. An illustration of these points came out at a meeting at IS 201 between the education task force of the New York City coalition and the 201 governing board and community. [2] The school was so hot that people were all but disrobing as time went on, and the subject of the heat finally came up. It turned out that this windowless school did not have properly working air-conditioning, and try as he did, the school's new principal (who admittedly had only been in office for two days) could not get any action from headquarters. Superintendent Donovan finally sent in a cadre of engineers to fix 201's air-conditioning, after a call from officials in the task force. This is how decisions get made in a bureaucracy that has no adequate means of finding out about conditions in its operating units and should therefore be reorganized so that it can.*

One federal official who deals regularly with the board made a similar observation: [3] "They don't really have centralization there," she said. "They have segmented baronies and fiefdoms that do not communicate with each other. There is no good information system. Livingston Street is somehow superimposed without really relating to the field. They have every conceivable experiment, but they are not well coordinated, rationalized, or always evaluated, and most of the evaluations are poor."

If the board had adopted standard monitoring, auditing, and budgetary techniques that permit meaningful evaluations, some of its inefficiencies and pathologies might have been minimized.

Most large organizations have imperfect systems of evaluation and control, and top decision makers have to formulate policies in conditions of uncertainty.[4] Moreover, coalitions of internal and external pressure groups exist in all organizations, and introduce their politics into major policy decisions. Some organizations, of course, are better run than others. Though top policy makers may never have enough information, there are techniques such as performance budgeting, auditing, and evaluation that produce fairly precise data on past programs. There are also new techniques—such as computer simulation—that allow decision makers to judge possible benefits and costs in advance. But many large business corporations, to say nothing of public school systems—and especially the New York City school system—make their decisions very crudely.

Dr. Marilyn Gittell and her colleagues wrote: "None of the advanced techniques of the planning-programming-budgeting system utilized so effectively in the federal government have

---

* The ordinary phone call from a principal often gets no action, and it was only when this élite group intervened—though not without feeling the brunt of Donovan's rage that they had visited one of "his" schools without permission—that something was done.

been introduced into the city school budget process. Such an approach allows for cost measurements on alternate programs as well as meaningful evaluation of performance. Public discussion of the present education budget at any stage is virtually impossible, and civic and interest group participation is severely limited. . . ." [5] To say that the New York City school system's policy makers did not have enough knowledge to evaluate past programs and make future policy, is understatement. They have been incapable of solving problems meaningfully and of long-range planning on important matters. And they have been equally incapable of overseeing the implementation of the programs that they do institute.

Most decision makers and staff personnel in the New York City schools are trained as teachers and supervisors, not as administrators. They might not be able to make good decisions even if they had access to informational devices that exist. Furthermore, interest in their careers and their units might lead them to neglect goals such as pupil achievement and desegregation. Outside administrators, with no vested interest in the existing structures, would benefit the system, even though they would have to win over many insiders to their ideas—a very difficult and tedious task.*

The practice of assigning former classroom teachers to positions at headquarters is partly responsible for the bureaucratic ineptitude. There are teachers in auditing, zoning, human relations, demographic research, programming and data processing, and guidance counselling, who have little or no technical training. Since they are paid out of their home-school budget allotments, those schools are deprived of the use of some of their money. Furthermore, "Teachers are chosen on the basis of rank favoritism," an inside school official reported. "People are specifically designated for headquarters assignments, they don't simply openly advertise the assignments. So somebody at headquarters has to know you and ask for you." The code behind this—that one has to have been a teacher to qualify for these positions—surely needs reconsideration.

An examination of the expense budget, showing who is assigned to headquarters and at what salary, indicates two categories of personnel—teachers and civil service employees.[6] In

---

* Administrative and technical "amateurism" are rampant throughout the system. Surely the civil service laws that produced this organized inefficiency could be changed.

the School Planning and Research Unit, for example, those with pedagogical backgrounds earn as much as $23,000, while a civil-service planner has a maximum of $14,000. There is generally a high turnover among these planners, as there is among well-trained technicians in other staff units, mainly because salaries elsewhere are higher and because of the inequities in the salary scale. The system promotes and gives higher salaries to untrained personnel.*

Interviews with headquarters officials indicate that there has never been any systematic or even impressionistic study to delineate the conditions that make for "good" and "bad" schools. Neither does the board have any clear criteria for defining a "good" principal or a "professional" performance. In early 1967, Deputy Superintendent Theodore H. Lang of the Office of Personnel announced a projected study of the qualities, training, and background that make for "successful" principals in ghetto schools.[7] Why has it taken so long? Since the 1930s reports and studies have recommended that such data be made available.†

That there is no effective auditing procedure helps explain why noncompliance among the field staff became such a well-established tradition and why there is so little response from headquarters. The traditional argument is that principals are "professionals" who cannot be subjected to the kind of supervision that might be called for in managing blue-collar or low-level white-collar personnel. They think of themselves as professionals, but their training, career interest, and the bureaucratic structure in which they function, make it hard for them to act professionally.

For a single, obvious example of the result of inappropriate training, many principals and teachers use traditional middle class curricula and instructional techniques to educate the Negro and Puerto Rican poor. Many don't understand the culture of these populations, and some of those who do reject

---

* In all fairness to the board, it has been hampered from hiring more highly paid technicians by the Bureau of the Budget, which has refused to grant it the funds.

† Numerous studies suggest that the principal's behavior toward his teachers, students, and the community may help determine the quality and effectiveness of school programs. Parent groups have felt this way for a long time, and the protests of ghetto parents against particular principals indicate how widespread this feeling has become. Yet this study seems to have never begun, let alone been used.

it.* One solution would be to change the curricula in the city colleges and to change standards for school staffing. The latter would require a drastic revamping of the civil service examinations, a change the board recognizes as essential but has failed to make. Teachers and principals should be recruited for ghetto schools on the basis of how well they understand and accept ghetto culture, as well as on the basis of traditional licensing standards and on their willingness to try out new instructional techniques.†

Since there is more behind the inadequacies of ghetto schools than inappropriate training, one solution is decentralization and community control, with parents, other community leaders, and local school officials (teachers) having powers to select superintendents, principals, and teachers through governing councils. Delegating such powers to laymen raises the usual protests about control by the "rabble," patronage, and the decline of the merit system. None of these charges need be valid if procedures for selecting and screening personnel are set up appropriately, and explicit standards of "expertise" developed. As it stands now, the Board of Examiners uses few measures of socially relevant expertise for service in ghetto schools. Furthermore, by refusing to develop standards of performance for principals, and enforcing them, the Board of Education and the examiners perpetuate this unprofessionalism.‡

If the board were to develop more rigorous and relevant performance standards for service in ghetto schools, perhaps many teachers and supervisors now there would not pass. Given the present civil service system, it would be difficult to transfer or remove unqualified school officials on the scale necessary to

---

* A top headquarters official reported to her colleagues that lack of curriculum materials, for example, on minority groups, is not the key problem so much as the teachers' ability to use the materials. "Many teachers simply do not know how to utilize these new books on minority groups," she said.

† One of the many techniques that was used in the HARYOU anti-poverty agency in Central Harlem was to teach English as a second language, building on the "language of the streets." There was no systematic evaluation of how effective this was, but the agency staff observed that the pupils were much more involved and highly motivated than they had been in regular public schools. Many of them seemed to improve significantly in reading and writing skills. This is now being done in some schools, after many years of resisting the idea.

‡ One would also hope that teachers and supervisors would be paid (in part) and promoted on the basis of their performance, or that at least performance would be measured and counted for something.

improve the schools. A massive retraining program, accompanied by decentralization, would help. Those school personnel who still fail to measure up to standards might be encouraged to transfer to schools in white middle class areas of the city or in the suburbs.* Meanwhile, there might very well be a concerted effort to recruit educators from other systems. Negro educators might well be induced to come to New York City to serve in its ghetto schools. There would be greater incentive if the kind of administrative and instructional reforms I am discussing were put into effect.

In June, 1964, when civil rights leaders proved to Gross and his top professionals how widely the principals had sabotaged the Free Choice Transfer Plan, there was much talk that headquarters should provide more leadership. Civil rights leaders asked why headquarters did not punish rebellious principals. "We cannot deny that some district superintendents and principals have done some of the things you report," a headquarters official said to civil rights leaders, "and it really worries me. But we cannot undermine our field people, who are, after all, professionals, by policing them." When it was suggested that the actions of field supervisors were unprofessional, the board still refused to punish them, and supervisors reportedly continue to subvert pupil-transfer programs with impunity.†

Now that decentralization is at issue, headquarters staff fear that they will meet even greater resistance if they push field supervisors too hard; some fear that their personal influence, their careers, and their units may be endangered.[8] Given the power of supervisory associations, such fears seem justified. District superintendents and principals are already rebelling, however, even without headquarters controls, perhaps because of this. The supervisors' resistance to such new concepts as educational complexes and parks and decentralization are examples.‡

---

* Some of the less competent, of course, would not be welcome in those areas.

† Many civil rights leaders and even some headquarters staff report this.

‡ The Council of Supervisory Association's objections to the board's delegation of authority and power to community governing councils in three decentralization experiments to select school staff for their districts, declaring it a violation of state education laws, is a most recent case of resistance. The CSA is trying to get the courts to declare the experiments illegal, and both the CSA and the teachers' union have been active in trying to persuade parents in the districts to reject the decentralization program.

There are other reasons for the lack of development and application of performance measures. Meaningful measures for the evaluation of complex professional tasks are difficult to formulate, especially since teaching effectiveness depends on many factors in addition to the actions and skills of school officials—for example, poverty, neighborhood and school conditions, and pupil backgrounds. This is not at all to take the view of many defensive school officials that the school system is doing all it can under impossible conditions. One defense that school officials often use against ratings and performance measures is precisely that too many external factors affect how well pupils do to warrant assigning much responsibility to teachers and principals. The result is that nobody inside the system takes the responsibility for the poor quality of education in ghetto schools, not to speak of other areas.

Performance Measures

Despite the many problems of interpretation, there are several possible measures of educational effectiveness. Instructional performance may be assessed by conventional reading and achievement test scores and measures of various aspects of psycho-social growth—for example, feelings of self-respect. Measures of supervisory effectiveness might include teacher morale, turnover, and absenteeism, number and percentage of suspensions, reading and achievement scores, and extent of community agitation regarding school conditions. Educators are still at a primitive stage in the systematic use of such indicators partly because there is no consensus on the goals of public education. If there is general agreement that the schools should develop basic skills that qualify for employment and a career, there is much confusion on other goals—training for "citizenship," social attitudes, the development of personal traits that will be functional for mobility and achievement. And there is even more disagreement on instructional methods and techniques. It is easier to apply techniques of cost-effectiveness analysis to the development of missiles systems, where the goals are fairly simple, clear and agreed upon, than in public education. But a major effort should nevertheless be made.*

* Cost effectiveness analysis, a technique for assessing the relative merits of alternative programs and policies, is now being used in governmental planning, especially in cities. In September, 1967, Mayor Lindsay contracted with Rand Corporation officials to set up "information systems" for all city agencies that would involve such techniques, and they are being used or considered for many other large cities.

Typically, outside groups have developed more imaginative ideas in this regard than board officials. Suggestions have been made by the Peoples' Board of Education, a militant citizens' group, in a paper analyzing the school budget.* One rather interesting suggestion there is that a series of vandalism indicators be kept on each school—number of broken windows, fires, and break-ins—as a measure of school–community relations.[9] The incidence of vandalism reflects many social forces in addition to the actions of school officials, but it may be a barometer of how well the schools are doing as well. There is wide variation, for example, in the incidence of such vandalism among schools within the same neighborhood and serving the same ethnic and socio-economic groups:

> PS 117 had 185 broken windows and JHS 120 had 410. Both in East Harlem—but 117 had just got rid of a principal nobody wanted.
>
> JHS 45, which operates a full-time center and a good one, had 309 broken windows—JHS 139 in Harlem, much smaller, had 1,379 broken windows (they have their third principal in five years, and 25% of the staff is absent every day).

Actually, the Board of Education does collect all sorts of data on these matters, through the Bureau of Educational Program Research and Statistics, headed by Dr. Joseph Justman, but the data are rarely if ever used to evaluate schools and programs. Justman does an ethnic census of pupils and teachers and has data on absenteeism, turnover rates, and teachers' salaries. His inventories are used in annual statistical reports, as well as in the board's many other reports and public relations brochures.

The board also has a Bureau of Educational Research, headed by Assistant Superintendent J. Wayne Wrightstone, which evaluates various board programs. Since 1966, this unit has been phased out gradually as the board has subcontracted its evaluation research to organizations such as the Center for Urban Education. It did evaluate such programs as the pairings and the More Effective Schools plan. There is also a Bureau of Curriculum Research, which deals with curriculum planning and development. The studies undertaken by these bureaus record reading scores, the extent of interracial and inter-class friendships among pupils, and other aspects of personal growth

---

* The Peoples' Board, discussed in Chapter Four, was formed in December, 1966, by Negro, Puerto Rican, and white leaders, in protest against the regular board's failure to reform the schools.

in experimental and newly desegregated schools, and there is an attempt to show how they are correlated with variations in class size, ethnic composition, money spent per pupil, and number of staff. But for the evaluations to be meaningful, they would have to include information on the neighborhood, administrative, and classroom settings in which the new programs were tried out, as well as more complete information on the background, past experiences, and social attitudes of school officials and pupils. All these factors affect what goes on in the classroom and the degree of success of school programs.

To illustrate the limited nature of the board's research in 1964, Dr. Justman completed a study of a sample of 934 Negro pupils attending sixth grade classes in sixteen slum-area schools in New York City to find out if there was any relationship between pupil mobility (as measured by number of schools attended between third and sixth grades) and changes in IQ and reading ability.[10] The following table summarizes his main finding:

No. of schools attended	Third grade IQ	Sixth grade IQ	Extent of decline
One	94.2	92.9	1.3
Two	97.6	97.5	0.1
Three	91.7	90.5	1.2
Four	88.0	84.0	4.0

The IQ scores of pupils who attended four schools declined more than those of pupils who attended fewer schools.

Justman inferred from the study that pupil transfers to secure racial balance were educationally harmful. "The findings tend to support arguments advanced by opponents of plans that involve transfer of pupils to provide better ethnic balance in a given school," he said in summarizing his findings to a *World-Telegram* reporter, who went on to remark: "Justman suggested that instead of bussing children away from their original schools, the board consider a sort of reverse-bussing procedure for youngsters whose parents frequently move from one part of the city to another. He would bus such pupils back to their original schools so they could continue their schooling without interruption." Would this mean that pupils who had moved out of the ghetto would have to go back?

Usually in quantitative studies that show that changes in one variable are associated with changes in another, it is necessary to investigate further to see whether still other variables may be involved. If the number of times pupils change schools seems associated with a declining IQ, the researcher then has to see if changing schools is really the cause or if there are other causes too. Among ghetto families, much moving around is usually associated with poorly educated, impoverished parents, broken families, and other conditions typical of slum life. Perhaps even more important, the low expectations that teachers have about the abilities of ghetto pupils, also contribute to low achievement levels. In other words, Justman's policy recommendations are not warranted by the limited data he presents.

A recent evaluation of Open Enrollment by the Center for Urban Education is another example.[11] It was found that though there was some variation among different receiving schools, Open Enrollment generally had little immediate impact on reading achievement. However, without data on the implementation (especially on how well the principals prepared staff, pupils and community), the findings have little administrative or scientific relevance.

One reason such studies are so badly done is that educational measurement is dominated by psychologists, who are more concerned with how they measure than with what they measure.[12] They are trained in laboratory and experimental psychology, and they do not have the tools for what is called "soft" or "messy" data. The board needs competent researchers —and especially research sociologists who are trained to deal with complex data. It does not have a single sociologist on its research staff, nor do most other school systems. The Center for Urban Education, to whom the board subcontracts evaluation studies, has many competent social scientists, but there is some question as to whether their recommendations are always acted on. (See, for example, Chapter Eleven on the educational complex studies.)

The board—partly for political reasons—does not gather relevant data. Systematic data on religion and the socio-economic status of pupils and school staff are not available. A social scientist who investigated the board's research procedures said: "On the religious information, one school official told us it had something to do with church and state. On socio-economic status, people in the school system felt it was too sensitive and threatening. This sort of thing usually has more to do with the asker's sensitivity than with the sensitivity of the person asked." In the 1940s and 1950s, civil rights organizations objected to the board's gathering racial data on grounds that they were not relevant to school matters. These groups have shifted their position since then.

The research is rarely anything more than a preliminary inventory of school conditions, and it does not deal extensively with the conditions for variations in school performance. One social science investigator referred to it as "public bookkeeping." * There are no studies on community relations, a key problem.

The School Planning and Research Unit does all the population projections, for purposes of building schools; as of this writing they did not have a single trained demographer. Though political pressures from civic groups and public officials often determine where schools will be built, City Planning Commission officials and parents groups have noted numerous mistakes in projection and school size.†

In some instances the data the board furnishes its outside evaluation studies are so inadequate as to preclude even the bookkeeping function of such studies. EQUAL summarized the Center for Urban Education's evaluation studies on the board's Title I programs, and noted the following: [13]

> Several Reports said that it was almost impossible to measure reading improvement because the Board's records were so messy and because so many different kinds of tests were being used. In the Center's Middle School Report it is found that the Board of Education uses six different instruments at different times, making comparisons almost impossible.
>
> Data received from the schools . . . were incomplete. In the junior guidance program, of 10 responding schools 4 schools did not report any test scores whatsoever; 3 schools reported scores which were only teacher estimates, and 3 schools had partial scores for reading and none in math.

Moreover, the board does little to collate data from other agencies with its own—for example, welfare data. The Human

---

* A group of social scientists commissioned by the city administration did a study in early 1967, evaluating the board's research.

† See the discussion in Chapter Twelve on the adequacy of the unit's research.

Resources Administration is now in the process of trying to coordinate these data for purposes of spotlighting where the greatest needs are for educational services, where the school system performs at higher and lower levels, and some of the reasons for variations in performance. The board could do much more analysis even of the little data it has. Instead of simply collecting descriptive statistics on staff and pupil characteristics, the board could analyze how variations in pupil achievement are associated with variations in class size, staff training, experience, and backgrounds, staff–pupil ratios, classroom composition (ethnic integration, single *vs.* multiple track), and money spent per pupil. Some of this kind of analysis is done on special programs, but it is difficult to justify not doing it throughout the system, for quality control and upgrading instruction and supervision. The first time it was done (in a very preliminary way) was by sociologists Eleanor Sheldon and Raymond Glazier in their book, *Pupils and Schools in New York City,* published in 1965.[14] But, there is nobody at headquarters systematically gathering information on "good" and "bad" schools throughout the system.*

Assuming that the board does nevertheless gather much information that is relevant for policy makers, there is some question of how much use is made of even these data. As in most organizations, politics play a predominant role in this regard. One social scientist from the team mentioned above reported that the work of "Wrightstone's unit is supposed to be relevant to policy decisions at the board level, but we could never get clear from him how this worked. When the board would start in on some new venture, say More Effective Schools, he'd start in devising evaluation designs, but we could not get clear what fed into new policy decisions in the first place."†

Indeed, the social scientists report that researchers and research data often have a tenuous status in the system. The social

---

* One statistic that Puerto Rican groups complain they no longer have access to is how many Puerto Rican pupils graduate from high school with what kinds of diplomas. The data have not been made available since 1964.

† If this group of social scientists from the city administration could not secure such information, one can imagine how difficult it is for civic groups. Attempts by civic groups and city officials to secure trend data on reading scores and other indicators of school quality have been unsuccessful, as of this writing. One would hope that the records of public agencies might be made available to the public.

scientists' comments ranged all the way from the charge that the integrity of research findings may not always have been safeguarded, to one that top researchers are sometimes ignored or not consulted by top administrators. One social scientist reported: "My main feeling about board research units is that they are insulated. They are not in a position to make what they do relevant to broader educational concerns. They have little to do with policy, and they are unhappy. And it doesn't look like research will have more of a role to play in policy-making in the future, either. The whole thing seems to be run at the behest of the superintendent."

This is a common state of affairs in large, tradition-bound organizations. Policy makers must be acutely sensitive to political pressures in deciding whether particular programs should be discontinued. Many decisions to continue or discontinue programs are made almost without reference to how they have gone in the past. For example, the board put into motion the approval procedure for renewing all its federally financed Title One programs in late August, 1966, several months before the evaluation reports were made public, and without the Council Against Poverty involved in the process.[15] "How can you have every single Title One program criticized the way it has been," said a staff person at headquarters, "and have them renew every single one, and figure that they make any use of the research?" *

Performance data in the area of personnel and staffing are used limitedly. Interviews with union officials indicate that few teachers are dismissed or transferred by their principals during the three-year probationary period, and the board rarely gives teachers unsatisfactory ratings. Fred Hechinger, education editor of the *New York Times,* reports that in the last five years only 170 regular teachers and only 82 substitutes out of 54,235 teachers

---

* There is a politics to this process as well. If the board had not asked for a renewal of these federal monies, it would have been criticized for showing little concern with upgrading ghetto school programs. Yet, in order to qualify for the money, it had to get some procedures underway for approving and administering the programs. The federal government's delays in providing some of the money made it imperative that the board act as quickly as possible. Indeed, the federal government often confronted the board with contradictory pressures and imperatives: it demanded that all federally financed programs be objectively evaluated and modified accordingly, yet it created delays and made it hard for the board to follow this demand.

in the system have been given unsatisfactory ratings, and in the last five years, the tenure of only 12 teachers was discontinued.

Usually, an unsatisfactory teacher is transferred, frequently from one ghetto school to another, but he is not given an unsatisfactory rating. The system faces a shortage of teachers who are willing to serve in ghetto schools. Many principals don't want the responsibility of defending an unsatisfactory rating for fear it may reflect negatively on them, because they don't want to be bothered, or because they are afraid of union harassment.

The practice of transferring unsatisfactory teachers may contribute to poor teaching performance in some ghetto schools. One south Bronx teacher kept his class of Negro children after school one day to lecture them on how lucky they were that the white community was treating them so well, suggesting that they should be grateful.[16] The children's parents complained to the principal, who immediately called the principal in Bedford–Stuyvesant under whom the teacher had last served to ask for further information and learned that he had done poorly there as well. A more candid system of teacher ratings might prevent this kind of thing.

The performances of principals are subject to even less measurement and control than those of teachers. Some district superintendents attempt to improve the performance of those principals who have poor community relations—when there are complaints from many parents—but a significant number do not. Gittell's survey of district superintendents' activities suggest that they generally spend much less time in supervising principals than they should, either because of other priorities or because of pressures from principals' associations and some headquarters personnel.[17] Frequently, a district superintendent checks on a principal only after his community relations have so deteriorated that parent group protest and agitation are rampant. There should be some administrative checks to blunt the poor community relations of principals before school–community tensions reach the boiling point.

Budgetary Planning

The New York City School system uses a lump sum, modifiable budget that systematically precludes administrative control. Once the board receives city, state, and federal funds for

some specified uses, it can shift these funds any number of times
without recording the shifts and without public hearings. The
practice came about as a result of a Memorandum of Understanding between the board and Mayor Wagner in 1962,* but
the memorandum, while freeing the board from the burden
of having to develop a line-by-line budget, clearly stated that
no shifting of money across functions (from curriculum to personnel, for example) could be done without public hearings.
Such an arrangement allows for substantial administrative flex-
ibilities, as contingencies inevitably develop that cannot be
planned for in advance and that demand changes in staff, space,
and other allocations. But a modifiable budget is a double-edged
sword. Given the nature of professional groups within the New
York City school system, this procedure may in fact have made
for more rigidity rather than less.

There was virtually no accurate accounting of the final
use of public monies. Even when officials from established
civic groups went to headquarters for an account of budgetary
shifts, they got it only with great difficulty, and were sometimes
insulted and ridiculed in the process. One of the top administrators of the Bureau of Business Affairs had acquired a reputation for being an obstinate guardian of the board's budgetary
records.[18] He would divulge nothing, except under extreme
pressure.†

* The political dynamics of the controversy around the memorandum
illustrate the informal alliance of powerful moderate groups and board
professionals. Officials of the Citizens Committee for Children, PEA, UPA,
ASPIRA, and the Citizens Budget Commission expressed great dismay in
1963 and early 1964 that the board kept violating the memorandum by
making major fund transfers without holding public hearings. Harold
Siegel, executive secretary of the UPA, and PEA officials had joined with
CCC, which led the fight to make sure that the public was informed before
such budget shifts were made. At some point in 1964, however, only the
CCC was actively engaged in this struggle for accountability. By 1967,
after he had served on the board for two years, Mr. Siegel was no longer
visible among the ranks of people who demanded a publicly accountable
budgetary procedure.

† When an official from one prominent civic group asked him for
data on how Title I funds had been spent over the period from 1965
through 1967, the reply was that those data were not available (which
they were not). The board's budgetary and fiscal records were so dis-
organized and unavailable to the general public that a university researcher
who had spent more than two years at the board on a foundation-sponsored
study (that included several other big city school systems) told board
officials that she would have to submit a negative report indicating the
unavailability of fiscal data for New York City. He then reportedly told

In drawing up its budget, the board estimates how much it will spend for personnel and teacher training; curriculum research and evaluation; instruction; design, construction, and physical plant; business and administration; the board; and the Superintendent of Schools. Contrary to the Memorandum of Understanding with Mayor Wagner, there is considerable shifting of funds, both within and across these areas. "This meant that scores of decisions were made to change the original allocations each year," explained a headquarters official, "and the professionals inside could easily shift funds from one to another area without having to clear this with the public or the board. People inside had a lot of power to make these changes." [19]

The practice was prevalent in Title I programs, as I described briefly in Chapter Seven. One board member made an informal investigation of how these funds were being spent. After a couple of days' work, he found that the professionals did with the federal money what they had always done with local funds; they shifted the funds without any public review and even without letting the board know what they were doing.[20] This board member sent a memo to Superintendent Donovan and Jacob Landers, coordinator of Title I projects, questioning the professionals' capacity to change the budget any time they wanted, deploring their irresponsibility toward the public, and asking how the board could ever justify this practice of the city. Donovan discussed this at the next executive session of the board. He explained that the many contingencies (staff, space, facilities) school programs face made it impossible to clear every change through public hearings and the board. Donovan won his case, and Board President Lloyd Garrison even stated publicly in April, 1967, when Mayor Lindsay said he wanted a line-by-line budget for the schools, that this would constrain the board and should not go through.[21]

On the theory that the board is accountable to the public to show how public funds are actually spent, this public agency falls far short of that fundamental obligation. Recent pressures from Mayor Lindsay for the board to institute program and performance budgeting may force a change in the old procedures, and such a change may at least lead to more efficiency. The board itself claims to have embarked on such budge-

---

her that they don't run the Board of Education for the benefit of researchers, a point with which I would generally concur.

tary changes with a group from the Stanford Research Institute, which would require the very line-by-line program–performance budgeting system that the mayor demands.

Public pressures to abandon the lump sum, modifiable budget procedure have mounted since 1966. The publication of a report by the Mayor's Temporary Commission for City Finances provoked civic groups and city administration officials into pressing for a change in board procedures. A report of Mayor Lindsay's Human Resources Administration that recommended new budgetary arrangements also stirred up interest.* [22] Citizen concern with how increasing federal monies under Title I were being spent also contributed. Finally, the shift of ghetto parent and white liberal groups from demands for desegregation to an emphasis on quality and administrative efficiency led to a natural alliance with the city administration and a high degree of receptivity to budgetary reforms. A new coalition has thus formed to force the board to rationalize and modernize its budgetary procedures.

Consider the following criticisms of board practice:

As we have observed ESEA in New York City, and particularly Title I, the following legislative mandates seem necessary to us:

1. We ask that you (the Sub-Committee on the Elementary and Secondary Education Act of the Education and Labor Committee of the House of Representatives) mandate that changes in budgeted program amounts approved for funding by the Office of Education exceeding 10% of their original budget be resubmitted through the same approval cycle. The appended list of New York City's Title I projects shows the comparison of the original budget as passed in a public hearing and two subsequent modifications made without public review. Projects were modified up to 400% from the original allocation. These comparisons were obtained only by extensive digging in the records of the Board of Education, since no procedures for review of modifications exist in the system. Such administrative changes, remote from public scrutiny, we understand to be widespread throughout the country.

2. We ask that you strengthen the role of community participation in planning in order to provide at least some checkpoints on Title I allocations. The present loose consultative relationships of the New York City Board of Education and the Council Against Poverty are ludicrously insufficient to relate planning for Title I to other educational projects and they make a mockery of community involvement and comprehensive planning. They in-

* This is known as the Sviridoff Report.

vite deception on the part of the Board of Education and are, therefore, potentially dangerous.

This is an excerpt from a testimony of Mrs. Nathan W. Levin of the Citizens Committee for Children, to inform Congress of the Board of Education's budgetary operations.[23] Mrs. Trude W. Lash, executive director of the committee, who was also chairman of the education committee of the Lindsay administration's Council Against Poverty, and her testimony is unusually well-informed about board practice.*

Much deception can take place under a modifiable budget arrangement, as Mrs. Levin's testimony suggests, and it has taken place, for instance, in the board's supposed use of some Title I funds for grade reorganization and desegregation programs. As the Citizens Committee for Children researchers noted:

> In the two years of Title I operation in New York City, approximately twenty percent of the total has been allocated for the reorganization of grade levels to a 4–4–4 system. This "reorganization" has been mandated as a way to effect racial balance in the schools by the New York State Department of Education in 1964, before ESEA existed. But when ESEA money was made available, $28 million went for this purpose—the largest segment ($17.6 million) for the creation of Comprehensive High Schools, whose actual inception is not yet scheduled. The funnelling of this money for routine school expenses seems to us inappropriate and a deliberate misreading of the educational intent of Title I that you wrote into the law.[24]

There is no clear record of how often this kind of misrepresentation took place or how prevalent it was, but perhaps in terms of its questionable legality, once is too much. Consider the following practice, as reported in the budget analysis of the People's Board of Education: [25]

> We organized a delegation of schools to go to the hearing to demand a pre-school program for a specific ghetto. Several years ago District 4 did this in Harlem. They did careful research, presented cogent testimony; the elected officials gave the delegation a standing ovation . . . The Budget Message increased the appropriation for pre-school programs but the schools in District 4 got none of the programs because the Board of Education decided that year they didn't have the necessary space.

* Some board members responded to the points made by these civic and city administration interests, but they have continued with their past budgetary procedures.

This document contains one of the most cogent discussions of the board's administrative and budgetary procedures that has yet appeared. It asks the following: What are the goals and priorities of the budget? Which specific schools will get each program? What results are the programs supposed to produce? Who is responsible? How is it decided if various programs are worth what they cost? What are the comparative values of different programs—variations in class size, staffing, per-pupil expenditures, use of nonteaching personnel, instructional methods, single *vs.* multiple track classes, segregated *vs.* desegregated schools, consolidation devices, forms and degrees of decentralization, and the like?

Examples of waste are legion, and many have been uncovered by the People's Board. They found, for example, from the board's proposed expense budget for 1967–1968, that it planned to spend $3,160,000 to supply three paperback books apiece for 550,000 children from kindergarten to sixth grade. This averaged out to $2.00 a book, while parents could get them for 35¢ and 50¢. They looked through the monthly calendar items of proposed expenditures for supplies and could find exact information only once. It was for 700 toy dump trucks at $7.95 each, several dollars more than at any local toy store. They fought against the board's continuing an Intensive Teacher Training Program (ITTP) with Title I money that was rejected by the city colleges, the Council Against Poverty, and ghetto and white parent groups, as a failure, but the board found funds from other sources.* One experience that several parents had as members of the local school board in West Harlem and Washington Heights deserves to be told in full:

> Three years ago, the board proposed an electrical modernization for JHS 139 in Harlem (due for replacement four years from that date). They planned to spend one quarter of a million dollars to rewire, and take two years to do it. The local school board had to spend three months convincing the board that all that was necessary was to change the light bulbs. Finally there was a compromise: half the building done each way. And hundreds of schools badly need repairs they can't get.[26]

---

* As the People's Board study reports: "Both City College, which ran the program last year, and the Council Against Poverty, which must review all Title I proposals, turned down this crash teacher training program as harmful to children of the poor. So the Board is now finding funds from other sources, and has arranged with another university, at one million dollars—last year it was only a $600,000 failure—to run it."

These are examples of the many wasteful programs that should have been dropped or changed, effective programs that shouldn't have been dropped but were, and cases where the public was not informed of the costs and benefits of programs or items. The inefficiencies were tremendous, and they still are.

Sometimes, the inefficiency shaded over into what seemed to be favoritism or even corruption in dealing with outside firms. One local school board member who happened to know a lot about musical instruments said that the board bought instruments for much higher prices than was necessary. He related that one company, a low bidder with a good product, was not given a large contract. "My friend told me that he was not only rejected," he said, "but he was rejected by the company that made one of the highest bids and that was asked by the board to make a judgment on who should get the contract. When I asked an involved board official about it, he shrugged his shoulders and replied that he felt he had to get somebody to help him decide who knew something about the values of musical instruments." [27]

The New York City school system suffers from a disease common to many public school systems, namely "undercontrol." It uses primitive procedures for budgeting, auditing, data processing, and evaluation. The information it produces is often not used by top policy makers and administrators. The result is that the system has functioned largely along traditionalistic lines, so that decisions are shaped not so much by administrative and technical expertise as through the informal friendships, cliques, and influence that constitute the internal and external politics of the system.

There is increasing recognition, at city hall, among citizen groups, and among some school officials and board members, that major changes in personnel, structure, and procedures are necessary. When Mayor Lindsay remarked on May 24, 1967, that the school system's traditional budget procedures are "archaic" and asserted that "there is a tendency, whenever someone else gives you the money, to become sloppy in your budget practices," he was expressing such a point of view.[28] The board is now beginning to institute the kind of program performance budgeting system that Mayor Lindsay and many management experts have suggested. It is of some significance that the board's efforts at reform have speeded up as outside pressures to do so have increased.

The Board's Change Agents

This is to suggest, then, that a pattern of "undercontrol" characterized most of the board's operations. The system was allowed to run in such a haphazard way and with such poor communication and information flows from the field to headquarters and among officials in field and headquarters units, that it is no wonder school programs were so poorly adapted to diverse local conditions. It was difficult for the system to learn from experience, because it had no way of knowing what its experience had been.

Ironically, this condition of undercontrol did not apply to those units that had been set up as "change agents" within the system. While most units at headquarters generally defended the status quo, in the past ten years three staff units were established for effecting changes. They included the Central Zoning Unit, the Human Relations Unit, and the Assistant Superintendent in Charge of Integration Activities. Officials in these units who carried out their mandate to innovate were often closely controlled in their activities and sometimes even treated punitively if they violated "unofficial policy," regardless of how much it might diverge from "public" policy statements. While these patterns of under- and over-control might seem contradictory, both patterns simply reflect the system's tendency to reinforce tradition: it rewards or deals permissively with those school officials who are not about to buck the status quo, and punishes those who do.

These units were the first of their kind in public school systems anywhere in the nation, and the professional staff in many of them are among the most progressive in the system. An analysis of their position and informal influence shows how a traditional bureaucracy handles officials who want change. *Human Relations Unit.* In the context of the broad discussion over the past few years about decentralization, increased community control and improved school–community relations, the Human Relations Unit is potentially very important. Yet, it cannot function in the present structure.

The mandated tasks of the Human Relations Unit are to promote programs among pupils, staff, and the community for better intergroup and school–community relations and to provide leadership and training for school–community coordinators, who are the staff personnel attached to each district superintendent's office. In addition, they are to cooperate with district superintendents and principals in developing human relations programs; to intervene as consultants when there is community conflict over the schools; to develop a resource center and library for materials on intergroup relations; and to develop curricula and encourage research. These activities are to be carried out in cooperation with the field superintendents and principals.

The unit was set up in 1961 in response to a recommendation by the board's Commission on Integration, pressures from the civil rights movement, and an outbreak of intergroup and interracial hostilities.* It started with a budget of only $75,000 for its first year, and a staff of five—three teachers on assignment and two administrative personnel.[29] As the school desegregation issue was more hotly contested and civil rights groups exerted more pressures, the unit expanded. By the spring of 1967 it had more than forty staff members with another two hundred auxiliary teachers under its control.[30] Some of the most progressive people in the school system are in it.

The racial controversies of the early 1960s, the rise in intensity of civil rights demands for desegregation, decentralization and better schools, and the threat the unit presented to tradition-bound administrators, led to periodic re-evaluations of its priorities. In fact, the unit has suffered for many years from a confusion of priorities. Its main function has been "fire-fighting" when relations between school officials and community groups, or among community groups themselves, are in acute conflict.[31]

Its long-range activities include working on evaluations of textbook materials and curriculum as they have to do with intergroup relations questions; conducting in-service training programs for teachers and supervisors to increase their understanding of race relations; and occasionally preparing staff, pupils, and communities for desegregation programs. (Some Dick and Jane readers show brown faces now.) Some of the unit's staff worked with curriculum specialists and top-level headquarters administrators to improve the content of textbooks; this has generally not posed serious problems; but it

---

* At this time there were several instances of desecration of Jewish cemeteries and synagogues, and damage to Catholic churches. Several ethnic groups had a stake in the unit, but the actual suggestion for it was made by Dr. Gardiner Taylor, the only Negro member of the board at the time.

has not produced much, since the unit's staff had little influence over curriculum people. Other functions did pose problems. In-service training programs implied to many school officials that they were not equipped to handle their jobs effectively— a valid assumption. Community and staff preparation also threatened school and headquarters officials.

The unit has a human relations coordinator for each borough, who, in turn, has a representative in most districts, though some superintendents successfully resisted this. The unit's staff for easing community tensions can only recommend to the principal and district superintendent involved. When a district superintendent refuses a recommendation, it may be passed on to the assistant superintendent in charge of integration activities, and ultimately to the superintendent, to act on. Often, no action is taken.[32]

District superintendents, on their side, report to the executive deputy superintendent at headquarters who deals with problems of school–community relations. This dual authority system creates much overlap, conflict, confusion, and buckpassing. A simple resolution to this administrative problem would be to have the assistant superintendent in charge of the unit be responsible to the executive deputy superintendent, just as field superintendents are, and not to the superintendent.

Each district office also had its own community relations specialist, referred to in the system as the school–community coordinator. He was responsible for many of the same activities as the human relations staff, and in the last few years, most coordinators coming into the system have been trained by the Human Relations Unit. In addition, the unit's staff held monthly conferences with the coordinators. Yet, the two groups often conflicted. The coordinators were generally chosen by district superintendents, to whom they gave their primary loyalties. They often sided with superintendents in resisting greater community involvement in school affairs for fear that it would lead to agitation, and functioned as a shield for superintendents against the unit's staff.[33]

If both groups were responsible to the same superior within the bureaucracy, their skills would be better used. Now there is administrative overlapping and confusion, with the coordinators responsible to the district superintendent and the human relations staff to a borough supervisor from headquarters. In situations of disagreement, the coordinator usually prevailed because of the district superintendents' power.* "Very few relations between the Human Relations person and the coordinator are positive," a headquarters official reported. "The coordinator mirrors the superintendent's status-quo desire, while the human relations person comes in more action-oriented. The coordinator and district superintendent tend to be public relations people, rather than human relations."

The unit has limited authority over administrators in the field and at headquarters. In fact, its staff has no real authority and power, and it is remarkable that the unit could do as much as it did. Despite the importance of its activities, the unit's director, Dr. Frederick Williams, had no superintendency rank until June, 1966, when he was finally appointed assistant superintendent, and its field staff had only teacher rank—this was the result of the resistance of principals and district superintendents to the setting up of a unit outside their control. When the unit was first established, superintendents were questioned on their views, and helped ensure that its powers would be limited.[34]

The board had not originally intended the unit to be so weak. Williams himself reports, for example, that they offered him a rank of either assistant or associate superintendent, but that he turned the offer down, thus not upsetting the district superintendents.[35] He had been a confidential secretary to former Board President Arthur Levitt and knew the internal politics of the system very well. He realized that his former position made him automatically suspect to some school officials, and hoped that his unit would become a more effective change agent by moving in a tactful manner. Its limited formal authority and his reluctance to buck tradition-bound administrators have been one of the unit's biggest problems.

* An unpublished board-sponsored study of 1964, based on interviews with human relations staff and community coordinators, documented their conflicts. Both sides agreed that their contacts were too infrequent and that they rarely shared experiences, despite the formality of monthly meetings. Furthermore, coordinators expressed little sense of loyalty to the human relations staff. One of the main complaints of coordinators was that the human relations staff did not give them clear-cut directions or suggestions about how to deal with new community conflict situations related to desegregation. Coordinators were thus both insulating themselves from the human relations staff because of loyalties to the district superintendent and expressing a need for more direction. Their quest for clear-cut answers to such complex social problems was a reflection of their own limited perspective.

The potential contributions of this kind of unit cannot be too much stressed. Community relations were important during the period of controversy over desegregation; they are even more important now with increasing parent dissatisfaction and demands for decentralization. Yet, the board constituted the Human Relations Unit in such a way that regardless of the talents of its staff, it could only be ineffectual.*

The main explanations for the unit's failures are clear. It was set up to reverse the school system's long insulation from the community and to change the social attitudes of many school officials. But the structure of the system, which gave rise to its insulation and the negative social attitudes, has remained the same—overcentralization, inbreeding, hierarchy, limited community-relations training, and careerism. The unit could not function adequately under such conditions unless it was given strong support from headquarters. Numerous interviews with headquarters and field officials, as well as with many citywide and local civic leaders, indicated that support was limited.

Large, bureaucratic organizations invariably develop mechanisms to dilute the potential influence of sub-units oriented toward innovation and reform. The units are isolated; they may be given limited resources; they may be made the scapegoats for problems that others rather than they have generated; and the ineffectualness of their staff may be blamed for their limited influence. All these patterns characterize the situation of the Human Relations Unit.

The Human Relations Unit can only function effectively with the cooperation of the district superintendents, who are ultimately the ones who invite in and dismiss the unit's staff. District superintendents may ask for outside help or they may prefer to "pass the buck" to headquarters. Unfortunately, they often call for help too late.[36] "District superintendents call frantically for help," explained a headquarters official, "after community tensions have deteriorated almost beyond repair. Their community relations are often bad, and they finally call in outsiders to set them right, but only on their own terms, which often doesn't help the situation." Human Relations Unit staff report that they are often asked for a quick "inoculation" of human relations to quiet tensions, and that they are evaluated by the extent to which they success-

---

* Williams' perennial caution probably contributed as well.

fully dampen "agitation." What is "agitation" to the superintendents, however, is often not that at all to the human relations staff, who define success in terms of how much increased communication takes place between school officials and all involved community groups, including the most militant.

The conflicts between district superintendents and human relations staff are affected by administrative conditions as well as ideological differences.[37] The dual authority pattern, the limited authority of human relations staff, and their "outsider" and staff status all contributed to conflict. Human relations staff were thus seen as one more headquarters intrusion, and perhaps one that reflected a capitulation to civil rights group pressures as well. In addition, the relationship was one of a staff specialist with only the formal status of a teacher giving advice to a more experienced and higher ranked administrator, which created a lot of tension.*

Another reason for conflict was that the human relations staff has a mandate to change attitudes, values, and practices of school officials, and thus places many officials in a defensive position. It was difficult enough for many teachers, principals, and district superintendents to deal constructively with criticism from citizen groups; when the criticisms came from the board's staff, they were deeply resented.† The general pattern, then, was one of deep suspicion and distrust toward the human relations staff.

One ghetto school case illustrates these points. The district superintendent asked for a human relations person to "improve the image" of a junior high school so that some of the white middle class who had just moved into a new co-op in the area would send their children there. The new residents were predominantly Jewish, were generally liberal, and many reportedly thought of sending their children to the school at first—then changed their minds, for what they said were educational and not racial or class reasons. The human relations staff worker, together with a trained social worker, built up an active parent association that included many middle class whites who became interested in and critical of school programs. This angered the district superintendent and principal, and they

---

* This kind of line-staff conflict is common in large organizations.

† "We are here to needle the establishment," said one human relations official, "and they don't like that." Another noted: "We are looked on as agents of change and therefore threatening."

called headquarters to order the staff out of the field. The human relations people involved were criticized at headquarters for what they had done.[38]

This case was typical of many, as reported by human relations and other headquarters staff. Field supervisors hoped that people from headquarters might be public relations agents for their schools to get more middle class whites to come in, but their and the human relations staff's ideas on how middle class whites could be persuaded were very different. When the whites as well as the Negroes and Puerto Ricans would take a more active interest in the schools and complain about their maintenance and how they were run, something that was inevitable with increased community participation, field supervisors complained that the human relations staff were stirring up "agitation." Many supervisors actually preferred to deal with the Negro and Puerto Rican poor, because they felt they could manipulate these people more easily than they could middle class whites.*

The conflict often centered on the differing definitions field supervisors and human relations staff had of the "community." Many superintendents and principals reportedly liked to deal with only the non-threatening groups in the community, while the human relations staff often took the position that all interested people had to be listened to. They did not agree with the supervisors' idea that the latter decide who should and should not represent the community; and they wanted to increase community participation in school affairs well beyond what progressive school officials cynically refer to as "setting up cake sales." They became demoralized when supervisors saw them as in alliance with or at least the patsies of "outside agitators."

My final illustrations of the unit's ineffectiveness in the present structure are taken from evidence on how it has prepared communities for desegregation and decentralization plans and conducted in-service training programs for school staff.[39] Even here, as in its "fire-fighting" activities, the unit is given little support. Though desegregation is no longer a key issue, evidence on the way it was handled is relevant for understanding the present decentralization controversy. In the years when

---

* Several headquarters people reported this. Many times, the only reason a supervisor called for headquarters help was to keep his schools from becoming completely segregated.

the unit's staff explained the board's policy on desegregation to parent groups, PAT-oriented citizens would often call headquarters to complain. They did not like what was being said, even though it was "official board policy." Headquarters officials did not relish any criticism from citizen groups implying that the board was in sharp conflict with them. During the heat of the desegregation controversy, there was a widespread feeling within the Human Relations Unit that the board would not reaffirm its own policy statements if there was sharp citizen criticism. Many of the unit's staff felt they were often undercut by headquarters simply for representing its policy statements. Members of the unit went out into the field and spoke at community meetings to win acceptance for desegregation, but if the going got too rough, they would often be called down back at headquarters.

That the unit and its staff are undercut by headquarters for representing board policy is a commentary on the system, and not primarily on the staff. It reflects the failure of the board to engage in any meaningful planning and community preparation, something just as likely to take place on the decentralization question as on desegregation, unless there is continued outside pressure for the board to mandate decentralization reforms. "It is not a question of more comprehensive preparation plans," said a headquarters official, "but of any. What we need is an approach to school–community relations."*

The board has a tradition of in-service training programs for teachers to help improve school–community relations, and the Human Relations Unit is supposed to help out informally in the program designed to train teachers in skills and attitudes

* Consider the following from the unpublished board study on the Human Relations Unit and desegregation in 1964: "There was a general recognition of the lack of any working plan. The announcements of policies, changes, or proposals in the integration field seem to catch the School–Community Coordinators off base too often and a feeling of hopelessness sets in. There is a kind of cynicism that pervades the atmosphere among the field staff, and its cuts across the entire structure of the school system from the top to the bottom . . . There is no overall plan for getting communities to accept change, for example, on the pairing plans. Timing of announcements creates paralyzing fears and anxieties and reactionary parent groups are having a field day. The Human Relations staff and Coordinators are somewhat overwhelmed by these developments, and needless to say are put into the position of trying to put out tremendous brush fires with buckets of water. There must be comprehensive overall plans worked out for securing modification of hostile attitudes and acceptance of changes in our school communities."

that will enable them to better adapt to conditions in ghetto schools. Teachers who complete their training in the program qualify for salary increases and are regarded within the system as more competent than those who do not. The program has now become mandatory since the board has realized its importance. But there are some fundamental inadequacies in the way it is carried out and in the philosophy on which it is based.

Since the board's community–relations problems involve primarily principals, district superintendents, and some headquarters officials, there are obvious drawbacks to limiting in-service training to courses for teachers—yet, human relations training is not yet mandatory for principals and district superintendents. The principals especially would benefit from in-service training programs, since the principals set the tone both for teachers inside and in their relations with the outside community. Programs for teachers should also be expanded; but community relations is a general problem and cannot be approached simply as a matter of teacher training.

Recognizing this, the board has started to consider various retraining techniques. Sensitivity training and role playing programs are now being considered.* A long-standing criticism of sensitivity training, as developed by its founders in the National Training Laboratory at Bethel, Maine, is that it focuses too much on attitude change and not enough on the need for changes in structure and administration.[40] A new set of performance measures and administrative controls for community relations skills would have to be instituted to give structural support to any attitudinal and behavioral changes that the school system might introduce, and these would have to come from the top.† One cannot effectively change the structure in any basic way without also changing the attitudes of the people in an organization, and the two must go on simultaneously. Simply to change the latter without also changing the former, is a questionable commitment of the school system's resources.

The Human Relations Unit suffers from the board's failures in this regard. Since policy has not been firmly set from the

* Role playing programs are a technique for changing basic values and attitudes and have been used in group psychotherapy.

† Social science consultants for business are full of examples of human relations training programs for first-line supervisors that have failed because there were no changes in attitudes and behavior at higher administrative levels.

top and the board has been more prone to political posturing than following through on strong commitments for change, the unit is vulnerable to cross-fires, periodic studies on its effectiveness, and scapegoating. Teachers and field supervisors see the administration vacillating continually on controversial policy issues. Headquarters officials frequently charge its staff with ineptitude and with encouraging agitation when they don't make headquarters "look good" or don't quiet down community protest. Many of the unit's staff view open conflict between community groups and school officials as a positive step toward better relations, while top headquarters officials view it with trepidation or cynicism.[41]

One way to increase the unit's effectiveness would be to decentralize it and place its staff under the control of the district office. If district-wide governing councils were set up throughout the system, including parent groups and outside institutions (universities, corporations, and foundations) as well as teachers and supervisors, the unit might serve as technical staff for the councils. This seems one of the most appropriate places to start decentralization. Many of the board's problems are community relations problems, which could best be handled at the local level; and it is administratively sound to lessen the present conflicts between the unit's staff and field supervisors.

If the Human Relations Unit were out in the field more, administratively as well as physically, its staff would have more chance to develop an understanding of the problems of teachers, principals, and superintendents, and school officials of the outlooks and skills of the human relations staff. Both parties might work together in the communities, and with no conflicting loyalties to bureaucratic superiors.*

It is doubtful whether this decentralization should take place right away, however. Since there are many principals and district superintendents now in the system whose community relations skills are very limited, and they would probably not perform much better under such decentralization than they do now, it would not be appropriate at all to decentralize the unit right away. If decentralization proves viable, and this would

---

*Students of administration often stress the importance of minimizing line-staff conflicts by more integration of central headquarters staff with operating (often field) units, and it has special relevance in this set of tangled and often ambiguous relationships.

involve many personnel changes at the supervisory level, the unit should then be decentralized.

A critical case that illustrates the tendency to make a scapegoat of the unit is the IS 201 controversy. When community protest reached a critical stage and a strike was called, some top headquarters officials claimed that they had been misinformed by the human relations staff, who had played an active role over the summer in trying to maintain communications between the community and school officials. Superintendent Donovan was very close to the situation in the weeks immediately preceding the public demonstrations, and met regularly with community leaders, so he may have been imputing blame to some human relations staff whose role was far less important than his own and the board's.* Actually, he was hamstrung himself by his board, which maintained final powers of decision and undercut the agreements he had made with community leaders. The protest was not primarily a result of ineptness of the human relations staff; it reflected the failure of the board, the superintendent, and the entire system to respond to legitimate community grievances, and their long history of mishandling this situation.[42]

The unit may have ended up the scapegoat because they were generally more progressive than many school officials and wanted to increase community participation to a degree that was not acceptable within the system. Some human relations staff made the political mistake of representing actual board policy to the community. Since policy was never really fixed and was always changing because of political pressures, those who were primarily interested in maintaining their good standing within the system never represented the board's advanced policy statements to the community and certainly did not take them too literally. The unit's role as an agent of change, taking board policy seriously, made it a lightning rod.

Another function of the Human Relations Unit must be expanded—preparing local schools, local communities, as well as the city as a whole, for innovation. This will not mean open hearings where polarized community groups will have just one more arena to continue their struggle or where all civic groups can attack the integrity of the Board of Education. It does mean

---

* Donovan reportedly claimed that he was poorly informed by his human relations staff about political dynamics in the area.

a much more intensive program of mobilizing local and city-wide support for those innovations that professional research and the politics of the situation warrant. Decentralization is first on the agenda. The board's continued failures on the desegregation issue indicate the need for more community preparation.

If the board is unable or unwilling to do this, other institutions should take over the job. There is evidence from the pairing controversy that indicates this is possible. The contrast between what the Human Relations Unit and the board were doing, and what an activist civic group could do, was evident in the weeks preceding the school opening in September, 1964. Mrs. Ellen Lurie, chairman of EQUAL, suggested to Superintendent Gross and his staff that the board have an open school week in the paired areas, with visits of pupils and parents from one paired school to another and with the clergy and other civic leaders participaing.[43] She also suggested that the board and other interested groups ask clergymen to give sermons the week before the opening of school on the moral significance of the pairings. The board found these ideas imaginative and worthy of trial, yet the extent of its public community relations effort was a series of spot TV announcements by Gross and Jacob Landers, the assistant superintendent in charge of integration activities, a few days before the opening of school.

The contrast between the board's and other civic groups' efforts in preparing for decentralization is even more marked. EQUAL and United Bronx Parents have prepared elaborate training materials to help parents develop skills in organizing, evaluating teachers and curricula, handling discipline and suspension problems, and evaluating overall school programs. This is essential if decentralization is to work, but the board has made little effort in this field. Because decentralization involves the transfer of power from the board to community groups, it is not likely the board will undertake this necessary task. This is one more reason, of course, for encouraging outside groups and institutions to do the job.*

---

* As of this writing, the Ford Foundation has developed plans to finance an institute for parent training throughout the city, to increase the expertise of civic groups in school affairs and in mobilizing greater parent and community participation.

Central Zoning Unit. Many of the same points I made about the Human Relations Unit's limited power and effectiveness apply to the Central Zoning Unit, set up in 1957 to deal directly with desegregation and school-utilization questions. The main function of the unit was to provide leadership in zoning decisions, and it has played a research and administrative role in all of the utilization and Open Enrollment programs. It investigated the feasibility of various zoning patterns under Open Enrollment, and it was then overseeing how and whether principals and teachers told parents about the availability of transfer plans.*

In the endless buckpassing that takes place when parents go to headquarters to inquire about school programs, the Central Zoning Unit, almost more than any other, is the end of the line.[44] One of its staff members reported: "The parents are often shunted to us by other headquarters and field people. In September, we have parents on chairs lining the halls right down here. I don't believe there is any other motivation to send them here aside from getting parents off somebody's back. We frequently send them back to the superintendent. 'I was just there,' they say. 'You're giving me the run-around.'"

The Central Zoning Unit had the same limited power and authority as the Human Relations Unit. Its director, Hillery Thorne, was only an acting director for three years, and was not appointed assistant superintendent and director of the unit until 1967. Thorne is a Negro, whose progressive views on desegregation have not always endeared him to traditional administrators. He was preceded by Dr. Francis A. Turner, who served from 1958 to 1963 and was more deeply attached to the neighborhood school concept.†

Under Turner, the Central Zoning Unit did little to push desegregation, since he often sided with white and middle class Negro populations who opposed the zoning of ghetto pupils into their schools. One member of the Central Zoning Unit confirmed what had been agreed upon by many civil rights leaders who pushed for Open Enrollment: "Frank Turner had a very sensitive attitude toward the neighborhood school." Turner

* Open Enrollment has been largely curtailed since June, 1967, especially at the high school level.

† Turner, also a Negro, was an assistant superintendent.

was regarded in civil rights circles, however, as honest and as a man who would always listen to civil rights groups' pleas for desegregation. Within the board itself, he was seen as a good administrator.

Theoretically, the Central Zoning Unit plays a major role in formulating zoning plans. But in actual fact, it cannot mandate any plans that the district superintendents oppose. Originally, the Subcommission on Zoning recommended that a headquarters unit be set up to make citywide zoning plans for desegregation and to override the veto power of the district superintendents who wanted to preserve their local authority. It never worked out this way.

There was virtual unanimity among the unit's staff we interviewed that they rarely take the initiative in formulating zoning changes. They all agreed that the impetus for zoning decisions came from the district superintendents, a pattern that the board was theoretically supposed to be moving away from. "We don't institute feeder patterns. The zoning boss of a particular school is the district superintendent," a staff member in the unit said. "Zoning proposals come to us from the district superintendent and our job is to review them for the various zoning criteria. Mostly we review the proposals of the field superintendent, who makes soundings through his local facilities. We are asked to review the integration potential of the prospective site, and to make recommendations."

Actually, several parties have been involved in zoning decisions. In addition to the district superintendent, local school boards, real estate interests, organized parent and civic groups, and a few headquarters groups such as the School Planning and Research Unit, divisional heads, and the assistant superintendent in charge of integration activities all take part. Local real estate groups play a significant role. They represent the interests of white homeowners or tenants, who frequently feel that they would like their children to attend schools only with other white, middle class children. Real estate pressures are exerted at every level, but especially on the district superintendent.

Even at headquarters, the Central Zoning Unit shares its authority with several other units. The School Planning and Research Unit is deeply involved in site location and zoning decisions and has generally been much more influential than the Central Zoning Unit. The assistant superintendent in charge of integration activities had more formal authority than the Central Zoning Unit until late 1967, and he sometimes represented its views to a district superintendent who refused to go along with zoning decisions that contributed to desegregation. Finally, the divisional heads could exercise some veto power over zoning decisions. Thus, the responsibility for final decisions was diffuse. It is little wonder, then, that when parents go to the board to get some information on a zoning decision, they are passed from one office to another without ever getting a satisfactory answer.

The fact that the power to initiate and veto zoning changes rests with the district superintendents suggests that the neighborhood school concept is still strong. Supposedly, it is board policy to use six criteria for site location and zoning decisions. One of them is integration; the others are distance from home to school, continuity of instruction, space utilization, topographical barriers, and transportation facilities. Different criteria may be given priority in particular decisions, depending on the district superintendent and his local constituency and upon their relationship with the headquarters staff.

The Central Zoning Unit has supported desegregation plans and is sometimes successful in getting zoning changes for that purpose, but it is often not successful, because policy is made elsewhere in the system. Members of the unit have a low rank and little power, and the diffusion of authority and responsibility in the field and headquarters units prevent any uniform zoning policies from being formulated or implemented.

Informal, personal relationships play an important role in determining who can make decisions, and the Central Zoning Unit sometimes has not been successful because its director and staff have not been influential with district superintendents and key headquarters personnel. This is partly because they have a reputation within the system for being progressive, but administratively they are seen as less than competent. Their relationship with tradition-bound officials improves, as they take on more of an advisory role.

One reason for the isolation of the unit's staff within the system was that it administered the implementation of Open Enrollment: it got mimeographed statements distributed to schools, and processed the parent applications directly, rather than having them returned to the principal or district superintendent.[45] The unit tried to minimize the subversion of the program by principals. Several Negro parents said that they got information from the unit's staff about which schools they might transfer their children to and which were good schools. The unit thus represented legitimate parent interests against those of principals and district superintendents who were discouraging transfers.

Another policing function of the unit was concerned with the tendency of principals in some predominantly white receiving schools to under-report the amount of space they had for incoming students from ghetto schools. A staff member reported: "White communities sometimes prefer to remain overcrowded than to have their kids transfer out or go to new fringe area schools. And sometimes you have to check out on a principal who is hiding space. It's a simple matter to check the registration and when there are too many rooms that are designated for special use, it begins to look pretty suspicious. And at this point we are oriented toward action on this sort of thing." This policing of field supervisors further undermined the unit's position.

The problems of the unit, then, related to the internal politics and codes of the system. District superintendents, for example, could not easily be challenged. "The district superintendents are very jealous of their power and they are very powerful," one staff member of the Central Zoning Unit reported. "If we disagree with them on a zoning problem, we are in no position to take it upon ourselves to deal with such a situation. It should be handled through channels."

No borough-wide, let alone citywide, zoning plan could ever be formulated, because the Central Zoning Unit's staff can only respond to specific zoning plans initiated by district superintendents. They enter into a zoning decision after a plan has been formulated and rarely go into any local situation without headquarters clearance. "We go into the community when we're invited," said a staff member. "The soundings of community groups come to us from district superintendents. Impressions seep through to us, but mostly we review the proposal of the field superintendent." The initiative in zoning is not from headquarters but rather from more status quo oriented interests in the field.

Often the neighborhood school concept is used in zoning decisions, because headquarters cannot veto a proposal put forth by a district superintendent. In a few instances where district superintendents develop new desegregative zoning plans, they are undercut by headquarters staff who are reluctant to arouse opposition. The board breaks away from the neighborhood concept when it feels it is "politically safe" to do so. But whenever there is any prospect of local resistance it backs off.

Assistant Superintendent in Charge of Integration Activities. Since 1964, the Central Zoning and Human Relations Units both borrowed their power from the assistant superintendent in charge of integration activities.[46] He had formal rank and could challenge a principal or district superintendent. A member of these units reported: "Sometimes we feel so strongly about a local crisis situation that we invoke Landers' authority and he will then intervene. If a district superintendent isn't moving where there are good prospects for integration we then report on this to Landers, and you see he's got a rank that equals theirs. He's an assistant superintendent himself, and sometimes Jack will try to budge them."

Landers was never popular with tradition-oriented field supervisors when he tried to urge them to comply with desegregation plans. In June, 1966, he became a special assistant to the superintendent, and a few months later, the coordinator of Title One programs. His replacement, Frederick Williams, was much more reluctant to exert influence on field supervisors who resisted desegregation; he referred to his approach as a "low key" one. To civil rights leaders and progressive school officials, "low key" meant little action. Williams remains as director of the Human Relations Unit, and may keep both units relatively powerless while making district superintendents autonomous.*

It doesn't matter too much, however, who occupies this position as assistant superintendent in charge of integration activities, from the perspective of how influential he might be in pressing for change. The position is hemmed in with all the constraints that most others in the system were, and any person who tries to innovate immediately confronts strong resistance

* For example, when asked by integrationist groups in Queens to support them by developing and implementing a plan to desegregate Andrew Jackson High School, located in a middle class Negro area and generally regarded as a "good" school, Williams replied that he was new in his position and had to investigate the local situation more. This was a widely discussed case, however, and the facts of the controversy were already well known to involved community groups and school officials.

from headquarters and the field and becomes isolated within the institution.*

The New York City schools are both too centralized and too decentralized, but in the wrong areas, and centralization and decentralization usurp each other's proper areas. Routine, minor decisions should be made locally, yet are made centrally. More significant decisions should be made centrally and implemented through strong central leadership—yet they are actually made locally. District superintendents are allowed to have negative veto power and to make policy on contested areas. The system thus works to subvert those units at headquarters that were mandated to change it. The mandate is really a charade, and most civil rights leaders recognize that. It is one of the reasons for their final disenchantment with desegregation.

The units designed for innovation that are discussed above have little stature or influence, and their staff are very much isolated within the informal structure of headquarters relations. They often engage in busy work, because they have no power to do anything else. The human relations staff might visit principals who were in trouble or advise other units on curriculum and textbook materials; these are important tasks, but perhaps less so than preparing communities for new programs or conducting major retraining programs with field supervisors. Central Zoning Unit staff spend much time on the administrative implementation of Open Enrollment or with their demographic data. These also are necessary, but not to the exclusion of initiating large-scale zoning plans for desegregation.

Many of the more idealistic and progressive staff in these units became demoralized. They would ask their director to represent their wishes for more formal authority and higher salaries. At one point in the 1965–1966 school year, members of the Central Zoning Unit's staff asked that they be given supervisory rank. The board refused, asking who it was that they supervised. They supervised no one, because the original recommendations of the Subcommission on Zoning had been

---

* In April, 1965, Landers prepared a booklet on educational parks in which he suggested that the controversial Canarsie-Flatlands site was ideally suited for a park. The board later turned down that site, and Landers did not endear himself to some headquarters administrators after civil rights groups quoted the booklet as one more justification for their demand.

subverted. The Human Relations Unit suffered from the same kind of handling.

History provides few examples of established institutions welcoming people or units whose purpose is to change the status quo. The New York City school system is no exception. Since its defective structure and the internal political alignments are not likely to be changed over the short run, it is very important to consider relocating these important functions. Perhaps the zoning might better be done by one of the city agencies—for example, the City Planning Commission. And many human relations functions might well be conducted through the Commission on Human Rights and the Human Resources Administration. The obvious advantages of locating these functions outside the Board of Education is that they could be performed in a more innovative way without being constrained by pressures from school professionals. Subcontracting important functions that the existing structure will never tolerate is perhaps one of the most significant strategies for innovation that could be followed, and this is so with regard to decentralization—to which we may now turn.

COMMUNITY RELATIONS

The pathologies and administrative problems I have described are played out in the board's relations with the community, which are not good and getting worse. When the board has listened, it hasn't known what to do. Some preliminary proposals for decentralization, and the organization of a few demonstration experiments to test these proposals, have been its main response.*

When civil rights groups and ghetto parents gave up on desegregation, they started to coalesce around the issues of the board's non-accountability and limited responsiveness to their grievances. The desegregation controversy dramatized the gulf between communites and their schools. The board has contributed to many of the problems. For example, although Superintendent Donovan had announced in the fall of 1965 that parents should have access to reading-score data, many parent groups had to struggle for months to secure these figures. When the Citizens Committee for Children requested information about suspensions and the board's disposition of the pupils, to "suggest different procedures for suspensions that would be in the best interest of the child, and to request educational, psychological, guidance and other services for all suspended children," it got little response.[1] "Whenever we asked for this

---

* See Chapter Thirteen for an extended discussion of decentralization and how the board has undercut these demonstration experiments.

information," CCC officials reported, "the authorities answered specific questions with general information." *

IS 201

The IS 201 controversy brought all these questions to the fore. The struggle between the community and the board over the location and zoning of that school, and over the appropriate role of local groups in school decisions, resulted in a coalition that included the mayor, the Ford Foundation, big business, universities, and state education officials, which supported the demands of ghetto groups for better schools through decentralization—which means, in principle, greater community control over the schools.[2]

The controversy began early in 1962, when the Board of Education decided to build a new junior high school between 127th and 128th Streets on Park Avenue. The purpose was to relieve overcrowding in the junior high schools of Harlem and East Harlem.[3] The community objected greatly to the location because it clearly meant the school would be segregated. Even the community faction that was opposed to desegregation objected to the site, since it was adjacent to the New York Central Railroad tracks and surrounded by depressing tenements and storefronts. In early 1962, there was a meeting of board officials and architects to develop plans for a windowless, air-conditioned building. When asked by Harlem leaders if the community had been notified, the answer was "no," but the board was sure the community would be delighted. Later that year, Local Planning Board No. 11 and the local school board sponsored a meeting, where community groups expressed strong opposition.

Construction began in 1964, and the board announced in late 1965 that the school would open on April 1, 1966. Dr. Bernard Donovan said at a public meeting in the spring of 1965 that 201 would be an integrated intermediate school,

---

* Arthur Clinton, Director of the Bureau of Attendance, informed officials from the CCC in October, 1966, that he could not give them data on the exact length of time of particular student suspensions, the grades of suspended students, the specific reasons for their suspensions, and what happened to them after the suspensions took place. He said that this information was not available centrally. It is also unavailable in the district offices.

following the guidelines of the Allen Report's proposed re-organization of the school system.[4] According to Harlem parents present at the meeting, he suggested that white students would be attracted by its special program and accessibility via the Triboro Bridge. He also alluded to having the school connected to a university and offering special programs.

In the fall of 1965, a committee of parents asked the board to describe the plans that had been made for integrating the school and for the special programs. "Mrs. Dorothy Jones, education director of the Protestant Council's Office of Church and Race, reported that no details were provided by the board at the time."[5] By the beginning of 1966, the board gave the community an answer: the school would have roughly 50% Negro children and 50% Puerto Rican children. Integrationists within the community were enraged.

The school's zoning was sharply contested throughout the spring of 1966.[6] Community leaders wrote: "On April 26, Mr. Schreiber [the district superintendent] announced a new feeder pattern for 201 whereby PS 24, 39, and 7 would be the principal feeder schools for 201 with some children coming in from 155 and 96. The purpose of the gerrymandered pattern, which dipped far south into East Harlem, but excluded elementary schools adjacent to 201 in the north, was to achieve a student body of 50% Negro and 50% Puerto Rican students. While the local school board had been informed of the change in zoning, they had warned Schreiber to discuss it with the community before making it public. The community, which was not in-volved in the zoning discussion, was furious. Not only was Schreiber refining his phony concept of integration, he was gerrymandering to achieve it, and without consulting the community groups and parents' associations, which had been working on the school for months. It is hard to conceive of a move calculated to generate more bad feeling within the East Harlem community. Schreiber's gerrymandering resulted in increased activity in community organization over the 201 issue. By now, the school had become a symbol of bad faith of the public school system and the contempt which its officials held for parents in the ghetto. It was also seen as a test of the board's good faith in moving to reorganize the school sys-tem to achieve integration."

The community was also irritated by the board's handling of

the naming of the school.[7] The community's historical account reports that "While the community was assured that no name would be chosen without its consultation, the Board of Education staff bulletin was published in October, 1965, referring to 201 as the "Arthur Schomburg School." Miffed by this breach of trust, parents began pressing for details on its program, the specifics of the zoning, the selection of staff, etc."

Though the school was scheduled to open on April 1, 1966, community protests forced a postponement until May 1, then June 1, then a month later for a summer program, and finally to September 12, the official opening day for the school year. By late spring and early summer, the parent and community committee and the board had become so stalemated that the committee appealed to Mayor Lindsay, the State Commissioner of Education, and finally to the United States Commissioner of Education, Harold Howe, to intervene. Nothing happened.

Some school officials met with the parents in attempts to settle the controversy. Jacob Landers, assistant superintendent in charge of integration activities, met with the Parents' Council on May 31, but reached no agreement with them on zoning, curriculum, or integration. On June 20, there was a meeting with the board, which produced no results.

Superintendent Donovan, Board President Garrison, and other school officials met with parents and community representatives on August 18 to discuss the impasse.[8] Parents reported that the board made the following claims: "That compulsory zoning of white children into the school would violate Board of Education policy against bussing children to achieve integration," and "that community power over the affairs of the school would be illegal, and that the board could not abdicate its responsibility toward the school." The Harlem representatives replied that "the board had already abdicated its responsibility, that this fact made it necessary for the community to have meaningful power." [9]

Superintendent Donovan then took over the negotiations and met regularly in Harlem with community representatives. Parents insisted that if the board could not integrate the school, it should give a community council working jointly with the school staff a veto power in the selection of school personnel and the right to participate in the making of school policy.[10] Superintendent Donovan agreed to replace Stanley

Lisser, who was slated to take over as principal, with a black, male principal, to be selected by the board and community representatives.* The board refused to back Donovan on either commitment, and Lisser began the year as principal. The school finally opened on September 21; demonstrations and picketing continued for another week, and parents clashed with the IS 201 teachers who backed Lisser and who refused to teach in the nearby PS 103 while 201 was closed and negotiations between parents and the board were going on.

After the board reversed Donovan and negotiations completely broke down, militant local groups, including SNCC, the Black Panthers, and other nationalist groups became involved. They had been invited in by the parents.†

The opening of school did not end the discussions. In late September, Dr. Kenneth Clark suggested that the administration of IS 201 and its feeder schools be subcontracted to universities in the area. Clark's proposal, along with many others, was ignored, and on October 20, the board released its own proposals, which included a citywide "task force" and an advisory council for 201. The Lindsay administration and the Ford Foundation, through its new president, McGeorge Bundy, became involved in the discussions, along with board officials, the United Federation of Teachers, and parent spokesmen. Ford was interested in urban development and public education and saw the reform of the New York City schools as central to that interest. And, of course, the mayor realized that the quality of the schools affected many other city problems and was a political question with which he had to deal.

Harlem leaders were approached by Board President Garrison to serve on the task force, but they all refused, on grounds that this was merely another stalling tactic by the board, that they didn't want yet another intermediary between them and the board, and that any program directed by the board would not succeed. Bundy withdrew because he had agreed to serve only on the condition that the ghetto community be represented.[11] The mayor and his staff were especially disappointed

---

* Ironically, Lisser claims that he had recruited many white parents from outside the area to send their children to 201. He was then undercut by headquarters officials who refused to entertain such a plan.

† Harlem CORE, reputed by some school officials to be among these groups, had been on the parents' negotiating team from the beginning.

by the failure of the task force, since they saw it as an opportunity to participate more directly in educational policy-making and to assume more power.

Despite the failure of the task force, the IS 201 controversy hastened the city wide mobilization of protest against the schools, which might otherwise have taken much longer to develop. The controversy precipitated a wave of demonstrations in other ghetto schools about the poor education there, and demands for more community power over staffing and curriculum. A Peoples' Board to watch over all the activities of the Board of Education was formed in December, 1966, composed of parents and activists from ghetto communities throughout the city. The Peoples' Board accelerated the protests throughout the winter and spring of 1967.

The 201 controversy shows that the board has become so insulated from the community that it could unwittingly help build the very coalitions that may eventually tear down the whole system. The making of decisions on the location, zoning, and naming of the school without consulting community groups beforehand; the promises that 201 would open as an integrated school, despite a location that precluded it; and the board's refusal to directly involve itself in the controversy until the last moment, sending instead headquarters officials who were not empowered to make final commitments—all this reinforced the community's distrust, galvanized its agitation, and prevented the sides from coming to an agreement.*

From the board's point of view, there was a logic to its actions. The board felt it could not honor demands for community power in the selection of school staff and the development of curriculum. State education laws supposedly prevented this.† Furthermore, the board was not certain who the "community" was, a perennial problem. Seeing a number of factions and leadership struggles, it delayed making any final decisions until it could see how these struggles within the community developed. However, community leaders report that the board

---

* "They make us into militants," a ghetto area leader explained, "and then they discredit us for being militants. We just cannot win. That's why we want to take over the whole thing."

† In September, 1967, the board decided that there was enough flexibility in the laws governing the selection of staff that it could delegate such powers to community groups. By that time, political pressures to do so were much greater than they had been the year before. The board's interpretation of the law has always been a function of politics.

did more than this, and that "attempts were being made in June by board officials to divide parents and community groups." [12]

Other interests took sides. The teachers' union, for example, got caught in the middle between the community and the board, as it invariably does. The board feared that the teachers' refusal to hold classes in 103 might increase the strength of parents, and the parents felt it would increase the board's power in the negotiations. The union was afraid of eventual community veto power over their appointments. Principals reacted in an even more protectionist way, accusing the parents of wanting to take over all staffing decisions. Mrs. Dorothy Jones of the Protestant Council reported: "That same day [that Donovan announced the reassignment of Lisser] thirty white principals of Central Harlem schools went into a state of panic. They held a meeting from which no formal statement was issued, but from which leaked the rumor that they were going to resign in a body if Mr. Lisser were not reinstated. It seems that these principals feared that the demand for a Negro principal at IS 201 and the superintendent's acceptance of this concept meant that they were all likely to be faced with demands that they be replaced." [13]

The white civic groups and the press also responded predictably. PEA and UPA both denounced demands for a black principal as a threat to professionalism, to the merit system, to integration, and to the integrity of the board against irresponsible attack and political meddling by a small band of outside agitators. They maintained that the leaders in the IS 201 struggle did not represent parents in the community and discredited the protest on these grounds. Yet, neither group had responded over the two years to protests by ghetto parents about the board's failure to act on their demands.

The press, as usual, supported the position taken by PEA, UPA, and the board. They misrepresented the parents as demanding either the bussing in of white children or total community control, and they dramatized the supposed "takeover," in their words, by the "militant, nationalist, racist forces of the community." The community's demands were both more complex and more tempered, and militant, activist groups had been called in only after negotiations had completely broken down.[14] That this protest was then turned into a political and public relations defeat by the press, moderate groups, and the board, indicates the continued powerlessness of ghetto groups.

However, it also indicated some failures of strategy on their part as well. Their demands for a black principal at a time when fears of Black Power had turned so many former allies from the movement, set them up to be maligned in the press and by powerful white groups. It was almost inevitable that they were charged with demanding "total control" and Black Power, although, in truth, demands for more community participation and for a veto power in the selection of the principal reflected years of frustration at having to deal with the board, and must be interpreted in a context of their experience with expanding segregation, lower reading levels, and the insensitivity of the school system to their pleas. Nevertheless, the result of their demand for a black principal was that the *New York Times* and almost all civic groups, let alone the school professionals, defeated them.

Board officials maintain that they have become increasingly responsive to the community over the past few years, acknowledging some of the legitimate complaints of IS 201 parents and others throughout the city. My evidence does not support this assertion.

Local School Boards

One of the ways the board has attempted to give citizen groups more access to school officials has been through the establishment of local school boards. The board was criticized in the late 1950s for not providing for adequate citizen participation in school affairs.[15] In 1961, the state legislature directed the new central board to reorganize its local boards in order to increase such citizen participation.[16] The new local boards began to operate in 1962–1963.

The Women's City Club investigated the structure, functions and powers of local school boards from 1962 to 1965, and found, during that period, increasing contact between the central and local boards, and that the latter were occasionally consulted on decisions affecting their districts.[17] They found also that relationships between local boards and district superintendents, parent associations, and their communities had greatly improved.

Despite this, "there is not yet [in 1965] full acceptance of local boards as officially interested parties by the professionals at headquarters." [18] Also, headquarters officials often made decisions and announced them publicly without notifying the local boards and failed to provide clear leadership on desegregation which contributed to local community resistance to even limited proposals. Local board members thought that headquarters often communicated indecision on desegregation questions and used public meetings of local school boards to pit groups against one another. A further problem was that local boards, especially in ghetto and fringe areas, did not include adequate representation of the Negro and Puerto Rican poor.

Local school board members felt they would only be influential if the system were decentralized. For example, less than 25% of the 48 board members interviewed regarded their contacts with headquarters as "good," another 50% characterized them as "bad." [19] Their specific comments reflected their deep frustrations: "Local board has important advisory role if staff of Board of Education accepts this," one board member said; "Professional staff not so good; they answer letters, but in double talk. Have to go to board to get straight answers from the staff," said another. They also commented upon the difficulty in reaching specific administrative personnel on specific problems.

Local school board chairmen were especially angry and demoralized about their powerlessness, and many complained that the central board did not take their deliberations seriously and failed to give them the necessary autonomy to respond to citizen complaints or initiate new programs. One chairman, after citing several examples of recommendations he and his board had made to headquarters that had never been acted upon, remarked: "The professional board is a great, ponderous glacier that creeps along, giving occasional warning signals as to their intentions. When you deal with them, you feel their hearing aids are turned off. It's such an enormous operation, like throwing spitballs at Gibraltar. There is no point at which the local school board and the citizenry are brought into the planning. . . . We feel we legitimize arbitrary decisions of the board."

Six local school board chairmen wrote to their colleagues on October 10, 1966: [20]

The six undersigned local school board chairmen met informally on September 26 to discuss what seems to us to be a continuing deterioration of the position of the local boards. We agreed that the time is ripe for the local boards to take the initiative in moving the system toward a pattern of organization in which the local boards would have a real function. . . . What we share as local school board members is the increasing irrelevancy in our work.

Feelings of alienation from headquarters were thus widespread. The Women's City Club report concluded: "There is already some evidence that frustration and a feeling of impotence have been responsible for some resignations from the boards. If they are not given what the members can regard as satisfying and meaningful functions to perform, it will be impossible to continue to get citizens of high calibre to be willing to serve." [21]

Many parent association presidents interviewed in the study expressed the same views. Nearly 40% stated that local boards had not contributed to running and improving the schools, and another 12% gave qualified answers to a question on the local boards' contributions. PA and PTA presidents from every borough except Staten Island commented at length on the powerlessness of local boards.* One PA president in Manhattan expressed a view held by many of her colleagues elsewhere: "Our PTA favors strengthening the local school boards. Since they are close to the schools, they should carry more weight than they do. On two issues the Board of Education gave the local board insufficient time to consider the matters and make recommendations. This makes a mockery of giving more weight and responsibility to the local board." †

These expressions of resentment reflected accurately the con-

---

* No parent association presidents were polled in Staten Island, where the UPA has no local chapters.

† Harold Siegel, the board's secretary, noted in a memo to then vice-president Alfred Giardino his evaluations of how the central board handled the local boards: "I do not think that the role of the Local School Board has been clearly articulated or thought out either by the board, its members, or the staff and the Local School Boards themselves. Is the LSB a voluntary agency such as say the PA, a community council, etc? Is it an advisory group to the board? to the district superintendents? Is its purpose the initiation of corrective action at the headquarters level? at the district level? Does it have a mediating role at the district level? As I have heard the board members relate to the Local School Boards, and to local board members, they conceive of the Local School Boards as being all of the above. . . .

straints imposed on local boards by headquarters. The consensus among several headquarters professionals and board members we interviewed was that local boards were an important "buffer" between them and the community—to explain headquarters policies (which turned out to be non-policies on controversial issues like desegregation), and to provide some release of community tensions and sentiments about school programs. The board also hoped that local boards would defend and represent it at the community level.* "After my appointment five years ago," a local board member from the Bronx reported, "I had a pep talk from the district superintendent that I now represented the Board of Education, what I said reflected on the board, and that I should be careful what I said and defend their policies." [22] The problem was that many local board members conceived their role differently, and they resented deeply the way they were so often undercut from headquarters.†

One aspect of the powerlessness of local boards was their relationship with their district superintendent, who was an ex officio member of the local board. District superintendents are generally more protectionist in their relations with the community and prefer more insulation than do local board members, for obvious reasons.‡

In recent years, local board members have encouraged legitimate parent protests, defining such actions as an essential part of their role to provide a meaningful link between the community and the schools. For example, Local School Board No. 4, in East Harlem, often protested board policies, and became so discouraged during the IS 201 dispute that they all resigned. Reverend Vincent Resta, acting as spokesman for the local school board, stated publicly in November, 1966, "The board has utterly refused to discuss the issues seriously

---

* This was different from the board's policy and public statements in which it expressed an interest in giving local boards more power.

† The central board sometimes seems oblivious to these frustrations, as indicated, for example, at one of the ceremonial teas held by the board for local school board members in late 1966. Several of the latter voiced sharp protests about their powerlessness, and Alfred Giardino, then Vice President, expressed surprise at the complaints.

‡ Superintendents, as educators, identify much more with other school officials within the system in many instances than they do with community groups, while the local board, as laymen, identify more with the community.

with us or with the parents. The board's proposal for us to set up a parent's committee to advise the school administration would make it nothing more than a glorified PTA." [23]

Local School Board No. 12–14 in West Harlem and Washington Heights became so discouraged at the board's rejection of its many desegregation proposals while not coming up with any of its own that it refused to hold hearings on the Gross Blueprint. In December, 1966, four of the nine members resigned.* [24]

The central board has felt that it could not give local boards any more power than they had. It wanted to keep down the level of community protest and conflict so that headquarters could get on with the main business of mandating reforms without too much further upset. From the central board's point of view, there are so many vested interests and opposition groups as it is, and there is so much protest over school programs, that if more community conflict arises, the board will never be able to push through needed changes. It seems to have equated giving local boards more power with creating more local vested interests who might block change and subvert the system.†

This policy has affected many local board appointments over the past couple of years. As Garrison noted, "During the last few months [April–June, 1966] our Board had vacancies to fill on all thirty local school boards and considered approximately 450 applications to fill these vacancies. In a number of cases, incumbents were not re-appointed." [25]

Selection. One of the most contested of the board's decisions in this regard was to renew Mrs. Ellen Lurie—an active member of Local School Board No. 6 in West Harlem and Washington

---

* Board members throughout the city have resigned for similar reasons, and other local boards have rebelled in similar fashion.

† Former Board President Lloyd Garrison defined the policy of ruling off activists in a letter to a local school board chairman: "It is not seemly or appropriate," he wrote, "for a local school board member to use his or her position as a fulcrum for the organization and stimulation of group activity directed against Board policies. We have taken the position that a Local School Board member, like any other citizen, is free to engage in activities of this sort but should in that event relinquish membership on the Local School Boards." One of the main problems with the statement is its disregard of what local school board protests actually indicated. Many board members who protested on desegregation were in effect doing so in the name of the central board's own policy statements, which the central board was not implementing.

Heights—for only one more year, despite the unanimous recommendation of the district's screening panel, backed by her local board colleagues and the district superintendent, that she be reappointed for a five-year term. Mrs. Lurie had supported the central board in its pairing proposals and had formulated numerous plans, along with her local board colleagues, for the desegregation and the more even utilization of schools in her district. However, she also helped to organize many militant public protests against the board's delay and inaction on the desegregation recommendations of the Allen Report.

Mrs. Lurie's defense of her actions in protesting the board's decision raises several general issues about its policies regarding the role of local boards. As she noted in a letter to Board President Garrison: "You say in your letter that you want a healthy and vigorous Local School Board system, composed of citizens who have been involved and active leaders in their communities. And yet you go on to say that Local School Board members should not stimulate group activity directed 'against board policies.' " [26] Mrs. Lurie also pointed out that the "stirring up" she did was aimed at pushing the board to implement its own policies, as contrasted with its professional staff who subverted them. Finally, she noted that it seemed unusual to deny the right of dissent and of mobilizing the opposition to local school board members who were powerless and never participated in formulating board policy.

The powerlessness of local boards results from the way they are selected, as well as from the informal rules their members must function under. The selection is made by the central board with a concern for limiting agitation, especially from the left, and to discourage local boards from participating in key decisions. Local board members are selected from a list of nominees made by a local screening committee, generally composed of community leaders. In integrated and fringe areas, however, and even in ghetto communities, the committees are often composed of middle class people who do not represent the Negro and Puerto Rican poor and may not be responsive to their interests. Furthermore, district superintendents often participate in the screening and selection of local board members to ensure that "troublemakers" are kept off.

Officially, the board states that it prefers the nominees to be civic leaders with an interest in and knowledge of school affairs. Unofficially, it has not always welcomed people who are too sophisticated about the workings of the system, because they might become "obstructionist" and veto headquarters and district superintendents' decisions. They might also question board policy and mobilize protests against it.

Militants and integrationists are usually kept off local boards. The following examples are typical: Both Reverend Lawrence Smith and Harold Dicks, articulate Negro leaders, have applied two years running for the local board in District 9 in The Bronx, and have been turned down with no reason given; the school board in Brownsville and Canarsie had only one Negro from Brownsville until 1967, and he was not strong on integration—now they have two.[27]

The composition of the screening panel and the scheduling of its meetings have been a discriminatory device throughout the city. "Meetings of local groups to discuss who should make up the screening panel were always held in the morning," a civic leader in District 9 reported.[28] "This past year [1966], through a tremendous effort, we got a change in the meeting time so Negro and Puerto Rican groups could come. And we got a Negro and a Puerto Rican nominated. Both turned out to be effective, but it was only by this great effort that we were able to get two of the nine people representing the sizeable Negro and Puerto Rican population here."

The Negro and Puerto Rican people who are finally chosen are often conservative middle class types with few ties to the poor. A Brooklyn civil rights leader gave an example: "The chairman of the local board (1966) in District 16 in Bedford–Stuyvesant is a middle class Negro. This individual does not believe in Open Enrollment or bussing and thinks they can build up their own neighborhood."

The interests of the poor or even the more radical middle class thus go unrepresented. "The local board in my district [No. 7] is generally not representative of the community," explained a Puerto Rican leader in the south Bronx, "and it does not know how the community feels or the real problems there. I applied to be on it but was turned down, since I am too controversial." "Mrs. Babette Edwards was very highly recommended by the screening panel in my district [No. 4]," reported a Harlem civil rights leader, "but was not appointed, and the board still has no representative from the district's eastern side.

The central board apparently will go to great lengths to keep some people off, as reported by a civil rights leader on Manhattan's Upper West Side. "Our district [No. 5] has had several openings the past year," this leader said. "At one time the names of Naomi Levine of American Jewish Congress and Rosalie Stutz of EQUAL were put up. The board turned down both, even though they are well informed people who have worked on school matters for years. Rosalie knows more about problems in West Side schools than almost anybody around, but she was seen as too militant. There still remains one vacancy on the local board, which they refuse to fill with either person, and they were the two top people recommended," he further asserted.

Supporting the central board in its dislike of activists is the screening panel, which often represents a limited part of the local district. "The way the screening panel is set up," explained one local school board member in the Bronx, "it can be controlled in individual districts by a small ingroup. Sayde Reiss managed to get many of the same people reappointed to the local school board in her district because of her control of the Mid-Bronx Community Council [a federation of white middle class moderate and conservative groups]."

The board did appoint some integrationists and some people of more liberal bent, but invariably these were people who were not very controversial in their communities. A majority of its appointments, even in integrated and ghetto areas, were conservative and moderate PTA and PA types. This reinforced the powerlessness of the Negro and Puerto Rican poor and may have encouraged more outside protest and agitation against the system.* The people the board implicitly supported in many districts such as Canarsie, the mid-Bronx, and central and south Queens had in some cases worked actively against desegregation. They were selected and reappointed on the grounds that they represented their communities. By that logic, it would then have been appropriate to have local board members in Harlem, East Harlem, Brownsville, the south and mid-Bronx, and Bedford–Stuyvesant, who represented their respective communities.

Ghetto and integrated communities are now more factional

---

* See Appendix for a partial list of activists on the left who were kept off, and those on the right who were chosen.

than white ones, sometimes making it difficult for the board to judge how large a constituency particular local leaders have. These communities are now in the process of developing strong civic and political organizations. If the board is to be a significant vehicle in that development, however, then its policy of excluding activists from local boards is self-defeating. Indeed, if the board increases the authority and responsibility of the local boards under decentralization, but continues to exclude activists, it may drain leadership out of the system and contribute to continued efforts to undermine the institution. Far from tending to decrease community tensions, this policy would activate militant elements by refusing to give them a voice. Such a strategy would result in neither reform nor survival.

Response to the Community. At present, several local boards are quite unresponsive to the interests of the whole community. Those who are responsive find themselves overruled by the system, and the effect is the same. The following two cases are illustrations.

The first is District No. 9, along the racial frontier in the southwest and mid-Bronx.[29] It contains at least three separate communities—one predominantly Negro, one a fringe area, and the third a predominantly white area. In this instance a coalition of the district superintendent, the local school board, and white middle class parent and civic organizations beat down attempts by the insurgent Negro and Reform Democrat community to press for desegregation and other reforms in the district. The chairman of the local board, Mrs. Sayde Reiss, was a long-time civic and political leader in the white community, with very close ties to the Democratic Party machine and to a federation of white organizations, the Mid-Bronx Community Council. The council was very influential in selecting local school board members.*

When school pairings were proposed in the district in early 1964, Parents and Citizens (PAC), a neighborhood school group, was formed. They worked actively, within the PAs in the white schools, against pairings, and campaigned to disaffiliate the schools from the UPA—whose position, they felt, was too equivocal. A predominantly white integrationist group,

---

* It also had the district superintendent's school-community coordinator on its payroll, hardly qualifying him to give impartial treatment to the expanding ghetto community.

UNITED (United Neighbors for Integration Through Education and Democracy), was formed to counter PAC.

The district superintendent and local school board chairman were much more responsive to PAC than to UNITED. Mrs. Lynette Teich, the leader of PAC, was always given free access to speak in schools, at parent association and local school board meetings. Since getting access to the schools required the principals' permission, and since the district was widely regarded as under the tight reins of its superintendent, Dr. Maurice Ames, one may assume that his principals were not opposed to PAC's views.*

The same courtesies were not extended to UNITED, the NAACP, or other local groups from the Negro community (Claremont), whose leaders had to struggle to get speaking time at local board meetings. "At one meeting, Mrs. Teich had written requesting speaking time," a local board member reported, "and rose first to the usual warm greeting from Mrs. Reiss. When a representative of UNITED rose next [she had also written requesting time], she was told there was no letter from her and she could not talk." †

In the fall of 1965, the board announced its intermediate school program. At the local board meeting called to discuss this, a leaflet was handed to people entering. It was a letter signed by Mrs. Reiss, expressing on behalf of the community the desire for a "moratorium on change"—that is to say that there would be no intermediate school programs to foster integration.

The Negro community had by this time shifted from an interest in integration to one in quality in ghetto schools. Its leaders asked that the reading scores for the schools in the district be made public, in accordance with Superintendent Donovan's public announcement to this effect. The local board, however, cited a letter it had received from Donovan,

---

* The close alliance of Mrs. Reiss and PAC was quite public, as indicated by the habitual warm welcomes to Mrs. Teich at local school board meetings. . . . "our honored guests," . . . . "we are so honored . . ." The relationship even extended to Mrs. Teich's playing in a key role in a plan to censure Reverend Keller, a board member with strong sympathies with the Negro community, and to Mrs. Reiss' arranging for a PAC-sponsored meeting with local politicians.

† Integrationist leaders had so much trouble getting speaking time that they took to sending their requests by registered mail. They still kept being told that the local board didn't get their letters.

leaving it to the judgment of local boards, and refused to give out scores, saying the information was not yet available.[30] Community groups protested and were supported by three local politicians, but to no avail.*

Mrs. Reiss then failed to call a public board meeting for several months in late 1965 and early 1966, and she said publicly on several occasions that one would not be called. "Let them cool their heels," she remarked. The fact that integration reports had been issued from headquarters that the community wished to discuss did not alter this decision.

Executive sessions were called, however, and at one of them Reverend Keller was formally censured for picketing a new school's ghetto location, distributing leaflets protesting the lack of public meetings, and discussing with the Negro community the proceedings of the local board's executive sessions. Keller was urged by the central board to keep his fights "within the family." †

Keller's censure mobilized the Negro and white integrationist groups, and when a local board meeting was finally called in March, 1966, three months after the last one, the board was met with a hostile community, which filed a complaint with the Commission on Human Rights, asking for the removal of the district superintendent and local school board chairman. William Booth, the commission's chairman, and board officials intervened, held a closed session with the Negro community, the local board, and the district superintendent, and drew up a list of agreements answering the community's many grievances.‡

There have been some changes since then. Two new local board members have been appointed—a Negro man and a Puerto Rican woman. Joe L. Jackson, the Negro, has been in continued conflict with Mrs. Reiss, who threatened several times to resign because of him and walked out of some public board meetings. She finally did resign in 1967.

The case is an extreme one, but it illustrates the degree to which one local board was unresponsive to the Negro and

---

* Assemblyman Seymour Posner, City Councilman Gelfand, and State Senator Harrison Golden. Mrs. Reiss later upbraided them for this in private, and one withdrew his insistence that the scores be made available.

† He had tried endlessly to do so, but with no results.

‡ It was necessary to reinforce this the following fall (1966), with another meeting and list of agreements.

Puerto Rican poor, a common pattern in many areas of the city.

The local board in the Harlem–Washington Heights areas of Manhattan, District 12–14, was perhaps more committed to desegregation than any other local board in the entire city. Its members included Mrs. Dorothy Jones, an activist Negro professional from Harlem, who was then a staff member of the City Commission on Human Rights, and Mrs. Ellen Lurie, who had worked as a community organizer and social worker in East Harlem before becoming chairman of EQUAL. This local board provided many desegregation plans for its district, but it was completely powerless and those on the board who were committed to reform became demoralized.

This board was constituted, like all others, in the fall of 1962. Its year-end report of August, 1963, indicated its dissatisfactions: "If at the end of this first year, many of us have a feeling of frustration, it is due to the rapidly increasing awareness of the need for change and the slowness of the process to bring such changes about." They later informed Lloyd Garrison, then vice president of the central board, that: "We are of the opinion that our frustration is partly due to the fact that the functions of the local school boards are ill defined. The 'Plan for the Revitalization of the Local School Boards,' was, we believe, never implemented in terms of specifics." [31]

In a statement for an open local school board meeting in their district, dated January 30, 1964, they gave a perceptive diagnosis of the board's failures on desegregation, complaining of

> the absence of bus supervision, of increased services, retraining of teachers to deal with different types of children, for those schools participating in the Open Enrollment program. The Local School Board has requested these services, but has not met with any success. We have noted that these essential needs for the receiving schools are not included in the expanded free choice transfer program.

They also expressed concern with "the lack of communication and consultation between the central board and the local school boards in developing its various plans for implementing a program of integration despite the reference in the December 6th report, to community and local involvement in discussing integration," and "that the changes (rezoning, changing feeder patterns, school linkage, Princeton Plan) were not spelled out more fully and specifically as to when, where, and how they would occur . . ." Their final charge "that sincere requests made by our principals, teachers, and parents are rarely even acknowledged, let alone acted upon," reflected a condition prevalent throughout the city.

Upgrading and desegregating the district's junior high schools was a major interest of this local board. Their frustrations in working on this problem were endless. In 1962, the two all-Negro junior highs, 136 and 139, had no principals. Finally, in February, 1964, the central board developed a plan to integrate three of the junior highs—JHS 164, which had roughly 10% whites; JHS 52, which had 85%; and JHS 115, which had 50%. The plan was poorly regarded. "This plan was so bad," a local board member related, "we could see that it would have the whole community up in arms and completely torn apart. We asked them to keep it quiet, and they even agreed. They themselves could understand what it would do." [32]

The local board then held a meeting attended by every major group in the community, from Harlem Parents Committee to PAT, to develop a plan. Finally, Mrs. Lorraine Addelston, principal at JHS 136, who had been opposed to previous plans, developed an idea with the help of the president and staff of the Bank Street School of Education to form a consolidated program for an educational institute for seventh graders in the three schools. Every junior high school principal involved was wholeheartedly in favor of the plan, as were civic groups.

> At this point, when there was real unity in the community, and the most hidebound groups had shown open minds in working together to this point, District Superintendent Shapp gave the story to the *World Telegram*. It was a bad leak at a bad time. Up to that point, the atmosphere in the community was wonderful, but the leak changed all that, and by March 19, 1964, when the institute plan was brought to the board, the PAT demonstration at city hall of March 15 had already taken place, and the board killed it in the usual way. We simply never heard from them. Subsequently, we developed other, less radical plans—still good, and certainly an improvement over the situation as it was, but we never got an answer to any of them.[33]

On March 7, 1965, after this and other plans were rejected by headquarters, the local board decided not to hold public hearings on the Gross Blueprint. They gave the following reasons: "We are not willing to hold hearings on proposals to which the Board of Education is not committed. . . . We need a specific detailed plan to set before our entire district which will not capriciously transfer any child from one existing segregated school to another." [34]

The next month, Sidney Rosenberg, the new district superintendent, developed the first of his many desegregation proposals that the central board rejected. At a local school board meeting on April 1, 1965, it was reported in the minutes that "Dr. Rosenberg reported on his proposed plan for quality integrated education for the junior high schools in north Manhattan which he had submitted to a meeting consisting of presidents of parent associations, principals, teachers, and local school board members. He mentioned that this plan had been rejected by a committee of associate superintendents, mainly on the grounds that people from Inwood would not send their children to JHS 164. . . . A lengthy and intensive discussion followed during which everybody agreed that, as it looks now, we are left with a status quo." Rosenberg developed other plans, many of them highly regarded by the local board and community groups, but none was accepted at headquarters.[35]

The minutes of this local school board contain numerous detailed references to requests, recommendations, and grievances regarding particular schools that were not acted upon by headquarters. In late 1965, the chairman finally released a letter to community groups, explaining why the local board had not held any public meetings during that school year:

> Over an extended period of time, inquiries and recommendations emanating from our open meetings have been transmitted to the Board of Education at Livingston Street, and only occasionally have we received word concerning reactions to, or the disposition of these matters. . . . The problem became particularly aggravated when in June of this year a number of critical proposals and inquiries were made regarding JHS 139, 115, and 164, the Capital Construction Budget, and related matters. . . . No satisfactory response has been received regarding any action taken. Early in November we reviewed the problem with Mr. Giardino. To date, no response has been received. . . . In the absence of adequate feedback from the Board of Education, there seems to be minimal value in conducting open meetings within our community. . . . Local School Board 12–14 would strongly welcome your

advice and counsel in its efforts to make the educational system more responsive to local needs.[36]

There is no adequate explanation for the Board of Education's refusal to answer the inquiries of this local board, though it may be that the diversity of populations within the district made the central board very wary of stirring up community conflicts. The district contains a large Negro community in Harlem; a racially mixed community in Washington Heights to the north; and a conservative white community called Inwood to the north of that, which has a large Irish Catholic population who, along with some Jews in Washington Heights, were opposed to desegregaton, and many of whom were followers of PAT. The Board of Education was more responsive to Inwood's demands than to those of integrationists.

Year-end reports of local boards indicate that these two cases are typical. Similar complaints of poor communications with headquarters and of the powerlessness of local boards have been made throughout the city. Though the Board of Education formally recognizes the importance of giving local boards more authority to make decisions, some Board of Education members are still very reluctant to do so, and they are moving with their accustomed caution on this matter. One result of the central board's inaction is that the system has come under increasing criticism and is now in danger of collapsing entirely, because few people in the city have confidence in it any longer. Central board members continue to assert that they have strengthened the local boards in recent years, but the vast majority of local board members and citizens apparently do not believe it.

Community Action Agencies

One of the reasons the board has been reluctant to give local boards more power has been its basic distrust of community action and protest in ghetto areas. Most tradition-bound institutions are quick to condemn protest activity as "irresponsible agitation," and the New York City Board of Education is no exception.

For example, in May, 1967, Senators Joseph Clark and Robert Kennedy held hearings in New York City to discuss the model cities program and to find out more about the quality of health, education, and welfare services in ghetto communities.[37] Superintendent Donovan did not appear but sent his representative, Jacob Landers, who had become familiar with the workings of federally financed anti-poverty programs. Landers said to the senators that "we do not believe that government funds should be used to foment attacks on other public institutions; we deplore the use of anti-poverty funds to mount sometimes violent attacks on the Board of Education and its personnel." * Senator Clark then replied: "This is typical of the attitude of a well-entrenched bureaucracy who oppose outside agencies coming into their areas of influence. This is what I've been finding all over the country—indignation running into entrenched and insensitive bureaucracies. Quite frankly, if these two groups continue to clash, they may destroy the poverty program and education with it." I believe that Clark's observations were much the more perceptive of the two.

Any kind of citizen or student protest against the authority of school officials is regarded as a threat to their professional integrity. After Judge Constance Baker Motley ruled in April, 1967,[38] that suspended pupils should have the right to legal counsel when they and their parents attended a meeting with school officials on the disposition of their case, one high school principal stated publicly that the courts had no right to question the professional judgment of the board. In June, 1967, a federal court order reinstated a seventeen-year-old student who had been removed from his position as co-editor of the school newspaper at Charles Evans Hughes High School in Manhattan. The student was co-author of an editorial accusing many teachers of lacking concern for students at the school and asserting that faculty and administration at Hughes "should not be ruled out as possible contributors to increasing tensions." The principal had fired the student from his job as editor after he and some fellow students distributed copies of the editorial outside the school premises. After the court ruling, Francis S. Moseley, president of the High School Principals' Association, stated: "We have entered upon sorry times when school discipline is almost daily made a subject of courtroom litigation. This is especially so when heads of schools can ap-

---

* Landers is widely recognized within the board as one of its most progressive staff members, with strong sympathies for the Negro and Puerto Rican poor. Even though he appeared as the superintendent's representative, it is fair to assume that most other board staff are considerably more insulated and protectionist than Landers.

parently expect to be abandoned by their superiors when litigation is begun." [39] As long as the power continues to remain in the hands of these school professionals, respect for civil liberties and tolerance for dissent and legitimate protest against inadequate school programs will be limited. The effect of this may be to stimulate the very revolution that school officials most fear.

Mobilization for Youth. If decentralization, the recently proposed solution to many school problems is to be successful, the Negro and Puerto Rican poor will have to organize themselves better than they have done so far and develop some expertise in school affairs. This is one of the many strategies now being followed by the Lindsay administration and the Ford Foundation, as it is to a lesser extent by the Office of Economic Opportunity (OEO) and the Office of Education (USOE) in Washington. Community development corporations, preschool parents' councils, the use of parents as para-professionals and teachers' aides, and Decentralization Demonstration Projects are all examples. These techniques of transferring power and authority to the poor can be successful only if school officials cooperate. Otherwise, they may become discredited just as desegregation was discredited and counter-coalitions may develop to defeat them, leading inevitably to a new surge of agitation and protest over the schools' insularity and declining performance.

There are contemporary lessons to be learned from a look at the Board of Education's response to past attempts by community organizations to improve the schools. Two anti-poverty agencies that have been deeply involved in the schools are Mobilization for Youth (MFY), serving Manhattan's Lower East Side Puerto Rican and Negro populations, and MEND in East Harlem.

Mobilization for Youth was one of the first agencies set up with anti-poverty funds for the express purpose of organizing the poor and correcting the failures of established institutions to deal with their problems. It used federal money, then, to protest the actions of governmental agencies, and it was attacked and nearly destroyed as a result. In 1964, MFY was charged with employing many communists on its staff, who were supposedly encouraging anarchistic, revolutionary activity; several people had to be removed, even though the red-baiting was not substantiated with evidence about their contemporary political affiliations. The institutions that MFY was trying to change were primarily responsible for the attacks, and the Board of Education was one of the main ones, since MFY staff were very critical of the schools.[40]

MFY workers helped organize a group of Puerto Rican parents, called Mobilization of Mothers (MOM), to protest conditions in the schools. They came into direct conflict with one principal, whom they later asked to be removed, along with the district superintendent. MFY supported the first school boycott on February 3, 1964, which created further conflict between them and the school system, and school officials were reputed to have said that if MFY supported such attacks on the schools, they must be "extremists" and "communist agitators."

The main conflict flared in late 1963 and early 1964 over protests by MOM about conditions in the schools. Their specific grievances were about the low reading levels of Puerto Rican children, and the hostility and defensivenesss of one principal when he was asked about what he would do to upgrade school programs. With the help of MFY staff, MOM suggested a number of specific programs—such as more remedial reading instruction, bilingual courses, home visiting for teachers, and provision of more books and homework assignments to help children learn more quickly to read and write. Many of these suggestions were not immediately acted upon by the principal or district superintendent.

As so often happens in conflicts of this kind, these substantive issues, on which some consensus might have been reached, became less significant than others. For MFY and MOM, the most basic issues were the lack of responsiveness of school administrators to parents' legitimate complaints about the schools' failure to upgrade programs. The school administrators felt that MFY was fomenting community conflict by stirring up false problems.

On January 27, 1964, local principals from the Lower East Side district sent a telegram to the president of the Ford Foundation, with copies to various other national and local officials, including President Johnson, Senators Javits and Keating, Representatives Lindsay and Green, Secretary of Health, Education, and Welfare Anthony J. Celebreze, and all major newspapers in the New York City area.[41] The principals demanded an immediate investigation of MFY and asked for the removal of one of Mobilization for Youth's top officials.

They alleged in the letter that MFY workers had become "full-time paid agitators and organizers for extremist groups." They further asserted that MFY had been "subverted from its original plan to war against delinquency into a war against individual schools and their leaders."

The principals' complaint was precipitated by a letter from MOM, which had been sent to school officials and the press, demanding among other things, the removal of a principal. It was not released by the press until a day after a story was printed reporting the principals' telegram.

On February 1, the local school board sent a telegram strongly supporting MFY. The local board said it believed

> that some of the activities of parent groups which have been questioned in the principals' telegram as "extremist," and as "work of agitators," may be the normal response of concerned minority group people who simply seek a better education for their children. We are on record as encouraging full participation by the parents of all children in the educational process.

Though released to the same papers as the principals' telegram, this letter was not published.

Meanwhile, Winslow Carlton, chairman of MFY's board, sent his own telegram to the Ford Foundation, commenting on the principals' telegram.[42] He said that the community group, not MFY workers, ultimately decided what it would do, and that the local groups agitating for better schools "are extreme in only one respect; they are extremely distressed about the inadequate education their children are receiving.*

The local school board then held a public meeting to explore the issues. One community leader observed that he had never seen so many Puerto Rican parents turn out for a meeting of this type before. "Usually it's the whites who run the show here. They are the ones who come to these meetings," he said.[43] The president of MOM noted at the meeting:

> We strongly refute the declaration made by the school principals of this neighborhood in the *New York Times* that we are "extremist" and "newcomers" in this city. We are organized through our own efforts and we will fight whenever necessary,

---

* Carlton noted also that there were groups in other sections of the city with the same distress and serious concern about the education of their children.

because we want our children, as American citizens, to receive better education and so to attain the realization of their ambitions.[44]

MOM was organized to secure better facilities and services for the children in their neighborhood, and they succeeded in getting an After-School Center set up at PS 140. They also developed a proposal for a cooperative Mothers' and Children's Center.

At the start of the 1963–1964 school year, the mothers began to be more concerned about the reading retardation of their children. Data on reading levels indicated that over 64% of the Puerto Rican eighth graders in the MFY area were three or more years retarded and one-third of the Negro eighth graders were.[45] Looking at the other end of the distribution, only 13% of the Puerto Rican eighth graders and 29% of the Negroes read at grade level or above, as contrasted with 53% of all others.*

MOM decided to hold a meeting at PS 140, and its president, Mrs. Maria Lorenzi, a member of their parent association, with four children in the school, invited the principal. He, in turn, contacted an MFY worker and questioned the representativeness of the group, which consisted of about ten active Puerto Rican mothers. He criticized the content and tone of Mrs. Lorenzi's letter of invitation, was angry that a group outside of the parent association called a meeting on education, and refused to meet without getting the permission of the district superintendent. A meeting was finally arranged between the principal and the parents, and later with seventy-five other mothers who had the same complaints.

The exchanges in these meetings precipitated the open conflict. The parents felt that the principal and superintendent were genuinely hostile. The principal began his talk to the predominantly Spanish-speaking group by saying that he would speak briefly "because you won't understand me anyhow." [46]

Some white mothers were present on one occasion, on the assumption that it was a local school board meeting, and they expressed shock at the principal's treatment of the parents. "He wouldn't dare talk to us that way," one white mother said. "You have to organize," she and her friends advised.

---

* One reason for the Puerto Ricans being farther behind than the Negroes was their language problem. Parents had asked for but were denied bilingual instruction for their children.

"Otherwise he'll think he can go on walking all over you." The meeting ended with the principal and the parents shouting at one another. Following the meeting, MOM drew up a petition to have him removed, to guarantee more meetings of parents with teachers and principals, to have more adults serve as monitors, replacing children in that function, and to have more textbooks and special homework assignments.[47]

At a later meeting, the district superintendent attacked the parents, describing the principal's response to them as analogous to the loving parent who scolds his children. She accused Mrs. Lorenzi, MOM's leader, of doing a "terrible, terrible thing" and reproached the parents for coming with "demands," insisting that "civilized" people should strive for cooperation in dealing with problems. "How dare you say that we must get a better method of education," she said. "New York City has the best method of education in the United States." At the same time she announced four changes, in line with the parents' demands, including acquisition of more books, giving more homework assignments, use of only the better students as monitors, and arrangements for teachers and principals to make themselves available to concerned parents.[48]

Local school officials' view of MFY, and their opinions of the ability of low income Puerto Rican parents to protect themselves, reflected the board's insulation. At meetings with MFY staff, principals characterized the parents as "sick and disturbed," guilty of "uncivilized expression," "simple," and "primitive." The superintendent argued that letting these parents participate in community affairs without "guiding" them is like "teaching children how to swim by dumping them in deep water." At one meeting she observed that the parents "were not ready for freedom." [49]

MFY staff felt school officials used a double standard, regarding the participation of middle class parents as distinct from lower class ones. At a meeting of white middle class parents protesting school desegregation plans, MFY officials said, the audience behaved like an angry mob, and yet the district superintendent did not question their right to behave that way. At a meeting of Negro and Puerto Rican parents, however, she made it clear that she considered that they were poorly informed and meeting only because they wanted to be troublesome.

MFY's philosophy—that lower income people should organize to improve their social conditions—conflicted with the school officials' view, that the increased militancy and organization of the Puerto Rican and Negro poor were the result of MFY's "rabble rousing." MFY was not alone: the coalition against the schools included citywide Negro and Puerto Rican groups, local parents, the local school boards, many social welfare professionals, and local community welfare groups such as LENA (Lower East Side Neighborhood Association). Some teachers also expressed sympathy with the parents. An unsigned telegram "from the majority of teachers" in one local school protested "accusations of inadequacies, insufficient ability, negative attitudes, and lack of academic preparation," in referring to their principal's treatment of the parents.[50]

School officials prepared a lengthy statement in their defense.[51] They mentioned the wholesome atmosphere in the schools, the many ways they had cooperated with MFY, the highly trained headquarters personnel whose recommendations were turned down or who were discouraged by MFY staff from playing a role in the schools, and the close relationships between the schools and the community. They pointed out that many of the teachers had lived in the neighborhood all of their lives. They attacked the demagogic tactics used by some MFY personnel in attempts to turn the community against the schools, the unwarranted attacks on school personnel and programs, the undermining of independent neighborhood agencies, the failure of MFY to include school personnel in its projects or when launching cooperative enterprises with parents, which undermined teacher and staff morale, and their unwillingness to join school officials when overtures were made.

The behavior of the principal and the district superintendent in the MFY case reflect a situation within the entire school system. Although a few principals and field superintendents relate skillfully to the Negro and Puerto Rican poor, they are a distinct minority. This is not to say that the majority lack skills as educators, or that they are less competent than their colleagues serving in ghetto schools in other large northern cities. The New York City teachers and supervisors are more able than those in many other large cities, but the skills these school officials have are more relevant for educating lower middle class or middle class white pupils than those in the ghetto. There are few educators who have both the educational competence and the social values to be effective in the ghetto, which is not to say that it is all their fault, or that the job is easy. Regardless of the complexity of the cause, however, school–community conflicts in the city's many ghetto areas are increasing rapidly, and something drastic must be done before violence becomes much more prevalent.

Solutions can be arrived at only when we fully understand the problem. The basic problem, of course, is that the children are not learning, and it is around that question that school–community conflicts keep escalating. Each side blames the other in a never-ending series of charges and countercharges. Ghetto parents demand that particular teachers and principals be removed for reasons of incompetence and negative attitudes toward minority groups; they demand that suspended pupils be given the right to legal representation and that the practice of suspensions be investigated; they demand that community groups be given more power and authority to participate in school decisions regarding staffing, curriculum, and programs; and they charge that many school officials behave in "unprofessional" ways and that the system does not account for how it spends the public's money or for its performance.

These pressures are, in turn, a response to the attitudes and practices of many individual school officials, who maintain low expectations regarding the learning potential and aspirations of minority group pupils, and adapt standards and programs to such expectations in a way that reinforces and perpetuates poor school performance. Furthermore, many school officials do not try to develop relationships with parents and community leaders in the ghetto, and they regard parents as not interested in their children's education and not educated enough themselves to participate meaningfully in school affairs. And some suspend and transfer pupils whom they regard as "problems" without taking into full consideration the pupils' rights; attempt to control parent associations; and work actively to cut off anti-poverty funds from those community action groups who mobilize parents to become more involved in and critical of school programs.

The actions of each side are conditioned by many forces. Parents are mobilized by civil rights groups, local activists, anti-poverty agencies, and even such established institutions as the city administration, foundations, and universities. The actions of school officials are affected by the bureaucractic pressures they face and the need to maintain order in the school, follow prescribed programs and instructional methods, and discourage community agitation.

It is not necessary to document all these points in any detail. Local civil rights and ghetto parent groups keep detailed files and records of parent complaints about teachers and principals. Their records contain numerous concrete accounts of what they legitimately regard as indignities to their children by teachers and principals. Parents' most serious charge, that their children are not learning, cannot be denied. And some school officials readily admit it and are willing to accept much of the responsibility.

Black parents are in the midst of a period of rising expectations. They have experienced years of frustration, in which they discovered there was no recourse from the actions of school officials. Increasing numbers of parents feel that education is one of the only ways their children can escape an oppressive way of life in the ghetto. And now many activists have been busy mobilizing them to protest conditions in the schools. We have the makings of a deepening and accelerating conflict.

Many school officials sincerely want to improve conditions in ghetto schools, as much as some parents and activists. The board's recent stress on early-childhood programs reflects this concern, as do its human relations, in-service training programs for school staff. The board has been increasingly more open about the low reading levels in ghetto schools and has made pre-school and elementary school programs its top priority.

But early childhood programs, better instructional methods, or efforts to change staff attitudes help in only a marginal way. More money for such reforms would, of course, be desirable. Basic organizational changes, however, are needed to re-vamp the entire school system. As long as the authority and power structure of the school system remain unchanged, human relations courses and new curriculum and instructional methods will not be very effective. Many teachers, principals, and district superintendents, even when they are well-equipped by training and have forward-looking views, and are skillful in dealing with the mounting demands and social problems they face, are hamstrung by the bureaucratic structure. Changing that structure must be the system's top priority.

This involves more than just decentralizing. It involves greater centralization of certain functions and more headquarters leadership as well. And it finally involves much more coordination of educational decisions with those of other city agencies, private institutions, and citizen groups. The failure of the schools is conditioned by and affects many other social problems of the city—housing, poverty, crime, delinquency, unemployment and manpower shortages, and deteriorating neighborhoods. Coordinated planning to deal with all these interrelated pathologies of the city is essential.

XI

DECISION MAKING, ADMINISTRATIVE STYLES, AND CRISIS MANAGEMENT

Those who will make the policy decisions about reorganizing the structure of the New York City schools will have to answer several questions: What role should the central board and the superintendent have in directing the change-over? Which powers should remain at headquarters, or be vested there, and which be delegated to local school boards? Which functions should be subcontracted to other agencies of city government, or to research and business organizations? And what should be the extent and speed of implementing the reforms? A look at how the central board has managed past innovations provides some guides.

Social scientists have used terms like "crisis management" and "fire department" administration to characterize managerial styles of large, bureaucratic organizations; and these terms fit the operations of the New York City schools perfectly.[1] The board's strategy for handling controversial innovations like desegregation has been one of *caution* and *minimal action,* hoping not to alienate the large block of white parents and school officials fearful of compulsory desegregation plans; of *deliberate delay and vacillation* in the face of cross-pressures from civil rights, moderate, and opposition groups, and of *ineffective planning and preparation* for the programs it finally implemented. This contributed to the polarizing of civil rights and opposition groups and resulted in a long stalemate. It is likely that the board will adopt the same strategy for handling decentralization, if it is given the power to manage its implementation, since the same kinds of political alignments and cross pressures will exist. Also, decentralization may proceed as a series of isolated experiments and be absorbed and discredited if its implementation drags along over a period of five to ten years. While parts of the old structure continue to operate, so too will the political base of status-quo-oriented professionals, and they will be in a strategic position to subvert this reform, as they did all others.

There is a danger of implying that these shortcomings are unique to the Board of Education, when in fact they are not. Most large, bureaucratic organizations have a tendency to avoid long-range planning for innovation, despite the availability of numerous administrative techniques (control systems, simulation, forecasting) that facilitate it.[2] Future events and conditions are difficult to anticipate: changes in client demands and outside institutions that impinge on organizations take place so rapidly, and in ways that are still so unpredictable, that it becomes difficult to engage in much meaningful long-range planning. In addition, the coalitions that often develop in large organizations have vested interests in maintaining their power and in avoiding the innovations that long-range planning implies.*

Nevertheless, the New York City Board of Education is a prime example of the short-range oriented, reactive, fire-fighting organization, and this acts to preclude the central board and superintendent from playing an effective role in managing future changes. The board's reactive, non-planning posture is illustrated by a number of delaying and temporizing strategies, including: lengthy public hearings, often held before shaping a policy position; studies and committees that sometimes simply hash over old studies, or often see any innovative plans diluted or discarded; hiring outside "experts" and "consultants" who develop innovative plans that are not used; insulation behind a wall of "technical" arguments as to why innovations are not feasible; trying a few local experiments when political pressures for innovation mount, rather than the city wide in-

---

* As social scientists Richard Cyert and James March suggest: "Organizations avoid uncertainty. They avoid the requirement that they correctly anticipate events in the distant future by using decision rules emphasizing short-run reaction to short-run feedback rather than anticipation of long-run uncertain events." See their *Behavioral Theory of the Firm,* Englewood Cliffs, N.J.: Prentice-Hall, 1963, p. 119.

novations that are needed; diffusing authority for formulating and monitoring the implementation of new programs across so many units within the institution that it is impossible to pinpoint responsibility for success or failure.

Top board officials continue to assert that interest group pressures limit the extent of innovation that they can institute, and point to the strong white parent opposition to desegregation as a case in point. However, the relationship between public opinion and board decisions is a reciprocal one and the board's actions and inactions contribute to as well as reflect an interest group politics that has severely limited the amount of desegregation that took place.

Crisis Management

Virtually every new desegregation program of any significance was put into effect only in the face of tremendous political pressure. On Open Enrollment, for example, despite all the studies and recommendations made by the board's own Commission on Integration, there was no move toward implementation until the board was confronted with what seemed like a massive show of unity and strength from civil rights groups, accompanied by a strike threat.[3]

Even after the plan was instituted, the normal workings of the system effectively diluted its implementation. Yet, by the mid-1960s, the board was putting the blame elsewhere by suggesting that Negro as well as Puerto Rican parents were not interested in transferring their children to predominantly white schools. Throughout the period the plan was in effect, the system was able to limit the numbers of transfers through its construction program and its juggling of utilization figures. A study in 1964 by the City Commission on Human Rights and interviews with civic group spokesmen and board officials indicate how much principals, district superintendents, and even headquarters personnel underreported the numbers of empty seats in "receiving" white schools, thereby subverting the board's own plan.[4]

In the next major desegregation controversy, over pairings, the same patterns of delay and subversion took place. At first, the board refused to develop any pairing plans except to say that a few pairings might be tried on an experimental basis.

Within two months of this statement the board, faced with another massive, citywide boycott, suddenly announced that it had a list of twenty pairings that might be tried—but it did not name the proposed schools.

The board gave numerous status-quo interests access to the decision-making process without having any firm data and commitments of its own. White middle class parent association leaders, district superintendents, and local school boards (which, because of the selection process, represented the white, middle class, neighborhood school position) were invited in to present their "research" and knowledge of local conditions as a basis for final decisions. The result of these meetings was that sixteen of the twenty proposed pairings were dropped.[5]

If the board had seriously considered pairings as a desegregation technique, it would have done its own research before inviting in such groups. Supposing that its research found the pairings viable, these groups would have been brought in later, not to help make the decision but in an attempt to mobilize their support and to secure further information about local conditions that would lead to more efficient and effective implementation.

Interviews with top board and UPA officials indicate that both groups felt they had made a major contribution to school desegregation by eliminating those sixteen proposed pairings and that the decisions had been made on a "technical" and "professional" basis. "Those meetings really helped us refine our criteria for pairings," reported a board official, "and saved us from a lot of mistakes. I am pleased with what we did. You ought to take a look at the original list and see how the white schools in each pairing that we dropped had already started to tip." But the board's own data on pupil enrollments in those schools indicate how invalid that judgment was: [6]

PERCENT OF WHITE PUPILS IN PREDOMINANTLY WHITE SCHOOLS IN PROPOSED PAIRINGS

			1960	*1965*				*1960*	*1965*
PS 100	Queens	97.0	96.6	PS 55	Brooklyn	98.2	93.2
PS 55	Queens	98.2	93.2	PS 219	Brooklyn	91.7	76.6
PS 68	Queens	85.7	89.2	PS 94	Brooklyn	92.4	85.0
PS 156	Queens	99.7	81.0	PS 108	Brooklyn	88.4	56.9

PERCENT OF WHITE PUPILS IN PROPOSED
HEARINGS *(Continued)*

			1960	1965				1960	1965
PS	34	Queens	96.8	86.6	PS	76	Brooklyn	87.8	71.2
PS	52	Queens	87.3	55.7	PS	242	Brooklyn	71.3	83.0
PS	35	Queens	82.0	69.7	PS	213	Brooklyn	96.6	72.5
PS	19	Queens	72.7	74.6	PS	40	Manhattan	91.7	85.7
PS	5	Queens	97.8	93.4	PS	70	Bronx	99.8	57.2
PS	121	Queens	78.5	64.3					

The board's figures indicate that at least 10 of the 19 predominantly white schools for which data are available were not tipping at all during their period, and 3 of these even increased their white enrollment.*

The board failed to develop citywide proposals for pairings. If large numbers of elementary schools were scheduled to be paired, this might have made the tipping criterion somewhat academic, since white parents thinking about pulling their children out of their schools would have had limited places to send them. Parochial schools are already overcrowded and so are private schools; and many parents might not have moved to the suburbs immediately. It would take at least money, trained and committed staff, and other ancillary services to make pairings work on a citywide scale; and it would take an extraordinarily efficient and flexible administration and strong leadership from the central board and top headquarters officials, both in monitoring how the plan was implemented and in mobilizing community and staff support.†

What was lacking in the board's handling of the pairing controversy was any kind of forceful conviction or advanced planning and preparation. The point is not so much whether pairings might have been an answer to the segregation and quality problems as that a particular style of temporizing prevailed.

* This original list contains nineteen pairings, all of them dropped, suggesting that a few more than those commonly reported had been under consideration.

† All these conditions, with the exception of the first, represent the elements of an entirely new system. Until such a new system is created, desegregation will probably not work, and civil rights groups have come to recognize that fact, as I indicated in Chapter Four.

The same pattern of limited innovation prevailed in school construction for fringe areas, another desegregation technique. Continued efforts by civil rights leaders and by officials of the Mayor's Commission on Human Rights to get the Board of Education to develop borough-wide and citywide construction plans all failed. The board's reasons for not engaging in such planning for changes in construction programs parallel those it gave in zoning controversies.[7] It claimed that there was much more political pressure against fringe area construction, including some from the Negro and Puerto Rican poor, than pressure in favor of it. It also pointed to the instability of fringe areas, the tremendous need for school space in ghetto communities, and the high transportation costs. The board, however, might have conducted an active community persuasion campaign to mobilize greater support for desegregation by explaining its benefits. It might have done more with its own professional staff. It could also have developed borough- and citywide construction plans and tried to negotiate site location and zoning decisions within the context of such plans.

There is little evidence that it did any of these things very extensively, and a lot that it did otherwise. Most site location decisions were made on a case-by-case basis without reference to any broader, area-wide plans. Had political pressures for fringe area schools built up more than they did, the board might have developed more plans. It was not about to play a leadership role on desegregation and much more often adopted a temporizing posture to see how the politics were developing. A change-oriented coalition could never develop in response to this posture, because many powerful groups who might have been in one could get no clear signals from the board that it was sufficiently committed to implement desegregation techniques efficiently, even if these civic groups came out in support of such a move.

Educational complexes, parks, intermediate schools, and the four-year comprehensive high school were also delayed and subverted. Very few intermediate schools have been built in fringe areas, where desegregation was possible.[8] Nine of the fourteen intermediate schools that were supposed to achieve ethnic balance did not; the four-year comprehensive high school concept was even more subverted, even though it has gained more and more national acceptance among professional educators. It was in this context that the Allen Report, commissioned by the board itself, recommended basic changes in the high schools.

The politics of the board's withdrawal on the comprehensive high school concept seem clear. The academic and vocational high school principals' associations opposed it, and opposition was very strong from the UPA and more conservative neighborhood school groups as well.[9] "You should have seen those UPA ladies from Brooklyn storming the board," a liberal board member reported. "From hearing them talk you'd think that Erasmus and some of those other high schools that they lay claim to are their sacred domains. It doesn't help to explain to them that a large and rising percentage of minority group kids already attend those schools and graduate with a general diploma that fits them for nothing." Though the board started a committee on the comprehensive high school in August, and invited the white middle class civic groups to participate, it never followed up. The board's actions on each of these controversies can be explained and justified in terms of the political pressures against innovation from opposition groups, but the fact remains that the board did very little to counter that opposition.

The decentralization controversy will spawn the same kinds of coalitions. Given the internal and external politics that come into play on every reform issue, it is clear that this board and superintendent are unable to manage effective innovation. Their incapacity has little to do with their social outlook or political skills, but is rather an institutional problem. The New York City Board of Education is literally a leaderless institution, and every board and superintendent of the past couple of decades has been consistently emasculated and subverted by the professional staff. It makes little sense to entrust the responsibility for formulating and implementing a decentralization plan to the board and superintendent alone. At most, they should be members of a commission that has such powers. Furthermore, their stated preference for a gradual, step-by-step approach in making the change should not be allowed to prevail.

Each case I have cited illustrates the complete inadequacy of the style that the board has invariably used in handling innovation and that it proposes for decentralization. It has led in the past to the isolation, subversion, dilution, and discrediting of the innovations, all the while that the board projected a positive image to many white liberal and moderate groups for having been the first big city school system in the nation to experiment with particular programs.

Local Experiments. The board's caution and indecision are best illustrated by its reluctance to embark on any "systemwide desegregation plans and studies." Sociologist Robin Williams, in a review of studies on factors affecting receptivity to desegregation plans in northern cities has noted in this regard:

> Any partial, selective plan that affects some areas and not others similarly situated and characterized, runs the risk of adding to tensions and conflicts.[10]

The issue of whether desegregation should be systemwide or local has been widely discussed by educational planners, school administrators, social scientists, and civic groups. The board has dismissed a systemwide approach as utopian. The rationale for the local-experiment strategy has been that it is better to try out new plans in just a few areas, see which ones work best, get the imperfections out of them, and then move on from there. They rarely move on.

Ironically, rather than contributing to more soundly based innovations, this piecemeal approach leads in the other direction. Accepting the premise that one can evaluate a new plan within a few years, just confining its existence and evaluation to a few "experiments" makes it almost impossible to tell what affects the degree of success or failure.

Usually, the extent of effectiveness of any new program depends largely on conditions in the school and community that had existed long before the program went into effect. Unless one implements a plan in many areas and assesses the effects of such factors as the extent of teacher and supervisor turnover, staff experience, training, and attitudes, pupil background and turnover, housing patterns, extent of demographic change, of parent participation, and the climate of school–community relations, the experiment is all but meaningless. The boards tendency to disregard these factors and to make judgments about the benefits of programs on very limited information has little justification other than a possible political one.

A paper by Dr. Herbert Gans, now at the Center for Urban Education (done in conjunction with the educational-complex project of Dentler and his colleagues), develops a number of convincing arguments for systemwide rather than local desegregation, and has immediate relevance for decentralization as well.[11] Gans recognizes the intrinsic differences between a "micro" local school or district situation and a "macro" citywide problem.

His arguments are as follows: (1) the difference in scale between a local school or district and the total system makes for little comparability when one wants to extrapolate from the results of a local experiment to the system as a whole. Since fewer people and institutions are involved in a local experiment, it cannot then be used for systemwide planning. (2) Furthermore, the difference in characteristics of the people and institutions as one moves from a local to a systemwide focus makes a local experiment of little relevance for the total system; and (3) there are some serious political disadvantages to local experiments. They may be used as substitutes for action, and they may throw protest groups off guard, since they indicate some effort at reform. Yet there is plenty of evidence that no changes are then built into the system as a whole, to continue the reforms on a bigger scale, even when the local experiments are considered successful—they are really little more than "tokenism." Thus, local experiments are an excellent delaying tactic, whether always planned for that purpose or not. If a local experiment does not succeed—as is often the case for reasons unrelated to the program—the board may then argue that it has no justification for trying it on a larger scale, let alone throughout the system.

A final political cost of local experiments is that they can be used as targets for opposition groups who may mobilize elsewhere in the city in preparation for the time when their schools might be used for an "experiment." Furthermore, people initially opposed to the program have the option of moving to another school district in the city where it is not in operation.

A good single example of the futility of a local experiment and of its limited relevance for citywide problems was the board's nationally known Higher Horizons program. A pilot project conducted in a single junior high school in West Harlem (JHS 43) received several hundred thousand dollars worth of services such as extra staff, reading specialists, and after-school programs. The results were quite dramatic: there were sharp increases in reading levels, IQ scores, in the numbers graduating from high school and going on to college; and there was a sharp decline in the drop-out rate. The program demonstrated that a lot of money and services, and a strong commitment on the part of the school staff to improvement in instruction, could raise pupil achievement.

The board decided to apply the techniques and services from the local experiment to a much larger number of schools, and titled the broad program "Higher Horizons." The original program was watered down and spread, and it immediately became ineffective. The administrative, financial, staffing, instructional, and other problems in Higher Horizons schools were qualitatively so different from those in JHS 43 that it was almost an absurdity to extrapolate from that single case to the new program, and the board's own evaluation data indicated how unsuccessful Higher Horizons was.*

For the board to argue, then, that local experiments are fiscally and administratively the soundest way to proceed with controversial innovations, is highly questionable. It may make sense politically, but it is very expensive and has no educational relevance beyond the single experiment.

Studies. The tendency of this board to overstudy all plans before making policy and to hold extensive hearings, further hampers the acceptance of innovations. There is nothing intrinsically wrong with studies and hearings. The issue is more how they are carried out, and with what planned or unplanned effects.

Both actions communicate the board's own indecision, to school officials and civic groups. When interests both inside and outside the school system realize that the board is uncertain, they increase their pressures. The reader may recall the comment of one civil rights leader (Chapter Four) that when it became clear that the board was overresponding to pressures, it invited more of them. This strategy gave school officials and civic groups continued opportunities to present their status quo views. The strategy cluttered the schools with so many projects, it was difficult to keep track of them all, let alone evaluate them. Finally, it left untouched the basic organizational structure of the system while meaningless studies were done on "local experiments."

One recurrent pattern is that the board's studies on local

---

* The problem with demonstrations is that so much money may be poured into them to make them work that the results cannot be extrapolated (within the budgetary constraints the board often faces) to the wider system. Furthermore, expectations may be raised by the single, successful demonstration that cannot be met on a wider scale.

experiments are not followed up until years later. Often the evaluations and the end of the program come at the same time, though in some instances like Higher Horizons, the board continues to publicize nationally how outstanding its innovative program is, several years after its own evaluation data indicate that the program failed.[12]

The pairing evaluations, for example, stirred little interest from the community and seem to have had no relevance for future policy decisions. Open Enrollment evaluations done inside the board were never released, and even respected outside professionals have never been given access to the data. Many knowledgeable insiders wonder what ever became of them, and some even doubt that they were ever done. Martin Mayer commented in a *New York Times* article:

> I think that open enrollment did make some positive difference in the accomplishment of the Negro children who rode the buses—but I can't prove it and neither can anyone else. The New York system swims in research, useless statistics and excessive documentation (copies of the Feinberg Oath, disavowing Communism, must be held in the files until the teacher's 80th birthday, etc.), but the schools have never kept for these open enrollment children the kind of records that would make strong assertions possible.[13]

The fact that the system is literally inundated with local experiments, studies, and evaluations might be interpreted as a sign of its receptivity to innovation. Since the studies are rarely consolidated and followed up, however, the opposite interpretation is suggested, namely, that they become too often a justification for inaction. When board officials say to protest groups that they are doing preliminary studies on particular programs, they are frequently buying time by communicating their good intentions, all the while deflating the militancy of these groups.

Board members sometimes complain that the New York City school system has too many experiments and that it would be better if few new ones were instituted in the immediate future. "If we could only consolidate what we already have," said a board member, "we'd be much better off." There is much merit in this point of view, but it was the board and its professionals who instituted most of the experiments, not the community.*

* The board set up an innovation unit at headquarters to devise new programs under Title III of ESEA, and there is the danger that this could simply further proliferate local experiments.

Hearings. The public hearing, another strategy this board uses for handling controversies, contributed substantially to a dampening of innovation. One would hope that a different strategy is used on decentralization. Hearings were used often, by many city agencies during the Wagner administration, to give officials a feeling for the politics and conditions in local communities, to give civic groups an opportunity to participate in governmental decisions, and, on highly controversial matters, to get city officials off the hook. Generally, few people showed up at hearings in the 1950s, and little controversy was generated by them. This has not been the case at all in the sixties.

The Board of Education resorted widely to holding public hearings on desegregation plans, and some board members now feel that there were too many hearings.[14] During the period of most intense controversy, scarcely a month went by without some dramatic public debates or hearings that led to increased intergroup conflicts, attacks on the board, and nit-picking discussions over the details of particular proposals. New York City liberals have an almost unlimited capacity for dissection of new ideas, and the more opportunity they have to engage in such activity, the more likely it is that innovations will be discredited and watered down and a strong opposition will develop.*

If this process were continued in debates over new decentralization plans, they might well meet the same fate as desegregation plans did. Fortunately, the board may have less to say on this matter of decentralization than it did on past issues, if the mayor gives strong leadership. It is unlikely—at least judging from his handling of other controversies—that the mayor will allow extended discussions to get out of hand.

It was not just the number of public hearings that dampened innovation, but the style. Board members hardly ever asked questions of people testifying, as are asked in congressional hearings to make the testimony more relevant and keep cranks out. Instead, they would sit quietly for twelve and sixteen hours at a time, presiding over their own and the programs' emasculation. One wonders why the board kept this up.

It is required by law to hold monthly public meetings and

---

* Legislators in Albany have in fact voiced their confusion in early 1968 at being presented with so many decentralization plans and not knowing who supported which ones. All they saw was one more example of New York City's fragmented politics.

to hold hearings on its budgets. Invariably, since desegregation was the key issue in the 1960s, those meetings and hearings would focus on particular desegregation plans.

Hearings did give the board further knowledge about particular local situations and often reminded them of important matters they had overlooked, but there were other ways the board could have secured much of the local information it needed. The board might have relied more on outside experts, and consulted with partisan parent groups in private. It has tended to do more of this in recent years, though it has yet to change its style of conducting marathon public hearings.

Public hearings helped to get the board off the hook on controversial plans and to justify its inaction, even if this were not necessarily the design.* After holding one of its marathon hearings (and they sometimes lasted from mid-morning until late at night), and watching the polarized factions fight it out to a standstill, the board could say that the community was too divided and that it had no mandate to move ahead. But one cannot reach such a conclusion if all the important facts are taken into account.

During the desegregation controversy, the board held hearing after hearing at both the local school board and citywide level, providing one more arena for warring citizen groups to renew their battles and public demonstrations, harden their positions, and increasingly rule out any prospects for finding compromise proposals on which they might agree. Hearings were thus an open invitation to the most militant elements on both sides to protest and demonstrate, rather than to work with the board in producing some workable plans. They led to a crystallization of opinion around one of two increasingly hardened positions, and pickets, demonstrations, and marches became the order of the day. A liberal board member once remarked, after a day of civil rights and neighborhood school groups' demonstrations outside the hearing room, that these two polarized coalitions deserved each other. A much more valid observation would have been that the board deserved both of them. It had contributed substantially to their frustrations, their militancy, and their pressure tactics.

The fact that the board held such long hearings and ordered

---

* Hearings were also a technique that kept protest groups busy. "If I took hearings seriously," reported a civic group professional, "I could do little else than write testimonies."

local school boards to do likewise—in the absence of any firmly stated central board policy—indicated to many groups that it had not yet made up its mind. What the board did—through hearings, studies, and press leaks—was to communicate its own indecision and ambivalence, and provide a further opportunity for the school system to be criticized and undermined, at a time when it was already suffering from a crisis of community confidence. All these effects—polarization of the community, the impression of indecision, and opportunity for criticism—resulted inevitably in a retreat to the status quo. With community polarization and board indecision, the moderates could then step in and push through their meliorist programs by showing that theirs was the only position that was politically and educationally sound. Their meliorist programs were readily absorbed or discredited by the system.

One theory about the board's use of hearings, then, is that it was too responsive to the public too early. Another theory, in seeming contradiction to the first, is that some board hearings were merely a "democratic ceremonial" to give an appearance of consultation. For example, the board would sometimes consult with moderate groups almost exclusively, put the machinery for implementation of programs into effect even before the hearings, and make its final decisions a week or two after the hearing day. Of course, if it were really responding to community opinion, it could not possibly digest all the testimony in such a short time. Some headquarters officials have even said that they no longer expect protest groups to believe that hearings have any other than a ceremonial function.

A more effective strategy for change would have been to conduct many more private meetings with civic groups, have some outside experts do preliminary studies, come to a firm policy position, conduct a community education and persuasion campaign, and then enlist the public's help in determining *how* rather than *whether* the plan would be implemented. Since it is very unlikely that board professionals can ever conduct such a campaign, this function should be carried out by other public agencies like the Mayor's Commission on Human Rights and the Human Resources Administration.*

The best way to ensure that hearings do not subvert decen-

---

* See my previous discussion on how the board's Human Relations Unit failed. No administrators or staff units at the board can carry on a campaign for change and survive politically within the system.

tralization in the future, as they did desegregation in the past, is to take the responsibility for consulting with civic groups out of the board's hands. This is not to say that consultation should be dispensed with, but rather that more skilled and committed leadership should be exercised. On the decentralization question, that leadership might best come from the mayor and the Ford Foundation, since they were the most directly involved in developing a proposal.

Technocratic Defenses Against Innovation. If the board was incapable of managing innov tion, partly because of its own limited resources and ineptness, the professionals were even more inept and resistant, and in an active way. They had a large and seemingly unlimited repertoire of techniques to deflate the demands of protest groups and discredit and subvert the implementation of those innovations that the board and superintendent put into effect. One widely used strategy was to retreat behind a wall of technical and administrative arguments as to why particular desegregation, staffing, or curriculum innovations could not be instituted.* It is important that these techniques be recognized and not be permitted to intrude on such innovations as decentralization and urban development programs in the future.

Examples of professional protectionism abound, especially in the school construction field. One dramatic case involved a verbal agreement Superintendent Gross made in the summer of 1964 with civil rights leaders to suspend all action on the construction of junior high schools still in the early planning stage—drawing up contracts with architects and builders, and actually beginning construction—pending later discussions between Gross, headquarters staff from the School Planning and Research Unit, and civil rights leaders, of the prospects for different locations to achieve more desegregation.[15]

The agreement was made in June, 1964, and civil rights leaders then did a study of all school sites in question. They came back a month later with a list of suggested changes, assuming that the agreement had been made in good faith and that there would be further discussions, but that was not the

* Social scientists have accumulated a lot of evidence on how many professional groups maintain their autonomy from legitimate client demands by such techniques, but more attention must be paid to this kind of "professional politics." It has perpetuated the powerlessness of the Negro and Puerto Rican poor in large urban centers.

case at all. Adrian Blumenfeld of the School Planning and Research Unit had gone ahead during that period, and civil rights leaders felt he had even speeded up the process, with actions toward expediting the construction of schools. When civil rights leaders protested that he had reneged on the agreement that he and Gross had made, he reportedly replied that he had a large staff of people who had to be kept occupied on what they traditionally do—namely, expediting the construction of schools—until he had definite plans for other sites. Further, he said, the architects' plans had been completed and all plans for buildings were already made final. He also said that if the board reneged on the agreements it had made with architects and construction firms, it could be sued. In other words, all the time that civil rights leaders spent gathering data for later negotiations with Gross and Blumenfeld, the expediting process for building schools in segregated neighborhoods, and thereby subverting the agreement to review the sites, was going on.

One of Blumenfeld and Gross's protective covers was the ground rule, suggested by Gross, that civil rights leaders not talk in public or even in private about the nature of the meetings. "That was our big mistake," reported a civil rights leader. "Not unless you continually expose what they are doing can you win. Otherwise, they have you over a barrel in the end. They have their interpretation of what went on and your case is weakened because you kept quiet about it. Many of us took detailed notes about what went on, but it would be their word against ours, and we don't have much of a chance under those circumstances."

By the time civil rights leaders found out what Blumenfeld had been doing, he was already approaching the actual construction stage, and the only recourse left was to boycott the sites, lie down on them, or stage some similar kinds of demonstration, and then be labelled extremist by the *New York Times*.

A general strategy Blumenfeld used with civic groups was to tell them how technical and complicated the planning and site-selection process was, implying that they would never understand it all. Since the public is generally ill-informed about this political process, and since they know so little about the administrative and technical considerations that affect board decisions at each stage, Blumenfeld and his associates could make it sound so technical that they had much freedom to maneuver. Parent groups throughout the city, for example, report that Blumenfeld often told them they would not get their school if they did not accept the site he designated.*

Misrepresentation of school data by the professionals has also been widely practiced. One headquarters official pointed out, for example, that three sets of utilization figures are kept— one for civic groups and two others for internal use.[16] The same school may be represented to outsiders who are pressing for changes as at 100% capacity, and to people inside the board as at 75 or 80%. Officials of the United Parents Association called the board on this a few years ago and were able to eliminate some of the misrepresentation. It still exists, however, and one administrator in the system reported that he habitually subtracts 15% from the utilization figures he receives from the School Planning and Research Unit when making plans for the zoning of schools. When challenged about the validity of their utilization data, school officials often reply that the space that is represented as filled (to civil rights groups) is being used for "administrative purposes," "shop and storage space," and the like.

At one private meeting of civil rights leaders with top board officials in June of 1964, for example, these leaders claimed that there were 700 empty junior high school seats in one middle class white area of The Bronx.[17] They were trying to press Gross to mandate an extension of Open Enrollment and were citing the board's own utilization data. For some unknown reason, perhaps to demonstrate to Gross how poorly informed civil rights leaders were, Blumenfeld corrected them and said that there were 1,200 empty seats † in that area. The public is thus very vulnerable to the exercise of professional power on a matter relating to a significant policy issue.

Part of the problem is not just misrepresentation. Some headquarters officials report that capacity figures for some schools are ten to twenty years out of date: they were not changed when seats were added or decreased.‡

* See Appendix A for examples.

† Classroom space is generally measured in "seats," which is shorthand for capacity measurements and not necessarily actual chairs.

‡ Misrepresentation is common, however, as suggested by one top headquarters official who reported that he and his colleagues were on the lookout for principals who "hide space."

Another form of misrepresentation that merits close examination involved the administration of reading tests. Several parents and school officials report that it is common practice for teachers in ghetto schools to give the same test more than once and record only the highest scores. Others say that pupils are drilled in test-taking to score well. Still others claim that some district superintendents press principals and teachers to follow such practices. One Harlem principal, for example, reported that he was under strong pressure from his district superintendent to have reading tests given several times, and refused to do so.

These practices are a direct result of community and administrative pressures to improve reading scores. Teachers and principals are concerned about making a good showing to their superiors, and the temptations to engage in such practices are apparently strong. The evidence suggests that this is widespread, and the following incidents, reported by a junior high school teacher, may well be typical: [18]

> The teachers will always know two or three weeks ahead of time when the tests will be given, and they often receive a copy of the tests. They then drill the kids in preparation. They'll take thirty or more words from the first vocabulary section of the test and drill the kids in those words a couple of days before the test. Then they'll take passages from the comprehensive part, change the names and a few words, and go over them. The kids come to expect this as par for the course. You turn out to be a bad fellow if you don't. They say: "Mr. So and So went over the test with us last year. Why don't you? We can't do very well if you don't go over it first. It's not fair."
>
> The time limit is distorted. We are told to be very strict with time limits in October but to give the kids time in May, to make sure they finish. Also, we are told to make sure the kids get it right. From hearing supervisors talking to each other, I know that the principal expects his teachers to do this.
>
> Teachers will give tests several times when they want to get rid of kids. This year they changed from a seven-eight-nine school to six-seven-eight. They graduated two classes, and those giving the tests were told by the supervisors to make sure all eighth graders got at least 5.0 scores so we can get them out of here. If he got below that score, a child was tested over and over until he reached that level. They'll do that with troublemakers too, [pupils] who [because of low reading ability] legally should be held back in junior high school another year.
>
> Teachers also help the kids. They are told to walk around the

room and help the children. In practice this means telling them words they don't know.

Up until the last two years the teachers have accepted all this with a deathly silence. Just now it's beginning to change, but it's hard. Three young teachers at one elementary school have openly sided with the parents in their protest against this practice, and they are being persecuted now by the other teachers in their school.

It may be difficult, then, to place much value on reading scores as an indicator of pupil performance, since one has no way of knowing how many different techniques were used to get the scores up. If there is no standardized test-giving procedure, the test results have limited relevance as measures of anything, and we are left with no adequate indicators of achievement.*

One possible way of minimizing these protectionist practices is to take away the board's jurisdiction over those functions where misrepresentation, manipulation of the public, and poor performances are most rampant. Demographic projections, site selection, community relations, administering reading and other achievement tests, and evaluation studies, are all functions that might well be transferred to other agencies. Any future decentralization reforms would do well to include recommendations for such transfers, unless the administrative changes permitted much more outside review and control over these functions than now exists.

The Use and Abuse of Experts

Since the lay board recognized in many instances how internal political pressures affected the judgments of its own headquarters staff, it might well have relied more than it did on outside "experts."

During the period of peak controversy over desegregation, the lay board was either disinterested or ambivalent on this matter. It was only when the controversy escalated in late 1963 that board members were willing to employ outside experts, partly as a political device to handle protest groups.[19]

The first time they did so, though it turned out to be a rather limited experience, was in September, 1963, under

---

* The Center for Urban Education's evaluation of the More Effective Schools program indicates that there was "cheating" on the part of teachers and principals in the administration of reading tests to raise the scores.

the threat of a citywide boycott. Board representatives asked civil rights leaders if they could furnish their own expert and come up with desegregation plans within forty-eight hours.[20] Civil rights groups called on Dr. Max Wolff, research director of the Commonwealth of Puerto Rico* and specialist on matters of de facto school segregation. Wolff came up with some general suggestions and guidelines, under the assumption that nothing more could be expected or produced in such a short time. He also proceeded under the assumption that he would be paid a consultant's fee for his services and would be contacted by board officials in a short time, giving their reactions to his preliminary work. Wolff was not paid, nor was he contacted by school officials for several weeks. When Wolff finally submitted a bill several months after he did his work, Gross released a statement to the press to the effect that Wolff was trying to hold up the Board of Education for a consultant's fee on work that was never contracted and was insufficient even if it had been.†

Wolff was the first outside consultant the board had used on the desegregation issue, and its treatment of him could hardly be considered as collegial.

The next board experience with consultants was in January, 1964. Three outside experts on desegregation and intergroup relations were called in for six months as advisors on civil rights matters. They included Dr. Dan Dodson, professor of educational sociology and human relations at New York University and long-time specialist on school desegregation matters; Dr. Edward S. Lewis, education director of the Urban League of Greater New York; and Dr. Antonia Pantoja, professor at the New York School of Social Work and leading official in ASPIRA, a Puerto Rican educational group.

Theoretically, they were at the board for all kinds of consultation services, especially on ghetto schools. The board indicated to them that it was interested in but not bound by their judgments. They, in turn, had access to top policy makers and, in fact, were present when a number of significant policy decisions were made.

---

* The Puerto Rican civil rights group described in Chapter Four.

† A follow-up press release by officials from the Public Education Association and the Anti-Defamation League supported Gross. In addition, ADL officials informed Wolf that he probably was too busy to serve any longer on its board and wouldn't it be a good idea if he resigned.

Each did separate studies while there and they made many recommendations that were generally rejected.*

They were concerned about what they defined as the board's capitulation to the white backlash, as evidenced by its high degree of receptivity—from February through May of 1964—to pleas from local parent groups not to have pairings in their schools. Had the board capitulated completely, the three consultants stood ready to make it a public issue by relating to the press the key events and maneuverings by which the board backtracked.

All three were powerless to change board policies or programs and had almost no voice in any decisions, big or small. Gross had even told some civil rights leaders shortly before the three came to the board that he didn't need or want any more outside advice, since he was going to have his own consultants in January. This led some civil rights leaders to become quite suspicious of these three consultants, feeling that they would be unable to keep their own interests clear of the board's. The consultants' hope was that they could interpret the civil rights groups' interests to the board and keep both sides working together toward some agreements.[21]

This might have been possible if the board had ever had any intention of using them in such a manner. Instead, the board all but forgot they were there. All three reported that they only saw Gross a couple of times each in the entire six-month period, even after he had used their presence to put off civil rights groups' demands. In fact, he once said to one of them: "A consultant blows in, blows off, and blows out."

While Gross apparently disregarded these consultants, James Donovan tried to use them to mobilize support from national civil rights leaders (but not Galamison and local groups) for a limited desegregation program. As one consultant noted: "James Donovan always wanted me to talk to Whitney Young or to Wilkins. This is James Donovan. He was oriented that way. He always knew that the national office would take a more conservative approach." This was what some local civil rights leaders had feared might happen. It didn't, but the fact that

* As one of the three noted: "Our most fundamental advice was not implemented." As he went on: "I kept saying to Jack Landers that there was no way to resolve some of the basic civil rights questions except by negotiation. He and Gross and the top brass took the position that they would not negotiate. I said, all right, don't call it negotiations, just at least sit down with them and tell them why you can't."

it was tried indicates how the board president, at least, defined the functions of such outside consultants.

In summing up their experiences, one consultant commented: "The board had never had outside consultants before, and they needed a critical look at themselves badly." To some extent, they actually got a critical look, in private exchanges and studies. According to the consultants, however, the board failed to act on what it heard.

A later use of consultants by the board was a contracted study it assigned to Dr. Robert Dentler and his associates from the Institute for Urban Studies, of Teachers College.[22] Dentler's research group had done all the demographic work for Commissioner Allen that formed the empirical basis for the policy recommendations in the Allen Report of May, 1964. One of the recommendations in the report was for more consolidated facilities, in the form of educational complexes and parks, to counteract the segregated school and housing pattern.

The Dentler work was done in the political context of ongoing meetings of the civil rights negotiating team and top headquarters officials. Civil rights leaders suggested in May and June of 1964 that the board bring in an outsider to make a study of complexes along the lines of the Allen Report recommendations.

It was finally agreed at these private meetings that Dentler do the study. He was identified with the Allen Report recommendations, and civil rights leaders felt he would favor new desegregation techniques. Some school officials were reportedly apprehensive about Dentler's doing a study because he was identified with this new desegregation and decentralization concept.

The initial contact with Dentler was made not by the board, but by civil rights leaders. As one recalled: "The initial request to Dentler came from members of our negotiating committee. A small delegation went to Teachers College at Columbia and asked Dentler if he would take this on. He agreed and said he would do it if the initiative came from the board." Board officials then contacted Dentler and he eventually was given a contract to do a six-month study, beginning in September, 1964, to explore the possibilities of setting up educational complexes in different parts of the city.

Civil rights leaders were apprehensive that the board might not cooperate with Dentler and might try to use his work in such a manner as to delay acting on their desegregation demands. They contacted him and asked that he give them a running account of everything he was doing. As one civil rights leader reported: "We insisted that Dentler give us his thinking, step by step, so that we could check it and see how and in what direction he was moving. We told him that otherwise, we were going to be very suspicious of what he was doing. We then asked to see his contract. The board didn't want us to see it and Dentler felt that it was inappropriate for him to do so and it was up to the Board of Education."

The political context in which Dentler began his work, then, was one that was fraught with suspicions on all sides. He tried, as an objective social scientist, though with openly stated commitments to desegregation, to maintain his integrity as a researcher by staying out of any differences between the board and civil rights groups. He was successful to the degree that civil rights leaders never questioned his integrity, nor did the board officials with whom he dealt.*

Despite his position as an objective researcher whose role was as a consultant, rather than policy maker, Dentler's work inevitably became an element in the politics of board–civil rights group negotiations. For example, weeks and months before he was to begin his work, school officials used Dentler's forthcoming study in their bargaining with civil rights leaders. As one civil rights leader reported: "One of the real hookers all summer long was that every time we came to a discussion of school construction and junior high school desegregation, Blumenfeld, Landers, or Gross would say something to the effect that our man Dentler was coming in in September and why don't we defer any conversations about that until he arrived. At the time, it seemed reasonable to most of us, but we soon saw it as a ploy that was used against us to delay any discussions when time was so important."

The turning point for civil rights leaders came in late September, at the first meeting the board called for Dentler and his colleagues to present their preliminary ideas to various civic groups. Civil rights leaders had been told that Dentler was actually hired to do a desegregation study. Yet, when he presented some preliminary plans for possible complexes it became apparent that many of the complexes he was proposing

* Namely, Gross, Blumenfeld, and Dr. Jacob Landers. Landers was the chief liaison person between Dentler and the board.

had no immediate desegregative effects. One civil rights leader, reflecting the restiveness of all of them, spoke up and asked what it was that Dentler had been contracted to do. She and her colleagues were under the impression, she said, that he was going to come up with some desegregation plans. Instead, she noted, he was proposing some complexes that didn't offer any desegregation prospects at all.

Later, in private meetings between top board officials and civil rights groups, Landers and Gross were both reported to have said that Dentler was the civil rights groups' man and that by his standards desegregation was not possible. This paralleled their use of the Dentler project in July and August when Gross, Landers, and Blumenfeld were reported to have said that in view of the fact that "their man" was to be engaged in a study on complexes it would not be pertinent to have any discussions about construction plans.

At one point in the early fall, civil rights leaders went to Dentler and asked him if he would look at their data on school capacity and utilization rather than relying just on the board's. They felt he was being given data that were a year out of date and sometimes without information as to which schools were slated to be closed down. Some feared that since they were not professionals in the field of demographic analysis and school planning, he would rely more on the data he got from Blumenfeld and his colleagues in the School Planning and Research Unit at the board.*

Thus the political setting of board–civil rights group relations as well as the internal politics of the board affected the research situation in which Dentler and his colleagues found themselves. It didn't matter what they did or what plans they came up with, they were invariably drawn into a situation where they were seen by both sides in terms of each's political imperatives and problems. Any researchers in this situation had to be viewed with suspicion, just by the political logics each side was following.

Dentler and his colleagues produced fourteen memoranda

---

* They were angry on one occasion, for example, when Dentler announced a particular cluster of schools for a complex in Queens only to have Blumenfeld report that one or two of the schools Dentler had listed were to be closed down. Dentler was reported to have said: "I have only gone on the data the board gave me. Why didn't you tell me these schools were to be closed down?" Blumenfeld then reportedly replied: "We gave you what you asked for."

by the end of their six-month contract period; and the main outcome of their work was that it was shelved by the board.

Dentler and his associates entered their agreement with the board in good faith, assuming that they would be given the data and entrée they needed, in return for which they would develop specific plans for complexes in various areas of the city that they chose to investigate.

Their contract called for an investigation into the feasibility of complexes without specification as to area. They chose Queens as an example of a relatively easy borough to desegregate and Brooklyn as a difficult one.*

Though the recommendations Dentler's research group made promised to improve the system on a number of significant counts—for example, to provide a means of administrative decentralization and increased accountability—and to desegregate it in some instances, they were never taken up. In fact, they were discredited by several top headquarters professionals who either had too much to lose if the Dentler project recommendations were acted upon or simply could not grasp the significance of what was being recommended.

Headquarters officials working in the desegregation field objected to the report on several grounds. First, it did not seem to offer much hope for desegregation. One top headquarters official, Dr. Jacob Landers, offered the opinion that this was due to the tendency of Dentler and his colleagues to circumscribe the boundaries of complexes in too narrow a sense. As long as complexes were conceived of as geographically contained units, argued Landers, they could never be effective as devices for desegregation. In fact, he argued, they would, if anything, limit it. Second, there was an objection to the Dentler group's concept of desegregation. It was felt that they conceived of it in static terms, without taking into account trends in outmigration of whites. There was also an objection to their use of "racial balance" criteria in the context of borough-wide

* Their work included much demographic analysis; suggestions for complexes throughout each borough; commentaries on how they would affect desegregation, if at all; a detailed discussion of proposed administrative arrangements for the complexes and of the curriculum they would have; and some other miscellaneous papers—one providing a methodological critique of the School Planning and Research Unit's demographic research and projections; one of the "600" schools; and the one I referred to above, by Herbert Gans, on the irrelevance of local experiments for system-wide change.

population distributions of Negroes, Puerto Ricans, and whites, when for some areas this was assumed to be quite misleading.*
Finally, there was strong objection to the administrative apparatus Dentler suggested which permitted more decentralization and accountability.

Another group who opposed the Dentler recommendations were Blumenfeld and Sachs in the School Planning and Research Unit. One basis for their objections was the fact that Dentler and his colleagues had been so criticial of their population projection techniques as they affected estimates of school plant needs in particular areas. An early memorandum Dentler's group presented to the board contained a number of insightful criticisms of assumptions used in the unit's demographic research. Blumenfeld and Sachs appeared at one meeting where this memorandum was presented and responded in a defensive way, just as they had to similar criticisms made by City Planning Commission officials. They kept to the argument that their research assumptions were "in line with board policy" and "the way it has always been done," though both points had limited scientific relevance.†

Dentler's recommendations were also rejected by the lay board and by all those headquarters professionals who feared that complexes would provide a means of decentralization different from the one they wanted. They were right in assuming that administrative decentralization was one of the study's most significant recommendations. The administrative arrangements for complexes that the Dentler report suggested provided means for, among other things, ensuring greater accountability for teacher and supervisor performance by relocating the administration of schools to the field and by ensuring closer and continuing review of classroom functions. The Dentler recommendations were criticized by the lay board and school professionals on grounds that they would create a series of little bureaucracies out in the field, each contributing to the same

---

* These were at best only partially valid criticisms, and some headquarters officials had to misrepresent Dentler's proposals to justify disregarding them.

† An indication of the intensity of their annoyance was suggested to me six months later when I called for an interview. When I first mentioned my affiliation with the Center for Urban Education, it was assumed that I was working directly with the educational complex team, and I was told to call back in a few months. Only after I identified my study as independent of the complex research was I granted an interview.

difficulties of communication of the community and field officials to one another and to headquarters as had the control board in the past.

This is to suggest, then, that the internal politics of the board and its conception of what community groups might accept, led to a shelving of the educational complex proposals. They could be used later on, as indeed they were, as an example of how even "experts" sympathetic to the desegregation cause failed to see much prospect for desegregation in New York City. This was to misinterpret the report and to quote it out of context, but nevertheless, it was done, and with some frequency, when school officials were under attack.

The way that headquarters officials treated the Dentler field staff is also quite revealing of the board's traditional ways of handling outside consultants. The kinds of data and entrée the group were asking for, as well as any recommendations they might come up with, were potentially so threatening to many groups inside the system that his group felt they were sometimes treated more like "foreign spies" than people under a Board of Education contract. So many "inside secrets" could potentially be let out if his staff were given too ready access to data and schools that they were not readily given much important information. At the same time, they were able to secure much data without cautious school officials ever knowing that they had.

Furthermore, the research had to be done within the context of board-imposed assumptions as to what were appropriate utilization rates for different categories and sizes of schools. The problem with this was that the board's assumptions were such as to limit sharply the prospects of desegregation. If middle or high schools were not allowed to go above a certain level of capacity during some interim period, while the necessary construction, renovation, and conversion to a more consolidated system were taking place, it was like saying that the board wanted desegregation without confronting the costs that a change-over to a desegregated system would entail.

Even more basic was the board's initial unwillingness to define the Dentler project in strictly desegregation terms. It was rather defined as a feasibility study on educational complexes, with desegregation as one focus. At the same time, board officials represented the study to civil rights groups, perhaps to buy time, as solely a desegregation study. When Dentler was originally questioned by civil rights leaders at the first private meeting with school officials and civil rights leaders (in which he presented his work) about his use of some of the board's traditional data and utilization assumptions and about the non-desegregative effects of some of his proposed complex plans, he had to restate the terms of his contract. They turned out to be somewhat different from the way they had been represented. Some civil rights leaders felt that board officials had duped them once again.

One of the most significant actions the board engaged in with reference to the Dentler recommendations was to throw them open to the arena of interest group politics, much as it had done with its own internally generated plans through hearings. A series of private meetings was set up by the board, starting in early October, 1964, to discuss particular memoranda from the complex study. At the intervention of Mayor Wagner, who was deluged with pressures from neighborhood school groups to turn back the board's efforts at "mandatory" desegregation, Gross was forced to call in representatives of these opposition groups to participate in the meetings.

The meetings became a vehicle for attack on the Dentler group's memoranda from all sides, and the criticisms were as prevalent from board officials as they were from Parents and Taxpapers or civil rights leaders. Dentler was placed in the role of chairman of the meetings, while Gross and other school officials played the same outside devil's advocate role as civic leaders present. The complex proposals, then, were defined initially with great skepticism as to their utility.

Given this private meeting format, there was no other way the complex proposals could have been handled. They might just as well have been presented at a public hearing, so systematically were they attacked. In fact, opening them for debate before neighborhood school groups was a way of helping the latter to go back to their communities with detailed arguments as to why they should resist the complex idea.

One might well conclude from this experience that though the board claimed to have entered into this contract in the best of faith, and some school officials undoubtedly did, its subsequent conduct indicated otherwise. Too many personal and organizational interests were threatened by some of the proposals. One has the impression that the board was not very committed to the complex idea from the outset but felt it was advantageous to go through with the contract for some side benefits that might be derived—e.g., it would buy time and help keep civil rights group pressures at bay; it would keep both civil rights and opposition groups busily engaged in analyzing the memoranda and off the board's back; and it would demonstrate once again that such "utopian" concepts are not the answer to the New York City school system's problems. There is little indication that the board was ever, at any time, very receptive to the educational complex idea.*

Still a fourth case is that of Dr. Cyril Sargent of CCNY, a professor and educational planner, who has worked under contract with the Office of Economic Opportunity in Washington to develop plans for educational parks in Washington, Philadelphia, and New York City. Sargent's work was contracted in the fall of 1966 and he worked with the New York City board for a year.[23] At the time he began working with the board, it was struggling along on a court case brought to Commissioner Allen by an integrationist group in east Brooklyn, asking for an educational park.

Allen had ordered the board several times to come up with its own plan for the area and it had asked for several postponements. Finally, it was able to refer to a forthcoming study of Dr. Sargent and gain several months more of grace. By the end of February, 1967, the study became available. It contained an imaginative "linear city" plan for the entire area of south and east Brooklyn, with urban renewal, shopping centers, and industrial development as well as the use of abandoned Long Island railroad tracks for a series of educational parks. The plan was presented at a private meeting of city and board officials and integrationist groups, and the latter were urged not to make it public at that time, for fear that strong opposition would be mobilized against it.

It was generally agreed that the linear city concept offered many more desegregation prospects because of its broader geographical expanse and its being linked with economic and community development plans than would the original idea that civil rights groups had put forward before. Yet, linear city was just a general concept at that time and no specific plans in-

---

* References to Dentler as a utopian sociologist are often made by headquarters officials.

volving particular schools and timetables had been formulated.

The use to which the board put Sargent's work is most revealing of its posture to this day. Originally, the board gained several months' grace in presenting a plan for Commissioner Allen and was able to represent Sergeant as having come to them from Washington, which was not completely the case. Even though Sargent was supported by federal funds, the requests that he investigate possibilities for parks came from specific cities. (The board made it sound as though this study had been assigned from Washington to cover New York City.)

After the preliminary Sargent report was presented in late February, 1967, the board demanded that Allen's stay on the construction of the seven segregated schools be lifted. They used Sergeant's report in this regard, implying that linear city was then a reality. It was only a reality as a general concept that had not been developed and specified, let alone implemented.

The integrationist group called for an additional hearing which was held in early March, 1967. Lloyd Garrison, then board president, talked at length about the urgent need for new elementary schools in Brownsville, about the probability of actually having linear city, and finally asked that the stay be lifted. John Silverberg, lawyer for the protesting parents, argued that Mr. Garrison only had a concept and even then had failed to mention how linear city could encompass schools that would take the place of the segregated neighborhood schools he was then requesting. He went on to suggest that with the money the board had available because of the stays on construction, the board could easily convert at least one junior high school in Brownsville to an elementary school and plan a small complex on the eastern side of the railroad track for linear city or a Flatlands park, if either became a reality.

Mr. Garrison then went into a private conference with his superintendent and the city's corporation counsel (Laughlin) who had accompanied him to the Albany hearing. They asked for a couple of weeks to come up with a plan and came up with one within six weeks. Their plan, however, involved using the Long Island railroad track for seven discrete neighborhood schools, six of which were named and a seventh referred to as intermediate school X. Part of the plan was to create a new educational park to serve pupils from neighboring East New York and parts of west Queens, but it left intact the middle school segregation in Brownsville which was the main point of contention in the case.

Meanwhile, there is no mention at all of linear city plans in the board's 1969–1974 long-range building program, even though there now exists a unique interagency structure to develop them. And while Sargent proposed the plans as a means of consolidation and shared school facilities for pupils from diverse subcommunities and ethnic origins, the board continues to put forth plans for small, discrete, segregated neighborhood schools along that track.

Civil rights leaders contacted Sargent privately when they heard that the board planned seven isolated schools along the track rather than shared facilities. Sargent was caught in the trying situation of having a contractual relationship with the board, with an opportunity to develop some meaningful plans, while the board was translating his plans into its traditional, neighborhood school policy. Civil rights leaders now question what kind of a contract he can have if his work continues to be used to put their legitimate demands in limbo and continues to be reinterpreted in such a way as to lose its intended impact.

One implication of all these cases is that professionals cannot be effective change agents for the New York City school system if they have any legal, contractual relation with the board. They only get used in whatever ongoing struggles it has with particular civic groups. And their new plans are invariably either rejected outright or watered down and completely redefined, to fit the traditional policies and internal politics of the system. The only role that outside professionals and experts can take, if they want to be effective change agents, is one in which they are outside the board's employ and not under any legal, contractual relation. This is essentially the role the Mayor's Decentralization Panel seems to have. There are serious difficulties in assuming it, however, the most important of which may be that one needs entrée to the system to secure the data necessary to formulate meaningful plans. It would not be easy for outsiders who are clearly recognized as interested in innovation to gain such admittance. They would have to offer the board something in return, and until the board becomes much more desperate than it is now about community protests against the system, there is little likelihood that outside experts can play such a role.

Absorbing Protest and Externalizing the Blame

My reviews of how the major desegregation controversies went and of the various strategies the board used in dealing with them suggest one mechanism that is common to all the events recounted. In each instance, the board was able to indicate its intentions to reform the system all the while it was gaining time, keeping protest groups preoccupied with what turned out to be "side issues" and defensive reactions, and eventually externalizing blame for the fact that more reforms were not forthcoming.

In other words, by conducting "local experiments," making advanced policy statements, doing studies, giving technical and administrative explanations as to why more change was not practicable, and employing outside experts, the board could "look good" to protest groups and the wider community. This gave the board a lot of time to delay any system-wide planning and implementation. The delay, in turn, contributed to more militant demonstrations and agitation from protest groups, thereby discrediting them with the more moderate and conservative community. And the fact that the board was so busily engaged in the actions I have outlined satisfied the powerful moderates that it was doing all it could to deal "responsibly" with the protests for change that it faced. The end result was always the same: no system-wide planning and innovation, and a basic failure to unlock a system that has thus far been able to absorb virtually every major protest that has been made.

Decision-Making Structure

The board maintains that it should oversee any decentralization plans tried in the future, and it urges moderation and gradualism in implementation, warning that otherwise there might be complete chaos. This assumes that the board is in control of the institution, that the gradualism strategy it has followed has been effective in gaining acceptance of innovations, and that they have been implemented efficiently. Much of the evidence presented in this study belies those assumptions. The system is already in a state of chaos, having been that way for many years, and the collision course on which it is now embarked in relations with the ghetto community demands that radical and rapid change take place immediately.

Gradualism, moderation, and local experiments have never

worked, as the board should know quite well. The present board is the perfect example of the failure of that approach.

The decision-making structure within the system followed the fragmented, baronial pattern outlined in Chapter Eight, with all the power blocs inside the system exercising their negative veto power in diluting innovations. When the board and superintendent had approved a new program, with all the good will imaginable, and reflecting the board's liberal ideology toward reform, it was passed down to the field and headquarters professionals and it was doomed. "We had a well-developed plan for Co-Op City," explained a school official. "It was approved by Donovan and the board in August of last year [1966] and there was a nine-month delay before anything happened. Everybody and his brother felt he had a veto power over the plan and wanted to put in his bit, and many acted as though there was no authority at all in the superintendent's office or in the board. The vocational and industrial arts guys have to look at it, then the divisions, then the School Planning and Research Unit. It got stalled there for two months while a man was out sick. You might think the board and superintendent never approved it. The same thing goes on all the time on many decisions, and it is especially bad on school construction. The man in charge of school construction finally left in utter frustration."

Sometimes valuable new ideas never even get to the implementation stage. One consultant summarized his frustrating experiences: "We sit down there with a committee of board members and professionals, and the first thing the professionals tell you is that this idea has already been tried in the city and does not work. It is like a conditioned reflex. You often hear the professionals remark at one of our conferences: 'Will you please let me finish what I have to say?' The man will finish, and then he literally pushes his chair away from the table and tunes out. He'll sit back and only enter into the conversation again to offer another comment that it can't be done. They often do not listen to one another and certainly not to outsiders."

One incident illustrates the extent to which the professionals diluted the authority of the board. A private meeting was called in early 1967 by Richardson Dilworth, president of the Philadelphia Board of Education, with the then president of the New York City Board, Lloyd Garrison, to discuss prospects for some joint planning on educational parks for the two cities. The meeting was only a preliminary one meant for exploring how they might work together, to be held in Garrison's law office. A person who was present described it as follows: "It seems that the whole professional hierarchy finally showed up. Every time the elevator stopped at Garrison's floor, another one of these men would step out. They introduced a negative note to almost every suggestion as to how we might proceed, and mind you this was just presented as a preliminary study, not for immediate conversion of the school system. The top brass gave a hundred reasons why the plan would not work here, and Dilworth got a real education on how the New York City school hierarchy work over and finally kill new ideas. After the meeting was over, Dilworth expressed amazement at how the professionals behaved, and at how little power Garrison had to stop them. Garrison looked thoroughly bewildered by the whole experience."

Virtually every major decision, on school construction, zoning, staffing, curriculum, textbooks, instructional methods, desegregation, and decentralization, is made or affected by large numbers of headquarters and field professionals. Authority and power are so diffused throughout the system that it is impossible to pinpoint responsibility, and the delays in getting programs ready for implementation are endless. This is characteristic of multilayered bureaucracies that are fragmented into numerous specialized units, but it nevertheless disqualifies the board from programming its own reform. The board has debated decentralization within its own ranks for close to ten years, and it has been embarked on a decentralization plan since 1965, but very little has been done. It probably never will, unless by other groups.

THE BOARD OF EDUCATION AND
NEW YORK CITY GOVERNMENT

The effectiveness of any future school reform will depend heavily on the mayor and the various city agencies. He should participate actively as a change agent, since the schools are inseparable from the many social problems that exist in the city and for which he has a major responsibility—poverty, segregation, inadequate health and welfare services, crime, delinquency, narcotics addiction, intergroup conflicts, and the fragmentation of municipal government.

The mayor and his administration could adopt several strategies. A key one is to press for the rapid and radical decentralization of the schools, accompanied by efforts to improve budgetary, staffing, construction, and other headquarters functions. Others include organizing parents in poverty areas and training them to function on local school boards, parent councils, and as para-professionals; improving teacher training by pressing the city colleges to update their curricula; mobilizing such established institutions as big business, foundations, universities, and labor unions into a new urban coalition to support decentralization and help improve ghetto schools; clearly labeling the present public school system as "sick" and unworkable, to dramatize for these institutions the many costs of their remaining relatively uninvolved in school reform efforts; setting up new, parallel structures to eventually put the existing system out of business; and embarking on total urban development programs (Model Cities, multi-service centers) that include education as one component. This is an ambitious program, but nobody needs to be reminded how acute the problem is.

Since improving and desegregating the schools cannot be done by the Board of Education alone, coordinated planning in terms of this last strategy has great significance. Urban planners generally agree that school reforms can best be carried out in coordination with programs for new housing, employment, industrial and shopping centers, mass transportation, health and cultural facilities, and colleges, as well as schools. A total urban redevelopment strategy is perhaps all that can prevent the city from becoming increasingly ghettoized. Hopefully, the private sector—such as real estate developers, banks, insurance companies, industrialists, and retailers—would be directly involved as well, as part of a new urban coalition to improve schools in the context of a general program for the social and economic development of the city, and especially of the ghetto.[1]

The mayor would have to forge such an urban coalition of established institutions and get it to work with local groups in poverty areas. Indeed, the political mobilization and training of citizens in poverty areas and the development of a new urban coalition are complementary strategies. Both are needed for greater clarity in expression of community demands and greater effectiveness in producing political pressure, something the city administration needs for political leverage to push the Board of Education, with its inner empires, toward "organizing itself out of business." * They will not do so unless confronted with a massive show of political power. Educational reform is thus a political matter and must be handled politically by the mayor.

Numerous studies have documented the isolation of the Board of Education from the rest of the city, preventing it from effectively using the vast resources of community groups and established institutions.[2] Since the New York City public schools have an annual expense budget of over $1 billion, more than 20% of the total city budget, and since the schools' failure has contributed to the city's other problems, it is incumbent

---

* This strategy would apply to other municipal agencies as well. They, too, should abandon their archaic bureaucratic structures to become more flexible and responsive to the populace they serve.

on the mayor to become increasingly involved in educational planning and reform to end this isolation.*

The mayor and other agencies have always been involved in some school decisions, since the Board of Education is fiscally dependent on the city administration. Its capital budget must be approved by the City Planning Commission, the Board of Estimate, the Site Selection Board, and the mayor.

Informally, the mayor, these agencies, and many other elected public officials as well (borough presidents, councilmen), have had considerable latitude in influencing school construction and zoning decisions—and in ways that hurt the city. "Somewhere along the line," an experienced City Planning Commission official said, "everybody gets into the act, and they all have different interests and standards." While a system of checks and balances helped prevent the concentration of power in the hands of a small number of officials, New York City's government shows a kind of pluralism run wild that prevents needed innovations, as various agencies veto one another's ideas.† [3]

Limited Interagency Coordination and Planning

While there may have been more planning in the latter years of the Wagner administration than earlier, city agency officials were generally agreed that the amount of coordinated planning was less than adequate. A top Housing Authority official reported: "The first thing I did when I got into this position was to set up an interdepartmental committee with the Housing Authority here and with the School Planning and Research Unit at the board. Formerly, we operated with an in-file letter from the board when we planned on opening projects. The board's letter would say that the present and planned facilities were adequate to the needs of the housing project we were opening. Often, this would mean that there would be no school around there for ten more years, and since I got this

---

* Few, if any, big-city mayors have been willing to become actively involved in school affairs, for obvious reasons. Virtually all proposed reforms have been a focus of intense conflict, as, for example, in the U.S. Office of Education's request of the Chicago Board of Education that it begin to desegregate its schools before federal monies under the 1964 Civil Rights Act became available. Mayor Daley intervened in that conflict, and he reinforced the segregated status quo by making the Office of Education

interdepartmental committee operating, it has been much more satisfactory. In fact, our go-ahead on housing projects now includes simultaneous plans for the school to service that population."

There are other city agency officials who recount case after case of limited coordination with the Board of Education. One suggested that the Board of Education was at least partly responsible: [4]

> What we certainly do need is coordination among schools, housing parks, all of that. I can give you the perfect example of absolute chaos, absolute lack of coordination, in the Bruckner Boulevard development in the Bronx. That was the matter of public and middle income, Mitchell–Lama housing just thrown in together. Poor design. Inadequate schools. No parks. No stores. And because of a lack of sophistication and lack of choice really open to Negroes, that whole project is becoming all Negroes. Whites are free to look for something better and they can because they have the option. The schools are so badly planned that the children from the middle income developments have to cross this eight-lane highway. Middle class whites are sensitive to their children's education problems, and they won't move in there, and that's what made the place available to Negroes. It goes like this: The schools are badly planned; it puts whites off; the Negroes move in. It's the same with Rochdale Village in Queens. All these developments. The schools were opened late and the whites tend to avoid it. The schools are always way behind.

Even when there was an attempt to coordinate planning, the Board of Education seemed sometimes unwilling and/or unable to provide adequate school space. The reasons for this relate to the politics of the site-selection process, as I will explore below.

Some city officials saw the board's internal operations as an obstacle to effective interagency coordination. "You take the 114th Street block in Manhattan," a top city official recalled. "The Wadleigh Junior High School wanted a playground from the Board of Education. Well, the board set up a

---

back down and contributing at least indirectly to Commissioner Francis Keppel's resignation.

† This dismal experience on school construction and other similar interagency functions has led many skeptics to look with great pessimism at Mayor Lindsay's attempts to establish superagencies, consolidating city government. There can be effective and ineffective interagency arrangements, however, and it is not valid to generalize from the ineffective ones that have dominated New York City government in the past.

meeting with Blumenfeld and his staff, HARYOU-ACT, and us, the Renting and Rehabilitation Authority. But I had to be the one to ask for the principal to be invited. The Board of Education people said: 'Oh, do you think that would be a good idea? Okay, let's ask him.' You see, there is something about their size and their armylike frame of mind. Even when it is a matter of *their* wanting the meeting, Blumenfeld's unit had to write a letter to [the Office of School Buildings]. It's very hard to get things moving with a structure like that."

The frustrations of this official, echoed by many others, were reflected in her concluding comment on prospects for getting agencies to work together: "The City Planning Commission, the Board of Education, and the housing executive committees should all be involved in the upgrading of neighborhoods, along with local people. The Planning Commission should assume responsibility for coordinating all this, but they don't. And the Board of Education is so jealous of its own prerogatives, that it is not an easy situation."

This poor coordination has contributed to the general deterioration of the schools and the city. Decisions by other agencies to proliferate low income housing projects in ghetto areas, to implement urban renewal programs that spread ghettos across the city, to develop industrial parks in key areas that might better be used for educational parks, and to establish mass transit lines that seriously limit prospects for consolidated schools, pupil transfers, and redistricting in some parts of the city, all hamper desegregation, balanced community development, and efforts to retain the white and Negro middle class.

The best example of this failure, though one that may be reversed, is the planning for new schools in central and south Brooklyn.[5] This is an area that has had a heavy influx of Negro and Puerto Rican families and the white middle class families have been moving out. In 1966, the Board of Education gave up on any school construction aimed at achieving desegregation despite an order from State Education Commissioner Allen to the contrary. However, in early 1967 a new urban redevelopment plan was developed by Dr. Cyril Sargent,* with support from city and federal officials, for the creation of a linear city complex throughout Brooklyn.† Since schools do

* Of the City College of New York.
† See Chapter Eleven for a fuller discussion of this.

affect and are affected by all other institutions, piecemeal educational planning makes little sense and may well be the least efficient way of proceeding in attempts to revitalize the city. Unfortunately, however, the interagency structure developed to institute the linear city plan is the only one of its kind in the city, and it has not yet gained widespread acceptance among civic groups and city officials, especially those at the board. "Some of my colleagues were scandalized at Sargent's suggestions, which are still very vague," said Joseph F. X. McCarthy, the school board's representative on the project. "But I'm not." [6]

The idea of establishing an interagency structure to improve planning and stabilize or even reverse demographic and socio-economic trends is not new. A number of civic groups involved in school desegregation first suggested it as early as 1957. Civil rights and liberal white groups in New York City have been divided on many school issues, but they have never disagreed on this one. The Urban League's plea for such an agency in its 1963 school desegregation report, for example, received the strong endorsement of such groups as the American Jewish Committee, the Public Education, and the United Parents Association.[7] Yet Mayor Wagner, who endorsed the idea, and other city officials, exerted no leadership for its implementation.[8]

Wagner was reportedly skeptical about the merits of creating one more agency to do what existing ones should, and might have done with enough political support. He was also reportedly unwilling to delegate any power to an agency that might compete with him as another "countervailing force" in city affairs. Mayor Lindsay has different views. Lindsay wants to consolidate and rationalize various city agencies and feels that there is little prospect of ever coming to grips with the city's problems without such changes. Wagner's criticism of Lindsay after the latter's first year and a half in office for being more concerned with the forms rather than the substance of government is indicative.[9] Wagner implies that Lindsay should get on with the business of governing and stop being so preoccupied with how the New York City government is set up; Wagner is content to follow tradition, while Lindsay is anxious to reform.

Wagner's failure to set up an interagency structure to limit demographic and socio-economic trends led to a complete absence of long-range, citywide educational planning. This reflected a common condition in New York City government. Traditionally there has been a respect for the autonomy and expertise of officials in agencies other than one's own, and a reluctance to question their decisions.[10] There has been a tendency to support actions of "sister agencies," unless they encroach on one's own autonomy and power, in which case they would be vetoed and discredited. And there has been a preference for ad hoc, informal bargaining in interagency relations, rather than for more formalized procedures for coordination and planning. These traditions have helped to fragment the city government. Increasing segregation, deteriorating housing and education, inadequate welfare services, the exodus of business and industry, traffic congestion, air pollution, and a deepening fiscal crisis are hard enough to handle with the city's limited resources. But to deal with them through an archaic municipal agency structure makes it impossible.

The fragmentation of city agencies is partly the result of vast changes in New York City's population and economic base. The increased social problems that they created required vastly expanded and improved services. Unfortunately, the new specialized city agencies that were set up, each with its coterie of professionals, may have generated more problems than they solved, because agency professionals saw citywide issues in terms of their own specialist logics. It was the story of the Board of Education all over again. The cases of Co-Op City in the northeast Bronx and of the Lincoln Center urban renewal project, cited in Chapter Two, indicate how poor planning has expanded the ghetto and hastened the social and economic deterioration of many areas in the city.

Many city officials who recognize the problem feel powerless, because the existing administrative structure of the city government prevents planning. Mayor Wagner, sensing the rising distrust of city government, increased the opportunities for citizen participation in governmental decisions in the late 1950s by setting up Community Planning Boards throughout the city. And public hearings were held more frequently.[11]

Few people appeared at the public hearings at first, but subsequently they became an arena where the factional politics of the city have been played out with increasing intensity. They went well beyond the point of merely providing a forum for democratic discussion. The Lower Manhattan Expressway and

the East River subway tunnel connecting Manhattan and
Queens, for example, have been debated for more than a decade. Many officials who had originally backed increased citizen
participation have had second thoughts.

A model of New York City government is suggested by the
previous discussion. It may be presented schematically as
follows:

1) *Demographic and Socio-Economic Changes in the City:*
   New, low income minority group populations.
   Rising expectations of minority groups, and whites' in-
   creasing fears of declines in services.
   Exodus of industry, business, and the white middle class.
   Declining fiscal base of the city.

   LEADING TO

2) *Increased Scope and Scale of Social Problems*

   DEMANDING

3) *More Planning and Rationalization of City Government*

   YET LEADING INSTEAD TO

4) *The Creation of Multiple, Fragmented City Agencies:*
   Growth of multiple power and decision centers and
   empire building, rather than confrontation with problems.

   LEADING, IN TURN, TO

5) *Narrow, Inadequate Solutions:*
   Limited or no interagency coordination.
   An absence of citywide or long-range planning with
   efforts at implementation.
   Buck-passing, avoidance of accountability by officials in
   any single agency; overlapping jurisdictions and inefficiencies.

   AND TO

6) *Further Exacerbation of Problems, Accompanied by In-
   creased Inter-group Conflicts Within the Community and
   Increased Feelings of Alienation and Distrust Toward
   City Government.*

These administrative pathologies may well have reached their
most acute stage in education. The Board of Education, perhaps
more than any other agency, is insulated from the rest of the
city—both from other agencies and from the populace. When

other agency officials or citizen groups protested against board policies or made requests to meet with board officials to work out controversial questions, they were often told that the board was an autonomous state agency and could not permit outside political interference. This was the case with desegregation, the development of school programs for poverty areas under Title I of the Elementary and Secondary Education Act of 1965, and on the linear city project. It might well occur in the implementation of the recently proposed decentralization reforms.

City Commission on Human Rights

One way to minimize the isolation of the Board of Education from other city agencies that have a significant contribution to make to decentralization and other reforms is to make clear what led to that isolation in the past. The agency that has been most concerned with questions of race relations and civil rights and is thereby in closest contact with problems in ghetto communities, is the City Commission on Human Rights. Yet, the commission, more than any other city agency, has been excluded from much participation in Board of Education programs for ghetto schools.

The commission participated in school desegregation controversies almost from their inception in New York City.[12] Set up by Mayor Wagner as a partial fulfillment of a campaign promise to give Negro and Puerto Rican populations greater representation and more of a voice in city government, the commission mediated between civil rights groups and city agencies, including the Board of Education. It often set up meetings during periods of crisis, for example when a citywide boycott was in the offing and when board and civil rights officials refused to get together on their own, and it was sometimes successful in working out an agreement. It has also commissioned studies of school programs and sometimes backed civil rights demands for reforms—for example, desegregation, selecting more Negro and Puerto Rican supervisors, and decentralization.[13]

The commission played a dual role as both mediator and representative of civil rights interests and was finally ignored by the Board of Education because of its emphasis on the latter. Its mediating efforts in such situations as the Ridgewood–Glendale Open Enrollment experiment in 1959, the threatened civil rights boycott in 1960 demanding an expansion of Open Enrollment, and other desegregation controversies, reportedly helped the board avert more prolonged and widespread confrontations with civil rights groups, while endorsing at least limited reforms.* [14] By 1963, however, under the chairmanship of Stanley Lowell, a former executive assistant to Mayor Wagner in the late 1950s, the commission had assumed an unequivocally critical position on the board's desegregation efforts.† [15] When the commission attempted to define its mediator role in late 1963 as one of pressing the Board of Education to desegregate the schools, it was excluded entirely by the board.

The board members and the commission had sharply contrasting definitions of the role the commission was playing and of the strategy that would best ease community tensions. Most members of the commission felt they were trying to help extricate the board from a situation that might blow up into continued civil rights boycotts and widespread community conflicts. They assumed they were playing a mediating role and giving support to the board for reform. "We were willing to go to bat for them if they would act in good faith," reported a commissioner, "but they never did. By the time of the boycott in 1964, the board felt that we were simply a voice of civil rights groups. Any suggestion for change from us was the equal of criticism."

This was quite an accurate perception of the board's views. Board members were unable and unwilling to perceive Lowell and the commission as trying to give them support, to get them off the hook. Yet, the commission was nowhere near as militant as civil rights groups and gave every indication of wanting to work out some compromise, much to the dismay of some civil rights leaders.

Since 1964, the commission has played a less influential role in public education controversies. Its staff have met monthly with the board's Human Relations Unit staff to discuss such matters as in-service training for teachers and supervisors, discrimination in examination procedures, and school–community

---

* See Chapter Four for an extended discussion of this period.

† Chairman Lowell, encouraged by a few members of his professional staff, and one of the few insiders in the Wagner administration willing to take a strong position favoring desegregation, was largely responsible for this activist posture of the commission. His influence at the Board of Education correspondingly decreased.

relations, but the meetings have little impact on school policies or encouraging needed innovation. Even with Mayor Lindsay's election in 1965 and his appointment of a new chairman of the commission, there has been little basic change. William Booth, the new chairman, has been an outspokenly militant leader in the NAACP, and he has made numerous statements condemning particular school practices. He has commented publicly that there has been discrimination against Negro applicants for supervisory positions, but he has not presented much data to back up the charge. He has pushed the board to put in more desegregated educational parks and encouraged greater decentralization. These are all pro forma actions, however, and there is no indication that the board takes them very seriously.*

The commission's main problem has always been its violation of a basic Board of Education and New York City government code by publicly criticizing the workings of a "sister agency." "The board's position about us," a top commissioner related, "was that we should be keeping civil rights groups in line." Even the liberal members of the board held to this view.†

A second significant aspect of this conflict between the commission and the board was that the commission had violated another board code that was in use at that time, namely, that educational policy decisions were not negotiable. There may have been some relaxing of the code, however, since James Donovan retired as board president in 1965.

One of the ironies in the commission's role is that though the board felt the commission had gone too far on the school desegregation issue, militant civil rights leaders felt that it was simply the mayor's buffer against the Negro and Puerto Rican community.[16] Some leaders from the ghetto felt that the commission represented white liberal interests who wanted to keep the lid on racial tensions while seeming to press for desegrega-

---

* The commission wobbled on the IS 201 issue. It backed Principal Lisser against attempts to get a black principal, while attacking the board for making false promises to desegregate the school. Then it failed to back the protesting parents and made a public statement saying "we abhor all extremists." Extremism was not the basic issue in 201.

† A commissioner recalled having had the following conversation in early 1964: *Commissioner:* "We are so shocked at what happened when the meetings with civil rights groups broke off and James Donovan refused to discuss any of the issues. I'd like to know where you stand." *Liberal board member:* "The board is very disturbed about the statements you have made about us in public. My colleagues and I are quite upset."

tion. Some commission staff shared this feeling and this accounted in part for its high turnover. "The staff finds there have been blocks as they try to press ahead," one such staff person noted in late 1965. "Lack of action. Actually, our role has been as the public relations arm of city hall. All the good people have left, because of dissatisfaction and disillusionment. Our major problem is institutional mediocrity and a fear of change with decision makers here. Don't rock the boat. It hits all divisions."

Basically, the commission can do no more than the mayor allows. Depending on how responsive Mayor Lindsay is to ghetto residents, there may be some prospects of increasing the commission's influence as an agent of change.* One of its major problems, however, that of giving a professional staff a chance to be competent, will have to be solved before it can ever have any significant impact.

Since decentralization is now the big issue, the commission might best encourage greater participation of ghetto populations in the decentralized school districts that are established. As an arm of the mayor it might also help in retraining school officials, and mediate between them and the community in situations of conflict. If the board and school professionals wish to resist decentralization to anywhere near the same degree that they did desegregation—as seems quite likely—they will persist in regarding the commission as another civil rights group encouraging irresponsible attacks on the integrity of the schools.

A key to its success will be the extent to which the mayor supports such efforts and is able to mobilize a large and powerful enough coalition to reinforce them. The community relations role would be the best one for the commission to play, especially in view of the Board of Education's continued failure to support its own Human Relations Unit. The mayor needs all the help he can get in improving communications between the schools and ghetto groups, and since he already has an agency set up to do that, one would hope that it is given the resources to carry out that mission. Otherwise, it might just as well drop its pro forma activities in education and use its limited resources more effectively in other areas.

* It has become increasingly clear that Mayor Lindsay is responsive to ghetto area needs, as indicated both by the many anti-poverty programs he has instituted through the Human Resources Administration and the New York Urban Coalition and by the reception he gets when he tours these areas.

City Planning Commission

The other agency most involved in school matters has been the City Planning Commission. In contrast with the Commission on Human Rights, it was a much more insulated, tradition-bound, and professional agency. Yet, it did have education staff who were committed integrationists, and they might have contributed to halting the steady drift toward increased segregation, if Mayor Wagner had given the Planning Commission much power. It functioned in an advisory capacity only, however, in relations with other agencies, developing some limited desegregation and urban renewal plans. But it is meaningless to develop plans unless they get implemented. "The commission doesn't have any power at all," one of its top professionals reported, "only to the degree that the mayor recognizes and is guided by it. If you are in a position of planning, you're 'non-operating' unless your recommendations become part of the guts of someone else's operations."

In addition to the constraints imposed by the mayor, the limitations of the commission's staff contributed to their ineffectiveness as an agent of change. Many were hesitant to exercise political influence with civic groups and other agencies for greater acceptance of their ideas, and in that sense they were personally responsible for not playing a stronger role.[17]

The City Planning Commission was mandated in 1937 to come up with a master plan for the city. By 1966 it had not come up with such a plan, though it intends to have one by 1968. Its limited legal authority, its staff, and the rapid demographic and socio-economic changes within the city, which dated long-range, citywide plans almost before they were formulated, all contributed to the delay. The commission's insulation from local community groups and its penchant for studying problems instead of acting have also contributed to its failures to come up with imaginative plans for the city. "I worked on the commission for three years," reported a social scientist in 1966. "I am trained in sociology and was there as a planner, but they had me coloring maps. It was stupid and meaningless. Most of the commissioners, let them be confronted with a Negro, and immediately they get so busy trying to figure him out 'as a Negro'—they don't even listen to what he is saying."

One prominent elected public official, distressed over opposition in his borough to attempts he had made to put low income housing projects in middle class white neighborhoods, went to the commissioners and top staff at the commission for help.[18] The gist of the Planning Commission chairman's response was: "We agree with you that you should fight to integrate those neighborhoods. But you know, we are up to our ears in problems here. It looks like it's just the thing for a study. We'd be happy to do one for you."

Mayor Lindsay commented several times, both during his campaign and in his first year of office, that the commission had not fulfilled its mandate.[19] His appointment of Don Elliott, a Reform Democrat and activist from Manhattan's Upper West Side, as new chairman, indicates an interest in revitalizing the commission.

Despite its powerlessness to become much involved in decisions of other agencies, the City Planning Commission has played an influential role in public education. Before 1960, all the demographic research for school planning and construction was done by the commission. One of the recommendations of several administrative studies on the Board of Education was that it set up its own demographic research and planning unit, which it did in 1960.[20] The commission has continued doing its population projections and has had many confrontations with the board on the adequacy of the latter's projections and planning.

The commission's main exchanges with the board have been over the construction budget. Its education staff has been critical of the board's construction planning and have voiced their criticisms publicly at each of the last four years' capital budget hearings.[21] In January, 1965, for example, the commission attacked the board's practice of continuing to build more segregated neighborhood schools, in contradiction to its own policy statements: [22]

> The Planning Commission was particularly impressed by the meaningful points made by many people on a number of basic facets of the school construction program. There was much discussion of integration, educational parks, the possibility of changing the basic organization of the grades from the present 6–3–3 system, the severe overcrowding of schools in certain neighborhoods as contrasted to considerable underutilization in other neighborhoods in the same Borough, and other key matters. We believe that the overall presentation underscored the Commission's strong recommendation to the Board to keep the building program, and

the new school buildings, as flexible as possible during this period of basic reconsideration.

At another point in the same statement, the commission pointed to the uneven utilization pattern, even within the same area of a borough:

> The Planning Commission wishes to call the attention of the Board of Education to the situation of extremely unequal utilization of the elementary and junior high school plants within the various boroughs. We will approach the Board for a more detailed discussion in the near future. At present, suffice it to say that latest Board of Education figures available to us indicate total overcrowding of 6,500 in elementary schools and 4,700 in junior high schools in The Bronx, while at the same time there are available seats totalling 12,000 at the elementary level and 1,000 at the junior high level in other parts of the borough. In Brooklyn, there is 19,600 overcrowding at the elementary level and 5,900 at the junior high level, while there is a total of 25,100 available seats at the elementary level and 3,500 at the junior high level. In Queens, there is 5,500 overcrowding in elementary schools and 2,700 in junior high schools, while there are 19,800 seats available in elementary schools and 3,300 in junior high schools.

For the commission to call these facts "to the attention of the board," and to suggest a pattern of "extremely" unequal utilization, was a very strong statement, especially in view of its traditions of inaction, delay, and doing more studies.

More important than any statements, however, was the degree to which the commission actually influenced board decisions. While it did have limited influence, in the sense of putting in or deleting particular schools from the budget, the commission was powerless to change basic Board of Education policy on construction.*

The CPC's critiques of the board's demographic projects was one area where they had some success and did change the board's construction programs. Their projections of school needs for particular areas of the city diverged significantly from those of the School Planning and Research Unit at the board, due mainly to differences in methodology.

---

* Some civil rights leaders claimed a victory after the above-quoted statement was released, suggesting that for the commission to criticize the board so publicly was an almost unprecedented act. It wasn't long before they realized that it was no victory at all, as the board continued to "build the schools where the children are," in apparent disregard for its own de-desegregation policy statements.

One such difference was that the commission's staff used ethnic breakdowns in their projections, while the board did not. "The vast differences in mortality between white and Negro populations could throw all their projections off and lead them to the wrong decisions regarding schools. We had to fight to get them to make this change," reported a commission official. "It's tough to get anybody at the board to admit that he might be wrong. This was an obvious error, but the people at the School Planning and Research Unit fought us hard."

A second criticism the commission's staff made was on the board's so-called "averaging method" for estimating how many seats per grade it would need in particular areas. This involved projecting on a five-year period of demographic experience without taking into account trends within that time. Low income housing projects sometimes got figured in twice, which led to inflated projections for many ghetto areas and over-building there.*

The commission's direct influence was its capacity to actually change the board's construction budget. Each year the board asked for more school construction funds than it would use for the period, to protect itself against budget cuts or delays in construction due to political controversies regarding particular sites. It was also to show "good faith" to civic groups who were protesting loudly that more schools were needed immediately for their neighborhoods.

The commission objected strongly to this procedure, because it resulted in the allocation each year of vast sums to the Board of Education's construction budget that went unspent, while other agencies and city services were in dire need.[23] Many commission staff felt that the board took advantage of the fact that education is such a high priority item and that there is a lot of "good politics" in showing that it is getting more and more money for construction, even though it couldn't spend the money immediately. The commission refused to permit the board to have such a backlog of funds and cut its budget accordingly. It cut $65 million from the budget in 1965, for example,

---

* Many of the same criticisms were made by Dr. Robert Dentler and his colleagues from Teachers College in their work on educational complexes. They suggested that "the scheme devised and followed for estimating future public school enrollments fails to account for intra-city movement and migration . . . includes no definite means for considering future ethnic composition by grade level . . . and the present procedures used to compute percent change in ethnic composition per community are unreliable."

and there was little the board could do to restore these funds.

Planning Commission officials felt the press had handled this issue in an unfair manner, often criticizing the commission for taking money away from such a vital city service, without ever going into the reasons for the decision. "We have tried again and again to get the press to write the story on how the board is both hoarding scarce city funds and not building schools in a rationalized way," reported a top commission official. "They keep turning us down and will not print the story. We are pictured as the bad guys who don't want more schools and are trying to introduce false economies, while the board is pictured as the good guys, trying to provide badly needed school space. The board's story is not the whole story by any means."

The commission also intervened at the local level, in particular site-location controversies. Both commission staff and board officials would attempt to pack local school board hearings, encouraging civic leaders and local school board members to endorse their chosen sites.[24] Commission officials educated parents in the technicalities of site-selection decisions, informed them of maneuvers board officials engaged in, and sometimes even won their point on particular sites. These officials were convinced that the board's research and sites not only failed to meet the needs of many areas, but actually made things much worse by building schools in a way that expanded the patterns of uneven utilization and segregation. "Blumenfeld at the board has no plan," a commission official related. "He is just trying to railroad through his chosen sites, selected without much logic in many instances. This is what has led to the chaos in the utilization picture—to over- and underutilization. He looks very good in the short run, since he gets lots of schools up. And he is highly regarded by board members. But in the end it is all ridiculous, because the schools are not located where they should be."

These confrontations between the commission and the board illustrate some of the obstacles to meaningful, borough-wide, long-range planning. The commission kept coming into conflict with the board, because it had formulated some plans, while the board had not.

Since the commission was subject to fewer community pressures than the board, it could enjoy the luxury of formulating some areawide construction plans without too much fear of reprisals. It was much more protected from constituency protests than the board was.

The board, on the other hand, was in a difficult position. A shortage of school space does exist, and at just the period in history when increased demands are being made on the school system in many other respects as well. Furthermore, the demographic changes in the city have been so rapid since World War Two that even if there were a more expeditious arrangement to push through construction decisions, the building and relocation of schools could keep up with population shifts only with great difficulty.

Notwithstanding all these inherited problems and existing pressures, the board's way of handling them has often exacerbated the trend toward overutilization in some ghetto and fringe areas, underutilization in many white areas, and expanding segregation. By refusing to build schools in fringe areas and overbuilding in segregated white and Negro communities, the board has forced a confrontation with the City Planning Commission, whose education staff are well aware of the consequences of these policies.

The commission, however, was not much more effective than civil rights groups in getting the board to build more schools that might be desegregated. It could influence decisions on particular school sites, but that was not the same as forcing basic changes in board policy.

The desegregation question is less immediately relevant now than in the early and mid-sixties, but the issues raised in the many confrontations between the Planning Commission and the Board of Education are very current. Overcrowding, underuse, poor demographic projections, and board manipulation of parent groups to secure poor sites, still exist.

One way to minimize these problems is simply to give back to the Planning Commission the school planning and research functions it had before 1960. "We should get rid of the School Planning and Research Unit," suggested a top school official. "It's too riddled with internal board politics, with the desire of staff within the unit to protect their careers and their skins, and with limited competence. I think this function really belongs in the Planning Commission." [25] Of all the functions now centralized at board headquarters, there is none that more merits being completely removed from the system than this.

The other major contribution the Planning Commission can make to future educational reforms is in such urban development programs as linear city. The commission can direct plans that are now recognized as essential. Since it has, now, a strong chairman who is close to the mayor, one would expect the Planning Commission to play a more active role in the next few years in revitalizing the public schools as part of a general program of community renewal.

One of the most promising recent developments for improving school and housing planning is a program initiated by former Board President Lloyd Garrison. Mr. Garrison has created a New York City Educational Construction Fund, designed to finance high-rise buildings, with apartments or offices above the schools. The income from the privately owned residential and commercial facilities would be used for debt service on bonds and notes which paid for school construction. Mr. Garrison has worked with civic and governmental officials to generate support for the state legislation necessary to develop the program.[26]

The program has many potential benefits. It would enable the board to build many more schools much faster than would otherwise be the case. It would help to revitalize subcommunities throughout the city. And it would facilitate a better integration of school and community by actually providing in many instances for housing on the premises for teachers and other local school officials. This is perhaps one of the most imaginative programs for coordinating school and housing construction that has yet been formulated in the nation's urban centers.

Site Selection Board

A key to understanding the political obstacles to educational planning and interagency coordination is the Site Selection Board, the agency that makes final decisions on the school construction budget. It is composed of the borough presidents, the director of the budget, the comptroller, the chairman of the City Planning Commission, and the commissioner of real estate.*

The range of interests represented is so diverse, as are the

---

* A Board of Education representative sits in but has no vote.

criteria used by each party for evaluating sites, it is no wonder that little coherent planning or school construction takes place. The real estate commissioner, the comptroller, and the director of the budget, are interested mainly in building on the cheapest sites available, regardless of the effect this may have on utilization, desegregation, and quality of school services. Their posture of fiscal conservatism may ironically lead to unnecessarily expanded school costs as well as heightened community tensions, as schools get built where they are not always most needed.

The borough presidents recommend sites in response to real estate, taxpayer, and civic group pressures.[27] As elected officials, they must respond to these interests, lest they lose considerable political support for future elections. The borough president of Queens, for example, perennially elected by a coalition of white real estate and taxpayer groups, responds to their pleas for local, segregated, neighborhood schools and to exclude low income housing projects from white middle class areas—e.g., Forest Hills, Elmhurst, and Flushing.*

The Board of Education, though somewhat more insulated from these pressures than borough presidents, nevertheless follows a policy of caution in selecting school sites.[28] "The board is mainly interested in expediency," reported a top city official who was a member of the Site Selection Board. "They often play along with people like the budget director. Blumenfeld is paid to expedite everything, because they know they need schools badly. Sometimes, their choices are poor, but they want to look good to everybody and keep out of hot water, rather than push for school sites that might really benefit various areas. That would take a political fight to get them through, and the board tries to avoid such fights."

The City Planning Commission probably comes closest to choosing sites that maximize desegregation, utilization, and community development considerations, but the Board of Education has much more power on site selection and often works through the borough presidents and other politicians to secure sites it feels will not upset too many interests.

One city official, hopeful of more planning than took place, suggested that the many pressures on members of the Site

---

* The same can be said of the Brooklyn and Staten Island borough presidents, and those from The Bronx before 1965 when Herman Badillo, a liberal, was elected.

Selection Board contributed to the problem. "The Site Selection Board is an absurdity," he explained. "The budget director, the director of real estate, and the comptroller are all only interested in the cheapest site and put in their two cents' worth. Then each borough president has to look good to his constituents and gets to put in an extra school, perhaps one that should have been in but was taken out, perhaps to make him look good putting it back in. The thing is a terrible mess. Everything is finally decided, just like you read in the textbooks, in a smoke-filled room. There are many trades and much wheeling and dealing. Everybody finally has to look good to his various constituencies and planning goes out the window."

These were the comments of an idealistic city planner, exasperated with the bargains, maneuvers, and hard realities of New York City politics that diluted many of the plans he had formulated. His idealism, however, has great practical relevance for the city, suggesting some reforms that might improve the functioning of city government as it affects the schools.

The politics of school construction are as follows: A multiplicity of local civic and real estate groups, each asking for more schools or additions to existing ones, exerts pressure on the Board of Education, the Site Selection Board, and politicians, with the latter frequently acting as intermediaries between the citizenry and appointed officials. These demands are often justified, considering the city's rapid demographic shifts, the severe overcrowding in some schools, and the limited planning by board and city officials.

At the same time, however, the very nature and intensity of the demands reinforces poor planning. The more city officials are confronted with demands for localized services, the more they are diverted from providing schools for broader, areawide needs. Demographic changes involve entire boroughs and often involve large sections of the city. They cannot be responded to effectively on a localistic, neighborhood basis. Indeed, it was the neighborhood school approach of the Board of Education that contributed so much to the uneven utilization pattern.

One solution to this dilemma of limited planning is much along the lines proposed by the Lindsay administration. It involves both greater consolidation of city government and more decentralization, two complementary changes. Consolidation would contribute to more planning that took into account the interrelatedness of housing, urban renewal, poverty, transportation, industrial, and education decisions.*

Decentralization, on the other hand, through the establishment of community corporations, local city halls, or their equivalent, would provide city officials with more information on local problems and a sounder basis for developing programs than in the past. It would also give the citizenry more opportunity for real participation in shaping governmental decisions, as opposed to the ordeal of testifying at numerous hearings that serve little purpose other than to make everybody involved more agitated.

One specific reform that is desperately needed is to consolidate the arrangements for reviewing school construction and site-location decisions. So many civic groups and city agencies review and re-review particular projects that the delays in final construction are endless and the demography and needs of local communities have often changed by the time the schools are finally built. One study indicated, for example, that it takes an average of seven years from planning to completion of construction in the public schools, and four years for parochial schools.[29]

There is even some question of whether the board should have anything at all to do with construction, since its own indecision and vacillation contribute to further delays. One top construction administrator at the board summed up his problems: "Now we're almost in business on a crash program of seventeen high schools. But it takes time for the board to make up its mind, and in the interim, various principals' associations have exerted pressures against the comprehensive high school. The board has not come up with programs yet. It's extremely frustrating waiting for the board to make up its mind. We could be out of the woods on the high schools in another couple of years, but meanwhile, we're delayed by the board's indecision. As for the intermediate school, the board has left the 5–3, 6–2 and 4–4–4 options up for grabs."

Perhaps the most appropriate arrangement would be for construction decisions to be made by the Public Works Commission, which takes care of most city construction. It is now headed by Eugene Hult, former executive director of the Office

---

* It might best be effected by the setting up of interagency establishments, as the mayor is trying to do.

of School Buildings at the Board of Education, and has on its staff Richard Bader, former education director of the City Planning Commission.* If that agency took over school construction responsibilities, at the same time that a new policy-making structure was devised for the Board of Education to minimize its indecisiveness, the city would benefit immeasurably.

Now that decentralization has become such a major issue, there is much discussion about how to cope with the problem of the sharing of power among school and city officials and the community. The superintendent is required by law to talk to the community and make the schools accountable for their performance. He is in a difficult position, however, because he has few people to whom he and the board members are willing to give responsibility for talking with the community. And it is unclear just who the community is, given the multiplicity of civic groups, many asking for different things. The mayor is also involved, and much of the controversy over decentralization centers around the question of who has the right to control the schools.

Council Against Poverty (CAP)

The most dramatic recent example of these dilemmas, as well as of the limited interagency coordination on education programs, is the emerging relationship between the Mayor's Council Against Poverty and the Board of Education. The council is a citizen agency set up to increase the participation of the poor in anti-poverty programs and to involve them directly in developing programs to upgrade city services and living conditions in ghetto communities. It was set up to give real meaning to what one city administration publication refers to as "the much used and even more abused phrase 'maximum participation of the poor.' " [30]

The council was established by an executive order from the mayor, effective September 15, 1966, which reflected the Lindsay administration's interest in planning and decentralization. It was intended to "eliminate the cumbersome anti-poverty structure that had hampered operations in the past." Indeed, numerous complaints from ghetto populations and city officials about the old anti-poverty agency were taken into account in

* Mr. Hult died since this was written.

setting up the council.[31] Its functions include setting overall goals and priorities for anti-poverty programs; allocating both federal and city funds for community development; overseeing the establishment of community corporations, which were to become umbrella groups for community action in all poverty areas; and making the final decisions on all programs and fund requests submitted by the community corporations. It is, in brief, the single policy-making organization for the city's anti-poverty programs.

The Council has attempted to work with the Board of Education in planning special education programs for children in poverty areas, funded under Title I of the Elementary and Secondary Education Act of 1965, which requires the joint development of programs by school boards and community action groups. It became apparent at the very outset that the Board of Education would maintain its traditional insulated posture and not cooperate in any joint planning.

The Title I programs for the 1966–1967 school year, for example, had been planned by the board alone. Preliminary and later evaluations of the previous year's programs were not made available to citizen groups until after the board had developed its plans for the coming year. There were hearings in August, 1966, but all the structuring of programs had already been planned. The council was determined not to let that happen again, and to make the board live up to the law.[32]

The first formal confrontation between the council and the board on the matter came in October, 1966, in an exchange of letters between Reverend H. Carl McCall, the council's chairman, and Board President Lloyd Garrison. McCall's letter outlined the failure of the board to comply with the law, advising the board that the council was therefore in no position to approve its proposals. McCall's letter and Garrison's answer, in full here, give some indication of the problem. McCall wrote as follows:

Dear Mr. Garrison:

As you know, Section 205 (a) (7) of the Elementary and Secondary Education Act of 1965 requires that Title I projects for educationally deprived children in low income areas be developed cooperatively by the local school board and the local community action agency. Before approving Title I projects the State Department of Education is, in the words of the statute, under a mandate to determine that:

Wherever there is in the area served by the local educational agency a community action program approved pursuant to Title III of the Economic Opportunity Act of 1964 (Public Law 88–452), the programs and projects have been developed in cooperation with the public or private non-profit agency responsible for the community action program.

The Council Against Poverty cannot in good conscience say that the Board's present Title I proposals were "developed in cooperation with" this agency.

The United States Office of Education requires that the community action agency state whether it was "consulted in the planning" of proposed Title I projects. This agency cannot so state because in the view of the Council Against Poverty adequate consultation did not take place. In the opinion of the Council, an opinion shared by the Office of Education and the Office of Economic Opportunity, cooperation means a genuine, day-to-day, working relationship in project planning and development. This did not exist.

The Office of Education further requires that this agency state whether the proposed Title I programs will "complement ongoing and projected anti-poverty programs in the community" and whether said Title I projects will "be effectively coordinated with the administration and operation of the community action agency's program." Again, this agency cannot answer that question in the affirmative. In spite of repeated requests, this agency has not received information sufficient to permit it to make an informed judgment. To this date, it does not know the Board's goals or priorities or even the specific areas and schools in which Title I projects are proposed.

We are therefore in no position to approve these project proposals.

If I may briefly recapitulate the history of this year's Title I projects, I think you may find it illustrative of the complete absence of cooperative planning. Although there was some preliminary discussion between staff members, the Title I projects were not developed cooperatively and were not received by the Economic Opportunity Committee, the predecessor to the Community Development Agency, until a few days before the Board's scheduled public hearing of August 17, 1966. The proposals were submitted in outline form with no indication of priorities, no statement of measurable goals, and no listing of disadvantaged areas to be served. In spite of the fact that the proposals had not been developed with our cooperation. Mr. James Dumpson, my predecessor as Council Chairman, requested on August 8, 1966 that the Council be given detailed answers to specific questions so that it might be in a position to make rational judgments on the merits. This request was renewed on August 17, 1966. However, the information was not received and on September 23, 1966, three days after assuming his office, George Nicolau, the new Commissioner for Community Development, renewed the request in a letter to Dr. Donovan. On September 27, 1966, Dr. Donovan stated that the information had been given to members of the Community Development Agency staff. But the information was of a preliminary and unsatisfactory nature and Mr. Nicolau renewed his request on October 11, 1966. To this date (Oct. 19) the requested information is still lacking, and if it is received now, it will be too late for intelligent action. . . .

Over the past year and a half there has been discussion of joint planning but very little action. I know that you agree with me that the time has come for that action so that the education system and the anti-poverty program, and the local communities, can effectively plan for the future of the city and its disadvantaged citizens.

Mr. Garrison's reply conceded shortcomings in past practice and said that the board wanted to cooperate from then on. He indicated agreement with McCall's desire for joint planning on Title I programs, suggesting that he, the other board members on its committee dealing with federally financed programs and Superintendent Donovan would be pleased to meet with the Council Against Poverty at a mutually convenient time and place. He went on to state that shortcomings in the way the Board had handled Title I planning with the Council in the past could hopefully be corrected and that they were due to the newness of the law for federal funding and to some of its ambiguities. Garrison was promising, then, that in the future, the board would cooperate with the council in planning all Title I projects. It did not always work out that way. While the board's administrator of Title I projects, Jacobs Landers, regularly attended meetings of the council's education committee, starting in March, 1967, instructions received from his superintendent and the board were that if the council did not like the prepared programs he presented, the board would feel free to adopt them anyway. "Landers always produced packaged programs," a member of the council reported. "The council could say yes or no, but it could not insert its own programs. We wanted to be consulted, not asked to rubber stamp." As Landers reportedly said at one meeting: "I hope that the education committee will approve the programs the board has developed. However, if the board feels that a program which has been rejected by the committee is worthwhile, it would have to go through with its plans to have the program." [33] This was not much of an indication of joint planning.*

The next showdown came in June, 1967, when the board repeated the non-consultative actions that it had followed the year before.[34] Board professionals received preliminary evaluations of 1966–67 Title I programs from their evaluation agency, the Center for Urban Education, on May 15. Citizen groups were as usual denied access to the reports, as were the board members and Council Against Poverty until just before the monthly board hearing on June 28. The board put in some amendments to its expense budget for more than $10 million of Title I programs to be passed at that meeting without any prior review. Board members were caught off guard to the same degree as were citizen groups and the council. As one board member related: "The professional staff seem to work it out every year that they present us with their plans so close to the time we have to make a decision, that it is almost too late to make any constructive comments. This year, I believe they told us that they were held up by the mayor's request for line-by-line budgeting. Last year it was another reason. It takes many years of experience before you can really understand how this bureaucracy works. Next year we are going to try to discuss the following year's Title I programs in January for the following September, rather than be put into this bind." Finally, the board scheduled public hearings in August on all its September Title I programs, after the programs would have been structured and set into motion for September.

Excerpts from a brief report compiled by Mrs. Marge Benjamin, research associate for the Citizens Committee for Children and consultant for the council's education committee, relate what took place: [35]

> Interim evaluations of current Title I programs have been made by research staff commissioned by the Center for Urban Education and were presented to the staff of the Board of Education on May 15, 1967. The lay board members received them over a month later, after the staff had already prepared tentative budget allocations for 1967–68, recycling some of the same programs. The

---

* A close reading of the law, however, especially its Gibbons amendment of 1966, spelling out the rights of boards of education and antipoverty agencies, indicates that the latter had little if any authority to develop programs or veto those of school officials.

evaluations were read by Mrs. Benjamin at Board of Education headquarters on June 20, 1967; a telegram was sent to Mr. Landers the following day, from Rev. McCall (Chairman of the Council) and Mrs. Lash (Chairman of its Education Committee), urging that the interim evaluations be made public and available to the members of the Education Committee to help them in making valid judgments regarding the use of Title I funds and allowing the community to judge between alternatives for next year.

The public hearing on Title I proposals and the receipt of the final evaluations are set for late August, which is too late, of course, for either to have any significant effect on Title I programs for 1967–68. There is every reason to believe that the pattern will follow that of the summer programs for 1967. The board voted on May 9 to accept the programs; the staff prepared a list of staff responsible for their implementation dated May 1.

Last summer it was "too late." This summer, there is still time for CAP Education Committee to give thoughtful consideration to the Title I evaluations and to press for revision of tentative plans for the coming year.

Two days later, on June 28, the board attempted to push through the amendment to its expense budget for an additional $10–15 million for Title I programs.³⁶ The following exchanges took place between Mrs. Lash and Mrs. Benjamin, representing the council, and Superintendent Donovan:

MRS. LASH: How would you propose, Dr. Donovan, to adopt this program tonight, then to have public discussion, then to consult the Council Against Poverty?

SUPERINTENDENT DONOVAN: Simply because tonight we're adopting a budget. We're not adopting a federal program. This we must do if we are going to organize the schools. We don't have to consult the Council Against Poverty in order to adopt a budget. When we come to make specific proposals on Title I, which are in the process of production now by Mr. Landers' office, they will go directly to the council for consultation.

MRS. LASH: You would not consider, then, these proposals under the early childhood education programs in the disadvantaged areas as program proposals?

SUPERINTENDENT DONOVAN: Well, I consider them as things we want to do in those areas but the distinct method of financing them will be in the specific proposal. It will come to the council. I don't think we have to discuss our budget. I think we only have to discuss specific proposals before we send them to the federal government.

Now let's assume for the moment that one of those proposals receives the disapproval of the council and you don't think it's a proper expenditure of federal funds, then that's the decision this board will have to make as to take the Council Against Poverty's decision on it or to go ahead with its plans. Then those will be discussed here late in August when all of it is ready for Mr. Landers' office. Meantime we have to indicate to the mayor programs that we as a board feel are proper for the children of the city.

MRS. LASH: You don't believe that you can weaken the council's role and then force it to then disapprove something that has already been presented? For instance, the employment of teachers rather than teacher aides or whatever the council might propose.

SUPERINTENDENT DONOVAN: I don't think we're weakening the council. I do think we're keeping the Board of Education strong.

MRS. LASH: That, yes—but I'm sorry but I have to disagree with you, Dr. Donovan, that the council will be put in a position, not consulting with the Board of Education but of either accepting what the Board of Education has decided to do with federal funds . . . You know, Dr. Donovan, that there has been a great deal of unrest in the local communities because they felt—rightly or wrongly—that they have no choice in the education of their children, that they are not being consulted and if they are consulted, it is only for show because all of the decisions have been made.

DONOVAN: I think consultation is a very fine process. I think we've had it with the local school boards in this city which are our first line of consultation. The second line of consultation is with the Council Against Poverty and its counterparts throughout the city. I don't see anything in this program in strengthening of early childhood education by giving a better teacher–pupil ratio, by putting people into kindergarten from the very area where they have asked to be put in as teacher aides, by giving more money for materials of instruction. I don't really see anything in here that can be argued against particularly as a program for young children, and I think we have a responsibility to say so, as a Board of Education.

LASH: Dr. Donovan, you know very well that you don't have to give me a lecture on whether early childhood education should or should not be strengthened. I do not protest the program. I protest the method. I think you're mistaken in saying that the council is only the secondary group to be consulted. As far as Title I funds are concerned, the council is the group that under law has to be consulted and I believe it was quite possible to ask the council or its education committee to convene a special meeting and to present to them this program before it was here presented publicly and I wish to enter my strong protest.

DONOVAN: Well, I wish, Mrs. Lash, to call your attention to the fact that the Council Against Poverty is the main public body to which this Board of Education directs its reports, but this Board of Education, by law, is the first body to make the proposals and it is then transmitted to the Council Against Poverty for consultation and for its suggestions.

I do also want to point out that what we're doing here to-night is not new. We stated this a couple of months ago in our statements to the Board of Estimate, in our public statements in the budget, in our original submission last January. Everything in here is a reiteration of what we've been saying for the last six months. It is really not new tonight, except to-night we're acting on it.

LASH: Except, Dr. Donovan, when you were questioned on Title I—and I think Mrs. Benjamin questioned whether in your budget the proposals were final that you were going to carry out next year—I believe you answered that this was simply the form in the budget and that the proposals themselves would of course be considered later. I believe I disagree with your interpretation of the law. I believe what you are implying is not consultation and I shall bring back to the council your answer. Thank you.

PRESIDENT GIARDINO: Well, I would like to say, Mrs. Lash, that I'm sorry that there's any misunderstanding on the procedures and I hope that it doesn't take away from the substance of the program that the board has commenced and I believe that perhaps you and many others are convinced is a very worthwhile program for so many children of our city. Personally, I'm sorry I didn't appreciate the fact that you felt that you had not been consulted early enough.

LASH: It's not a feeling, Mr. President. It is a fact. As you know from the many times I've appeared before you, I wholeheartedly believe in strengthening early childhood education but after last year's discussion, on the role of the council as far as the programming of Title I funds is concerned, we received from the board written assurances that in the future the consultations with the council would be held before any public discussion of programs would take place.

After Mrs. Lash concluded her questioning, her associate, Mrs. Benjamin, added a few questions for further clarification:

MRS. BENJAMIN: I don't want to belabor the point that Mrs. Lash made on behalf of the Council Against Poverty, namely that the law states that the council is to be consulted in the formulation of Title I projects, but I would like clarification of one point and that is the use of the word "structuring" the use of schools for fall, and I wonder if this could be defined so that we might judge how this is different from setting programs into motion.

DONOVAN: I don't think there is much difference between structuring and setting programs. By structuring we mean we have to appoint teachers, we have to organize classes, we have to get schools—what we call organized for the fall, so that they can begin to teach children. The specific programs by which we're going to do it or the specific use of federal money for those programs is being developed now by Mr. Landers' office and will be the subject of discussion.

If we find at a point that there is a federal program that does not receive approval from the Council Against Poverty and our board does not think it should pursue the case after that, then we will have to change these funds and use other funds and we have constantly used that kind of modification— but right now, we have to organize schools for September and that must be done now. We can't wait until September to do that kind of organization.

BENJAMIN: But, I think your words were before that you wouldn't set a program into motion without having a public hearing in August and yet you just said that structuring the schools is tantamount to putting programs into effect.

DONOVAN: What we said was, we wouldn't send any federal proposals for federal funding in until we had the public hearings. But right now we have to organize the schools. I cannot wait until August.

BENJAMIN: You're going to announce the proposals, but you're not going to send them in.

DONOVAN: We're going to right now organize the schools for September and August. We're going to have public hearings on the use of federal monies to help us with these programs.

BENJAMIN: But, meanwhile you're going to set the programs into motion.

DONOVAN: Yes, Ma'am. The schools have to be organized. That's correct.

The issues involved here are somewhat more complex than they may seem to either side. The board was faced with some administrative imperatives. The superintendent was required to organize the schools for the fall, something he and his predecessors had been doing for many years. If he did not take care of this matter, there was every likelihood that even more than the usual chaos would prevail. At the same time, he had to comply with the federal law (ESEA), which stated that Title I programs had to be developed in cooperation with the community action agency involved and that evaluations had to be done on the previous year's programs and made the basis for restructuring them for the coming year. The time pressures for doing all this were unusually tight. It took a while to do the evaluations, write them up, and then interpret them. Furthermore, the Council Against Poverty had just recently been formed, and many of its local community groups, organized through community corporations, were uncertain about what programs they wanted. Some groups were still in the process of formation, and many did not have the information or expertise to make criticisms of existing programs and suggestions for new ones that would be in their own self-interest. Most did not necessarily know what their community's self-interest was.

Nevertheless, from the council's point of view, reflecting that of many citizen groups, the board was handling the Title I question as it had handled so many others, in complete disregard of the rights of civic groups. The law did, after all, state that the public should be consulted in the development of Title I programs and that the programs should all be evaluated and the evaluations taken into account in planning those for the next year.

Evidence on this controversy suggests that the Board of Education at least partly disregarded the spirit and intent of the federal law. It used traditional organizational strategies—delaying the formulation of a program until it was too late for any citizen review; informing the board members on the program at the last possible moment; maintaining a façade of consultation through citizen groups in the form of "democratic ceremonials" while refusing to invite them in on any joint planning basis. And it did this despite a federal law and an increasingly enraged citizenry who were opposed to that style.

Furthermore, though the New York City Board of Education may have behaved no differently from other boards around the nation on most civil rights and poverty controversies and may even have been a bit more progressive than many, that was not the case with Title I programs. At least one member of the House Committee on Education and Labor had some comparative observations to make on New York City's handling of the program, relative to that of other cities. As Rep. William Ford of Michigan noted to Mrs. Nathan Levin and Mrs. Marge Benjamin, representing the Citizens Committee for Children of New York City: "I would just like to make one observation. You have touched on this many times, and I don't think we are confessing to anything, that you live in one of the cities that does the poorest job under the Economic Opportunity Act. My first experience with the Detroit program is that it has been relatively trouble-free. I hope in judging the cooperation between the educational system and the community action program that you will look out to the experience of some other large cities across the country, and I am not even prepared to guess why it is working in Detroit and not in Cleveland, New York, Los Angeles, and in other places. As an outsider—Mr. Scheuer [Bronx Congressman] can't say this and he might take issue with me—your record in New York is not distinguished in that regard." [37]

Several recent developments, however, indicate that the Council Against Poverty may become a significant change agent, especially if prodded by its own education committee, by poverty area groups, and by city administration officials. In August, 1967, for example, the council was instrumental in pushing the Board of Education to decentralize $13.5 million of its $69 million Title I federal funds. This meant that local poverty area groups, usually the education committees of the community corporations, could develop Title I programs for schools in their area, in collaboration with their district superintendents. Twenty-one of the twenty-six poverty areas had satisfactory "sign-offs" * of decentralized Title One proposals for the 1968–1969 school year.

The council's education committee, composed of various representatives from all the designated poverty areas, and with the strong support from the Education Action Division staff of the Human Resources Administration, has continually prodded the Board of Education to permit more community participation in developing the Title III, Title I, career ladders, teacher training, after-school study centers, and pre-school programs. They have also urged the board to develop better programs in these fields. The council and the Educa-

---

* Local community groups and district superintendents worked together in these districts to develop Title I proposals. The term "sign-off" was used to indicate those cases where the two parties were able to agree on the final proposal for Title I funding.

tion Action Division may still be of only nuisance value, but they have begun to decentralize the schools and to organize and train parents to protest for more decentralization and accountability and to be able to evaluate school programs, offer constructive help and criticism to school officials, and develop their own proposals for new programs.

The Mayor

It is quite apparent that the mayor is a key figure in the educational politics of New York City and that any future improvements in the schools will be largely contingent on the leadership he provides. Mayor Wagner refused to become involved in most school controversies, and the most important consequence of his limited involvement was that it strengthened the power of inside professionals at the board. The fact that he received an award from the Public Education Association at the end of his three terms of office, for contributing so much to the cause of professionalism and excellence in the city school system, only attests to the strength of civic group support for Wagner's position. A coalition of "educationist" - oriented "good government" groups—for example, the Public Education Association, the Ctizens Budget Commission, the Citizens Union, the United Parents Association, the City Clubs—as well as school professionals and some politicians, reinforced Mayor Wagner's desire to remain uninvolved in school controversies.

One of the only ways for decentralization and other needed reforms to get through would be for Mayor Lindsay to intervene very actively in school affairs. The levers that Lindsay would need are a staff with both professional and political legitimacy and strong community support. As the mayor in a city whose school system spends more than 20% of the city's budget, he has every right and is in fact obligated to evaluate how the board spends its money. Board members and school professionals may continue to protest that the school system is an autonomous, state agency, but the mayor has control and a final say about how effectively they are functioning.

The board has been unable to maintain control, abdicating power to school professionals, who have become increasingly responsive only to themselves. For Mayor Lindsay to do so, with the help of his own professional staff, would counter the power of school professionals for the first time in many decades.

There is no other wedge into the system. The thirty school

boards are documentably powerless, and the central board has limited power over its professional staff, for all the reasons outlined in this study. The Board of Education thus functions as a closed system, and the only hope for innovation is through the intervention of outside parties.

Such outside intervention by the mayor would effect more professional and lay review and control over the school system's operations, would counter the protectionism of inside school professionals whose programs, procedures, and codes have become outdated and inefficient, and would encourage more long-range planning by forcing more coordination between the board's projects and those of other city agencies.

Specifically, there are many actions the mayor and his staff might undertake. One would be to keep pressing the board to institute new budgetary procedures, preventing it from having the luxury of receiving its money in lump sums, dividing them up without extended public review, making continuous modifications, and then never giving any accounting of how they were spent. The mayor's staff might help develop many specific programs for the budget, based on evaluations of past programs, and they might keep in close contact with those outside institutions that do the evaluations.

The mayor might also participate in the setting up of some decentralized demonstration schools, bringing in business, university, labor, and civic organizations as co-participants. Such schools might be administered in a manner that kept them autonomous of the bureaucratic structure of the system. This is the only way that local experiments may be effective.

It is apparent that Mayor Lindsay has reversed the policies of his predecessor, Mayor Wagner, by becoming increasingly involved in school matters. He announced his intentions early and has generally kept to them. In April, 1966, he shocked school officials by asserting at a meeting of the Public Education Association that the city was not getting a full return on its expenditures for education. He said then that he would insist on a performance budget. Later, in September, 1966, during a controversy over IS 201 in East Harlem, he accused the Board of Education of "clumsy" handling of the dispute with parents and charged that the board had isolated itself from the public. Though the board accused him of intrusion, the mayor said he would not, in the future, stay out of school controversies.[38] Later in the fall, the mayor made reference to Commissioner

Booth's charge that the Board of Education had discriminated against Negroes and Puerto Ricans in its selection procedures for supervisory positions.

The extent of the mayor's intervention increased in the spring of 1967. In late March, the state legislature, reportedly against the wishes of Commissioner Allen and the Board of Regents, asked Mayor Lindsay to submit a proposal for decentralization that would include a plan for breaking up the New York City school system into five districts. The avowed purpose of such a plan was to give the city an extra $54 million in state aid by assuming that the city's school system, while administered by a central board, actually constituted in the five boroughs the equivalent of five school districts. School state aid is allocated on a formula based in part on the real estate valuation in each school district, and districts with a high value of real estate receive less aid than those with a lesser realty value. The Lindsay administration contended quite correctly that the heavy concentration of high-value real estate in Manhattan and Queens inflated the city's overall real estate valuation, having the effect of cutting down on the amount of school aid the city received as a whole. Commissioner Allen and the Board of Regents were able to defeat this plan, arguing that such reorganization would, in effect, block the effective decentralization of the schools, hamper efforts at integration across borough lines, and introduce political interference by the borough presidents, who would appoint three of the members of the borough-level boards. They claimed further that it would decrease the central board's flexibility in attempting to solve education problems on a citywide basis. Equally as important, they felt that increased bureaucracy at the borough level would hamper any efforts of the board to increase citizen participation in school affairs.[39]

Though the five-borough plan was defeated, the legislature's demand that the mayor formulate a decentralization plan was not, and soon a mayor's decentralization panel was set up to develop its own plan by December 1, 1967, independently of whatever plan the board developed. Allen complained that this procedure would make it difficult to "get and hold good people on the board," but this study has already suggested that the competence of the board is irrelevant within the existing system.

The mayor had other preliminary plans as well, as possible specifications of his decentralization proposals, including subcontracting to colleges, universities, foundations, and business certain aspects of the administration of local schools and districts—for example, staffing, curriculum, budgeting, instruction, and community participation. The old good-government coalition immediately protested. The UPA sent a telegram to Allen, saying: "Decentralization is a policy matter, properly the responsibility of the city Board of Education, not the mayor or the state legislators. It should not be tied to state support." [40] A couple of weeks later, when the mayor announced his intention to replace the board's "lump sum" budget with a "line-by-line" budget, the Public Education Association charged that the action "is a dismal climax to a series of moves to downgrade the New York City Board of Education."

Superintendent Donovan, meanwhile, charged that Mayor Lindsay was trying to by-pass the Board of Education to "get more power to control the city's schools." [41] He conceded that the board's decentralization plan was just a beginning and as yet "doesn't go far enough." But, he added, "the mayor has plans, too, and they go too far." The mayor answered the charges by suggesting that one could argue the question of his right to present his own decentralization plan. "The fact of the matter is," he continued, "that this was the insistence and the condition of the state legislature, and we'll live up to it."

On April 14, the mayor took a further step toward greater involvement in school affairs. He tightened city hall's control of school funds by demanding that the board change to a "line-by-line" budget. This meant that the board could not shift funds across functions—for example, from staffing to construction—without getting prior city hall approval. The reaction was immediate and expected. "Lump sum budgets enable the board to shift amounts from one function to another with relative flexibility and expedition," Board President Lloyd Garrison said. "In the past, such shifting of funds under the line-by-line budget was a time-consuming process, both for the board and the budget officials, and we regret the reversion to it." Dr. Frederick C. McLaughlin, director of the PEA, urged the board to "resist every attempt to substitute political guesswork for educational judgment in the formulation of policy for the public schools." [42] This assumed that there was adequate "educational judgment" in the present system, and that the system allowed such judgment to prevail.

Mindful of the strength of civic and governmental groups opposed to his actions, the mayor attempted to allay fears of these groups in a major speech before the PEA's coordinating committee on April 28. He promised school autonomy and defended his action in abandoning the practice of granting lump-sum budget allocations to the board, asserting that his proposed change to a "program" budget would improve fiscal accountability while preserving the administrative flexibility of the board.[43]

Later developments reinforced the fears of those groups who wanted to keep city hall out of board affairs. On May 1, Lindsay appointed Dr. David S. Seeley, formerly an assistant commissioner in the U.S. Office of Education, as his chief policy advisor on educational matters, to fill a post outlined in a report prepared by Mitchell Sviridoff the previous fall for reorganizing city government. Seeley was directly responsible to Sviridoff, administrator of the Human Resources Administration, a city agency that oversees, among other programs, about a fourth of the federally supported pre-kindergarten programs operated in the poverty areas of the city. As a *New York Times* reporter noted: "There is some fear among education officials that the administration may attempt to widen its authority to include the remaining programs now run by the school system." [44]

As of this writing, the mayor has continued his rather steady course of public criticism of board procedures. He disclosed on May 24 that he had asked the city's budget director to look into the Board of Education's spending practices with a view to obtaining a better return. He said in a press interview that he was "in the dark" about the value of many of the programs and services that make up the proposed $1.2 billion school expense budget for 1967–1968, and described the school system's traditional budget procedures as "archaic." He said his goal was an improved budgeting procedure for the city as a whole that would make it possible to analyze whether objectives were being achieved. Reiterating that the city schools spent far more on the education of each pupil than other school systems did, he said it was only natural to ask whether the money was being spent well.[45]

Since May, 1967, Mayor Lindsay has pressed for educational reform through various city agencies and through his New York coalition. The Human Resources Administration, the mayor's superagency dealing with anti-poverty, manpower, welfare, education, and narcotics problems, has been especially active in this regard. All the social-change strategies I discussed at the beginning of this chapter have been pursued by HRA, with varying degrees of success, in education. HRA's Office of Educational Liaison, under David Seeley, for example, has been the mayor's main agency working to get the greatest possible acceptance within the city and among legislators for decentralization. Seeley's office has also worked on improving city college programs, helping initially to decentralize some Title I programs, setting up a citywide citizens committee to support school reforms, develop the education component of Model Cities programs, of linear city, and coordinating all city administration efforts to improve the schools.

HRA's Education Action Division, under Commissioner Thelma Johnson, has also played a key role in pressing for school reforms. This division is the staff unit for the Council Against Poverty's education committee and has been relentless in its efforts to organize parents in poverty areas, train them to write proposals and evaluate school programs, develop new school programs on its own, improve HRA's Headstart program, and continually prod the Board of Education on all programs connected with ghetto schools. Just as the Office of Educational Liaison has worked more to mobilize the support and resources of established institutions and white middle class groups, so has the Education Action Division worked with poverty area groups to train and organize them.

Other HRA units as well have worked on educational reform activities—for example, the Manpower and Career Development Agency on the career ladders program for para-professionals, the Program Planning and Development Unit on early childhood programs and the formulation of administrative and curriculum materials for decentralized school districts.*

Several issues are involved in this emerging confrontation of the mayor and the board. A first is that he sees administrative and political decentralization as a major strategy for school

---

* Much of this activity has just been getting underway (starting in late 1967 and early 1968) and it is too soon to make many evaluations as to its effectiveness. It certainly represents a marked departure from the limited participation in school affairs of the Wagner administration and is generally much more ambitious than the educational reform efforts of any other city administration in the nation.

reform and has pushed to have his own voice in the formulation of decentralization plans for consideration by state officials. His concerns are that the school bureaucracy needs to be rationalized; that it must become more responsive to the needs of the citizenry and the unique conditions of particular communities in ghetto areas; and that he, as mayor, has a direct responsibility to ensure that decentralization in fact takes place. The board agrees with him that some decentralization is necessary, but it does not subscribe to nearly as much decentralization as he does, nor does it feel that he has any legal right to usurp its legally mandated powers to develop plans and oversee their implementation.

A related issue is the mayor's strong conviction, supported by recent studies on the board's budget and much current thought regarding "systems management" * and municipal agency budgeting, that the board must convert to what is now referred to as a Planned-Program Budgetary System (PPBS). The board is moving ahead on new budgetary programs as well, along parallel lines, and some board members feel that they had developed these programs on their own initiative, just as they had their decentralization programs, before the mayor became involved in these matters.

Perhaps the most basic issues of all relate to the mayor's legal rights to become involved in school affairs and the fact that his increased involvement does mean greater city hall control. There is some ambiguity in the mayor's relations with the board. Under the law, the school system is regarded as an autonomous arm of the state and the Board of Education is answerable to the State Education Commissioner and the Board of Regents. The board has not been effective, however, as an agent of reform, even though it has become quite clear to most involved civic and governmental groups that reforms are long overdue. Furthermore, the mayor does appoint the nine unsalaried members of the board, and he has some stake in how the school system functions.

Indeed, the mayor's stake in how effectively and efficiently the school system performs is quite substantial. Since school pro-

---

* "Systems management" is a technique for administering large organizations through the use of advanced mathematical and statistical techniques for gathering information on all the relevant internal and external factors that affect the degree of success of various programs. It is becoming more widely used in business and public institutions.

grams relate so directly to other city functions and problems it has become increasingly difficult for the mayor not to become involved. "With the school now at the center of all social goals," notes Fred M. Hechinger of the *New York Times,* "from urban renewal to integration, from the battle against poverty to the creation of a manpower pool for a changing labor market—educational policy holds the key to a city's future. For a mayor, the success or failure of the schools thus becomes a matter of his own political life and death. The danger under present conditions is that the traditional independence of the schools is subtly turning insulation against political interference into isolation from political power." [46]

The weight of evidence presented in this study—on the bureaucratic pathologies of the Board of Education and on the powerlessness of the board and superintendent as well as many community groups to effect change—justifies the course the mayor is now taking. Admittedly, such a strategy on any mayor's part involves many potential political costs. Civic groups, school professionals, and civil service personnel from other agencies object quite strenuously to such mayoral involvement. They are part of an "old coalition" and interpret such involvement quite correctly as a threat to their power.

In addition, the mayor may run the risk of appearing to be too much oriented to the demands of a single segment of the population. However, all taxpayers have a stake in the schools and suffer from their failures. The extent of his success will depend on how clearly he can show that the white middle class, as well as the Negro and Puerto Rican poor, are victimized by the schools.

Finally, the mayor may run a risk if he proposes radical decentralization plans before enough pressure and support to do so have built up from community groups. It is not clear how much of that there is at the present time, even though it may be increasing. Furthermore, there are so many different interests and points of view among community groups that the mayor may not find a large coalition favoring any single course of action.

There is another way of looking at the mayor's role, however. Community groups have become fragmented in part because they despair of seeing any improvement. If the mayor were to give some strong indication that he intended to reform the schools, he might well galvanize a coalition among

many groups, both white and Negro, who have become so dissatisfied with the performance of the public school system. He
might be the catalytic agent for a new and more unified interest
group politics that in turn would give him ample political
justification for what he was doing.

State Education Officials

Mayor Lindsay's intervention would have a greater likelihood of success if he had the backing of State Education
Commissioner Allen and his staff, the Board of Regents, and the
state legislature and governor, all of whom must cooperate in
pressing for the legislation necessary to decentralize the schools
and change their staffing procedures. There is certainly a possibility of such a coalition developing, especially since Commissioner Allen and the Board of Regents have viewed the
increasing unrest in the ghettos and the continued evidence
of poor school performance with much concern.

Allen's role in the past, however, has not been significant.
On the desegregation issue, for example, he was not able to
mobilize the board toward much reform. The two times he
did intervene directly, in his request in May, 1963, for a desegregation plan, and in the Allen Commission Report of 1964,
the board did not implement his recommendations except in
the most piecemeal way. Allen was reportedly subjected to
political pressures that prevented him from influencing the
board, even when he became directly involved.[47]

A coalition of upstate and big-city neighborhood school
legislators has encouraged Allen to move slowly in enforcing
the implementation of desegregation plans for New York City,
lest one of the many neighborhood school bills they brought
to the legislature get passed. Thus far, all these bills have been
kept in committee, but their existence and the active efforts
of this neighborhood school coalition to pass them have made
it clear to him that if he moves too rapidly there may be
strong opposition. He had also reportedly been subject to pressures from some of the governor's staff not to intervene in
New York City school affairs. There is always the possibility,
then, that the governor and state legislature might undermine
the authority and legitimacy of Allen's office if his actions
were too "out of line" with their concept of what was politically acceptable.

An example of how Allen's powers could be diluted was the educational parks controversy in east Brooklyn. Allen was so impressed with the demographic analysis presented by the lawyer and researchers for the protesting integrationist group that he issued a stay order in the summer of 1966, preventing the Board of Education from building any more segregated schools in the area. He gave the board several months after the hearing to come up with its own plan. When the board informed him a few days prior to the December 1, 1966, deadline date that it had been so preoccupied with the ramifications of the IS 201 controversy that it could not come up with a plan by then, and when it then reported that Dr. Cyril Sargent was doing a study on the problem, he complied with its request for an extension until February. Since then it has turned the Sargent study into a shield for continuing its traditional, neighborhood school construction, and there is no indication that Allen is intervening to force an end to the board's delaying tactics.

Allen and his staff, then, have followed a cautious strategy. Individually, Allen is one of the most reform- and innovation-minded State Education Commissioners in the nation, and his views on desegregation especially have been unusually progressive and far-reaching. But the political pressures on him have been so great that he has hesitated to use all the powers of his office for fear that he would undermine himself, his position, and his agency by the backlash he would create.

Yet, there is at least a partial way out for him, and that is to align himself with reform-minded mayors like Lindsay and work with them to create new, change-oriented coalitions. The desegregation issue, one on which Allen intervened more than any other State Education Commissioner and yet stumbled just the same, has become less salient for the present. Most community groups, however, continue to bemoan the state of the schools, feel their children are not being educated and that the board is not responsive to their complaints. Allen now has an obligation as well as an opportunity to intervene in such a situation.*

Public education controversies in New York City without

---

* Since this was written, Allen's position has changed markedly. On the decentralization issue, contested in the state legislature throughout the spring of 1968, Allen played a very active role in urging that the present lay board be dissolved and that a radical decentralization plan be enacted.

the mayor and State Education Department playing a major role have been a classic case of what conflict theorists refer to as a "no win" game. All participants, including school officials, have been victimized.

If the city's diverse populations can be mobilized around the slogans of upgrading quality and making the school system more accountable and responsive to its clients, they can force Lindsay's and Allen's intervention and improve prospects for reform on such questions as decentralization, educational parks, personnel and examination procedures, curriculum development, the use of indigenous populations in the schools, and teacher training. None of these innovations is possible, however, without the development of a large enough coalition to force Lindsay and Allen to intervene. Conversely, such a coalition may never develop unless top city and state officials are willing to take some risks by intervening "before the fact" to show their commitments and good will.

The New York City school system as presently constituted is basically defective, no longer functioning at an acceptable level of effectiveness. It will never be reformed from within, but neither will it be reformed from without unless a new coalition including Allen and Lindsay begins to force some changes that school officials themselves have failed to implement over many years and decades of increasing failure.

This discussion of what might be is not entirely academic. A much more concerted effort at direct intervention in New York City school affairs by both the mayor and state education officials is just getting underway. It centers around the decentralization plan that the mayor's panel developed in November, 1967, and the politics surrounding controversy over that plan are likely to shape the workings of the schools for many years to come.

XIII

❦

ALTERNATIVE REFORM STRATEGIES AND PUBLIC SCHOOL SYSTEMS

We have presented a case study of the public schools' failure in the nation's largest city. Though public officials, school administrators, and civic groups in other large cities have often looked to New York City for ideas on how to improve public education, they've looked to the wrong place. The New York City schools have failed in ghetto areas, in most desegregated communities, and in many white ones as well. One out of three pupils in the system is a year or more retarded in reading and arithmetic, and the gap between their achievement and national standards widens as they remain in school. In 1966, 12,000 pupils were suspended, 30% of the teachers were "permanent substitutes" without standard licenses; 89,227 pupils attended overcrowded schools while 99,872 were in underused schools. High drop-out rates, teacher strikes, deteriorating community relations, and increasing criticism from business of student unpreparedness are indicators of the failure of the schools.

Public education was for previous ethnic groups a prime means for social mobility, but for the Negro it tends to block mobility and to increase socio-economic and racial segregation. By its failure to educate Negro pupils from the ghetto, public education has reinforced many personal and social problems—crime, delinquency, wasted human resources, and urban decay. Improving the public schools may be one of the only ways to break what Kenneth Clark refers to as the cycle of pathology in our large cities[1]—poor education, menial jobs or unemployment, family instability, and group and personal powerlessness.*

Two main reform strategies have been adopted—compensatory education programs and desegregation. Many of the programs were first instituted in New York City and none has worked for more than a small number of pupils. The Coleman Report, *Equality of Educational Opportunity,* the U.S. Commission on Civil Rights Report, *Racial Isolation in the Public Schools,* and other recent studies indicate that compensatory programs have resoundingly failed thus far and may never work because of the rigidity and incapacity of school officials, and conditions in the ghetto.[2] Evidence is mounting that desegregated education under some conditions (more than 50% white pupils; teachers and principals who accept and know how to teach lower-class Negroes) can substantially raise achievement levels of Negro pupils and not lower those of whites.† But the experience of every big city throughout the nation is that most whites and school officials will not accept desegregation and have successfully beaten it down. Changing neighborhoods and segregated housing create further obstacles and given the fact that big cities face so many other related problems at the same time (fiscal, housing, poverty, welfare, crime, class and racial conflict, governmental) and because the country has committed itself to Vietnam and the space program in preference to its cities—the situation seems almost hopeless.

Yet new strategies for revitalizing public education and cities are proposed. The major proposals include radically decentralizing the existing public school systems in large cities (as put forth by the mayor's Decentralization Panel for New York City); setting up competing, alternative forms of public and private education; and establishing metropolitan school systems that involve the consolidation of inner cities and adjacent suburbs. The first two abandon the quest for desegregation over the short run, assuming that it will be possible only, if at all, after the education of ghetto pupils is substantially upgraded. The third assumes that ghetto schools can never be

* Compulsory school attendance laws seem an anachronism in ghetto areas where regular attendance may even be harmful to pupils who keep experiencing failure, fall farther and farther behind, and keep being exposed to teachers and principals who are untrained, not empathic, and uncommitted to teaching the children.

† This is usually in small and medium-sized suburbs, as for example, White Plains, New York; Evanston, Illinois; and Berkeley, California.

improved much, and that the mounting evidence on the failure of the compensatory approach necessitates a direct confrontation with the desegregation problem, regardless of the political difficulties.[3]

Decentralization

One thing that distinguishes the New York City system from all others, and may require different strategies, is its immensity. Other big-city systems have many of the same administrative shortcomings—inbreeding, overcentralization, buck-passing, overconformity to rules, crisis management, and insulation from parents—but none has them on the same scale. There has been much discussion in recent years of whether the city is governable, and many of the arguments that say it is not can be applied to its schools. The present study leads me to the conclusion that the existing bureaucratic structure of the school system in New York City is no longer viable and must be scrapped. The question is what should take its place and how the change should be effected.

Unlike his predecessor, Mayor Lindsay assumed the burden of dealing with this question when he established a Decentralization Panel on April 30, 1967, under an act of the 1967 State Legislature. It was to develop a plan for "the creation and redevelopment of education policy and administrative units . . . with adequate authority to foster greater community initiative and participation in the development of education policy . . . to achieve greater flexibility in the administration of the schools." [4] The panel made its own study of the system, gathered materials from other investigations, and informally attempted to enlist the support of all influential civic, community, and professional organizations for its proposals before they were finally made public.*

The report called originally for the radical decentralization

---

* The panel included McGeorge Bundy, president of the Ford Foundation, as Chairman; Alfred Giardino, president of the New York City Board of Education; Francis Keppel, a former U.S. Commissioner of Education and then president of General Learning, Inc.; Antonia Pantoja, professor of social work at the New York School of Social Work and one of the leaders of the Puerto Rican community in the city; Mitchell Sviridoff, then administrator of the Human Resources Administration and later to be Vice President of National Affairs in the Ford Foundation; and Benetta Washington, a leading Negro educator. The panel's report soon became known informally as the Bundy Report.

of the system into between thirty and sixty relatively autonomous districts, to be run by local community school boards, partly chosen by the parents and partly by the mayor and a central educational agency. The local boards would have substantial power over staffing, curriculum, budgetary, and educational policy decisions, while headquarters, freed from the detailed operation of the schools, would have "important powers of service, support, and review," and "would be free to carry out overall policy and planning functions which at present it cannot handle effectively." * The report also calls for the elimination of the Board of Examiners, eliminating many local tests and eligibility lists, and the substitution of the National Teachers Examination and State Certification.†

A key recommendation of the panel is that the change-over take place rapidly and be in effect throughout the system by 1970. The board, while expressing general agreement that the system should be decentralized, feels that headquarters should oversee the decentralization and that it should retain the power to enforce citywide standards, do evaluations of all programs, and provide leadership for all local districts for long-range improvements in curriculum, staff recruitment, instructional methods, and administration.‡

Also, the board objects to the proposed timetable, wants more policy-making powers to remain centralized at headquarters, and urges gradualism under the guise of moderation, warning that only chaos would result from radical change implemented too rapidly.[5]

Gradualism, moderation, and local experiments have never worked. The recent history of public education in New York is sufficient proof of the failure of that approach. If the system is not substantially and quickly decentralized, it will absorb,

* Bundy Report, *Reconnection for Learning*, Introduction. It would also have citywide responsibilities for specialized education—schools for handicapped and advanced pupils, high schools—and would encourage citywide desegregation programs through an incentive fund that provided additional monies to participating districts.

† New York City is the only city in the state that has refused to abide by state certification standards alone. Its own local tests and licensing procedures have contributed substantially to many staffing problems—inbreeding, shortages, and delays in licensing and placement. See Chapter Eight.

‡ The mayor restored these powers to the central board, in a letter to the governor, the state legislature, and the Board of Regents, after the initial report took them away.

isolate, and discredit whatever limited reforms are effected.

A compelling argument for decentralization is that the board, as an institution, has not been responsive and accountable to its clients. It is an insulated, rigid, and tradition-bound bureaucracy; its officials have enjoyed autonomy, and band together to protect it; the system's clients attend compulsorily, and there is no alternative system for the great majority of citizens. The panel's supporters claim that its plan would make the school more open, flexible, and competitive, and they assume that these changes will provide a new setting in which classroom education would be improved, by relaxing many bureaucratic constraints and releasing the energies of teachers and supervisors.

Discussion and debate on the details of the plan went on for many months and brought opposition from the board, the school professionals, the United Federation of Teachers, some white civic groups, and, more mildly, from national civil rights leaders.*

The meliorist posture of all these groups prevailed, just as it had on desegregation. The board's long rebuttal to the Bundy Report, released a day after it came out, and its own decentralization plan released a few months later, called for more headquarters leadership and for the retention of a central board.[6]

One of the board's justifications for having a citywide system was that school problems are citywide and can only be dealt with by an interagency approach.† It has already been noted, however, that the board has failed to develop cooperative relationships with many city agencies, so the argument that it has such interests is irrelevant. To assume that interagency cooperation can take place with the existing bureaucratic structure of the school system is wishful thinking.

---

* Public hearings and meetings indicated a repetition of the same differences between national and local civil rights groups that existed on desegregation. The national organizations were more tentative in their support of the plan than ghetto groups and expressed concern that it might further limit desegregation and reinforce the political strength of extremist Black Power leaders.

† The board's rebuttal to the Bundy Report begins: "The fact is that educational efforts are weakened because of the inadequacies of other governmental actions, especially in the fields of housing, employment, welfare, sanitation, and recreation. The board has repeatedly emphasized the interrelationships of these fields with education, and the urgency of comprehensive citywide plans for coping with the ravages of discrimination and poverty which virtually affect the efforts of the schools to provide quality education for all students."

Because this is the first major decentralization plan proposed for big-city schools, and it may have national implications, other objections should also be considered. The most significant bear on questions of desegregation, standards, staffing, curriculum, administrative efficiency, outside political pressures and patronage, and ethnic conflicts.

Segregation and Separatism. One of the things that most disturbed critics of the plan was that it seemed to promote further pupil and staff segregation, leading to black and white separatism. It was ironic that the white liberal groups (UPA, PEA) and supervisory associations who had been so gradualist on desegregation became suddenly concerned about it.[7]

I have demonstrated that desegregation has not even begun to be achieved in New York. In addition to the demographic, fiscal, staff, and space * factors that prevented it, it has to be said that most white groups and school officials did not want it, and that the school bureaucracy subverted and discredited whatever local experiments were tried, just by its normal workings.† Civil rights groups finally concluded that to continue working for desegregation within the existing structure was futile, given the combination of power blocs and the lack of efficiency and accountability.

Notwithstanding the fact that there may be increased pressure from the federal government for desegregation over the next several years, it would be important to decentralize the schools as rapidly as possible.‡ Actually, the Bundy Report's proposed incentive fund to be administered by headquarters would grant $2\frac{1}{2}\%$ budget increments to districts that promote desegregation. Furthermore, the mayor suggests limiting the number of districts to thirty and empowering the City Plan-

---

* By space factors I mean that severe overcrowding limited prospects of desegregation, especially at the high school level. Even this overcrowding, however, was partly the result of the board's vacillation on its high school policy and consequently on its building program.

† Active subversion, of course, was also rampant.

‡ Increased federal pressure for desegregation is likely as the evidence accumulates that desegregation does more than compensatory programs to upgrade the reading levels of ghetto pupils, not to mention its positive effects on the self-image of Negro pupils and on the racial attitudes of Negroes and whites. Decentralization may actually help desegregation by fostering the kinds of radical administrative reforms without which there can never be "good" education, desegregated or otherwise. Without the increased accountability that decentralization would bring, desegregation alone, however, would not work well.

ning Commission to draw up the district lines. It would be desirable if the newly decentralized districts did not reinforce segregation and if they were also consistent with economic necessities.* There may actually be more prospects for desegregation in a decentralized school system, since there would be more accountability for performance, and the large headquarters bureaucracy and its many veto groups who subverted previous desegregation plans would have been pared down.
Staffing. Even the supporters of the plan expressed grave concern about the prospects of adequately staffing the ghetto schools.[8] If schools have to compete for staff, and if headquarters is no longer authorized to decide where teachers will serve, there is the danger that teachers may choose white middle-class schools, or if they are filled, suburban schools. Albert Shanker, the president of the United Federation of Teachers, has predicted, for example, that "thousands of teachers' will leave the city school system if the decentralization proposals are adopted without alteration.†

An argument for the plan is that it will stimulate strong parent interest and leadership, and that teachers who may presently feel their functions are hampered by bureaucratic controls may be attracted to a classroom situation where these constraints are relaxed. There are at least two additional arguments against central staffing. First, principals develop their own local leadership styles and should be permitted to select teachers who fit that style, assuming that it is acceptable to the local board and community and brings results. Second, if headquarters has the authority to help districts with staffing problems, the districts will have little incentive to recruit a larger para-professional group, many of whom could take over instructional responsibilities in the near future.
Local Parent Participation. One fear that many teachers and union leaders have is that "irresponsible, Black Power extremists" may take over local boards and intimidate their teachers. There have been anti-Semitic attacks on teachers in some ghetto schools over the past year, and there were attempts by some local

---

* There are obvious economies of scale that would not be met if districts were made too small.

† One reason for their leaving would be because they fear being held accountable to parents and the wider community for their performance. However, many private schools are able to recruit good teachers, and they are responsible to parents.

leaders at IS 201 to "screen" teachers after the 1967 strike; concern over the anti-Semitism is legitimate, but fear of parents' and community leaders' screening is another story.

Relations between teachers and ghetto parents are severely strained in New York City. The size, the rigidity, and the militaristic nature of the school bureaucracy are one reason. The frustrations that people inside or outside the system feel in trying to deal with the bureaucracy often lead to power-seeking behavior that spreads distrust at all levels. Teachers and parents, both victims of this system, have been taking it out on each other, and the ultimate victim is the child. The teachers, frustrated by the board's failure to provide adequate facilities for the so-called "disruptive child" who they felt prevented any learning from taking place in ghetto schools, initially demanded the right to remove these children from their classes, charging the board with neglect. Many Negro and Puerto Rican parents were enraged by this demand and countercharged that incompetent and poorly motivated teachers are mainly responsible for the poor education of their children. Both have a point. The board is developing procedures to give better services to children who are judged disruptive, but it has not yet developed adequate procedures to remove, retrain, or supervise more closely incompetent teachers. The union is more powerful than the ghetto parents.

Decentralization might minimize these mutual animosities between teachers and parents. The more control people feel they have over the institutions that affect them, the less likely they may be to turn to extremist politics. When people become involved as active participants in the institutions, they develop much more of a stake in making them work than in tearing them down.[9]

It is fruitless, however, to simply transfer power from the Board of Education to the community without training the community to use the power effectively and judiciously. Though decentralization itself is a technique for increasing community participation and leadership, there still must be some training mechanism built into the implementation of the plan to help local school boards and community leaders develop expertise in education and administration.

An effective training program would involve bringing in outside experts in school administration, curriculum, instructional methods, and similar fields in education, as well as community organizers, to do the training. Parents and school board members would have to develop an expertise in technical education matters that was somewhat commensurate with their new power and responsibilities. Other programs, training para-professionals from the ghetto parent population, and setting up career ladders for them whereby they can move up to more responsible positions within the schools as teachers' aides, and eventually as licensed teachers, are also necessary.*

There must be a system of checks and balances to prevent local leaders who are not representative of the large community or responsive to its interests from taking over. The plan empowers the mayor and a central education agency to select five of the eleven local board members with the provision that community groups who object to the mayor's and central agency's powers may petition to select all eleven local board members.

Some opponents of the plan charge that control over local board appointments could become a patronage pot for the mayor. Since the interests of future mayors cannot be predicted, even those groups who approve Lindsay fear what his successors might do with this prerogative.

Standards and Quality. Opponents of the plan suggest that decentralization would invariably lead to a decline in standards, especially in the ghetto schools which have so much difficulty in securing adequate staff. Union officials, supervisors, the board, and some white civic groups charge that standards might be lowered and become more parochial.

With the vastly increased powers that local boards would have in establishing curriculum, ordering textbooks, and the like, this is possible. Given the mobility within the city, and between the city and suburbs, it is important that the central agency be empowered to set and enforce standards which would apply to all districts and schools within the system. In fact, the plan calls for that, while at the same time minimizing the politics of headquarters curriculum officials who have limited

---

* Some initial career ladders programs are now being run by the city administration (through the Human Resources Administration, Mayor Lindsay's anti-poverty agency) and the Board of Education, and are being funded by the city and federal governments. These programs are for public service careers in schools, hospitals, and social welfare agencies.

experimentation and innovation in the past by hamstringing local schools officials.*

Some critics of the plan, comparing the proposed ghetto school districts to segregated Negro districts in other cities, suggest that there cannot be quality education under such conditions. Such comparisons may or may not be relevant; it would depend on the resources the decentralized districts can mobilize—parent training programs, para-professional staff, and active participation by universities, business, labor, and the city administration.

Despite the prospect for such resources, critics have correctly pointed out that the plan actually says little about quality. However, the panel was not mandated by the state legislature or the mayor to do this. Its primary purpose was to develop a decentralization plan that might create a new climate of trust and harmony in relations between school officials and the community, and among school officials themselves, and thereby increase the likelihood that innovations in curriculum, instructional methods, staffing, and administration, could gain more acceptance. Clearly, at least within the existing system, more money and new programs alone are not the answer.

Increasing Ethnic Conflict. Many Reform Democrats, white liberals, and moderate civil rights leaders fear that the decentralization plan would pit Negro and Puerto Rican groups against each other for control over the local boards and tear the ghetto communities wide open.† This is based on the city's experience of increasing conflict between these groups for control over poverty programs, a conflict exacerbated by the limited funds available and some administrative problems at city hall in organizing and staffing its anti-poverty agency.

One strong proponent of this view, Bronx Borough President Herman Badillo, has reportedly asserted that while he favors decentralization, he fears that handing over power to

---

* The politics of headquarters officials are minimized by delegating much more authority to the districts and to local schools for developing curriculum than is now the case.

† This fear is based on the assumption that the more power that local groups in poverty areas have, the more demanding they will become of the city administration. Supposedly, they will end up fighting one another for scarce services even more than they do now because local leaders will have to demonstrate that they are able to get more services for their people with the increased power that they have.

the community will promote political power struggles between Negroes and Puerto Ricans, and with white groups too.[10]

The plan assumes that parents' concern with their children's education will prove stronger than ethnic hostilities and power-seeking. The view of Badillo and liberal Democrats is that power-seeking is inevitable, especially among the poor, and that one should not encourage its uglier aspects. Some of this power-seeking, however, is a direct consequence of the insulation and bureaucratic red tape of the Board of Education and other municipal institutions. If the plan is properly implemented, probably there is a good chance that local community groups will become more rather than less united. Ethnic, racial, and class conflicts are a political fact of life, but they can be handled better when people have more rather than less power.*

Creation of Numerous Bureaucracies. Many liberal groups also fear that decentralization will simply replace one mammoth bureaucracy with thirty smaller ones, which will become just as rigid and, given the substantial duplication of functions, will be much more costly to run than the existing system. Each local district will develop its own constituencies and vested interests and ten or twenty years from now, when pressures mount for a new, perhaps more consolidated structure, the decentralized system will have become too entrenched to allow for the change.

This argument can be made against any organizational change. Assertions about vested interests and constituencies are true. However, there may be more flexibility built into the decentralized districts and many more checks and balances than exist at the present time. The situation is in itself more flexible when decisions are made locally and when community groups can more easily hold school officials accountable for their performance.

The potential benefits of the plan are clear. It would break up the monopolistic power of headquarters, increase the adaptability of the schools to local conditions, and allow them to be more receptive to innovations. Competition between districts might improve the performance of individual schools. Violence and political extremism might be less likely, if the schools provided ghetto populations with a better opportunity to de-

---

* All these problems would have to be considered by the transition unit the mayor set up to oversee the reforms.

velop their own leadership. The plan might also help the Negro and Puerto Rican poor to develop a sense of pride in their communities. Most important, it gives the poor, both black and white, the power to shape their own institutions, something they have never had before.

However, the Bundy Report ignores a number of vital questions. One is the staffing of local school boards, which must have the resources to fulfill their expanded responsibility. If they do not have such resources, it is entirely possible that teachers and supervisors will subvert the local boards as they have the central board. Also there must be some established procedure for retraining and getting rid of incompetent teachers and supervisors. The Bundy Report maintains the existing tenure system, doubtless for political reasons, since other civil service personnel would probably side with the teachers and lobby to defeat any other plan.* It also fails to develop any procedure for handling "disruptive," racist, and inept teachers, or supervisors, who contribute substantially to the schools' failures in the ghetto.

The problem of incompetent teachers and supervisors stems in large part from the fact that the city colleges have not been responsive in their training programs to changing conditions in the city. The success of decentralization will depend a great deal on the extent to which the mayor's staff and the board can improve the course programs in the teacher training institutions.

The Bundy plan assumes that the existing school system is salvageable, that it can be reformed by a shift of authority and power, provided one can also mobilize business, labor, universities, foundations, the city administration, and civic groups to improve curriculum, staffing, and administration. There is serious question of whether one can mobilize such a coalition, displace the vested interests at the Board of Education who are opposed to radical decentralization, or retrain teachers, principals, and district superintendents if decentralization does go through.

The failure of past reforms has led some people to think that reform is hopeless and that we must start entirely new systems. One should note in this regard the experiences of administrators and community leaders in three demonstration

---

* They would probably also vote against Lindsay in greater numbers than in the last election, should he run again.

districts set up in July, 1967.* Their dealings with board headquarters reinforce the fears of those who feel that reforms
within the New York City school system can't work. Despite
orders from the board and superintendent that headquarters
officials make every effort to cooperate with the districts in
setting up their decentralized programs, the normal workings
of the system, as well as deliberate sabotage from high levels,
contributed to many problems in staffing, securing space and
facilities, and planning for the future. The demonstration
units were treated like any other district or local experiment, and
that was synonymous with preventing them from working
effectively.

A study by Thomas Minter, temporary staff member of the
Ford Foundation's decentralization panel, documented these
problems.[11] He reported that the project participants had no
way of knowing or anticipating how much power the superintendent and the board were going to allow them to exercise,
whether the superintendent's interpretation of a request represented the board's position, or if the board even knew of some
of the problems the demonstration projects were experiencing.
The unit administrator in Ocean Hill–Brownsville, for example,
reported that general information about the schools had not
been made available to him as late as August 25, even though
the unit began operations in early July. "Solutions to problems
were hammered out individually," he recalls, "as they arose,
instead of having been anticipated in advance planning sessions between the superintendent or his representatives and the
project administrators." He also reported publicly that top
headquarters officials at the Bureau of Personnel had sought
to dissuade teachers from applying for jobs in his district.

Similar problems have occurred in other districts, and though
one might argue that poor communications between headquarters and district offices exist in many organizations undergoing
decentralization and might be improved in this case, the long
history of failures of administrative reform in the New York
City schools may suggest a strategy that abandons efforts at

* The units included IS 201 and its feeder schools in East Harlem;
JHS 65 and its feeder schools on Manhattan's Lower East Side in the area
between the Brooklyn and Williamsburg bridges, the so-called Two Bridges
Experimental School District; and junior high schools 271 and 178 and
their feeder schools in the Ocean Hill–Brownsville section of east Brooklyn.

changing the system, except in combination with other strategies.

The Bundy Report does not allow for multiple forms of public and private education. Different forms of decentralization should be tried to give ghetto residents more initial choice and to discover as rapidly as possible what types are most effective. In New York City, for example, there are some good prospects for upgrading ghetto education through the use of small, storefront schools. The Urban League has been running its own prep school in Central Harlem to train high school drop-outs for college and work. Preliminary experience indicates that they have been much more successful than the public schools were in preparing ghetto school drop-outs for college and for work. The school system itself has some preliminary programs to encourage high school students in ghetto areas to go on to college, giving them additional instructional help. Mayor Lindsay's Human Resources Administration has other programs of a similar nature.

Competing and Alternative School Systems

Though the Bundy Report would give parents more power, their options are still limited since they and their children remain captive clients of the public school system. Indeed, the inability of ghetto parents to escape the educational monopoly of the diseased public school system is at the heart of the problem. Other more radical strategies have been proposed that would be more difficult still to implement. They involve setting up a variety of small, competing school systems, to be administered under various auspices.

Ironically, conservatives as well as radicals advocate this approach—for example, Dr. Milton Friedman, the University of Chicago economist who worked as Barry Goldwater's adviser in the 1964 national election campaign, and William F. Buckley, Jr., as well as Paul Goodman and many New Left writers—and for similar reasons. They point out that public education, an institution that was established for egalitarian and democratic reasons, has now turned into an instrument that perpetuates inequality. The stratification of neighborhoods limits children from mixing with others from different class and ethnic backgrounds; the "good" public schools are in the high income neighborhoods. The schools in the central cities that have the largest low income populations are also those with the biggest bureaucracies that in turn perpetuate rigid hierarchy and conformity.

Proponents of this strategy suggest that competitive enterprise instead of the monopolistic situation that now exists would not only expand options for the consumer, but it would stimulate greater efficiency and innovation in all schools, promote a healthy variety of schools, and introduce flexibility into school systems. Flexibility is especially important in procedures for licensing and paying teachers. "If one were to seek deliberately to devise a system of recruitment and paying teachers calculated to repel the imaginative and daring and self-confident," writes Milton Friedman, "and to attract the dull and mediocre and uninspiring, he could hardly do better than imitate the system of requiring teaching certificates and enforcing standard salary structures that has developed in the larger city and state-wide systems. . . . The alternative system would resolve these problems and permit competition to be effective in rewarding merit and attracting ability to teaching." [12]

There are several ways to set up such competing systems. One is to give parents tuition grants or vouchers redeemable for a specified maximum sum per child per year if spent on "approved' schools. They could, if they desired, supplement this allowance. Private schools might be set up with foundation money, or under federally financed programs—for example, under Titles I and III. They might even be run by private enterprises and on an experimental basis. If they proved successful, they might attract more funds, staff, and students, and others might be established. The schools would be subject to state standards for curriculum and the licensing of some staff, and they would move toward very small class size and individualized instruction.

Another possibility is for public agencies to begin subcontracting with private groups and institutions to manage schools. The federal government, universities, private corporations, teachers, parents, neighborhood anti-poverty boards, and other agencies, might all set up their own schools in competition with, or under contract to, the school board.

Some social critics and students of urban education have developed specific plans in this regard. Paul Goodman, for example, has suggested establishing "mini-schools" for children in the elementary grades.[13] These schools might include as few as twenty-eight children, four teachers, and no administrators, and they would not have any standard curriculum or licensing procedures.

Other ways of opening up the schools include contracting out basic reading and arithmetic instruction to educational entrepreneurs—for example, firms manufacturing new technological aids, such as talking typewriters, television, and computer consoles. These firms would be paid by the results they got (improved reading and arithmetic scores) and would have an incentive to innovate, while the parents would be free to keep their children in conventional school programs or have them instructed outside on released time. Another technique would be to have a system of "home" and outside schools, for purposes of desegregation, with some activities organized on a cross-school basis throughout the year.[14]

Metropolitanization

Most decentralization plans assume that though desegregation is desirable, it can come about only after ghetto schools have been upgraded. It is conceivable, however, that as many integrationists maintain, the oppressive social conditions of urban ghettos will never permit such improvement, and that much lower standards will always prevail, regardless of plans for increased community participation, small schools, improved teacher training and instruction, and all the other paraphernalia of compensatory education programs. Urban education experts generally agree that the goal of high quality education for ghetto children and the goal of school desegregation are inseparable, at least over the long run.[15] Desegregation is increasingly unattainable in most of the nation's largest cities, however. Anthony Downs has recently pointed out that at present rates of increase, the center cities of several major metropolitan areas, including Chicago, Philadelphia, St. Louis, Detroit, Cleveland, and Baltimore, will have school systems approaching 90% Negro by 1983.[16] New York City, we would regretfully add, may not be far behind. And there is little evidence to suggest that these trends can be reversed without a radical change in the socio-economic and political forces that bring them about.

It is in the context of these projections, as well as of the mounting evidence of the failure of compensatory education programs, that federal officials and urban affairs experts are increasingly mentioning metropolitan-area regional planning and the creation of educational parks linking inner-city and suburban school systems as a possible solution to the problems of declining quality and increasing segregation in the inner city.

Given the rapid development of what the urban planner, David Lewis, refers to as the "Open Form" metropolis, this strategy has much to commend it.[17] As Lewis notes, the old insulated shape of cities has been blasted open by new transportation systems, and inner cities and adjacent suburbs have become a federation of interdependent centers—industrial, commercial, and residential, extending work and leisure options.

The mass of Negroes in the urban ghetto, however, remains insulated from these developments, and one of the key problems of the next several decades will be to enable them to exercise the same options that middle class whites will have. One way to do so is for the federal and state governments to cut off aid for housing, school, health, and other public service programs that stress suburban exclusion and ghetto improvement without desegregation.

The two major fields in which the federal government might plan an important role are housing and schools.[18] Instead of helping to build more ghettos by providing funds for low cost housing only for slum areas, as it has in the past, the federal government must provide housing for the poor throughout metropolitan areas. Providing adequate space, decent housing, and needed services for ghetto residents will be virtually impossible, given the rapid growth of urban Negro populations, unless many of them have opportunities to live elsewhere.

One strategy would be for the federal government to provide financial incentives for suburban desegregation. Large amounts of federal and state aid to local government for housing and education might help weaken the incentives to exclude poor people from suburbs. If substantial Title I and III monies were made available to suburban communities on the basis of how many school-age children from low income families were attending their schools, for example, there might be less resistance to admitting them. The federal government could authorize additional public service grants so that new low income families would not add to local tax burdens. Other approaches might include rent supplements for the poor in existing housing, making greater use of suburban housing in managing the relocation of people displaced by urban renewal in the central cities, and the development of model cities programs in central cities and suburbs that worked together in joint planning. The more federal funds allocated for metropolitan areawide plans and for cooperation between central cities and suburbs, the better the prospects for relieving the central cities of an intolerable burden of poverty, social pathology, mounting political conflict, constant threat of violence, and the inability to provide adequate services for their populations.

Educational parks on the fringes of inner cities linked with adjacent suburbs are among the proposals now under consideration in Washington. They would probably never be accepted by the general public, especially suburbanites, simply as a desegregation device, but their chances might be improved if additional school and community services were included in the package.

Prospects

It is one thing to list and discuss academically the range of solutions for urban education problems, but it is quite another to suggest what the prospects actually are for any of these reforms. The only one that may have much chance of going through, and then probably only in attenuated form, is the Bundy plan. Despite the mounting dissatisfactions of school officials as well as civic groups with the "system," the coalition against many parts of the plan is large indeed, including the United Federation of Teachers, the Public Education Association, the United Parents Associations, and the Council of Supervisory Associations. When one adds up the objections of these and other groups, the prospects for a watering down of the plan seem likely.

The future of the Bundy plan (or modifications of it) will depend largely on the legislation that gets passed. Some of the proposed legislation (none of which was subject to public discussion in the first few months after the report was released) does offer the prospect for limited reform. One item allows the local school boards to contract out schools to business, universities, or other outside corporations. If this were passed, it would provide the climate for shaking up the system.

The alternative-school-systems approach has almost no active constituency now, with no prospect that it will pick one up in the immediate future. The difficulties of pushing through even a modified and watered-down version of the Bundy plan would be compounded if one tried to secure legislation for this more radical strategy. The only way it could be followed over the short run would be in an individualistic and piecemeal way, by securing foundation or anti-poverty funds for demonstration schools. Institutional, system-wide change is necessary, however, and piecemeal changes would not accomplish that. Proponents of the strategy argue that the Bundy plan will not do that either, but they have not yet worked out a political strategy to gain legitimation of their approach.

One distinct possibility is that either a watered-down version of the original Bundy plan or a Board of Education substitute will be mandated, and that the schools will get worse in the chaos of carrying it out. The school system may actually need to slide further downhill, so that the community dissatisfaction and social tensions will force more radical measures for reform. The New York City Board of Education, like most big city boards and municipal agencies in every field, is engaged in at best a holding action, and there are sound political grounds for limiting their capacity to do even that. The fact that such strong opposition developed in response to the Bundy plan indicates that as much as the schools have failed, and as dissatisfied as many civic groups and school officials are, they still see the costs of radical change as greater than those of maintaining the status quo and continuing this holding action. They must come to believe the opposite, if a strong enough coalition is to develop to give the mayor and the state legislature the mandate to push through radical reforms. A decentralization plan, perhaps almost any plan that shakes up the system, may lead to that effect.

The metropolitanization solutions are probably the most difficult of all to establish. Most suburban residents, no matter how progressive they may be in social outlook, would strongly resist any federal program that dispersed poor Negroes from the inner city or set up educational parks and districts linking the city and adjacent suburbs. Also, there may be little support from Negro leaders in inner cities for such a move. Many feel that they are just beginning to gain power in city government, and they fear that regionalism and metropolitan government may well dilute that power. It must be remembered also that conditions in the adjacent suburbs of New York City —Yonkers, Mount Vernon, New Rochelle, and even Hempstead—are becoming more like those in the city; merging with them might offer few benefits. The fact that lower middle class whites have settled in these suburbs in increasing numbers might only contribute to further problems in gaining acceptance for such an approach.

Is There an Answer?

I would conclude, then, that there may be no solution for the failures of big cities and urban education over the short run, and that conditions will probably get worse before they improve. Meanwhile, all that can be done is to press for piecemeal and politically attainable programs, without raising expectations that they will substantially reverse the downward trend of the past. I believe that decentralization, both of the schools and of other aspects of city government, in combination with strong citywide leadership (to set standards, adjudicate intergroup conflicts, and engage in long range planning), is the general approach we should take.

The main drifts in American society have clearly been in the other direction, toward bureaucratic centralism, and in many instances with positive results. The development of a stronger federal government since the 1930s has helped mitigate some of the economic and social dislocations of our rapidly changing society, has helped to break down narrow, provincial customs, and has helped override segregationist local interests in the civil rights struggle. Most twentieth century liberals still subscribe to this trend.

It may have limited relevance unless accompanied by decentralization, however, when one seeks to revitalize the nation's largest cities—the centers of our most acute domestic problems. Bureaucratic centralism in the management of municipal systems has become dehumanizing, inefficient, rigid, and undemocratic to an extreme. If you are a Negro in an urban ghetto, you are regarded not as a person but in the context of how some city[19] bureaucracy must deal with you as a "case" or a "client" to be recognized. If our public schools and other municipal institutions are to actually serve the public, it seems reasonable to make them more responsive and accountable and to give the public more power in setting policies. This is what every black and white citizen deserves in a democratic society.

Ironically, other large cities seem to be moving in precisely the opposite direction. Hartford, Boston, and other communities have begun to set up metropolitan consolidation programs, and various federal agencies (for example, the U.S. Civil Rights Commission and the Office of Education), as well as such civil rights groups as the NAACP, are urging reform in this direction. Superintendent James F. Redmond of Chicago has recently developed a plan, which was accepted by his board, that calls for a massive effort at integration, through extensive transportation, educational parks, "magnet" schools so glamorous that they will lure suburban residents back to town, and city–suburban exchanges—all carried out on such a scale that eventually "there would, in effect, be no neighborhood schools." Dr. Phillip M. Hauser, University of Chicago sociologist, has called the Redmond plan "a wonderful step in the right direction." Meanwhile, Dr. John H. Fischer, president of Teachers College, Columbia University, has labelled the diametrically opposed Bundy plan as "splendid" and "wholly desirable." [20] Many interested citizens and public officials may well become more confused as to what urban education is all about.

There need not be any contradiction in the two plans, if either could be carried out. In fact, the metropolitan consolidation approach may be best implemented if the inner cities decentralize. Suburban districts would not be consolidating with entire big city systems, but rather with particular districts, usually those with Negro and Puerto Rican pupils. The administrative problems of effecting such consolidations might be much easier to handle through negotiating with decentralized districts in the big cities, or with central headquarters bureaucracies that have been liberated from all the red tape and entanglements that now exist in New York City. The fact that legislation has been written to permit such consolidations (if it ever passes) under a decentralized system of public education in New York City indicates city hall's awareness of the complementarity of these approaches.

Ultimately, it would be essential to deal with many factors in addition to the bureaucracy, if one were to improve the New York City schools. These would include the training of teachers and administrators, the technology of teaching, the quality of people choosing careers in public education, and the institutions and interest groups now involved in school decision-making. What exists now in New York City is sick bureaucracy, false professionalism, irrelevant and outdated curricula and instructional techniques, some school staff who are poorly trained and often of narrow, parochial outlook, and only the bare beginnings of outside coalitions.

THE NEW URBAN COALITIONS STRATEGY

One of the main reasons that protest groups were so unsuccessful in pushing the board toward reform was that they did not have the active support of many established and powerful institutions—big business, the city administration, universities, foundations, and the labor movement. These institutions have the resources to help change the school system, but have been committed either to limited reform, to maintaining the status quo, or, in most cases, to a posture of non-involvement. This left a power vacuum in public education and contributed substantially, if indirectly, to the school system's capacity to absorb protest and externalize the blame without changing its outdated and ineffective programs.

The factional and stalemated politics that I have analyzed on the desegregation question, then, resulted from the fact that civil rights groups and their white liberal allies did not have the political resources and leverage to force innovations. The only way that future reform will be possible will be through the development of a new urban coalition that includes ghetto groups and these established institutions.

Proponents of the new urban coalition strategy, for example, city hall, must recognize the forces that have limited the participation of these institutions in the past so that they can be reached during this critical period through the most appropriate inducements. In many instances, these institutions simply had other priorities, and they were not particularly sensitized to the problems of the schools. If they were, they did not see what role they could appropriately play, or they were repelled from playing any role by the Board of Education.

The universities are a case in point. Teachers College trained more people for service overseas and in underdeveloped nations than it did to work in the ghettoes of New York City. Until very recently, its relations with the Harlem community were either non-existent or severely strained. For example, it developed plans in 1964 to use one of the public schools for experimental purposes, drawing pupils from all over the city.

The school, PS 125–36, was to be located on the edge of Morningside Park, adjacent to West Harlem (122 Street), yet the local residents were not initially consulted.

The city colleges and city university have been more involved than Teachers College in local school matters, but until recently, and even now, their participation as change agents has been limited. A few activists and reformers on the faculties of Yeshiva University, NYU, CCNY, Hunter, Queens, and Brooklyn College were involved in action programs—for example, teacher training, curriculum development, new instructional methods, parent participation, and desegregation—but very little institutional commitment existed. University administrators generally give a higher priority to teaching, research, and writing, than they do to service. One action-oriented professor at a city college remarked, for example: "There was quite a lot of unhappiness at the university about people being out in the community and involved in local controversies. 'What are you doing out there?' they ask."

The city colleges have not only failed to play a role as change agents, they have actively obstructed school reform by failing to revamp their teacher training courses in light of the vast demographic and socio-economic changes in the city in recent decades. They are almost as responsible for the schools' failures as are board officials, since they trained most of these officials. If there is a New York City education establishment, it includes top administrators and faculty in the city colleges as well as board professionals. The links between the two are often quite close, with city college people serving on examining boards in the schools, and many board officials maintaining their affiliations with the colleges—for example, as adjunct professors.

In spite of these ties, there has been limited coordination of teacher training programs with board planning. Each institution has functioned as an island, and they must be reconnected.

Big business has been even more withdrawn from participation in school affairs than the universities, even though corporate executives realize that the city schools are not meeting their manpower requirements. "One department store had to interview 14,000 applicants before they could find 1,000 who were qualified for part-time Christmas work," reported a New York City business leader, "and this is quite common in many big corporations." The biggest users of the school system's graduates are banks, insurance companies, and large department stores. Many have given up trying to deal with the schools, and under pressure from the federal, state, and local governments to hire more blacks and Puerto Ricans, they have developed their own training programs to raise the literacy levels of minority group applicants. "We hire qualifiables rather than qualified people," a top Wall Street banking executive reported, "and we train them to make up for for the schools' failures."

Both university and big business spokesmen explain that they have been inactive in school reform efforts before, not only because they have other goals, but also because of their habitually negative experiences with board officials. "We have had so much trouble with Livingston Street," related a city college professor. "There was a guy down there who would always say when we brought some new programs 'get it cleared,' and he would run from office to office until he got a no." "You talk with the board, and nothing happens," recalled another. "It's a bureaucracy par excellence. There's such inertia in that kind of structure."

Big business withdrew for many other reasons as well, for example, to protect its economic and political interests. Top Wall Street executives report that on one occasion they had come close to lodging public protests about the failures of the schools but decided not to when they realized that they managed the pension funds of the teachers' union and supervisory associations. These businessmen were also wary of becoming involved for fear that they might be identified as having partisan loyalties—for example, as supporting Mayor Lindsay on decentralization. Meanwhile, an important resource for change is lost to the city.

All of these potential change agents must be activated. The inducements for their participation must be raised. Big business and universities have a lot to gain, since neither can function adequately in a setting of social unrest, conflict, and riots. The manpower needs of many large companies might be better met. Furthermore, publishers and companies in the soft and hardware fields of educational technology realize that the public schools are a large and expanding market. These companies have to be concerned with school administration and programs to ensure that their technologies are used effectively.

Until such an urban coalition is activated, and city hall

is one of the most logical parties to do so, controversies over school reform will get played out in the same futile way that the desegregation and decentralization issues were. Civic groups will become polarized and fragmented, they will dissipate their limited resources fighting one another, the moderates will protect the board from "extremist" attacks that the board itself provoked, and the school system will lumber along in its own inimitably cumbersome way, contributing further to the academic retardation of children and to poor school–community relations. There is no conceivable reason why this should be allowed to continue. Perhaps a clearer perception by city hall, business, and universities of its political dynamics and of the costs of its continuing may help activate them to form a new coalition and press successfully for badly needed reforms.

A particularly difficult problem however is the quality of people going into public education. In New York City, as elsewhere, they tend to be from predominantly lower middle class origins, with a provincial, parochial outlook that limits their capacity to flexibly adapt to the rapid demographic and socioeconomic changes in the city and makes them almost unreachable through in-service training programs. Those who have been in the system a long time are afraid of occupational obsolescence, yet are incapable of adapting to change. How to recruit a wider variety of social types into public education is a major problem that will have to be faced.

The failure of the schools is also conditioned by the failure of many other urban institutions. Restructuring of the school system must therefore be part of a total urban development strategy that involves the simultaneous revitalization and reform of transportation, recreation, cultural facilities, housing, and the economies of subcommunities throughout the city. Interagency planning is a necessity and must be assisted by the private sector. The proposed solutions are complex, but so are the problems.

The nation clearly must change its priorities and allocate more resources to revitalizing our moribund schools. Otherwise, the schools will surely fail, and with them our entire social order.

Appendix A

STORIES OUT OF SCHOOL

Many assertions we made about board practices were only documented with one or two examples in the text and we feel it is important to give a few more. This is to suggest that the situations described are quite prevalent, and not unique to particular schools or districts.

1. Local school boards—demoralized and powerless.

> *LSB No. 6, West Harlem–Washington Heights–Inwood;* letter of resignation of its four senior members to board president Garrison, December 19, 1966:
>
> . . . We have received close cooperation and support from our District Superintendent, Dr. Sidney Rosenberg, and his dedicated staff. But, because of the lack of responsiveness on the part of the central Board of Education, our service has turned out to be extremely frustrating and disappointing. . . . Time and again, we have made specific suggestions for the improvement of education in our district. *We not only did not get any significant action, we often did not even get a response!* [Underlining theirs] . . . Our continuation would only perpetuate the illusion that we are engaged in productive and substantial dialogue with the Board of Education about the educational needs of our community and how they can be met. [Followed by chronicle of four specific experiences where the Board of Education thwarted local school board requests for school improvements and desegregation, rarely if ever replying to them.]

LSB No. 5, Upper West Side, member:

You take the issue of PS 69. We gave the board five pages of single spaced recommendations for a More Effective School. Donovan said: "Oh, it's an excellent plan, etc." but we never heard of it again. . . On the West Side High School situation, with Brandeis High School eventually opening at almost 200% capacity, we sent letters, called up board members, had meetings, complained, issued statements to papers, but the decisions were usually made without any reference to what was going on.

LSB No. 4, East Harlem; all members resigned in late 1966; Rev. Resta, a member, testifying at public meeting:

We did not represent the community, because of our real lack of power. In this IS 201 dispute in our district, when there were meetings of the parent negotiating committee with the borough president, the district superintendent, and the board, we were not even informed, no less invited. And afterward, the board expected us to continue functioning as the spokesmen of the community.

LSB No. 14, Brooklyn, member:

My first real action was in discovering that a school really did have rusty water, as the parents claimed. They had gotten nowhere with complaints, so I went to the papers. The water was fixed, but I found out that going to the papers was something you never, never do.

East Elmhurst, Queens, where they had school pairings; interview with parent association official:

The local school board came into a terrible amount of abuse. They didn't give any information, and they didn't have any. They've finally worked out now that if you want some definite information, you let them know two weeks in advance. It takes them that long to get it and they really try.

2. Local school board selection—militants kept off.

LSB No. 29, Southeast Queens, civic leader:

I am on the screening panel in my district and we nominated eight persons in order of preference. The board selected numbers four and eight. They select who they want. For the last two times, the screening panel has nominated the same person in the number one position, and both times she was passed over. I believe the reason is that they don't take fighters, people known to be against board policies.

LSB No. 9, Mid-Bronx, civil rights leader:

I apply every year for the local school board, and now I do it just for the principle. The screening panel is usually chosen well to ensure that the "right" kind of people get chosen. Usually three people interview each applicant for ten or fifteen minutes. Last time, a PAC member and lawyer was chairman of the panel and insisted on personally interviewing me. He gave me the third degree from eight to ten one evening, wanting me first to admit there was no school segregation, and second to state that I would go against the Negroes and the civil rights movement if necessary, because of my position on the board.

Central Brooklyn, civil rights leader:

Mrs. Marjorie Hoover was not appointed to the local school board, after a very high recommendation. She is a militant person in our community. I feel she is quiet respectable and acceptable, but of course, she has strong views on integration and things like that.

3. The non-availability of reading score data to parents, after superintendent's order that they be made available.

LSB No. 4, East Harlem, local school board member:

It was always like pulling teeth. Our local school board did some good by informing parents when Donovan's order came that they could demand the scores. When this was done parent associations could get them, although grudgingly. Even then the principals could give them a hard time and the district superintendent gave an equally hard time in enforcing Donovan's order.

Brooklyn, CORE leader:

As far as I know, local groups had no general figures before they were published in the *New York Times* this week [December, 1966]. Parents could get individual schools, but groups like CORE could certainly not get anything.

4. Giving reading tests more than once, distorting scores.

South Bronx, Puerto Rican leader:

I know that reading scores are doctored, and that in PS 5 many failed and were asked to take the tests again and again.

Brooklyn, civil rights leader:

In JHS 271, they gave the reading test three times and then

modified the results before they'd send them on to the board. This was told by a teacher friendly to us.

5. Pupil suspensions and transfers; rights of pupils not respected.

LSB No. 4, East Harlem, local school board member:

Discipline-problem kids were shifted back and forth between the schools, whenever it got too much at one of them. There were instances where principals would suspend kids and then they would be totally forgotten about, while the parents waited for notice that the child could return to school.

Citywide, Leader of large Puerto Rican organization:

We handle individual parents who come in to complain, mostly over suspensions and transfers to 600 schools. We often can't do much, it's so impossible, and often just depends on how the district superintendent feels that week. We usually call the principal or guidance counsellor and if the school is obviously wrong, we can get the kid back in. But all that that does is make them more careful with the records the next time, and they get rid of the kid anyway.

Brooklyn, CORE official:

I was with a mother today whose child was suspended. The reason given was that he was late a lot and cut some classes fairly regularly. Is that really grounds for suspension before you even ask why he is late and why he is cutting those particular classes?

Ruling by Justice Constance Baker Motley, U.S. District Court, in suspension case against Board of Education:

As a result of a review of the testimony, exhibits, and records produced by the district superintendent, this court finds that a "guidance conference" can ultimately result in loss of personal liberty to a child or in a suspension which is the functional equivalent of his expulsion from the public schools or in a withdrawal of his right to attend the public schools.

6. Principals contributing to school–community conflict; mistreatment of pupils and parents.

Harlem, Local school board member:

The new principal of PS 125 whom they took out of retirement addressed the first parents' meeting as if they were somewhat less than first graders. She was so excited to see what exciting things the science classes were doing. They were studying -a- ther- mom-e-ter. A thermometer is what you measure temperatures with. My husband just walked out, he was so insulted for those parents.

Citywide, Puerto Rican leader:

One principal asked me to come to discuss ways to improve attendance by Puerto Rican children, complaining that he couldn't get the parents there to discuss the problem. I asked: "Do the parents ever come to school?" "Yes," he said. "They come every day, twice—to bring the kids and to pick them up. They won't even wait outside. They come in to dress and undress their children and disrupt what we are doing. I have to shoo them out every day!" "If you really wanted to talk to them," I said, "you should take advantage of their being there and ask them to stay a minute to talk about their child." The general attitude is that parents are wanted at the school exactly when and only when the school wants to see them. By then, they don't want to go at all.

Mid-Bronx, Local School Board Member:

The principals present a façade of cooperation but by and large they buy off parents by giving them jobs, like giving flowers to the teacher. Any real complaints from parents are waved aside as being untrue or unimportant. Principals also stand between any real contact of teachers to parents.

7. Teachers.

Albert Shanker, UFT President, at public meeting on IS 201:

We must be able to tell parents about the problems of teaching in ghetto schools and how often we resort to the techniques of survival that we all know about but rarely mention—throwing a kid out of the classroom, telling him not to come back because we haven't learned to cope with him.

Manhattan, white middle class high school student:

I have an old German teacher. She always wants the room to be silent and has no qualms about insulting a person directly. She calls you names—knucklehead, things like that. She would tell you, "shut up!" "shut your face", "you disgust me."

For awhile, we had a sub who said of the Negro kids "I have never seen such animals." She once said something about "miserable monkeys."

HRA commissioner:

When I was visiting a ghetto school recently and attending

an auditorium program, the principal and teachers told me: "Don't they sing and play beautifully." "Yes," I said, "but why can't they read?" They were insulted.

Mid-Bronx, civil rights leader:

We had a case here where a teacher dismissed the few white children in his classes and kept the Negro kids after school lecturing to them that they are nothing, will never be anything, and anything they have they owe to the white man. This was done twice and the parents were in a furor. I went to all the kids and parents and had the kids all write in their own words what was said. The principal was at first reluctant to do much but then called the school in Bedford–Stuyvesant where the man had last taught and hanging up the phone said he'd go along with anything the parents wanted. He stopped teaching there, but we could not get his license revoked.

Bedford–Stuyvesant, CORE official:

My daughter and I discussed the school in The Bronx where the teachers are picketing because of student attacks. She explained that some kids really have a chip on their shoulders, but many times the teachers goad them into doing something. One teacher kept making fun of a kid's clothes in front of the whole class, and just kept at it and at it. . . . At one school, a teacher grabbed and threw a first grader. When the parent complained, she was told a teacher would never do anything like that; it's unprofessional. No respect is shown to parents.

Manhattan, Local School Board Member:

My child has just been put into the audio-visual group, which means that he was excused from some classes to learn to run the audio-visual equipment. This is an honor earned for good grades, but in ghetto schools, the worst kids get to do this and be monitors, thus getting them out of the teacher's hair; but making the possibility of them ever learning anything more remote.

8. Headquarters manipulation of parents on construction.

Mid-Bronx, local school board member:

We had some meetings on the site for PS 84 and Blumenfeld from headquarters told us in the form of an ultimatum that if not PS 84 here, then he'd build the school in Brooklyn instead. He couldn't threaten the parents that way.

LSB No. 9, Mid-Bronx, civil rights leader:

Blumenfeld frightened parents right out of integration on the site for JHS 148. Many parents objected to the 1st site he offered as not providing for integration. He then came willingly to a parents' meeting to insist without discussion: "If you don't want that original site and demand an integrated school then it will have to be north of Fordham Road." It wasn't even what was said but how it was said. There was no explanation, no encouragement, no realistic discussion of the distance involved (Fordham Road is not really far away) and above all no room left for discussing alternatives and they did exist. The whole incident frightened the parents and they insisted on a neighborhood site and refused to discuss an integratable site.

East Harlem, Puerto Rican leader:

Blumenfeld has no respect for the ghetto. The best example of his double dealing was in the IS 201 dispute where he explained carefully in the spring how the school was being built there purposely because of the integration possibilities across the bridge. Then later he dared to tell them that it would be integrated by having some Puerto Ricans and some Negroes. He must have thought that the parents would have forgotten the original promise over the summer.

9. Frustration at dealing with headquarters.

Southwest Queens, parent association official:

The parents of PS 289 were upset because of severe overcrowding. They were trying desperately to find ways to get more seats for the school. Fifteen blocks away there was a white majority school, PS 161, that had a completely empty fifth floor. The parents of 289 asked if they could use that fifth floor until a new housing project in the 161 area was completed. They were refused, first because who could ask pupils and teachers to walk up five flights, and then because the seats were reserved for the new middle income project kids. They then asked if they could use the Boys High annex and were turned down. They then asked for another story in the building and were told the foundations would not support it. They found a school in Far Rockaway where it had been done, but the board still claimed it was impossible. Even on the question of portables which they asked for, they were told it was impossible. When they finally threatened to boycott, they got some action from Donovan. The board does not listen to talk and only responds to pressure, and only then when it is public and they are being watched.

East Elmhurst, Queens, white middle class parent association official:

There is a general feeling against the board from all sides in this area. It is nearly impossible to get copies of the things the hearings are on. If you go to 110 Livingston Street, you can get everything, but you really have to work to find it. You spend an entire day going from one office to another, being nice to all the clerks and secretaries, or properly angry at all the officials. Sometimes you can resort to a little stealing. But all these things are printed so nicely at public expense, they should be distributed and never are. Our local school board feels this way too. Too often they end up looking like fools because parents manage to find things out that they should be told automatically.

10. Pairing sabotage.

Long Island City, Queens, parent association leader:

After the Jackson Heights pairings, parents from PS 111 and 112 in Long Island City went to the board with the support of the district superintendent asking that these two schools be paired. They met with resistance at the board, but it was finally allowed. Nothing, however, was said to counteract the fears fanned by PAT or the natural questions parents had. They had to do all that themselves, list the advantages, doorbell ringing, etc.

Mid-Bronx, parent association leader:

When pairings were proposed in 1963, the Mid-Bronx Community Council (with close ties to the school–community coordinator from the district superintendent's office who was on the council's payroll) called meetings protesting. The district superintendent and the local school board chairman wrote outraged letters against them, and they were dropped. Nothing positive came from school people.

11. Techniques to preserve segregation.

Upper West Side, Manhattan, parent association leader:

Until six or seven years ago, the Upper West Side was gerrymandered terribly, but now it is nearly all east-to-west and therefore as integrated as you can make it. Of course the classes are still segregated within the school.

Mid-Bronx, civil rights leader:

JHS 145 opened in September, 1965, physically unready and one of the most poorly staffed in the city. It had a 10% white population, many in the fast track classes. Last June (1966) the fast track kids were offered the option of electing Hebrew as their language and then choosing from two other schools where it was given. This gave an out to most of the whites and also quite a few Negroes and Puerto Ricans who caught on and elected Hebrew.

Brooklyn, civil rights leader:

In Brooklyn Heights I know a woman who lived in the same building with a white family whose child went to PS 7, the white school, while the Negro child and others in the building went to PS 8. This happened all over the city.

West Harlem, white parent:

I live at West 126th Street in the one integrated building in the project. My kids were assigned to PS 129, one of the best in the area. Later, when I was working with a tenants' group, I realized that the kids in the next building, all Negro and Puerto Rican, had been put in PS 80, a very bad and old school.

Harlem–Upper West Side, local school board member:

The old district went from 106th Street on the east side up to 125th. Coming west, it went up to 133rd and down to 110th. It was obviously gerrymandered and completely segregated.

Mid-Bronx, civil rights leader:

There are Negro pockets in areas close to predominantly or all white schools, yet the schools stay that way, for example PS 114 and 162. And the school construction pattern is such as to keep kids within the ghetto junior highs, while other junior highs, for example 117 and 82, remain nearly all-white.

12. Reverse Open Enrollment.

The late Mrs. Dorothy Fulmer, a white middle class parent from Sheepshead Bay, Brooklyn, organized fifty white parents to send their children to PS 20, a ghetto school in the center of Bedford–Stuyvesant. The program went through, but only after much harassment from the board. Excerpts from her story:

From a background of personal experience, we claim that the Board of Education in New York City has deliberately delayed and attempted to completely frustrate a plan of voluntary

school integration which we helped to create. . . . Our two
sons, ages eight and nine years, currently travel daily by bus
from our home in segregated white Sheepshead Bay [Brooklyn]
to P.S. 20 some five miles north of our home. . . . Simply
by talking to other parents in our immediate area [February,
1964] we were able to get 150 signatures of support for our
project. But even with this backing we received no satisfaction
from the Board of Education. . . . We hired a bus, loaded
it with eighty-five children and on boycott day (March, 1964)
sent the busload to a 100% black segregated school in Bedford–Stuyvesant. . . . We were refused entrance. Dr. Galamison quietly remarked that black mothers in the South had been
"sitting in" for integrated education for a number of years.
Much to our surprise, as we had planned a friendly visit,
we announced to Mrs. O'Daley (assistant superintendent)
that we were a "white sit-in for integration" and we marched
past her into the school. Once inside, the police blocked our
entrance into classrooms. We were herded into the auditorium. . . . At an open hearing dealing with integration efforts at Board of Education headquarters, James Donovan,
then president of the board, was asked from the floor, "What
do you intend to do about the white parents who want to
send their children to Negro and Puerto Rican schools?" His
curt reply was, "That bunch of phoney fakers—they're not
going to send their children anywhere." . . . After struggling
since February of 1964, finally in June Dr. Calvin Gross, then
superintendent, signed a directive allowing the children to
attend P.S. 20 on a plan of "extended" Open Enrollment. . . .
The response of the Board of Education during the months
since "reverse" open enrollment has become official policy has
been disheartening. We petitioned the board that P.S. 20, as
a pilot school for an experiment in integrated education, be
given special benefits (such as paired schools and More Effective Schools receive). Such action would link quality education and integration and would encourage more parents to
participate in the integration experiment. To the date of this
writing nothing has been done to implement our request.

We also bombarded the board with requests to do a first-
class public relations job on the P.S. 20 project. Eventually the
board ran an article in the Staff Bulletin, which is read by
staff members and not by the parents we are trying to reach.

The method used by the board to seek applications for
transfer is half-hearted at best. An ambiguously worded flier
was prepared, loaded with such technical jargon that the

average parent found it unintelligible. . . . Principals were instructed to reproduce this flier on their own schools' mimeograph machines and distribute it to the children. We informed the board that our prior experience had shown little cooperation on the part of principals in all-white schools. When we tried to transfer our own children, the principal would not send us transfer papers sent to him by the board.

A survey we conducted indicated that very few parents had received the transfer flier. When we protested to the Board of Education we were informed that the board had no way to force principals to follow through on their instructions! . . .

Our struggle continues to be one of action against Board of Education bureaucracy and hypocrisy. That the struggle is far from its completion is attested by these memories our activity has produced.

We remember marching three days in a row outside a jail in Long Island City where our pastor was incarcerated. We saw him handcuffed and carried away in a paddy wagon. His crime—trying to integrate the public school system.

We saw a police horse push a child through a plate glass window during a demonstration outside the Board of Education headquarters in downtown Brooklyn—and we saw the child's blood flow. Headlines the next morning read, "Teenage Gangs Riot."

And we remember a youth named Ronald who was arrested during a demonstration and charged with assaulting a police officer. One month after his arrest, we saw Ronald again. He was in the army. The judge had given him the choice of serving a sentence for assault or enlisting. It is little wonder that Ronald chose the latter course. Such is the high price of the Northern struggle for integration.

> From Chet and Dot Fulmer, "The Struggle for Reverse Integration: the Board and the Bus," *Renewal,* October–November, 1966, pp. 14–16.

13. Queens Desegregation. "What's so disturbing is that almost *anything* will work in Queens . . . pairings, complexes, parks, anything. We have a large Negro middle class in Hollis, and places like that are lovely sections."—white parent leader.

Rochdale Village:

A middle income co-op apartment complex built on the Jamaica racetrack site; 85% white and surrounded by the South Jamaica ghetto. Rochdale's sponsors, the United Housing Foundation (UHF), gave the city suggestions for three school sites, two for elementary and one for a junior high. . . . In March, 1962, when construction was beginning there were two wooden schools—PS 110 and 161—each very near to a suggested site for new elementary schools. A few Rochdale parents noted early in 1962 that as construction was beginning on one site, it was going faster on the other site—farther away from the co-op. Assuming that both schools were meant for Rochdale children, they asked why the farthest away was going up first. . . . The UHF sent back "vague and unsatisfactory answers," and as they sought out school officials and parents in the area Rochdale co-opers found that the first school, PS 80, was meant as a replacement for the two old schools (in the ghetto). The second new school, PS 30, would be for white Rochdale children. Where would the Rochdale children go while waiting for the second school to be ready? Bussing was suggested as a possibility. Also suggested was that the wooden schools could stay open and the Rochdale children might use PS 80 in the meantime. . . .

Bussing seemed an unnecessary hardship to Rochdale parents. The alternative seemed highly unfair to the South Jamaica community. In either case the end result would be two segregated schools within one housing project, while the immediate situation remained uncertain.

A committee of Rochdale parents was formed. They were most anxious to work with the Negro community and very willing to accept the board's leadership in attempting that as well as other things. "We would have done anything the board wanted," recalled a parent leader.

They got no help from the UPA, whom they had approached, and were completely frustrated in their meetings with board officials. They proceeded on their own to establish contacts with the South Jamaica community and ran joint informal workshops. Eventually, the Rochdale committee acting jointly with ghetto parent groups at PS 161 and 110 asked the board to make both new schools integrated—with half Rochdale and half community. The board accepted, though one of those active at the time recalls, "We were never certain up to the last minute, and we felt we had to always keep pressuring to make sure it got done."

Soon after beginning its activity on elementary schools, the committee found that JHS 72, to be built on the third donated site, was still in the site acquisition and planning stage. Not

only did this seem illogical, but it again raised the question—
where will our children go in the meantime? The committee
pointed out to board officials that the board's own figures
showed that the nearby junior high schools were operating at
well above capacity. And Mr. Blumenfeld at one meeting had
admitted to them that these figures were distorted, with the
real classroom capacity even lower. Ultimately they appealed
to State Education Commissioner Allen, through whose efforts
they succeeded in reopening the budget and including funds
for construction of JHS 72.

There were still problems of getting sufficient funds and
services to make integration work in the two elementary
schools and in JHS 8, a predominantly Negro school where
Rochdale children would go while JHS 72 was being built.
With great effort and much cooperation from the principals of
JHS 8 and PS 30, and the district superintendent, Dr. Ryan,
they were somewhat successful.

Rochdale offered to the board an opportunity with built-in
answers to the problems they claim to face in bringing about
integration. There was a naturally integrated school population formed by whites buying into the area—quite the opposite
from the typical unstable, transitional area. The new housing
and antiquated schools necessitated new schools and new zoning. The sites had been donated to the board, eliminating
delays and difficulties there. The white population was not
opposed to all integration, having bought into an integrated
housing development. And there was an active group of leaders
in the white community willing to work under the board's
leadership to counter the fears whites would have concerning
the quality of predominantly Negro schools.

Yet the initiative at all times came from the parents, not
the board. It was the parents who saw the opportunities for
desegregation, while the board's actions were fostering a segregated situation. It was the community leaders who began and
carried through the community relations work in both communities (predominantly white Rochdale and black South
Jamaica) and between them, seeking out fears and intelligently
answering them with little help or direction from the Board
at any stage. And finally it was the community that initiated
the programs needed to make it all work, including the final
appeal to outside institutions. [Universities came in to help.]
The result could hardly be anything but the skepticism that

parents in this area express concerning the sincerity of the board's commitments to "quality, integrated education."

Andrew Jackson High School:

In an area near Rochdale, school and community leaders have been fighting what they consider a losing battle for several years to maintain an integrated Andrew Jackson High School. These leaders point out that Jackson is a good school. Well over 50% of its graduates go to college, its parent organization is active and concerned, its faculty experienced, and its program solidly academic, including courses in six languages. In March, 1967, a group of white parents from Staten Island's PTAs visited the school to study its apparent "success formula."

Moreover, Jackson is a well-integrated school, fed primarily from Negro and white middle class areas, some of which—Laurelton for example—are integrated. Community leaders in Laurelton have undertaken housing programs in recent years to prevent the kinds of instability that leads to a transitional area, and credit Jackson's presence with contributing to the stability of the community.

For several years the trend has been unmistakably toward an increased Negro enrollment. By 1967, the school was roughly 50% Negro, compared with 27% in 1960. At the same time, Negro students account for only 15% of the total population of Queens high schools.

At least since 1963, parents and community leaders have been asking the board for a comprehensive plan for rezoning Queens high schools for a better racial balance. The board's response has been to study the matter. Three new high schools were built since then and during the construction of each one parents and community leaders were led to believe that the rezoning would follow the construction. It never has.

What has been done is re-assigning Negroes who would attend Jackson to other high schools. The total effect has been to reduce the enrollment of Jackson to slightly below its capacity. At the same time, the five high schools nearest to Jackson are all overcrowded. Board projections for 1967–1968 indicated that Francis Lewis High School would be at 167% capacity; Martin Van Buren at 134%; Jamaica High School at 139%; and Springfield Gardens at 130%.

A movement developed to "save" Jackson as a good, integrated school. The leaders involved saw the only solution as that of assigning white students from the solidly white sections nearby. In 1966, Dr. Donovan also recognized ". . . the answer to Jackson's ethnic problems can and should be found by re-zoning of high schools. This should not only involve move-ment of Negro and Puerto Rican pupils . . . but also the movements of others [whites] . . . into Andrew Jackson."

As no rezoning plans were forthcoming, the parents filed suit with State Education Commissioner Allen to force the board to act. On February 9, 1967, Allen ordered the board to prepare a plan by May 1, 1967, to meet the problem by the following September. On March 9, 1967, Donovan announced a plan to gradually reduce Jackson's enrollment to 2,000, to set up a music and art program to attract voluntary transfers from all over Queens, and to encourage the city to set up a com-munity college nearby. Finally, a new high school is to be built in Holliswood, north of Jackson, which Donovan claimed would "provide a more effective opportunity for integration."

These plans were not reported to Allen or to the com-munity's attorney at that time, despite a letter from the at-torneys (to which they received no reply) asking specifically that, if these were to be the board's answer to Allen, they file them immediately to give time for challenging what would be effective in September.

The reaction of integrationist groups was suspicious and angry. They viewed the reduction of capacity as unconscion-able, in light of the overcrowding in the surrounding schools. One parent leader, familiar with the schools' methods for handling troublemakers, fears the voluntary transfer to the special music and art program without entrance requirements will prove an easy out for principals anxious to get rid of behavior problems. Some read into the mention of a com-munity college in the area an unmentioned long-term plan to phase out the school entirely and use the building for this purpose. Many teachers began expressing uncertainty about the board's intentions, and the UFT publicly supported the integrationists' position.

The plan to build Holliswood High School seems the ul-timate confirmation of a long-held suspicion that the board will never send white students into a school that is more than 50% Negro and Puerto Rican—even if those Negroes and Puerto Ricans are middle class and even if it is necessary to build a new high school in order to keep the burden of traveling on the Negro population.

The president of the Committee of Parents and Friends of Andrew Jackson High School expressed their views at a local school board meeting, asking Dr. Donovan to exhibit some of the good faith he has been verbally passing about. . . . Here in Queens, the board has an ideal situation. It can prove its integrity and its desires to balance the schools racially. Instead, it exposes its true views. . . . How can the board ever justify honorably a situation like this one?

14. University faculty frustrated at trying to deal with the board and gain acceptance for innovative programs.

Professor:

We had a bilingual program to use Spanish to teach English and it never got off the ground. The schools stopped us cold. The district superintendent would not allow it. We took it to the board and got various reasons for the negative decision. First, they said they did not want to countermand the decision made at the local level. Finally, we went to Loretan who said we could run the program in any area but the district where we were set up. . . .

We were going to train non-English-speaking aides to build the children's vocabularies, have them begin to read simple Spanish—what is called a reading readiness program. They were to be taken out of class—perhaps fifteen minutes a day, and taught to sight read. Then they were to switch to English after they had doped out the symbol system. The reason the district superintendent gave for not approving the program was that there was no time to take the child out of the classroom—that "even if it's play activity, it is important at that age!" . . . Delays are always there. If you ask to have a program, and they want it in writing, they will always find an error on page three, or some such trivial reason to stop it. Then you get delay on the local level. As far as the board is concerned, life is long, and short-term projects are short.

We had After-School Reading Centers run in the Lower East Side, Mobilization for Youth area. We wrote to the schools, asking them to nominate children who needed help.

We set a limit for each school, due to the limited number of staff people, and had lists of children for four of the five junior high schools covered, but the fifth kept delaying. We could have gone ahead with the program but would have had clinicians not working at full capacity, which would have been scandalous in an area where 90% of the kids need remedial help. So we waited and waited, and this was not just a matter

of the principal's tardiness. The clinicians were treated badly
when they went into the schools, told to select the children on
their own, which was a left-handed way for showing disdain
for the whole project. After some months we told the clinic
director to get the names by a certain date or we would increase the number from the other schools to fill the limit.
The principal reacted in a most violent way possible. He wrote
an answer "comparing the Kennedy assassination to the note
the clinician wrote." Then the school officials formed a united
group against the common enemy, and the district superintendent ordered that none of the schools should send children
unless the order was rescinded. So MFY had to back down,
after totally wasting four months of the clinic's being opened
but unable to give services.

We have not worked too closely with the Board of Education partly because the board has not always been terribly
receptive. Even the attitude about the campus school has been
"take a load off our backs" not "what can we learn together?"
It is not as if the board is making any effort to use the program's experience to their own best advantage—it's more so
they can say "look at the cooperation. Look what we're doing."

Professor:

The Board of Education was so uncooperative with city hall
officials about giving out information on its Title I programs that HRA called me, saying they had tried to get information from the board for a month. What a ridiculous
situation—having to call a professor for public information.

Professor:

I had a project at Mobilization for Youth, setting up skill
centers, self-directed and self-correcting prescriptive teaching.
Because we couldn't get anything done through the schools, we
had to do the program in the summer. The board made us
rent space and wouldn't give it to us "to give a program to the
kids." The program was very successful—one to two years
growth in six weeks. Ford did an unannounced site visit, visiting a class of under-achieving, behavioral-problem type kids,
and all of them were perking like mad. The Ford people were
amazed, and asked: "Why aren't you doing this in the schools?"
We answered that we didn't know. In October, the year before, we had put in a proposal. In November, we were told to
resubmit it with fifteen copies. The following February, after
much prodding, we finally learned it had been turned down at
the board. The memo said it was not adequately tested. When

we tried to pinpoint who had turned it down, we could not.
We were not even able to find who had been sent the fifteen
copies.

15. Big-business executives who tried to work with the board.

Vice presidents of a large bank:

We try to hire as many people from the Negro and Puerto
Rican group as we can. We have been very, very disappointed
at the schools' failure to turn out high school graduates who
can even read and spell, and we have a training program to
raise their levels of literacy. We have sat in on meetings with
school people, but they just set up their committees and do
their studies. And it takes them so long to pass on anything,
that after awhile, we got very discouraged and stopped meeting
with them.

Officials in a large business association:

One very large corporation reported to us through its personnel
department that it had to interview 10,000 applicants to find
1,700 who were qualified for the lower level white collar jobs it
had available. All kinds of businesses are suffering in this city
as a result of not being able to get people to fill these positions.
We had a meeting with Donovan and he said he would produce
1,000 poor kids from the ghetto for one of our training programs so they could get good jobs, and he ended up producing
only a few hundred.

16. The Educational Experience: treatment of middle class white
pupils, in advanced classes in integrated schools.

East Side, Manhattan, junior high school, mostly white middle
class; teacher:

The seventh-grade social studies teacher in our school requires, at least twice a semester, a long paper from each of her
pupils—twenty-five or thirty typed pages. She teaches the top
class in the grade. She's always carrying a few of these papers
around with her, I suppose it makes her feel important. But I
know for a fact she doesn't read them; she grades them A, B, C,
or whatever, based on the child's latest exam.

White middle class public teacher, who teaches in a mostly
white junior high with the highest reading-score average in the
city:

Would I send my son and daughter to private school if I
could get them in? In one minute flat. I believe in public

schools, in principle, but I'd swallow my principles because they're no good for the kids.

Upper West Side, Manhattan; white middle class parent:

For one year, I was an active member of the PTA. I didn't work on rummage sales, but with some others I listened to parents' complaints and talked to the principal about them when the parents were afraid to, if that was necessary. We were careful to assure the principal that we were sure the problems weren't of his making or any other individual's, but felt he'd want to know when parents were upset about something. The principal likes his PTA to keep busy with rummage sales. Eventually he had two of my children called out of their classrooms and brought to the school nurse, who inspected their faces and hands for cleanliness. The children's teachers were shocked; the children were puzzled and embarrassed, and told me about it with tears in their eyes. We are in a different school district now, and I'm through with PTAs. We've applied to private schools, but we'd need a scholarship and I don't think we'll get it.

East Side, Manhattan, junior high school, mostly white middle class; teacher:

Maria, who's in the bottom class in seventh grade, screams obscenities. That's her bit. Her regular teacher was absent one day and another teacher took the class. She'd been in the school for ten years, but Maria didn't recognize her, and apparently having a stranger disturbed Maria. She began to curse the teacher out, starting with four-letter words and working her way up. The teacher sent for the principal. He just walked into the classroom, told the teacher in a stage whisper "The police know all about her," and walked out.

White middle class teacher and parent:

Last year, when my son's kindergarten teacher and I had the official parent–teacher conferences, she could talk about only two things: (1) her complaint that he wasn't "adjusted to the group"—that is, he "doesn't sit still"—and (2) "Why can't he do representational paintings?" He was doing representational and every other kind of painting at home at that time, but he disliked that teacher so much that by the end of the year he wouldn't do *any* painting in school. On the first day of first grade—under a different teacher, of course—he painted a big, complicated, representational picture, which she put up on the wall. That teacher has never mentioned whether he sits still—apparently she doesn't feel it's a problem. I hadn't

tried to change his kindergarten teacher for another, because
from what I heard and saw they were all pretty much alike,
and I know what a hassle it is to try to change anything.

Manhattan, white middle class parent:

Mrs. A. was my older child's first-grade teacher last year, so I
carefully registered my youngest daughter late so I could talk
to the assistant principal when there wasn't a crowd around to
hear, and make sure she got a different first-grade teacher. That
sort of thing usually works, but in this case it didn't: Mrs. A.
had been changed from a regular first-grade teacher to a first-
grade reading teacher, and she goes around to most of the first-
grade classes. She has the children come up to her desk, stand
by it, and read from the book that's flat on the desk. My daughter has shoulder-length hair. It falls into her face when she
bends her head forward, and she pushes it back. Mrs. A. is very
disturbed by this, she's asked me if I want my daughter to go
blind, she constantly tells her she should cut her hair or wear
it in braids—which she doesn't want to—and once she had the
entire class sing a song to my daughter about "you should wear
ribbons in your hair." My daughter could read a little before
she started first grade with Mrs. A. but now, in March, she
doesn't know the alphabet any more.

Manhattan, white middle class parent:

My daughter, who's in the "middle school," had a French
teacher who left in the middle of the year. They brought in a
Spanish teacher to teach French, who couldn't pronounce the
difference between *les cheveux* and *les chevaux,* and who said
la main as though it were the northeastern state. My daughter
began *un*learning the good accent she'd got from a French
friend of ours. I went to the guidance counsellor to see what
could be done—she got very angry, said "My goodness, it used
to be we just gave the children busy work for the first three
weeks of school. Now if there's one minute the children aren't
learning, the parents have a fit." I couldn't believe it. Eventually, I went to the assistant principal, and now my daughter
is in a French class with the unruly children, but the teacher
has a good accent and knows the language, and she lets my
daughter go to the library, and study during the "hygiene"
lessons the other children get once or twice a week.

Upper West Side, Manhattan; elementary school, white middle
class parent:

My children's day at school begins with all the several hundred lining up, by class, in the gym. "Teaching assistants"

scream at them—yes, scream—and blow whistles, and don't allow a line to move out toward the classrooms until each child in the line is standing still and quiet. Yes, these are children from the first grade up. They then go to the classrooms, two by two, in lines, silently—in theory. Predictably, there are kids who won't take it, and run and horse around going through the halls. So they have more teaching assistants, and teachers, at various points in the hallways, who do some more screaming and blow more whistles. Substantially the same thing happens in the lunchroom: children are marched in, they're not allowed to leave the table to go outside when they're finished but must wait until an adult dismisses the entire table (about fifty kids) —and of course the kids respond to this by either feeling intimidated and "good" or rebelling and feeling "bad." Same story in the playgrounds. I'd like to know what the schools feel they're teaching children in this military atmosphere. It isn't citizenship, it isn't love and respect for other people. Don't even ask me what I think about what goes on in the classrooms.

Upper West Side, Manhattan; elementary school, white middle class parent:

For some time, Mrs. X. has had a reputation among parents as a terrible teacher. Any time of the day you happen to pass her classroom you could hear her yelling at her pupils—mostly telling them to be quiet. Everyone I know went to great lengths to avoid getting her for their children—she teaches first grade. Two years ago Mrs. X. got angry with a little black girl in her class and closed her in a closet in the classroom. Then Mrs. X. was called home, and left without releasing the child from the closet. After school was over an older child passing the room heard a child's sobbing, and went to investigate. She found this little girl in the closet. The small girl said—between sobs—that she couldn't come out because Mrs. X. had told her not to. It took some persuading, on the part of the older child, to get the little one to come out. The little one's mother went to the principal about this, and he assured her that everything would be taken care of. Nothing seemed to happen. Then the PTA president got an anonymous letter, naming no names, but describing the incident. It was decided that this should be read to the next general PTA meeting, and I was supposed to be in the audience to suggest some sort of decent action; I'm sorry to say I couldn't get there in time. I heard what happened: the letter was read, and all the comments from the floor added up to a denunciation of the mother and the PTA leaders for choosing such a method of presenting the case. The principal got up and said a letter had been placed in the teacher's file and she had been warned that this should not happen again. That's as far as it went; the teacher is still teaching first graders. Last year a white mother who knew the story found her child assigned to Mrs. J.'s class for the coming year, and made up her mind for private school.

Parent:

Our close friend had her child at PS 199 in Manhattan. He was in the third grade, but the mother knew he could not read well at all. Suddenly she heard that he was reading at third grade level. Dorothy knew this was not true, so she went down to the school and finally the teacher said: "Yes, that's true. When we tested him he only read at the first grade level, but I figured that he just must have had a bad day." This is the reverse expectations problem you have with the teachers and the white middle class kids. Sometimes, it's great for them, but the parents have no idea how the kid is doing. Dorothy took her son out of 199 and put him in private school.

Parent:

Gloria's daughter was in a class with a new substitute teacher brought in in February. The teacher was inexperienced and could not handle kids. The mother complained, and her daughter was removed from class one day for making a comment to her friend sitting next to her that the teacher could not manage the class and had bad attitudes to the kids. Her daughter came home hysterical and when Gloria went to school to protest the following day, the principal scolded her: "How dare you discuss the teacher's qualifications with your child?" Gloria tried to explain that she was a parent and was trying to listen to her child's complaints and help her. That teacher is still there and the parents are still unhappy, but they are afraid to protest.

Tenth-grader:

In the seventh grade, I had a French teacher who was very strict. She didn't seem to be a very good teacher. She yelled at us all the time, gave us homework assignments and didn't go over them. She started to lose control over the class, started to teach less and yell more. One day, she was standing in the hall, talking to another teacher and the late bell hadn't rung yet, so I ran down the hall to return a flute to another teacher, taking about a minute or two. And when I got back, she was still standing there talking, and went in and sat down. When she came in, she wanted me to write her an apology for leaving her room after I'd come in, and an explanation for why I'd done so. She didn't like something on the note I wrote, and so she made me write it over again. Finally, I had to write it over three more times before she finally accepted it. I don't remember all the reasons but once it was because I hadn't skipped two lines between the end of my explanation and my signature. So I missed two French classes just writing these notes for her.

Seventh-grader:

I hate school. I have teachers who ask us to write stuff twenty-five times, if we do something wrong. My friend George who is such a smart guy mostly sleeps in class, he's so bored with what goes on. We don't learn anything.

Andrew Lenihan, white middle class pupil, twelve years old:

A Breath of Life

Inside all the classes
Abides a deep stifled dark,
A closed tight world
Of closed tight thought,
Not a bit of life
Nor life's blood, thought,
No breath of light penetrates,
Stubborn, stubborn rule
A world of thought could be,
But not a one penetrates
Stubborn, stubborn rule.

Appendix B

MEMO TO SOCIOLOGISTS

It may be useful to summarize New York City's experience in much more abstract terms than those used in this book, which was not written primarily for sociologists. The advantage of an abstract schema is that it suggests some of the key variables that one must manipulate to get social change.

Most of the sociological propositions one can generate, summarizing New York City's experience, relate to its *pluralism,* its consequent *political fragmentation,* and its *massive school bureaucracy.* The main consequence of these conditions, of course, is *inaction,* which is what this book is all about. Consider the following:

1. The *larger* the city population, the more *heterogeneous* it is, and the wider its *geographic spread,* the more *fragmented* its populace becomes. There are so many interest groups, because people have so many divergent loyalties—community, ethnic, racial, class, and religious. It is difficult to form coalitions from such diversity.

2. This *fragmentation* and *pluralism* prevent *action* and *innovation.* The city is composed of a series of veto groups that play off against one another, and the result is a *stalemated politics.* There are no bases for the crystallization of large enough interest groups to press through innovation effectively. This permits encrusted, tradition-bound institutions like the New York City Board of Education to continue unchallenged, regardless of their many inadequacies.

3. The more the interest group fragmentation, the more the cross-

pressures on city agency officials and the more caution and vacillation they show in leadership.

4. Fragmentation, intergroup conflict, and ineffective leadership reinforce one another. The more conflict and cross-pressure, the more caution by city officials; but the more their caution, the more uncertainty among groups as to what the power structure is and how to move it, and the more fragmentation.

5. Interest group fragmentation is affected by other conditions: (a) the extent of fragmentation of city agencies—as fragmentation increases, there is less coherent planning, more unevenness and inefficiency in distribution of services, authority and responsibility are diffused, and the various groups intensify their fight with one another for their share; (b) the extent of scarcity—the more the scarcity, the more intergroup conflict and weak city leadership there are, and they lead to increased conflict. Everybody is fighting it out for the crumbs. City agency officials are simply sharing the poverty and responding to pressures of the moment.

6. The extent of consolidation of power within the school system and in city government bears directly on prospects for innovation: the greater the consolidation, the greater the likelihood of innovation. The city can only be energized for change if there is a coalescence of interests—among civic groups, within the school system, and in city government. New York City is an extreme case of the balkanization of city government, the school system, and the civic groups.

7. The basic problem then becomes: How to energize a school system and a city to innovation when several institutional obstacles stand in the way, namely:

(a) Fragmentation at all levels;

(b) Chronic scarcity of money, staff, and school space; and

(c) Leaders who react mechanistically to cross-pressures. Meaningful innovation demands that unusually far-sighted leadership emerge. It has yet to do so in most major cities.

MODELS OF BUREAUCRACY

Social scientists have developed models of different types of organizations, in an attempt to characterize their administrative structures and styles. Two polar types are the authoritarian and the professional. The Prussian military, the Roman Catholic Church, and the industrial corporation are examples of the authoritarian type. The prototype of the professional organization has been the university. Civil service organizations have generally been closer to the authoritarian; and partly because of this they do not foster or encourage professional behavior among their functionaries.

The following chart depicts both models; the New York City school system fits the monocratic, authoritarian one. The chart provides an encapsulated summary of the system's many characteristics that would have to be changed radically for reform to take place:

Authoritarian, Monocratic Model	*Professional Model*
High degree of centralization (even of routine operating decisions).	Flexible centralization (to set standards and provide leadership; but with many routine and non-routine decisions decentralized).
Authoritarian leadership ("boss rule").	Professional leadership ("collegial rule").
Hierarchy (many levels, "tallness").	Limited hierarchy (few levels).
Assumed omniscience of top officials (accompanied by).	Flexible, consultative relationships with top officials. (accompanied by).
Hierarchical, "upward" orientation of field staff, with periodic tendencies toward widespread rebellion and noncompliance.	Lateral, "collegial" orientation; no problems with rebellion; internalized professional standards regulate performance.
Complete discipline enforced from the top down.	Colleague groups informally enforce conformity to professional standards; administrative looseness; limited emphasis on authority based on office.
Responsibility owed from the bottom up.	Responsibility to live up to professional standards that one has internalized as inner controls.
High degree of specialization (departmentalization, parochialism; separate units function by their specialist logics; fail to be concerned with the broader organizational implications of their actions and their politics).	Limited, flexible specialization (free, open communications; little separatism and departmental chauvinism).
Recruitment and promotion practices that reinforce adherence to traditional bureaucratic codes (inbreeding).	Regular recruitment of outsiders.
Fragmentation of authority and power of top administrators,	Consolidation of power and authority at top; extradepart-

despite centralization (separate power blocs corresponding to major subunits—divisions, bureaus, separate levels) ; each bloc is a veto group, opposing changes that threaten its position.

Weak chief executive.

High degree of politicalization of bureaucratic functionaries (function as political bureaucrats; oriented toward *extrinsic rewards* of power, status, promotion, to the exclusion of professionalism.)

Limited planning (segmental, localistic, short-range reactivity, fire-fighting) .

mental ties result in more commitment to organization-wide goals than to personal career and empire building.

Strong chief executive.

High degree of professionalism oriented toward *intrinsic rewards* of professional recognition and status.

System-wide, long-range planning.

Many elements in the authoritarian model have been typical of all New York City government, and not just of the Board of Education. Greater centralization and decentralization are essential to improve their functioning. *Centralization* (the formation of superagencies) permits more and better planning, stronger top leadership, and limited overlap, duplication, interagency conflict, ambiguity of roles, and buckpassing. It creates serious administrative (coordination) problems, of course, that must be handled.

Decentralization forces more accountability, introduces greater flexibility in decision-making, and gives citizens more power and rights. It can take place within a framework of more consolidation and planning at the top, though not without some tensions. Yet, centralization and decentralization are complementary strategies and contribute to each other's effectiveness. What exists now is arbitrary and chaotic centralization, and decentralization by default and in rebellion against a central authority that serves no meaningful function, and is itself powerless.

Bibliography

I. General Works (Books and Articles)

David Alison (pseud.), *Searchlight: An Exposé of New York City Schools*, New York: Teachers Center Press, 1951.

Edward C. Banfield and James Q. Wilson, *City Politics*, Cambridge, Mass.: Harvard University and M.I.T. Press, 1963.

Edward C. Banfield, *Big City Politics*, New York: Random House, 1966.

Chester I. Barnard, *The Functions of the Executive*, Cambridge, Mass.: Harvard University Press, 1938.

Warren G. Bennis, *Changing Organizations*, New York: McGraw-Hill, 1966.

Charles Bidwell, "The School as a Formal Organization," in James G. March, ed., *Handbook of Organizations*, Chicago: Rand McNally, 1965.

Kenneth E. Boulding, *Conflict and Defense*, New York: Harper, 1963.

Robert S. Cahill and Stephen P. Hencley, eds., *The Politics of Education in the Local Community*, Danville, Ill.: Interstate Printers and Publishers, 1964.

Richard O. Carlson, *Adoption of Educational Innovations*, Eugene: Center for the Advanced Study of Educational Administration, University of Oregon, 1965.

Kenneth B. Clark, *Dark Ghetto*, New York: Harper, 1965.

John Henrik Clarke, ed., *Harlem, a Community in Transition*, 1st ed., New York: Citadel, 1964.

James S. Coleman, *Community Conflict*, Glencoe, Ill.: Free Press, 1957.

James B. Conant, *Slums and Suburbs*, New York: New American Library, 1964.

James B. Conant, *The Comprehensive High School*, 1st ed., New York: McGraw-Hill, 1967.

Ronald G. Corwin, *A Sociology of Education*, New York: Appleton-Century-Crofts, 1965.

Robert Crain, *The Politics of School Desegregation*, Chicago: Aldine Publishing Co., 1967.

Michel Crozier, *The Bureaucratic Phenomenon*, trans. by author, Chicago: University of Chicago Press, 1964.

Richard M. Cyert and James G. March, *A Behavioral Theory of the Firm*, Englewood Cliffs, N.J.: Prentice-Hall, 1963.

Robert A. Dahl, *Who Governs?*, New Haven: Yale University Press, 1961.

Midge Decter, "The Negro and the New York Schools," *Commentary*, September, 1964.

Robert A. Dentler, Bernard Mackler, and Mary Ellen Warshauer, eds., *The Urban R's*, New York: published for the Center for Urban Education by Praeger, 1967.

Robert A. Dentler, *American Community Problems*, New York: McGraw-Hill, 1968.

Dan W. Dodson, two position papers: 1. *Power as a Dimension of Education*, 2. *The Creative Role of Conflict in Intergroup Relations*, prepared for The Center for Human Relations and Community Studies, New York University, 1963.

Dan W. Dodson, *How Realistic is the Goal of Desegregated Education in the North?*, lecture delivered at the New School for Social Research, February 20, 1964.

Dan W. Dodson, *The School Superintendency and the Civil Rights Revolution: Irresistible Force—Immovable Object*, Center for Human Relations and Community Studies, New York University, 1964.

Robert Dreeben and Neal Gross, *The Role Behavior of School Principals*, unpublished report, Graduate School of Education, Harvard University, August, 1965.

Robert Dreeben, *On What is Learned in School*, unpublished M.S., Harvard University, March, 1966.

Peter F. Drucker, *The Practice of Management*, 1st ed., New York: Harper, 1954.

Peter F. Drucker, *The Effective Executive*, New York: Harper, 1967.

Amitai Etzioni, *Modern Organizations*, Englewood Cliffs, N.J.: Prentice-Hall, 1964.

Estelle Fuchs, *Pickets at the Gates*, New York: Free Press, 1966.

Nathaniel L. Gage, ed., *Handbook of Research on Teaching*, Chicago: Rand-McNally, 1963.

John W. Gardner, *Self-Renewal*, 1st ed., New York: Harper, 1964.

Marilyn Gittell, *Participants and Participation*, New York: Center for Urban Education, 1967.

Marilyn Gittell, ed., *Educating an Urban Population*, Beverly Hills, Calif.: Sage Publications, 1967.

Nathan Glazer and Daniel Moynihan, *Beyond the Melting Pot*, Cambridge, Mass.: M.I.T. Press, 1963.

Paul Goodman, *People or Personnel?* New York: Random House, 1965.

Barry Gottehrer, *New York City in Crisis*, prepared by the New York *Herald Tribune* staff under the direction of Barry Gottehrer, New York: D. McKay Co., 1965.

Scott A. Greer, *The Emerging City*, New York: Free Press, 1962.

Neal Gross and Robert E. Herriott, *The Professional Leadership of Elementary School Principals*, unpublished report, Graduate School of Education, Harvard University, April, 1964.

Nat Hentoff, *The New Equality*, New York: Viking, 1964.

Nat Hentoff, *Our Children are Dying*, New York: Viking, 1966.

Nat Hentoff, "Profile on Mayor John Lindsay," *The New Yorker*, October 7 and 14, 1967.

Neil Hickey and Ed Edwin, *Adam Clayton Powell and the Politics of Race*, New York: Fleet Pub. Corp., 1965.

Walter A. Hill and Douglas M. Egan, eds., *Readings in Organization Theory: a Behavioral Approach*, Boston: Allyn & Bacon, 1966.

Edward Hollander and Marilyn Gittell, *Six Urban School Districts*, New York: Praeger, 1968.

John C. Holt, *How Children Fail*, New York: Pitman, 1964.

John C. Holt, *How Children Learn*, New York: Pitman, 1967.

Hubert H. Humphrey, ed., *Integration* vs. *Segregation*, New York: T. W. Crowell, 1964.

Ralph B. Kimbrough, *Political Power and Educational Decision-Making*, Chicago: Rand McNally, 1964.

Gordon J. Klopf and Israel A. Laster, eds., *Conference on Integration in the NYC Public Schools*, proceedings, New York Bureau of Publications, Teachers College, Columbia University, 1963.

Herbert R. Kohl, *36 Children*, New York: New American Library, 1967.

William Kornhauser, *The Politics of Mass Society*, Glencoe, Ill.: The Free Press, 1959.

Jonathan Kozol, *Death at an Early Age*, Boston: Houghton-Mifflin, 1967.

Law and Society Review, v. II, No. 1, November, 1967, issue on de facto segregation.

League for Industrial Democracy, An Anthology of Essays: *The Urban School Crisis*, United Federation of Teachers, AFL–CIO, New York, 1966.

Rensis Likert, *New Patterns of Management,* New York: McGraw-Hill, 1961.

Seymour M. Lipset, *Political Man,* 1st ed., Garden City, New York: Doubleday, 1960.

Theodore J. Lowi, *At the Pleasure of the Mayor,* New York: Free Press of Glencoe, 1964.

Joseph P. Lyford, *The Airtight Cage,* 1st ed., New York: Harper, 1966.

Raymond W. Mack, *Our Children's Burden,* New York: Random House, 1968.

Martin Mayer, *The Schools,* 1st ed., New York: Harper, 1961.

Martin Mayer, "Close to Midnight for the New York Schools," *The New York Times Magazine,* May 2, 1965.

Martin Mayer, "What's Wrong with our Big-City Schools?" *Saturday Evening Post,* September 9, 1967.

Matthew Miles, ed., *Innovation in Education,* New York: Bureau of Publications, Teachers College, Columbia University, 1964.

A. Harry Passow, ed., *Education of the Disadvantaged,* New York: Holt, 1967.

"Mini-School Districts," The Reporter's Notes, *The Reporter,* November 30, 1967, p. 8–11.

Wallace S. Sayre and Herbert Kaufman, *Governing New York City,* New York: Norton, 1965.

Peter Schrag, *Village School Downtown,* Boston: Beacon Press, 1967.

Patricia C. Sexton, *Education and Income,* New York: Viking, 1961.

Patricia C. Sexton, *The American School,* Englewood Cliffs, N.J.: Prentice-Hall, 1967.

Patricia C. Sexton, ed., *Readings on the School in Society,* Englewood, Cliffs, N.J.: Prentice-Hall, 1967.

Eleanor B. Sheldon and Raymond A. Glazier, *Pupils and Schools in New York City,* New York: Russell Sage Foundation, 1965.

Eleanor B. Sheldon, James R. Hudson, and Raymond A. Glazier, "Administrative Implications of Integration Plans for Schools: Open Enrollment in New York City," in Albert J. Reiss, Jr., ed., *Schools in a Changing Society,* New York: The Free Press, 1966.

Herbert A. Simon, Donald W. Smithburg, and Victor A. Thompson, *Public Administration,* 1st ed., New York: Knopf, 1950.

Roger Starr, *The Living End: The City and its Critics,* New York: Coward-McCann, 1966.

Svend, Ranulf, *Moral Indignation and Middle Class Psychology,* Copenhagen, 1938.

Bert E. Swanson, *Current Trends in Comparative Community Studies,* A Report on the 1961 Kansas City Conference on Community Policy-Making, Kansas City: Community Studies, 1962.

Karl E. Taeuber and Alma F. Taeuber, *Negroes in Cities,* Chicago: Aldine Pub. Co., 1965.

Victor A. Thompson, *Modern Organization,* New York: Knopf, 1965.

"Civilizing the Blackboard Jungle," Education Section, *Time Magazine,* November 15, 1963.

Richard J. Whalen, *New York: A City Destroying Itself,* New York: Morrow, 1965.

II. Journals

The Center Forum, news about the Center for Urban Education, New York.

IRCD Bulletin, a bi-monthly publication from the Eric Information Retrieval Center on the Disadvantaged, Yeshiva University, New York.

Integrated Education, published bi-monthly by Integrated Education Associates.

Learning Together, articles on integrated education, published by Integrated Education Associates.

Law and Society Review, published by Sage Publications, Inc.

Renewal Magazine, published by the Chicago City Missionary Society and the New York City Mission Society.

Saturday Review of Literature, Education issues since May, 1963.

III. Newspapers

Amsterdam News
Daily News
Long Island Star Journal
New York *Herald Tribune*
New York *Post*
New York Times
Village Voice
West Side News
World-Journal Tribune
World-Telegram

IV. Board of Education Reports

Expense Budget for the Fiscal Year 1966–1967.

Summaries and Details of Recommendations Submitted by the Superintendent of Schools, Budget Estimate for 1968–1969.

Staff Bulletin, The Public Schools of New York City.

Annual Reports of Local Boards, 1963 to present.

The Education Park: What Should it be? Educational Specifications for the Northeast Bronx Education Park, City School District of the City of New York, August 1966.

Report of Joint Planning Committee for More Effective Schools to the Superintendent of Schools, May 15, 1964.

Evaluation of the More Effective Schools Program, Summary Report, Bureau of Educational Research, September 1966.

Evaluation of the Community Zoning Program, Summary Report, Bureau of Educational Research, September 1966.

The Open Enrollment Program in the New York City Public Schools, Progress Report, September 1960 – September 1963.

Progress Report on Implementation of Recommendations Contained in the Report of the Sub-Commission on Zoning, February 24, 1959.

New Programs and Practices, A Report from the Schools, Office of Instruction and Curriculum, 1966.

Community Data Book, Brooklyn, 1967–1973 School Building Program, prepared in the Programming Section, Dr. Morris Nelson Sachs, Director, June 30, 1966.

Community Data Book, Compilations, Tabulations and Projections, Enrollment-Capacity, 1966–1967 School Building Program, Queens, prepared in the Programming Section, Dr. Morris Nelson Sachs, Director.

Community Data Book, Compilations, Tabulations and Projections, Enrollment-Capacity, 1966–1967 School Building Program, Manhattan, prepared in the Programming Section, Dr. Morris Nelson Sachs, Director.

Community Data Book, Compilations, Tabulations and Projections, Enrollment-Capacity, 1966–1967 School Building Program, The Bronx, prepared in the Programming Section, Dr. Morris Nelson Sachs, Director.

Supporting Schedules, 1963–1964 Budget, School District of the City of New York, April 25, 1963.

Toward the Integration of Our Schools, Final Report of the Commission on Integration, June 1958.

Toward Greater Opportunity, A Progress Report from the Superintendent of Schools to the Board of Education, dealing with Implementation of Recommendations of the Commission on Integration, June 1960.

Report of the Committee on Integration, Part I, Zoning, Human Relations, Teacher Personnel, February 1963.

Progress Toward Integration, September 1 – November 30, 1963 and Plans for the Immediate Future, Interim Report, December 1963.

Action Toward Quality Integrated Education, May 1964.

School Integration in New York City, 1964–1965, Questions and Answers, September 1964.

"600" Schools, Yesterday, Today and Tomorrow, Committee Study, a Report to the Superintendent of Schools, June 1964 – February 1965.

A Five-Year Crash Program for Quality Education, An Attack on Unemployment and Poverty Through Improved Educational Opportunity, October 1964.

Toward Quality Secondary Education, Recommendations on the Reorganization of the New York City High Schools, A Report to the Superintendent of Schools, December 1964.

Blueprint for Further Action Toward Quality Integrated Education, Recommendations of the Superintendent of Schools to the Board of Education, Proposals for Discussion, March 1965.

The Educational Park In New York City, Concept for Discussion, April 1965.

Implementation of Board Policy on Excellence for the City's Schools, Submitted to the Board of Education by Dr. Bernard E. Donovan, Acting Superintendent of Schools, April 1965.

Action for Excellence, Recommendations of the Superintendent of Schools to the Board of Education on Grade Level Reorganization, January 1966.

Toward Excellence in Teaching, Report to the Superintendent of Schools by the School–Community Committee for Educational Excellence, January 1966.

Programs for Potential and Actual Dropouts, for Early School Leavers for Employed, Underemployed and Unemployed Youth and Adults, Board of Education, Spring 1966.

Staffing of J.H.S. 145, A Review and Analysis, Paul Warner, Principal, December 15, 1965.

The Educational Park In New York City, Concept for Discussion, April 1965.

Decentralization Statement of Policy, March 30, 1967.

Memorandum to Members of the Board of Education from Alfred A. Giardino, March 13, 1967.

Memorandum to all Assistant Superintendents and all local school board chairmen from Alfred A. Giardino, Chairman, Committee on Local School Boards and Progress of Decentralization.

Report of Committee Recommendations from Abraham P. Tauchner, Assistant Superintendent, District 16, to Bernard E. Donovan, Superintendent of Schools.

Ethnic Distribution of Pupils in Regular Elementary and Junior High Schools, September, 1957.

Ethnic Distribution of Enrollments in New York City Public Schools, by Schools, as of October 31, 1960.

Special Census of School Population—Composition of Register, February 8, 1965.

Summary of Proposed Programs, 1967–68, Title I—Elementary and Secondary Education Act, August 30, 1967.

V. Evaluations of the Board of Education

Cresap, McCormick, and Paget, *The New York City Board of Education Organization of the School System,* unpublished management consultant study, August 1962.

Institute of Urban Studies, *Fourteen Memoranda on the Educational Complex Study Project,* Robert A. Dentler, Executive Officer, Teachers College, Columbia University.

New York City Department of Education, *Report to the Regents and the Commissioner of Education of the State of New York and to the Mayor of the City of New York,* Max J. Rubin.

Reconnection for Learning, New York City Mayor's Advisory Panel on Decentralization of the New York City Schools, 1967.

Reorganizing Secondary Education in New York City, Education Guidance and Work Committee of the Public Education Association, October 1963.

Mark Schinnerer, *A Report to the New York City Education Department,* New York, 1961.

State Education Commission Advisory Committee on Human Relations and Community Tensions, *Desegregating the Public Schools of New York City,* A Report for the Board of Education of New York City, May 12, 1964.

George Strayer and Louis Yavner, *Administrative Management of the School System of New York City,* Volumes I and II, October, 1951.

The City of New York, Board of Education: *Organization and Management of School Planning and Construction,* Report of the City Administrator, February 1959.

American Jewish Congress, *From Color Blind to Color Conscious,* A Study of Public School Integration in New York City, September 1959.

The Public Education Association, *The Status of the Public School Education of Negro and Puerto Rican Children in New York City,* October 1955.

Urban League, *A Study of the Problems of Integration in New York City Public Schools since 1955,* September 1963.

The Center for Urban Education, *Expansion of the More Effective School Program,* Evaluation of New York City Title I EDUCATIONAL projects 1966–1967, by David J. Fox, September 1967.

Daniel E. Griffiths, John S. Benben, Samuel Goldman, Laurance Iannaccone, Wayne J. McFarland, *Teacher Mobility in New York City,* A Study of the Recruitment, Selection, Appointment, and Promotion of Teachers in the New York City Public Schools, Center for School Services and Off-Campus Courses, School of Education, New York University, August 30, 1963.

Daniel E. Griffiths, Richard C. Lonsdale, Laurance Iannaccone, Samuel Goldman, *A Report of Recommendations on the Recruitment, Selection, Appointment and Promotion of Teachers in the New York City Public Schools,* Center for Field Research and School Services, New York University, 1966.

VI. City, Federal Studies

U.S. Commission on Civil Rights, *Equal Educational Opportunity in America's Cities: Problems and Programs for Change,* A National Conference sponsored by the U.S. Commission on Civil Rights, November 16–18, 1967.

The Corde Corporation, *The Education Park,* Report to the School District of Philadelphia, January 1967.

The Corde Corporation, *A Report on the Education Park,* 1967.

Rogers, Talioferre, Kostritsky, Lamb, *Linear City and Cross Brooklyn Expressway,* Baltimore, Md., September 13, 1967.

Alpern, Robert, *Pratt Guide,* A Citizens' Handbook of Housing, Planning and Urban Renewal Procedures in New York City, Community Education Program, Pratt Institute, Brooklyn, New York, 1965.

City Planning Commission, *Staten Island Development,* Policies, Programs and Priorities, Comprehensive Planning Report, New York City, June 1966.

Temporary Commission on City Finances, *Toward Fiscal Strength,* Second Interim Report, November 1965.

Temporary Commission on City Finances, *Blueprint for Fiscal Improvement,* Third Report, June 1966.

Temporary Commission on City Finances, *Better Financing for New York City,* Final Report, August 1968.

Equality of Educational Opportunity, Office of Education, Washington, D.C., 1966 (Coleman Report).

VII. City Agencies

CITY COMMISSION ON HUMAN RIGHTS OF NEW YORK CITY

Statement by Stanley H. Lowell at the end of the meeting between the Board of Education and the Civil Rights Groups, August 27, 1963.

Agreement Reached by Representatives of the Board of Education and the City-Wide Committee for Integrated Schools at meeting at City, September 5, 1963.

An Analysis of the Interim Report on School Integration Issued by the NYC Board of Education, September 1963, as compared with the Recommendations in Commission on Human Rights Policy Statement on School Integration issued July 1963, December 16, 1963.

Memorandum to all city agencies and to all interested civil rights groups, September 13, 1963.

A Tale of Two Boroughs, A School Integration Success Story, September 1961.

"Can New York Integrate its Public Schools?" by Stanley H. Lowell, *American Unity,* published by the Council for American Unity, January-February 1961.

Statement on Selection of School Sites and Establishment of School Zones adopted by the Commission on April 25, 1963.

Policy Statement on School Integration Adopted at Commission Meeting, July 25, 1963.

A Chronology of Some Important Events Concerning Progress Toward School Integration During Recent Months, January 9, 1964.

CITY PLANNING COMMISSION

1966–1967 Draft Capital Budget and Capital Improvement Plan for Ensuing Five Fiscal Years, January 3, 1966.

VIII. Interest Groups Publications

AMERICAN JEWISH COMMITTEE

The Elimination of De Facto Segregation in the Public Schools of New York City:—Principles and Practice, by Israel A. Laster, Associate Director, July 1961.

Elements of the New York Chapter Experience with School Integration in New York City, by Israel A. Laster, August 1962.

News, January 1965.

News, March 1965.

Testimony of New York Chapter American Jewish Committee at New York City Board of Education Integration Hearing, April 1965.

Testimony on Behalf of the New York Chapter of the American Jewish Committee—Presented at Board of Estimate Hearing on Disposition of Flatlands Development Site, September 1965.

The Application of Federal Aid to the Educational Park, Prepared by Irving Levine, Director of Community Relations, New York Area Office for distribution at the New York Conference on the

Educational Park held at Brotherhood in Action, November 30, 1965.

AMERICAN JEWISH CONGRESS

Analysis of the pamphlet, "The Psychiatric Aspects of School Desegregation," published by the Group for the Advancement of Psychiatry, 1957, prepared by Naomi Levine, director of the Program Department, American Jewish Congress, May 1963.

Speech, "Integration in the Public Schools of New York City," by Naomi Levine, Associate Executive Director, American Jewish Congress, September 1964.

Article, Memorandum from Program Department, by Mary Flynn, from *The Reporter Dispatch,* White Plains, New York, Monday, October 19, 1964.

Resolution by the Metropolitan Council, American Jewish Congress on the "Blueprint for Further Action Toward Quality Integrated Education," Recommendations of the Superintendent of Schools to the Board of Education dated March 5, 1965.

Statistics on Racial Composition of Elementary and Junior High Schools Involved in Transfer of 14,700 6th graders to Junior High Schools, Memorandum from American Jewish Congress, March 10, 1965.

Agenda, Executive Committee Meeting, Metropolitan Council, September 29, 1965.

Draft Statement on Use of Classrooms at the Roosevelt Jewish Center for Public School Purposes, October 13, 1965.

Agenda, Metropolitan Council Meeting, Chairman, Murray A. Gordon, October 13, 1965.

Joint Program Plan for Jewish Community Relations, National Community Relations Advisory Council, 1965–66.

News Release on decentralization, February 20, 1968.

CITIZENS' COMMITTEE FOR CHILDREN

Letter to Assistant Superintendent Francis A. Turner, Chairman, Committee on Integration, New York City Public Schools, from Mrs. Trude Lash, Executive Director, Citizens' Committee for Children, April 10, 1963.

Statement by Trude Lash, Executive Director of Citizens' Committee for Children, on the Superintendent's Interim Report on Progress Towards Integration, January 13, 1964.

Letter to Dr. Calvin E. Gross, Superintendent of Schools, Board of Education, from Mrs. Melvin Harburger, Vice-Chairman, Education

Section, Mrs. Trude Lash, Executive Director, Citizens' Committee for Children, June 16, 1964.

Letter to the Editor, *New York Times,* from Mark A. McCloskey, Charlotte E. Winsor, Algernon D. Black, Rose Goldman, July 14, 1964.

Letter to Dr. Calvin E. Gross, Superintendent of Schools, New York City Board of Education, from Mrs. Trude Lash, October 15, 1964. 20th Anniversary Report, 1944–1964.

Statement of Mrs. Nathan W. Levin, Chairman of the Educational Services Section before the Sub-Committee on the Elementary and Secondary Education Act of the Education and Labor Committee of the House of Representatives, March 18, 1967.

Report on School Suspensions, April 5, 1967.

A Brief History of the Intensive Teacher Training Program, April 10, 1967.

"A New State Constitution can mean a Brighter Future for New York's Children," recommendations to the 1967 State Constitutional Convention, May 24, 1967.

Letter to Mrs. Shelly Umans, Director, Title III Office, February 12, 1968.

Letter of resignation from Mrs. Trude Lash to Edwin Greenidge, Chairman, Council Against Poverty, February 8, 1968.

Tentative Evaluations, Title I Programs for School Year, 1966–67, Marge Benjamin, June 26, 1967.

COMMONWEALTH OF PUERTO RICO

"School Integration: A Puerto Rican View," an address before the Conference on Integration in New York City Public Schools at Teachers College, Columbia University, by Joseph Monserrat, Director, Department of Labor, Migration Division, Commonwealth of Puerto Rico, May 1, 1963.

EQUAL

Brief Description of Activities in Local Communities, April 23, 1964. A Report on the meetings with the Board of Education, an open letter from Ellen Lurie, Chairman, *EQUAL Newsletter,* July 1964.

School Integration—Rumor vs. Fact Sheet, September 1964.

Letter to Dr. Calvin E. Gross, Superintendent of Schools, New York City, from Emily Delbaum, re Paired Schools, P.S. 148, Jackson Heights, N.Y., and P.S. 127, E. Elmhurst, New York.

Report to the Community by Civil Rights and Other Groups on the Current Status of their discussions with the Board of Education concerning school integration, October 13, 1964.

Report on meetings with Dr. Calvin Gross, November 23, 1964.

School Integration and the Board of Education, Report II from Ellen Lurie, *EQUAL Newsletter,* December 1964.

"The Community and the UFT," by Rosalie Stutz, *EQUAL Newsletter,* July 1967.

Research for Action, Bulletin No. 2, February 15, 1967.

Research for Action, Bulletin No. 1, December 10, 1966.

Letter to Emanuel W. Klein, president, Parents' Association of Stuyvesant High School, from Rosalie Stutz, January 2, 1966.

Statement by Warren Lyons, age 15, relating to what he calls a "Jim-Crow" type graduation ceremony, July 11, 1966.

Release, October 27, 1966.

Board of Education Hearing on Title I Proposals, November 14, 1966.

Release, November 15, 1966.

Recommendations for Use of Federal Education Funds, December 10, 1966.

"Decentralization of the New York City Public Schools," *EQUAL Newsletter,* February 1967.

Statement to Board of Education on Decentralization, March 7, 1967.

Statement Prepared for Educational Park Hearing, Board of Education, June 16, 1965.

Statement on EQUAL's Position Concerning the Allen Report and the School Shutdown, January 28, 1965.

What are the Essential Ingredients of a Good Desegregation Plan? February 4, 1965.

School Integration and the Board of Education, Report III from Ellen Lurie, March 1965.

Statement to Board of Education Hearing April 14, 1965.

Release, EQUAL Terms Board of Education Implementation of Integration Policy "A Colossal Hoax," April 29, 1965.

Statement by Stanley Leyden, submitted to Local School Board, Districts 25–27 on May 4, 1965.

Proposed EQUAL's Statement of Policy, May 27, 1965.

Ballot and Nominating Committee Slate for Members-at-Large of Steering Committee, May 27, 1965.

Statement Prepared for: Educational Park Hearing, Board of Education, June 16, 1965.

An Open Letter to Friends and Members of EQUAL from Ellen Lurie, Chairman, October 1965.

Statement before the City Planning Commission Capital Budget Hearing, by Ellen Lurie, Chairman, December 13, 1965.

Summary of Major Recommendations of Committees on School Reorganization and Some Initial Reactions from EQUAL, January 1966. Letter from Ellen Lurie, January 26, 1966.

Summary of Remarks on Proposed Capital Budget 1966–1967 Joint Public Hearing of Board of Estimate and City Council, presented by Ellen Lurie, Chairman, February 17, 1965.

Our Analysis of "Action for Excellence," February 24, 1966.

Report on 1966 Summer Reading Program, by West Side EQUAL, Reading Reform Foundation, Hudson Neighborhood Conservation, Summer 1966.

Statement to Board of Education, Mrs. Rosalie Stutz, Chairman, September 19, 1966.

EQUAL Newsletter, September 1966.

Release, October 27, 1966.

Recommendations for Use of Federal Education Funds, December 10, 1966.

Summary and Analysis of Evaluations of New York City Board of Education Title I Programs, 1965–66 as conducted by the Center for Urban Education and as extracted and edited by EQUAL's research committee, Bulletin No. 1, *Research for Action,* December 10, 1966.

HARLEM PARENTS COMMITTEE

Views, Monthly publication, May 1965 to present.

Suggested Planks for a Community Platform on Political Action.

Memorial to U.S. Commission of Education, October 21, 1965.

The Education of Minority Group Children in the New York City Public Schools, 1965 (The Black Paper).

JUNIOR HIGH SCHOOL PRINCIPALS' ASSOCIATION

A Proposal for Integrating the Junior High Schools, Memorandum to the Board of Education, the Superintendent of Schools, *et al.,* from James G. Murray, President, March 1965.

NAACP

Statement of the National Association for the Advancement of Colored People, 13 New York City Branches, before the Board of Education of the City of New York, prepared by Frederick Jones, New York City Branch Representative and State Education Chairman, and June Shagaloff, Special Assistant for Education, National NAACP.

Report for 1964, NAACP Legal Defense and Educational Fund.

NAACP and CORE statement to the New York City Board of Education and Superintendent of Schools on Commissioner Allen's Report, May 28, 1964.

NAACP 55th Annual Convention Resolutions, June 22–27, 1964. Press release, June 15, 1964.

NAACP statement on the School Desegregation Proposals, March 9, 1965.

PUBLIC EDUCATION ASSOCIATION

Reorganizing Secondary Education in New York City, Committee on Education, Guidance and Work, October 1963.

Integration in the Public Schools of New York City, *Special Report Card,* February 1964.

Desegregating the Public Schools of New York City, Report Card, June 1964.

Statement of Organizations Attending Meeting of PEA Coordinating Committee on Integration and School Improvement for 1964–65, September 2, 1964.

The Conference on Quality Integrated Education, Draft Critique of Dr. Bernard Donovan's "Action for Excellence," April 1965.

70th Annual Report, 1965.

Four-Year High School Committee's Report, January 17, 1966.

Toward Excellence in Teaching, Summary prepared by the PEA, Feb. 28, 1966.

Follow-up Memo to members of the Coordinating Committee from Mrs. Adele B. Tunick, October 13, 1966.

High Schools for a Changing World, Committee on Education, Guidance and Work, February 1, 1967.

Statement of the Public Education Association on the Decentralization of Authority and Responsibility in the New York City School System, presented by J. Lawrence Peel, Vice-President, March 8, 1967.

UNITED PARENTS ASSOCIATIONS

Parent Action in School Integration, by Gladys Meyer, 1961.

Statement by Harold Siegel, Executive Director, United Parents Associations, at the public hearing in relation to selection of Members of the Board of Education, the Association of the Bar of the City of New York, December 2, 1964.

Statement by Harold Siegel, Executive Director of the UPA, on Educational Parks, June 16, 1965.

News Release, Florence Flast, President, October 13, 1965.

UPA statement on the Intermediate School, December 6, 1965.

Statement by Mrs. Florence Flast, President of the UPA, on the Superintendent's Proposals for Reorganization at the Board of Education Hearing on March 11, 1966.

Statement by Mrs. Beatrice D. Steinberg, Vice-President of the UPA, at the Capital Budget Hearing, City Planning Commission, City Hall, on December 13, 1965.

Statement by Mrs. Florence Flast, President of UPA at Expense Budget Hearing at Board of Education, December 21, 1965.

United Parents Associations' Policy on Decentralization, January 8, 1968.

News Release, January 14, 1968.

School Parent, September 1963 to present.

"Report of Visitation to Transferred 6th and 9th Grades, February, 1965."

Letter to Harold Howe, Commissioner of Education, Washington, D.C. from Florence Flast, President UPA, May 27, 1966.

Statement by Mrs. Florence Flast, President of UPA, before the Senate Standing Committee on City of New York, in Regard to Proposed Structure and Organization for School Decentralization, Feb. 14, 1968.

U.P.A. *Study of Supply Procedures in the Public Schools,* February 5, 1968.

MILTON GALAMISON

Proposal on Decentralization, submitted to Dr. Sol Gordon and Dr. Harry Gottesfeld of Yeshiva University, June 13, 1967.

UNITED BRONX PARENTS

Catalogue of Training Materials, prepared by Parent Leadership Training Program, United Bronx Parents, September 1967.

WOMEN'S CITY CLUB OF NEW YORK

"Statement of Women's City Club on Comprehensive High Schools Before the Board of Education Hearing," Mrs. Alexander A. Katz, Chairman, Education Committee, May 24, 1967.
Strengthen or Abolish?, 1960
Performance and Promise, 1966

CITIZENS FOR A BETTER SOCIETY

Open letter to the Board of Education, April 14, 1965.

DR. MAX WOLFF

Statement before the Board of Education, A Discussion of the Concept of the Educational Park and the Specific Suggestions made by the Acting Superintendent of Schools, June 16, 1965.
The Educational Park, A Decisive Step Toward Improved Public Education.
Educational Park Development in the United States, 1967, A Survey of Current Development Plans, The Center for Urban Education, August 1967.

UNITED FEDERATION OF TEACHERS

UFT Statement on Decentralization, Prepared by Albert Shanker, President, based on Policy Established by UFT Executive Board.
Critique of the Bundy Report, UFT Proposals, Need for More Funds, United Action, November 1967.

ASSOCIATION OF ASSISTANT PRINCIPALS

Recommendations for a Reorganization of the New York City School System, 1968.

NEW YORK CITY PEOPLE'S BOARD OF EDUCATION

Publications, People's Board.
Analysis of the Proposed 1967–1968 Executive Budget as it Pertains to Public Education, *1967*.

ARCHDIOCESE OF NEW YORK

"Report of the Superintendent of Schools," 1965–1966.
"Catholic Schools are Integrated," statement of the Right Reverend Monsignor George A. Kelly, Secretary for Education, Archdiocese of New York, Public Meeting, Board of Education, August 17, 1966.
Statistics for all Elementary and Secondary Schools, Archdiocese of New York, October 1966.

Survey, conducted by the New York Archdiocesan Superintendent of Schools, February 1967.

Bulletin of the Superintendent of Schools, June 1967.

Report of the Superintendent of Schools, 1967–1968.

THE MAYOR

Memorandum: Background and Summary of New York City School Decentralization Plan, February 26, 1968.

Letter to Nelson A. Rockefeller, Governor, and Members of the State Legislature, and Members of the Board of Regents, from John V. Lindsay, January 2, 1968.

Statement by David S. Seeley, Director of the Mayor's Office of Education Liaison in Hearings on the structure of Proposed Decentralization School System held on February 21, 1968 before Committee of the Senate and Assembly of New York State.

Analysis of Proposed Legislation for the Decentralization of the New York City School System.

Proposed Legislation for the Decentralization of the New York City School, Recommendations of the Bundy Panel as modified by the Mayor in his proposals of January 2, 1968.

IX. Interviews

Roughly 1,100 over the period from July 1964 through March 1968. Interest-group leaders, parents, board officials, city, state, and federal officials.

NEGOTIATING TEAM FOR PARENTS OF I.S. 201

Sequence of Events Surrounding I.S. 201, September 24, 1966.

BOYCOTT COMMITTEE

History of P.S. 36–125 Controversy.

Source Notes

Introduction

1. George Strayer and Louis Yavner, *Administrative Management of the School System of New York City*, October 1951, v. I, II.

2. See Chester Barnard, *The Functions of the Executive*, Cambridge: Harvard, 1938; Herbert A. Simon, *Administrative Behavior*, New York: MacMillan, 1947; and Max Weber, *The Theory of Social and Economic Organization*, tr. A. M. Henderson and Talcott Parsons, New York: Oxford, 1947, pp. 324–41.

3. Herbert A. Simon, Donald W. Smithburg, and Victor A. Thompson, *Public Administration*, New York: Knopf, 1950, pp. 58–64.

4. The New York *Post*, November 18, 1967.

5. Public statement by Superintendent Donovan in 1967.

6. Kenneth Clark makes this point in his unpublished paper, "Alternative Public School Systems: A Response to America's Educational Emergency," prepared for the National Conference on Equal Educational Opportunity in America's Cities, sponsored by the U.S. Commission on Civil Rights, Washington, D.C., November 16–18, 1967.

7. For a similar point of view, see Edward Hollander and Marilyn Gittell, *Six Urban School Districts*, New York: Praeger, 1968.

8. Amitai Etzioni, *Modern Organization*, New York: Prentice-Hall, 1964.

9. Norton Long, "The Local Community as an Ecology of Games," *American Journal of Sociology*, v. 64, no. 3, 1958, pp. 251–61.

10. William Kornhauser, *The Politics of Mass Society*, Glencoe, Ill.: The Free Press, 1959.

11. U.S. Civil Rights Commission Report, *Racial Isolation in the Public Schools*, 1967; U.S. Office of Education Report, *Equality of*

Educational Opportunity, 1966; and several papers given at the U.S. Civil Rights Commission conference on cities, November 16–18, 1967. See especially, *How Evanston, Illinois, Integrated* ALL *of its Schools,* prepared by Gregory C. Coffin, Superintendent of Schools, Evanston, Illinois, and *School Desegregation in Berkeley: The School Superintendent Reports,* prepared by Neil V. Sullivan, Ed.D., Superintendent of Schools, Berkeley, California.

12. Richard J. Whalen, *A City Destroying Itself,* New York: Morrow, 1965; and Barry Gottehrer, *New York City in Crisis,* prepared by the New York *Herald Tribune* staff under the direction of Barry Gottehrer, New York: D. McKay, 1965.

13. Max Weber, *The Methodology of the Social Sciences,* tr. and ed. Edward A. Shils and Henry A. Finch, Glencoe, Ill.: The Free Press, 1949; and Alvin W. Gouldner, "Anti Minotaur: The Myth of a Value-Free Sociology," in Irving Louis Horowitz, ed., *The New Sociology,* New York: Oxford, 1965, pp. 196–218.

I   *The Failure of Desegregation . . .*

1. *Toward the Integration of Our Schools,* Final Report of the Commission on Integration, Board of Education of the City of New York, 1958, p. 25.

2. The board's many reports on desegregation include the abovementioned and *Toward Greater Opportunity,* A Progress Report from the Superintendent of Schools to the Board of Education, June, 1960; *Report of the Committee on Integration,* Part I, February 15, 1963; *Progress Toward Integration,* Interim Report, December, 1963; *Action Toward Quality Integrated Education,* May 28, 1964; *School Integration in New York City, 1964–1965, Questions and Answers,* September, 1964; *Blueprint for Further Action toward Quality Integrated Education,* Recommendations of the Superintendent of Schools to the Board of Education, March 5, 1965; *Implementation of Board Policy on Excellence for The City's Schools,* April 28, 1965; *The Educational Park in New York City, Concept for Discussion,* April, 1965; *Action for Excellence,* January 18, 1966.

3. *Ethnic Distribution of Pupils in the Public Schools of New York City,* the Central Zoning Unit of the Board of Education, March 24, 1965, and June 15, 1966.

4. *Improving Ethnic Distribution of New York City Pupils,* Jacob Landers, Assistant Superintendent, Office of Integration, May, 1966.

5. *Desegregating the Public Schools of New York City,* A Report for the Board of Education of New York City by the State Education Commission Advisory Committee on Human Relations and Community Tensions, May 12, 1964, p. 3.

6. *Study of the Effect of the 1964–1970 School Building Program*

on Segregation in New York City's Public Schools, unpublished study, the City Commission on Human Rights of New York, March 26, 1964, and further analyses by the authors.

7. *Desegregating the Public Schools of New York City, op. cit.,* p. 6.

8. *The Status of The Public School Education of Negro and Puerto Rican Children in New York City,* Presented to: The Board of Education Commission on Integration, Public Education Association, assisted by the New York University Research Center for Human Relations, October, 1955.

9. *Toward the Integration of Our Schools, op. cit.*

10. Irving Goldaber, *The Treatment by the New York City Board of Education of Problems Affecting the Negro 1954–1963* (unpublished Ph.D. dissertation, New York University, 1964).

11. *Daily News,* December 24, 1957.

12. *Daily News,* December 24, 1957.

13. Interviews with NAACP and Parents Workshop officials.

14. Interviews with civil rights leaders.

15. Interviews with NAACP and Parents Workshop officials.

16. *The Amsterdam News,* December 20, 1958.

17. *New York Times,* September 15, 1959.

18. Interviews with civil rights leaders and school officials.

19. Interviews with civil rights leaders and school officials.

20. *New York Times,* July 7, 1960.

21. Interviews and Goldaber, *op. cit.,* pp. 194–199.

22. Allen edict, *New York Times,* June 19, 1963.

23. Interviews with civil rights leaders.

24. *New York Times,* December 11, 1963.

25. *New York Times,* February 10 and 14, 1964.

26. *New York Times,* February 8, 1964. The American Jewish Congress position on pairings was announced in the *New York Times,* December 25, 1963.

27. *New York Times,* February 14, 1964.

28. *New York Times,* March 17, 1964.

29. *New York Times,* May 29, 1964.

30. Interviews with civil rights leaders and attendance at their meetings.

31. *New York Times,* January 29, 1965.

32. *Amsterdam News,* April 17, 1965.

33. *New York Times,* April 24, 1965.

34. Interviews with civil rights leaders and observation at their meetings.

35. Dorothy S. Jones, "The Issues at I.S. 201: A View from the

Parents' Committee," *Integrated Education,* v. IV, No. 5, October–November, 1966, pp. 18–27.

36. *New York Times,* December 20, 1966.

37. Jacob Landers, *Improving Ethnic Distribution of New York City Pupils,* City School District of the City of New York, May, 1966, p. 28.

38. *Ibid.,* p. 34.

39. *Policy Decisions on Comprehensive High Schools,* Board of Education of the City of New York, November 29, 1967.

40. *An Evaluation of the Transitional Middle School in New York City,* Center for Urban Education, August 31, 1966.

41. Interviews with civil rights leaders and school officials.

II *Demographic and Housing Patterns*

1. Data from the board's census on the *Ethnic Distribution of Pupils in the Public Schools of New York City* (March 24, 1965), cited from the Department of City Planning Newsletter, October, 1962, and based on the 1960 *Census of Population.* The 1964 data are from the *New York City Population Health Survey,* Population Characteristics, 1964, New York City Department of Health, April, 1966.

2. *New York City Population Health Survey, op. cit.,* Table I.

3. Seymour Sudman and Norman Bradburn, *Social Psychological Factors in Inter-Group Housing*—Results of a Pilot Test, National Opinion Research Center, May, 1966, p. 10.

4. *New York City Population Health Survey, op. cit.,* Table III.

5. *Ibid.,* Tables V and VI.

6. Data for 1950 and 1960 are from the Census of Population; 1964 data from the *New York City Population Health Survey, op. cit.,* Table I.

7. *Census of Population, op. cit.*

8. *World Journal Tribune,* November 9, 1966, p. 26.

9. From testimony of Staten Island parents and politicians at Board of Estimate and City Planning Commission hearings, 1964 and 1965.

10. From same testimony.

11. *New York City Population Health Survey, op. cit.,* p. 1.

12. From interviews, observation, and Community Data Book, School Planning and Research Division, New York City Board of Education, Queens, 1967–1973, School Building Program, June 30, 1966.

13. Testimony of Randolph Rankin, Jamaica NAACP, at City Planning Commission Hearing, December 13, 1965.

14. *Census of Population.* Since there are no religious data in the census, this judgment about the majority of new whites in Queens during the 1950's is partly impressionistic, and based in part on the substantial increase of whites from German and East European origins during these years.

15. *New York City Population Health Survey, op. cit.,* Table I.

16. From the *Special Census of School Population,* Board of Education of the City of New York, October 31, 1967, p. 5.

17. Interview with white civic leader in Queens.

18. Interviews with several Rochdale residents, and Harvey Swados, "When Black and White Live Together," The *New York Times Magazine,* November 13, 1966, pp. 47 ff.

19. Interviews in Rochdale.

20. Interviews with integrationist leaders.

21. *New York Times,* February 13, 1968.

22. The City Commission on Human Rights of New York, unpublished *Report on Background Material for Commissioners on School Construction Programs,* January 1, 1965. Material was compiled by the City Planning Commission.

23. *New York City Population Health Survey, op. cit.,* Table I.

24. *Special Census of School Population, op. cit.,* p. 5.

25. *Census of Population, op. cit.*

26. These materials come from interviews with civil rights leaders and parent groups.

27. Interviews.

28. City Commission on Human Rights, Background Material, *op. cit.*

29. *Special Census of School Population, op. cit.,* p. 5.

30. *New York City Population Health Survey, op. cit.,* Table I.

31. *Special Census of School Population, op. cit.,* p. 5.

32. *West Side News,* February 15, 1968.

33. *Community Data Book,* School Planning and Research Division, New York City Board of Education, Manhattan, 1967–1973, School Building Program.

34. Data obtained from the Chancery, New York City.

35. These are rough estimates, developed by the research department of the Protestant Council.

36. These judgments were made on the basis of interviews with five top Catholic school officials and a review of parochial school data that they and the Board of Education's Bureau of Attendance generously provided.

37. Interview with an official from the Catholic Inter-Racial Council.

38. Interview with a Bronx developer.

III   *The Neighborhood School Movement*

1. See Allan Blackman, "Planning and The Neighborhood School," *Integrated Education*, August–September, 1964, pp. 49–56, for a general discussion of the neighborhood school concept.

2. *Ibid.;* also Max Wolff, John H. Fischer, "Educational Parks," in the U.S. Civil Rights Commission Report, *Racial Isolation in the Schools*, 1967; and the U.S. Civil Rights Commission's *Educational Parks*, 1967, The Educational Park in New York City, Board of Education of the City of New York, April, 1965.

3. See the report prepared for the City Commission on Human Rights of New York, *Study of the Effect of the 1964–1970 School Building Program on Segregation in New York City's Public Schools*, March 26, 1964, unpublished. The main findings of this study were released to the press and never refuted by the board. They documented in detail the board's continued building of segregated schools.

4. *Desegregating The Public Schools of New York City*, a report prepared for the Board of Education of the City of New York, by the State Education Commissioner's Advisory Committee on Human Relations and Community Tensions, May 12, 1964, p. 28.

5. *Implementation of Board Policy on Excellence for The City's Schools*, submitted to the Board of Education by Dr. Bernard E. Donovan, Acting Superintendent of Schools, April 28, 1965, p. 7.

6. Interview with headquarters official.

7. Interviews with board members.

8. See Seymour Sudman and Norman Bradburn, *op. cit.*

9. *New York Times*, May 6, 1960, and September 3, 1964.

10. Interviews with civil rights leaders and school officials.

11. Interviews.

12. PS 145 in Manhattan was one such case, as written up in the *West Side News*, November 26, 1964.

13. *New York Times*, June 2, 1959; and September 13, 1959.

14. *Ibid.*

15. *New York Times*, September 15, 1959.

16. Order from State Education Commissioner James E. Allen, *New York Times*, June 19, 1963.

17. *New York Times*, October 22, 1963.

18. Board of Education policy statement of June 14, 1963.

19. *New York Herald Tribune*, September 11, 1963.

20. Interviews with local civil rights and neighborhood school leaders.

21. Interviews with PAT and civil rights leaders.

22. *New York Times*, September 9, 1964.

23. *Long Island Daily Press*, September 30, 1963.

24. *New York Times,* September 2, 1964.

25. *New York Times,* September 10, 1964.

26. Interviews with neighborhood school leaders and parent association spokesmen.

27. Interviews.

28. *Long Island Star Journal,* October 24, 1964.

29. See Kurt and Gladys Lang, "Resistance to School Desegregation Among Jews," in *Sociological Inquiry,* Winter, 1965, pp. 94–123; and David Rogers and Bert Swanson, "White Citizen Response to the Same Integration Plan: Comparisons of Local School Districts in a Northern City," *Sociological Inquiry,* Winter, 1965, Vol. 35, No. 1. This section is a revised version of the Rogers and Swanson article.

30. Interviews with residents in the area.

31. Rogers and Swanson, *op. cit.,* p. 111.

32. *Ibid.,* p. 112.

33. This outlook is commonly associated with high F (authoritarian) personalities, as first spelled out in detail in Theodore W. Adorno, *et al., The Authoritarian Personality,* New York: Harper, 1950, pp. 224–41; Seymour M. Lipset describes this outlook among working classes in his *Political Man,* Garden City, New York: Doubleday, 1960, chapt. 4. See also Daniel Bell, ed., *The Radical Right,* Garden City, New York: Doubleday, 1963, chapt. 3, 4, 13, and 14, for analysis of middle class politics that proved helpful for the one in this book.

34. Daniel Bell, ed., *Ibid.* Especially pp. 69–77 and 260–64.

35. Interview with a West Side Reform Democrat official.

36. These data on the civilian review board vote, by election district, are from the *World Journal Tribune,* November 9, 1966. Dr. Marilyn Gittell of Queens College and the City University of New York very kindly made available data she had compiled on the ethnic characteristics of residents in the election districts.

37. Observation at this meeting and interviews with CORE officials.

38. William Kornhauser, *The Politics of Mass Society,* Glencoe, Ill.: The Free Press, 1959, chapts. 1–4.

39. See Clark Kerr and Abraham Siegel, "The Interindustry Propensity to Strike," in Arthur Kornhauser, Robert Dubin, and Arthur Ross, editors, *Industrial Conflict,* New York: McGraw-Hill, 1954, pp. 191–203, for a discussion of the relation between the absence of intermediate social structures and extremist politics among miners, longshoremen, sailors and loggers.

40. See Scott Greer, "Individual Participation in Mass Society," in

Roland Young, ed., *Approaches to the Study of Politics,* Evanston, Ill.: Northwestern, 1958, pp. 329–43.

41. Karl Mannheim, *Man and Society in an Age of Reconstruction,* London: Kegan Paul, 1940; and Ortega y Gasset, *The Revolt of the Masses,* New York: W.W. Norton, 1932.

42. James Coleman, *Community Conflict,* Glencoe, Ill.: The Free Press, 1957, pp. 15–16.

43. Kornhauser, *op. cit.,* p. 61.

44. See Seymour M. Lipset, Paul F. Lazarsfeld, Allen H. Barton and Juan Linz, "The Psychology of Voting: An Analysis of Political Behavior," in Gardner Lindzey, ed., *Handbook of Social Psychology,* Boston: Addison Wesley, 1954, v. II, pp. 1140–43; and Lipset's *Political Man, op. cit.,* chapt. 7.

45. A summary of the effects of ecological factors on the formation of groups is in George Homans and Henry Riecken, "Psychological Aspects of Social Structure," in Lindzey's *Handbook, op. cit.,* pp. 801–805.

46. New York *Post,* August 11, 1965.

47. Interviews.

48. *New York Times,* September 6, 1964.

49. *New York Times,* September 9, 1964.

50. New York *Post,* August 11, 1965.

51. Attendance at that hearing, and at many others where PAT protesters appeared.

52. *New York Times,* March 13, 1964.

53. New York *Herald Tribune,* September 13, 1964.

54. Interview with PAT leader.

55. Canarsie in Southeast Brooklyn is an example.

56. Interview with PAT leader.

57. Interviews with white parents.

IV *Civil Rights Organizations*

1. Speech by a civil rights leader at a meeting of civil rights organizations.

2. Interviews and attendance at meetings.

3. Numerous summaries have been made of that case and its implications. See Dorothy Jones, "The Issues at I.S. 201: A View From the Parents' Committee," *Integrated Education,* v. IV, No. 5, October–November, 1966, pp. 18–27; and Gertrude Goldberg, Yeshiva University, *IRCD Bulletin,* Winter, 1966–1967.

4. *New York Times,* December 21 and 22, 1966.

5. Interviews with Parents Workshop and NAACP officials.

6. Interviews with these officials.

7. Interviews with Harlem Parents Committee officials. See also its monthly publication, *Views,* for a compendium of "horror stories" on ghetto schools.

8. Harlem Parents Committee, *Harlem Black Paper,* 1965.

9. Interviews with civil rights leaders.

10. Interviews with CORE and NAACP officials.

11. Interviews with civil rights officials.

12. *New York Times,* December 10, 1963.

13. Interviews.

14. *New York Times,* March 9, 1965.

15. Interview with NAACP official.

16. Interviews with Urban League officials.

17. Interviews with Urban League officials.

18. Interviews with Urban League officials.

19. Interviews with CORE branch officials.

20. Interviews with civil rights leaders.

21. Attendance at meetings of Harlem CORE.

22. *New York Times,* September 4, 1963.

23. Interviews with civil rights leaders. New York *World Telegram,* March 30, 1964.

24. Interviews with civil rights leaders.

25. Interviews with civil rights leaders. See also the *New York Times,* February 12, 1964.

26. Interview with civil rights leaders.

27. Interviews and *New York Times,* February 15 and 27, 1964.

28. *New York Times,* March 30, 1964, and interviews.

29. See footnote four in Chapter Three on the report. Allen Report.

30. Interviews with civil rights leaders.

31. Interviews.

32. *New York Times,* June 16, 1964.

33. Interviews and attendance at civil rights meetings.

34. Interviews. See also the *New York Times,* July 31, 1964, and August 3, 1964.

35. Interviews and the *New York Times,* January 1, 1965.

36. This assessment of the politics of the situation is shared by some civil rights leaders negotiating with Gross.

37. Interview with civil rights leader.

38. *New York Times,* November 14, 1964; and January 29, 1965.

39. Attendance at meetings, and *New York Times,* November 24, 1964.

40. This section is based primarily on interviews with top Puerto Rican leaders. See also the *New York Times,* for a report on

Negro–Puerto Rican conflicts in 1967, especially June 20, July 13, and October 6, 1967.

41. Interview with Puerto Rican leader.

42. Interview with Puerto Rican leader.

43. Interview with Puerto Rican leader.

44. Interview with East Harlem leaders.

45. Interview with civil rights leader.

46. Interview with civil rights leader. We interviewed those civil rights leaders whom at least one board member wanted to use to split the national office leaders from local leaders.

47. Interview with civil rights leader.

48. Interview with civil rights leader.

49. Interview with civil rights leader.

50. Interview with civil rights leader.

51. Interview with civil rights leader.

52. Interview with civil rights leader.

53. *New York Post,* January 18, 1967. The school page of the *World Journal Tribune* had many stories of such union–parent, joint protests from November through the winter months. This partnership, initiated by top union officials who were afraid of losing parent support, dissolved in the spring, after teachers started to demand the right to remove "disruptive children" from classrooms.

54. Interviews with Irving Levine. American Jewish Committee pamphlets.

V   *The White Liberals*

1. Kenneth B. Clark's views are expressed in his book, *Dark Ghetto,* New York: Harper, 1965, pp. 228–34. Clark's comments pertain mainly to the ambivalence of white liberals on civil rights issues.

2. Interviews with members of the committee. Also analysis of its minutes.

3. Interviews and pamphlet prepared by the American Jewish Committee, *What Parents Should Know About The Basic Values of School Integration,* etc., published by the Urban League of Greater New York, and New York chapter of the American Jewish Committee.

4. Kenneth B. Clark, *Dark Ghetto, op. cit.,* chapt. 6.

5. Interviews with members of the committee.

6. From the minutes of meetings.

7. Interviews.

8. Attendance at conference meetings. I attended almost every

meeting of the conference from March, 1964, until it disbanded in 1966.

9. Attendance and interviews with those attending.

10. Attendance and interviews.

11. Interviews.

12. Interviews with Jewish and Catholic officials. Since the Board of Education does not take a religious census of students, one can make only gross judgments on this question.

13. Interviews with Jewish leaders in New York City.

14. Interview with Jewish leader.

15. *Analysis of the Board of Education's January 29, 1964, Plan to Integrate the New York City Public Schools, and Additional Proposals Submitted* by the Metropolitan Council of the American Jewish Congress, February 14, 1964.

16. Interview.

17. Interview.

18. Interview.

19. Interview.

20. The American Jewish Congress and other Jewish organizations pursued this strategy with their constituents.

21. Interviews with parents in receiving school districts.

22. Interview with civil rights leader.

23. Interview with civil rights leader.

24. Interview.

25. Interview.

26. Interview.

27. Interview.

28. Interview.

29. Interviews.

30. Interviews with officials from other Jewish organizations and civil rights leaders.

31. Interview with Jewish civil rights leaders.

32. Protestant Council statement supporting quality integrated education, by Reverend Norman van Meter, education director, June, 1964.

33. Interviews with Protestant leaders.

34. Attendance at board hearing.

35. Attendance at breakfast meeting.

36. Interviews.

37. Citizens Committee for Children, Twentieth Anniversary Report, 1964.

38. Interview.

39. Telegram from Mrs. Marshall Field, president of the CCC, to Board President James Donovan, January 31, 1964.

40. Attendance at the meeting.

41. Letter to Mrs. Rose Shapiro, member of the Board of Education, from Mrs. Trude Lash, executive secretary of CCC, August 23, 1963.

42. Interviews with civic group professionals.

43. Interview with board official.

44. Interviews with EQUAL members and officials.

45. Observation from attendance at a public hearing, 1966.

46. *Research for Action,* Bulletin No. 1, December 10, 1966, EQUAL.

47. Interview with Jewish leader.

48. *New York Times,* November 12, 1967.

49. *Ibid.*

VI *The Moderates*

1. Estimates made by UPA officials.

2. Interviews with officials of civic groups, school officials, civil rights leaders, and parents.

3. *The Status of the Public School Education of Negro and Puerto Rican Children in New York City,* presented to the Board of Education Commission on Integration, prepared by: The Public Education Association, assisted by the New York University Research Center for Human Relations, October 1955.

4. *Amsterdam News,* December 20, 1958, Judge Justine Wise Polier decision.

5. E. Franklin Frazier, *Black Bourgeoisie, The Rise of a New Middle Class in the United States,* Glencoe, Ill.: The Free Press, 1957.

6. Interviews with UPA officials. These are obviously only crude estimates.

7. Interviews with UPA officials and attendance at delegate assembly meetings.

8. UPA Report, dealing with integration, discussed at an October, 1963, delegate assembly meeting.

9. UPA memo, January, 1964, to local Parent Associations.

10. Memo from Mrs. Adele Tunick, UPA President, to Parent Associations, February 25, 1964.

11. Interviews with UPA officials.

12. Statement by Harold Siegel, executive secretary of UPA, on the Superintendent of Schools' Plan for "Quality Integrated Education," June 4, 1964, p. 3. See also UPA's Delegate Assembly Statement on intermediate schools, December 6, 1965.

13. UPA delegate assembly statement, October, 1963.

14. Press release on the integration crisis in the New York City schools, April 20, 1964.

15. See, for example, UPA Draft of Statement on the Superintendent's Proposals for Reorganization, for presentation at Board of Education hearings, March 11, 1966.

16. Attendance and observation at the annual UPA conference, January, 1967.

17. Sol Cohen, *Progressives and Urban Social Reform,* Bureau of Publications, Teachers College, Columbia University, 1964.

18. See PEA study, *The Status of . . . , loc. cit.*

19. See *Reorganizing Secondary Education in New York City,* Committee on Education, Guidance and Work, Public Education Association, October, 1963; and *High Schools for a Changing World,* February 1, 1967, same PEA Committee.

20. *Reorganizing Secondary Education in New York City, op. cit.,* p. 8.

21. Statement of the Public Education Association on the Decentralization of Authority and Responsibility in the New York City School System, March 8, 1967.

22. PEA statement on bussing in Special Report Card, February, 1964.

23. Interviews with PEA officials.

24. Interview with civil rights leader.

25. Sol Cohen, *op. cit.,* p. 222.

26. *Ibid.,* p. 225.

27. *Ibid.*

28. Interviews with union officials.

29. See, for example, Kenneth B. Clark, *Dark Ghetto,* New York: Harper, 1965, chapt. 6.

30. Interviews with parents and union officials.

31. *The American Teacher,* December, 1966.

32. *Toward the Integration of Our Schools,* Final Report of the Commission on Integration, Board of Education of the City of New York, 1958, pp. 14–17.

33. Interviews with union officials. This happened in the spring of 1965.

34. Interviews with union and school officials.

35. David J. Fox, *Expansion of the More Effective School Program,* Center for Urban Education, September, 1967.

36. *New York Times,* March 17, 1967.

37. Interviews with civil rights and liberal white officials about the press.

38. Interviews with civil rights and white liberal leaders.

VII *The Board and Its Top Decision Makers*

1. *Facts and Figures, 1967/1968, NYC Public Schools,* p. 77.

2. The board's preliminary policy statement, Decentralization: Statement of Policy, March 30, 1967, indicates how centralized it is; and see Marilyn Gittell, *Participants and Participation,* Center for Urban Education, 1967.

3. Some of these pathologies are discussed briefly in *Reconnection for Learning,* Report of the Mayor's Advisory Panel on Decentralization of The New York City Schools, 1967, especially pp. 11–14. This report also makes clear, however, that the problems are not confined to ghetto areas, as indicated, for example by Table IV in Appendix C, p. 106, where data are presented on the percent of academic diplomas granted in nonspecialized academic high schools with the highest white population. They range between 28.7 and 57.9% of their total enrollments.

4. Attendance at the board's public hearings on the comprehensive high school, May 24, 1967. Statements by EQUAL, the Women's City Club, and the PEA all make this point; interviews with top school officials confirm it.

5. See, for example, Peter Schrag's discussion of Boston in *The Village School Downtown,* Boston: Beacon, 1967, chapt. 3.

6. Interview with influential white civic leader.

7. See source note No. 2, Chapter One, for a list of board policy statements on desegregation. See also, *Improving Ethnic Distribution of New York City Pupils,* Jacob Landers, School District of the City of New York, May, 1966; and Eleanor B. Shelton and Raymond A. Glazier, *Pupils and Schools in New York City: A Fact Book,* New York: Russell Sage Foundation, 1965, chapt. 6.

8. See, for example, *New Programs and Practices,* 1966 Directory, Office of Instruction and Curriculum, Board of Education, City of New York, September, 1966; and *Summary of Proposed Programs, 1967–68,* Title I, Elementary and Secondary Education Act, August 30, 1967.

9. See, for example, Edmund Gordon and Adelaide Jablonsky "Compensatory Education in the Equalization of Educational Opportunity," a report to the U.S. Commission on Civil Rights, November 17, 1967, pp. 13–16. The board's own evaluation indicates no significant improvements in reading scores.

10. Interviews with board members and school professionals.

11. Interviews with civil rights leaders and school officials.

12. Interviews with civil rights leaders and school officials.

13. Interviews with school officials. Some board members and

school professionals regarded Mrs. Kohler as a "meddler" and as "too aggressive."

14. Interviews with people who helped gather the signatures for one board member.

15. Interviews with civil rights and moderate leaders.

16. Interviews with civil rights leaders and black school officials.

17. Interviews with school officials.

18. Interviews with school officials. Board reports on its committee system.

19. Strayer and Yavner, *op. cit.*, chapt. 19.

20. *A Report of Recommendations on The Recruitment, Selection, Appointment, and Promotion of Teachers in The New York City Public Schools,* Center for Field Research and School Services, New York University, 1966. Giardino's reforms are reviewed in the *Staff Bulletin,* The Public Schools of New York City, February 20, 1967, pp. 1 *ff.*

21. Interviews with board members. See also the *New York Times,* November 19, 1963.

22. Interviews with board members. This point is also made in the endless management studies of the system, especially Strayer and Yavner, *op. cit.*; Cresap, McCormick, and Paget, *The New York City Board of Education, Organization of The School System,* August, 1962, II. Proposed Organization Plan. See also, Gittell, *op. cit.,* chapt. 2.

23. Interviews with school professionals and civic leaders.

24. Interviews with board members.

25. Interviews with school officials.

26. *New York Times,* March 1 and 5, 1965, and interviews with school officials.

27. Interviews; attendance at public hearings on Title I; and for example, the letter from Mrs. Florence Flast, President of the UPA, to U.S. Education Commissioner Harold Howe, May 27, 1966, describing the practice of favoring parochial schools at the expense of public schools with Title I funds.

28. Interviews with school officials.

29. Materials for these personal histories come from interviews with board members; *Who's Who;* and the New York *Herald Tribune,* March 7, 1965.

30. Interviews with school officials and board members.

31. Interviews with civil rights leader and board member.

32. Interviews with school officials and board members.

33. Interviews with school professionals and board members.

34. *New York Times,* December 12, 1963.

35. Interviews with board members and school officials.

36. Interviews with IS 201 leaders. See the report, *Sequence of Events Surrounding Community Involvement With Public School 201,* September 24, 1966, a history of the controversy prepared by the Negotiating Team for Parents of IS 201.

37. Interviews with board members.

38. See source note No. 2, above. This was not a decentralization plan, but only a preliminary policy statement.

39. Interviews with city and school officials.

40. Interviews with school officials.

41. Interviews with school officials.

42. *World-Journal Tribune,* November 9, 1966, excerpts from a speech given by Giardino.

43. Interviews with board members.

44. Interviews with civil rights leaders.

45. Interviews with board members.

46. Interviews with civil rights and white civic group leaders.

47. Interview with board member.

48. Interviews with school officials; *New York Times,* March 4, 1965; and Fred M. Hechinger, "Who Runs Our Big City Schools?" *Saturday Review of Literature,* April 17, 1965.

49. Materials that follow come from interviews with board members, civic leaders, and school professionals.

50. *New York Times,* December 5, 1964.

51. Gross's letter to Allen, asking about the order, and the *New York Times,* August 26, 1963.

52. Interviews with school officials, board members, and civil rights leaders, *New York Times,* January 20, 1964.

53. Interview with person attending the conference.

54. *New York Times,* January 5, 1964.

55. *New York Times,* May 1, 1964.

56. *New York Times,* March 6, 1965.

57. Memo from Superintendent Donovan to deputy superintendents, district superintendents, and heads of bureaus, on *A Planning–Programming–Budgeting System. . . ,* May 1, 1967.

58. Interviews with school officials.

59. Interviews with school officials.

60. Interviews with school officials; private meetings of UPA and school officials; and attendance at board hearing on the comprehensive high school, May 24, 1967.

61. Interviews with school officials.

62. See the remarks on the board's proposed 1966–1967 capital budget by EQUAL, February 17, 1966, analyzing the board's 4–4–4 grade reorganization efforts.

63. Testimony by Superintendent Donovan at this capital budget

hearing of the Board of Estimate and City Council, February 17, 1966.

64. See, however, his memo of May 1, 1967, to Deputy Superintendents, District Superintendents, and heads of bureaus, indicating his intention to set up a Planning-Programming-Budgeting-System.

65. Interviews with parents and civil rights leaders.

66. Charles E. Bidwell, "The School as A Formal Organization," in James March, ed., *Organizations,* Chicago: Rand McNally, 1965, pp. 996–1003.

67. Interviews with school officials.

68. See, for example, studies mentioned in source note No. 22.

69. Interviews. *New York Times,* August 15 and September 19, 1961.

70. Statement by the Board of Regents, 1961.

71. Interviews with board and school officials.

72. Interviews with school officials.

73. Interviews with top school officials.

VIII *The Professional Bureaucracy*

1. Chester I. Barnard, *The Functions of The Executive,* Cambridge, Mass: Harvard, 1938, chapt. 12.

2. See Victor Thompson, *Modern Organizations,* New York: Knopf, 1961; Michel Crozier, *The Bureaucratic Phenomenon,* Chicago: University of Chicago Press, 1964; Robert K. Merton, "Bureaucratic Structure and Personality," in his *Social Theory and Social Structure,* Glencoe, Ill.: The Free Press, 1957, pp. 195–207; Chester I. Barnard, "The Functions and Pathologies of Status Systems," in William F. Whyte, ed., *Industry and Society,* New York: McGraw-Hill, 1946, pp. 46–83; James Worthy, "Organizational Structure and Employee Morale," *American Sociological Review,* April, 1950, pp. 169–79; F.L.W. Richardson and Charles Walker, *Human Relations in an Expanding Company,* New Haven: Labor and Management Center, 1948; and Warren G. Bennis, *Changing Organizations,* New York: McGraw-Hill, 1966. My "sick bureaucracy" model was derived from these works.

3. For social science writings on "bureaucracy" and "professionalism," see Howard M. Vollmer and Donald L. Mills, eds., *Professionalization,* Englewood Cliffs, N.J.: Prentice-Hall, 1966.

4. W.W. Charters, Jr., "The Social Background of Teaching," in N.L. Gage, ed., *Handbook of Research on Teaching,* Chicago, Rand McNally, 1963, pp. 718–723.

5. A case study written up for civil rights groups.

6. Marilyn Gittell, *op. cit.,* chapts. 4–6; and *Reconnection for*

Learning; Cresap, McCormick, and Paget; Shinnerer; and Strayer and Yavner, all *op. cit.*

7. Interviews with school officials, principals.

8. See Eliot D. Chapple and Leonard R. Sayles, *The Measure of Management,* New York: Macmillan, 1961. The term "bottom-up" management was originally coined by a business executive, William B. Given, Jr., of the American Brake Shoe Company, in his book, *Bottom-up Management,* New York: Harper & Brothers, 1949.

9. Interviews with school officials.

10. Interviews with headquarters officials.

11. See Cresap, McCormick, and Paget, *op. cit.,* chapt. 2, p. 18; and Strayer and Yavner, *op. cit.*

12. These are not hypothetical examples, but come from many actual situations.

13. Interviews with teachers, principals, and parent association officials. See also the *UPA Study of Supply Procedures in the Public Schools,* United Parents Associations, February 2, 1968.

14. Interview with a teacher from one of the academic high schools.

15. *A Report of Recommendations on the Recruitment, Selection, Appointment, and Promotion of Teachers in The New York City Public Schools,* Center for Field Research and School Services, New York University, 1966.

16. *Staffing of JHS 145: A Review and Analysis,* Paul Warner, Principal, 1966, mimeographed statement.

17. *The Status of the Public School Education of Negro and Puerto Rican Children in New York City,* prepared by the Public Education Association, October, 1955; *A Study of the Problems of Integration in New York City Public Schools Since 1955,* Urban League of Greater New York, September, 1963; and Eleanor B. Sheldon and Raymond A. Glazier, *Pupils and Schools in New York City,* New York: Russell Sage Foundation, 1965.

18. Interviews with school officials and parents, and minutes of Local School Board 12–14. Letter to Dr. Sidney Rosenberg, district superintendent, from M. Sylvester King, Bank Street College of Education, February 16, 1966, on the run-down and chaotic state of JHS 139.

19. Interview with headquarters official.

20. Gittell, *op. cit.,* chapt. 4; interviews with field officials and local school board members.

21. See two articles by Martin Mayer that deal with these questions: "Close to Midnight for the New York City Schools," The *New York Times Magazine,* May 2, 1965; and "What's Wrong with

City Schools," *The Saturday Evening Post,* September 9, 1967, pp. 21 *ff.*

22. Interviews.

23. Interviews.

24. Interviews with teachers and supervisors.

25. Interview.

26. Mortimer Kreuter, "The Teacher in The Brown Paper Bag," *The Urban Review,* May, 1966.

27. Gittell, *op. cit.,* Appendix B.

28. Gloria Channon, "The More Effective Schools," *The Urban Review,* v. II, No. 1, February, 1967, p. 24.

29. The workings of the Board of Examiners have been considered in most management studies of the board. See, Strayer and Yavner, *op. cit.,* chapt. 19; Mark Schinnerer, *A Report to the New York City Education Department,* New York, 1961, pp. 41–53; *Reconnection for Learning, op. cit.,* Part III, pp. 44–52.

30. Wallace Sayre and Herbert Kaufman, *Governing New York City,* New York: Russell Sage Foundation, 1960, p. 426.

31. *A Report of Recommendations on the Recruitment, Selection, Appointment, and Promotion of Teachers in the New York City Public Schools, op. cit.,* p. 2.

32. *Staff Bulletin,* The Public Schools of New York City, February 20, 1967, v. V, No. 8.

33. *A Report of Recommendations . . . , op. cit.,* pp. 26–29.

34. Gittell, *op. cit.,* p. 12.

35. Letter from principal to Garrison, and memo by headquarters official about the matter.

36. Interviews with civil rights leaders and school officials.

37. Strayer and Yavner, *op. cit.,* chapt. 19.

38. *Ibid.*

39. For a sophisticated, social-science discussion of personnel testing, see Marvin D. Dunnette and Bernard M. Bass, "Behavioral Scientists and Personnel Management," *Industrial Relations,* v. 2, No. 3, May, 1963, pp. 115–31.

40. Interviews with board members.

41. Interviews with school officials, and *Reconnection for Learning, op. cit.* Part III.

42. Interviews with social scientists who had studied the civil service procedures of the board.

43. Interviews with board members and school officials.

44. Interviews with headquarters officials.

45. Cresap, McCormack, and Paget, *op. cit.,* Part II.

46. Interviews with school officials.

47. Gittell, *op. cit.,* chapt. 2.

48. Interviews with field supervisors. See also "Administrators on School Integration," Council of Supervisory Associations, *Integrated Education,* June–July, 1964, pp. 30–34.

49. Interviews with school officials.

50. Jacob Landers, *Improving Ethnic Distribution of New York City Pupils,* May, 1966, p. 28.

51. Interviews with parents, field, and headquarters officials.

52. Interviews with school officials.

53. *The Open Enrollment Program in The New York City Public Schools,* Progress Report, September, 1960 – September, 1963, prepared under the direction of the Open Enrollment Committee.

54. Unpublished materials from the board's preliminary data evaluating the community zoning plan include: A Report of the Reactions of the Three Assistant Superintendents Involved to Certain Aspects of The Community Zoning Program; and Interviews with Principals of the Eight Paired Schools, Bureau of Educational Research, June 10, 1965. The "official," published version is *Evaluation of The Community Zoning Program, Summary Report,* Office of Educational Research, Board of Education of The City of New York, September, 1966.

55. Interviews with Brooklyn Heights parents and school officials.

56. Interviews with civic organization officials.

57. Interviews with school officials.

58. Interviews with school officials.

59. *Toward Quality Secondary Education,* Recommendations on the Reorganization of the New York City High Schools, A Report to the Superintendent of Schools, New York City Public Schools, December, 1964.

60. *New York Times,* May 27, 1967.

61. Materials collected by union officials.

62. *Report of Visitation to Transferred 6th and 9th Grades,* United Parents Associations, February, 1965, p. 1.

63. *Ibid.*

IX   *Administrative Controls*

1. For some recent writings on systems analysis, see Chadwick J. Haberstroh, "Organization Design and Systems Analysis," in James G. March, ed., *Handbook of Organizations,* Chicago: Rand McNally, 1965, pp. 1171–1213; Walter A. Hill and Douglas Egan, *Readings in Organization Theory,* Boston: Allyn & Bacon, 1966; and Warren G. Bennis, *Changing Organizations,* New York: McGraw-Hill, 1966.

2. *New York Times,* April 1, 1968; and attendance at the meeting.

3. Interview with federal official.

4. Richard M. Cyert and James G. March, *A Behavioral Theory of the Firm,* Englewood Cliffs, New Jersey: Prentice-Hall, 1963.

5. The Temporary Commission on City Finances, City of New York, *Governing the Public Schools,* Staff Paper 9, August, 1966, p. 20.

6. Interviews with school officials and board members.

7. Staff Bulletin, Board of Education of the City of New York, March 13, 1967, p. 2.

8. Interviews with school officials.

9. *Analysis of the Proposed 1967–1968 Executive Budget As It Pertains to Public Education,* New York City People's Board of Education, 1967.

10. Joseph Justman, A. Harry Passow, Miriam Goldberg, and Abraham J. Tannenbaum, eds., *Education of the Disadvantaged,* New York: Holt, 1967; and the *World-Telegram,* February 23, 1965.

11. David Fox, *Free Choice-Open Enrollment,* Center for Urban Education, New York, 1967.

12. See Marvin D. Dunnette and Bernard M. Bass, "Behavioral Scientists and Personnel Management," *Industrial Relations,* v. 2, No. 3, May, 1963.

13. *Summary and Analysis of Evaluations of New York City Board of Education Title I Programs, 1965–66,* Research for Action, Bulletin No. 1, December 10, 1966, EQUAL.

14. Sheldon and Glazier, *op. cit.*

15. Interviews with members of Mayor Lindsay's Council Against Poverty, the anti-poverty agency. See also, Chapt. Twelve.

16. Interviews with parents in the area.

17. Marilyn Gittell, *Participants and Participation,* Center for Urban Education, 1967, Appendix B.

18. Interviews with civic leaders.

19. Interview with headquarters official. See also, Gittell, *op. cit.,* chapt. 4.

20. Interviews with headquarters officials.

21. *New York Times,* April 15, 1967.

22. *Developing New York City's Human Resources,* report of a study group of the Institute of Public Administration to Mayor John V. Lindsay, V. I., June, 1966. (Generally known as The Sviridoff Report.)

23. Statement of Mrs. Nathan W. Levin, chairman of the Educational Services Section before the Subcommittee on the Elementary and Secondary Education Act of the Education and Labor Committee of the House of Representatives, March 18, 1967.

24. CCC statement on Title I.

25. *Analysis of the Proposed 1967–1968 Executive Budget, op. cit.,* p. 3.

26. *Ibid.,* pp. 4 *ff.*

27. Interview.

28. *New York Times,* May 24, 1967.

29. Interviews with school officials.

30. Interviews; and from the Expense Budget for the Fiscal Year 1966–1967, Board of Education, City School District of the City of New York, p. 11.

31. From an unpublished Board of Education study on the Human Relations Unit and school–community coordinators, February, 1964; and from interviews.

32. Interviews with school officials.

33. See footnote 31.

34. Interviews with school officials.

35. Interviews with school officials.

36. Interviews with school officials.

37. From an unpublished board study (see footnote 31) and from another unpublished study subcontracted by the board, April, 1967, and interviews.

38. Interviews.

39. Interviews.

40. For a review of arguments supporting and criticizing sensitivity training, see Harold Lazarus and E. Kirby Warren, eds., *The Process of Management,* Englewood Cliffs: Prentice-Hall, 1968, Part Five.

41. Interviews with school officials.

42. IS 201 history, prepared by Negotiating Team for Parents.

43. Interviews with civil rights leaders.

44. Interviews with Central Zoning Unit staff.

45. See, for example, *The Open Enrollment Program in The New York City Public Schools,* Progress Report, September, 1963.

46. Interview.

X *Community Relations*

1. Citizens Committee for Children, memo on school suspensions, April 5, 1967.

2. My historial account draws heavily on a document prepared by the coordinating committee of IS 201.

3. IS 201, Sequence of Events Surrounding Community Involvement with PS 201, memo by Negotiating Team.

4. *Ibid.,* p. 2.

5. Interviews. Also *Ibid.,* p. 2.

6. *Ibid.,* p. 2.

7. *Ibid.,* p. 2.

8. *Ibid.,* p. 4.

9. *Ibid.,* p. 4.

10. *Ibid.,* p. 4.

11. Interviews.

12. This comes from the 201 historical account and from interviews with community leaders.

13. Dorothy S. Jones, "The Issues at IS 201; A View from the Parents Committee," *Integrated Education,* v. IV, No. 5, October–November, 1966, p. 25.

14. Interviews with community leaders.

15. The Women's City Club followed up its first study, *Strengthen or Abolish?,* 1960, with *Performance and Promise,* 1966, a thorough study of local school boards.

16. Women's City Club, *Performance and Promise,* p. 1.

17. *Ibid.,* p. 14.

18. Statement by a local school board member at a meeting of local school board members, Women's City Club, April 22, 1967.

19. Women's City Club, *op. cit.,* p. 10.

20. Memorandum to Local School Board Chairmen, October 10, 1966, signed by six local school board chairmen.

21. Women's City Club, *op. cit.,* p. 56. When local board members were asked to give specific suggestions for changes, 31 of the 66 mentioned giving the local boards more power (p. 32). The finding that follows on PA presidents' views regarding local school board contributions is from *Performance and Promise,* p. 31; and the quote from the Manhattan PA president is cited from *ibid.,* p. 33.

22. Interview with local board member.

23. New York *World Journal Tribune,* November 2, 1966, p. 29.

24. Letter of resignation, written December 19, 1966.

25. Letter from Lloyd Garrison to Kenneth Josey, chairman of Local School Board No. 6, June 24, 1966.

26. Letter from Mrs. Ellen Lurie to Lloyd Garrison, September 1, 1966.

27. Interviews with civil rights and white civic leaders.

28. Interviews with civil rights leaders.

29. This account comes from interviews with parents, civic leaders, and school officials.

30. Letter from Superintendent Donovan to the local school board.

31. Letter to Lloyd Garrison from members of local school board 12–14, November 19, 1963.

32. Interviews with local school board members.

33. Interview with local school board member.

34. Letter from Kenneth Josey, chairman of local school board

12–14, to explain the board's decision against holding public meetings.

35. Minutes of the executive session, local school board 12–14, April 1, 1965.

36. Letter from Josey, calling a special executive session, December 9, 1965.

37. *New York Times,* May 10, 1967.

38. United States District Court, Southern District of New York, Victor Madera, Ramiro Madera and Manuela Madera, Plaintiffs, against Board of Education of the City of New York, *et al.,* 67 CIV. 635, New York, New York, April 10, 1967, Constance Baker Motley, United States District Judge.

39. *New York Times,* June 10, 1967.

40. Report by MFY on "Principal's Dispute with Mobilization for Youth," February 19, 1964. Also, report prepared by principals of Districts 1–4, presenting the bases for the telegram of January 27, 1964, requesting an investigation of Mobilization for Youth and the dismissal of a top MFY official, February 24, 1964.

41. Telegram sent by the principals to those people, January 28, 1964. Much of this material comes from reports prepared by MFY and the principals.

42. Statement by Winslow Carlton, January 31, 1964.

43. The *Village Voice,* February 20, 1964.

44. From the MFY report, *op. cit.*

45. These data were compiled by MFY from board figures.

46. MFY report, p. 7.

47. *Ibid.,* p. 8.

48. *Ibid.,* p. 10.

49. *Ibid.,* p. 12.

50. *Ibid.,* p. 16.

51. Report prepared by principals of Districts 1–4, *op. cit.*

XI *Decision Making . . .*

1. Richard M. Cyert and James G. March, *A Behavioral Theory of the Firm,* Englewood Cliffs, New Jersey: Prentice-Hall, 1963.

2. *Ibid.,* chapt. 3.

3. Irving Goldaber, *op cit.* Goldaber's dissertation indicates that the board never acted on desegregation plans until it was confronted with a massive show of strength by civil rights groups.

4. *Study of the Effect of the 1964–1970 School Building Program on Segregation in New York City's Public Schools,* The City Com-

mission on Human Rights of New York. Interviews with civil rights leaders, March 26, 1964.

5. Interviews with UPA and school officials.

6. These figures come from *Ethnic Distribution of Enrollments in New York City Public Schools, by Schools, as of October 31, 1960;* and Board of Education of the City of New York, *Special Census of School Population,* February, 1965.

7. Interviews with officials at the City Commission on Human Rights.

8. See Chapters One and Eight.

9. Interviews. Attendance at the public hearing on the comprehensive high school, May 24, 1967.

10. Robin M. Williams, Jr., *Factors Affecting Reactions to Public School Desegregation in American Communities,* unpublished paper prepared for the Conference on Racial Issues in Education, Greystone Conference Center, New York City, March 31–April 1, 1964, p. 51.

11. Herbert Gans, Memorandum No. 7, *Experimental* vs. *System-Wide Introduction of the Educational Complex,* Institute of Urban Studies, Teachers College, Columbia University, December, 1964.

12. Interviews with civic leaders and school officials on how some of the latter were publicizing Higher Horizons after negative data were in.

13. Martin Mayer, "Close to Midnight for the New York Schools," *The New York Times Magazine,* May 2, 1965, p. 35.

14. Interviews with board members.

15. Interviews with civil rights leaders and school officials.

16. Interviews with school and UPA officials.

17. Interviews with civil rights leaders.

18. Interviews with teacher.

19. Interviews with school officials and civil rights leaders and an examination of the correspondence between Wolff and school officials.

20. *New York Times,* December 28, 1963.

21. Interviews with consultants, school officials, and civil rights leaders.

22. Interviews with Dentler project staff, civil rights leaders, and school officials.

23. Interviews with consultants and civil rights leaders.

XII *The Board of Education . . .*

1. See, for example, the paper by David Lewis. See also footnote 2, chapt. 13.

2. The most recent studies that assert this position are Marilyn

Gittell, *Participants and Participation* (See Bibliography), and *Reconnection for Learning* (See note 3 for Chapter Thirteen).

3. Interview with top city official.

4. Interview with a housing official.

5. Interviews with parents and city officials.

6. *New York Times,* November 13, 1967.

7. Interviews with civic leaders.

8. Interviews with city officials.

9. Interviews with city officials.

10. Interviews with city officials and civic leaders.

11. Interviews with city agency officials.

12. Interviews with many commission staff and commissioners.

13. CCHR studies—see, for example, Harold Goldblatt and Cyril Tyson, *Pupil Evaluations: An Ethnic Study;* October, 1962; Gerhart Saenger, *The First Year of the Open Enrollment Program,* June, 1961; *Report on Three Demonstration Projects in the City Schools,* May, 1968.

14. Interview.

15. Interview with a commissioner.

16. Interviews with civil rights leaders.

17. Interviews with city agency officials, and civic group leaders.

18. Interview.

19. *New York Times,* November 27, 1965.

20. Interviews with city agency officials.

21. Interviews with Planning Commission officials.

22. CPC attack on board construction.

23. Interviews.

24. Interviews.

25. Interview with board member.

26. Interviews; and *New York Times,* July 16, 1967.

27. Interviews with city officials.

28. Interviews with city officials.

29. Interviews with parochial and public school officials.

30. Bulletin of the Human Resources Administration of the City of New York, December, 1966, p. 2.

31. Interviews.

32. Interviews with CAP officials and school officials.

33. Attendance at meetings of CAP education committee.

34. Interviews with CAP officials.

35. CCC, Margaret Benjamin.

36. From Board of Education stenographic notes of a public meeting.

37. *Elementary and Secondary Education Amendments of 1967,* Hearings before the Committee on Education and Labor House of

Representatives, Ninetieth Congress, First Session on H.R. 7230, Part 2, pp. 1572–1573.

38. *New York Times,* April 15, 1967.
39. *New York Times,* March 31, 1967.
40. *New York Times,* April 1, 1967.
41. *New York Times,* April 3, 1967.
42. *New York Times,* April 14, 1967.
43. *New York Times,* April 28, 1967.
44. *New York Times,* May 1, 1967.
45. *New York Times,* May 25, 1967.
46. *New York Times,* April 9, 1967.
47. Interviews with state officials.

XIII *Alternative Reform Strategies* . . .

1. Kenneth B. Clark, "Alternative Public School Systems: A Response to America's Educational Emergency," prepared for the National Conference on Equal Educational Opportunity in America's Cities, sponsored by the U.S. Commission on Civil Rights, Washington, D.C., November 16–18, 1967.

2. U.S. Civil Rights Commission Report, *Racial Isolation in the Public Schools,* 1967; U.S. Office of Education, *Equality of Educational Opportunity,* 1966; and the many papers delivered at the U.S. Commission on Civil Rights conference, especially Edmund Gordon, "Compensatory Education in the Equalization of Educational Opportunity"; David K. Cohen, Policy for the Public Schools; Compensation or Integration; Thomas F. Pettigrew, "The Consequence of Racially Isolated Schools: Another Look"; and Michael W. Kirst, "What Types of Compensatory Education Programs Are Effective?"

3. See *Reconnection for Learning,* report of the Mayor's Advisory Panel on Decentralization of the New York City schools, 1967. Several papers delivered at the National Conference on Equal Educational Opportunity in America's Cities, sponsored by the U.S. Commission on Civil Rights, Washington, D.C., November 16–18, 1967, suggest proposals for reform. They include: David K. Cohen, "Policy for the Public Schools: Compensation or Integration?" Irwin Katz, "Desegregation or Integration in Public Schools? The Policy Implications of Research"; Kenneth B. Clark, "Alternative Public School Systems: A Response . . ." (see Note 1 above) ; Thomas F. Pettigrew, "The Consequences of Racial Isolation in the Public Schools"; David Lewis, "The New Role of Education Parks in the Changing Structure of Metropolitan Areas"; and Bernard J. Frieden, "Can Federal Programs Help Negroes Leave the Ghetto?" See also Christopher Jencks,

"The Public Schools are Failing," *The Saturday Evening Post*, April 23, 1966; and Paul Goodman, "Mini-Schools: A Prescription for the Reading Problem," *The New York Review*, January 4, 1968.

4. *Reconnection for Learning, op. cit.*, Preface.

5. *Statement of the Board of Education and the Superintendent of Schools Re Recommendations Made by the Mayor's Panel,* November 9, 1967. This seven-page statement contains the board's main objections to the Bundy Report.

6. *Ibid.*

7. See Reverend Milton Galamison's letter to the editor of the *New York Times,* April 13, 1968, in which he explains quite clearly that the educational establishment has used "the corpse of the integration movement, killed by that very establishment, as a shield against community control."

8. This objection, and the ones that follow, are developed in the board's initial statement criticizing the Bundy Report, as well as by other opposition groups.

9. William Kornhauser, *op. cit.*

10. *New York Times,* December 4, 1967.

11. Thomas Minter, unpublished paper on the three demonstration districts, the Ford Foundation, September, 1967.

12. Milton Friedman, *Capitalism and Freedom,* Chicago: University of Chicago Press, 1962, p. 96; William F. Buckley, Jr., in the New York *Post,* January 13, 1968; and Goodman and Jencks citations referred to in source note No. 3.

13. Goodman, *op. cit.*

14. James S. Coleman, "Toward Open Schools," *The Public Interest,* Fall, 1967, pp. 20–27.

15. Coleman Report, U.S. Civil Rights Commission Report, separate papers at U.S. Civil Rights Commission conference by Clark Pettigrew . . .

16. Anthony Downs. "The Future of American Ghettos," paper delivered at the American Academy of Arts and Sciences Conference on Urbanism, Cambridge, Mass., October 27–28, 1967.

17. David Lewis, *op. cit.*

18. Bernard J. Frieden, *op. cit.*

19. Paul Goodman, *People on Personnel,* New York: Random House, 1963.

20. *The Reporter,* November 30, 1967.

Index

ABOUT THE AUTHOR

DAVID ROGERS is Associate Professor of Sociology and Management in the Graduate School of Business Administration of New York University. *110 Livingston Street* was researched while he was Senior Research Sociologist at the Center for Urban Education in New York City, a research and development laboratory chartered by the New York State Board of Regents and set up under a grant from the U.S. Office of Education. Professor Rogers is presently working on a study of urban coalitions in several large American cities.

Dr. Rogers is a Bostonian, and has lived in New York City for ten years. He received his A.B. and Ph.D. in sociology at Harvard and has taught at Columbia. He lives in Manhattan with his wife and two sons.